Cost Control Handbook

Second edition

FOR KAREN

AND

FOR CHRISTINE

AND THEIR

BRIGHT YOUNG FUTURES

Cost Control Handbook

Second edition

R M S Wilson

A Gower Handbook

First published 1975 by Gower Press Limited

Second edition published 1983 by Gower Publishing Company Limited, Aldershot, Hants, England

Wilson, R.M.S.
Cost control handbook.–2nd ed.–(A Gower handbook)
1. Cost control–Handbooks, manuals, etc.
I. Title
658.1'552 HD47.5

ISBN 0-566-02250-8

Set in Press Roman by Supreme Litho Typesetting, Ilford, Essex.

Printed and bound in Great Britain by
Robert Hartnoll Ltd. Bodmin, Cornwall

Contents

Foreword

by
William Hyde
President (1980–1981)
The Institute of Cost & Management Accountants
(incorporated by Royal Charter)

Recent years have shown a marked change in the demands that industry, commerce, and the public service make on both accountants and managers. This change is reflected particularly in the increasing importance of management accounting in which the emphasis is on the effective use of resources and which is exemplified by the demand for more meaningful cost control information.

Cost control has, therefore, become a major focal point in managing organizations. The whole of the organization and its needs should be seen as the context within which cost control takes place. It can no longer be regarded as the peculiar concern – suggested by many text books – of the factory manager and the works accountant. If the accountant can work as a full member of the management team, it is clear that his specialized creative and analytical skills can be put to profitable use. This must be the case wherever there is an increasing realization of the essential part that soundly based systems of cost control play in attaining organizational objectives.

This book takes the reader through the various steps by which an overall perspective of cost control can be established and employed. It shows how, for instance, the manager can use cost information – compiled to his own specifications – in his problem-solving activities so that his decisions may help in securing corporate aims. Major techniques and their application are covered and the overall treatment of the subject should be of great value to practising managers.

This handbook reflects the forward-looking view of the Institute and is in line with its objectives and policies of promoting maximum effectiveness in industrial, commercial and other undertakings. We are indebted to the author, Richard Wilson, for compiling it in such a clear, systematic and integrated way.

Preface

It is pleasing that the continuing demand for this book (since it initially appeared in both Britain and the United States in 1975) has resulted in the publisher's request for this revised edition.

The book aims to be useful to busy managers who require clear explanations of cost control aims and methods. The changes made for the new edition are designed to contribute to this aim. For instance, a new Introduction has been written to set the book's subject matter into a corporate decision-making context, and there are new Preambles to two of the three main sections of the book: the Preamble to Part Two examines the impacts of uncertainty and inflation on cost control; and the Preamble to Part Three deals with the (behavioural) impacts of implementing systems for controlling costs.

Redundant material has been eliminated and new sections added to various chapters such as in Chapter 6 on performance measurement, in Chapter 7 on output budgeting, in Chapter 10 on non-production standards, in Chapter 11 on variance analysis in physical distribution, in Chapter 16 on energy cost control, and in Chapter 17 on cost-based bid pricing.

Chapter 13 (Management Audit) is new, and Chapter 15 (on Research and Development) has been re-structured to incorporate material on network analysis and project control.

More attention is given in this edition to organizational considerations and to broader matters than one normally envisages in the context of cost control. However, there continues to be in this edition, as in its predecessor, a set of worked examples and illustrations showing how cost control techniques can be developed and used in different situations. (Since these examples are intended to show the ways in which cost control techniques can be applied, the figures used in them – such as wage rates – should not be assumed to be either accurate in a contemporary sense or a matter of historical record. This is not their purpose.)

Finally, throughout the book (whether at the end of individual chapters or at the end of each main part) there are newly-added annotated references to further reading on each major issue covered.

If this revision continues to help managers to see some of their problems in a new light, and to help illuminate their solution, then its purpose will continue to be well-served.

University of Sheffield

Dick Wilson

Acknowledgements

The following publishers/writers were kind enough to grant me their approval to reproduce copyright material:

David E. Hussey and Pergamon Press Ltd. for Figure 8.2 ('A Generalised Planning Model') from D.E. Hussey, *'Introducing Corporate Planning'*, Oxford: Pergamon. 1971.

Business Books Ltd. for Figure 16.5 ('Optimum Maintenance Chart') from H.V.M. Steward, *'Guide to Effective Maintenance Management'*, London: Business Books. 1963.

The British Institute of Management for Figures 9.21–9.24 based on tables in F.C. de Paula, *'Accounts for Management'*, London: Management Publications Ltd. for B.I.M. 1955 (revised ed. 1965); and for information in Chapter 12 on interfirm comparison extracted from Management Information Sheet number 3, January 1969 (revised 1973).

Gower Publishing Company Ltd. for Figures 14.5(a) and 14.5(b) ('Monthly Analysis of Labour Turnover' and 'Reasons for Leaving') from the Industrial Society's book, *'Design of Personnel Systems and Records'*, London: Gower, 1969, and for Figure 13.2 ('System Capability Factors') from M.G. Christopher, et al. *'Distribution Planning and Control'*, Farnborough: Gower, 1977.

R.G. Bassett and *Accountancy* for Figure 18.4 ('Vehicle Control Report') in modified form, plus an argument that generally follows the lines of that contained in R.G. Bassett, 'Costing and Pricing of Fleet Operations', *Accountancy*, Vol.83, No.947, July 1972, pp.22–25.

David M. Scott (of P.E. Consulting Group Ltd.) for Figure 5.2 ('Quality Cost Report') taken from a paper presented by Mr. Scott at a P.E. Seminar entitled 'Profit from the Financial Management of Quality'). (This paper is reprinted in B. Folkertsma (ed.): *'Handbook for Managers'*. London: Kluwer-Harrap. 1972.)

The Institute of Cost and Management Accountants for several items from *'The Terminology of Cost Accountancy'*, London: I.C.M.A. 1966, (Revised ed., 1974), used in modified form in the Glossary.

Her Majesty's Stationery Office for several items from H.M. Treasury's booklet, *'Glossary of Management Techniques'*, London: H.M.S.O. 1967, used in modified form in the Glossary; and for Figure 17.10 (Form P11D) which is Crown copyright material.

Sir Isaac Pitman and Sons Ltd. for Figure 15.15 ('Network'), and Figure 15.16 ('Bar Chart') from K.G. Lockyer, *'Factory Management'*, London: Pitman, 2nd Edition. 1969.

Macdonald and Evans (Publications) Ltd. for Figure 8.5 ('Fixed Budget'), Figure 9.13 ('Process Cost Sheet'), and Figure 11.10 ('Direct and Indirect Overhead Cost Summary') from W.W.Bigg, *'Cost Accounts'*. 8th Edition. 1963.

McGraw-Hill Book Company for Figures 17.1–17.3 from P. Carroll, *'Overhead Cost Control'*, New York: McGraw-Hill. 1964 edition.

Martin S. Downer, ACMA, MCIT, Controller – Management Information Services, Freight Transport Association, and the Editor of *Accountants Weekly* for Figures 18.7–18.9 (with modifications) and an argument based on that contained in Mr. Downer's article, 'Profitable Use of Company Transport', *Accountants Weekly*, 15 December, 1972.

Prentice-Hall, Inc., for Figures 9.16–9.18, 10.2, 11.6 and 11.9 from C.T. Horngren, *'Cost Accounting – a managerial emphasis'*. Englewood Cliffs, N.J.: Prentice-Hall. (1st Edition). 1962.

The Editor of *Accountancy*, for Figure 15.3 ('Types of R and D and Distinguishing Criteria') from Tony Buckland's article, 'Can You Account for R and D?', *Accountancy*, Vol.85, No.968, April 1974.

Allan Witts (of the School of Economic Studies in the University of Leeds) for the illustration on the pricing of material issues contained in Chapter 9.

The Financial Executives Institute (U.S.A.) for Figure 4.6 ('Controllership and Treasurership Functions Defined by F.E.I.') from *The Controller*, May, 1962.

The American Institute of Certified Public Accountants for Figure 4.7 ('Job Description: Controller') from E.B. Cochran: 'What is a Controller?', *Journal of Accountancy*, July, 1955, (pp.46–53), and for Figures 10.3–10.8 (from L.G. Rayburn: 'Setting Standards for Distribution Costs', *Management Services*, Vol.2, No.2, March-April, 1967. (pp.42–52).

The Planning Executives Institute (U.S.A.) for Figure 8.16 ('Statement of Duties and Responsibilities of the Budget Director').

The English Universities Press Ltd. for Figure 4.12 ('Predictability of Behaviour Patterns') from Stafford Beer's *Cybernetics and Management*, London: E.U.P. 2nd ed., 1967. (p.18).

The Editor of *The Journal of Business Finance & Accounting* for Figure 4.14 ('The Business Organisation as a System') from E.A. Lowe: 'The Finance Director's Role in the Formulation and Implementation of Strategy: A Framework for Financial Strategy', *Journal of Business Finance*, Vol.4, No.4. Winter, 1972. (pp.58–70).

Elsevier Scientific Publishing Co. for Figures 9.1 ('The system/product/project life cycle') and 9.2 ('Total life cycle cost') from B.S. Blanchard: 'Life Cycle Costing – A Review', *Terotechnica*, Vol.1, No.1. 1979. (pp.9–15).

Hutchinson Publishing Group for Figures 15.8–15.12 from I. Holden & P.K. McIlroy, *Network Planning in Management Control Systems*, London: Hutchinson Educational, 1970.

Richard D. Irwin, Inc., for the basis of the discussion of variance analysis for distribution cost control in Chapter 11 contained in L.G. Rayburn: *Principles of Cost Accounting with Managerial Applications*, Homewood, Illinois: Irwin, 1979. (pp.453–6).

The Macmillan Company (U.S.A.) for Figures 13.3–13.6 based on material contained in B. Berman & J.R. Evans, *Retail Management: A Strategic Approach*, New York: Collier-Macmillan, 1979.

The Institute of Internal Auditors for the *Statement of Responsibilities of the Internal Auditor* reprinted in Chapter 13.

The Director of the Centre for Interfirm Comparison for Figure 18.10 ('Road haulage – factors affecting the vehicle operating cost/revenue ratio') which appears in H. Ingham and L.T. Harrington, *Interfirm Comparison*, London: Heinemann, 1980, (p.75), and Figure 18.18 ('Pyramid of main distribution cost ratios') from *Distribution Cost Comparison – Proposals*, C.I.F.C., August, 1980.

The Editor of *Management Accounting* (published by the National Association of Accountants, New York) for Figures 16.7–16.9 from B. Gold: 'Practical Productivity Analysis for Management Accountants', *Management Accounting* (U.S.A.) Vol.61, No.11, May 1980. (pp.31–5, 38 and 44).

At the University of Sheffield the main burden of preparing the typescript for this edition, in the face of tight time limits, fell on the very capable shoulders of Mrs Marie Boam who coped with her usual enthusiasm and competence. My indebtedness to her is very considerable.

At Gower Publishing Malcolm Stern's guidance and sponsorship has proved invaluable in the development (and appearance) of the revised edition, as has the editorial skill of Ellen Keeling.

As well as expressing my gratitude to all those named above for their generosity and help, I cannot omit reference to the vital role played by my wife, Gillian, in providing the supportive environment that allowed this revision to be written.

R.M.W.

Introduction

Whilst the title of this book might suggest that it is intended for an audience composed of accountants in general, or cost accountants in particular, this is far from being the case. It is a book for managers: whether he has a specific responsibility for production, administration, marketing, or some other activity, each manager must have a well-developed awareness of the basic methods of financial control if he is to perform at a high level of effectiveness.

Such an awareness will tend initially to be related to a manager's immediate area of specialism. The argument of the book starts from the premise that cost is synonymous with *sacrifice*, and it is assumed that managers will wish to minimize (in so far as they are able) the sacrifices involved in achieving given outcomes. However, their awareness really needs to extend beyond the area of functional specialism to embrace the interfaces with other specialisms, since minimizing costs in any one area is more than likely to cause an increase in the costs of another area. It is beneficial, therefore, to consider cost control in an overall corporate context so that the impacts of different courses of action on the organization as a whole can be seen.

Let us develop this perspective a little to consider managerial functions within a corporate context. In a typical manufacturing-marketing company one will find the various functions that are considered individually in Part Three of this volume, namely:

Administration
Research and development
Manufacturing
Marketing (order-getting)
Distribution (order-filling).

These functions can be categorized in this way as a result of their differentiated roles: i.e. each one does something different. (It is vital to recognize, however, that the role of any one is irrelevant when removed from its location amongst the others.) But there are other ways in which one can classify managerial functions that emphasize common activities across the range of departmental functions noted above. Perhaps the best known is the approach that identifies:

Planning
Organizing
Directing
Staffing
Innovating
Co-ordinating
Controlling
Communicating

as the main managerial functions. Whether one is a marketing manager or a data-processing manager, it is necessary to carry out these functional activities within every department.

It is possible to summarize the purpose of any functional breakdown by focusing on the overall task of management, which can be defined as acquiring and allocating available *means* (i.e. resources of one kind or another) in order to accomplish desired *ends* (i.e. goals), subject to whatever constraints exist. At every stage in the execution of this complex task it is necessary for problems to be solved. (What products shall we produce? In which markets should we operate? How much should we produce? Is preventive maintenance cost effective? Should the company continue to operate its main-frame computing facility? What level of customer service should the distribution function aim to offer? Should there be a basic research allocation within the R & D budget?) And the solving of problems requires that decisions be made, and every decision has cost implications. Hence this book!

Financial information is a major input to the decision-making process, but it is vital that the information is provided in a way that:

(*a*) is relevant to the decision that has to be taken (i.e. suits the decision-maker's requirements, rather than the convenience of whoever is providing it); and
(*b*) is understood by the decision-maker (who should be made aware of any underlying assumptions or known causes of poor reliability).

Since the accounting function represents an overhead cost in every organization, it is not unreasonable for its existence to be justified by a level of service that meets the above criteria. It is not acceptable in terms of the philosophy of this book for an organization's accounting function to retain the traditional preoccupation with fiduciary and stewardship responsibilities and do nothing more. Those responsibilities have an importance, but it is argued that the accountant has a greater responsibility to understand the decision-maker's information needs and then to seek to satisfy those needs.

An appropriate way to summarize the approach of this book is through the following steps of a problem-solving sequence:

1 Is the organization effective?

Do we mean the whole organization, or a particular division?
What is meant by 'effective'? (For example, are costs too high and profits too low?)
From whose point of view are we looking?

2 If not, why not?

How can we establish the actual level of effectiveness? (For example, is it highlighted by a budget variance?)
Can we devise a model of the situation that indicates the causes of good or bad performance?
What criteria are used to identify 'good' or 'bad' performance?
Can we define the problem?

3 How can the performance be improved?

Can we generate alternative solutions?
Will those alternatives actually work?

4 Can we select the best alternative solution?

How do we evaluate alternatives?
(Can the criteria from step 2 be applied quantitatively?)
What are their financial implications?
How do we actually choose?

5 Having made a choice, can we devise a means of implementing it?

What are the organizational problems (e.g. training)?
What are the cost aspects?

6 Following implementation, how do we evaluate the effectiveness of the solution? ... Which takes us back to step 1 in an iterative manner.

In the remainder of the book much attention will be devoted to commercial (i.e. profit-making – or at least profit-motivated) organizations that produce tangible physical outputs. This is not to suggest that the approach put forward and the techniques themselves are not also suitable for commercial *service* organizations, or that the methods cannot be applied – subject to various modifications – to *non-profit* organizations (whether charitable, institutional, or governmental).

Service organizations obviously cannot have an inventory of their market offering: in one respect this saves the costs of holding stocks, but in another it means that any service potential that is not realized (such as when a hairdresser has 30 minutes with no customers) is lost revenue. By their very nature services are perishable, and it is rather difficult in many instances to define the outputs of a service organization. For example, what is it that an insurance company does that is a definable, measurable output analogous to the outputs of manufacturing companies? If quality control is important in service companies how is this to be measured and controlled?

As for non-profit organizations, most of these are also providers of services, and many have to arrange their affairs so as to maximize the service outputs (however they are defined) from a given budget. This requires careful cost control, so the ideas in this book have a distinct relevance to such organizations even though their motives are non-commercial.

FURTHER READING

Anthony, R.N., and Dearden, J., *Management Control Systems,* Homewood, Illinois: Irwin, 4th ed. 1980.

(A valuable text that brings together many control techniques in the context of a realistic organizational setting.)

Anthony, R.N., and Herzlinger, R.E., *Management Control in Nonprofit Organizations,* Homewood, Illinois: Irwin, Rev. ed., 1980.

(This does for non-profit management that which Anthony and Dearden does for commercial management. An excellent book.)

Barnard, C.I., *The Functions of the Executive*, Cambridge, Mass.: Harvard U.P., 1938.

(A classic that still has a lot to teach us.)

Dale, E., and Michelon, L.C., *Modern Management Methods*, Harmondsworth: Penguin, 1969.

(A very readable guide that introduces in a lucid way many quantitative and behavioural ways of thinking about management.)

Rappaport, A. (ed.), *Information for Decision-Making*, Englewood Cliffs, N.J.: Prentice-Hall, 2nd ed., 1975.

(A helpful set of readings on a range of key issues.)

Starr, M.K., *Management: A Modern Approach*, New York: Harcourt, Brace, Jovanovich, 1971.

(Very good, but for the reader who is willing to read seriously.)

Welsch, L.A., and Cyert, R.M. (eds), *Management Decision Making*, Harmondsworth: Penguin, 1970.

(An excellent set of articles on how managers behave in relation to decision making.)

Part One

COSTS

1

Costs and their Behaviour

WHAT IS COST?

The ubiquity of cost was highlighted in the Introduction: everything that a manager does, as well as many things that he fails to do, has an associated cost. This is not to suggest that the costs of taking (or not taking) a particular course of action are all identifiable or measurable. But this begs the question of what is meant by the idea of 'cost'.

Cost is characterized by the word sacrifice and, as such, it is very much in management's interests to control and reduce where possible the sacrifices involved in achieving desired results. In this broad sense cost is equivalent to sacrifices of various types, although they are not all reflected in a company's cash flow. Let us briefly consider some of the concepts of cost that we are certainly all familiar with intuitively, if not more formally.

Non-financial costs are those costs that are not directly traceable through a company's cash flow. (Whilst such costs certainly involve sacrifices and they may lead eventually, in complex ways, to a reduced cash flow in the future, they do not represent immediate cash outlays.) Psychic costs are a good example: these are the costs of mental dissatisfaction such as one might find in the lowering of the workforce's morale following a 5 per cent (rather than 10 per cent) pay rise, or on the part of manager B when C is promoted on the retirement of A. Another non-financial cost is that associated with a diminution of a company's public image if it is guilty of acts of pollution, unfair trading etc. (This cost would be reflected in a fall in the value of a company's goodwill – if only we had a satisfactory way of measuring this.)

Non-cash costs are financial sacrifices that do not involve cash outlays at the time when the cost is recognized. Two important examples of this concept are to be found in charges for depreciation and in the idea of opportunity cost.

When a long-lived asset, such as a major item of plant, is acquired for cash this transaction clearly entails a cash outlay, but since the purchase price is almost certainly deemed to be at least equivalent to the value of the asset to the business at the time of purchase there is no diminution of value, hence no sacrifice (other than in terms of financial flexibility), and hence no cost. However, as the plant is used it will physically wear out, or otherwise lose value (e.g. due to its reducing market value, or due to reasons of technological obsolescence), and this is seen as being the depreciation cost to be charged against the revenue of the business on a periodic basis. Thus depreciation charges are costs, but these costs do not represent an outflow of cash at the time the costs are recognized.

Every manager, and consumer, is accustomed to the problem of trying to cope with limited resources, which means that one is invariably unable to do all the things that one would like to do. This is the setting within which opportunity cost is most apparent: if you allocate your scarce resources to one purpose you also allocate the same resources simultaneously to another purpose. One forgoes the potential benefits of strategy X if one applies one's resources to strategy Y, and these *forgone benefits* constitute the opportunity cost of strategy Y (i.e. the sacrifice involved in pursuing Y is given by the benefits that one has to forgo by not pursuing X). It will be apparent that there is not a cash outlay corresponding to the opportunity cost of a given situation.

Cash costs are those sacrifices that are reflected in actual cash outflows. Thus when one pays one's fare for an immediate journey by some form of public transport the cost (i.e. that which one gives up) is incurred at the same time as the cash expenditure. In a corporate setting it is a reasonable approximation to equate operating expenses (excluding depreciation) with cash outlays, provided stock levels are not fluctuating in anything other than a minor way.

Business transactions usually involve both reward (or revenue) and sacrifice (or cost), with the difference between the two being gain (or profit). Thus

Reward – Sacrifice = Gain
Revenue – Cost = Profit.

In measuring the outcome from business activity this general concept of sacrifice must be simplified by being expressed in numerical terms in order that it can be manipulated in a company's accounting system. The common denominator in business is money, and it follows that cost is best represented in financial terms, despite the inherent limitations of this. (See the Preamble to Part Two, pp.114–20, for a discussion of the problems stemming from the use of the money measure in times of changing price levels).

It is important to realize that the term 'cost' only has meaning in a given context – there are different costs for different purposes, and no single cost concept is relevant in all situations.

ELEMENTS OF COST: DIRECT AND INDIRECT COSTS

If the object of interest for identifying and measuring cost is to determine how much sacrifice is involved in manufacturing a particular product, then initially one can define the three elements of total cost:

Materials
Labour
Expenses

All of these may be direct (i.e. specifically related to a given cost unit) or indirect (i.e. not specifically related to a given cost unit).

If one takes any product – such as a pair of shoes – it will be seen to consist of various inputs. Leather and thread are obvious examples of material inputs, and a labour input is necessary to make these materials into the final product. Such inputs are termed *direct costs* of the product because they are readily traceable to specific units of the product. But there are many more costs involved in making and marketing goods that are not so readily identifiable as being direct. Machinery must be used to manufacture shoes, yet the cost of using machines is considered to be a direct cost only if it can be easily measured and related to the output of shoes, and only if the machines in question are used purely for making shoes. Similarly, the cost of incidental items (such as glue and nails) can only be considered direct costs if they are used in making a particular type of shoe and their usage per unit of product can be measured. However, it is generally found that it is not worth attempting to trace the usage of incidental materials to specific units of output, and in most situations the cost of such items is considered to be an indirect cost (i.e. not directly associated with particular units of output).

Similar reasoning applies to indirect labour: a storekeeper will issue direct materials to be made into a finished product, but it would be extremely expensive and time-consuming to attempt to relate precisely the effort he spends in issuing a given type of material to the final cost of the product into which this material is incorporated.

Indirect expenditure (or overhead) covers a wide range of items that are listed in detail in Chapter 2. At this stage, however, it is important to note that the directness or otherwise of a cost depends on the base (or cost unit) to which it is related. A sales representative's salary is indirect with regard to the various products that he sells, but it is a direct cost if one is interested in the total cost of his sales territory. In the same way the costs of distributing various products to wholesalers may be indirect with regard to the goods themselves, but direct when one is concerned with costing the channel of distribution of which the wholesalers are part. A further example is the hiring of a crane which, if hired by a contractor for a given site, is a direct cost of that site's operations, but if it were hired for the general use of a factory it would become an indirect cost of the various activities of that factory.

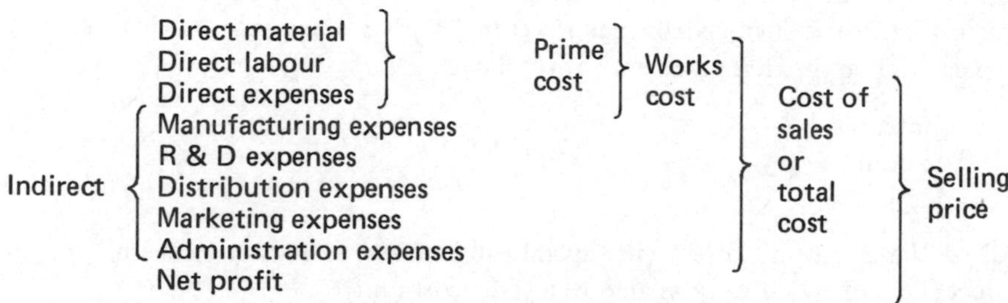

Figure 1.1: Elements of cost (using a product-costing approach)

As shown in Figure 1.1, expenses can be classified by function within a broad product-costing framework composed of all three elements of cost – material, labour, and expenses.

Direct product costs are collectively termed *prime cost* and, with the addition of manufacturing overheads, this becomes *works cost*. When the other overhead expenses are added we arrive at *total cost* (or cost of sales), and the difference between this and sales revenue is *net profit*. Gross profit, in contrast, is the difference between works cost and sales revenue. The information in profit statements is often classified as being either 'above the line' or 'below the line', and this distinguishes between those items giving rise to gross profit on the one hand, and those that reduce gross profit to net profit on the other.

Figure 1.2 shows a simple profit and loss account of the type that is often found in practice illustrating the major categories of cost. In order to demonstrate how much is hidden in aggregated figures, the data in Figure 1.2 is exploded into greater detail in Figure 1.3 which indicates the type of detail one needs if costs are to be successfully controlled.

XYZ LTD Profit and loss account for the year to 31 December, 19XX

	£'000	£'000	£'000
Sales revenue		1 000	
Works cost of goods sold		520	
Gross profit			480
Distribution expenses	90		
Marketing expenses	110		
R & D expenses	50		
Administration expenses	75		
			325
Net profit before tax			£155

Figure 1.2: Simple profit and loss account

VARIABLE COSTS

Prime product costs (direct material and direct labour) tend to vary in direct proportion to the level of activity (i.e. rate of production or sales) within a business. If the cost of leather for a pair of shoes is £1, then the cost of leather for 10 000 pairs of shoes will be £10 000. If the direct labour input is 50p per pair, then the labour cost to make 10 000 pairs will be £5 000. These are examples of *variable costs*. (It should be apparent that, with certain exceptions, variable costs are *fixed* per unit of output but are variable *in total* in relation to the level of output.)

When a factory is operating at, or near, full capacity it may be necessary for overtime to be worked and this will put the unit direct labour cost up to, say, 75p per pair of shoes produced. In such a situation the proportional relationship between direct labour cost and output still exists, although it is no longer strictly proportional. (Capacity is the topic of Chapter 3.)

The relationship between variable cost and output is demonstrated in Figure 1.4. Overhead costs are often variable – varying with the changes in the volume of activity, but they cannot be directly related to units of output.

FIXED COSTS

In contrast to variable costs, some costs do not vary in relation to the level of output during a given period of time. For example, a managing director's salary will not tend to vary with the volume of goods produced during a period, and interest payable at 10 per cent pa on a loan of £50 000 will not vary with

XYZ Ltd Detailed profit statement for year to 31 December 19XX

	Total		Product A		Product B		Product C	
	£'000 actual	% of sales	£'000 actual	% of sales	£'000 actual	% of sales	£'000 actual	% of sales
Sales	*1 000*	100.0	*200*	100.0	*300*	100.00	*500*	100.0
Direct material	260	26.0	40	20.0	100	33.33	120	24.0
Direct labour	160	16.0	30	15.0	50	16.67	80	16.0
Manufacturing expenses	100	10.0	20	10.0	25	8.33	55	11.0
Works cost	520	52.0	90	45.0	175	58.33	255	51.0
Gross profit	480	48.0	110	55.0	125	41.67	245	49.0
Distribution expenses	90	9.0	20	10.0	30	10.00	40	8.0
Marketing expenses	110	11.0	25	12.5	35	11.67	50	10.0
R & D expenses	50	5.0	15	7.5	15	5.00	20	4.0
Administration expenses	75	7.5	30	15.0	15	5.00	30	6.0
Total expenses	325	32.5	90	45.0	95	31.67	140	28.0
Net profit	155	15.5	20	10.0	30	10.00	105	21.0

Figure 1.3: Detailed profit and loss account

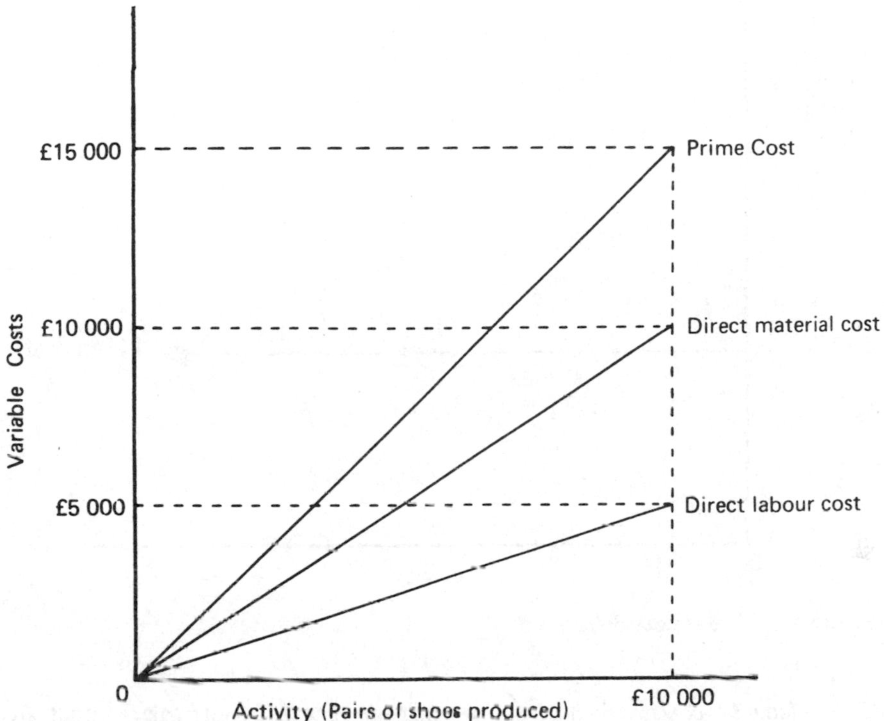

Figure 1.4: Variable cost behaviour

the level of a company's activity. Such costs are termed *fixed costs*. The time period is important because a managing director having a salary of £20 000 in 1982 – which is a fixed cost of that year – may earn £25 000 in 1983, which will be a fixed cost of that year. This difference is not due to variations in the level of output, but is rather due to the passage of time: fixed costs vary over time and not with the level of activity. (However, if one relates fixed costs to output the fixed cost *per unit of output* will vary according to the level of output. In this respect it appears variable even though, in total, it is a fixed amount.)

The basic behaviour of fixed cost is shown in Figure 1.5, but it is of greater value in connection with cost control to analyse fixed costs in the following way:

1 *Committed costs*. Costs that are primarily associated with maintaining the company's legal and physical existence, and over which management has little (if any) discretion. Insurance premiums, rates, and rent charges are typical examples.

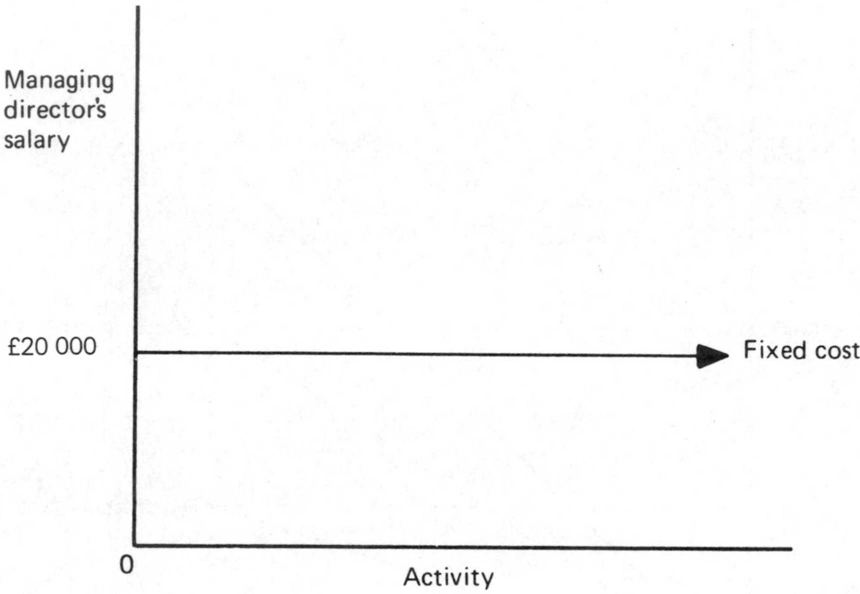

Figure 1.5: Fixed cost behaviour

2 *Managed costs.* Such costs are management and staff salaries that are related to current operations but which must continue to be paid to ensure the continued operating existence of the company.

3 *Programmed costs.* Costs that are subject both to management discretion and management control, but which are unrelated to current activities. R & D is a good example, and it will be apparent that these costs result from special policy decisions.

By classifying fixed costs in this way, and combining the result with variable cost data, Figure 1.6 can be compiled. This shows the major constituents of total cost in a way that reflects policy rather than function. (A similar analysis can be carried out on the revenue side of the profit equation.)

Being associated with time rather than with output, fixed costs will accumulate irrespective of a company's level of activity – insurance premiums, rent, and salaries will all be payable even though there is no output. On the other hand, variable costs will not accumulate at all in the absence of business activity because it is only business activity that causes them.

From a decision-making point of view, whether a cost is fixed or variable will depend upon the decision under consideration, and this will determine the appropriate time-span and hence the nature of the cost.

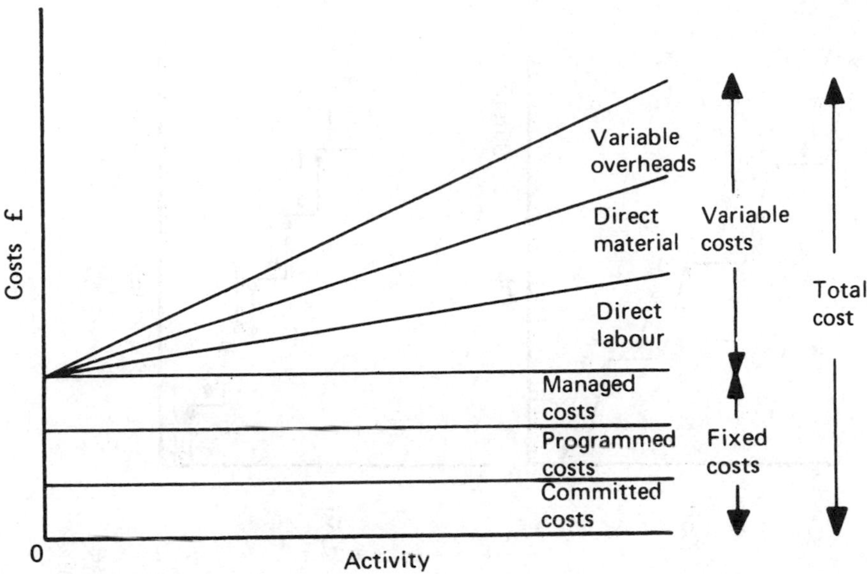

Figure 1.6: Classified cost pattern

MIXED COSTS

Certain costs are of a hybrid nature being partly fixed and partly variable. An example is found in telephone charges – the rental element is a fixed cost, whereas charges for calls made are a variable cost. Figure 1.7(a) illustrates this behaviour pattern, and Figure 1.7(b) shows the semi-variable cost behaviour that would be found if new telephones are installed as the level of business changes.

Some mixed costs are characteristically semi-fixed. Up to a given level of output it may only be necessary for a factory to work one shift and it may only need one foreman – a simple instance of a fixed supervisory cost. However, beyond that level of output it may be necessary to start a second shift and recruit a further supervisor, and this gives rise to the stepped cost pattern of Figure 1.7(c). Maintenance costs payable on a contract basis would tend to follow the pattern of Figure 1.7(d) if more machines are bought as output increases.

With mixed costs the question arises of whether to treat the cost as partly fixed and partly variable, or as wholly fixed or wholly variable. The answer must depend on the degree of variability of the cost itself and the level of activity.

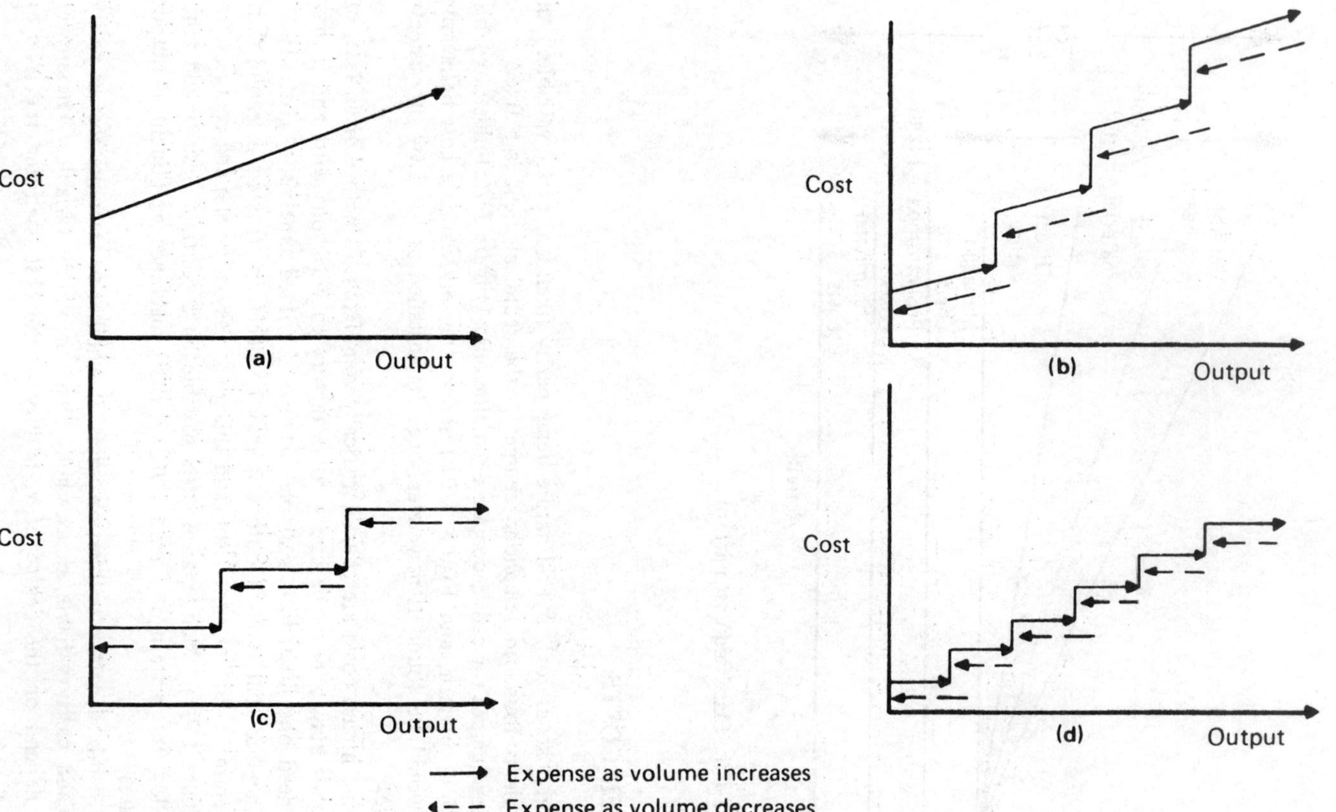

Figure 1.7: Cost behaviour patterns

SEPARATING FIXED AND VARIABLE COSTS

The total cost at any level of operations is the sum of a fixed cost component and a variable cost component. If the variable cost per unit of a particular item is £1.25, fixed costs for the period are £10 000, and the output of the period is 12 000 units, then the total cost will be:

Total cost	=	Fixed cost	+	Variable cost
£25 000	=	£10 000	+	£(12 000 × 1.25)

When the values of the fixed and variable components are unknown it is possible to estimate them so long as the total costs are known for any two levels of activity. The procedure is as follows:

1. Deduct total cost at the lower of the two levels from total cost at the higher level. Since fixed costs do not vary with volume, the difference must be entirely composed of variable costs.
2. Divide the difference in cost by the difference in volume (i.e. units produced) to give the unit variable cost.
3. Multiply one observed level of activity by the unit variable cost and deduct this from the total cost of that level to give the fixed cost component.

The following example will clarify the method fully:

Total cost at output of 15 000 units per period:		£25 000
Total cost at output of 10 000 units per period:		£20 000
Difference	5 000 units	£5 000

The unit variable cost is therefore £5 000/5 000 = £1.

At the higher level of activity the variable cost must be 15 000 × £1 = £15 000. Since total cost is £25 000 it follows that fixed costs must be £10 000. (This answer can be checked by applying the same reasoning to the lower level of activity.)

This method is simple and rather crude. More refined statistical techniques can be applied to obtain more precise results. One such technique is the method of least squares which involves plotting several observed levels of cost and their associated levels of activity on a scattergraph (see Figure 1.8) and then applying statistical analysis to fit the best line through these points. Fixed costs are given where the fitted curve cuts the vertical axis, and the variable cost element is found by dividing the balance of the cost at any volume by the volume itself.

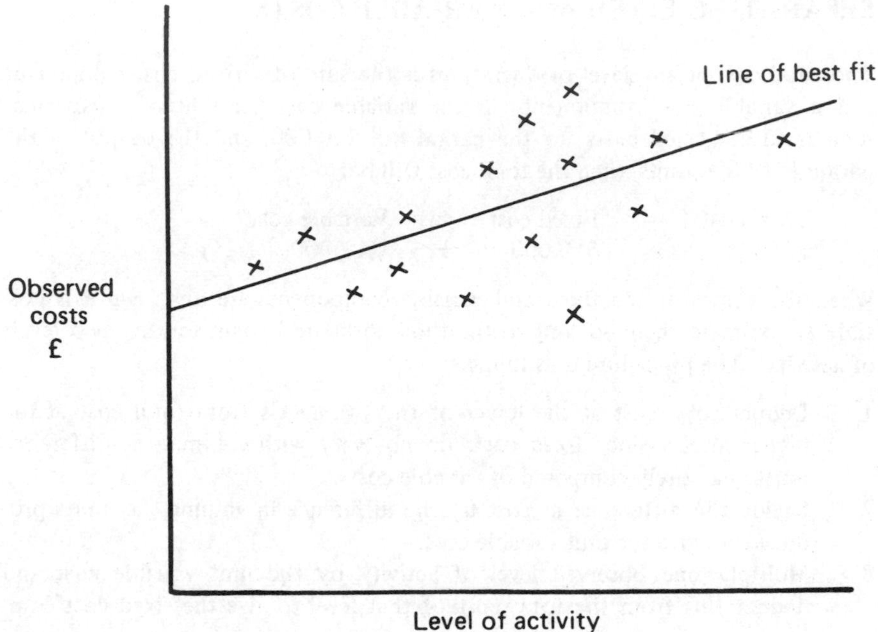

Figure 1.8: Scattergraph

USEFULNESS OF THE FIXED-VARIABLE SPLIT

The importance of separating variable from fixed costs stems from the different behaviour patterns of each, which have a significant bearing on their control: variable costs must be controlled in relation to the level of activity, whilst fixed costs must be controlled in relation to time. From a decision-making point of view, it is also important to know whether or not a particular cost will vary as a result of a given decision.

By taking a company's (or division's) total fixed cost curve and plotting it (as in Figure 1.9(a)), and then adding the variable cost curve for the expected possible levels of activity in a forthcoming period, the total cost curve shown in Figure 1.9(b) is obtained. Alternatively, if the variable costs are plotted initially (Figure 1.9(c)) and then the fixed costs added (Figure 1.9(d)), the same total cost curve is obtained but by another means.

Because fixed costs must be incurred even when there is no activity, the fixed cost curve (and hence the total cost curve) cuts the vertical axis above the origin, and this results in the total cost curve being proportional – but not strictly proportional – to the level of activity.

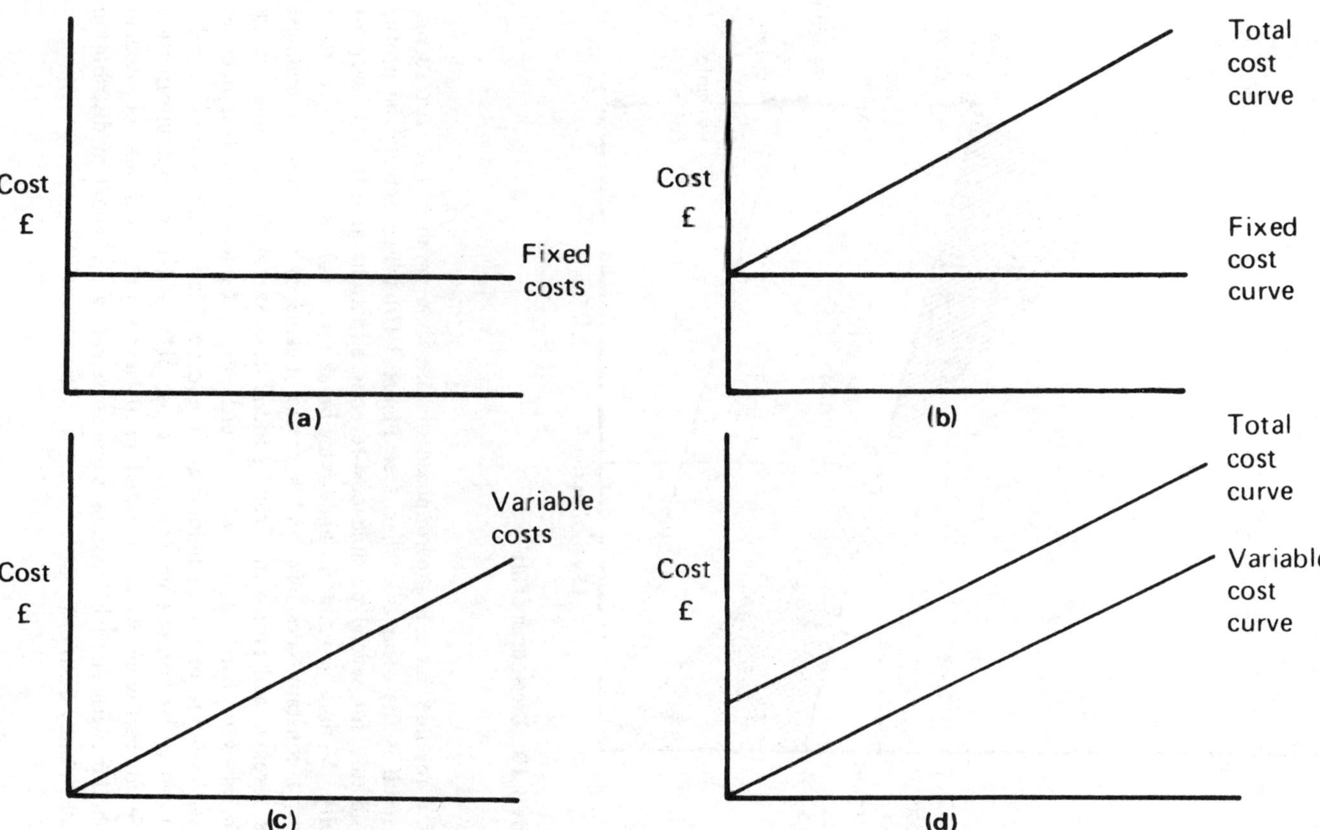

Figure 1.9: Total cost curves

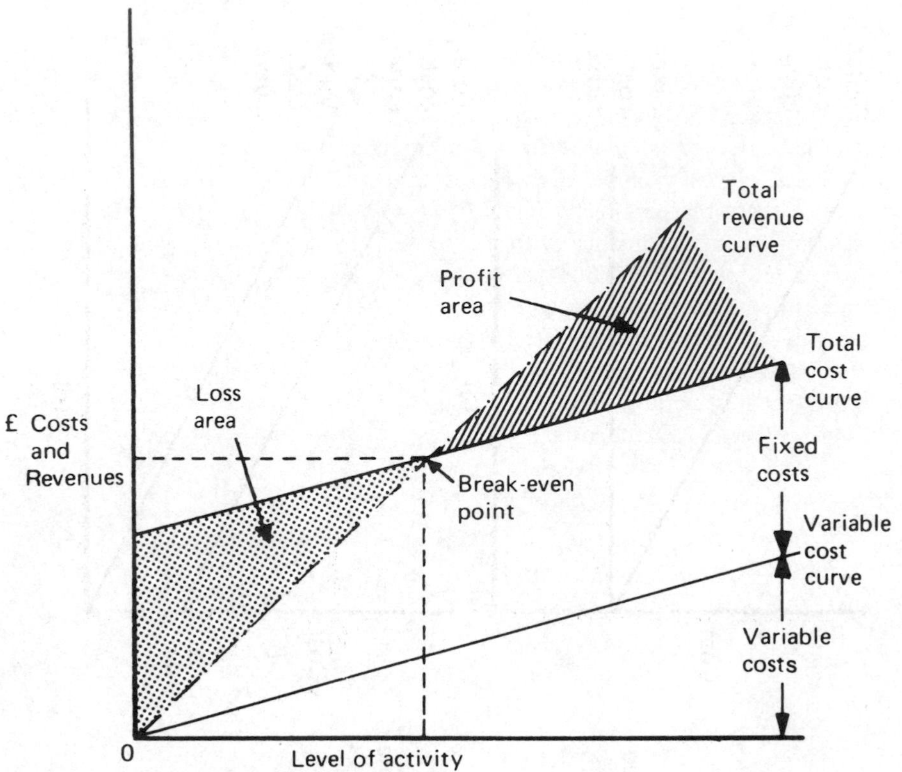

Figure 1.10: Break-even chart

If a revenue curve is superimposed on the same graph as the cost curves, the result is the break-even chart (see Figure 1.10) which depicts the profit/loss picture for several possible cost-revenue situations at different levels of activity. Various assumptions underlying break-even analysis – such as constant prices, a constant sales mix, and a greater degree of independence amongst costs, revenue, and profits than can be found in most real-life situations – make the break-even chart a basic tool. Nevertheless, provided its user appreciates the static nature of this technique he should be able to employ it effectively.

In particular, break-even analysis is useful as a background information device for reviewing overall cost and profit levels, but it can also be used in connection with special decisions such as selecting a channel of distribution or make-or-buy decisions.

SUMMARY

Cost is synonymous with sacrifice, but its precise definition will depend on the situation in which a measure of sacrifice is required – different cost concepts are relevant to different sets of circumstances.

There are only three elements of cost: materials, labour, and expenses. Any of these can be directly related to a cost unit or indirectly related. Costs that change in accordance with the level of activity are termed variable and have a different behaviour pattern from fixed costs which only vary with time. Some costs are partly fixed and partly variable, but it is possible to separate the two types by statistical means. Break-even analysis and other techniques that are relevant in the context of cost control are based on these important distinctions between variable costs and fixed costs, and between direct costs and indirect costs.

2

Overheads — A Problem Area

WHAT ARE OVERHEADS?

An *overhead cost* is one that is essential in some way to a company's operations, but which cannot be related in a direct way to units of output. The case of the storekeeper given in Chapter 1 (page 9) is a typical example of an overhead cost. This is an example of an indirect labour overhead cost – overhead costs are, by definition, indirect costs. *Overhead* is the aggregate of indirect material costs, indirect labour costs, and indirect expenses. In other words, any cost that is not covered by one of the elements of prime cost (which is made up of direct material, direct labour, and direct expenses – see Figure 1.1) is part of the overhead. (Synonyms for overhead that are in current use are 'burden' and 'oncost'.)

Example

The receipt of a straightforward order from a customer for an item carried in stock will give rise to a whole array of overhead costs. Amongst these are:

1 Interpretation of customer's order
2 Transcription of order onto a standard form

3 Checking of customer's credit rating
4 Checking inventory for stock availability
5 Picking item from stock
6 Packing item for despatch to customer
7 Despatch
8 Preparation of invoice
9 Related book-keeping
10 Collection of amount due from customer.

If the item is out of stock it may be necessary to add a large number of additional overhead cost activities to the list. In particular the following should be considered:

1 Checking design
2 Issuing production order
3 Scheduling production
4 Setting up machines
5 Expediting production
6 Inspecting items produced
7 Materials handling activities
8 Warehousing finished goods.

INCREASING IMPORTANCE OF OVERHEADS

In general terms the importance of overhead costs to a particular company will depend on the size of that company along with the nature of its product range (hence its technology) and the characteristics of the markets it serves.

Complex manufacturing processes for products involving advanced technology, coupled with long channels of distribution (e.g. manufacturer/wholesaler/retailer/consumer), will tend to be associated with a high level of overheads in the factory, in the laboratory, in the administrative system, and in the marketing operation.

Conversely, simple products that are sold direct to consumers from a base of low capital investment will tend to be associated with a low level of overheads.

The importance of overhead costs is increasing because the proportion of total costs that are of an indirect nature is growing. This trend is shown, for instance, in the steady rise in the proportion of employees engaged in administrative, clerical, and technical work in manufacturing industry in Great Britain. The current figure is in excess of 25 per cent of those employed, and a similar pattern exists in the U.S.A.

Characteristics of this increasing importance of overhead costs include:

1 Large-scale operations
2 Specialization
3 Product diversification
4 Competitive pressures
5 Widening markets
6 Technological development
7 Automation
8 Increasing complexity.

Advanced technology demands a large amount of capital investment if it is to be successfully incorporated into manufacturing processes and products. This must inevitably take place in an atmosphere of complexity, and this is associated with a high proportion of indirect costs.

As the level of automation increases, it will bring a higher level of capital investment per employee, and the amount of overhead cost will become increasingly important. Automation entails a reduction in direct labour costs and an increase in overhead costs, an increasing proportion of which will be of a fixed nature (e.g. depreciation charges, equipment rental/lease payments, etc.). An increasing number of machines requires an increasing amount of maintenance, and whether this is carried out internally or by maintenance contracts with suppliers of equipment, it will lead to further overhead costs.

CATEGORIES OF OVERHEAD COST

Overhead costs can be categorized in various ways depending on the purpose. The basic classification of such costs into fixed, variable, and mixed categories along the lines of the discussion in Chapter 1 should be readily appreciated. It should be noted, however, that the fixed/variable split is not the same as the direct/indirect split: variability relates to cost behaviour, whereas directness is concerned with the identifying of specific costs with a given cost unit.

Examples of fixed, variable, and mixed overhead costs are the managing director's salary, salesmen's commission payments, and telephone charges respectively.

An alternative form of categorization is that of overhead costs into *natural* and *functional* groups.

A natural cost is one that is classified according to its basic nature: salaries is one example, and under a natural costing system all salaries would be gathered together as a total for this item. The same would also be done for motor expenses, professional charges, postage payments, and so forth.

The categorizing of costs according to their nature is not very useful from a cost control viewpoint. (The reasons behind this statement will be explored more fully in Chapters 4 and 6, but it will suffice at this point to emphasize that cost control can only be effective if individuals are held responsible for the costs over which they have authority. Whilst the managing director of a company ultimately is responsible for the natural cost category labelled 'salaries', he cannot be expected to control this item in the way that a departmental manager can control the salary cost of those who are employed in his department.) Another basis is therefore desirable – the functional basis.

The major activities in most companies are grouped under the headings of:

Administration
Marketing and selling
Distribution
Manufacturing
Research and development

These are the *functions* according to which overhead costs can be allocated and controlled under the functional cost framework. Many costs – such as salaries – will be found in all functional areas, but others – such as directors' fees – will be quite specific to one function.

Natural costs can be allocated to functional cost categories on a cause-and-effect basis. The natural cost heading of 'rents for buildings' may total £10 000, but on inspection it may be found that this is made up of four particular items of cost:

	£
Rent of laboratory	2 500
Rent of warehouse for finished goods	5 000
Rent of flat for managing director	1 000
Rent of warehouse for raw materials	1 500
Total of natural cost heading	10 000

Functionally, therefore, these constituent cost items will be allocated as follows:

Item of cost	*Function*
Laboratory	R & D
Finished goods warehouse	Distribution
Managing director's flat	Administration
Raw materials warehouse	Manufacturing

Figure 2.1 illustrates the way in which overhead costs (of the fixed, variable and mixed varieties) can be classified under functional expense headings. Within

these headings, of course, it is convenient to use natural cost categories so that all the salaries for the administrative function are listed together, and so on for office expenses, etc.

When classified in this way (i.e. as a *chart of accounts*) the full range of overhead cost-incurring activities that are carried out by the company can be seen at a glance. Furthermore, thought, discussion, and other considerations that lie behind the compiling of a detailed chart of accounts should give all concerned a greater appreciation of the workings of the company coupled with an explicit awareness of the particular overhead activities (hence costs) that are the responsibility of the respective functional heads.

It is important that the chart of accounts is agreed by management and compiled with its full cooperation. This is so because the chart should represent the desired operational framework of the company (albeit in abstracted form) and is consequently much more than a mere accountant's book-keeping convenience.

The over-riding limitation of the chart shown in Figure 2.1 is that it fails to show the *purpose* of the various expenses. (It shows what expenses were incurred, under which functions they were incurred, and thus – implicitly – by whom they were incurred, and one could easily ascertain when they were incurred, but there is no real clue as to *why* they were incurred.) In Chapter 8 (on budgeting) this point will be developed further since the approach that emphasizes the purpose for which different expenses are incurred is termed *output budgeting*. There will also be further references to it in Chapter 15 (on project management aspects within R & D).

Once compiled, the chart of accounts serves as the list of overhead account headings that make up the basic book-keeping system (normally contained in the *nominal ledger*), and indirect costs will be debited (and sundry receipts credited) against the appropriate account. (To be complete this chart requires the addition of direct costs and revenues, and assets and liabilities.)

In classifying overhead costs, two points in practice are worthy of emphasis:

1 There is disagreement among managers and accountants concerning whether or not certain costs are direct or indirect. A common example is overtime premiums (e.g. the 'half' in 'time and a half') paid to direct production workers. There is no definitive answer – the treatment of such items must be a matter for individual companies.
2 Closely related to the above point is the fact that some direct costs are treated as overheads because it is *impossible* to associate them with units of productive output (e.g. supervisory salaries), whereas other direct costs may be treated as overheads because it is *inconvenient* to trace them to units of output (e.g. glue, electricity consumed, etc.).

CHART OF ACCOUNTS: CLASSIFIED OVERHEADS

ADMINISTRATION	*R & D*	*MANUFACTURING*	*MARKETING*	*DISTRIBUTION*
Salaries	*Salaries*	*Salaries*	*Salaries*	*Salaries*
Directors	Executives	Executives	Executives	Executives
Executives	Technical	Clerical/secretarial	Representatives	Clerical/secretarial
Clerical/secretarial	Clerical/secretarial	staff	Clerical/secretarial	staff
staff	staff	Hourly paid	staff	Hourly paid
Temporary staff	Hourly paid	*Expenses*	*Commission*	*Expenses*
Expenses	*Expenses*	Travelling	Executives	Travelling
Travelling	Travelling	Motor	Representatives	Motor
Motor	Motor	Entertaining	Agents	Entertaining
Entertaining	Entertaining	Other	*Royalties payable*	Other
Other	Other	*Departmental*	*Expenses*	*Transport*
Office expenses	*Laboratory*	*expenses*	Travelling	Fleet supervision
Stationery	Services	Progress	Motor	Road fund tax
Telephone and telex	Consultants' fees	Goods inwards	Entertaining	Insurances
Postages	Safety costs	Time-keeping	Other	Painting and
Mail room/reception	Cleaning	Tool room	*Office expenses*	lettering
Cleaning	Maintenance	Production control	Stationery	Garage expenses
Hire of equipment	Hire of equipment	Purchasing	Telephone and telex	Vehicle running
Maintenance of	Consumable items	Personnel	Postages	costs
equipment	Sundry materials	Drawing office	Cleaning	Vehicle
Depreciation of	Samples	Maintenance	Hire of equipment	maintenance
equipment	*General*	Quality control	Maintenance of	costs
EDP expenses	Patent cost	*General*	equipment	Vehicle hire charges
Data preparation	Trademark costs	Training costs	Depreciation of	Depreciation
Operating costs	(Royalties	Services (eg,	equipment	*Warehousing*
Systems and	receivable)	boilerhouse)	*General expenses*	Rates and rent
programming	Subscriptions	Waste disposal	Training costs	Insurances
Stationery	Training costs	Heat, light, power	Recruitment	Hire of equipment

Financial expenses
- Audit fees
- Bank charges
- Interest payable
- Directors' fees
- Superannuation
- Secretarial/registrar
- Insurances

General expenses
- Training costs
- Heat, light, power
- Subscriptions and donations
- Security
- Personnel and welfare
- Canteen expenses
- Legal and other charges
- Hire of premises
- Rates
- Maintenance
- Amortization
- Telephone and telex
- Insurances
- Rent and rates
- Depreciation

- Insurances
- Rent and rates
- Protective clothing
- Fire and safety equipment
- Security
- Laundering
- Cleaning
- Sundry materials
- Scrap
- Telephone and telex
- Canteen expenses
- Subscriptions
- Hire of machinery
- Depreciation of machinery

- Subscriptions
- Hire of premises
- Maintenance
- Amortization
- Bad debts
- Legal expenses
- Discounts given
- Insurances
- Sales administration

Promotion expenses
- Sales samples
- Catalogues/price lists
- Advertising agency fees
- Media costs
- Production costs
- PR fees and expenses

Marketing research
- Agency fees
- Data processing charges
- Subscriptions

- Maintenance of equipment
- Depreciation of equipment
- Stocktaking costs

Despatch
- Packing and packaging
- Sundry materials
- Carriage outwards
- Insurances
- Maintenance of equipment
- Depreciation of equipment

General
- Canteen expenses
- Telephone and telex
- Training costs
- Heat, light, power

Figure 2.1: Chart of accounts: classified overheads

SUMMARY

Overhead costs are those that cannot be traced directly to units of output. An increasing proportion of costs are of this indirect nature for various reasons (mainly relating to technological developments).

Whilst the classification of overhead costs according to their behaviour patterns (over timc in the case of fixed costs, against the level of activity in the case of variable costs, and in relation to both time and activity in the case of mixed costs) is of fundamental significance, another important way of categorizing these costs is under natural and functional headings. In a cost control context the latter category (functional classification) is more useful than the former (natural classification).

The chart of accounts is the basis of both overall cost control and of the accounting system.

3

The Importance of Capacity

THE CONCEPT OF CAPACITY

The aims of both society and management are usually best satisfied by the efficient utilization of manufacturing capacity. Investment in productive assets – factories, machines, etc. – that are not used within reasonable limits of their potential capacity suggests an absence of sound judgement in their selection. Furthermore, profits are reduced in proportion to the cost of the unused capacity when this situation exists.

By far the majority of manufacturing organizations begin as small firms, but their success and their growth into large undertakings will depend to a large extent upon the way in which they utilize their available capacity. A given level of investment in plant and equipment can only facilitate a limited output. When the level of activity approaches this limit a decision must be taken in connection with the desirability of further investment, and this will depend on such factors as:

1 The market demand for the company's output.
2 The amount of new investment proposed.
3 The link between 1 and 2 – the ability to make effective use of additional capacity.

A company's capacity determines its level of fixed costs. For this reason fixed costs are often termed *establishment costs* – i.e. they are incurred to support an organization of a given size for a given period of time. The maximum level of output that can be supported will (in principle at least) be given when there are three 8 hour shifts working 7 days each week for 52 weeks a year. The minimum level of output from a particular level of fixed costs that one would *usually* expect to encounter is one shift working up to 40 hours each week for about 48 weeks each year.

The frequently-met imperative 'spread your overheads' can be vividly illustrated from these two examples of capacity utilization. If a company has an establishment cost (i.e. fixed overheads) of, say, £200 000 per annum and it operates at maximum capacity with 100 machines, then it will use 873 600 machine hours per annum.

Total = hours per shift × number of shifts × days × weeks × number of machines
873 600 = 8 × 3 × 7 × 52 × 100

In contrast, the use of only one shift for 40 hours per week over 48 weeks gives 192 000 machine hours.

Total = hours per week × number of shifts × weeks × number of machines
192 000 = 40 × 1 × 48 × 100

The fixed overhead cost per machine hour in the first case is:

$$\frac{200\,000}{873\,600} = 23\text{p}$$

and in the second case it is:

$$\frac{200\,000}{192\,000} = £1.04$$

The range is great. If it takes 4 machine hours to produce a final product that has a variable cost (direct labour input plus direct material input plus an apportioned element of variable overhead) of £2.00, the full product cost at maximum capacity will be:

Variable cost + (machine hours × fixed cost rate)
£2.00 + £(4 × 0.23) = £2.96

At the lower level of capacity utilization the full cost of a unit of production will be:

£2.00 + £(4 × 1.04) = £6.16

If selling price per unit is £6.25, the profit consequences (assuming that at least 873 600 ÷ 4 = 218 400 units can be sold) would be:

At maximum capacity utilization (£6.25 – £2.96) × 218 400 = £718 536
At low capacity utilization (£6.25 – £6.16) × (192 000 ÷ 4) = £4 320

These extreme examples – despite their obvious artificiality – indicate quite clearly the importance of an efficient utilization of available capacity.

It is necessary, however, to consider further the way in which capacity utilization (which is equivalent to the level of productive activity or output) can be measured and to relate this to cost behaviour. Both the behaviour of costs and the utilization of capacity are important factors in considering the whole question of cost control, and, subsequently, cost reduction.

MEASURING CAPACITY – CRITERIA OF CHOICE

Variable costs are proportional to the level of activity and fixed costs *per unit of output* are *inversely* proportional to the level of activity (whilst being constant in total within a specified period and range). But how can this level of activity best be measured? And should the same measure be used for variable costs as for fixed costs? Is it better to use a measure based on inputs (such as machine hours) or one based on outputs (such as units of finished product)? Whatever basis is chosen, should it be expressed in physical terms or in financial terms?

In the simplified case of a single product firm, it is easy to use a measure of activity expressed in terms of physical units of output, but in multiproduct firms this would be tantamount to adding apples to pears. As a result, factors such as the following should be considered in selecting a unit of measurement:

1 The cause of cost variability (where this is relevant), which may be labour hours, machine hours, or units produced, bearing in mind that some costs (e.g. machine depreciation) do not vary in accordance with some measures of activity (e.g. labour hours).

2 The adequacy of control over the basis selected. An index of activity that is based on actual labour hours, for example, will vary with the level of efficiency experienced and is thus not a uniform base. Standard labour hours (see Chapters 9 and 10) provide a better base since they do not fluctuate with effort.

3 The independence of the unit of activity selected. Ideally this unit should not be affected by variables other than volume. On account of fluctuations in the level of prices caused by inflation it is generally preferable to use a physical unit of measure such as units of output or machine hours.

4 The ease of understanding. This is important but it must not cause an inappropriate basis to be selected merely because it is easier to understand than an appropriate one. (An *appropriate* basis in this context is one that facilitates the determination of cost behaviour in relation to capacity utilization.)

The level of output (or volume of activity) of a company is often expressed as a percentage of capacity (where full capacity is equal to 100 per cent.) This concept can also be used to describe the level of activity within a single productive department of the company. For this measure to be meaningful it is necessary to express both the level of output and full capacity in common terms (such as direct standard labour hours, units of output, etc.) under the criteria discussed above. But what constitutes full capacity?

MEASURING CAPACITY – BASES

The following four major bases can be used:

1 Normal activity
2 Expected activity
3 Practical capacity
4 Ideal capacity

In practice only the first two have general applicability for the reasons given below.

Normal Activity

This can be defined as the rate of activity needed to meet average sales demand over a period that is sufficiently long to cover seasonal, cyclical and trend variations in the pattern of demand for the company's products. (A period of 3–5 years is commonly taken as being suitable.) Such a rate of activity will be influenced very largely by market factors in conjunction with the physical limits of plant capacity. If sales do not vary much from year to year, this base will be equivalent to expected activity (see next section), and a rule of thumb is to take normal activity to represent 75 per cent – 90 per cent of practical capacity (see below).

Since the rates set on the basis of normal activity are intended to last for several years, it follows that they will be unaffected by variations in the annual level of overhead costs from year to year. This means that, for the duration of the base period, there will be uniformity of product cost so far as overhead allocations are concerned, and this obviates the requirement for repeated revisions of overhead absorption rates as constituent costs vary over time. Furthermore, if cost-based pricing methods are employed, the adoption of normal activity as the base avoids unnecessarily changing prices following variations in overhead rates.

An illustration will show how a measure of capacity based on normal activity over 4 years can level out fluctuations in cost levels and simplify pricing decisions where cost-plus pricing is used.

Figure 3.1 shows, for each of the 4 years, the output, overheads, and annualized overhead rate per unit of output.

Year (A)	*Units of output* (B)	*Overheads* (C)	*Overhead per unit* (C) ÷ (B) = (D)
1	30 000	£45 000	£1.50
2	40 000	£50 000	£1.25
3	60 000	£66 000	£1.10
4	50 000	£60 000	£1.20
	180 000	£221 000	£1.23

Figure 3.1: Annual overhead rates

Year (A)	*Overhead per unit* (B)	*Direct cost per unit* (C)	*Total cost* (B)+(C)=(D)	*Price* (E)	*Profit* (E)−(D)=(F)
1	£1.50	£3.00	£4.50	£5.18	£0.68
2	£1.25	£3.00	£4.25	£4.89	£0.64
3	£1.10	£3.00	£4.10	£4.71	£0.61
4	£1.20	£3.00	£4.20	£4.83	£0.63

Figure 3.2: Data for pricing

It is assumed in Figure 3.2 that the cost of direct inputs (i.e. prime cost) remains constant per unit at £3.00 and that price is set at total cost (column (D)) plus 15 per cent. (Thus price per unit in year 1 is equal to $\frac{115}{100} \times$ £4.50 = £5.18.) This pricing policy results in the unit profit figures shown in column (F).

The summary of Figure 3.3 shows the annual profit figure that results from the policy of basing price on costs, which in turn are based on annually computed overhead absorption rates.

Now let us consider the outcome if the overhead rate is set at £1.25 per unit for all of the 4 years, and the selling price per unit is set at £5.00. (This, of course, presumes that the normal activity averages out at 45 000 units per annum, and the absorption rate is calculated on the assumption that overhead costs for the period will amount to £225 000 (i.e. £225 000 ÷ (45 000 × 4) = £1.25).)

Year (A)	*Units of output* (B)	*Total cost* (C)	*Total Revenue* (D)	*Total profit* (D)−(C)=(F)
1	30 000	£135 000	£155 400	£20 400
2	40 000	£170 000	£195 600	£25 600
3	60 000	£246 000	£282 600	£36 600
4	50 000	£210 000	£241 500	£31 500
	180 000	£761 000	£875 100	£114 100

Figure 3.3: Summary on annual rate basis

By adopting a normal activity basis there is no need to revise annual overhead rates, and consequently there is no need to revise product costs (i.e. direct costs plus overhead rate = £3.00 + £1.25 = £4.25). When cost-plus pricing is used there is no need, therefore, to revise prices for the duration of the base period (unless, of course, direct costs vary). This pattern of stability is portrayed by Figure 3.4 which shows that the averaging process results in overheads of £225 000 (column (C)) being charged against revenue in contrast with actual overheads of £221 000 (see column (C) of Figure 3.1). Despite this over-absorption, under the assumed conditions, the longer-term characteristics of the normal capacity base have resulted in profits of £135 000 whilst the annualized basis with all its variations has led to profits of only £114 100.

Year (A)	*Units* (B)	*Applied overheads* (B)×£1.25 =(C)	*Direct costs* (B)×£3.00 =(D)	*Total costs* (C)+(D) =(E)	*Total revenue* (B)×£5.00 =(F)	*Profit* (F)−(E) =(G)
1	30 000	£37 500	£90 000	£127 500	£150 000	£22 500
2	40 000	£50 000	£120 000	£170 000	£200 000	£30 000
3	60 000	£75 000	£180 000	£255 000	£300 000	£45 000
4	50 000	£62 500	£150 000	£212 500	£250 000	£37 500
	180 000	£225 000	£540 000	£765 000	£900 000	£135 000

Figure 3.4: Normal activity base

Expected activity

The expected activity (alternatively known as expected annual volume) is the rate of activity that is expected to prevail over the next year (i.e. it is the annualized basis illustrated in the previous section.) This method is considered to be more appropriate than normal activity when environmental conditions prevent reliable forecasts being made for periods in excess of one year. As with the normal activity method, expected activity may be expressed as a percentage of practical capacity (see next section).

A representative example would be that of a small jobbing engineering company. By the very nature of its operation it would be impossible to predict a normal level of activity for 3–5 years. It is difficult to do this even for one year, but an estimate can be made on the basis of available resources (i.e. on the basis of available inputs) as opposed to output. If one department in the company has 10 capstan lathes in use and these are used for 40 hours each week for the equivalent of 48 weeks per year, then the total potential machine capacity is given by:

$$\begin{array}{lcccccc} \text{Total} & = & \text{hours per week} & \times & \text{weeks per year} & \times & \text{number of machines} \\ 19\,200 & = & 40 & \times & 48 & \times & 10 \end{array}$$

An allowance must be made for machine breakdowns, routine maintenance, waiting time, etc., and let us assume that this is 20 per cent. The measure of potential expected activity (expressed in machine hours) for the department now becomes:

$$19\,200 \times 4/5 = 15\,360$$

Further allowances would have to be made if overtime (positive allowance) or labour disputes (negative allowance) are to be accommodated.

This example relates labour hours to machine hours in that 19 200 is the measure of available direct labour hours (equals 100 per cent) and 15 360 is the equivalent measure of available machine hours (equals 100 per cent of expected activity but only 80 per cent of ideal capacity – see below).

Practical capacity

This measure represents the maximum level of activity at which a company can *realistically operate at full efficiency*. This allows for unavoidable operating interruptions (such as the need for maintenance work to be carried out and waiting time) which means that practical capacity is less than ideal capacity – see next section. Nevertheless, the concept of practical capacity is an introspective engineering concept that pays no attention to current (or expected) demand conditions. The effectiveness of the measure depends on stability of demand giving stability of operations. In other words, given a ready market for its output and no distribution problems, practical capacity is that level of activity at which most managements would wish to operate.

Ideal capacity

This is the maximum number of operating hours that could be available ignoring the stoppages due to downtime, repairs, etc. No attention is paid to demand conditions which emphasizes the artificial nature of the measure. It represents a theoretical ideal that can be used as a benchmark: for example, practical capacity is usually taken to be 75 per cent to 85 per cent of ideal capacity. (The earlier example of 3 shifts working 7 days each week all the year round is an example of an idealized measure of capacity.)

Relationship between the different concepts of capacity

The relationship amongst these concepts of capacity is shown in Figure 3.5. (Normal activity is, for simplicity, taken to include expected activity in this diagram.) Between the 100 per cent maximum of ideal capacity and the more realistic practical capacity there is a gap due to inevitable but acceptable interruptions, considered from the viewpoint of the industrial engineer. A further gap exists between practical capacity and normal capacity which allows for the contingencies of uncertainty and environmental fluctuations.

Whilst ideal capacity is beyond human attainment, judgement is both important and necessary in selecting a capacity base from amongst the other three. Care must also be taken in specifying the unit of measurement to be adopted – machine hours, units of output, or whatever. In this respect the criteria for selecting a base measure for fixed costs may not be the same as those behind the selection of a base measure for variable overhead costs. These latter costs should be linked to an activity base that most closely reflects fluctuations in variable overheads. (If variable overheads are mainly composed of indirect labour costs of one type and another, it would follow that labour hours represent a better base than do, say, units of output.) Since fixed costs (in total) only vary with time rather than with the usual bases of activity measurement (such as machine hours), it is recommended that these be related to a base that best reflects the physical capacity that the fixed costs support. This permits a measure of capacity utilization to be readily derived. To take a simple example, machine hours may represent the physical capacity constraint of a company. If total available machine hours for a period are 10 000 and the fixed costs for the same period are £20 000 this gives an overhead rate for fixed costs of £2.00 per machine hour. If only 7 500 machine hours are used it is possible to measure the establishment cost of having idle capacity:

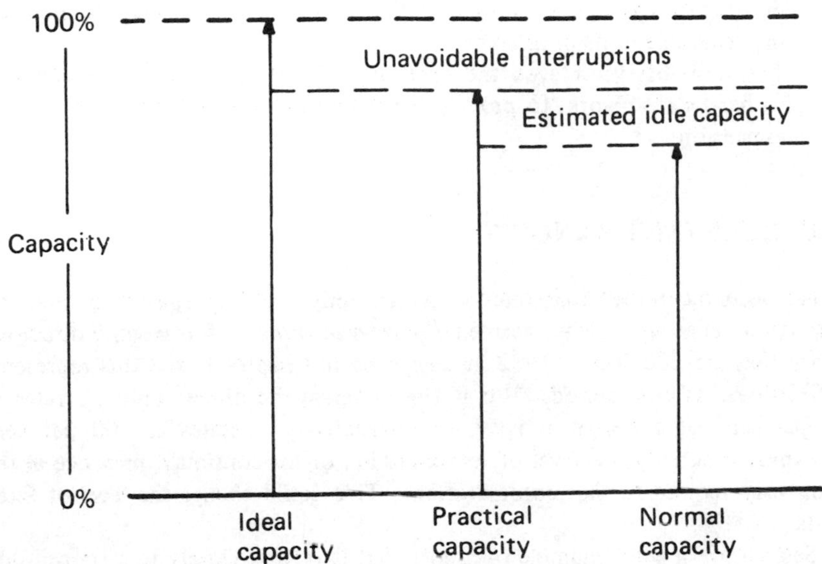

Figure 3.5: Capacity measurement

Capacity	10 000 machine hours
Establishment cost	£20 000
Establishment cost per hour	£2.00
Hours used	7 500
Hours unused	2 500
Establishment cost of unused hours	2 500 × £2 = £5 000.

This example demonstrates that fixed costs determine the limit of available productive capacity, and the cost of not being able to make full use of these facilities can easily be worked out.

In a cost control sense it must be pointed out that little – if anything – can be done in the short term to control the costs of providing capacity. This discussion has been intended to show the importance of relating costs to a capacity base as a check that the best use is being made *under prevailing conditions* of the capacity that is available. There are limitations on the effective use of capacity, and amongst the most frequently-met reasons for this are the following:

1 The difficulty of predicting the exact times that may be required to perform new manufacturing operations.
2 Unavoidable delays – repair schedules, emergency repairs, absenteeism, waiting time – that cause hold ups (or bottlenecks) in one part of the

production cycle even though another part of the cycle may be proceeding according to its programme.

3 The desirability, or even the necessity, of having some reserve capacity to handle rush work, to provide for emergencies, and to anticipate future expansion.

THE RELEVANT RANGE

It has been mentioned that fixed costs are only fixed in relation to time and through a range of activity, termed *the relevant range*. A managing director's salary may be £20 000 in 1982 as suggested in Chapter 1, and this represents a fixed cost of that period. But if the company he directs only operates at 10 per cent of expected activity, or alternatively operates at 200 per cent of expected activity, his level of remuneration or his continued presence at the helm may require further consideration. This could change the level of fixed costs.

Salaries are a good example of a cost that is related closely to responsibility and the size of an undertaking. For this reason top management in a large company earns more than its counterpart in a small one. Costs of an establishment nature are related to the size (hence capacity) of an organization, and this relationship can be expressed in the concept of the relevant range.

A factory may be geared up to producing between 60 000 and 100 000 units of output per period, and its fixed costs will be a major determinant of this potential. However, if output falls below 60 000 units it may be necessary to close down part of the plant, dismiss executive staff, and cut fixed costs in other ways as well. On the other hand, if output exceeds 100 000 units, the need for further investment in plant and equipment, executive recruitment, and so forth must be considered – i.e. an increase in the level of fixed costs must be contemplated. (Obviously temporary fluctuations in demand will not result in drastic alterations in the capacity base, but prevailing trends over several periods are likely to have this outcome.)

Graphically the situation is shown in Figure 3.6. Fixed costs will not change when output is within the relevant range of 60 000 to 100 000 units per period. However, at either end of this range a change in the level of fixed costs is quite possible. From this it will be appreciated that discussions of capacity (other than those concerned with further investment in new capacity or, alternatively, divestment of existing capacity) will be in relation to the relevant range.

Within the context of variable costs there is also a relevant range. Figure 1.4 illustrated variable cost behaviour in a very fundamental way. However, the variable cost curve is likely to be curvilinear (as in Figure 3.7) rather than

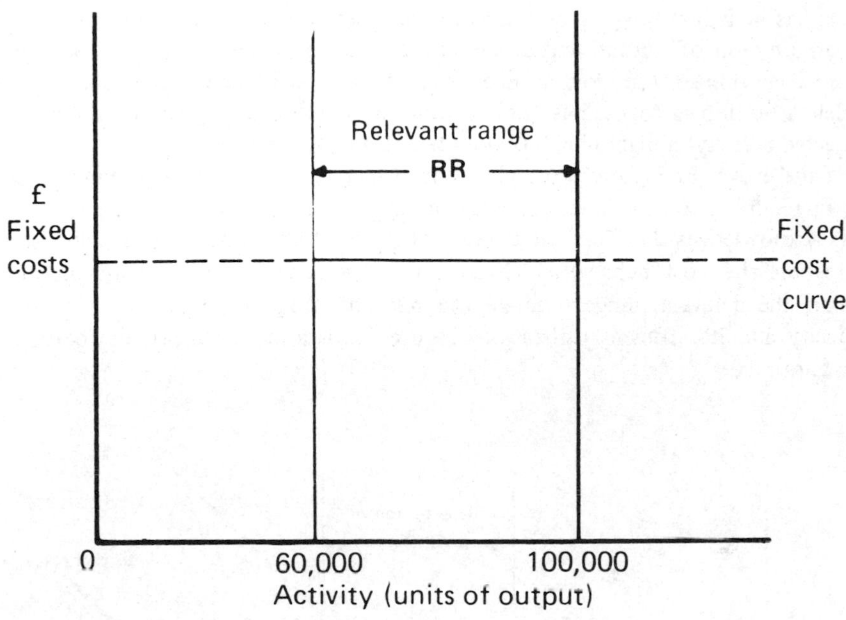

Figure 3.6: Relevant range – fixed costs

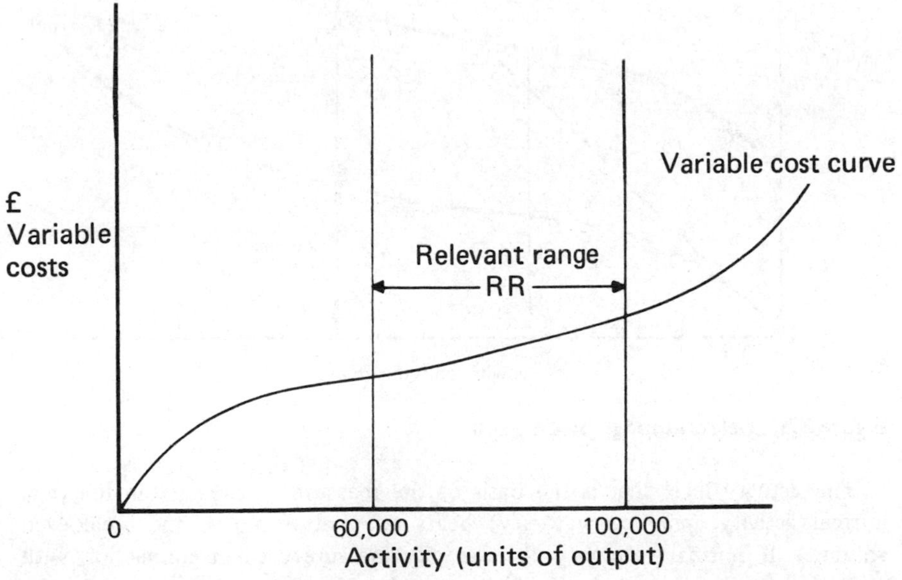

Figure 3.7: Relevant range – variable costs

linear (as in Figure 1.4). It is conventional practice to treat variable costs as a linear function of output within the relevant range on the basis that a section from a curvilinear function approximates to a straight line. The section on which attention is focused is the relevant range representing the extremes of expected activity: a high of 100 000 units and a low of 60 000 units.

If the curves of Figures 3.6 and 3.7 are superimposed on to a revenue curve (as in Figure 1.10) we have the relevant range break-even chart of Figure 3.8. This acknowledges the fact that a wide range of activity is possible, but concentrates on the cost behaviour patterns, revenue function, and profit picture within the relevant range. Since the relevant range is related to available capacity and its efficient utilization, Figure 3.8 is a more realistic device than is Figure 1.10.

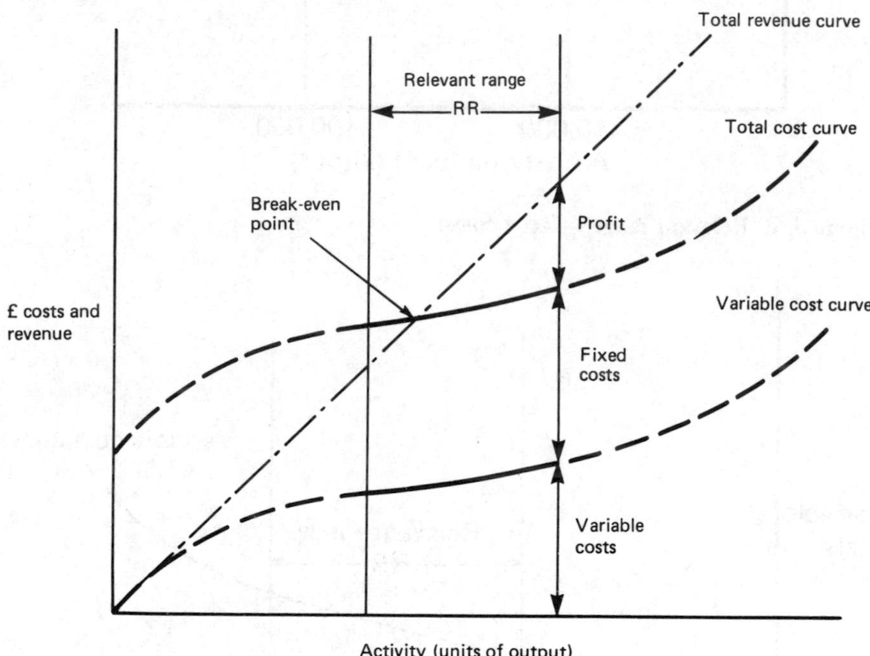

Figure 3.8: Relevant range profitgraph

The activity level that is the basis of the measure of capacity in use (e.g. normal activity, practical capacity) bears no relationship to the break-even volume. If normal volume is the capacity measure used in connection with spreading fixed overheads it should be considerably higher than the break-even point – hopefully towards the right-hand side of the relevant range in Figure 3.8.

BALANCING CAPACITY

A major decision faced by every company relates to the scale of operations to which it should aspire. But the effective scale of operations – or capacity – does not solely depend upon the capacity of the parts: it depends very largely on the way that management puts these parts together. The ideal combination of productive resources is that combination that leaves no part with capacity in excess of the other parts. Balance must be achieved.

Unfortunately, it is virtually impossible to achieve perfect balance with the result that bottlenecks arise in one area of activity whilst excess capacity exists simultaneously in another. A vital point to observe from this tendency is that the bottleneck – the limiting factor – sets the constraint against which operations must be evaluated. The following example clarifies this point.

A company produces three products, X, Y and Z, with the variable cost and revenue characteristics shown in Figure 3.9. On the basis of the profit

	Product X	Product Y	Product Z
Selling price	£4.86	£3.70	£9.87
Direct material cost	1.46	0.80	1.89
Direct labour cost	0.86	0.94	2.72
Variable overhead cost	1.73	1.22	3.85
Total variable cost	*£4.05*	*£2.96*	*£8.46*
Profit contribution	£0.81	£0.74	£1.41
Profit contribution percentage of sales	16.7	20.0	14.3

Figure 3.9: Cost and revenue characteristics

contribution as a percentage of sales, product Y is the most profitable and product Z is the least profitable. It will be observed that this ranking order has been derived in the absence of fixed cost allocations so it does not relate to the best use of available capacity that these costs represent.

Let us suppose that the processing time for each unit of each product (in hours) represents the limiting factor and is:

Product X 1.72 process hours per unit
Product Y 1.90 process hours per unit
Product Z 2.88 process hours per unit

It will then be seen that the profit contribution per process hour – as a measure of the efficiency with which available processing capacity is utilized – is:

Product X	£0.81 ÷ 1.72	= £0.47
Product Y	£0.74 ÷ 1.90	= £0.39
Product Z	£1.41 ÷ 2.88	= £0.49

This reverses the ranking order: product Z now appears as the most profitable whilst product Y emerges as the least profitable. It follows that, since Z makes the most efficient use of available capacity as represented by the limiting factor of process hours, sales of Z should be encouraged in preference to sales of X or Y.

If a total of 117 648 process hours represent the limit of normal capacity (i.e. after allowing for unavoidable stoppages and uncertainties), it would be possible – subject to demand, availability of raw materials, labour, etc. – to produce the output of products X, Y and Z with the following profit consequences:

Product X	117 648 ÷ 1.72	= 68 400 units × £0.81	= £55 404 profit
Product Y	117 648 ÷ 1.90	= 61 920 units × £0.74	= £45 821 profit
Product Z	117 648 ÷ 2.88	= 40 850 units × £1.41	= £57 599 profit

This demonstrates conclusively that concentrating on product Z is the most profitable use of capacity. If either product X or product Y were made to the exclusion of the other two products, plant capacity (measured in process hours) would have to be increased before the profit figure reached the level achieved by product Z with the existing capacity. If plant capacity is increased, the level of fixed costs would also increase, and this would make a comparable profit figure of £57 599 from products X and/or Y even harder to achieve.

The limiting factor could be labour, materials, time, plant, money, management, or equipment availability depending upon the circumstances of any given company at a particular point in time.

SUMMARY

Efficient utilization of productive capacity is desirable from the point of view of both society and management.

Capacity determines a company's level of fixed costs (or establishment costs) for a given period of time within a specified range of activity – the relevant range. A relevant range exists for variable costs as well as for fixed costs, and the break-even chart that is built up on the basis of cost behaviour patterns through the relevant range is a more useful device that the basic model described in Chapter 1.

Measurements of capacity can be of various types: normal, expected, practical, or ideal. In inflationary conditions it is better to use expected volume measured in physical rather than financial terms.

Since it is impossible to balance productive resources in most instances in anything approaching an optimal manner, it becomes necessary to evaluate the best use of available capacity by considering the limiting factor. (When several limiting factors operate together as constraints, mathematical programming techniques can be applied.)

4

Cost Control

INTRODUCTION TO CONTROL

Since control is a process whereby management ensures that the organization is achieving desired ends it can be defined as a set of organized (adaptive) actions directed towards achieving a specified goal in the face of constraints.

To bring about particular future events it is necessary to influence the factors that lie behind those events. It is the ability to bring about a desired future outcome at will that is the essence of control. In this sense it can be seen that control itself is a *process* and not an event. Moreover, the idea of control can be seen to be synonymous with such notions as adaptation, influence, manipulation and regulation. But control is *not* synonymous with coercion in the sense in which the term is used in this book. Nor does it have as its central feature (as so often seems to be thought) the detailed study of past mistakes, but rather the focusing of attention on current and, more particularly, on future activities to ensure that they are carried through in a way that leads to desired ends.

The existence of a control process enables management to know from time to time where the organization stands in relation to a predetermined future position. This requires that progress can be observed, measured, and re-directed if there are discrepancies between the actual and the desired positions.

Control and planning are complementary, so each should logically presuppose the existence of the other. Planning presupposes objectives (ends), and objectives are of very limited value in the absence of a facilitating plan (means) for their attainment. In the planning process management must determine the organization's future course of action by reconciling corporate resources with specified corporate objectives. This will usually involve a consideration of various alternative courses of action and the selection of the one that is seen to be the best in the light of the objectives.

In seeking to exercise control it is important to recognize that the process is inevitably value-laden: the preferred future state that one is seeking to realize is unlikely to be the same for individual A as for individual B, and that which applies to individuals also, within limits, applies to organizations. Only man can decide what future outcomes he wants to bring about, and in specifying these he sets goals for organizations.

In seeking to exercise control the major hindrances are uncertainty (since the relevant time horizon for control is the future, which cannot be totally known in advance) and the inherent complexity of socio-economic and socio-technical systems (such as business organizations). If one had an adequate understanding of the ways in which complex organizations function, and if this facilitated reliable predictions, then the information stemming from this predictive understanding would enable one to control the organization's behaviour. In this sense it can be seen that information and control have an equivalence.

Behind the presumption, therefore, that we can control anything there is an implied assertion that we know enough about the situation in question (e.g. what is being sought, how well things are going, what is going wrong, how matters might be put right etc.). But do we actually know these things?

WAYS OF KNOWING

Let us consider ways in which we know, think we know, or seek to know about the behaviour of phenomena within the organizational world (see Figure 4.1).

It is readily apparent that not all our beliefs about the world can be defended on logical grounds. For example, many of our ideas are held because society takes them for granted, or because a particular point of view has been put to us so many times that we no longer question it. Many ideas with this lack of a logical pedigree are to be found amongst the average individual's set of basic beliefs, even though contrary evidence exists in the empirical world (if only we would relate this to our beliefs).

There are many ways in which we seek to justify the things we believe in. The means for this may be found in statute or common law, religious dogma, political ideology, social norms and conventions, or through scientific endeavour. If we consider the bases of many of the decisions made in our everyday lives

{ Statute
{ Common law

Political ideology

Religious dogma

{ Social norms
{ Cultural conventions

Common sense

Hunch
Gut-feeling

{ Old wives' tales
{ Adages
{ Conventional wisdom

Experience

Empirical evidence

Authority

Logical argument

Scientific endeavours

Figure 4.1: Ways of knowing

we are likely to find that these reflect very questionable 'ways of knowing': e.g. hunch, conventional wisdom, old wives' tales, gut-feeling, and common sense. Although experience in its various forms lies behind these ways of knowing, they all exhibit a conspicuous lack of explanatory or predictive rigour.

Ways of knowing that are rather more satisfactory in terms of explanation and prediction include:

(*a*) empirical evidence in the form of, for example, statistics, financial statements etc., provided the basis of compilation is known and is acceptable;
(*b*) experience that is evaluated to try to allow for the necessary limits to any one individual's experience and the bias (both intentional and perceptual) that is inevitably present;
(*c*) citing authority, although 'expert' evidence should not be accepted in an unquestioning manner since the degree of authority of a particular source may tend to depend on status or position rather than on genuine expertise;
(*d*) logical argument and inference; and
(*e*) scientific theory-building through which knowledge is critically tested and evaluated as it is built up into a generally acceptable view of part of the world.

The main thrust of relevance to us is that given by (*e*), with (*a*)–(*d*) being taken into account as necessary.

At their simplest theories explain facts: they can tell us what is known and thus guide our decision making. More formally, a theory can be defined as a set of systematically interrelated concepts, definitions, and propositions that are advanced to explain, predict, prescribe and control the behaviour of phenomena.

The discussion that follows builds itself around the set of relations in Figure 4.2.

A good decision-maker can be said to be a man with good theories. This may conflict with the emphasis put on 'practicality' by unenlightened, defensive individuals who are only too aware of their own ignorance of the behaviour of organizational phenomena.

Theories are not unrelated to facts – the adequacy of our scientific knowledge can be measured by the degree to which fact and theory have been merged. It is the interplay of ideas (theory) and facts (data) that makes science into a going concern, so if scientific theories of organizational problem solving and control seek to comprehend what is known in order to derive a set of principles or action-guides to enable managers to run their affairs more effectively (or, to put it another way, if theories are concerned with knowing) it follows that those who dismiss the relevance of theories must be recommending a policy of *not* knowing. The practical man (operating without a theoretical base) is thus the man who does not really know what he is doing.

Theory and facts are two sides of the same coin, so to emphasize one (or merely to neglect the other) is potentially dangerous if one fails to appreciate that sound practice will be facilitated by valid theories, and valid theories must be grounded in the empirical world of organizational activity.

The purposes of theory are often given as aiding explanation and prediction. But there are other purposes, at a higher (i.e. more ambitious) level – namely prescription and control. Let us look at each of these four in turn.

Explanation

Theories seek to explain the behaviour of variables in order that we might come to *understand causal sequences*. This emphasis on causal relationships should not lead us to expect that precise cause-and-effect rules will emerge and be applicable under every potential set of circumstances.

One can only suggest (with at best a stated probability) that a particular outcome will occur when a number of specified variables interact in a defined organizational situation.

A theory that gives a satisfactory level of explanation of the behaviour of a particular phenomenon is deemed a paradigm (i.e. a generally acceptable statement of understanding), and this in turn provides a focus for research activities in a situation in which it would otherwise not be known which facts to seek

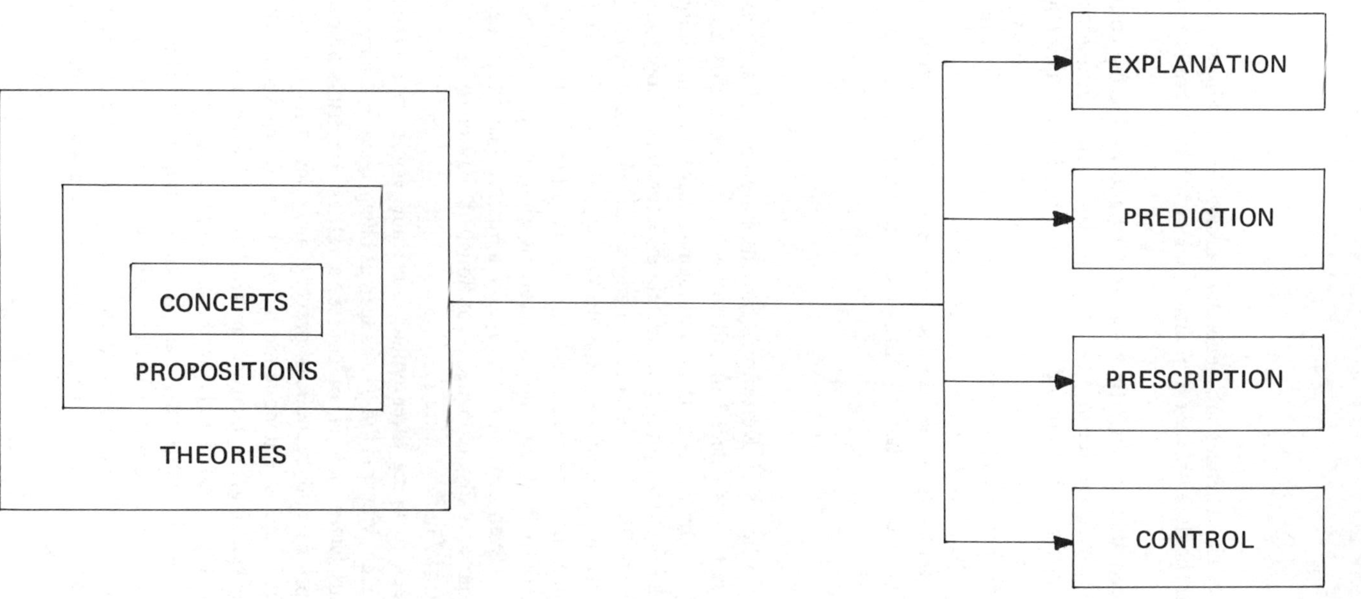

Figure 4.2: The structure and purpose of theories

to discover. The social sciences are generally lacking in paradigms, and this absence has clouded the development of politics and sociology as well as management theory.

It has been argued that the key to both creating and evaluating courses of managerial action and policies lies in understanding the system in question (i.e. being able to *explain its behaviour*, rather than just predicting it). One may be able to predict the behaviour of a system without being able to explain it, e.g. by extrapolating from its past behaviour. The ability to explain, however, necessarily involves the ability to predict. In addition, and of greater importance, the ability to explain provides the basis for redesigning a system in some fundamental way in order either to eliminate problems or to improve the system's effectiveness.

Prediction

If one subscribes to Charles F. Kettering's famous statement, 'I am interested in the future because that is where I intend to live', then the ability to predict the future that one might have (or that one might create) becomes important. The experience of the past may give us some help in determining how to proceed into the future, but we tend to be constrained by our own experience (in the sense that we tend to see, and to do, what we know), and since there is no way in which we can influence the past there should be a limit to the amount of effort that is applied to it as opposed to applying that effort to attempts to predict the future. (Even rewriting history, or adjusting last year's accounts, does not change what actually happened – although it may cause us to behave in a rather different way in the future.)

The future is seen as being threatening, uncertain, vague, treacherous, unknown, and value-laden, whereas the past is seen as being certain, secure, factual, and value-free. This latter view is, of course, a rather simplistic one to hold because our perceptions and prejudices prevent any view that we may hold from being value-free, and our understanding of events of the past will never be total. Nevertheless, a great many organizations fail even to attempt to predict future conditions and merely wait to accept whatever future comes along. It would seem desirable (in terms of improving both efficiency and effectiveness) to attempt to develop better theories of organizational control in order that managers might be better equipped to predict whatever the future may have to offer and hence to plan to achieve whatever seems feasible in the predicted circumstances.

Prescription

Even when predictive or explanatory theories are able to anticipate the outcomes of actions it is still necessary to choose amongst alternative courses of action (e.g. where the available alternatives are mutually exclusive, or where a rationing situation exists). Ethical considerations and value judgements must be taken into account in such a situation in order that the values of decision-makers may be aligned with the available alternatives.

It is in this domain that the inadequacies of our existing knowledge really show through. Who is to say what is 'best' in any situation? The values of individuals and society are continually being modified, as well as the public's ethical expectations of business (and of other formal organizations). If the decision-maker of today is arrogant enough to make a choice that will affect the next generation it may prove to be the case that he makes faulty assumptions about that generation's needs. But if today's decision-maker neglects to make any choice (other than the choice to do nothing) this will also have an impact on the next generation which may be unable to take whatever action may be necessary to improve their lot due to the passage of time.

Behind these comments is the presumption that at any point in time people may know what they want even if they may not know what they, or another generation, may want at another point in time. However, it is too often assumed that the nature of man's needs or desires is known when it is more probable that we do not really know what we want, or what anyone else might want. A knowledge of values and desires is logically essential to good decision making, but an awareness of real human values only seems likely to emerge from people who have freedom of choice in the absence of ignorance or other constraints. If this is the case, it follows that the empirical determination of current values is beyond our ability to achieve. Perhaps the only logical way to proceed in the light of this ignorance is to state very clearly all the assumptions that are made regarding values, and all other variables, when attempting to predict the future. In this way the assumptions can be varied on an experimental basis to test their likely impact on desired outcomes.

It is a chastening thought that whilst we have developed very elaborate ways of doing things, e.g. via advanced technology, we have not developed ways of justifying in ethical terms what we actually do.

Control

The ultimate level of attainment for a theory is to enable us to *control the behaviour of those phenomena in which we are interested*, which gives a means for solving problems in a most effective manner. If we understand the behaviour of the phenomena (and are thus able to make reliable predictions), and if we have a clear idea of what we are seeking to achieve, then theories should be able to help us reach our objectives by facilitating adaptive behaviour. (By manipulating the behaviour of variables within our control we can counter any external disturbance, provided our understanding of the situation allows us to predict it, and hence meet our objectives. A validated, predictive theory of cause-and-effect relationships should give us the opportunity to exert pressure on the causes to influence the effects in a way that will lead us to a desired future position.) This is highly ambitious, but also highly desirable since it caters for an improved way of knowing that can improve our problem-solving ability and so lead us towards improvements in organizational effectiveness and control.

INSIDIOUS CONTROL

In large organizations there are a number of insidious and unobtrusive controls to be found. These are all the more dangerous and powerful because they are so deceptive. Their deceptiveness is shown in their *not* causing participants to feel their presence – there is no feeling of being oppressed by a despot. Instead there is perhaps just the experience of conforming to the logic of a situation, or of performing in accordance with some internalized standard.

Beyond this source of 'control' there are other sources. To the extent that the behaviour of members of organizations is controlled, i.e. appears to be regular and predictable, such regularity may derive from the norms and definitions of subcultural groups within the organization rather than from official rules and prescriptions. The idea that organizational rules constitute the blueprint for all behaviour within organizations is not a tenable one.

Nevertheless, the most significant form of power within organizations is the power to limit, guide and restrict the decision making of organizational personnel such that even when they are allowed (or obliged) to use their own judgement they do not deviate from official expectations. In part this is due to the organization's structure, which can be seen as a series of limitations and controls over members' decision making, and which results from powerful, senior organizational personnel choosing what the structure should be (and hence determining who is allowed to do what).

It is something of a paradox that modern man is freer from coercion through the power of command of superiors than most people have ever been, yet men in positions of power today probably exercise more control than any tyrant ever had. This is largely due to contemporary forms of power exercised within organizations and by organizations in society. There is a distinct trend that places less reliance on control through a fixed chain of command, whilst placing more reliance on indirect forms of control. Let us pursue this in greater detail.

Forms of control have changed with the passage of time, and these forms have had impacts not only within organizations but also through them on contemporary society.

Organizations have taken advantage of a variety of control mechanisms from time to time, ranging from ones that are obviously bureaucratic in nature, e.g. command authority and discipline, to ones that are quite unbureaucratic (such as the controlling power that is rooted in expert knowledge).

Let us consider the range of control mechanisms:

1 The prototype (bureaucratic control) is the authority exercised through a *chain of command* in which superiors give subordinates instructions which must be obeyed. This coercive form of control has strong military overtones, and an essential element is rigorous discipline that must be enforced through coercive sanctions. Such discipline is not usually a characteristic of contemporary industrial life.

2 The establishing of explicit regulations and procedures to govern decisions and operations gives a programmed form of control. Discipline is involved in this mechanism also, and close links can be seen between the idea of a set of rules that must be followed and the idea of following orders via a chain of command. However, explicit rules do restrict the arbitrary exercise of power by superiors because they apply to rulers as well as to the ruled.

   In specifying rules on how to behave in particular circumstances it is unlikely that all possible situations will be catered for. It follows that rules should ideally be related to the principles underlying decisions rather than to particular decisions – thus specifying *criteria* for decision making will be less restrictive than the stipulating of *how* specific decisions should be made.

3 Incentive systems constitute a further control mechanism. Salaries and career advancement clearly make individuals dependent to a large extent on the organization that employs them, thereby constraining them to submit to the authority exercised within that organization.

   Incentives are often tied directly to performance, piece work rates and sales commissions being the most obvious examples. However, performance measures can be developed for most organizational roles and adjustments in salary levels and promotion decisions will depend at least to some extent on measured achievements.

4 Technology provides a control mechanism in two forms:

   (*a*) production technology constrains employees' performance, thereby enabling managers to control operations (e.g. the speed of an assembly line can be used to regulate productivity);

   (*b*) the technical knowledge possessed by an organization's 'technocrats' gives them the ability to understand and perform complex tasks and thereby maintain control of a situation. Management is thus able to control operations, albeit indirectly, by hiring staff with appropriate professional/technical skills to carry out the required responsibilities.

This reduces the need to use alternative mechanisms, such as detailed rules or close supervision through a chain of command.

5 Expert knowledge is a vital requirement in managing organizations. (It could even be argued that successful management comes about through the exercising of control over the basic knowledge.) It follows that recruiting suitable technocrats is a key mechanism for controlling the organization. If technically-qualified individuals are selectively recruited and if they have the professional ability to perform assigned tasks on their own, then if the organization gives such individuals the appropriate discretion to do what needs to be done, within the broad framework of basic policies and administrative guidelines, it should be possible for control to be effective.

6 The allocation of resources (including personnel) is the ultimate mechanism of organizational control since this facilitates certain actions and inhibits others.

Within most organizations one will find several of these mechanisms of control in operation, yet there seems to be a trend towards a decreasing reliance on control through a chain of command and an increasing reliance on indirect forms of control, e.g. via recruitment policies. Incentive systems and machine technologies are perhaps the most prevalent mechanisms of contemporary organizational control: control via recruitment and resource allocation is indicative of the likely future pattern.

At this point it is worth clarifying the distinction between the process of control on the one hand, and controls on the other.

CONTROL VS CONTROLS

In the language of management the word 'controls' is not the plural of 'control'. Not only would it be wrong to assume that more 'controls' would automatically give us more 'control', it would be assuming they meant the same thing – which they do not.

'Controls' has the same meaning as measurement, or information, whereas 'control' is more akin to direction. 'Controls' is concerned with means whilst 'control' is concerned with ends, and they deal respectively with facts (i.e. events of the past) and expectations (i.e. desires about the future). From this it will be appreciated that 'controls' tend to be analytical and operational (concerning what was and is), and 'control' tends to be normative (concerning what ought to be). A summary of key differences is shown in Figure 4.3.

The increasing ability, especially with the availability of computing power, to develop 'controls' has not necessarily increased our ability to 'control' organizations. If controls are to lead to control they must encourage human actors to behave in a way that facilitates adaptive behaviour on the part of the organization as a whole.

Σ CONTROLS $\neq$ CONTROL
Δ CONTROLS $\neq$ Δ CONTROL

CONTROLS	*CONTROL*
• Parts (∴ simple)	Wholes (∴ complex)
• Measurement →	Direction
Information	
• Measurable symptons	Unmeasurable causes
• Means	Ends
• Present/past orientation (∴ facts)	Future orientation (∴ expectations)
• Positive (what was/is)	Normative (what ought to be)
• Efficiency	Effectiveness
• Hardware (machines, physical processes)	Software (through human actors)

Figure 4.3: The different focus of control and controls

The complexity and uncertainty of the control problem are apparent when, for example, controls reveal that 'profits are falling'. But this does not indicate how one might (or should) respond – indeed, it would not be possible even to identify the whole array of potential responses! What is needed, therefore, if control is to be effective, is a basis for forming expectations about the future, as well as understanding about the past, that will enable us to combine these in order that we might behave in an adaptive way by either anticipating external changes and preparing to meet them, or by creating changes.

From this arises the basic question, 'How do we control?' In large part this is resolved by the answer to another question, 'What do we measure in order to control?' Care must be taken in measuring the key elements in any situation rather than those elements that lend themselves to easy measurement. ('Controls' are only helpful in 'control' if they are designed in the context of the overall control problem.)

Pareto's Law has a bearing on this matter – the '80/20 rule' aims to show how one might allocate one's effort, i.e. resources, to achieve the best results.

Within business organizations many critical factors are either non-measurable or go unmeasured. For example, how does (or should) one measure the ability of an organization to attract or retain capable managers? This is more important to survival etc., than last year's reported profit, but it cannot be quantified even though it is distinctly tangible. 'Controls' can only handle facts, i.e. observed events that are capable of measurement and quantification. There are no facts about the future, which is the temporal dimension of 'control', and there are many key control phenomena that are beyond our measuring competence. Furthermore, measurable facts are largely internal, whilst the environmental phenomena that give rise to the need for control are, by definition, external. (See Chapter 6.) But let us now return to considerations relating to the planning and control of costs.

Some advantages of planning and control that are at once apparent are:

1 The preparation of a plan involves clarification and a careful consideration of the role of each individual and function within the company.
2 Individual managers are obliged to consider how their departments can contribute to objective attainment and how their performance in doing this (i.e. their degree of success) can be evaluated.
3 Every participant is made aware of what the company is trying to achieve and what his part is in the facilitating plan.
4 Company policies must be brought into line with the requirements of objective accomplishment.
5 Objectives must be carefully thought out, quantified, and communicated to all concerned.
6 Management is encouraged to think ahead in a systematic way.
7 Plans provide a better basis from which to grasp new opportunities as they arise.
8 A starting point is provided for the development of standards of performance.
9 The facility for taking corrective action if circumstances change is given.
10 A basis is provided on which to build an information system.

As with control, planning may be either overall and covering the whole organization, or, alternatively, specific to one segment of the company. Where comprehensive planning exists it is usually based on a reconciled amalgamation of a series of specific plans for different segments of a company. (Chapter 8 deals with budgetary planning in greater detail.) Whether or not the plan is comprehensive, it will play the same role in the logical cycle of control which involves:

1 Planning what is to be achieved.
2 Putting the plan into effect.
3 Evaluating the success of the plan in achieving its intended purpose.

This cycle is developed later in this chapter.

Within this framework cost control exists to ensure that costs are kept in line with the requirements of stated plans in the company's endeavours to achieve its objectives.

At the heart of cost control are:

1 Information
2 Action

Information is required on the desired level of performance, the actual level of performance, and the variance (which is the difference between actual and desired performance). Action is necessary to put current plans into effect as well as to modify future activities (if necessary) to make sure that performance is in line with plans and standards, thereby leading to the attainment of objectives. The mere act of extracting a variance is *not* control – it is simply one small step in the whole control cycle: the action that follows this extraction of information is much more important.

Accounting information is essential to control in several ways, for example:

1 As a means of communicating plans, policies, performance levels, etc., in a quantified manner.
2 As a means of motivating members of the organization by clearly specifying what is to be achieved and measuring success in this direction.
3 As a means of reporting results as a basis for evaluating individual performance.
4 As a basis for further planning.

In the light of this it is apparent that accounting reports – at a minimum – should be presented in such a way that those concerned with cost incurrence can understand them fully and react to them in the appropriate manner. More particularly, accounting control reports should:

1 Show their recipients what is expected of them (i.e. their expected level of performance).
2 Show what their actual level of performance is.
3 Indicate whether performance is getting better or worse.
4 Provide a basis for investigating deviations from plan in order that causes can be established and future actions modified accordingly.

Before developing this discussion any further it is helpful to distinguish between *cost control* and *cost reduction* because they are quite separate activities. Cost control, as we have seen, is concerned with keeping costs at their planned level (i.e. conforming insofar as possible with existing standards and plans). In contrast, cost reduction is concerned with setting cost levels at the mimimum acceptable level by looking at ways of improving the standards that provide the benchmarks for cost control. Cost reduction may be achieved by value engineering techniques, method study, work measurment techniques, incentive schemes, revised layouts, etc.

If management misguidedly sets cost standards that are beyond attainment by current methods, etc., this will not lead to cost reduction: poor morale is a more likely outcome, with resultant labour problems. Conversely, if loose standards are set (i.e. standards that can be attained by a poor level of performance) cost control may be effective, but the overall level of costs will be at a most inefficient level.

It has been established that control must be exercised over the level of cost performance, and this requires a consideration of both direct and indirect costs.

Total indirect (or overhead) costs amount to a most significant proportion of total costs, but despite this fact it is found that many individual overhead items are small in relation to direct labour and direct material costs. Controlling these latter costs is generally more straightforward than is the case with overhead costs: it is easier, for example, to establish a direct material standard (e.g. the amount of glass needed to make a milk bottle) than it is to compute a standard indirect labour cost for repairing a faulty machine. The basic ideas of cost control are the same for indirect as for direct costs, but the techniques differ because:

1 The limited size of some overhead costs does not warrant intricate controls.
2 Responsibility for various overhead items belongs to different people.
3 The behaviour of overhead items varies enormously.

Nevertheless, many indirect costs behave in a similar manner to direct costs (e.g. routine activities such as warehousing, packing, and many repetitive clerical functions). Insofar as costs (whether direct or indirect) have a behaviour pattern, as shown in Figure 1.4 (i.e. a variable cost behaviour pattern) it will generally be possible to control them by the use of standards and variance analysis. (See Chapters 9–11.) However, those indirect costs that are of a different nature will need to be controlled by flexible budgets drawn up in accordance with the principles of responsibility accounting. (See Chapters 6–8.)

The existence of standards of performance (whether in the form of standard cost targets or budgeted levels of performance) makes possible the practice of *management by exception*. Under this principle only those variations from planned performance that are considered significant (or exceptional) are followed up. In most instances these items will tend to be few in number, and this procedure saves the focusing of effort on the majority of items that are under control (i.e. the performance of which is satisfactory). Chapter 10 deals with the setting of tolerance limits to permit management by exception in connection with cost control.

COST CONTROL, ORGANIZATIONAL PLANNING, AND RESPONSIBILITY ACCOUNTING

Costs can only be controlled if they are related to the organizational framework: in other words, costs should be controlled in accordance with the concept of responsibility – a cost should be controlled at whatever level it is originated and initially approved by the individual who did the initiating and approving. In this way it will be clear that certain costs are the responsibility of, and can only be controlled by, the chief executive of a company (such as corporate public relations expenditure) whereas others are controllable by responsible individuals at lower levels of the organizational hierarchy (e.g. a departmental manager will be responsible for the salary expense of those who work within his department, and a foreman will be responsible for the cost of consumable materials used in his productive department. Strictly, a foreman should only be held responsible for usage rather than prices due to his lack of control over the latter). As was pointed out in Chapter 2, cost control can only be effective if individuals are held responsible for the costs over which they have authority. This is the essence of responsibility accounting, and it will be covered at length in Chapter 6.

At this stage, however, it is important to distinguish between costs that are controllable at a given level of managerial authority within a given period of time, and those that are not. This distinction is not the same as the one between variable costs and fixed costs. For example, rates are a fixed cost that are uncontrollable – for a given time period – by any managerial level, whereas the annual road licence fee for a particular vehicle is a fixed cost that is controllable by the fleet manager who has the power to dispense with the vehicle. In the same way the insurance premium payable on inventories is a variable cost (fluctuating with the value of the inventory from month to month) that is not controllable at the storekeeper level, but it is controllable at the level of the executive who determines inventory policy (subject, of course, to the environmental vagaries of such factors as consumer demand which can never be removed).

Controllability is affected by both managerial authority and the element of time – a short-run fixed cost will be a long-run variable cost. (Thus the managing director's salary is fixed for 12 months, but variable thereafter.) All costs are controllable to some extent over the longer term, even if this involves a change in the scale of operations or a relocation of the company.

The problem of distinguishing between controllable and uncontrollable costs is more difficult in relation to overheads as opposed to direct costs. It is vitally important that costs be regulated at source, and this means that for many overhead items the beneficiary of cost incurrence is very often not the person to be charged with the cost. Obvious examples are overhead services –

maintenance, the personnel department, post room/switchboard facilities – from which all members of the company derive benefits, but for which cost responsibility is accorded to the respective supervisors and managers of these service functions.

In a control sense, overhead absorption rates and full product costs (made up of direct labour cost, direct material cost, and applied overhead) are not helpful. These rates and product costs must be broken down into their constituent parts and these parts must be controlled at source. It is impossible for one manager to control an overhead *rate*, but it is possible for him to control those specific costs over which he has authority.

To sum up so far, the approach to cost control that is based on the concept of responsibility accounting involves designing the cost control system to match the organizational structure in order that it reflects realistically the responsibilities of departmental managers, supervisors, etc. (This method of tackling cost control is reflected in the way Figure 2.1 is compiled: it permits the collecting and reporting of costs in such a way that the performance of organizational sub-units can be evaluated.) In devising an accounting system for securing cost control that accords with the organizational structure it will usually be found necessary to define more closely the duties of responsible individuals, and various responsibilities will have to be re-assigned in order to give a logical structure to an organization that may have grown in a haphazard manner. All subsequent organizational changes that lead to changes in individual responsibilities should be accompanied by suitable modifications to the cost control system.

Since costs result from the actions of individuals, it is of value in most organizations to have an internal audit function to see that the actions people take leading to cost incurrence are within their agreed authority.

An example can be taken from the order-invoicing process in relation to which the following questions might be asked:

1 Who causes purchase orders to be raised?
2 How are purchase orders initiated?
3 What control exists over their initiation?
4 Do those who sign purchase orders on behalf of the company have authority appropriate to the value of each order?
5 Who in the company can sign purchase orders?
6 Are all orders authorized?
7 What checks are there on authority, etc?
8 Why do delays arise in passing invoices for goods received for payment?
9 What is the procedure for approving these invoices?
10 Is this procedure adhered to?
11 Do goods delivered correspond with goods ordered?

12 Whose responsibility is it to ensure that goods delivered correspond with goods ordered?
13 What is done when errors arise in deliveries?
14 Are extensions on invoices checked?
15 Who is responsible for checking invoice extensions?
16 Would a sample check be sufficient?

The list could be much longer, but the above points illustrate the need to review in a fairly rigorous manner the procedures behind cost incurrence.

A FRAMEWORK FOR A COST CONTROL SYSTEM

Costs are incurred in acquiring and converting inputs into outputs, and control is necessary to keep costs within limits of efficiency. The company itself acts as the converter (or conversion unit) that transforms inputs into outputs.

Figure 4.4 illustrates a simple corporate input-output system in which various input factors (such as capital + labour + materials) are converted into desired outputs (such as goods and services). Whilst these inputs and outputs may be of a physical nature, it is essential to appreciate that many are not: aspirations and knowledge are non-physical inputs and consumer satisfaction and job satisfaction are examples of intangible outputs.

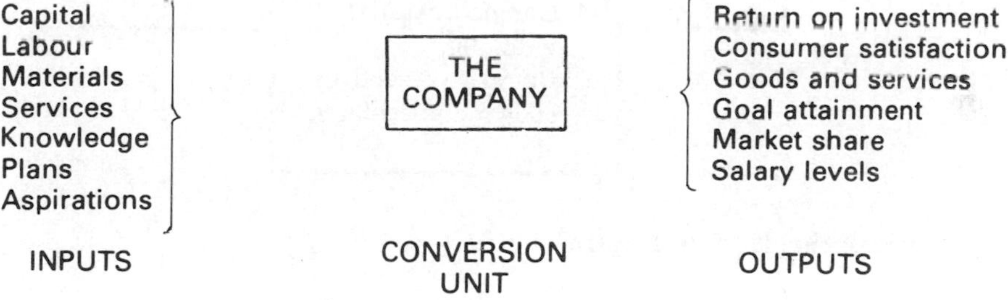

Figure 4.4: A simple corporate system

If this idea of an input-conversion-output system is applied to control we have a basis for the design of a cost control system. This is illustrated in Figure 4.5 and can be seen to consist of three major inputs: objectives (or desired ends); policies (or prescribed constraints); and plans (or means to ends within constraints). The planning phase takes the various resources that are available to the company (sales force, plant and equipment, materials, and so on) and allocates these in the best available way in line with requirements for the attainment of objectives. Detailed workloads must be established and standards must be set for comparative purposes. This is followed by the execution stage: the plan is put into effect. The major output in this simple framework is an observed level of performance.

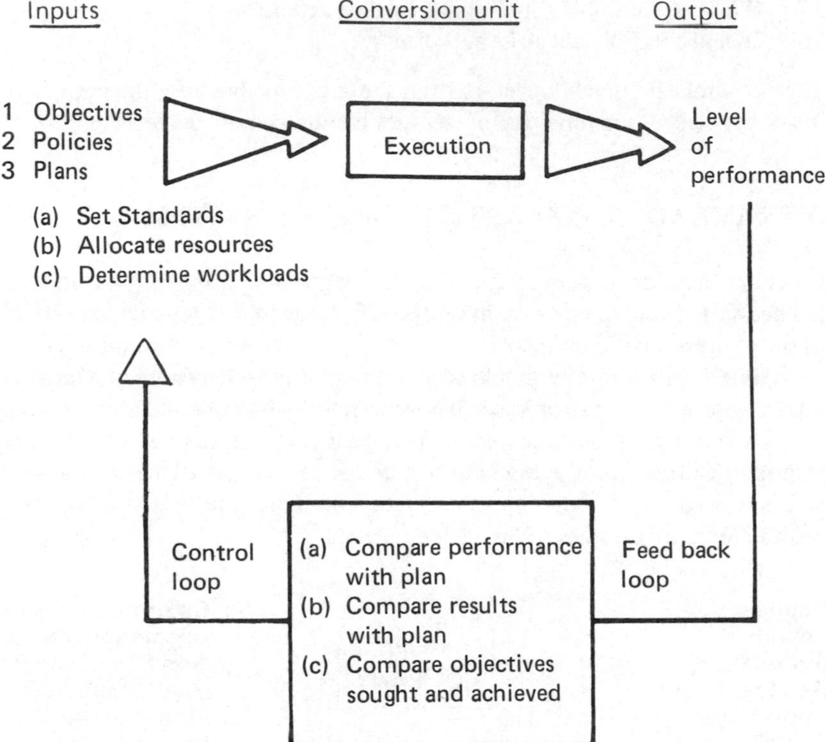

Figure 4.5: A simple control system

Measures of performance are fed back to the decision maker and compared with the desired levels of performance. This can take place at various levels: for example, an individual salesman may have been expected to sell 500 kitchen units in a given period which would have been his contribution to the brand's market share result which, in turn, would have played its part in striving for an overall rate of return on investment (ROI). Thus there can be a series of comparisons: one at the level of salesman performance; one at the level of the results of the brand; and one at the level of objective attainment.

In measuring output it must be realized that performance measurement has more than one dimension. Consequently, in relation to inputs and the efficiency of their conversion into outputs, it is appropriate to ask:

1 How much was achieved?
2 How good was this achievement?
3 How much did it cost?

The need for quantitative, qualitative, and financial evaluations of performance becomes clear if one imagines a production unit that operates an incentive scheme related only to the number of items manufactured. High quantity will tend to be at the expense of quality, and this will tend to mean a high rate of rejects resulting in high rectification or scrap costs. A more suitable approach would be to reduce costs by constraining quantity by a specified level of quality. This theme will be taken up again in the next chapter.

Following the performance measurement step in the cycle it remains to correct deviations from plan (or to modify the plan to accommodate the deviations). This completes the control loop, which is, of course, a continuing feature of the company's existence. However, the time interval between the measurement of performance and taking corrective action should be kept to a practicable minimum: monthly reports concerning overtime costs are probably too infrequent – weekly may be better; but daily reports of accrued debenture interest are too frequent – monthly reports would suffice in most instances. A balance must be struck between requirements and feasibility.

ORGANIZING FOR COST CONTROL: THE ROLE OF THE CONTROLLER

The individual who is most likely to have the prime responsibility in the typical organization for the design and operation of its control systems is the controller. It is probable that the holder of this office may be called by another title, such as chief accountant or management accountant, but it is important to consider the distinction between the controllership function and what may be termed the treasurership function of accountants.

Figure 4.6 gives the standard definition of the distinction between these functions and Figure 4.7 expresses the controller's role in the form of a job description.

In part the need for a controller stems from the increasing size and complexity of organizations, but it also arises from the increasing availability of planning and control techniques. However, despite the fact that the controller is responsible for designing and operating control systems for all aspects of the organisation, his own role (other than in relation to his own department), is a staff one rather than a line one. This requires that he refrain from making other people's decisions for them even if he has had to report to them on the consequences of alternative choices in a given decision situation.

The first formal official statement of the responsibilities of the corporate treasurership function was approved by the Board of Directors of Financial Executives Institute (established in 1931 as Controllers Institute of America) at its meeting in French Lick Springs, Indiana, on May 17, 1962.

For many years the Institute and its predecessor body had published an established list of functions of controllership. The newly approved list of treasurership functions was developed coincident with the change of scope and name of the Institute from Controllers Institute to Financial Executives Institute. (See *The Controller* for May, 1962: "CIA becomes FEI", page 228.)

FINANCIAL MANAGEMENT

CONTROLLERSHIP	**TREASURERSHIP**
PLANNING FOR CONTROL To establish, co-ordinate, and administer, as an integral part of management, an adequate plan for the control of operations. Such a plan would provide, to the extent required in the business, profit planning, programmes for capital investing and for financing, sales forecasts, expense budgets and cost standards, together with the necessary procedures to effectuate the plan.	PROVISION OF CAPITAL To establish and execute programmes for the provision of the capital required by the business, including negotiating the procurement of capital and maintaining the required financial arrangements.
REPORTING AND INTERPRETING To compare performance with operating plans and standards, and to report and interpret the results of operations to all levels of management and to the owners of the business. This function includes the formulation of accounting policy, the co-ordination of systems and procedures, the preparation of operating data and of special reports as required.	INVESTOR RELATIONS To establish and maintain an adequate market for the company's securities and, in connection therewith, to maintain adequate liaison with investment bankers, financial analysts, and shareholders.

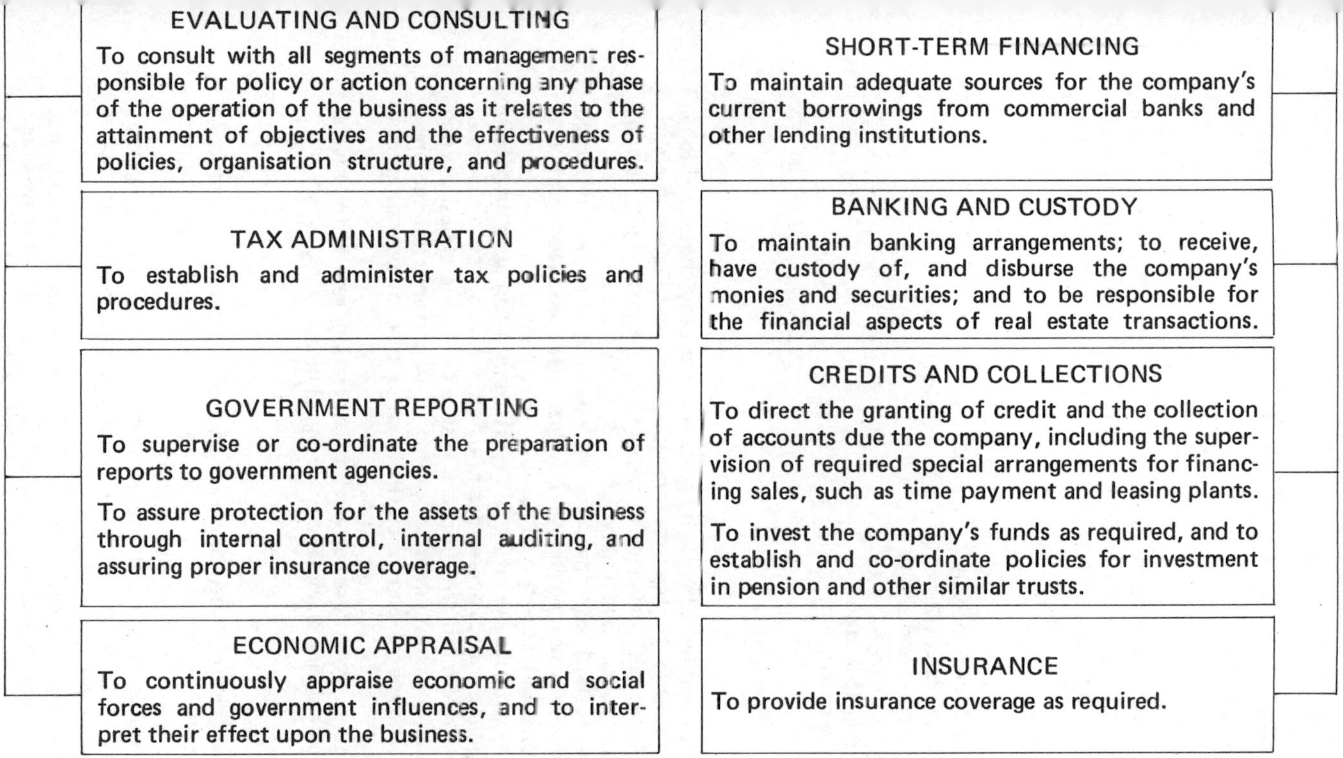

EVALUATING AND CONSULTING

To consult with all segments of management responsible for policy or action concerning any phase of the operation of the business as it relates to the attainment of objectives and the effectiveness of policies, organisation structure, and procedures.

TAX ADMINISTRATION

To establish and administer tax policies and procedures.

GOVERNMENT REPORTING

To supervise or co-ordinate the preparation of reports to government agencies.

To assure protection for the assets of the business through internal control, internal auditing, and assuring proper insurance coverage.

ECONOMIC APPRAISAL

To continuously appraise economic and social forces and government influences, and to interpret their effect upon the business.

SHORT-TERM FINANCING

To maintain adequate sources for the company's current borrowings from commercial banks and other lending institutions.

BANKING AND CUSTODY

To maintain banking arrangements; to receive, have custody of, and disburse the company's monies and securities; and to be responsible for the financial aspects of real estate transactions.

CREDITS AND COLLECTIONS

To direct the granting of credit and the collection of accounts due the company, including the supervision of required special arrangements for financing sales, such as time payment and leasing plants.

To invest the company's funds as required, and to establish and co-ordinate policies for investment in pension and other similar trusts.

INSURANCE

To provide insurance coverage as required.

Figure 4.6: Controllership and treasurership functions defined by FEI

JOB DESCRIPTION: CONTROLLER

Report to: The president

Basic function

Assists the president and his principal executives to obtain maximum profits; spearheads the joint development of realistic operating and investment plans and standards, and administers a system of positive follow-up and controls.

Supervises

Manager of controls and analysis
Manager of industrial statistics
Manager of procedures and audits
Manager of cost accounting
Manager of general accounting
Manager of office services

Specific duties

PLANNING

1 Develops and publishes the ground rules for company short- and long-range planning and the general procedure to be followed by each function. Works with department heads to co-ordinate their planning with company policies and objectives.
2 Reviews and clears all cost standards and measures of activity proposed by departments for use in plans and budgets. Initiates studies of areas where measures are not felt to be reliable.
3 Combines the proposed plans of all departments. Appraises the effects on profit, financial and market position, and the progress anticipated. Evaluates the realism of the proposed plan against general business and industry conditions. Summarizes points of importance for the president and recommends action on the master plan of operations and investment.
4 Issues monthly projections of current operating results for several months ahead, relating changes to the original plan.

FOLLOW-UP

5 Develops and ensures timely issue of control reports to the president and his principal executives. Administers a system of supporting reports to underlying levels of supervision.
6 Performs periodic review and appraisal of operations, involving study of performance in all operating areas and determination of factors underlying poor or good results.
7 Conducts a monthly review meeting with the president to bring out significant operating results and action points. Assists the president to prepare for his own follow-up meetings with key operating executives.
8 Works with all levels of supervision to develop understanding of quotas and budgets, the use of control reports, and the technique of holding review meetings on their own performance.

Figure 4.7: Job description – controller

OTHER

9 Reviews major pricing proposals for maximum profitability and thorough analysis of volume effect.

10 Conducts general accounting, cost estimating, cost accounting and payroll activities, ensuring adequate control over sources of basic data and conformance with government contract requirements. Issues necessary statements, reports and special statistics.

11 Co-ordinates the development of, and publishes, all inter-departmental procedures and all manuals and procedures with control significance; audits conformance to such procedures and manuals. Initiates steps to simplify procedures and cut costs.

12 Provides necessary office services.

13 Administers a report control system covering all recurring reports in the company.

Figure 4.7 (concluded)

If the controller is to execute his staff role satisfactorily for all areas of his organization he must become familiar with the nature of the various departments – engineering, R & D, marketing, manufacturing, logistics etc. It is from the point of view of the operating managers located within these departments that the quality of the controller's service will be determined: if he is not supplying information that helps them to perform more effectively given their problems as they see them, then the controller in turn is not performing effectively. The link between information and action cannot be stressed too highly: the controller supplies the information, but if it is to lead to appropriate action it must be relevant to the circumstances within which the action must take place.

It will be apparent from the last paragraph that the idea of divisional or functional controllers is one that has frequently found favour in recent years. In a decentralized organization it is probable that a centralized controllership function will lack an adequate understanding of divisional activities, or that the controller's staff will not have empathy with the operating personnel. The outcome is likely to be a sub-optimal basis for effective control.

On the other hand, if each division has its own controller, there is a higher likelihood of a closer link between information and action. (A variation on this theme that has not spread as widely as one might have anticipated, for reasons that are not wholly clear, is that of functional controllers. The idea of a marketing controller is well established, and the idea of a physical distribution controller also has support, with the holders of such posts being responsible for providing a planning and control information service for their functional superiors.)

If one thinks about the reporting relationship between a divisional (or a functional) controller and, in the first place, his divisional superior and, in the second, his head office superior, one sees the main inhibition to successfully employing this idea. A divisional controller cannot help having divided loyalties, and this puts him at risk in terms of being trusted and hence in terms of being effective in his divisional role.

A CHECKLIST ON COST CONTROL

1 Is the costing system adequate in general terms?
2 Does information from the cost control system highlight the critical factors that govern the company's success in achieving its objectives?
3 Do good relations exist between the accounting staff and line management? (If not, why not?)
4 Is cost control information geared to the requirements of responsible individuals?
5 Do control reports cover both financial and related causal factors?
6 Are cost control requirements and reports discussed with recipients?
7 Are control reports brief, simple to read, and relevant?
8 Are actions taken on the basis of these reports?
9 Are control reports used to indicate relative efficiencies?
10 Is the cost control system more complex (hence more expensive) than is necessary?
11 Do all employees understand the cost implications of their work?
12 Do all employees have cost targets (where relevant)?
13 Do all who require it receive cost information?
14 Do those individuals charged with various costs really have control over these costs?
15 Do recipients of control information know how to extract the most essential facts?
16 Are responsible individuals aware of the need to plan their activities?
17 Are cost controls established according to the nature of the tasks?
18 Are deviations reported rapidly?
19 Do controls conform to the organizational structure?
20 Are controls flexible and economical in operation?
21 Do controls help to explain variances and to indicate the corrective action that is required?
22 Does the cost control system have the active backing of top management?
23 Is the system seen as being an essential part of the company's management process?

24 Does the basis of measuring desired performance reflect those aspects of output and input that are important?
25 Do responsible individuals who are held accountable play a full role in setting cost levels?
26 Is the principle of management by exception followed?
27 Are results measured in accordance with the same units of measurement in which the standards are set?
28 Do the benefits of the cost control system outweigh its costs?
29 Are unnecessary reports eliminated, and are new ones introduced only when clearly needed?
30 Is the control system revised each time an organizational change takes place?

SUMMARY

Control is the major managerial function and is concerned with such tasks as setting objectives, formulating policies, drawing up plans, deciding amongst alternative courses of action, and monitoring performance in order to achieve objectives.

Control and planning are complementary and necessary to each other. Cost control exists to ensure that actual costs correspond to planned costs. Information and action are central to effective cost control.

Cost control is quite a different activity to cost reduction and the two must not be confused.

Whilst the control of direct costs is relatively straightforward (e.g. via standard costs), the control of overhead costs presents various problems and requires different techniques. It is not possible to control any apportioned cost: costs can only be controlled at source by those responsible for their origination and authorization. Controllability will be determined in part by managerial level and in part by the time period.

Internal audit procedures are a valuable supplement to any cost control system.

The company can be thought of as an input-output system, and this concept can provide a useful basis for designing a cost control system.

A company's cost control system can be tested for adequacy in relation to the checklist on control.

APPENDIX: SYSTEMS ANALYSIS FOR CONTROL

The aims of this appendix are:

1 To explain what a system is and to identify its components and behaviour patterns.
2 To suggest a classification of systems based on problem solving.
3 To consider the number of possible different states of a system, and the control implications of this.
4 To relate systems analysis to the idea of control.

The idea of a system has assumed more and more importance in recent years – e.g. economic system, ecological system, social system, transport system, solar system, political system. Systems are pervasive and appear everywhere.

The common link through all of these differing systems is that each is an assembly of interconnected elements that functions as a collective whole. Their extremes of size are worthy of note: at one extreme is the solar system (containing the sun and its planets), beyond which is our galactic system which spreads into the observable universe which contains other galactic systems. At the other extreme are the physicist's atomic systems and the biologist's cell system.

Systems appear in an hierarchy, with large systems encompassing the smaller systems. This gives us the idea of resolution levels from which to analyse systems. At different levels of resolution particular systems as such may be observed for the first time. At that level the way the system in question behaves as a whole may be observed, but it may be necessary to proceed to a higher level of resolution to identify the elements contained within the system and the ways in which these elements interact and behave. Each element thus becomes identifiable as a separate system which can in turn be resolved into its own elements at the next (higher) level of resolution.

By changing the level of resolution we change the time and space dimensions in which systems are observed and analysed. As we proceed to higher levels of resolution we tend to look in greater detail over shorter time spans, and as we lower the level of resolution we tend to observe broader issues over longer time horizons. This gives us the means to focus on different problems. The 'Resolution graph' (Figure 4.8) illustrates this point.

The ubiquity of systems resulted in the emergence of general systems theory which seeks to provide an integrative framework for the analysis and understanding of all kinds of systems. (This can be linked to 'Ways of knowing', see pp. 48–54.) Almost anything we care to name may be termed a 'system' as long as we define its characteristics and relationships carefully enough to enable us to classify it.

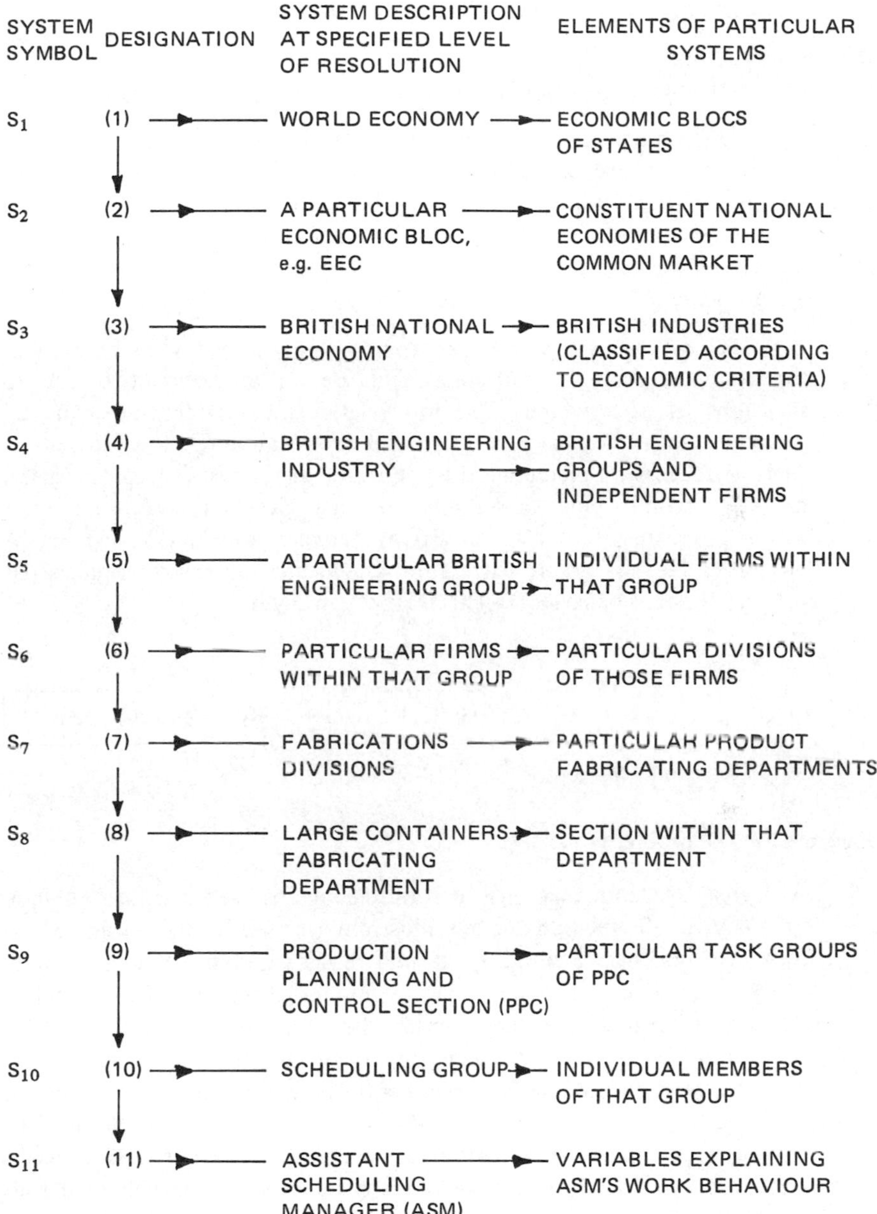

SYSTEM SYMBOL
DESIGNATION
SYSTEM DESCRIPTION AT SPECIFIED LEVEL OF RESOLUTION
ELEMENTS OF PARTICULAR SYSTEMS
S1
(1)
WORLD ECONOMY
ECONOMIC BLOCS OF STATES
S2
(2)
A PARTICULAR ECONOMIC BLOC, e.g. EEC
CONSTITUENT NATIONAL ECONOMIES OF THE COMMON MARKET
S3
(3)
BRITISH NATIONAL ECONOMY
BRITISH INDUSTRIES (CLASSIFIED ACCORDING TO ECONOMIC CRITERIA)
S4
(4)
BRITISH ENGINEERING INDUSTRY
BRITISH ENGINEERING GROUPS AND INDEPENDENT FIRMS
S5
(5)
A PARTICULAR BRITISH ENGINEERING GROUP
INDIVIDUAL FIRMS WITHIN THAT GROUP
S6
(6)
PARTICULAR FIRMS WITHIN THAT GROUP
PARTICULAR DIVISIONS OF THOSE FIRMS
S7
(7)
FABRICATIONS DIVISIONS
PARTICULAR PRODUCT FABRICATING DEPARTMENTS
S8
(8)
LARGE CONTAINERS FABRICATING DEPARTMENT
SECTION WITHIN THAT DEPARTMENT
S9
(9)
PRODUCTION PLANNING AND CONTROL SECTION (PPC)
PARTICULAR TASK GROUPS OF PPC
S10
(10)
SCHEDULING GROUP
INDIVIDUAL MEMBERS OF THAT GROUP
S11
(11)
ASSISTANT SCHEDULING MANAGER (ASM)
VARIABLES EXPLAINING ASM'S WORK BEHAVIOUR

Figure 4.8: Levels of resolution – a resolution graph

In seeking to define a system there are two aspects to consider:

(*a*) the system itself;
(*b*) the point of view, perceptions and purpose of the system's analyst.

The systems analyst's purpose will generally relate to the solution of a problem – he is unlikely to analyse a system for its own sake, but through a better understanding of the workings of a system we can seek to apply that knowledge to problems concerning the system (or its sub-systems or supra-system). It is possible to identify three general types of problem that systems analysis can help to resolve:

1 *Problems of analysis* which are essentially concerned with prediction; for example, given the particular structure, or arrangement, of the institutions of society and their interrelationships, or the departmental groupings of a business enterprise and their couplings, the problem of analysis focuses on predicting the behaviour of interest (e.g. profit, sales, national income, political stability) of that given structure. In other words problems of analysis consist of deriving from one known set of properties (i.e. the system's structure) knowledge about further properties (i.e. the system's behaviour). This is shown in Figure 4.9.

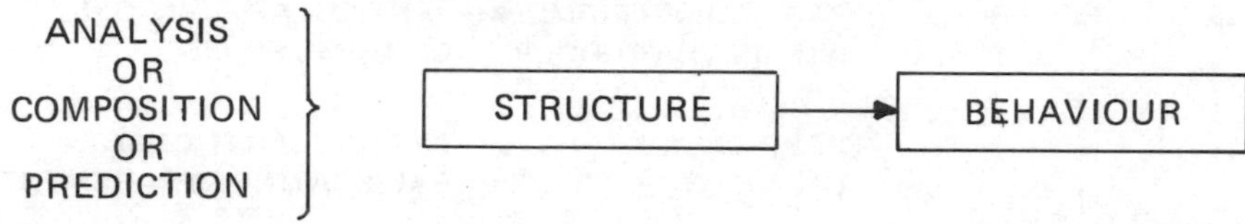

Figure 4.9: The problem of analysis

A great deal of management literature concerns itself with the problems of analysis. Simulation models illustrate this well. For example, the Systems Dynamics Laboratory at MIT has carried out a great deal of analysis of global systems using computer-based simulation models. Amongst the variables included within these models are natural resources, population levels, industrial investment and production, pollution etc. The effects of different policies relating to these variables can be simulated by setting different values/levels/states for each and then letting the computer calculate the possible range of future consequences. It seems from this work that the outcome of many policies is potentially disastrous for mankind. See Figure 4.10.

2 *Problems of synthesis*, which are to a large extent the converse of the problems of analysis (see Figure 4.11). Thus, given a particular behavioural outcome (either observed or prescribed), the problem of synthesis is to

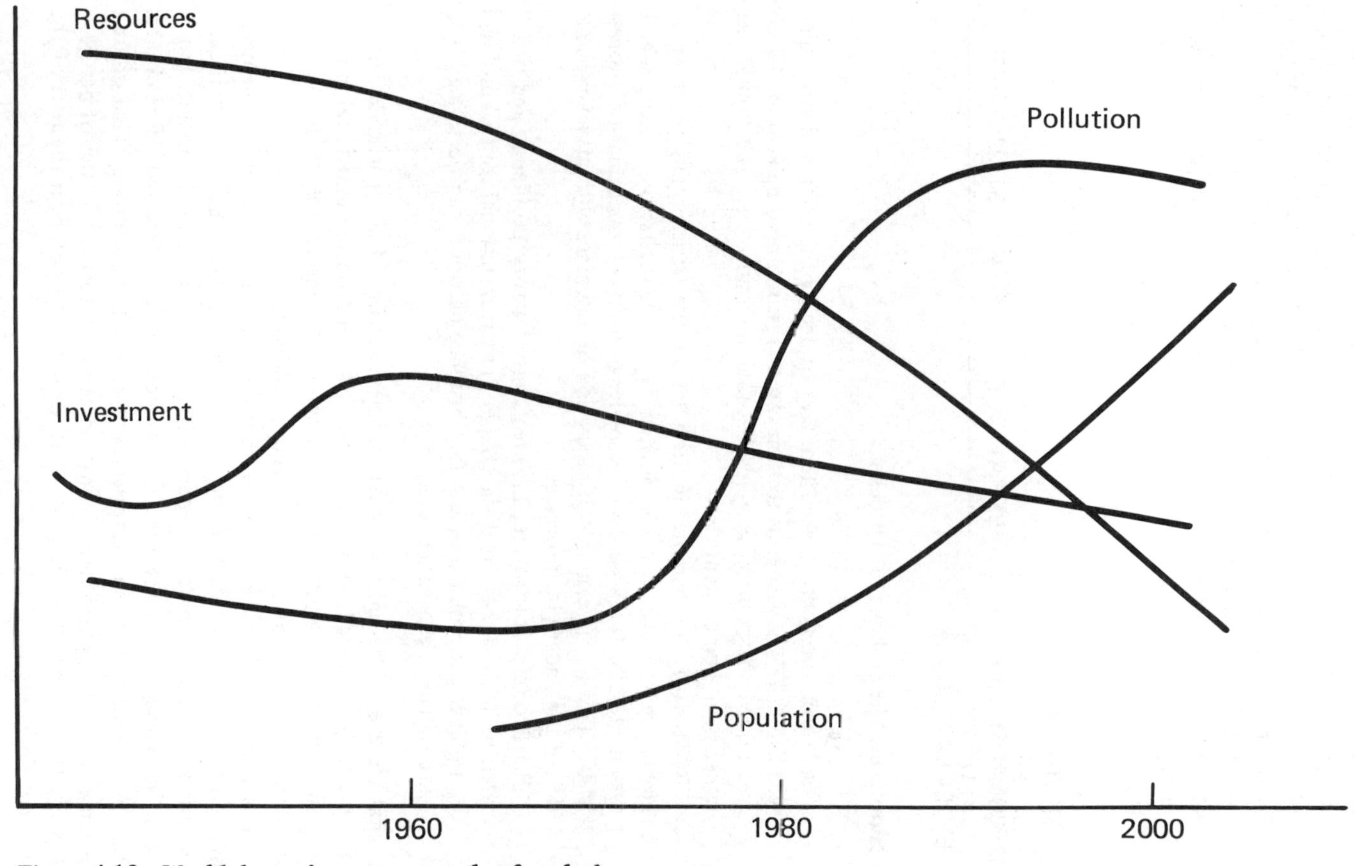

Figure 4.10: World dynamics – an example of analysis

identify the structure (in terms of the kinds of elements and their relationships) that is necessary for realizing the particular behaviour. Problems of synthesis, therefore, are concerned with finding explanations of given or desired behavioural outcomes. To put this another way, the problem of synthesis is to find a means to a given end (as opposed to the problem of analysis which seeks to determine the end of given means). Programming methods are an example of a means of solution to a pròblem of synthesis.

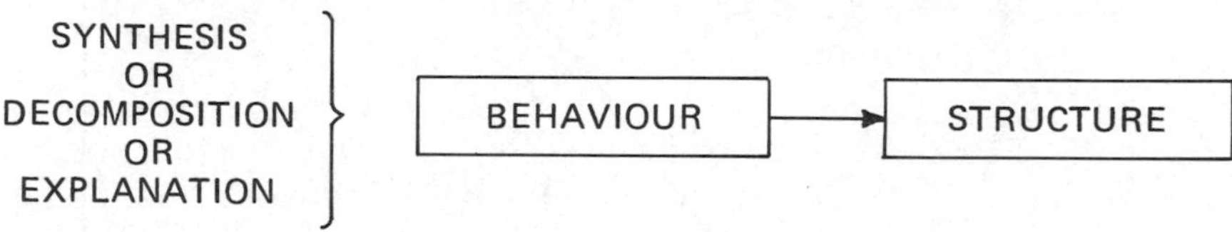

Figure 4.11: The problem of synthesis

3 *'Black box' problems.* We often have to deal with systems about which we have little knowledge as to their internal structure or behaviour. These are termed 'black box' systems because we know only the boundaries rather than their contents.

By studying the outputs that result from the transforming of observed inputs we can gain some understanding of the behaviour of the whole system despite the absence of knowledge of the transformation process itself. This is one example of prediction of outcomes without an explanation of the underlying processes.

Black box problems are, in effect, investigatory problems, and it will often be necessary to treat the study of an organizational control problem as a black box problem in the first instance before it can be refined into one or other of the earlier categories.

A vital feature of defining a system is the selection of the particular set of elements to be included within it. This will depend on the individual analyst, who can draw the system's boundary wherever he wishes. By redefining the boundary the analyst can vary the level of resolution.

It is necessary, however, to limit the scope of any study to the elements that interest us, and to exclude from consideration those that do not directly concern us. The system's boundary divides it from its environment, but it would be wrong to assume that environmental factors are not of relevance. They provide stimuli (often expressed as threats and opportunities) that prompt responses from the system itself. (Environmental factors – or states of nature – cause particular behaviour patterns – strategies – to occur on the part of the system under study.)

If we assume that any given system is seeking to achieve a dynamic equilibrium in its environment as it moves along a trajectory towards some desired goal, then if there is a change within the environment it becomes necessary for the system to adapt its behaviour to accommodate that change. (This is, in fact, the essence of control.) *Homeostatis* is the name of this equilibrium condition.

Since all environmental factors do not have equal relevance to the behaviour patterns of given systems we can logically segregate such factors into two groups:

(*a*) the general environment, containing factors that do not influence the system's behaviour at the chosen level of resolution; and

(*b*) the substantial environment, which contains all those factors that are likely to influence, and be influenced by, the behaviour of the system in question during the time period under consideration.

Systems are characterised by coherence, pattern and purpose. In other words:

1 The elements are connected in an interdependent way, and act as a whole.

2 The elements are organized rather than random, even though the pattern may be very complex.

3 The collection of elements exists to do something, and thus its behaviour can be studied as its elements, and hence the system itself, change state over time in response to environmental disturbances.

Question: Why is a box full of marbles not a system?
Answer:

1 Marbles are not linked or connected in a way that adds wholeness.

2 The box of marbles does not behave as a system – it has no purpose.

3 Adding or subtracting a marble makes no difference to the assembly or its properties.

As man's knowledge of elemental parts of his world has increased it has become apparent that he needs to address issues concerning the interactions amongst these parts – and the consequent complexity that is such a conspicuous feature of whole systems. Synthesis (or bringing together) becomes the focus of attention, as opposed to analysis (or the breaking down of phenomena into their components). The systems approach, or systems thinking, is concerned with wholeness and complexity. Behind his orientation is a desire to gain greater control over what is happening in, and to, man-made organizations and socio-technical/socio-economic systems.

It has become clear that no one specialist can tackle and resolve the problems of wholeness and complexity on his own: the need for multi-disciplinary or cross-disciplinary approaches is essential.

Can we adequately conceive of complexity? There are some schools of thought (e.g. KISS – Keep It Simple, Stupid) that fail totally to recognize the true complexity of socio-technical systems: simplistic solutions are insufficient for resolving complex problems.

A system's complexity is reflected in the number of different states each variable can exhibit, and the appropriate measure is termed the system's *variety*.

Even in a seemingly simple system there are very many different states that could be exhibited. It follows that it is difficult to predict how even a simple system might behave due to the interaction of variety and uncertainty.

If we have just one light bulb this can be either 'on' or 'off', so its variety is 2. When we have two light bulbs the variety doubles to 4, and this becomes 8 with three bulbs, 16 with four bulbs etc.

What is the general rule for calculating the variety of a system with *n* components?

Number of 2-state components	*Number of different system states*
1	2 or 2^1
2	4 or 2^2
3	8 or 2^3
4	16 or 2^4

For any set of 2-state components there are 2^n possible different system states where n is the number of components.

To take an everyday example, a pack of 52 playing cards can be dealt out in many different ways. The sequence in which the cards are dealt will vary, assuming the cards are shuffled between dealings. The total number of ways is 52! (i.e. $52 \times 51 \times 50 ..... 3 \times 2 \times 1$). This gives a number larger than 10^{67} which is a measure of the variety of this simple situation.

Following the idea of variety we get the law of requisite variety (W. R. Ashby). This is central to the idea of control, and relates to the fact that systems can exhibit a very large number of different states. If one is to be able to cope with a system's variety it is necessary to have at least as many behavioural states available as has the system. Or, from a slightly different point of view, if the system is to survive in a hostile and dynamic environment it must be able to counter every environmental threat and take advantage of environmental opportunities: the system must have as many strategies as there are states of nature.

As well as variety, complex systems appear to possess more than just the combined properties of the individual components: the idea of a *Gestalt* is present in living systems so that the whole is greater than the sum of the parts. This extra 'something' refers to the system's emergent properties, or the behaviour patterns that are within the capabilities of the system although they may be beyond the ability of any of the elements or sub-systems of that system.

But is the emergent behaviour predictable or not? In the case of a deterministic system this will tend to be the case (e.g. traffic lights), but for more complex systems (e.g. BP Ltd) their behaviour patterns are probabilistic (see Figure 4.12).

This is compounded by the fact that socio-economic systems are open systems (i.e. they take in and give out materials, energy and information across their boundaries in a continuing sequence of exchanges with the environment). In contrast a closed system is one that has no exchanges with its environment, but simply functions through interactions amongst its components. It is characteristic of closed systems that they will always follow the same route to a final state, whereas open systems exhibit *equifinality*. This describes the fact that many different routes can be taken to arrive at a given end state, and there is not just one single way to run an organization to achieve a specified goal. (This is not to say, of course, that none of the alternatives is to be preferred to the others).

In order to achieve control it is necessary to have the following:

(*a*) a goal state (i.e. a desired, specified, future state);
(*b*) a system that is capable of reaching the goal state (i.e. it has the particular state in its repertoire);
(*c*) some means of influencing the system's behaviour, which presupposes we know something about the connections between the means of influence and the system's behaviour.

Control will not come about through our simply watching, measuring and recording what the system does. It is necessary to understand something about the causal connections between inputs and behavioural responses (outputs), and the feedback links between outputs and (revised) inputs.

If we only seek to establish links between inputs and outputs we are not really achieving control. What we are doing is specifying inputs in the expectations that they will produce the desired outputs, which is termed open-loop control. However, the quality of inputs, or their mix, might change for reasons beyond our predictive ability. If we do not sense this the output will not be the expected state.

The need thus arises for a feedback loop by which the actual output values are regularly compared with the desired output values, and the differences, if any, are examined to isolate causes. Following from this adjustments may be made to the input values in order to influence outputs, or the expected output values may be modified (reflecting an initially optimistic, or pessimistic, setting). This gives us closed-loop control. Figure 4.13 illustrates this.

A number of points about closed-loop, or feedback, control are worth making. In the first place variances between actual and desired outputs are unlikely to be eliminated at the first attempt. Lags are usually to be found

SYSTEMS	SIMPLE	COMPLEX	EXCEEDINGLY COMPLEX
DETERMINISTIC	WINDOW CATCH	ELECTRONIC DIGITAL COMPUTER	EMPTY
	BILLIARDS	PLANETARY SYSTEM	
	MACHINE-SHOP LAYOUT	AUTOMATION	
PROBABILISTIC	PENNY TOSSING	STOCKHOLDING	THE ECONOMY
	JELLY FISH MOVEMENTS	CONDITIONED REFLEXES	THE BRAIN
	STATISTICAL QUALITY CONTROL	INDUSTRIAL PROFITABILITY	THE COMPANY

Figure 4.12: Predictability of behaviour patterns

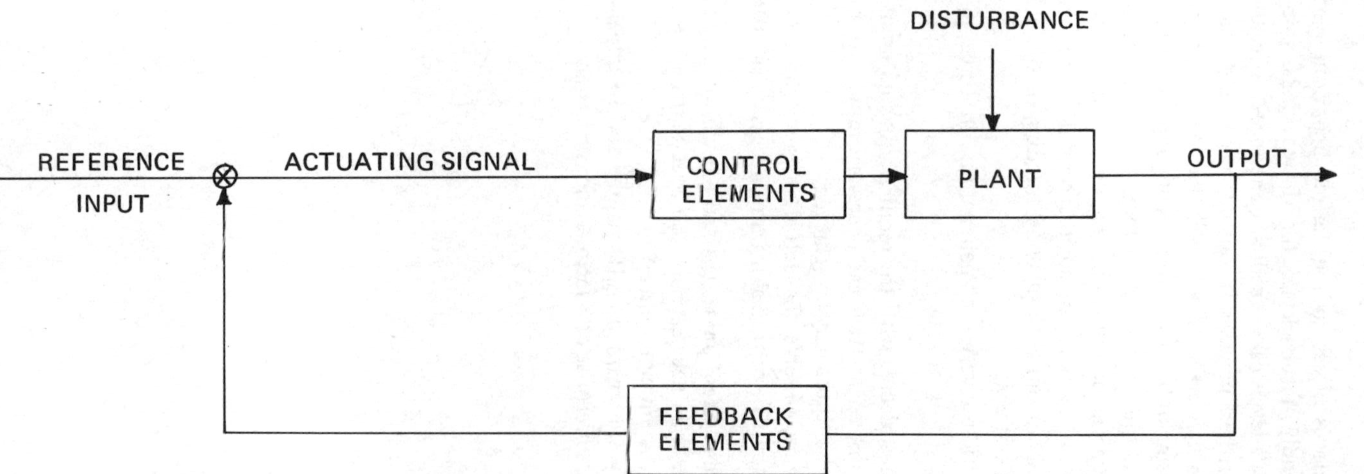

Figure 4.13: A feedback control system

as the system moves closer to the desired behaviour pattern with successive iterations. Secondly, feedback can be of two kinds: positive (through which increases in output levels cause feedback messages to result in additional inputs which lead to further increases in output levels, and vice-versa for decreases); or negative (in which case the feedback message acts to produce the opposite impact, so increasing outputs lead to reducing inputs etc.).

The ultimate type of control system, involving a multitude of feedback loops, is a cybernetic or self-regulating one. This, however, in the context of designing control systems for socio-economic/socio-technical systems, begs many questions about our level of understanding of the behaviour and internal workings of such systems.

Manual regulation involves human actions in three phases of the control process:

(*a*) someone must decide what the required outputs should be;
(*b*) someone must ensure that the necessary inputs are provided in order that the required outputs may be achieved;
(*c*) someone must observe the actual outputs and compare these with the desired outputs prior to making any necessary adjustments to the inputs.

In a self-regulating system phases (*b*) and (*c*) will be carried out automatically, although it will still be necessary for the goal of the system (hence the outputs) to be specified by an outside source.

As a summary statement of this chapter and its appendix Figure 4.14 portrays the business enterprise as a socio-economic system.

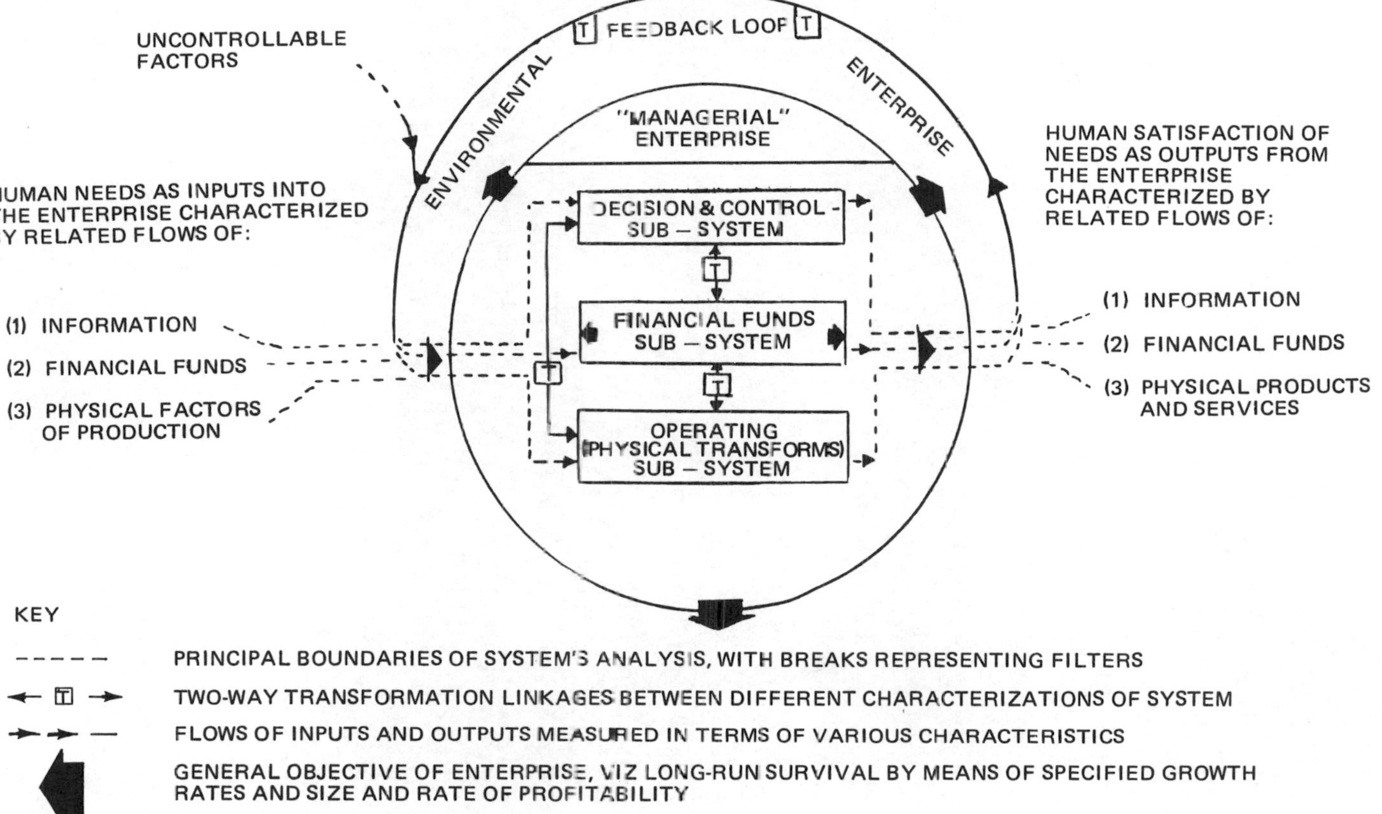
'SUBSTANTIAL' ENVIRONMENT TO THE ENTERPRISE
T
FEEDBACK LOOP
T
UNCONTROLLABLE FACTORS
ENVIRONMENTAL
ENTERPRISE
"MANAGERIAL" ENTERPRISE
HUMAN NEEDS AS INPUTS INTO THE ENTERPRISE CHARACTERIZED BY RELATED FLOWS OF:
(1) INFORMATION
(2) FINANCIAL FUNDS
(3) PHYSICAL FACTORS OF PRODUCTION
DECISION & CONTROL - SUB – SYSTEM
FINANCIAL FUNDS SUB – SYSTEM
OPERATING (PHYSICAL TRANSFORMS) SUB – SYSTEM
HUMAN SATISFACTION OF NEEDS AS OUTPUTS FROM THE ENTERPRISE CHARACTERIZED BY RELATED FLOWS OF:
(1) INFORMATION
(2) FINANCIAL FUNDS
(3) PHYSICAL PRODUCTS AND SERVICES
KEY
PRINCIPAL BOUNDARIES OF SYSTEM'S ANALYSIS, WITH BREAKS REPRESENTING FILTERS
TWO-WAY TRANSFORMATION LINKAGES BETWEEN DIFFERENT CHARACTERIZATIONS OF SYSTEM
FLOWS OF INPUTS AND OUTPUTS MEASURED IN TERMS OF VARIOUS CHARACTERISTICS
GENERAL OBJECTIVE OF ENTERPRISE, VIZ LONG-RUN SURVIVAL BY MEANS OF SPECIFIED GROWTH RATES AND SIZE AND RATE OF PROFITABILITY

Figure 4.14: The business organization as a system

5

Quality Control

INTRODUCTION

Profit is, as well we know, the prime measure of business success. This results from the sale of goods and services *of an acceptable quality* at a price that exceeds cost.

It is clear that management must consider very carefully the level of quality that is to be offered by its products (as indicated by the perceived value for money that this represents in the eyes of actual and potential consumers), as well as their price and cost levels. This shows a need for balancing these dimensions.

The value for money provided by a given product can be increased by improving those qualities that consumers desire (and are willing to pay for) such as a choice of different colours, and eliminating those qualities that are of little or no value to consumers – such as elaborate packaging.

As an alternative, value for money can be increased by reducing the cost of the product to the consumer whilst offering him the same potential benefits from his consumption. In this context the cost of the product to the consumer should be related to the life of the product: for a durable item this will be composed of the following categories of cost:

1 Initial outlay
2 Operating costs

3 Servicing costs
4 Out-of-service costs
5 Premature replacement costs

Aspects of cost reduction are obviously of importance but this chapter is concerned with aspects of quality.

QUALITY CONTROL

Quality relates to function, and from this it will be seen that, since the function of an item is to achieve its intended purpose, quality can be defined as *fitness for purpose*. A high quality item, therefore, is one that fulfills its purpose very well. This may or may not be related to *precision*: if it is not, then striving for high precision in manufacturing (as evidenced by tight tolerances and so forth) will tend to raise costs rather than improve quality. This is wasteful.

Reliability is closely associated with quality, the former referring principally to the ability of a product to continue functioning over a period of time, whilst the latter suggests acceptance at a particular point in time. It would be unrealistic to consider them apart.

The control of quality is of special importance because quality affects the relationships that the company has with consumers, suppliers, and various official organizations (most notably local authorities under the terms of the legislation relating to fair trading, weights and measures, and trades descriptions). In addition, quality affects the efficiency of internal operations: the early discovery of defective quality in units of output will lead to a rapid correction, and this should prevent serious losses in both financial terms and in terms of customer goodwill.

Customer goodwill depends on customer approval of the many dimensions of the company's output – including quality. This in turn depends upon:

1 The establishing of standards relating to such product characteristics as durability, size, function, finish, and appearance.
2 The existence of appropriate means within the organization to ensure that these standards are adhered to.

It is important to realize that quality control is not just concerned with detecting substandard work, but also with its *prevention*. This requires that quality control procedures in the case of each new product are planned in accordance with the operation sequence and method of manufacture. It is also helpful if quality control specialists are consulted in the design phase. This is more clearly apparent, perhaps, if the earlier statement that quality represents fitness for purpose is considered as this encompasses two interrelated but distinguishable aspects of quality:

1 Quality of design, which is determined by the degree of achievement of the specified purpose of the design itself.
2 Quality of conformance, which indicates the extent to which the product complies with the design.

A poor design can never lead to high quality, although poor workmanship can easily debase a good design. This again highlights the role of precision.

As the degree of precision is increased, then the relationships shown in Figure 5.1 will tend to prevail. When precision is at a low level it is likely that demand will also be at a low level and, consequently, price will be low. Increases in the degree of precision cannot be fully matched by increases in price: revenue will increase at a decreasing rate (as shown by the price curve) with the result that increasing precision brings with it smaller and smaller acceptable increases in price. In contrast, costs of manufacturing behave in quite the opposite manner: as precision is increased so do costs increase, but at an increasing rate. Figure 5.1 shows these relationships graphically with the difference between the price curve and the cost curve being the contribution, and this is also plotted. When price is equal to cost (at points A and C) it is evident that contribution must be nil. The contribution can be increased from nil at point A to a maximum at point B (where the price and cost curves are furthest apart), by

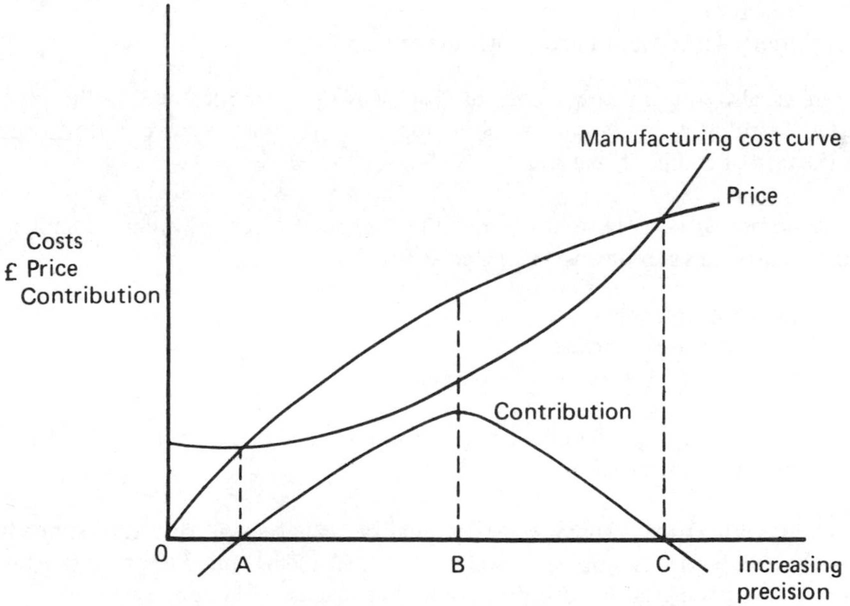

Figure 5.1: The effects of precision

increasing the precision, but beyond this point the contribution falls as precision is needlessly increased. Beyond the extremes of points A and C the contribution is negative, and this demonstrates that very low precision as well as very high precision is undesirable.

This has given us an insight into the financial aspects of one dimension of quality, but there are many other financial considerations involved in assuring consumers of a given level of quality. Basically, the cost factors involved can be broken down under the following headings.

1 **Failure costs.** Those costs that could have been avoided if the product had been made to an acceptable level of quality. Typical examples of this category of costs are:

(*a*) scrap
(*b*) rework
(*c*) reinspection
(*d*) sorting of rejects
(*e*) losses on sale of substandard items
(*f*) servicing of customers' complaints
(*g*) extra operations
(*h*) selective assembly
(*i*) downtime
(*j*) after sales service (under guarantee or warranty)

There is also the unknown cost of lost sales opportunities due to the company acquiring a reputation for poor quality or for poor relative performance in the face of competitive goods.

2 **Appraisal costs.** Those costs that the company incurs in order to limit its failure costs. Inspection and testing costs for:

(*a*) Incoming materials
(*b*) Manufacturing processes
(*c*) Products at all stages of manufacture and use

fall into this category, as do the costs of providing and maintaining the necessary equipment such as gauges.

3 **Prevention costs.** Those costs of quality management that the company incurs in order to optimize its total quality cost. This will cover such matters as the cost of special investigations into the causes of failure costs, the costs of training personnel in the control of quality, and the cost of providing quality reports.

It has been estimated that up to 12 per cent of total corporate turnover is spent in one way or another (as suggested above) on quality assurance activities. If this cost level could be reduced *whilst maintaining the same quality level* it would lead to a rapid improvement in business profits.

One approach to reducing quality control costs is to consider initially the total costs incurred in the various quality control activities. Figure 5.2 illustrates a useful format for recording and reporting these costs.

Extreme accuracy in completing a cost report such as that of Figure 5.2 is less important at this stage than is identifying the principal quality cost areas in order to arrive at a reasonable estimate of their annual value.

From this analysis of quality costs it will probably emerge that a small number of sources account for most of the costs. For example, scrap and rework costs may represent a high proportion of the total, or possibly excessive after sales service costs may be found. Efforts should then be directed to finding the causes of these high costs.

Once the causes have been found steps should be taken to bring them under control – at least to the extent that their effects on the major quality cost categories are minimized.

THE ROLE OF INSPECTION

Whilst all those engaged in manufacturing and marketing should be concerned with quality, inspection usually exists as a separate department that is mainly concerned (within the overall quality control framework) with making tests and measurements.

In order that inspectors may have the necessary freedom to secure the observance of quality standards, they should not be placed under the jurisdiction of foremen or works managers. Their independence is of paramount importance in the event of conflict. The chief inspector should report at a high level, and much will depend on the structure of the company, the nature of the products, and the emphasis that management wishes to place on quality.

On a day-to-day basis inspection may be a function of the distribution department (in which event the inspectors will accept or reject finished goods on the basis of whether or not they can be sold); or it may be a function of the marketing department (with a similar criterion); or a function of the plant manager. Ultimately, of course, inspection – and all other aspects of quality control – is the responsibility of the chief executive. In operational terms it is important that responsibility for each aspect of quality is clearly established so that each person knows what is expected of him. In addition to the inspectors, many other people are concerned directly with quality: there are the design engineers, purchasing personnel, foreman, and operatives. The

COMPANY ....DATE................

DIVISION..DEPARTMENT/UNIT................

TOTAL QUALITY COST ESTIMATE (12 MONTHS EQUIVALENT)

Category	*Item*	£	*Per cent total*	*Per cent turnover*
Failure (internal)	1 Scrap 2 Rework 3 Repair 4 Excess operation time 5 Excess production 6 Corrective operations 7 Tooling revision 8 Give aways 9 Troubleshooting 10 Design changes 11 Down grading			
Failure (external)	1 Warranty 2 Customer service 3 Customer returns			
Appraisal	1 Purchase acceptance 2 In process acceptance 3 Outgoing product approval 4 Quality 5 Inspection tools 6 Reliability monitoring 7 Quality audits 8 Training 9 Quality records 10 Outside appraisal services 11 Customer liaison			
Prevention	1 Design quality improvements 2 Vendor quality improvements 3 Plan product/process controls 4 Plan acceptance jobs 5 Conformance quality improvement 6 Evaluating consumer satisfaction 7 Quality education 8 Executive quality reporting			
Grand total			100	
Turnover				100

Figure 5.2: Quality cost report

control of quality is going to be of more immediate concern to top management in some industries (such as drugs) than in others (such as construction).

From this background discussion it is now appropriate to consider the specific purposes of inspection within a quality control framework. Essentially, there are five major purposes:

1 To ensure that standards for materials, components, and finished goods are adhered to. It costs as much to produce a defective unit of output as it does to produce an acceptable one and it can cost more if one allows for rectification costs. Similarly, to produce goods of a quality that exceeds the relevant standard creates unnecessary costs. (An example of this is the coating of steel sheeting with heavier layers of tin than are necessary for a canning process.)
2 To permit the correction of defects as they arise. For instance, castings that are too large can be machined down to size; batches of some chemical products can be reblended; etc.
3 To grade the units of outputs. Eggs are an obvious example, as are 'seconds' (i.e. substandard but saleable products such as shirts, shoes, socks, ceramics, linen goods, etc.).
4 To provide information on the efficiency of supervisors and operatives in various departments. It may become apparent through inspection that the most suitable materials are not being used, or the wrong grade of labour is employed, or training is needed, or the incentive payment scheme is inadequate in rewarding good workmanship, or tolerances are too tight, or that the maintenance of machines must be improved, etc.
5 To check the quality (and quantity) of output in connection with a payment by results (PBR) or piecework payment scheme. The inspector in this case should record the total number of units inspected per operative, distinguishing between the number that are accepted and the number rejected. Defects can then be related to men and machines and causes sought.

It should always be borne in mind that inspection adds nothing (in terms of value) to the finished product, and therefore no more inspection should be done than is necessary to accomplish its intended purpose.

Since product quality (for a given design) depends largely upon the materials used, the plant facilities and processes, and the skill of both operatives and management, inspection must be related to:

1 Incoming raw materials lest defective materials be processed or inadvertently paid for.
2 Incoming consumable items – such as maintenance supplies.
3 Incoming components.

4 Manufacturing processes.
5 Storage facilities (in connection with perishable items).
6 Suppliers' manufacturing/storage facilities.
7 Work-in-progress – the first-off of each batch as a minimum requirement to prevent further processing of unsatisfactory items.
8 Finished goods – the product should meet consumers' requirements with regard to mechanical performance, finish, cleanliness, and so forth.
9 Gauges and other measuring devices.

Inspection cannot always be carried out at every stage of production, so management should establish *control points* where errors may be detected before serious losses occur. The number and location of control points will be determined by the nature of the products and processes involved. The last operation in each production department is frequently selected prior to items passing on to another department for further attention.

Given these features of the inspection function let us now consider who should carry them out. Four alternatives are identifiable:

1 Professional inspections. In the case of complex products, and certainly in the case of checking gauges and related equipment, as well as in many other instances, it is advisable to have full-time inspectors acting as a staff service function to the production departments.
2 Worker inspection. With skilled men who are able to work to prescribed tolerances on a voluntary basis it should be possible to discover defects at an early stage with less cost than in item (1) above. However, dangers exist in the presence of indifference, carelessness, or incompetence. This function can often be combined with packing goods for shipment to customers.
3 Automatic inspection. This exists in the case of interlocking or coupling parts (i.e. where one part must be fitted to another in the assembly of the finished product). Since the acceptability of each individual item depends on fit the defective units will be immediately identifiable.
4 Machine inspection. A simple example of machine inspection is the weighing of items of output: if an item is either underweight or overweight it is set aside. This method can also be applied to other physical dimensions such as length and thickness.

The next consideration must be an answer to the question: 'How much should be inspected?' This raises two problems.

1 What percentage of materials, components, or finished products should be inspected?
2 What method should be used to determine the proper amount to inspect, and following this, how should one judge the whole batch on the basis of the results of inspecting a sample?

When manual work is involved it is usually necessary to inspect every piece of work (e.g. typesetting in the case of a book, or typing a letter). Essentially, however, this decision will depend on the importance of the work – even auditors do not consider it necessary to inspect every ledger entry before giving their blessing to a set of accounts. In the situation where automatic or semi-automatic machines are used, it should only be necessary to inspect a part of the output.

Sampling methods should also be considered for other reasons. To inspect 100 per cent of items produced or materials received in to stock is very costly, and in some instances it is not possible to test every item produced; e.g. stress testing on some products – such as glass bottles – leaves the product unusable. It becomes advisable to make use of statistical techniques. The typical questions that need to be answered are:

1 How large a sample should be inspected?
2 How should the items in the sample chosen for inspection be selected from the total?
3 When the number of defective items in the sample has been determined how can the number of defective items in the total be estimated?
4 What is the possible or probable percentage of error in the estimate of the total number of defective items?
5 What percentage of defective items in the sample is sufficient to justify the rejection of the entire lot?
6 How can the number of defective items in various samples be charted over time in order that unfavourable trends may be detected and the causes corrected?

Statistical quality control can supply all the answers, and whilst it would take a specialist text to look at all the implications of these questions, the next section considers the broad approach that should be adopted.

STATISTICAL QUALITY CONTROL

Statistical quality control (SQC) is based upon the established fact that the observed quality of an item is always subject to chance variability. Some variability in the observed quality of an item will be due to assignable causes which exist beyond the boundaries due to chance causes. (Assignable causes are, by definition, identifiable and steps can be taken to remove them. Examples include faulty raw materials, mechanical faults, etc., that are characteristics of the productive processes themselves. In contrast, chance causes are uncontrollable and cannot be removed. Examples are the occasional blemish in a piece of cloth due to a broken thread, an irregular bore hole through a piece of metal due to the operative's failure to clear shavings away before drilling, and so forth.) The major task of SQC is to distinguish between assignable and chance causes of error in order that the assignable causes may be identified, their cause discovered and eliminated, and acceptable quality standards maintained.

Even with automatic machine-produced items there will be chance variations around, for example, the required thickness of a component. This can be illustrated by thinking of a component that has a specified thickness of 1cm with a tolerance of 0.005cm, so this means that the acceptance levels are those within the range 0.995–1.005cm. If the process is under total control (i.e. no assignable variations exist) the following pattern (see figure 5.3) may emerge after 63 units have been examined and measured and expressed in the form of a *frequency distribution*.

This data can be plotted in the form of a *histogram* as in Figure 5.4. (This diagram can easily be converted into a bell-shaped curve that is known as the *normal distribution* and which has special properties.) Given that the machine is producing normally (i.e. it is under control) the average thickness of each component will be 1cm with the majority of variations falling within the range 0.995–1.005cm. When the process is under control in this manner the variability of product quality can only be affected if the production process itself is altered in some way. Let us suppose that components produced by the machine are inspected at regular intervals and that the average value increases

Thickness (cm)	*Number of observations* (frequency)
0.993	1
0.994	1
0.995	2
0.996	3
0.997	5
0.998	7
0.999	8
1.000	9
1.001	8
1.002	7
1.003	5
1.004	3
1.005	2
1.006	1
1.007	1
	63

Figure 5.3: Frequency distribution

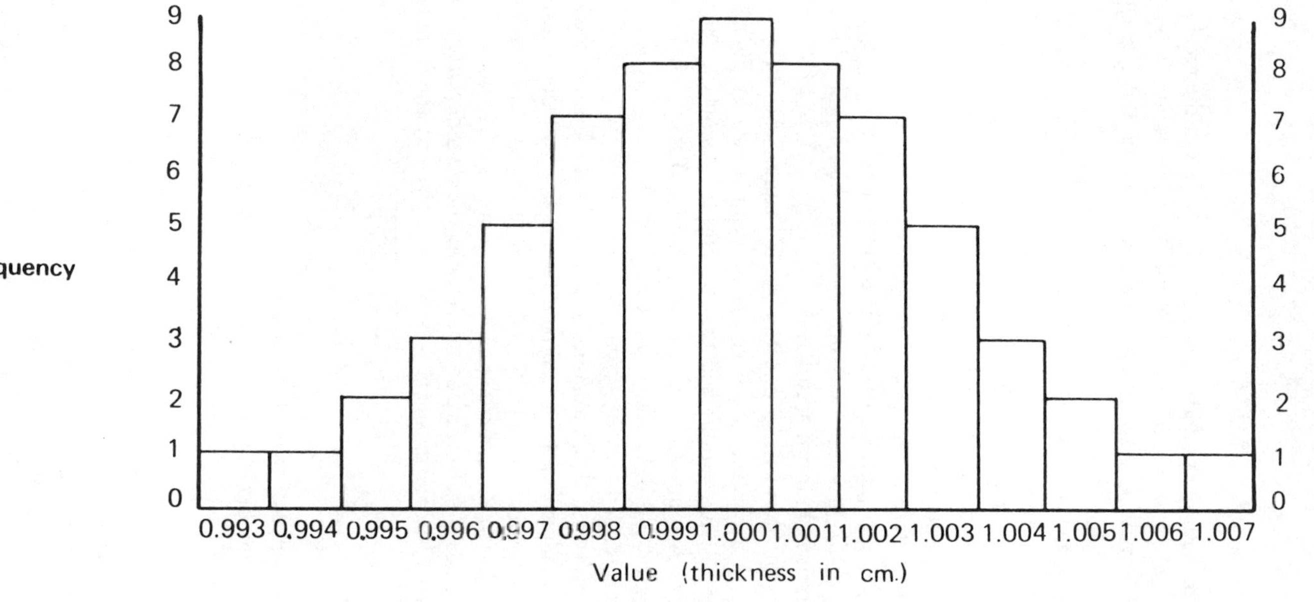

Figure 5.4: Histogram

to 1.002cm with a range of 0.996–1.008cm. In this event the machining operation would be said to be out of control and the process should be stopped until the cause (which may be a worn cutting tool) is found and corrective action taken.

The quality of units of output can, of course, be measured in various ways, but when we are concerned with mass-produced items it is usually expedient to measure quality by a fairly simple characteristic of the item under consideration. The width of a screw, the hardness of a bearing, or the strength of a material are representative examples.

Once the characteristic of quality is specified, SQC proceeds by checking samples of a specified (and statistically predetermined) size at regular intervals of time. The whole procedure is mathematically based and provides a check within predetermined limits of accuracy.

As pointed out above (in connection with Figure 5.4), the histogram can be converted into a continuous curve of the type shown in Figure 5.5. The highest number of observations will tend to cluster around the specified value which represents the highest point of the curve. There will be a reducing number of observations both above and below this specified value. This spread of observations is termed the *dispersion.*

In the case of a 1cm thick component it has already been noted that, whilst the process is under control, the average thickness of all observations will be 1cm, despite variations around this value. The average (or central) value is represented in statistical terminology by $\bar{x}$ (known as 'bar x'), and the spread or dispersion can be measured by computing the *standard deviation* (represented by the lower case Greek letter sigma – σ) which is given by the formula:

$$\sigma = \sqrt{\sum \frac{(x - \bar{x})^2}{n - 1}}$$

Where: x is the value of each observation
n is the number of observations
Σ (capital sigma) means 'the sum of ...'

It is found that the proportion of observations falling within various limits (as given by a specified number of standard deviations on either side of $\bar{x}$) is constant for processes under control *whatever the process.*

Between one standard deviation below the mean ($\bar{x}$) and one standard deviation above it (i.e. within the range $+\sigma$ to $-\sigma$) there will always be 68.27 per cent of observations; between $+2\sigma$ and -2σ there will always be 95.45 per cent of observations; and between $+3\sigma$ and -3σ there will always be 99.8 per cent of observations.

If a tolerance limit of $\pm 3\sigma$ is taken as being acceptable, then in a process that is under control 998 out of every 1000 observations will fall within this

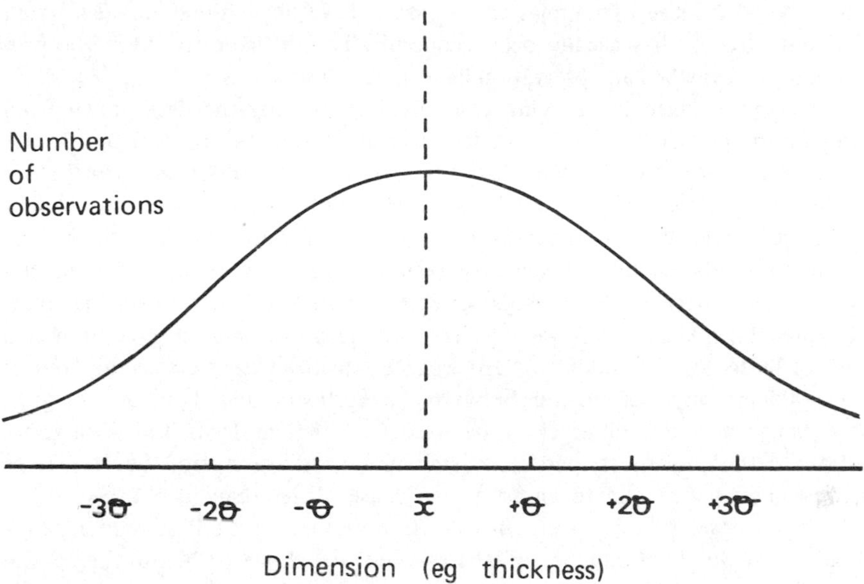

Figure 5.5: Normal distribution

range. This situation exists when pure chance alone causes variation in 2 units out of every 1 000 and such variations cannot be assigned or removed. However, should more than 2 units in a sample batch of 1 000 be found to be defective, then the process is almost certainly out of control and an assignable cause should be found and corrective action taken.

The size of the sample that should regularly be taken will depend upon the required degree of accuracy, with a larger sample for a given value of σ being required the higher the desired degree of accuracy. (Interested readers are recommended to follow up this topic in any basic statistical text such as M. J. Moroney, *Facts from Figures*, 2nd edition, Penguin Books, 1953.)

Actually applying SQC to a production process can be divided into two stages. The first stage requires $\bar{x}$ and σ to be determined. The process average, $\bar{x}$, is the specified dimension (e.g. thickness of 1cm), and the process standard deviation, σ, can be computed from a series of observations (when no variations due to assignable causes can be detected) by using the formula given on p. 96. From a knowledge of the values of $\bar{x}$ and σ it is possible to specify *control limits*. In practice, the limits given by:

$$\bar{x} \pm 3 \frac{\sigma}{\sqrt{N}}$$

where N is the size of samples to be taken, have been found satisfactory in the sense that it has usually been economically justifiable to check the production process when an observation lies outside these limits.

The second stage in applying SQC involves plotting the data drawn from samples to see whether or not their means lie within the control limits. (A sample size of 15 is very often used with satisfactory results.) A *control chart* of the type depicted in Figure 5.6 is extremely helpful in this task.

Figure 5.6 illustrates various points that have already been mentioned. It relates to several samples, taken at regular intervals over time, of 5 items per sample, with the mean (or average) of each sample being plotted on the chart. The predetermined central value is 1cm in thickness, and the predetermined control limits are 1 ± 0.009cm. An extra control device is a *warning limit* at 1 ± 0.006cm: any observation between 1 ± 0.006cm and 1 ± 0.009cm gives a warning, but any observation beyond 1 ± 0.009cm leads to investigative action as the process is then considered to be out of control (i.e. variations are assumed to be due to an assignable cause rather than to chance, with a very high degree of certainty). Investigation may also arise if a trend appears, if an unusually large number of observations are above or below the central value, or if several observations are near a control limit. Figure 5.6 does not suggest the need for any investigation as the process appears to be under control with all observations lying well within the control limits and all within the warning limits. It should be emphasized, of course, that tolerance limits should not be less than the control limits otherwise corrective action would not result if observations exceeded allowable tolerances but were within the control limits. Suitable tolerance limits for the situation shown in Figure 5.6 might be 1 ± 0.01cm.

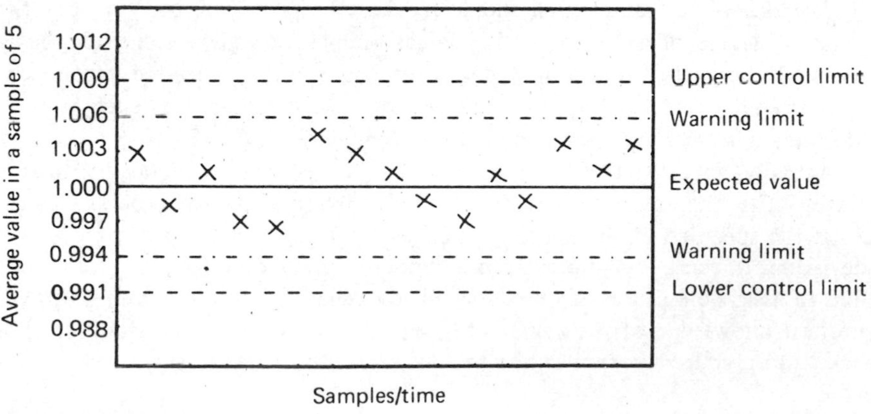

Figure 5.6: Statistical control chart

These basic principles of SQC can be applied in areas other than production. An example is given of a control chart for monitoring advertising expenditure as a percentage of sales in Figure 5.7. The standard of performance that is expected is that advertising expense will be 8 per cent of sales revenue, but random causes (i.e. chance) can make this figure vary from 6 per cent to 10 per cent of sales revenue. If the range of 6–10 per cent represents 3 standard deviations on either side of a mean of 8 per cent (i.e. $\bar{x} = 8$ with confidence limits of $\pm 3\sigma$), then observations would be expected to fall within this range in 998 out of 1 000 cases.

However, when an observation falls outside these limits two opposing hypotheses can be put forward to explain the situation:

1. The observation is the freak 1 out of 1 000 that exceeds the control limits by pure chance, and the company still has the situation under control.
2. The company has lost control over the situation due to some assignable cause such as a new competitor entering the market.

If hypothesis (1) is accepted it is unnecessary to investigate – with the risk that something has actually happened to cause the situation to fall out of control. On the other hand, if hypothesis (2) is accepted and investigations are begun into assignable causes there is always the risk – albeit very small – of the first hypothesis being correct and hence investigation being unnecessary.

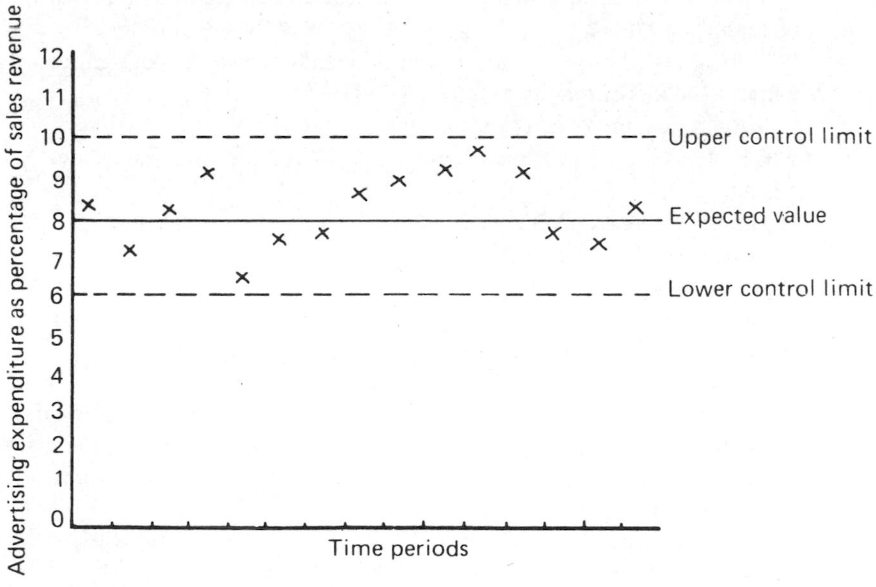

Figure 5.7: Advertising control chart

CLERICAL QUALITY CONTROL

It should not be overlooked that much of the work carried out in offices is 'productive' and quality control can often be applied to the company's advantage.

The quality of clerical work can be checked by examining all the work, or by means of a sample of the work drawn at random, or by means of SQC. Checking 100 per cent of the work is equivalent to doing it all twice (or employing twice as many people to do it once) and is not recommended. Random sampling is a reasonable compromise between doing a full check and doing no checking. SQC is better than both these other methods and can often be carried out along the lines suggested in the last section. (This topic will briefly reappear in Chapter 14.)

QUALITY CONTROL CHECKLIST

1 Are quality control standards for all materials, components, and products regularly reviewed?
2 Are tolerances, allowances, finish, and other requirements necessary and appropriate?
3 Can the specification requirements be raised to improve quality without increasing cost?
4 Will lowering the specification requirements reduce costs significantly without the loss of quality?
5 Can quality be improved by using new processes?
6 Will a change in inspection requirements affect the rate (hence cost) of rejects?
7 Is defective work excessive?
8 Are causes of defective work noted?
9 Is product performance in the field evaluated?
10 Could quality control costs be reduced (without sacrificing quality) by reducing or eliminating some inspection procedures?
11 Does the company use SQC? (If not, why not?)
12 Is the company paying for costly inspection at other sources when these could be more economically performed at the company's own premises?
13 Are inspection activities scheduled in such a way that they do not hold production up?
14 Are quality control ideas applied throughout the company rather than being confined to the production sphere?
15 Do the benefits from using quality control procedures exceed their cost?

SUMMARY

Costs and quality must be balanced in an attempt to achieve a fitness for purpose that represents good value to the consumer.

Quality and reliability go hand in hand, and the quality control process is concerned as much with preventing the appearance of substandard units as with detecting such units. This requires a consideration of both the quality of design as well as the quality of conformance. Precision is not necessarily equivalent to quality.

The recommended technique is statistical quality control (SQC) which has as its major objective the maintaining of quality levels without having to carry out 100 per cent checks. SQC involves inspecting only a fraction of the output of a process and this keeps the costs down whilst improving the efficiency of inspection. In addition, SQC ensures early detection of faults, with the minimum of delay in restoring control, and this has the effect of keeping wastage to a very low level.

When a process is under statistical control it is possible to accurately specify product quality by selecting the limits within which, say, 95 per cent of the output will fall. This permits accurate prediction which is beyond the reach of 100 per cent checks. SQC can readily reflect changes in quality caused by changes in the production process.

It is important to realize that the principles of quality control in general, and of SQC in particular, can be applied throughout the company to a variety of activities.

FURTHER READING FOR PART ONE

Benston, G.J. (ed.), *Contemporary Cost Accounting and Control*, Encino, California: Dickenson, 2nd ed., 1977.
(A valuable collection of articles that covers many relevant issues.)

Bierman, H. and Dyckman, T.R., *Managerial Cost Accounting*, New York: Macmillan, 2nd ed. 1976.
(A good comprehensive text that adopts a decision emphasis, but mainly intended for people who already have some background in accounting.)

Bonini, C.P., Jaedicke, R.K. and Wagner, H.M. (eds), *Management Controls: New Directions in Basic Research*, New York: McGraw-Hill, 1964.
(Despite its age this is still a relevant set of papers that constitutes a significant landmark in thinking about control.)

Emery, F.E. (ed.), *Systems Thinking* (in 2 vols), Harmondsworth: Penguin, 2nd ed., 1981.
(Whilst heavy going in places these volumes offer valuable insights into the functioning of living systems.)

Hart, H., *Overhead Costs: Analysis and Control*, London: Heinemann, 1973.
(This short book looks at the nature of overhead costs, the hows and whys of overhead apportionment etc., with a strong emphasis on linking UK company practices to an evaluative framework.)

Horngren, C.T., *Cost Accounting*, Englewood Cliffs, N.J.: Prentice-Hall, 4th ed., 1977.
(This is the standard international textbook on cost accounting.)

Johnson, R.A., Kast, F.E. and Rosenzweig, J.E., *The Theory & Management of Systems*, New York: McGraw-Hill, 3rd ed., 1973.
(An introductory text that covers a wide range of relevant ideas.)

Miller, D.W. and Starr, M.K., *Executive Decisions & Operations Research*, Englewood Cliffs, N.J.: Prentice Hall, 2nd ed., 1969.
(A classic that retains much of its early relevance.)

Moore, P.G. and Hodges, S.D. (eds), *Programming for Optimal Decisions*, Harmondsworth: Penguin, 1970.
(A convenient but demanding set of articles on aspects of mathematical programming.)

Salaman, G. and Thompson, K. (eds), *People and Organizations*, London: Longman, 1973.
(An intriguing collection of material on behavioural issues in organizational control.)

Salkin, G. and Kornbluth, J., *Linear Programming in Financial Planning*, London: Haymarket, 1973.
(One of the few books that looks at LP from the accountant's perspective: to be recommended.)

Schoderbek, P.P., Kefalas, A.G. and Schoderbeck, C.G., *Management Systems*, Dallas, Texas: Business Publications, 1975.

(A clear and comprehensive introductory book on management systems that looks at the organizational issues.)

Sizer, J., *An Insight into Management Accounting*, Harmondsworth: Penguin Books, 2nd ed., 1979.

(The most widely-used British introductory book: very readable and lucid.)

Skousen, K.F. and Needles, B.E. (eds), *Contemporary Thought in Accounting and Organizational Control*, Encino, California: Dickenson, 1973.

(A highly readable collection of articles that deal with the context within which accounting's role is to be found.)

Part Two

OVERALL COST CONTROL

Preamble to Part Two

Environmental Impacts

An organization's performance is profoundly influenced by the elements contained within its environment. In turn, of course, the organization also has an impact on its environment: there is a mutual dependency.

It is not far-fetched to argue that the very survival of an organization depends critically upon the willingness of its environment to sustain it. The reality of this can be seen if one considers how any organization draws all of its resources from its environment: financiers and other investors must be persuaded to back the company; 'technocrats' and those with other categories of skill must be encouraged to work for the company; individuals must be influenced to purchase the market offering; suppliers must be willing to provide goods, services and premises; society (in its various forms – such as government departments, local authorities, communities, the law, pressure groups, etc.) must be willing to –at least – tolerate the company's activities; and so on. In return the company must be willing and able to meet the requirements of each of these parties: consumers must be satisfied with their purchases; shareholders must receive dividends; the law must be upheld; society must not be abused; employees must be treated correctly; suppliers must be paid on time; etc., etc. If any key group withdraws its support the future of the company is bound to be in doubt.

It is the role of a control system to predict events that are likely to occur within the environment in order that the company may meet any challenges (or take advantage of any new opportunities). A company's costs are largely made up of payments to the suppliers of various types of factor inputs, and it is a function of a cost control system to anticipate any increases in input prices to enable the company to either re-negotiate (possibly with an alternative supplier) or arrange its finances so that it has the resources to meet higher input prices.

Figure I on the facing page illustrates the influence of external factors along the lines of the above discussion.

Two environmental factors that warrant particular attention given the subject matter of this book are risk and uncertainty on the one hand and inflation on the other.

RISK AND UNCERTAINTY

The essence of management is decision-making – the process of choosing among various courses of action. Such decisions relate to *future* outcomes, and therefore involve considerations relating to risk and uncertainty.

Views of the future are of four types:

(*a*) ignorance;
(*b*) certainty of outcomes (although choices must still be made among various strategies);
(*c*) risk – probabilities being assignable to possible outcomes; and
(*d*) uncertainty – unable to assign probabilities.

The latter two views are the most usual, and in the case of uncertainty, the decision-maker requires reliable criteria to help him choose among options, since their consequences cannot be predicted with confidence. This problem can often be solved through the collection of more information, which means that the cost of this information must be balanced with the possible losses due to uncertainty if it is not collected. Further assistance is given by the adoption of a systematic approach to decision-making, such as that contained in the following steps (which are a slightly modified version of those given on p.3):

1 Define the problem to be solved, and the specific desired objectives.
2 Determine alternative solutions (i.e. possible courses of action).
3 Analyze the consequences of each alternative by computing (in so far as possible) the costs and revenues of each.
4 Select the alternative that is most desirable.
5 Transform the decision into effective action.
6 Appraise the results.

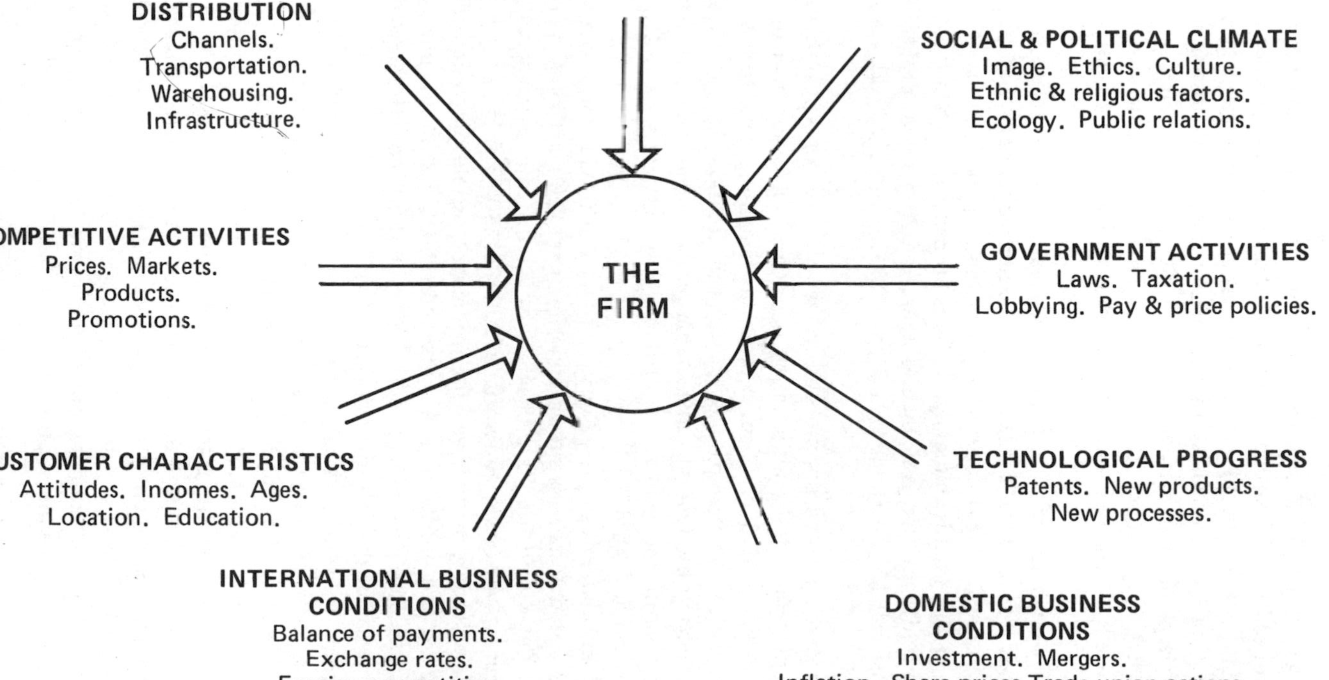
SUPPLIERS' BEHAVIOUR
Capital markets
Labour markets
Goods & services markets
DISTRIBUTION
Channels.
Transportation.
Warehousing.
Infrastructure.
SOCIAL & POLITICAL CLIMATE
Image. Ethics. Culture.
Ethnic & religious factors.
Ecology. Public relations.
COMPETITIVE ACTIVITIES
Prices. Markets.
Products.
Promotions.
THE
FIRM
GOVERNMENT ACTIVITIES
Laws. Taxation.
Lobbying. Pay & price policies.
CUSTOMER CHARACTERISTICS
Attitudes. Incomes. Ages.
Location. Education.
TECHNOLOGICAL PROGRESS
Patents. New products.
New processes.
INTERNATIONAL BUSINESS
CONDITIONS
Balance of payments.
Exchange rates.
Foreign competition
DOMESTIC BUSINESS
CONDITIONS
Investment. Mergers.
Inflation. Share prices.Trade union actions.

Figure I: The influence of external factors

In the risk situation, *probability theory* is central in rational decision-making. The probability of a particular outcome of an event is simply the proportion of times this outcome would occur if the event were repeated a great number of times. Thus the probability of the outcome 'heads' in tossing a coin is 0.5, since a large number of tosses would result in 50 per cent heads and 50 per cent tails. (It is characteristic of these probabilistic outcomes that they are determined by chance, and that the events to which they relate are *random* events.)

The probability of an outcome is a measure of the certainty of that outcome. If, for instance, a sales manager is fairly confident that his division will be able to sell 10,000 units in the forthcoming period, he may accord a probability of 0.8 to this outcome (i.e. he is 80 per cent certain that 10,000 units will be sold). By simple deduction, there is a 20 per cent probability that the outcome will be something other than 10,000 units (i.e. 100 – 80 = 20 per cent).

One development from probability theory is the concept of *expected value*. This results from the multiplication of each possible outcome of an event by the probability of that outcome occurring, and gives a measure of the *pay-off* of each choice. An example should make this situation clear.

A company has two new marketable products, but only sufficient resources to manufacture and market one of these. Estimates of sales, costs, and profits are as shown in Figure II.

The calculations are very simple. If sales of product A amount to £1,000, the associated costs – as shown opposite – are £500, and thus the profit is also £500. But there is only a probability of 0.1 that this outcome will eventuate, giving an *expected value* (or profit) of £50 (i.e. £500 × 0.1).

This procedure is followed for the other possible outcomes of product A sales, costs, and profits, and the expected values of each outcome summated to give an expected pay-off of £740. (This is nothing more than a weighted arithmetic average of the data given in Figure II.)

In contrast, product B has an expected pay-off of £1,395, and this choice is, therefore, the better one of the two – provided that profit is the desired objective, as measured by the pay-off computation.

Apart from the externally given economic and physical conditions surrounding a decision (i.e. the 'states of nature'), the decision-maker's own attitudes towards the alternatives must also be taken into account. His scale of values will determine the desirability of each possible course of action, whereas the conventional prediction systems merely assign probabilities.

'Desirability' has connotations of 'best' and 'utility', and can be measured by the formula for expected utility:

Expected utility = (Probability of success × Value of success)
– (Probability of failure × Cost of failure).

	Sales	Costs	Profit	Probability	Expected value
	£	£	£		£
PRODUCT A	1000	500	500	0.1	50
	1250	600	650	0.4	260
	1500	700	800	0.3	240
	1750	800	950	0.2	190
				1.0	£ 740
PRODUCT B	2000	800	1200	0.2	240
	2300	950	1350	0.4	540
	2500	1050	1450	0.2	290
	2700	1150	1550	0.1	155
	3000	1300	1700	0.1	170
				1.0	£1395

Figure II: Decision information

The general approach to problem-solving – the decision theory framework – is a central part of *management science*. ('Management science' is not synonymous with 'operations research'. The former is a broader concept than the latter, and embraces computer technology as a science in addition to operations research.) This consists of a variety of techniques that are essentially quantitative and aid management in both long- and short-term planning by establishing relationships between the company's objectives and resources.

Uncertainty arises from a lack of previous experience and knowledge. In a new situation it is possible for uncertainty to be attached to factors such as the following:

(*a*) date of completion;
(*b*) level of capital outlay required;
(*c*) level of sales prices;
(*d*) level of revenue;
(*e*) level of sales volume;
(*f*) level of operating costs; and
(*g*) taxation rules.

Inevitably, decision-making under conditions of uncertainty is more complicated than is the case under risk conditions. In fact, there is no single *best* criterion (such as expected pay-off) that should be used in selecting a strategy. Of the various available techniques, company policy or the decision-maker's attitude will determine that which is selected. Four possible criteria are given below, and these can be related to the following problem:

Let it be assumed that Minworth Limited has two new products, A and B, but only sufficient resources to launch one of these. The relevant states of nature relate to competitive activity: no matter which product is launched, it may be assumed that the competition will:

(*a*) do nothing; or
(*b*) introduce a comparable product; or
(*c*) introduce a superior product.

On the basis of past experience and current knowledge, the management of Minworth Limited attach probabilities of 0.25, 0.5, and 0.25 respectively to these states of nature. In the light of these alternative conditions, the profit of each strategy can be shown in a *pay-off matrix* (Figure III).

This matrix shows that if product B is launched and a comparable competitive product is introduced, a profit of £20,000 will be made, and so forth for the other five possible outcomes. The best decision would *appear* to be to introduce product B and *hope* that competitive action does not change. But is this so?

STRATEGY	*STATE OF NATURE*		
	Do Nothing	*Introduce Comparable Product*	*Introduce Superior Product*
LAUNCH A	£40,000	£30,000	£20,000
LAUNCH B	£70,000	£20,000	£0

Figure III: Pay-off matrix

Maximin – criterion of pessimism

The assumption underlying this technique is that the worst outcome will always come about, and the decision-maker should therefore select the largest pay-off under this assumption.

In the pay-off table (Figure III), the worst outcome is £20,000 for strategy A, and £0 for strategy B. It follows that strategy A should be pursued – it is the maximum minimum (i.e. maximin). The philosophy is that the actual outcome can only be an improvement on the profit from this choice.

Maximax – criterion of optimism

This is the opposite of 'maximin', and is based on the assumption that the best pay-off will result from the selected strategy. Referring again to Figure III the highest pay-offs are £40,000 and £70,000 for A and B, respectively. Strategy B has the highest maximum pay-off, and will be selected under the maximax criterion.

Criterion of regret

This criterion is based on the fact that, having selected a strategy that does not turn out to be the best one, the decision-maker will regret not having chosen another strategy when he had the opportunity.

Thus, if strategy B had been adopted (see Figure III) on the maximax assumption that competition would do nothing, and competition actually did nothing, there would be no regret; but if strategy A had been selected, the company would have lost £70,000 – £40,000, or £30,000. This measures the *regret*, and the aim of the regret criterion is to minimize the maximum possible regret. A regret matrix (Figure IV) can be constructed on the above basis.

STRATEGY	*STATE OF NATURE*		
	Do Nothing	*Introduce Comparable Product*	*Introduce Superior Product*
LAUNCH A	£30,000	£0	£0
LAUNCH B	£0	£10,000	£20,000

Figure IV: Regret matrix

The maximum regret is, for strategy A, £30,000, and for strategy B, £20,000. The choice is therefore B if the maximum regret is to be minimized.

Criterion of rationality – Laplace criterion

The assumption behind this criterion is that, since the probabilities of the various states of nature are not known, each state of nature is equally likely. The expected pay-off from each strategy is then calculated, and the one with the largest expected pay-off selected.

For strategy A, the expected pay-off under this criterion is:

$$(40{,}000 \times 0.33) + (30{,}000 \times 0.33) + (20{,}000 \times 0.33)$$

which equals £30,000; and for strategy B it is:

$$(70{,}000 \times 0.33) + (20{,}000 \times 0.33) + (0 \times 0.33)$$

which is also equal to £30,000. In this example, neither strategy is therefore preferable under the Laplace criterion.

In addition to these four criteria, the more involved methodology of *game theory* can be adopted.

INFLATION

In contrast to physical units of measurement (such as metres, kilogrammes, and specific gravity) monetary measures do not remain constant over time. When the value of the monetary unit declines (i.e. when monetary prices increase) we have a state of inflation.

But what of the accounting aspects of inflation? Accountants generally ignore changes in the price level in presenting their financial reports, with the result that measures of the financial position are distorted because they are recorded at historical cost, rather than adjusted for changes in the purchasing power of money.

The measurement of profit, for example, is a complex task in the presence of inflation. By adhering to the original cost of an asset in computing depreciation charges, values that relate to distant time periods (i.e. those when fixed assets were purchased) are confusingly added to costs, or deducted from revenue, of current purchasing power.

A further complication is the failure to record gains or losses from holding monetary items or being in debt during periods of changing price levels. It is widely accepted that holding cash and other monetary items during periods of inflation results in real losses, but conventional accounting practice is not to report these losses.

Another major area of impact of price-level changes is that of inventory valuation, and the computation of the cost of goods sold during a period. This has a most important significance in profit determination, and it is generally recognized that a big step forward will be made in financial reporting if some means of reducing the effects of inflation were incorporated into these reports.

Changes in price may be general, due to an overall change in the purchasing power of money, or specific, caused by economic factors affecting the product or commodity in question, irrespective of general price changes.

In the case of most companies, these two changes are likely to act together, and the questions that must be asked are:

1 Should allowance be made for inflation in financial reports to outsiders?

2 If so, should the necessary adjustments be partial (relating especially to stock valuation and the depreciation of fixed assets on a replacement basis), or complete?

3 In either case (i.e. partial or complete adjustment), should the adjustments be incorporated into the formal accounting system, or should they be supplementary?

4 How can inflation be handled in internal reports and in a company's management accounting system?

Without going too deeply into the technical accounting procedures involved in making adjustments, but accepting the argument that such adjustments should be made, both partial and complete adjustments will now be considered from a financial reporting viewpoint, (and it will not have escaped some readers' notice that the Foreword to this book was written by the man whose name is enshrined in the 'Hyde Guidelines' on this topic), and then we will look at the management accounting aspects of accounting for inflation.

Partial adjustment – stocks

Under the accountant's convention of conservatism it is acceptable to write inventory values *down* from cost to market value, but it is not generally acceptable to write inventories *up* to market value. (The same applies to marketable securities and investments.)

If inventories are to be shown at 'cost' rather than market value, the controller has some choice in establishing this cost. He may choose one of the following bases:

1 Specific identification. This is seemingly exact, but expensive, and often impractical.

2 Last-in first-out (LIFO). This method values the inventory as if the units most recently added (i.e. last-in) were the first used (i.e. first-out), even though this may not be the case. The closing inventory is thus assumed to consist of the oldest units, and valued accordingly. If the size of the inventory remains constant from period to period, the valuation will also remain constant, regardless of what happens to the replacement or market price of the inventory items. Conversely, the cost of goods sold will be valued at the cost of the most recently purchased units. (This may not represent *current* costs, since it is the cost of the most recent purchases, and this is not necessarily the same as current cost.) LIFO is essentially an artificial method that results in inadequate information for balance sheet purposes.

3 First-in first-out (FIFO). The assumption of the FIFO system is that the first units purchased (at their original cost) are the first ones issued

from stock. In this way it generally accords with the physical flow of goods, and the last purchased items are assumed to be on hand at the end of the period, and valued on the 'most recent cost basis'.

4 Weighted average. This is a compromise procedure whereby each purchase is lumped with the former inventory balance so that a new average unit price can be derived to value both subsequent issues from stock, and also the closing inventory. (This is a *moving* weighted average basis.)

In addition, inventories may be valued on the base stock principle, or on the basis of their adjusted selling price. However, these methods are not to be recommended, but a good many technical problems are avoided if inventories are valued on the basis of *standard costs*, and the inventories revalued each time the standards are revised due to changing prices.

Considering the LIFO and FIFO methods, the latter obviously more nearly matches the physical flow, and by valuing the closing inventory on the basis of the most recently purchased items, the FIFO inventory is more closely related to the current market conditions at the year end than is the LIFO inventory. In fact, it is possible to have a LIFO inventory that represents costs of 20 or 30 years ago, and which is unlikely to have any relation to current costs.

When the physical size of the inventory increases, the LIFO inventory is increased by the current cost of the units added, and over a period of growth, the inventory value will be composed of a number of *layers* – a new layer being added each year. If the physical inventory then declines, the most recent layer will be removed first in accordance with the LIFO principle. This process has a peculiar effect on the profit and loss account if the physical inventory is, in times of inflation, reduced to a very low level, since the cost of the older as well as of the newer units will be charged against revenue as the cost of goods sold, and this will result in a significant increase in reported profit because the cost of these older units will be lower than their current cost.

The relative importance of these 'inventory profits' varies widely among different companies, but LIFO has a more important influence on profits when:

(*a*) material cost constitutes a relatively large part of total product cost;
(*b*) the inventory is relatively large; and
(*c*) the manufacturing cycle is relatively long.

While LIFO results in the most recent costs being charged against revenue (i.e. 'matched') as cost of goods sold, FIFO charges relatively old costs against revenues: the LIFO method takes changes in the price level into consideration, and the FIFO method tends to overstate the profit during times of inflation. (This overstatement results from not adjusting the cost of goods sold to current prices during a period of inflation, so FIFO understates the cost of earning the revenues, and thus overstates the operating profit by failing to separate the gain from holding inventories through periods of rising prices from the true operating profit.)

LIFO charges current cost against revenue, which means that operating profit is usually reasonably measured, but the effect of price changes on the closing inventory valuation is completely ignored. The basic difference between this means of determining profit and the FIFO method is that the latter includes the gain from holding inventory during times of inflation, whereas LIFO excludes this gain. Both procedures are deficient, since the FIFO inventory is acceptable in current cost terms but not in terms of cost of goods sold. In contrast, LIFO values the inventory in an unacceptable manner, but results in a reasonably realistic statement of the cost of sales.

For best results, a compromise is necessary, such as valuing inventory on a FIFO basis and the cost of goods sold on a LIFO basis, or valuing inventory on a current cost basis and the cost of sales on a LIFO basis.

From the viewpoint of decision-making, historical inventory figures are irrelevant, since only the current market prices have significance. However, in adjusting historical costs to current costs, the gains due to inflation should be clearly separated from the operating profit.

Partial adjustment – fixed assets

The fixed assets of most companies will have been acquired at various times extending over many years. Price fluctuations may result in the unadjusted original cost of these assets being a questionable base for either the computation of depreciation for profit measurement, or their valuation for balance sheet purposes.

It is desirable that depreciation charges measure the *economic cost* of operations, and this can only be the case if depreciation is expressed in terms of the same purchasing power as the revenues earned during the period to which it relates.

The initial purchase price (i.e. cost) of a fixed asset is a significant measure of the economic value of that asset *at the time of purchase.* Changes in the price level will subsequently cause this cost figure to lose its significance as a measure of value. (It is worth pointing out that, although the depreciation mechanism charges out the *cost* of an asset over its useful life, it does not – and is not intended to – provide for the *replacement* of that asset. If depreciation was intended for replacement purposes, it would indicate that the company had committed itself to replacing existing assets with similar items, which presupposes that both means of manufacture as well as products manufactured are to continue unchanged into the long-term future, regardless of changing environmental conditions.)

If adjustments are to be made to historical measures of cost, it can be argued that this permits subjective judgement to be made on the part of the controller, which is considered to be undesirable. But even if no adjustments are made, subjective judgement will have been used initially in estimating the length of life of the asset. It is thought better to revise original cost figures on the basis of judgement than to accumulate data that are objective but useless.

Three bases for the computation of depreciation, hence asset values, can be envisaged:

(*a*) *Unconverted cost*: When the price level is stable, the depreciation charge may be satisfactorily based on the unconverted original cost. This results in revenue being charged with depreciation that is expressed in terms of the same purchasing power as the revenue. Consequently, this charge against revenue approximates to the expired cost, or expired value, of the fixed assets used during the period.

(*b*) *Converted cost – specific index*: If the price level is rising due to inflationary pressures, adherence to unconverted original cost will lead to a false measure of depreciation. This is so because, with rising prices, historical depreciation does not measure the expired value associated with earning the revenues of the period – to this extent it causes profit (in *monetary* terms) to be overstated, and means the company is failing to maintain its assets in *real* terms (i.e. in terms of constant purchasing power).

By using a specific index of the cost of each type of fixed asset in use, their original costs can be converted into current costs. This will give a measure of the real economic sacrifice of utilizing the assets in question, although it may be a tedious exercise if there is a wide range of assets purchased at different times.

(*c*) *Converted cost – general index*: This method avoids the intricacies of the previous section by applying a general index of the price level to all fixed assets, thereby converting the capital cost of the assets and the related depreciation into terms of current purchasing power.

Each of these last two procedures has advantages and disadvantages that must be related to a company's particular circumstances if the most useful one is to be selected.

Complete adjustments

The majority of proposals for dealing with the problem of inflation and financial control have been confined to the effects of inflation on fixed assets and stocks. This means that the effects of inflation on holders of money and money assets (e.g. debts) have been ignored to a large extent, but it is in relation to such money assets that the most severe effects of inflation may be felt.

It is, therefore, desirable to consider the impact of price-level changes on *all* items in the accounts – capital, reserves, assets, and current liabilities. Conversions should be made in accordance with a *general* index of purchasing power, rather than a *specific* index for either a specific industry or specific items. The basis of accounting would still be actual cost, but all items appearing in financial statements would be converted into monetary terms of the same purchasing power (i.e. actual cost × appropriate year's index).

Advocates of complete adjustment usually recommend that converted sets of financial statements should *supplement* rather than *replace* the conventional accounts (i.e. balance sheet and profit and loss account).

In a period of inflation, the effect of these adjustments is to increase the book value of the assets and to decrease the reported profit for the year. This decrease in profit results from both the increased depreciation charge and the upward adjustment in other expense items. In periods of deflation, the reverse would be found, but in either situation it is imperative that a clear distinction be drawn between *real* and *monetary* gains or losses.

Inflation cannot be ignored, and only by using price indices to allow for its effects can management realistically study trends and make valid comparisons over time.

Management accounting issues

Within the management accounting domain we are up against the problem of forecasting probable costs (and revenues) for such purposes as:

budgeting,
project selection,
wage negotiations,
cash flow analysis,
pricing decisions,
contract costing.

The greater the change in the price level the greater is the contraction of the decision-making horizon. This compression – which has inflationary as well as uncertainty causes – is vividly illustrated when one considers that price level increases of 2–3% per annum could generally be accommodated within the usual annual budgeting cycle, but if inflation is running at 24% per annum this is equivalent to compressing over seven years of annual 3% rises into one single year.

If budgets or standards are to be set on the basis of price levels at the beginning of the financial period in which they will be applied they will rapidly become out-of-date with inflation at the level of recent years. Alternative approaches are to regularly revise budgets and standards to keep them current, or to anticipate the inflationary increases for the forthcoming financial period and base the budget on anticipated monetary figures. (This may assume a straight line relationship between inflation and time, or alternatively a step function might assume that particular price increases will occur at particular points in time.)

Regular revisions to budgets or standards are tedious so many management accountants prefer them to be prepared in a way that anticipates likely cost increases. (It is better to do this by considering individually each head of expenditure rather than aggregate expenditure since inflation does not strike in a uniform way across the board.) When it comes to explaining any discrepancy between actual cost levels and budgeted cost levels part of the explanation will often be that inflation at x% was anticipated but, in the event, it ran at y% (where y is greater than x). The key to budgetary control in inflationary times is via the *physical* usage of resources rather than the *monetary* usage, so it is necessary to eliminate the effects of inflation by reducing *money* measures to *real* measures for purposes of performance measurement.

We shall return to this theme in Chapter 8 and later chapters.

FURTHER READING

Carter, C.F., Meredith, G.P. and Shackle, G.L.S. (eds), *Uncertainty and Business Decisions*, Liverpool: Liverpool University Press, 2nd ed., 1962.
(An interesting collection of papers from the first symposium held in Britain on this theme.)

Cox, B. and Hewgill, J.C.R., *Management Accounting in Inflationary Conditions*, London: I.C.M.A., 1976.
(The best introductory guide on this subject, based on the deliberations of an I.C.M.A. Study Group.)

Dickinson, J.P. (ed.), *Risk and Uncertainty in Accounting and Finance*, Aldershot: Gower, 1975.
(An advanced reader for the enthusiastic specialist.)

Gee, K.P., *Management Planning and Control in Inflation*, London: Macmillan, 1977.
(A relatively brief but rigorous treatment of the subject; recommended to the specialist.)

Kaufman, G.M. and Thomas, H. (eds), *Modern Decision Analysis*, Harmondsworth: Penguin, 1977.
(An excellent set of readings that cover decision-making under uncertainty and applications of decision analysis in business and non-profit organizations.)

Moore, P.G. and Thomas H., *The Anatomy of Decisions*, Harmondsworth: Penguin, 1976.
(This is as good an introduction to the field of decision-making under uncertainty as one is likely to find.)

Scapens, R., *Accounting in an Inflationary Environment*, London: Macmillan, 2nd ed., 1981.
(A clear discussion of the developments in this field from the 1920's to the 1970's, with an emphasis on recent developments).

Sizer, J. (ed.), *Readings in Management Accounting*, Harmondsworth: Penguin, 1980.
(A major theme through several items in this compilation is how to handle inflation.)

Sizer, J., *Perspectives in Management Accounting*, London: Heinemann, 1981.
(This is a personal anthology that focuses strongly on the theme of countering inflation).

6

Responsibility Accounting and Performance Measurement

RESPONSIBILITY ACCOUNTING

In analyzing organizations with a view to securing control over them there are five key variables to which one must pay attention. A change in any one of these will have consequences for one or more of the others (on a *mutatis mutandis* basis rather than a *ceteris paribus* basis). These variables are:

(*a*) the task of the organization (i.e. the purpose to be served by the outputs from the organization);
(*b*) the technology of the organization (i.e. the means whereby the inputs are converted into outputs);
(*c*) the structure of the organization (i.e. the roles, rules, etc.);
(*d*) the people of the organization (including their expectations, career development, etc.); and
(*e*) the environment of the organization (i.e. those factors beyond the organization's boundary).

In this section we will be concerned with aspects of (*c*) – the structure, as reflected through individuals' assigned responsibilities.

If a company is organized in such a way that lines of authority are clearly defined, with the result that each manager knows exactly what his responsibilities are and precisely what is expected of him, then it is possible to plan and control costs in order that the performance of each individual may be evaluated and, hopefully, improved. In addition, a meaningful basis can be given to the design of the reporting system if it is geared to areas of responsibility.

That is the essence of responsibility accounting which is a system of accounting that is tailored to an organization so that costs can be planned, accumulated, reported, and controlled by levels of responsibility within that organization. Responsibility accounting requires that costs be classified by:

1 Responsibility centre (see next section).
2 Their degree of controllability within their responsibility centre (on the premise that each responsible individual in an organisation should only be charged with those costs for which he is responsible and over which he has control).
3 Their nature.

This approach to classification will facilitate:

(*a*) self-appraisal by lower and middle management;
(*b*) subordinate appraisal by top management; and
(*c*) activity appraisal (by which top management might evaluate the performance of the overall range of corporate activities).

However, it is essential to the success of any control system that an individual is only held responsible for results when the following conditions prevail:

(*a*) that he knows what he is expected to achieve;
(*b*) that he knows what he is actually achieving; and
(*c*) that it is within his power to influence what is happening (i.e. that he can bring (*a*) and (*b*) together).

When all these conditions do not occur simultaneously it may be unjust and ineffective to hold an individual responsible, and it will be impossible to achieve the desired level of organizational performance.

From the above comments it will be apparent that targets or results should be compiled in a way that reflects one individual's 'uncontaminated' performance. Thus manager A's budget should contain a clear set of items which are deemed to be controllable at his level of authority, and a further set of items that are either fixed by company policy or are otherwise beyond manager A's influence. These latter items are uncontrollable from A's viewpoint, and his performance should not be assessed in relation to costs over which he has no control.

Control reports should be suited to the various areas of individual responsibility, and as one moves further up the managerial hierarchy more items will be contained, albeit in summary form, in reports prepared for each level since more items are controllable as the scope of managerial responsibility enlarges. Top management will therefore receive a summary of all items of income and expenditure.

Such summary reports can do little to rectify past mistakes, but by indicating exceptions to plans they can ensure that causes are investigated and appropriate corrective actions are taken to help in preventing future mistakes. The appropriate orientation should clearly be to the future rather than to the past.

A *responsibility centre* is made up of the various cost and revenue items for which a given individual is responsible. It is consequently a personalized concept that may be made up of one or more of the following:

(*a*) a cost centre;
(*b*) a profit centre; or
(*c*) an investment centre.

Let us look at each of these in turn.

A *cost (or expense) centre* is the smallest segment of activity, or area of responsibility, for which costs are accumulated. In some cases the cost centre may correspond with a department, but in others a department may contain several cost centres. The milling machines in a machine shop can be viewed as one cost centre of an engineering company, but the machine shop will also have other cost centres within it, such as turret lathes and auto-robots. A cost centre is not essentially a personalized concept, but it may be any specified area of activity for which it is desired to accumulate cost data, and may be of any of the following types:

1 Production cost centre, such as assembly departments and finishing departments.
2 Service cost centre, such as personnel, accounting, and utility departments that are necessary but not directly productive.
3 Ancillary manufacturing centres, such as those concerned with producing packing materials.

A cost centre may be created for cost control purposes whenever management feels that the usefulness of accumulating costs for the activity in question justifies the necessary effort.

Only input costs are measured for this organizational unit: even though there is some output, this is not measured in revenue terms. Thus a production unit will produce x units at a given total (or unit) cost, with the output being expressed either as a quantity or in terms of input costs.

It is conceivable that the converse situation might exist in which a manager is held responsible for the outputs of a centre, as measured in monetary terms, but is not responsible for the costs of the goods or services that the centre sells. Such a unit would be termed a *revenue centre*, and some branch sales offices might be of this form.

A *responsibility centre* is a development of the cost centre concept based on personalized responsibility. The machine shop that contains the cost centres referred to above (milling machines, turret lathes, and so on) will be under the control of a foreman: he is the responsible individual and the whole shop is his responsibility centre. The purpose of assigning costs to responsibility centres is to permit cost control which can only be achieved by personalizing responsibility for costs in departmental heads and supervisory staff. In contrast, the purpose of accumulating costs by cost centres is to charge each unit of product passing through that centre with a portion of the centre's costs. Cost control and product costing are separate activities that require separate concepts and procedures, and the two should not be confused.

A *profit centre* is a segment, department or division of an enterprise that is responsible for both revenue and expenditure. This is the major organizational device employed to facilitate decentralization (the essence of which is the freedom to make decisions).

Amongst the arguments favouring decentralized profit responsibility are:

(*a*) a divisional manager is only in a position to make satisfactory trade-offs between revenues and costs when he has responsibility for the profit outcome of his decisions (failing which it is necessary for many day-to-day decisions to be centrally regulated);
(*b*) a manager's performance can be evaluated more precisely if he has complete operating responsibility;
(*c*) managers' motivation will be higher if they have greater autonomy; and
(*d*) the contribution of each division to corporate profit can be seen via divisional profit reports.

The advantages of profit centres are that they resemble miniature businesses and are a good training ground for potential general managers.

Before setting up profit centres, however, the following points should be considered:

(*a*) profit centres require extra record-keeping (e.g. measuring output in revenue terms);
(*b*) profit centre managers should have some control over the quantity and quality of outputs, or the relation of outputs to costs;
(*c*) profit centres should not be built for such service functions as internal audit which exist to satisfy top management's wishes rather than as providers of desired inputs into operating sub-systems;

(*d*) profit centres are not needed if outputs are fairly homogeneous (e.g. cement) since a non-monetary measure of output may be adequate; and
(*e*) profit centres can create a spirit of competition within an organization that could cause friction rather than co-operation amongst centres which may not be in the organization's total interest, or it may cause too much interest in short-term profits at the expense of long-term results.

An *investment centre* is a segment, department or division of an enterprise that is not only responsible for profit (i.e. for revenue and expenditure) but which also has its success measured by the relationship of its profit to the capital invested within it (i.e. profitability). This is most commonly measured by means of the rate of return on investment (ROI).

The logic behind this concept is that assets are used to generate profits, and the decentralizing of profit responsibility usually requires the decentralization of control over many of a company's assets. The ultimate test, therefore, is the relationship of profit to invested capital within a division. Much of its appeal lies in the apparent ease with which one can compare a division's ROI with earnings opportunities elsewhere – inside or outside the company. However, ROI is an imperfect measure and needs to be used with some scepticism, and in conjunction with other performance measurements.

If one considers the formula by which one might compute ROI it will be seen that two aspects are involved:

$$\frac{\text{SALES}}{\text{INVESTED CAPITAL}} \times \frac{\text{NET INCOME}}{\text{SALES}} = \frac{\text{NET INCOME}}{\text{INVESTED CAPITAL}}$$

$$\text{Capital Turnover} \times \begin{matrix}\text{Percentage}\\ \text{Margin on Sales}\end{matrix} = \text{ROI}$$

Much will depend on how one measures the capital base on the one hand and the profit (or income) on the other.

Taking the capital base first, the alternatives that may be used include:

(*a*) total assets available, irrespective of their individual purpose;
(*b*) total assets employed, excluding idle or excess assets (such as vacant land or construction in progress);
(*c*) net working capital plus other assets; and
(*d*) shareholders' equity.

It has traditionally seemed reasonable that operating managers should be more concerned with the management of assets than with their long-term sources, so (*a*) – (*c*) have been preferred to (*d*).

Apart from this issue of which base to use there is the issue of valuing the elements contained within whichever base is selected. For example, assets can be valued on the basis of:

(*a*) historical cost;
(*b*) net book value (as opposed to gross book value);
(*c*) net realisable (disposal) value;
(*d*) replacement cost; or
(*e*) the net present value of expected benefits from the assets' use.

Choice is clearly problematic.

Next, let us look at the income figure. This might be taken to be either:

(*a*) a direct cost-based (or contribution) measure; or
(*b*) an absorption cost-based measure.

Whatever figure is taken for income should be consistent with the investment base. Thus, if an asset base is used interest should not be deducted from earnings.

The obvious generalizations that can be made about the ROI formula are that any action is beneficial provided that it:

(*a*) boosts sales;
(*b*) reduces invested capital; or
(*c*) reduces costs (whilst holding the other two factors constant).

In other words, any increase in percentage margins or capital turnover without worsening the other will enhance ROI. For example, if top management decides that a 20 per cent ROI is required, but current performance is:

$$\frac{\text{Sales}}{\text{Invested Capital}} \times \frac{\text{Net Income}}{\text{Sales}} = \frac{\text{Net Income}}{\text{Invested Capital}}$$

$$\frac{100}{50} \times \frac{9}{100} = \frac{9}{50} \text{ or } 18\%$$

it is possible to reach the desired ROI by either increasing the profit margin through reduced expenses:

$$\text{i.e.} \quad \frac{100}{50} \times \frac{10}{100} = \frac{10}{50} \text{ or } 20\%$$

or by decreasing the asset base:

$$\text{i.e.} \quad \frac{100}{45} \times \frac{9}{100} = \frac{9}{45} \text{ or } 20\%$$

The question arises, of course, as to what ROI rate is reasonable? It seems clear that profitability should be adequate to:

(*a*) give a fair return to shareholders in relation to the level of risk involved;
(*b*) provide for normal replacement of assets;
(*c*) provide, in times of inflation, adequate reserves to maintain the real capital of the business intact;
(*d*) attract new capital when required; and
(*e*) satisfy creditors and employees of the likelihood of the organization's continued existence.

This list excludes growth, showing that a return above the minimum rate necessary to cover the above points is necessary if growth is to take place. Nevertheless, it does give a basis from which to determine a standard ROI which permits:

(*a*) the comparison of performance over time; and
(*b*) the evaluation of alternative investment possibilities.

Establishing standards of performance against which individuals can be held accountable, and which motivate individuals towards goal-striving behaviour, is a difficult problem. In essence it should be solved by specifying what standards should be under prevailing conditions. Apart from the internal aspects noted above it will lead to better ROI standards if account is also taken of:

(*a*) the ROI achievements of successful competitors within the same industry;
(*b*) the ROI of other companies operating under similar risk and skill circumstances;
(*c*) the position of the company within its own industry, bearing in mind the prevailing degree of competitiveness;
(*d*) the level of operating risk faced, with higher risk usually requiring a higher ROI from the investor's point of view; and
(*e*) the 'expected' ROI as seen by such groups as the financial establishment, creditors, trades unions, etc.

There is nothing to suggest that external ROI results are indicative of real efficiency in operations, so regard must be had to that which is feasible as well as to that which has been achieved in the past.

Apart from ROI an investment centre may be assessed on the basis of *residual income*. This can be defined as the operating profit, or income, of an investment centre less the imputed interest on the assets used by the centre. An example can indicate the difference between the two approaches. If Division A and Division B operate in the same type of business with the same circumstances, but Division A's performance is assessed by ROI and Division B's by residual income, we might have the picture shown in Figure 6.1. If the manager of Division B was to maximize residual income he would expand his activities as long as his division earned a rate in excess of the imputed charge for invested capital. In other words, the manager of Division B would expand as long as his incremental opportunites earned 16 per cent or more on his incremental assets.

		DIVISION A	DIVISION B
		£	£
(1)	Operating income	25 000	25 000
(2)	Imputed interest at 16% of assets		16 000
(3)	Operating assets	100 000	100 000
	ROI [(1) ÷ (2)]	25%	
	Residual income [(1) – (2)]		9 000

Figure 6.1: Residual income vs ROI

In contrast, if managers were expected to maximize ROI this would induce managers of highly profitable divisions to reject projects that might be highly acceptable from the point of view of the organization as a whole. Thus the manager of Division A would be unhappy to accept a new project returning less than 25 per cent since this would reduce his average ROI even though 16 per cent is regarded by top management as an acceptable rate. The residual income manager, as we have seen, would accept all projects earning 16 per cent or more.

In the same way that setting a target ROI is problematic, so is establishing the rate to impute in measuring residual income. The critical questions are:

1 What rate should be specified?
2 When, and by how much, should it be altered?
3 Should the same rate be used in each division?

It seems likely that a uniform imputed rate will cause overall ROI to tend towards that rate, which will probably be lower than is otherwise attainable. A portfolio approach, therefore, which recognises that returns are a function of risk, is likely to be more satisfactory and is likely to result in different divisions having different desired rates of return depending on the relative investment risks of each.

CONTROLLABLE AND UNCONTROLLABLE COSTS

The value of the controllable/uncontrollable cost split is primarily found in fixing responsibility and measuring efficiency. Time is an important ingredient in this context since all costs are controllable at some organizational level if a sufficiently long time-span is taken.

Controllable costs are those that can be directly regulated by a given individual within a given time period. As already discussed, however, (p.61) the controllable/uncontrollable cost split does not correspond with the fixed/variable cost split, and examples were given at that point to illustrate the distinction.

The division of costs into controllable and uncontrollable categories is important in order that performance levels may be evaluated and also for securing the cooperation of managers at all levels. The manager who is involved in planning his performance level in the knowledge that those controllable costs for which he is responsible will be monitored, accumulated, and reported, is likely to be motivated towards attaining his predetermined level of performance. In this way it can be seen that the collecting of controllable costs by responsibility centres serves as a motivating force as well as an appraisal mechanism.

Whilst the ideal procedure is for each responsibility centre to be assigned those costs over which it has sole control and for which it is therefore responsible, in practical terms this cannot usually be achieved. It is rare for an individual to have complete control over *all* the factors that influence a given cost element. For example, a foreman cannot have control over wage rates since these are typically determined through negotiations between unions and management (subject to any legal restrictions such as those imposed by the Labour government's Prices and Incomes Policy of the mid-1960s, or the Conservative government's Pay and Price Code of the early 1970s). Nevertheless, the foreman will be held responsible for the total wage bill of his department which means that he must attempt to control his costs by varying the number of hours worked. In formula terms:

$$H \times R = B$$

where: H = hours worked
R = wage rate
B = wage bill

Both R and B are given: R is determined by union-management negotiations beyond the foreman's control, and B is his predetermined budget level for a period. In order to meet this budget level the foreman must concentrate on that factor that is largely within his control: the number of hours worked. This example is very simplified and it will be apparent that many complications can arise. Perhaps the most obvious is the need to consider overtime premiums. Thus:

$$(N \times R1) + (O \times R2) = B$$

where: N = normal hours worked
$R1$ = normal wage rate
O = overtime hours worked
$R2$ = overtime wage rate
B = wage bill

If an urgent job requiring unplanned overtime working must be done, then the only way that the foreman can hope to stay within his budget (B) is to reduce the planned hours required to perform the scheduled work, but with an increased rate of output (i.e. fewer hours but higher productivity per hour).

This in turn, however, may not be easy to achieve because the labour input per unit of output may be largely determined by fairly tight standards set by the company's industrial engineering department. Furthermore, the number of units that must be produced (and hence the total labour costs within the responsibility centre) may be affected by the output of other departments, by the availability of raw materials, by the level of finished stocks, by the level of consumer demand, and so forth. In such a situation the foreman should focus his attention upon the speed and efficiency with which work is done, eliminating in so far as he can such factors as avoidable waiting time.

The use of standard costing can be one way of distinguishing the controllable from the uncontrollable costs for a given responsibility centre. Ideally, a labour standard will specify what the direct labour cost per unit of output *should be* having taken into account the effects of wage rates, product design, types of material to use, etc., and other factors over which the foreman has no control. The reported difference between standard labour cost and actual labour cost then represents (at least in theory) the effects of the foreman's actions for which he must be held responsible.

Apart from those costs over which a responsible individual actually has control, his responsibility centre may be charged with costs that are beyond his direct control and influence but about which management wishes him to be concerned. A good example is the cost of a company's personnel department: an operating manager may be charged with a proportion of the personnel department's costs on the grounds that either:

1 He will be careful about making unnecessary requests for the services of the personnel department if he is made to feel somewhat responsible for its level of costs; or
2 He may try to influence the personnel manager to exercise firm control over his department's costs.

Allocating general overheads to responsibility centres is done by many companies which practise responsibility accounting and which therefore recognize that such costs are beyond the control of those to whom they are allocated, on the grounds that each responsible individual will be able to see the magnitude of the indirect costs that are incurred to support his unit. There is a major disadvantage that should be seriously considered: the manager of a small responsibility centre incurring directly controllable costs at his level in a given time period of, say, £10 000 may be allocated £45 000 of general overhead costs. In relation to the overall level of overhead costs the manager may feel that those costs for which he is responsible are so insignificant that he may give up trying to control them. The point to note is that each cost must be made the responsibility of whoever can best influence its behaviour, and allocating costs beyond this achieves at best very little from a control viewpoint, and may be distinctly harmful to the cost control effort. (Since a specific example of uncontrollable costs has not been given so far the general overheads of £45 000 referred to above can be used as a suitable example. For control purposes the costs that are being considered are the costs that can be directly influenced at a given level for a specified time-span.)

Controllable costs are not the same as direct costs. For example, the depreciation of equipment is a direct cost of the department that uses the equipment, but this cost is determined by company policy rather than by the head of the department, and can therefore be regarded as an uncontrollable cost at this level. Similarly, as we have seen, allocations of indirect costs are not controllable because the amount of cost allocated to a department will vary in accordance with whatever formula is used for allocation and not in accordance with whatever action has been taken by the responsible manager whose department is being charged.

In some instances the distinction between controllable and uncontrollable costs is largely a matter of judgement, whereas in others it may be affected by the procedures used within an organization. This can be illustrated in relation to maintenance costs: an allocation of maintenance costs to an operating department is an uncontrollable cost of that department, but if each responsibility centre requesting maintenance work is charged on the basis of an hourly rate for the maintenance work carried out at the request of the head of that responsibility centre, then this maintenance charge is clearly a controllable cost of the responsibility centre concerned.

Whilst the head of a responsibility centre may not have sole responsibility for a particular cost item, this item may reasonably be considered to be controllable at his level if he has a significant influence on the amount of cost incurred, and in this case his responsibility centre can properly be charged with the cost. This is one aspect of the wider problem that arises because few (if any) cost items are the sole responsibility of just one person. Guidelines that have been established for deciding which costs can appropriately be charged to a responsibility centre are, in summary:

1 If an individual has authority over both the acquisition and the use of a cost incurring activity, then his responsibility centre should bear the cost of that activity.
2 If an individual does not have sole responsibility for a given cost item but is able to influence to a significant extent the amount of cost incurred through his own actions, then he may reasonably be charged with the cost.
3 Even if an individual cannot significantly influence the amount of cost through his own direct action, he may be charged with a portion of those

elements of cost with which management wishes him to be concerned in order that he may help influence those who are more directly responsible.

ORGANIZATIONAL ASPECTS OF RESPONSIBILITY ACCOUNTING

It has been observed that individuals perform more effectively when specifically charged with the responsibility for particular tasks. Fixing responsibility is a fundamental prerequisite to responsibility accounting and entails deciding who is to be responsible for what and to whom. Organizational charts are useful if properly detailed. Apart from showing the chain of command (i.e. who reports to whom) such a chart should also include a schedule defining the duties of those individuals and any limitations to their authority. In this way responsibilities can be unambiguously assigned, and this knowledge clearly communicated to all concerned. Figures 6.2, 6.3 and 6.4 illustrate various aspects of organizational charts.

Figure 6.2 illustrates the clerical staffing of a small manufacturing organization by grade: *E* is the most senior clerical grade and *A* is the most junior. Responsibility can be delegated in accordance with denoted clerical seniority. Dating charts is important as they tend to change at frequent intervals.

The structure depicted in Figure 6.3 is of a financial controller's department in a fairly large organization. This specifies the functions that must be performed but gives no details of staffing. A development from this outline structure is given in Figure 6.4 which represents a possible marketing organization structure, giving more detailed duties within each functional area.

The implications of fixing responsibility, and of implementing control via responsibility centres, are:

1. The organizational structure must be clearly defined, and responsibility delegated so that each person knows his role.
2. The extent and limits of functional control must be determined.
3. The responsible individuals should be fully involved in preparing plans if they are to be held responsible for results.
4. Responsible individuals must be serviced with regular performance reports.
5. Means must be established to enable plans to be revised in line with actual performance in such a way that responsible individuals are involved.
6. Every item should be the responsibility of some individual within the organization.

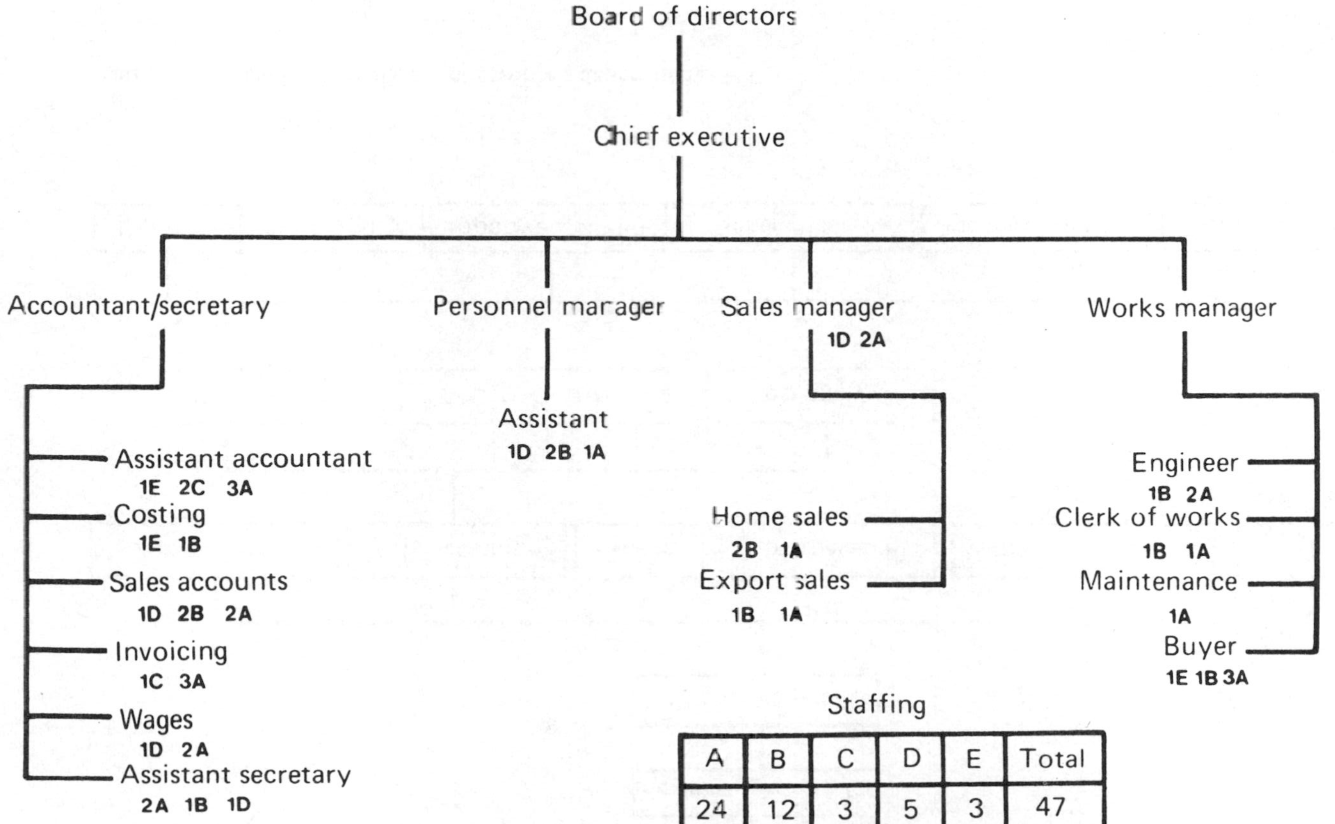

A	B	C	D	E	Total
24	12	3	5	3	47

Figure 6.2: A simple organization chart

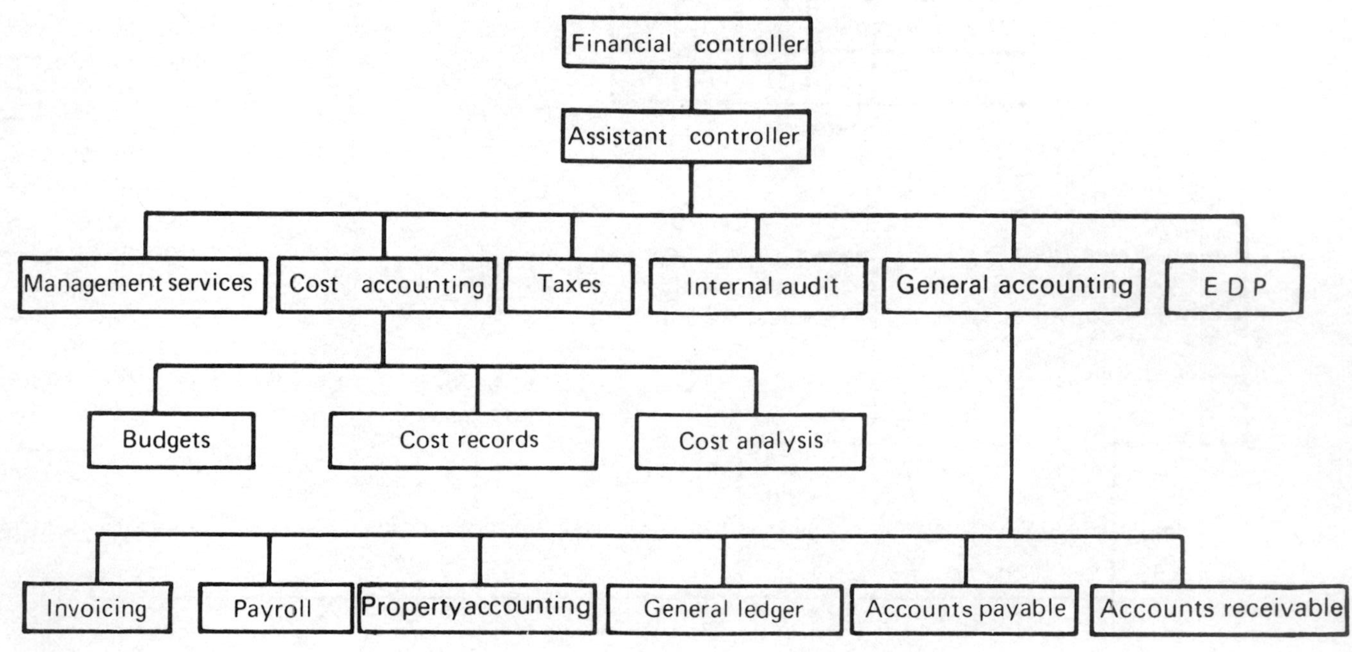

Figure 6.3: Organization chart – controller's department

MARKETING DIRECTOR
Function
Responsibility centres
Activities
A
Product planning
1 Product management
2 Packaging
3 Pricing
4 Servicing
Product selection
Styling
New product development
Specifying product mix
B
Advertising and promotion
1 Advertising
2 Sales promotion
3 Merchandising/display
4 Public relations
All aspects of advertising, promotion, and public relations with the exception of corporate image.
C
Sales operations
1 Domestic sales force
2 Export sales force
3 Sales office
Field selling, reporting, setting sales quotas, sales analysis, sales forecasting, etc.
D
Physical distribution management
1 Warehousing
2 Transport
3 Inventory management
Selection of distribution channels. Stock control. All other activities necessary to gain required distribution.
E
Marketing information and research
1 Library/information service
2 Marketing research
All aspects of marketing intelligence. Research studies. Model building.

Figure 6.4: Marketing organization structure

The ability to delegate is one sign of a good manager, and responsibility accounting facilitates this. However, it is essential to recognize that an individual can only be held responsible when he knows not only what he is expected to achieve, but also how well he is performing, and it must be within his power (at least to some extent) to regulate what is happening. If all these conditions do not exist simultaneously it may be unjust and ineffective to hold an individual responsible, and the desired control will become impossible to secure. But if the necessary conditions are present, and if delegation of responsibility also exists, it should be found that the act of passing responsibility down the line to the lowest levels of supervision gives these advantages:

1 It helps to create an atmosphere of cost consciousness throughout the organization.
2 It tends to get cost control action quickly without delays resulting from the need for a senior executive to receive a monthly report before decisions can be made.
3 It helps to give all levels of management a sense of team spirit with a common purpose.

PERFORMANCE MEASUREMENT

The level of performance of a responsibility centre from a cost control viewpoint can be evaluated by obtaining answers to 3 pairs of questions:

1 *Quantity*. How much was accomplished?
How much should have been accomplished?
2 *Quality*. How good was that which was accomplished?
How good should it have been?
3 *Cost*. How much did the accomplishment cost?
How much should it have cost?

As shown in Figure 4.5, performance may be judged in terms of inputs and outputs, and a good measure of performance is one that indicates the *efficiency* of the conversion process by which inputs are transformed into outputs.

Performance measurement presupposes a standard of comparison. An obvious example comes from the comparison of actual results with budgeted results – the latter being the predetermined standard of performance. Standards can be compiled for almost every business activity, such as:

1 Number of customer complaints
2 Production costs
3 Unit costs of handling and transporting products
4 Market share

5 Employee turnover
6 Downtime
7 Unfilled orders
8 Return on investment
9 Percentage of late deliveries of orders
10 A variety of cost/revenue ratios.

Any standard can only be an effective aid to cost control if it is seen to be equitable: those who are being judged (i.e. the responsible individuals whose performance is being measured) must be consulted in the setting of standards (Chapter 10 deals more fully with the setting of standards) otherwise no attempt may be made to reach them if they are considered to be either too high or too low. This ruins any attempt to control costs.

An important aspect of performance appraisal is found when the individual is aware of what was expected of him and how well he has done: this permits *self-control* at lower levels of management to be effective, and this serves to motivate as well as providing a basis for *subordinate appraisal* by senior management, and *activity appraisal* by top management.

The concept of performance measurement is a simple one to comprehend, but it can only be put into practice if plans are carefully prepared before decisions are made. In the absence of a plan (expressed in terms of cost standards and budgeted levels of performance) there is no benchmark for evaluating the performance of segments of the company, individuals in responsible positions, or of the company as a whole, and attempting to improve them. The existence of standards of performance eliminates many of the opportunities and excuses for poor performance, and provides a reference point for improvements.

Measuring the performance of the various types of responsibility centre (i.e. cost, profit and investment) will usually focus on financial aspects of organizational activity. This will not always be appropriate, although it tends to be the general case that managers are held accountable in terms of quantifiable performance rather than performance that is qualitative (such as employee morale or public relations). However, let us look in rather more detail at the role of profit in relation to performance measurement.

The role of profit

The amount of profit an enterprise earns is a measure of its effectiveness if that enterprise has a profit objective. (In this sense we can define effectiveness in terms of achieving that which one sought to achieve.)

Since Profit = Revenue (Output) − Cost (Input) it can be seen to be a measure of efficiency also in that it relates outputs to inputs. Thus an organization having revenue of £100 m. and costs of £60 m. is more efficient than one in the same industry, having revenue of £100 m. and costs of £70 m., since the former uses less input to produce a given output.

There are two particular forms of efficiency that are worth mentioning in passing – and it should be noted that the term 'efficiency' itself is strictly a limiting example of the idea of productivity in that an efficient system is one in which the ratio of outputs to inputs is optimal. Bearing this in mind, the two forms to note are:

(*a*) *technical* efficiency, in which one seeks to maximize the output from a given volume and mix of inputs; and
(*b*) *economic* efficiency, in which one seeks to minimize the input cost for a given level and mix of outputs.

It is highly desirable that an organization should be both efficient *and* effective, and profit is able to measure both of these attributes. But this should not cause us to overlook the significant difference between efficiency and effectiveness.

In essence effectiveness is an externally-oriented notion, which contains clear value preferences: in other words, if we are effective to the extent that we achieve that which we set out to achieve, then it is clear that someone must have specified that desired end, and this involves exercising preferences and is thus value laden. Our best definition of effectiveness is concerned with an organization's ability to bargain with various groups in its environment in order to obtain power over resources, and in this light it follows that the more acceptable are an organization's actions (and their outcomes) to these groups, the more effective is the organization. Hence effectiveness is really judged by those whose demands the organization is striving to fulfil. (Those groups within the organization's environment that possess resources which are sought by the organization will determine the extent to which the organization and its actions are acceptable – thus the extent to which it is effective.) Effectiveness can be seen to be more a socio-political notion than an economic or technological one.

In contrast, organizational efficiency is an internal standard of performance. The question whether that which is being done should be done is not posed – but only how well it is being done.

The ratio of resources used to output produced measures efficiency as we have seen and is (almost) value-free and independent of any criteria that might be used to evaluate inputs and outputs. To some extent, however, it seems that efficiency has come to be valued for its own sake. But unwanted activities cannot be of real value however efficiently their production may be organized, hence it is significant to have an agreed strategy that incorporates preferences before one embarks on productive transformations.

Despite its ability to act as a measure both of effectiveness and efficiency, profit is a less than perfect measure because:

(*a*) it is a monetary measure, and monetary measures do not measure all aspects of either input or output;
(*b*) the standards against which profits are judged may themselves be less than perfect; and
(*c*) at best, profits are a measure of what has happened in the short-run, whereas we must also be interested in the long-run consequences of management actions.

Nevertheless, profit measures can still play a distinctly valuable role in the control effort. For example:

1 A profit measure can provide a simple criterion for evaluating alternatives. (Although it will be necessary to take into account many factors other than profit in making a choice amongst alternative courses of action, on the face of it option *A* is more attractive than option *B* if *A* will produce more profit than *B*.)
2 A profit measure will permit a quantitative analysis of alternatives to be made in which benefits can be directly compared with costs. (Assuming a market exists for an enterprise's output, these benefits will be measured by the revenue flow from its sale.)
3 A profit measure can provide a single, broad measure of performance in that it is arrived at after all financial costs and revenues have been taken into account, and it thus subsumes many other aspects of performance.
4 Profit measures permit the comparison of performance to be made over time for one organization, or comparisons at a point in time to be made for a group of organizational units (e.g. divisions or competing firms within an industry), even if they are performing dissimilar functions. This is not possible with other measures, although it may be necessary to standardize accounting practices in measuring profits for this purpose, and to ensure that the valuations of assets are made on the same bases.

This all sounds very promising, but we need to bear in mind the limitations of the profit measure. Amongst these are:

1 Organizations have multiple objectives and will often forgo profit opportunities in order to avoid conflict over some other objective (or constraint), such as the desired image for the company, or some ethical standard.
2 Social costs and benefits are excluded from corporate profit figures. At best profit is a measure of an enterprise's success as an economic entity, but this does not measure that enterprise's net contribution (or cost) to society, such as the training programmes it might offer, or the pollution it might cause.

3 As already mentioned, profit measures typically measure current rather than long-run performance: actions can be taken to improve the former at the expense of the latter (e.g. by cutting advertising, R & D, training, and maintenance budgets).

4 Profit is an inadequate basis for comparing organizations' relative performance or for monitoring one organization's performance over time. The real test is actual versus target profit, but we are really unable to specify this latter figure in any sensible way because it should be based on profit potential and a company's profit opportunities are not all identified. It follows that an apparently high profit figure, even when this corresponds with the target figure, may in reality be poor when related to missed opportunities.

5 Accounting rules are also inadequate since they often do not permit the recording of economic reality. (Costs should reflect the use of resources, but accounting practice does not allow this to be measured when it values assets on the basis of historical cost rather than their opportunity cost, i.e. current value in an alternative use, which has an impact on the depreciation charge etc.)

6 Profit measures are not applicable in certain segments of a business, notably those that incur costs but do not generate revenue (unless a transfer pricing system is introduced to impute revenue flows). Examples of these types of segment are R & D, legal department, personnel department, and the accounting department.

Let us broaden our perspective on effectiveness and consider measures that go beyond profit and profitability.

Can we define for any type of organization what is effective and what is not? Early organizational analysts talked of such criteria as:

(*a*) profit maximization;
(*b*) high productivity;
(*c*) good employee morale; and
(*d*) provision of an efficient service, as sufficient to indicate effectiveness.

But these criteria are inadequate because:

(*a*) organizations behave ineffectively from some points of view if a single criterion is used; and
(*b*) organizations fulfil multiple functions and have multiple goals, some of which may be in conflict. It would be inappropriate to assess an organization's performance on the basis of any one criterion.

The difficulty, as will be apparent, lies in identifying those multiple criteria that are necessary and sufficient to ensure corporate well-being and survival. One way is via the application of 'Pareto's Law'.

Pareto's Law (or the 80/20 rule) is widely thought to apply to a range of situations in which most of the behaviour or value of one factor is deemed to depend on only a little of another factor. For example, it is often asserted that 80 per cent of inventory movements within an organization are attributable to 20 per cent of items stocked; 80 per cent of sales volume comes from 20 per cent of customers; or 80 per cent of profits are derived from 20 per cent of product lines. The main point here, of course, is that one can effectively control an inventory if one can focus attention on the critical 20 per cent of active items, or one can control the level of sales if the key customers are properly serviced. This can be greatly beneficial in terms of both cost savings (through eliminating unnecessary control effort on the 'insignificant' 80 per cent of items that only make up 20 per cent of stock issues) and improved organizational effectiveness (due to better control of the key elements).

The application of Pareto's Law is known by a number of different names. Perhaps the most frequently-encountered are: key variables; critical success factors; and key result areas.

To illustrate the idea further we can consider a generalized example, and then a number of specific industry examples.

Figure 6.5 identifies for each main sphere of activity the factors that are likely to be of some major significance to corporate performance. Each factor has financial implications, and if they can be controlled it is probable that the overall company can be controlled.

Sphere of Activity	*Critical Factors*
ENVIRONMENT	Economic – interest rates – inflation rates – concentration Political stability
MARKETING	Sales volume Market share Gross margins
PRODUCTION	Capacity utilisation Quality standards
LOGISTICS	Capacity utilisation Level of service
ASSET MANAGEMENT	Return on investment Accounts receivable balance.

Figure 6.5: A general example of key variables

Within specific industries there is likely to be considerable variation in key variables, as Figure 6.6 illustrates.

FOOD PROCESSING
1 New product development
2 Good distribution
3 Effective advertising

MOTOR VEHICLES
1 Styling
2 Efficient dealer networks
3 Tight control over manufacturing costs

LIFE ASSURANCE
1 Development of agency managerial personnel
2 Effective control of clerical staff
3 Innovation in creating new types of policies

OIL
1 Decentralization
2 Liquidity
3 Government-business relationship
4 Societal image
5 New ventures (to broaden its base)

Figure 6.6: Specific industry examples of key variables

As a slight variation on the theme the (US) General Electric Company gives a classic illustration of one organization's attempt to identify the major variables that management needs to monitor if total company performance is to be controlled. Eight key result areas were determined in accordance with the following criterion: 'Will continued failure in this area prevent the attainment of management's responsibility for advancing General Electric as a leader in a strong, competitive economy, even though results in all other key areas are good?'

The eight variables that met this requirement are shown in Figure 6.7.

1 Profitability
2 Market position
3 Productivity
4 Product leadership
5 Personnel development
6 Employee attitudes
7 Public responsibility
8 Balance between short-run and long-run goals.

Figure 6.7: General Electric's key result areas

Whilst these eight factors might seem to be generally applicable, it is their precise definition within the context of a particular company's activities that determines how critical they are. This highlights a fundamental aspect of designing any control system: it must be highly 'situational' if it is to be effective. In other words, it must be tailored to the specific characteristics of the situation, which means this company's objectives, this company's operations, this company's managers, and this company's environment.

The General Electric approach seeks to balance two conflicting tendencies: on the one hand, the diffusion of effort over multiple goals and the failure to perform as well as might be expected in any one area; and on the other hand, the tendency to emphasise one particular goal with the result that other goals are not attained.

The most common tendency in commercial enterprises is to focus on the short-run maximization of net profit (or sales) without considering the damage that this might do to the long-run position (e.g. by postponing repairs or maintenance work; by cutting back on advertising, or on research, training or quality control expenditure; by deferring capital investment outlays; or through exhortations to employees to increase productivity). Short-term 'gains' achieved in this way tend to be illusory because the subsequent need to make up lost ground, e.g. via heavier advertising or training in later periods, more than outweighs short-term gains.

To the extent that effectiveness is a multiple criterion we must avoid the trap of focusing too sharply on one contributing factor. It would be a mistake to assume that effectiveness would be assured through selecting and training the right people. We can define effectiveness in terms of a system's capacity to:

(*a*) survive, adapt, maintain itself, and grow – regardless of the functions it fulfils; and
(*b*) to achieve (*a*) through its bargaining position with its environment in relation to the acquisition of resources.

Effectiveness is likely to result if the following steps are carried out:

(*a*) internal or environmental changes are reliably sensed;
(*b*) relevant information on these changes is transmitted to those parts of the system that need to respond;
(*c*) the transformation process is adapted in accordance with the information flows;
(*d*) internal changes are stabilized and undesired by-products reduced;
(*e*) outputs are generated in line with the perceived environmental changes; and
(*f*) feedback is obtained on the success of changes through further sensing of the environment and internal workings of the organization.

Conversely, of course, failure will tend to come about if:

(*a*) there is either no sensing or unreliable sensing;
(*b*) there is a failure to inform relevant parties of changes;
(*c*) there is failure to adapt the organization's transformation processes;
(*d*) there is a failure to achieve stability and to cope with the impacts of change;
(*e*) there is failure to generate the appropriate outputs; and
(*f*) there is a failure to obtain feedback.

This line of thinking emphasises the need to acquire resources and to use them effectively, rather than the frequently-met obsession with efficient allocation (on the assumption that the existence of resources is given and non-problematic).

It is helpful in this context to think in terms of a coalition of interested parties, each of which wishes to achieve something but can only do so through organizations. However, each party may have different criteria for evaluating a given organization, and these criteria may or may not be compatible. In the (likely) event of incompatibility it is necessary for the organization to decide which group's requirements it will attend to and which it will ignore. Favouring one group inevitably offends another, and this can threaten the survival of the coalition because it puts at risk the organization's bargaining power over resources from at least one part of its environment, i.e. that relating to the offended group.

Evidence suggests that increasing organizational size may be associated with increasingly inconsistent interests amongst parties to a coalition, i.e. as an organization becomes larger it will tend to attract more attention and to establish coalitions with a wider range of groups. The likelihood of clashes will tend to increase accordingly, but the balance of power in any bargaining position will also change as one party grows.

Since effectiveness depends on responding to demands from interest groups within the organization's environment in accordance with these groups' relative importance at any given point in time, it is necessary to be able to assess the relative potency of these demands and to determine how they conflict and constrain the organization's actions. An approach to this end is to be found in the following sequence of steps:

1 Establish which groups are relevant to the organization's continued functioning; i.e. determine which resources and activities are critical to the company and which individuals do, or could, provide the resources needed to carry these out.
2 Since all groups will not be of equal importance, attach weights to their relative power; i.e. identify the critical resources through step 1, and rank them according to their degree of importance.

3 Determine the criteria or values by which each group evaluates the organization; e.g. impute this from their behaviour, or ask representatives of the groups about the criteria which they use.

4 Apply the criteria identified in step 3 to the organization's activities and ascertain the outcomes in terms of groups' preferences. Particular attention should be paid to outcomes that satisfy: (*a*) the most important groups' criteria; and (*b*) some groups' criteria, but not those of other groups.

This procedure forces the organization to recognise explicitly the action base of its behaviour.

CODING

To enable the performance of each responsibility centre to be measured, a procedure must exist for correctly classifying items of expenditure and collecting together all items to be charged to a particular responsibility centre. This is facilitated by a coding scheme linked to a chart of accounts.

The figures relating to actual performance must be accumulated and summarized in exactly the same manner as in the plan if comparisons are to be valid.

Each cost centre should have its own code for cost accumulation/allocation purposes, and this must fit in with the overall accounts code for the company in such a way that all the constituent cost centres of a responsibility centre can be linked to that responsibility centre. Within each cost centre every item of expense should be given a distinct allocation based on a code list. This list will reflect the chart of accounts because related activities under the control of a single individual will have linked codes.

One can envisage a coding scheme based on 10 digit codes in the following manner:

XXX	XXXX	XXX
Cost centre	Main account	Subaccount

The first three digits make up the cost centre code, and all cost centres within a particular responsibility centre could have their codes commence with the same digit. Taking an example based on Figure 6.3, the general accountant's responsibility centre can be seen to have six constituent cost centres which might have codes as shown overleaf:

Code	*Cost centre*
341	Billing
342	Payroll
343	Property accounting
344	General ledger
345	Accounts payable
346	Accounts receivable

In this example the first digit (3) could relate to the financial controller's department, the second digit (4) to the general accountant's responsibility centre, and the third digit (1–6) to the specific cost centre. (Depending on the size of the organization, there may be a need to have a variation on this to accommodate, say, billing as a responsibility centre instead of simply a cost centre, and this could be achieved in various ways – such as the addition of a fourth digit to this part of the code.)

The next four digits of our 10 digit code refer to the main account, such as personal expenses, which might have the code 1200. And the final three digits represent the subaccounts, which could be as follows:

Personal expenses: Main account 1200	
Car: depreciation subaccount	450
Car: running expenses	451
Hotel expenses	452
Fares	453
Entertaining: domestic customers	454
Entertaining: overseas customers	455

If this scheme was adopted it is easy to see that the code 343 1200 453 relates to fares paid on behalf of a member of the general accountant's staff dealing with property accounting. This approach to coding has an obvious bearing on computerized accounting systems, and expert advice should bc taken to ensure the feasibility of any desired coding scheme. Once a scheme is agreed and installed, all items of expense should be coded as near to source as possible: thus purchase requisitions (hence purchase orders and eventually suppliers' invoices) should be coded when raised, personal expense claim forms can be preprinted with appropriate codes, and so forth.

This suggested approach has certain advantages in that it enables the same subaccount codes to be used regardless of the particular cost or responsibility centre. In other words, account code 1200 451 will always refer to *personal expenses: car running costs* regardless of cost centre. This means that a listing of all items under account code 1200 451 can be produced to show the *total* costs of running company cars and/or reimbursing employees for using their own cars on company business. In the same way, the use of a cost centre code permits a listing to be made of only those costs that are relevant to a specified cost centre, and similarly for a responsibility centre, and so on for a function or division.

Flexibility can be built into a coding system by using 1200, 1300, 1400, etc., as the main account codes in order that 1210, 1220, etc., and even 1201, 1211, 1221, and so on, can be subsequently added to accommodate either new expense items or items that were overlooked when the system was first devised. (The same argument applies to departmental and subaccount codes of course.)

The chart of accounts that forms the basis of a coding scheme must be one that truly represents the structure of the responsibility accounting system. Such a chart would not be the same as the one illustrated in Chapter 2 (Figure 2.1) because that chart is simply a listing of functionally classified overhead expense items rather than a listing of cost elements under the responsibility criterion.

CHECKLIST ON RESPONSIBILITY ACCOUNTING

1. Are individuals' responsibilities clearly defined without duplication?
2. Is the assigned authority in line with delegated responsibility in all cases?
3. Is delegation properly carried out?
4. Is the organization chart current, adequately detailed, and available to all staff?
5. Could any organizational grouping be reorganized to reduce costs or improve effectiveness?
6. Are there too many non-productive jobs?
7. Are objectives – both corporate and departmental – established and communicated?
8. Are key assignments rotated? Should they be?
9. Is management successsion planned?
10. Are responsibilities divided in such a way as to permit a budgetary measurement of individual effectiveness?
11. Are all responsible individuals called upon to explain variances in their areas? Are follow-ups checked?
12. Is every necessary function unambiguously assigned to a responsibility centre?
13. Are responsibilities specific and understood?
14. Is there any overlapping of responsibilities?
15. Does each individual within the organization have one – and only one – boss?

16 Does an adequate coding system exist so that all cost items can readily be recorded in their proper account?
17 Does the chart of accounts accurately represent the organizational structure *as it is* rather than as it perhaps should be?
18 Arc all items of expense recorded in accordance with the lowest level or area of operations to which they can be directly related?
19 Are all needless allocations/apportionments/prorations avoided?
20 Are all changes in responsibilities made with a clear understanding of their impact on the part of all concerned?
21 Are all cases of promotion, salary increases, and disciplinary action approved by the immediate superior of the responsible individual?
22 Do all disputes over questions relating to authority and responsibility receive prompt and careful consideration?
23 Are accurate standards set for each measurable and controllable cost element?
24 Are all costs clearly split into their controllable and uncontrollable categories (bearing in mind the level of authority and the time span)?
25 Is cost consciousness encouraged throughout the organization?
26 Do cost controls correspond with areas of organizational responsibility?
27 Is the performance of each responsible individual regularly measured, monitored, and reported?
28 Are the plans/standards used in performance measurement adequate and sufficiently accurate?

SUMMARY

Responsibility accounting is a system that is geared to the organization structure so that costs can be planned and controlled in accordance with individuals' responsibilities.

This system requires that costs be clearly classified by responsibility centres. In contrast to cost centres that exist to enable product costs to be compiled, responsibility centres are personalized to enable control to be effective through specified decision-makers.

An individual can be held responsible only for costs that are within his control (at a given level in the organization for a given period of time). The distinction between controllable and uncontrollable costs is of fundamental significance. However, it is rarely found that any individual has sole and total control over any element of cost. Nevertheless, allocated costs are beyond the control of those to whom they are allocated.

For responsibility accounting to be effective it is necessary for the organization structure to be unambiguously defined in such a way that everyone involved knows his own responsibilities and how his role interfaces with the roles of others. Once this has been achieved, a chart of accounts should be drawn up to reflect these responsibilities, and a coding scheme devised to ensure that all costs are charged to their correct account.

Performance measurement is a central feature of any control system, including responsibility accounting. But actual performance must be related to a plan or standard of *desired* performance if efficiency of operation is to result and improvements are to be made.

Amongst the items listed on pp.381–3 for further reading, the following are especially recommended:

Anthony and Dearden;
Boyce and Eisen;
Goodman;
Pfeffer and Salancik.

7

Reporting Systems

INTRODUCTION

A system of reporting is vital to any cost control endeavour as a means of bringing information to each level of management in order that responsibilities to the organization may be fulfilled. This is especially important in the case of decentralized organizations since this forces the delegation of authority and the assigning of responsibility with the result that each manager must account for his performance.

Reports must be designed to suit the various areas of organizational responsibility, and as one moves further up the managerial hierarchy more cost items (albeit in summary form) will be reported at each level since more costs are controllable as the scope of managerial responsibility is widened. Top management, therefore, will receive a summary of all costs, composed of controllable costs at each subordinate level, plus those relevant to the top level. Such reports can do little to rectify past mistakes, but by indicating exceptions to plan they can help in ensuring that an investigation into causes will aid in preventing mistakes from recurring in the future. The orientation of a good management reporting system is clearly towards the future rather than the past.

In general terms, how effective a manager is in his job will tend to depend upon how much, how relevant, and how good his information is, and how well he interprets and acts upon this information. Basically, the manager needs information to:

1 Assist him in decision-making.
2 Indicate his performance and achievement.
3 Aid him in making plans and setting standards.

As is frequently observed, the manager may not know the precise information he needs or, alternatively, what information is available. In such a situation it is the responsibility of the accountant (or financial controller) to observe the types of information requirements a manager may have (based on, for example, the types of decisions made by the manager in question), and to suggest alternative reporting arrangements and procedures, with a specification of the information that is currently available, along with information that could be available, and an indication of both the means and costs of supplying it all.

The process of collecting, analysing, and using information is essentially the same in any size of business, whether for routine purposes or for special projects. What does vary, however, is the *method* of collection and analysis. The difference is usually found in the relative employment of manual, mechanical, and electronic data-processing systems. The increasing rate of adoption of EDP should ensure that fewer managers in the future have any cause to complain about insufficient, inaccurate, or delayed information.

Some of these topics will now be pursued further in greater detail, starting with the characteristics of cost control information.

CHARACTERISTICS OF CONTROL INFORMATION

Information for control purposes should be compiled upon the basis of the following characteristics and requirements:

1 Relevance
2 Selectivity
3 Accuracy
4 Timeliness
5 Accountability
6 Simplicity
7 Yardsticks of comparison.

The above items will be discussed in detail on the following pages.

Relevance

In determing *what should be measured*, relevance is a prime consideration. Beyond this the first, and perhaps most obvious, requirement is that whatever form of measurement is used it must be common to both the preparation of plans and the monitoring of performance, and it must also help in interpreting the level of achievement.

It is usual to measure only material factors – those that are readily expressed in production or financial terms. But it is important that certain non-material factors are seen to be relevant in indicating the performance of responsible individuals throughout an organization. Examples of these non-material factors might include quality levels, the number of new customer accounts opened, the speed of service, the market share details, absenteeism, productivity, and so forth.

Both internal and external information (as well as financial and non-financial) should be gathered if it has a bearing on improving the level of an individual's performance, and hence the level of performance of the whole organization.

The information presented for control purposes should be relevant in the sense that no manager is presented with information relating to matters over which he has no control.

Selectivity

Control can collapse if management endeavours to control too much, with the result that the really important issues become submerged in a mass of irrelevancies, or initiative is sapped by the requirements of over-zealous control systems.

In any series of elements to be controlled, only a small fraction in terms of elements will usually account for a large fraction in terms of results. This relationship is known as *Pareto's Law*, with one example being the frequently-met 80/20 rule by which 80 per cent of an organization's costs are absorbed by 20 per cent of its products, or 80 per cent of its sales are accounted for by 20 per cent of its customers (see pp.142–3).

Identifying the critical elements of performance that exert the greatest influence on the attainment of predetermined performance levels is a very fundamental task of management control. It is generally considered that between four and six factors constitute the causes of corporate success, provided the company is able to select the appropriate factors *and* do these four to six things extremely well. In practice, many organizations attempt to control many factors that are unimportant in a control sense because their behaviour patterns follow those of other more essential factors. Information systems must attempt to highlight the critical factors that govern an organization's success.

Accuracy

Even if information flows are not highly precise, it is essential that their degree of accuracy is known. If inaccurate information is presented for decision-making purposes, unknown to the decision-makers, it will not be surprising if the wrong decisions are made. Provided that the extent of any inaccuracies is made known to decision-makers, it should be possible to make due allowances for these inaccuracies in making decisions.

Spurious accuracy should be avoided at all times. This is caused by giving an unwarranted appearance of accuracy by calculating estimates to several places of decimals, or giving estimates as single figures (known as *point estimates*) rather than as ranges. For instance, the cost per ton of a material *X* may be estimated to be £58.6743 for the forthcoming financial year. Four places of decimals in this estimate suggest that the manager making the estimate has a clearer view of the future than is likely to be the case. It may be better to state the future price per ton of material *X* to be between £58.00 and £60.00. Probability analysis is useful in this context. A manager may be able to estimate the information shown in Figure 7.1.

Material X

Price per ton	*Probability*
£55	0.00
£56	0.05
£57	0.10
£58	0.20
£59	0.30
£60	0.20
£61	0.15
£62	0.00
	1.00

Figure 7.1: Estimates of future prices

These data (Figure 7.1) can be interpreted in the following way: the manager in question is certain that the price per ton of material *X* in the next year will not be as low as £55 (probability of 0.00) or as high as £62 (also with a probability of 0.00). He is fairly certain, however, that the price will be around £59 and he estimates that there is a 3/10 chance of it actually being £59, and a 2/10 chance of it being £58 and a similar chance of it being £60.

In other words, in 7 cases out of 10 the manager would expect the price per ton to fall within the range of £58–£60, and extending the argument further, in 10 cases out of 10 he would expect the price to be within the range of £56–£61, although he acknowledges that there is a relatively low degree of likelihood of the price being below £58 or above £60 (with probabilities of 0.15 in both cases).

If it is desired to present a single point estimate, then the concept of *expected value* should be used. The expected value of an outcome of an event is nothing more than the weighted arithmetical average of all the possible outcomes. (See also the discussion in the Preamble, p.110. Taking the data of Figure 7.1, the expected value of the price per ton of material *X* can be computed as shown in Figure 7.2.

Material X		
Price per ton	*Probability*	*Price × probability = expected value*
(1)	(2)	(1) × (2) = (3)
		£
£55	0.00	0.00
£56	0.05	2.80
£57	0.10	5.70
£58	0.20	11.60
£59	0.30	17.70
£60	0.20	12.00
£61	0.15	9.15
£62	0.00	0.00
	1.00	£58.95

Figure 7.2: Expected value of future prices

Specifically, Figure 7.2 shows that the expected value of £58.95 is the most likely outcome even though Figure 7.1 suggests that £59 has the highest individual likelihood of occurring (with a probability of 0.3). The difference is that there is a 0.7 chance of the future price of material *X* *not* being £59 (which is equal to 1 – probability of occurrence = 1 – 0.3 = 0.7), as individual probabilities (as in Figure 7.1 or column (2) of Figure 7.2) do not take account of other possible outcomes. The expected value concept, on the other hand, makes explicit allowance for other possibilities by weighting each possible outcome (i.e. future price) by its probability of occurrence. The result is that the most likely outcome is specified – given that various outcomes are possible with stated degrees of likelihood.

Timeliness

Information flows should be up-to-date in order that any necessary control action may be taken before the events that form the subject of the report are of purely historical interest. A guideline to the frequency with which information should be reported is that the period of time between reports should be the shortest in which management can usefully intervene and in which significant changes in performance are likely. The particular conditions facing individual organizations will, of course, vary and this particular variation will determine the precise period between information flows.

The controller's inherent desire for complete accuracy must not be allowed to frustrate management's desire for information by delaying the communication of information. If there exists an unnecessarily long time-lag between actual events and the reporting of these events, then there may be a need created for corrective action that is more drastic than if such action had been taken earlier on the basis of more promptly produced control information. Furthermore, delays in supplying information for control purposes may well cause higher levels of management to become involved – and hence those further removed from actual events needing correction – than would otherwise have been the case.

Accountability

This follows in many respects from relevance (see above). It is essential to the success of any financial control system that an individual is only held responsible for results when the following conditions prevail:

1 That he knows what he is expected to achieve.
2 That he knows what he is actually achieving.
3 It is within his power to regulate what is happening (i.e. what he is held responsible for must be within his control).

Information must therefore be keyed to those individuals who are responsible for achieving specified results.

Simplicity

It will often be found simpler – and hence more satisfactory – to have information related to such units as hours, units of electricity, miles, etc., rather than having everything expressed in terms of money. This has the distinct advantage that comparisons of usage will not be confused or rendered invalid by inflationary price chances.

As a result of both their training and temperament, accountants can generally find their way through masses of figures, observing detailed interrelationships, drawing conclusions, and knowing exactly what the figures represent. But as many non-accountants are unable to do this, the onus is placed squarely on the shoulders of the accountant to remove unnecessary complexity and technical trivia in order to provide information in a simple manner (consistent with its purpose) so that it can be understood by those who must act upon it.

Yardsticks of comparison

Information appertaining to actual results should be related to a yardstick of performance – a predetermined plan, budget, or standard. In the absence of this comparison there can be no meaningful basis for evaluating achievements and hence no effective way of enabling management to control operations.

From this discussion it will be seen that management information for cost control must observe the important features of any control system:

1 Accountability
2 Controllability
3 Selectivity.

In addition, the information used for cost control should be checked for four vitally important qualities:

1 Impartiality
2 Validity
3 Reliability
4 Internal consistency.

Information flows are the primary centres of attention for systems designers, and if the resultant systems are to be of value then they must be based on – and carry – information that is intelligible, timely, clearly specified, sufficiently detailed and complete, and accurate to an acceptable standard. Vague figures thrown out by an unplanned system are inadequate in attempting to secure proper control over costs. In considering the design of any information system, three fundamental questions arise:

1 What information should be provided?
2 In what form should this information be supplied?
3 To whom should this information be made available?

These questions lead us to a consideration of reporting systems themselves.

CHARACTERISTICS OF REPORTING SYSTEMS

An effective management reporting system is one that uses the available information flows to control the company's activities in accordance with objectives and plans. Important elements of the process of controlling costs are the devising, compiling, and constant revising of an adequate and up-to-date system of reports. This should result in better decision-making, faster action, greater managerial flexibility, and vastly improved coordination. But it should be borne in mind that no system can be more effective than either its designer specifies it to be or its users are capable of making it.

In essence, management reporting implies the preparation and presentation of comparative information that must be interpreted in such a manner as to stimulate decision-making. Reports are one of the means by which an organization's activities can be coordinated with a view to evaluation, policy formulation, and so on. Such reports can range from daily analyses of materials, labour utilization, and salesmen's calls, to annual reports on the overall business, and they may be expressed in physical operating terms or in financial terms.

Reports constitute a vital means of communication, and in developing them and deciding on their frequency, the controller must attempt to assess their ultimate utility to their recipients. In specifying what is to be reported at each level of management – especially at lower levels – the controller must pose the three questions noted at the end of the last section and also add a fourth: what are the necessary and controllable factors relevant to the level of authority under consideration?

The level of management in question will determine whether reports need to relate results to long-term plans, expressed in aggregates, or whether they simply need to relate results to cost standards in great detail. The principles of cost control are the same for these extremes, representing top management at one extreme and supervisory management at the other, but the form of report is different.

The adoption of a structured approach to reporting, with results being reported by areas of responsibility, enables top management to view the results and efficiencies of individual departments in the light of their contribution to overall performance and objectives. It may be found, however, that the need for control action on the part of top management indicates a failure to achieve control at a lower level – as in the case of time-lags.

The characteristics of good reporting systems for securing cost control follow largely from the characteristics of control information given in the previous section. These characteristics include:

1 Timeliness
2 Clarity
3 Facilitation of follow-up
4 Yardsticks of performance
5 Simplicity
6 Succinctness
7 Implications.

The above items will be discussed in detail on the following pages.

Timeliness

Reports should contain *current* information.

Clarity

Regardless of the technical soundness and accuracy of a cost report, it will not be well received unless it is clear, concise, and understandable to the non-accounting executive. Readability in financial reporting should ideally be given the same emphasis as an advertising agency gives to copy writing. Readability and clarity require that very careful consideration be given to the volume of information that should be presented in a report, and also to the terminology that should be used in it. The contents of a report should be so set out that it is inviting to those who must read it. This can be achieved – at least to some extent – by:

1 Using short sentences
2 Avoiding technical jargon
3 Clearly labelled headings
4 Clarifying all item descriptions
5 Spacing items well
6 Making good use of tables, figures, and charts
7 Breaking-up whole pages (e.g. by diagrams).

Facilitation of follow-up

Follow-up (as will be discussed later in this chapter) provides the controller with one of his greatest opportunities to serve management. It is only after a report has been published that it becomes of real value: the controller's job does not end when he has produced it. Reported results should be discussed between recipients and compilers as a preliminary step towards future decision-making.

The uses to which control reports are normally put fall into four categories, namely:

1 To spot things that are going wrong, thereby permitting corrective action to be taken before serious loss results: this is the most fruitful and constructive use of control information.
2 To spotlight what has already gone wrong and to guide management in picking up the pieces and trying to cut the losses that result from failure.
3 To determine exactly how and why failure has occurred, and to suggest the steps that might be taken to prevent its recurrence: this is highly

constructive as mistakes need not be repeated even though they may not always be avoided in the first place.

4 To find out who is to blame for failure, which, in itself, is not a very constructive use of control information.

It is worth noting that deviations from plan can – and do – arise because of inadequacies in the plan itself. For instance, errors in a budget may be due to incorrect assumptions, or to carelessness, or to changing conditions that have rendered the original plan obsolete.

Yardstick of performance

A reported figure in isolation of a benchmark has little meaning. Comparison is necessary for appraising performance.

The best yardsticks in cost control are standard costs and budgets. To be of maximum value, these yardsticks should have the confidence of those whose performance is to be measured, and the best way to build this confidence is for those responsible for results at a particular organizational level to be fully involved in developing the appropriate yardsticks.

Simplicity

Too much detail is more likely to cause confusion than to create enlightenment. A suitable degree of simplicity should be built in – provided that this does not lead to summaries that are too broad to permit understanding. A balance between broad summarising that gives perspective and supplying sufficient detail to permit understanding (hence action) should be sought. A well-balanced summary statement should provide sufficient clues for items that are out of line (i.e. the exceptions) to lead to analysis behind the summary figures when it is considered to be necessary. Any item that has a high degree of variability, or a high probability of deviating from plan, should be shown separately instead of being aggregated in a summary.

Simplicity can be achieved by such means as:

1 Eliminating unnecessary figures.
2 Avoiding technicalities that are not essential.
3 Rounding figures – e.g. £384 275.89 can be rounded to the nearest whole £ to give £384 276, and then to £384 000 when reduced to the nearest £1 000.

Succinctness

Succinctness is a great virtue in reporting. This is a very tangible aspect.

Implications

On an intangible plane, a major contribution made by an adequate reporting system is that the recipient of a report is made to pause and think over the contents of that report and its implications for the organization.

When considering who should receive control reports it is important to appreciate that reports are issued to *individuals*, rather than to *departments*, in order to stimulate action and to keep people informed. Thus individuals with specified responsibilities should receive reports relating to these responsibilities, and their superiors should be informed by receiving copies of these reports.

Within the framework of cost control, reports should be designed such that they:

1 Are oriented towards the user taking into account both his level and his function.
2 Give as much information as possible in *quantitative* terms, and flow both ways in the organization (i.e. up and down).
3 Are based on a flexible system that allows quick changes to meet new conditions.
4 Are oriented towards operations rather than towards accounting convenience.

It is often found, however, that the information systems on which managers in most organizations have to base their cost control decisions are inadequate and ineffective. Various reasons account for this failing, of which the following are the most frequently met:

1 Many systems are geared to one level of authority only: if this level is that of supervisory management, then reports will cover, *inter alia*, labour analyses that are essential for operational control at shop-floor level, but top management cannot be expected to make much use of this information at its own level in attempting to devise strategies.
2 Information flows are unrelated to individual responsibilities, with the result that action does not follow the reporting of facts because those facts are not linked with specific people.
3 A preoccupation with financial information draws attention away from other essential information about the organization, such as physical output, customer complaints, and so forth – and since these non-financial factors give rise to the financial outcome at the end of the day, it is clear that they are extremely significant.
4 The production of long, highly-detailed reports instead of brief statements that highlight major items and pinpoint areas of trouble prevents the exercising of management by exception, and hence uses executives' time inefficiently.

5 The focusing of attention on internal information, and ignoring external information, can result in a company missing profitable opportunities for growth and development.

Reporting systems that are nothing more than glorified accounting systems or systems that were designed many years ago for an organizational structure that has since changed considerably, are incongruent with the needs of dynamic cost control. The realization of this fact could be the starting point for redesigning the organization's entire reporting system.

INTERPRETATION AND FOLLOW-UP

Interpretation is the essential link between measurement and decision-making. Demands on executive time are usually such that it is important that reports both present *and* help to interpret the situation: this could lead to better decisions as well as saving executive time.

It should again be emphasized that cost reports have no value in themselves: their value lies purely in forming a basis for action on the part of their recipients.

The *meaning* of a cost report should never be obscure, even though the *significance* of its content may be. The significance of reported results lies in the interpretation of the information presented – this is largely a management skill. To the fullest extent possible, however, management reports should be designed so that interpretation is made comparatively easy and management's attention is focused only on the exceptions that require remedial action. At the time when he forwards cost reports to their recipients, the controller should review, analyse, and comment upon the content of his reports. In fact, the controller's department should have a definite programme to follow up the issuing of cost reports. This programme should cover the allocation of responsibilities to include:

1 The analysis of reports in order that significant deviations may be identified and investigations commenced into their causes. Exceptions should always be the focal point for analysis and interpretation. To aid in this task information can be displayed graphically (as discussed later in this chapter): for instance, the behaviour of overhead cost incurrence in relation to the level of productive activity could be plotted in an attempt to facilitate a rapid understanding of the situation prior to decision-making.

Trends can also be shown graphically – and since they develop very gradually over time, this could be of great value since trends will not be apparent from any one set of periodic reports. Any trend that is discovered should be reported to operating management and a decision made as to whether or not further analysis might be helpful. If the trend is short-term in nature and due to known, temporary fluctuations, then less concern may be felt than if it is a long-term trend caused by a variation in the basic conditions that underlie established methods of operation.

2 Arranging informal meetings with operating management to discuss points relating to cost reporting procedures and the contents of the reports. In particular, the following points could be covered:

(*a*) Individual managers' understanding of cost reports
(*b*) A review of variance analysis
(*c*) Standards of performance.

Efforts should be made – on the part of the controller – to develop an understanding of the activities and problems of operating departments, and also to encourage informal relationships to enable him to render the most helpful service he can to operating management.

3 Holding group meetings to follow up cost reports. For example, a general works manager might meet with all his subordinate managers and supervisors, in the presence of the controller, to discuss the overall plant position as well as specific departmental variances. Such a meeting should be arranged and directed by line management, but the participation of the controller (or a senior member of his staff) should ensure that a cost conscious attitude is encouraged as well as a high level of understanding of reported results. In order to play a useful role in group discussions, the controller must be both willing and able to explain things in down-to-earth terms to appeal to operating management's commonsense.

SOME EXAMPLES OF CONTROL REPORTS

To achieve his responsibility for communicating essential facts to management at all levels within the organization, it is necessary for the controller to have a very clear conception of the purposes, possibilities, and limitations of the many different types of statements and reports that could be used, and also to understand the problems and viewpoints of their users to make sure that they in turn appreciate the true meaning, as well as the limitations, of the reports that are prepared for them.

Typical examples of control reports can be grouped, as shown on the following page, into three categories – profitability reports, cost reports, and sundry reports.

1 Profitability reports by:
(*a*) Product
(*b*) Division
(*c*) Area
(*d*) Customer group
(*e*) Channel of distribution
(*f*) Whole organization
(*g*) Every profit responsibility centre.

2 Cost reports of:
(*a*) Labour analyses – direct labour
(*b*) Labour analyses – indirect labour
(*c*) Productive labour variances
(*d*) Non-productive labour variances
(*e*) Direct expense analysis
(*f*) Productivity analysis – direct labour
(*g*) Overtime payment analysis
(*h*) Analysis of spoilt work, rework, and scrap
(*i*) Material analyses
(*j*) Manufacturing overhead analysis
(*k*) Administrative cost analysis
(*l*) Marketing cost analysis (order-getting costs)
(*m*) Distribution cost analysis (order-filling costs)
(*n*) Product costs
(*o*) Cost of production
(*p*) Cost of sales
(*q*) Cost analyses for every responsibility centre and their constituent cost centres.

3 Sundry reports on:
(*a*) Orders received
(*b*) Orders delivered
(*c*) Overdue deliveries
(*d*) Backlog of orders at month-end
(*e*) Material yields
(*f*) Cash receipts
(*g*) Physical output
(*h*) R & D progress report
(*i*) Values of inventions
(*j*) Special studies
 (i) analysis and interpretation of problems or trends indicated by other regular reports
 (ii) studies directed towards finding cost reduction opportunities

(iii) adding/dropping product lines
(iv) make or buy decisions
(v) overhead allocation exercises
(vi) cost/volume/profit analyses, etc.

(*k*) Statistical analyses – trends, ratios, etc.

These reports may be compiled for an accounting period (such as a month, a quarter, or a year) or for more frequent periods (such as a week, a day, or an hour) for key factors. Statistical reports may or may not be integrated with the regular accounting reports.

The style of reports themselves, as we have seen, should facilitate understanding. Above all, the conventional debit-credit pattern should be avoided. Possible formats are given in Figure 7.3 and Figure 7.4. Frequently it will be found useful to add percentages and ratios in appropriate places in reports. To a large extent, however, this will depend upon the needs and personal preferences of recipients.

Figure 7.3 gives an example of a cost report relating to a small factory, and this shows a comparison between cumulative budget and cumulative actual results, with the variances being classified into favourable (or credit) variances that arise when actual costs are less than budget, and unfavourable (or debit) variances that arise when actual costs exceed budgeted costs. Some of the aggregated information on this statement would need to be disaggregated to enable proper cost control to be applied: the most notable examples are direct material and direct labour which should be detailed in accordance with the productive output and analysed along the lines of standard costing procedures.

The example of Figure 7.4, relating to a branch office of a marketing organization, shows the distinction between fixed and variable costs. The variable portion of the budgeted allowance for an item should be adjusted for comparative purposes to correspond to the actual volume of sales obtained during a given period of time.

CHARTS

As indicated in the last section, cost information can often be presented in chart form, by means of graphs and diagrams, as well as in conventional tabular format. This permits relationships, trends, and comparisons to be grasped more readily on account of their visual impact. A selection of different types of charts will now be considered.

Budget report			*Date*		
Item	*Amount this week*	*Total to date 26 weeks*	*Budget for 26 weeks*	*Budget comparison*	
				Above	*Below*
	£	£	£	£	£
OUTPUT (at Prime Cost)	5 000	140 000	154 000		14 000
Consumable Stores	35	740	690	50	
Maintenance	112	2 470	2 600		130
Canteen	73	1 820	1 750	70	
Welfare & Safety	28	630	605	25	
Pension Fund	30	750	740	10	
Holiday Pay	250	3 700	3 900		200
Indirect Labour:					
Cleaning	48	1 120	1 150		30
Inspection	140	3 300	3 100	200	
Stores	210	5 400	4 988	412	
Materials Handling	105	2 750	2 600	150	
Telephone, etc	25	530	490	40	
Insurance	10	250	275		25
Recruitment & Training	90	560	650		90
Stationery	45	800	745	55	
Rent & Rates	80	2 000	2 000	—	—
Depreciation	85	2 210	2 210	—	—
Direct Materials	1 648	48 127	57 232		9 105
Direct Labour	1 986	62 843	68 275		5 432

Figure 7.3: Factory cost report

Budget Report

Branch ______________ *Period* ______________

	Budget factors		*This month*			*Year to date*
	Fixed	*Variable*	*Budget*	*Actual*	*Over (under)*	*Over (under)*
	£	£	£	£	£	£
Net sales						
Salaries: Executive Sales force Clerical *Recruitment costs* *Office expenses:* Rent & rates Heat & light Stationery Telephone, etc. Insurances Depreciation Postage Other *Field expenses:* Travelling Entertaining Accommodation						

Figure 7.4: Office expense report

Bar charts

Bar charts (as shown in Figure 7.5) enable magnitudes to be compared visually in a very simple manner with the length of the bar being directly proportional to the value it represents. The basic *bar chart* of Figure 7.5 shows a straightforward comparison of the level of indirect labour costs for each of five different years. This overall level of costs can be broken down into its constituent parts – such as downtime, maintenance, labourers and storekeeping elements – and these parts can be shown in a *component bar chart* as illustrated in Figure 7.6.

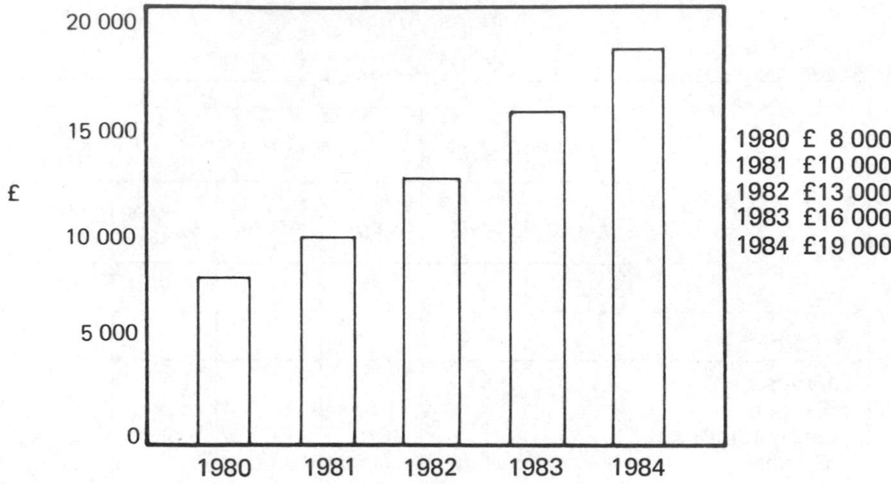

Figure 7.5: Bar chart: indirect labour costs

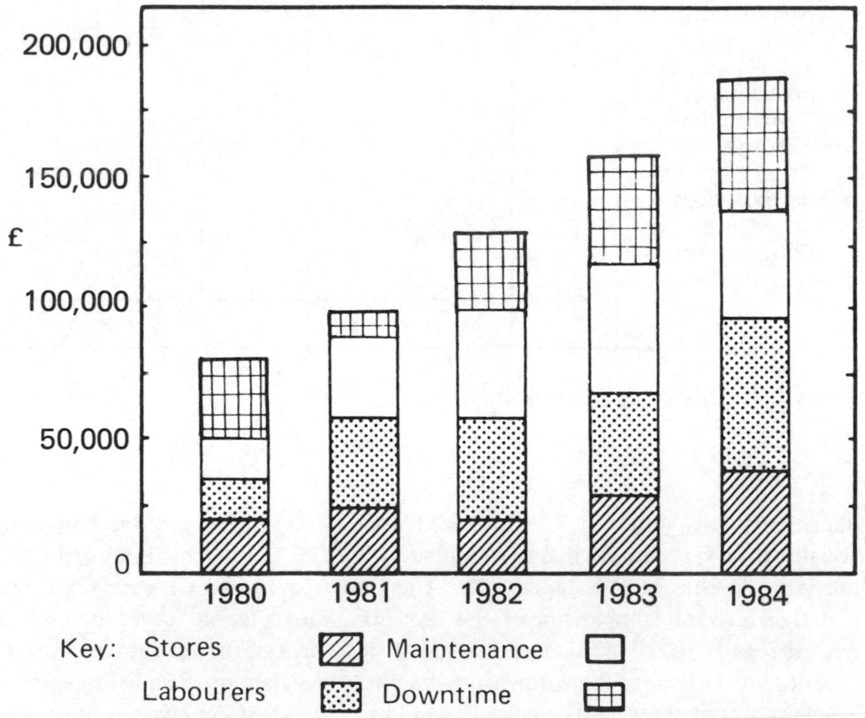

Figure 7.6: Component bar chart: indirect labour costs

A further variation is to compile a *percentage component bar chart* such as that shown in Figure 7.7. This chart differs from Figure 7.5 and Figure 7.6 in that the vertical scale is expressed in terms of percentages rather than in terms of money. The result is that the bars themselves are all the same height (which is equivalent to 100 per cent of whatever the cost of indirect labour for a particular year happened to be). The proportion of the whole that each constituent cost element represents can then be shown. For 1981, for example, the overall level of indirect labour cost was £100 000 (as shown in Figure 7.5). This is made up in the following way (see Figure 7.6):

	£
Downtime	10 000
Maintenance	30 000
Labourers	30 000
Stores	30 000
TOTAL	100 000

The percentage make-up of this total is easy to compute:

	Per cent
Downtime	10
Maintenance	30
Labourers	30
Stores	30
TOTAL	100

This analysis is portrayed in Figure 7.7.

Figures 7.6 and 7.7 clearly show in their respective ways how the composition of indirect labour cost varies from period to period. This facilitates the monitoring of trends.

A variation on the bar chart theme is the *multiple bar chart* as shown in Figure 7.8. This type of chart enables related items to be compared: the illustration relates the cost of factor inputs to the value of output of a manufacturing organization, with the difference being *value-added*. Essentially this is a compound of two simple bar charts.

In all compound and multiple charts it is, of course, vitally important that a clear key is given and all items properly identified. This requirement becomes increasingly important with more complex charts – and especially with the extreme example of a bar chart which is a multiple component bar chart.

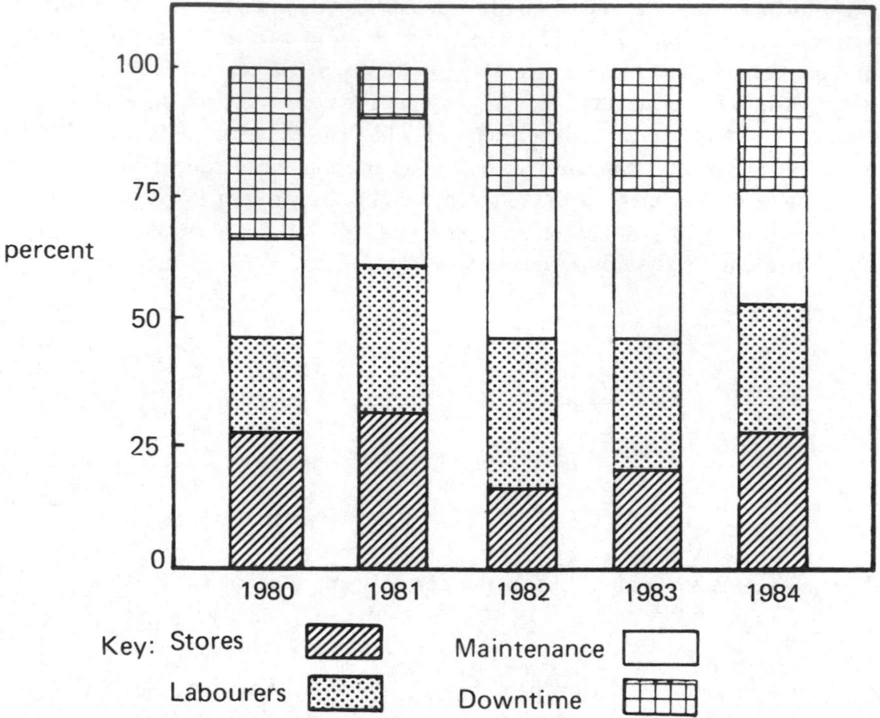

Figure 7.7: Percentage component bar chart

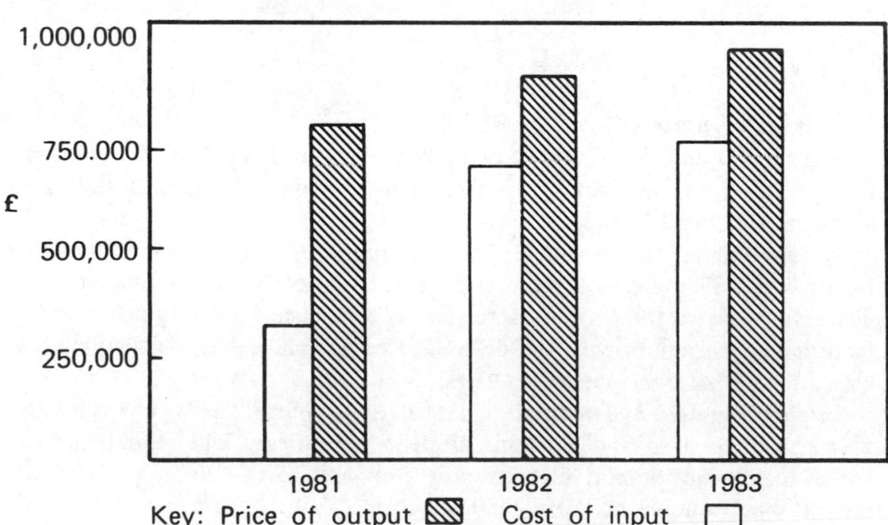

Figure 7.8: Multiple bar chart: value added

Pictograms

A pictogram is a pictorial bar chart that shows variables in a highly simplified manner. Symbols are used to represent the data – in Figure 7.9 a simplified picture of a lorry is used to portray the increasing size of a company's distribution fleet over time.

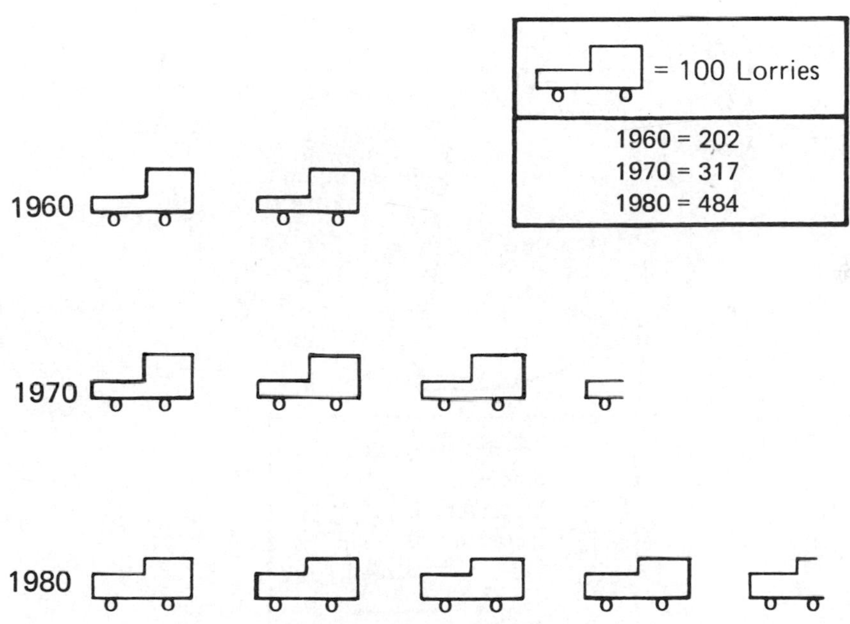

Figure 7.9: Pictogram: size of delivery fleet

Pie charts

Pie charts are similar to component bar charts in that they show the relationships between parts and wholes. Figure 7.10 illustrates this with reference to the make-up of each £1 of a company's sales revenue. It should be noted, however, that it is more difficult to visually compare one chart with another in the case of a pie chart than is found in the case of component bar charts.

Frequency curves

One particular type of frequency diagram, a histogram, was illustrated in Figure 5.4. This chart, as was explained in Chapter 5, portrays the frequency with which different values of a variable are observed. We can construct a

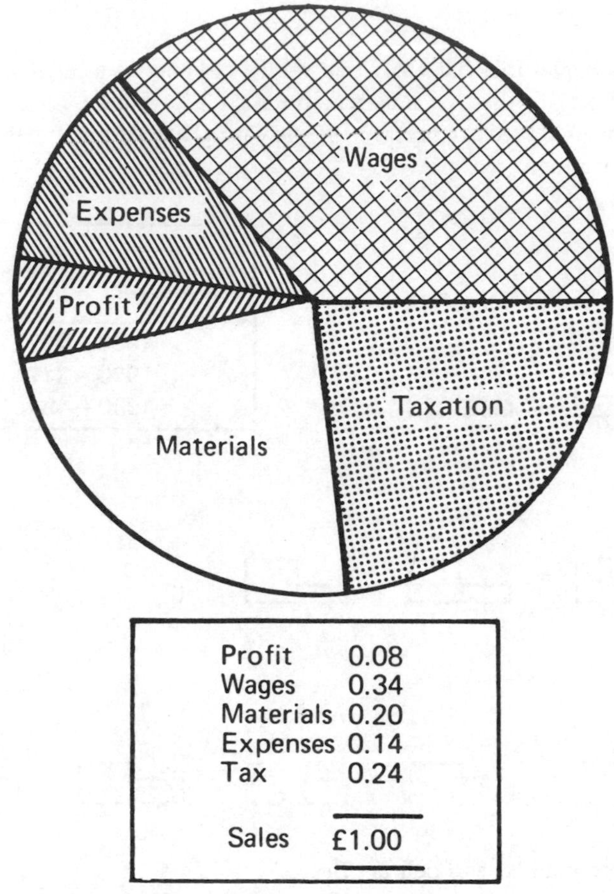

Profit	0.08
Wages	0.34
Materials	0.20
Expenses	0.14
Tax	0.24
Sales	£1.00

Figure 7.10: Pie chart: analysis of sales revenue

histogram on the basis of the frequency distribution of Figure 7.11 (which is compiled on the assumption that the predicted outcomes of Figure 7.1 actually occurred). The histogram from this data is shown in Figure 7.12.

By joining the midpoints of each rectangle in a histogram one can construct a *frequency polygon.* Figure 7.13 illustrates a frequency polygon based on the histogram of Figure 7.12. The frequency polygon is a simplified version of a histogram, but a variation is to construct a *cumulative frequency curve* (known as an *ogive*). The cumulative frequency of the observations of Figure 7.11 is shown in Figure 7.14, and the corresponding ogive is shown in Figure 7.15.

Variable (Price of material X)	*Number of observations*	=	*Frequency*
£55	0		
£56	5		
£57	10		
£58	20		
£59	30		
£60	20		
£61	15		
£62	0		
	100		

Figure 7.11: Frequency distribution of material costs

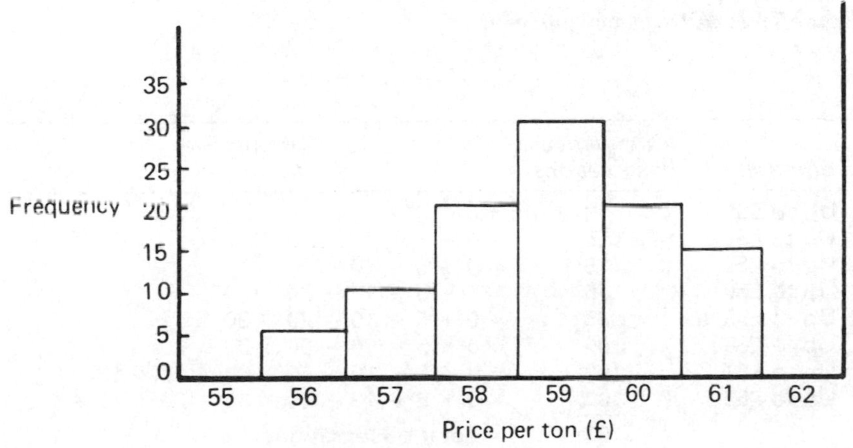

Figure 7.12: Histogram showing material cost

Ogives can be drawn to show either the actual cumulative frequency distribution of observations or their percentage cumulative frequencies. By coincidence (because 100 observations were assumed), Figure 7.15 is the same as the corresponding cumulative percentage frequency curve for the data of Figure 7.14. Comparisons between cumulative frequencies should be made only for *percentage* cumulative frequencies.

Graphs

It is usually quite an easy matter to draw graphs for each of a large number of variables. The general procedure is to plot the variable under consideration

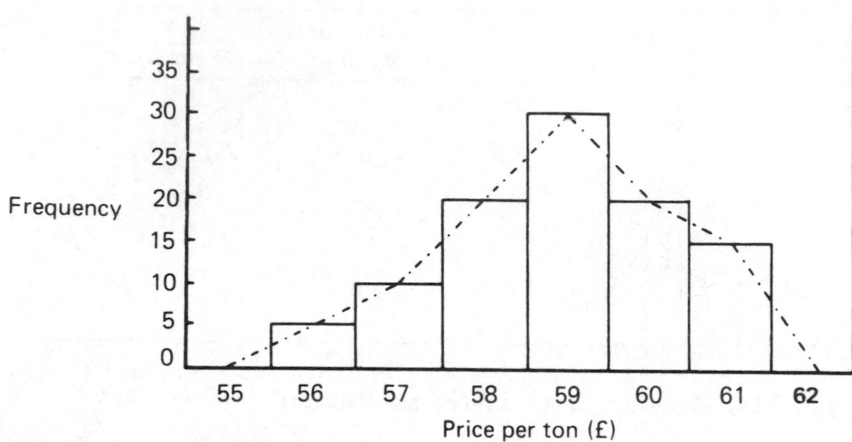

Figure 7.13: A frequency polygon

Variable	*Cumulative observations*	=	*Cumulative frequency*
Up to £55	0	= 0	
Up to £56	5	= 0 + 5	
Up to £57	15	= 0 + 5 + 10	
Up to £58	35	= 0 + 5 + 10 + 20	
Up to £59	65	= 0 + 5 + 10 + 20 + 30	
Up to £60	85	= 0 + 5 + 10 + 20 + 30 + 20	
Up to £61	100	= 0 + 5 + 10 + 20 + 30 + 20 + 15	
Up to £62	100	= 0 + 5 + 10 + 20 + 30 + 20 + 15 + 0	
	100	= Total observations	

Figure 7.14: Cumulative frequency distribution

(e.g. cost of a particular item) over time or against a level of activity. An example is given in Figure 7.16 of indirect labour cost over time. (Compare this with Figure 7.5.) As an additional piece of information, Figure 7.17 shows the relationship between the level of indirect labour costs and the (assumed) level of output.

More than one curve can be plotted on a graph, with the result that total indirect labour cost can be analysed as shown in Figure 7.18 which is known as a *band curve chart*. (This should be compared with the component bar chart of Figure 7.6.) This type of chart can also be constructed on the basis of percentages (compare with Figure 7.7).

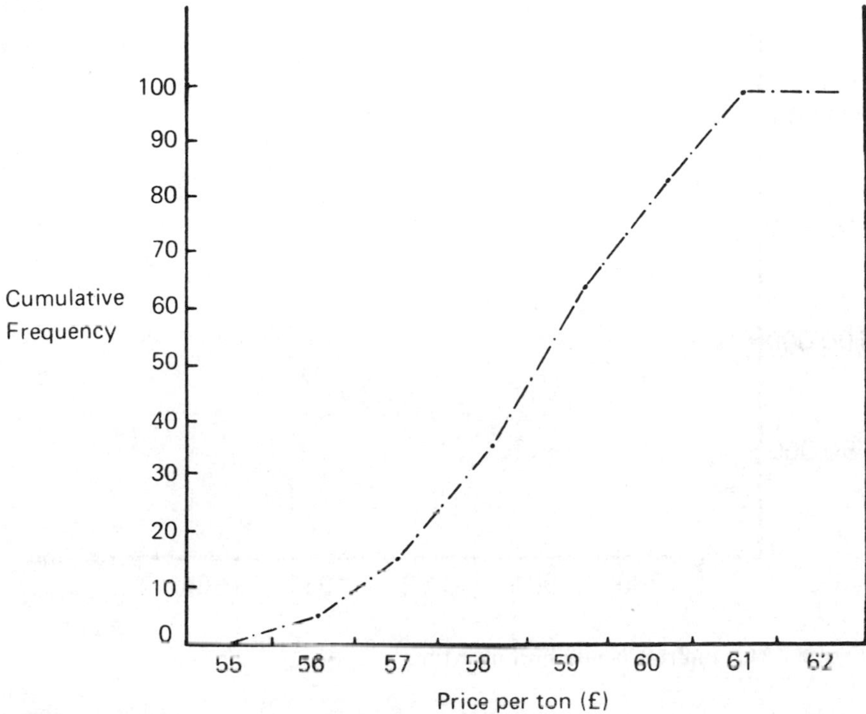

Figure 7.15: Ogive

Finally, a *scattergraph* (Figure 7.19) can be drawn by plotting available observations of variables that are thought to be related (e.g. the behaviour of heating costs is assumed to vary in accordance with the temperature) in order that the degree of correlation (i.e. degree of correspondence) may be computed. A 'line of best fit' can be fitted to the observations by one of a range of techniques, such as the method of least squares, which are described and explained in all basic statistical textbooks.

Other types of chart

Details of more complicated or specialized charts (including those drawn with logarithmic scales on one or both axes, Lorenz curves, Z charts, and so forth) can be found in most statistics books. But the simple illustrations given in this chapter demonstrate that graphic presentation can convey far more to a reader than can a page of figures even though the latter may be accompanied by a page of explanation.

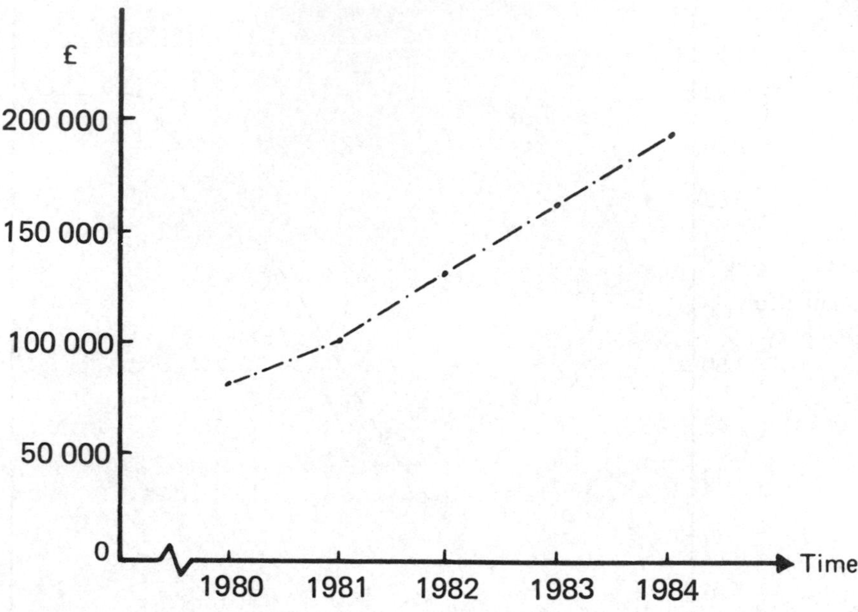

Figure 7.16: Indirect labour cost over time

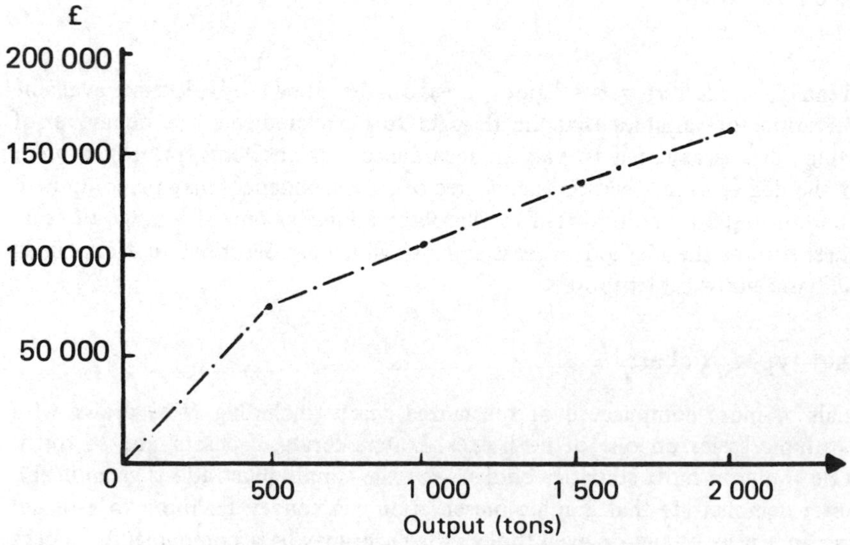

Figure 7.17: Indirect labour cost against output

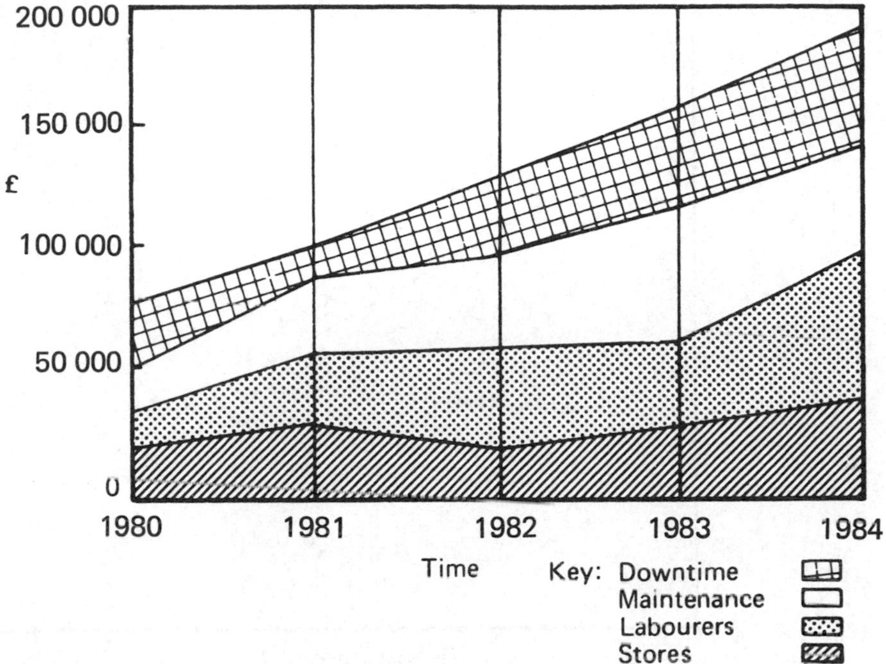

Figure 7.18: Band curve chart

Guidelines on using charts

Guidelines exist for employing charts. For instance:

1. Charts should be kept simple.
2. Charts should be used whenever a point is to be dramatized or otherwise emphasized.
3. Charts should be used to add impact and aid understanding in oral presentations.
4. Charts should be used whenever it is necessary to show patterns and trends over time or against the level of activity.
5. Charts should be used to show correlations – such as that between the level of output and the amount of scrap.

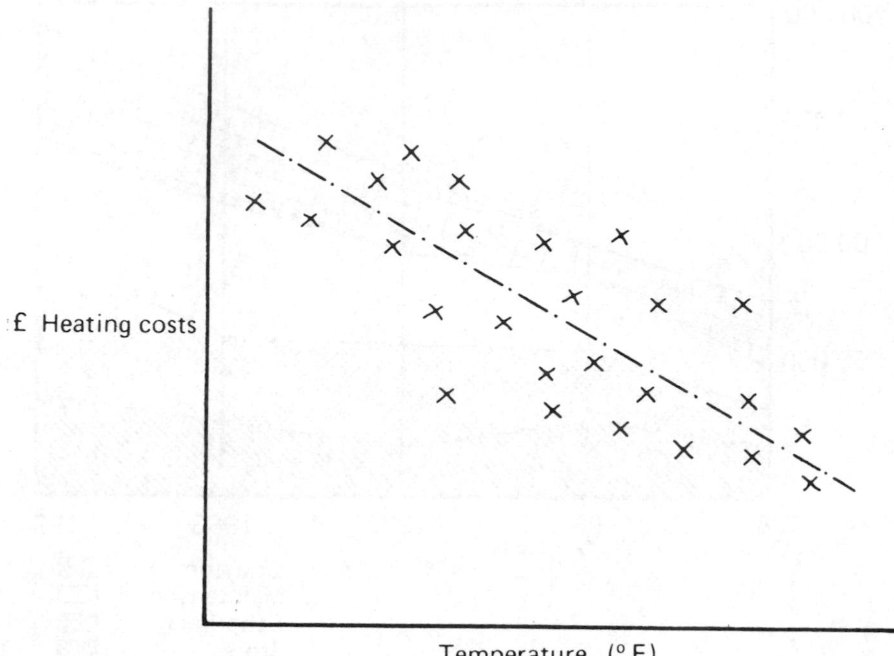

Figure 7.19: Scattergraph

CHECKLIST ON REPORTING SYSTEMS

1 Is information presented in such a way that it assists in decision-making?
2 Does information indicate each responsible individual's achievements and level of required performance?
3 Does the information presented to him enable the individual manager to make plans and set standards?
4 Do reports present both results *and* – insofar as possible – the reasons behind these results?
5 Are past *and* present levels of performance emphasized in reports?
6 Is the reporting structure flexible?
7 Are established goals and other standards stressed as benchmarks in reports?
8 Is information about the future given in reports?
9 Is information of a non-financial nature reported where it has relevance to financial outcomes?

10 Is information on external conditions (as they might bear on a particular organization's operations) given in reports?
11 Is each report oriented towards its recipient, considering both his level and function?
12 Do reports give as much information as possible in quantitative terms?
13 Do reports flow both ways in the organization?
14 Are reports suitably succinct?
15 Are recipients of reports urged to consider fully their content and to discuss this with colleagues and staff?
16 Is an appropriate and known degree of accuracy secured in reported information?
17 Does management realize that the study of management information and reporting systems is not necessarily concerned with computers?
18 Is it understood that more data in reports does not in itself mean more information for management?
19 Does the controller know that management's information needs cannot all be predetermined by systems studies? (Does management know this?)
20 Is it appreciated that for information to be instantly available does not necessarily increase its value or usefulness? And that frequent reporting does not necessarily mean that information is thereby more useful?
21 Is management by exception practised in designing and compiling reports?
22 Are reports understood?
23 Is unnecessary detail eliminated from reports?
24 Do reports call the attention of higher levels of management to those situations that cannot be controlled at lower levels?
25 Is each report that is produced really necessary?
26 Can reports be condensed, or combined one with another?
27 Can the frequency of issue of reports be altered?
28 Is an interest in the reporting system maintained at all levels of management?
29 Can significant figures be produced and communicated between normal reporting dates?
30 Are regular review meetings held to consider reports, results and the adequacy of reporting systems?
31 Are attempts made to explain variations from plan in an *upwards* direction in the organization before criticism proceeds *downwards* to the source of variation?
32 Are the duties and responsibilities of all those concerned with producing reports clearly defined?
33 Is the chart of accounts compatible with the requirements of the reporting system?

34 Are controllable expenses segregated from those that are non-controllable?
35 Are results reported in the same manner in which managers plan and think about their operations?
36 Are reports presented in an easy-to-read format?
37 Is appropriate use made of ratios and percentages?
38 Are figures in reports rounded whenever possible?
39 Is follow-up properly planned?

SUMMARY

The design and installation of a responsibility reporting system is a major undertaking for any organization. More important than technical accounting refinements are general management backing and the adoption of responsibility accounting principles. The structure of the organization and individuals' responsibilities should be reflected in the chart of accounts and hence in the system of reports.

Management reporting is not an end in itself. It is the heart of the communications system, and the effectiveness of the reporting system will largely determine the control that management has over its operations.

An organization's reporting system must be tailor-made for the organization, but certain characteristics (relating to accuracy, simplicity, clarity, timeliness, relevance, facilitating follow-up, succinctness, and the presence of yardsticks of performance) are common to all good reporting systems.

Follow-up is more important than reporting itself, and this can be aided considerably if good relations are developed between operating management and the controller's department.

Charts in their various forms, are valuable in highlighting reported results.

Amongst the items listed on pp.381–3 for further reading, the following are especially recommended:

Anderson, Schmidt and McCosh;
Bentley;
Emery;
Goodman and Reece.

8

Budgeting

THE PLANNING PERSPECTIVE

If a company's activities are not to be aimless they must be given some direction. This can come from answering such questions as:

1 What products is it proposed to produce and market?
2 What machinery and factory facilities are required?
3 What type of materials are required, and where can they be obtained?
4 What rate of expansion is aimed for?
5 What future development is intended?
6 What level of staffing is required in the field, the factory, the laboratory, the offices?
7 What level of overhead expenditure is to be incurred?

It is one of the functions of budgetary planning to ensure that suitable answers are given to these and many other questions.

Budgeting is a management tool used for shorter-term planning and control. Traditionally, budgets have been employed as devices to limit expenditure, but a much more useful and constructive view is to treat the budgeting process as a means for obtaining the most effective and profitable use of the company's resources via planning and control.

Briefly, the budgeting process consists of establishing objectives for the whole organization, devising plans and standards of performance for every area of activity, comparing actual results with planned results, and the taking of corrective action on the basis of significant variations from planned results. (Setting standards is dealt with in detail in Chapter 10.)

In compiling a comprehensive budgetary plan it is vitally important that *all* dimensions of a company's operations be considered. Each activity has an impact on many other activities – thus the level of scrap has an effect on the availability of raw materials, the quantity of acceptable finished goods, the level of piecework earnings, etc. Budgeting can be seen as a major aid to communication, and the process should enable each manager to see how his area of activity fits in and contributes to the whole. In this way management is put into a position whereby it can anticipate change (at least to some extent) and thereby be prepared to adapt to meet it. For example, a production manager's decision to alter the level of work-in-progress stocks, or a marketing manager's decision to change the terms under which a particular product is sold, can be traced through the entire budgeting system to show the effects of such decisions on the operations of other departments and on the company's overall results.

Figure 8.1 illustrates, in outline, the overall budget planning framework. This is only one of the two aspects of the budgeting process that must be considered:

1. Budgetary planning – the predetermination of a course of action in such detail that every responsible unit can be guided by it.
2. Budgetary control – the converse of planning, by which results are compared with desired standards of performance and any necessary action taken accordingly in relation to significant deviations.

In this book we are essentially concerned with short-term cost control, but this must be viewed (as shown in Figure 8.1) against a long-term planning horizon. Corporate objectives are the focal point over any time span: they establish the basic rationale and purpose of the company's existence. Objectives must be capable of attainment if they are to have any relevance, and this requires that they be specific and quantified. 'To achieve a 10 per cent net of tax rate of return on investment' is specific, as is 'to secure a 25 per cent market share within 5 years for product X'. But 'to be profitable' is too vague to guide operations.

Following from a statement of objectives, a corporate long-range (or strategic) plan can be built up. A generalized model of this is given in Figure 8.2.

This planning model highlights the distinction between current operating activities (shown on the left-hand side and equivalent to short-term budgeting) and future strategic activities (shown on the right-hand side and the subject of a long-term plan). Immediate managerial concern is likely to be with *market penetration*, by which efforts are made to sell more of an existing product range

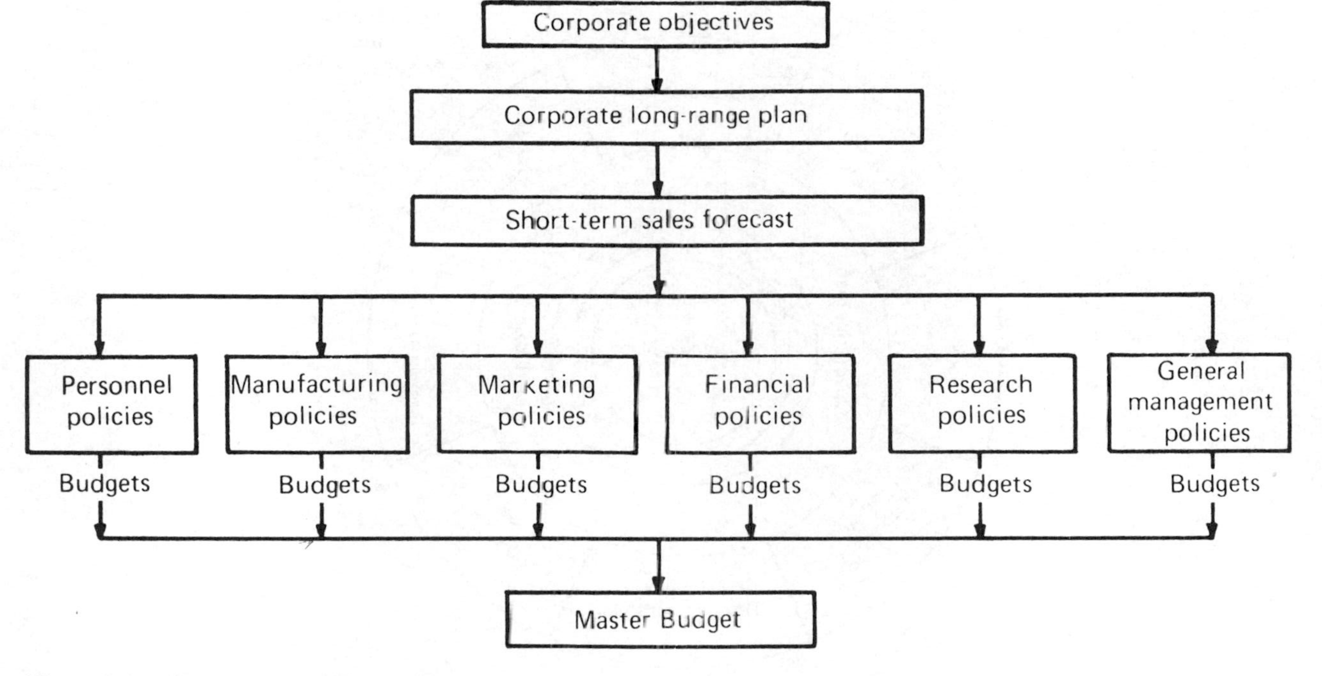

Figure 8.1: The budgeting process

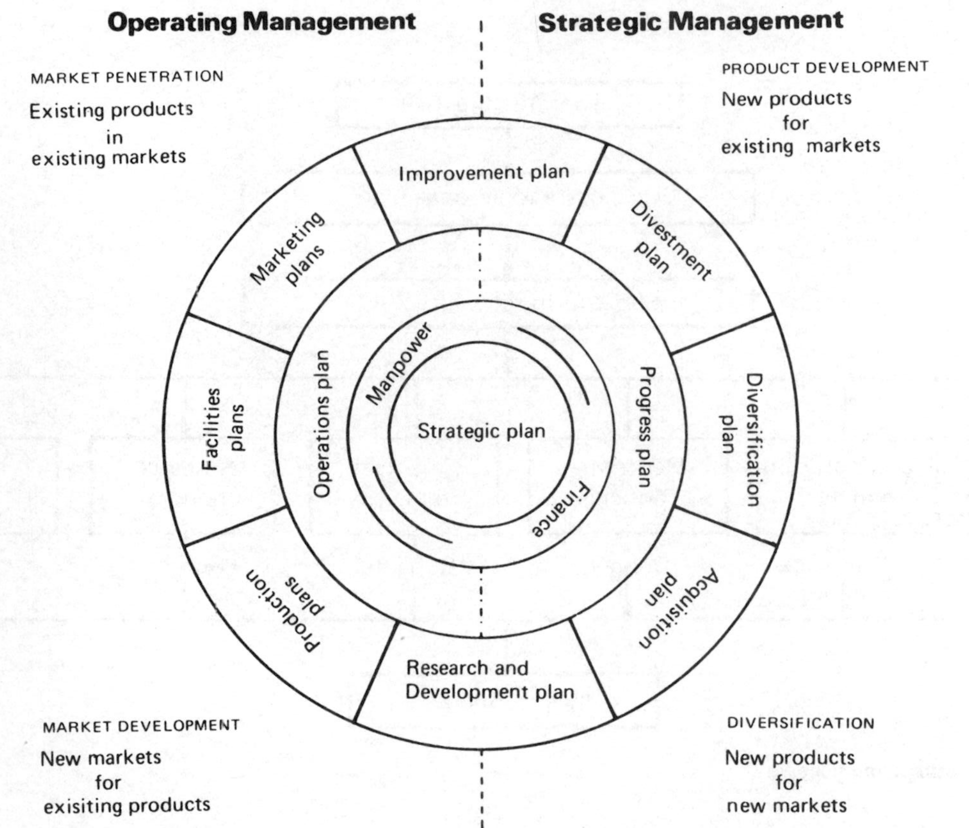
Operating Management
Strategic Management
MARKET PENETRATION
Existing products in existing markets
PRODUCT DEVELOPMENT
New products for existing markets
Improvement plan
Marketing plans
Divestment plan
Facilities plans
Operations plan
Manpower
Strategic plan
Finance
Progress plan
Diversification plan
Production plans
Acquisition plan
Research and Development plan
MARKET DEVELOPMENT
New markets for exisiting products
DIVERSIFICATION
New products for new markets

Figure 8.2: A generalized planning model

in existing markets, or *market development*, by which new markets are sought and exploited for existing product lines. In contrast, strategic managerial interest is likely to be more in the areas of *product development* (new products for existing markets) and *diversification* (new products for new markets). Both product development and diversification may be facilitated by the acquisition of other companies, so it will be apparent that such decisions are exceedingly complex.

Figure 8.2 is circular to show that all parts of the model are interdependent. The core of the model – the strategic plan – guides all the constituent parts in objective striving behaviour. Resources such as funds and manpower must be planned, acquired, developed, and allocated between current and future activities in such a way that there is balance within the total corporate plan.

Whilst operating management will principally be involved with developing operating plans for marketing, production, and facilities, with strategic management concentrating on acquisition, divestment, and diversification plans, both R & D and improvement plans are of common interest. From an operations viewpoint, the 'D' (or development) of R & D will tend to dominate, whilst from a strategic viewpoint the emphasis will tend to be on 'R' (i.e. research) in relation to products, materials, processes, and possibly to the overall technology, which may take the company into a completely new area of business activity. The improving of all operations and functions is a total management responsibility whether this is achieved by improving the productivity and efficiency of current operations or by redirecting future efforts towards a more effective attainment of objectives.

The other dimensions of Figure 8.1 (the budgeting process) will be dealt with in a later section in this chapter. The purpose of this section is to give a broad planning perspective to show how the budgeting process improves operations because it is a continuing effort to get the company's activities carried out in the best way by anticipating change and adapting to it.

Changes in the economy (such as varying rates of interest) as well as in competitive behaviour (such as price alterations or the introduction of new products) can – at least to some extent – be anticipated, and appropriate courses of action can then be determined in an attempt to counter these changes. The alternative to anticipation and adaptation is to be so preoccupied with one crisis after another that no attention is paid to the possible future courses of action available to the company.

By planning ahead, the management of a company will have a better basis for understanding the company's operations in relation to its environment which should lead to faster reactions in the face of developing events, thereby increasing the company's ability to perform effectively. Even though the future actions of, say, competitors cannot be predicted with perfect accuracy, the most probable alternatives can be considered and the company can consider *in advance* how it will respond to whichever comes about. (This is known as contingency planning.)

Furthermore, the budgeting process helps in the attaining of internal coordination. Decisions on every aspect of the company's operations affect costs and profits in some way, and the budgeting process provides an overall, integrated view of the cost and profit consequences of the company's activities.

Budgeting, as suggested in Figure 8.1, has an impact on policies within the company, and the master budget becomes the expression of managerial policies that must be transformed into effective action. This requires, of course, that those who are to be held responsible for the outcomes of events have been allowed to participate fully in drawing up the budgeted plan of action. (The budgeting process corresponds with the company-wide application of responsibility accounting as discussed in Chapter 6.) Budgets are especially important when a high degree of delegation is found if a company is decentralized into, for example, divisions that are geographically separated.

The other side of planning, as already mentioned, is control, and budgetary control follows the general principles of cost control that were discussed in Chapters 4 and 6.

THE SETTING OF BUDGET LEVELS

The way in which a budgeted level of performance is set will depend in part on the nature of the item in question and in part on the type of business in which the company is involved.

For example, in a mass-manufacturing situation, with lots of identical units of output being produced, standard costs can be established for direct materials, direct labour, and also for manufacturing overheads. (This topic will be dealt with at greater length in the next two chapters.) In contrast, in a jobbing shop it will not be possible to use standard costs because each job will vary. In the first case the budgeted cost of goods produced can be computed as:

Unit standard cost × Number of units produced

In the jobbing shop instance it will be much harder to estimate budget levels precisely due to the lack of standards and the variety of work. (It was stated in Chapter 3, however, that one of the objectives of the management of a jobbing shop will be to keep it working throughout the year at a specified level of activity – such as 85 per cent of available capacity, and that the labour and variable manufacturing overhead elements can be estimated on this basis, and the cost of materials will probably follow an established pattern.)

In a mass-marketing situation a similar argument applies to product costs based on what is termed the *case-rate principle*. This considers the cost of selling one unit of the basic product – that is, the smallest delivery unit, which may be an outer containing 12 or 24 items in the case of a grocery line, or a single item in the case of, say, a washing machine. Another example can be taken as the sale of products/materials by units of weight or volume, but the same case-rate principle applies. 'Case-rate' refers to the sum of money available for promotion and advertising once all other charges have been deducted. This follows from the observation that, for a well-established branded product, the manufacturing, selling, and distribution costs will be known (i.e. standardized to a large extent, or else highly programmed), and that the company will therefore be able to calculate the case-rate once allowance has been made for the required profit margin. Let us assume that the percentage breakdown for a case of canned vegetables is:

Selling price		100%
Manufacturing costs	50%	
Selling/distribution costs	15%	
Promotion and advertising	15%	
Profit margin	20%	
Total		100%

For a case sold to the grocery trade at £2.00 the cost profile is therefore:

Selling price		£2.00
Manufacturing costs	£1.00	
Selling/distribution costs	£0.30	
Promotion and advertising	£0.30	
Profit margin	£0.40	
Total		£2.00

The manufacturing costs will tend to be based on standards developed for an assumed level of sales. If a sales level of 250 000 cases is forecast for the next planning period, the overall profit/cost profile for this product line on the case-rate basis would be:

Sales revenue		£500 000
Manufacturing costs	£250 000	
Selling/distribution costs	£75 000	
Promotion and advertising	£75 000	
Profit margin	£100 000	
Total		£500 000

Changes in raw material prices, product formulation, trade margins, labour/

commission rates, and so forth, will all affect this profile, but its purpose is simply to give an overall approximation of cost and profit levels.

Another broad approach is to estimate overall cost levels for a forthcoming period on the basis of *cost per order received*, with profit being a residual. The rationale behind this type of approach is that overhead expense 'standards' can be developed (albeit in a very approximate manner) for each major category of cost in relation to orders, and then these relationships can be used to build up a cost profile for a projected level of sales activity. Let us take the example of a particular type of chair sold at £10 per unit. A cost profile is shown in Figure 8.3, and this can be repeated for each product line until an overall summary for the entire company can be derived.

	£	£
Sales: 100 000 @ £10		1 000 000
Orders received: 1 000		
Therefore average value per order = £1 000		
Order-processing cost per order	20	
Distribution cost per order	100	
General administrative cost per order	50	
Sales/marketing cost per order	30	
Total general and administration cost per order	200	
Manufacturing costs:		
Prime costs	500 000	
Manufacturing overheads	100 000	
General and administrative (1 000 @ £200)	200 000	
Total costs		800 000
Profit		200 000

Figure 8.3: Cost profile – cost per order basis

A further variation (*ratio analysis*) is to estimate future cost profiles as a projection of past ratios of net sales revenue. This is illustrated in Figure 8.4 for an anticipated increase of net sales revenue from £1 000 000 to £1 500 000.

(£'000's)	Current year		Budget for next year	
	Amount	Percentage of net sales	Amount	Percentage of net sales
Net sales	1 000	100.00	1 500	100.00
Cost of sales	650	65.00	975	65.00
Gross profit	350	35.00	525	35.00
Operating expenses:				
Distribution	70	7.0	105	7.0
Selling	100	10.0	150	10.0
Promotion and advertising	40	4.0	60	4.0
R & D	60	6.0	90	6.0
General and administrative	70	7.0	105	7.0
Total	340	34.0	510	34.0
Operating profit	10	1.0	15	1.0
Other income (net)	10	1.0	15	1.0
Net income (before tax)	20	2.0	30	2.0
Tax provision	10	1.0	15	1.0
Net income = Profit	10	1.0	15	1.0

Figure 8.4: Cost profile – ratio basis

This approach, along with the other two approaches suggested above (case-rate principle and cost per order basis), fails to allow adequately for:

1 The fixed cost – variable cost split and the different behaviour of individual components of total cost. (This is especially evident in Figure 8.4 where a 50 per cent increase in sales activity is incorrectly taken to mean that a proportionate variation in all cost figures will follow due to a rigid continuation of historical ratios that were built up in relation to – and will only adequately relate to – a given level of past activity.)

2 Future expectations – the methods merely extrapolate the past with the result that any inefficiencies included in historical ratios and cost rates are perpetuated into the future. No allowance is explicitly made for realistically-assessed future conditions and cost-behaviour patterns.

3 Detailed planning of specific activities. This is omitted due to an emphasis on overall aggregates.

One solution to setting budget levels that largely overcomes the objections mentioned above is to work in two directions in the budgeting process. At the top management level an initial view of possible cost and profit levels can be derived for various possible sales level/product mix combinations by using an aggregative rule of thumb method. Such a method might be a variation of one of those listed above that makes some allowance for future expectations and also for the existence of a fixed cost base.

At the same time, a more thorough grass-roots approach can be adopted whereby responsible individuals at the lowest level of delegated authority compile detailed budgets which are passed upwards and consolidated at subsequent levels in the organizational hierarchy until the overall picture can be compiled in summary form (supported by very detailed schedules) for comparison with objectives and also with top management's aggregate bird's-eye estimates. The grass-roots approach is infinitely more useful in achieving better coordination and also more valuable in demanding a more rigorous approach to defining the purpose of segments of the business, identifying alternative courses of action, and evaluating outcomes in order to select the best. But how is this total budget made up? The next section answers this important question.

THE MASTER BUDGET

Most organizations are too large to permit the detailed planning of all their activities in one budget, so it becomes necessary to use a summary approach that is contained in a *master budget*. Essentially the master budget is a consolidated summary of all the detailed budgets showing their outcomes in terms of their contribution to overall results.

The sales forecast is the starting point for preparing a budget. Sales revenue, stock levels, production requirements and hence most costs and, more especially, profit, all follow from a given level of sales activity. If the sales forecast is grossly inaccurate then the entire budget plan will be wrongly balanced. A sensible approach is to acknowledge that more than one level of sales is possible, so consideration should be given to alternatives.

The sum of sales requirements plus changes in stock levels of finished goods gives the production requirements for the period being budgeted. Once it is determined, the level of productive activity becomes the starting point for the direct materials, direct labour, and manufacturing overheads budgets. To some extent the purchasing and manpower budgets follow from these production plans: they also depend to some extent on the purchasing and manpower requirements of other functions within the company.

A budgeted cost of sales schedule can be drawn up on the basis of the manufacturing cost of expected sales. The marketing activities necessary to achieve the expected level of sales will be budgeted in accordance with the resources and actions that are necessary to ensure that the sales forecast (in terms of volume, value, and product mix) is achieved. This requires the budgeting of order-getting costs (such as advertising and selling) on the one hand, and order-filling costs (such as transport and warehousing) on the other.

Closely related to both marketing and production operations are the design and R & D functions which must be budgeted in accordance with policy requirements.

An overall administration budget can be compiled so as to include such cost-incurring items as personnel management, training, secretarial activities, general services, and the directorate. And, finally, a financial budget can summarize the whole package in the form of five budgeted statements:

1 Budgeted cash statement
2 Budgeted profit and loss account
3 Budgeted balance sheet
4 Budgeted funds statement
5 Capital budget

It may be useful to itemize more fully the constituent elements of the master budget. These elements are:

Sales budget This should show volume sales by item, by region, by channel of distribution, and (on a quota basis) by salesman, in a fully reconciled manner. The physical quantities can be extended in accordance with the proposed price list to show revenue by product line, sales territory, and so forth.

Selling expense budget Included within this heading will be salesmen's salaries, commissions, expenses, and related administrative costs.

Distribution budget Transportation, freight charges, stock control, warehousing, wages, expenses, and related administration costs make up this budget. The level of activity and the level of service must both be specified in advance.

Marketing budget Apart from details of all advertising, promotional activities, public relations, marketing research, customer services, and so forth, the marketing budget can also include a summary of the sales, selling expense, and distribution budgets.

R & D budget This will cover materials, equipment and supplies, salaries, expenses, and other costs relating to design, development, and technical research projects.

Production budget The aim of the production function will presumably be to supply finished goods of a specified quality to meet marketing demands. The distribution budget will specify finished goods stock levels, and this can be related to the sales budget to give detailed production requirements. Following from this it is necessary to consider a series of subsidiary budgets:

1 Raw materials budget. paying appropriate attention to desired stock levels.
2 Labour budget: ensuring that the plan will make the required number of employees of relevant grades and suitable skills available at the right times.
3 Maintenance budget: involving a decision between preventative or remedial maintenance.
4 Quality control: whilst not a production responsibility, must be budgeted in accordance with production plans to ensure its adequacy.
5 Manufacturing overheads budget: covering items such as consumable materials and waste disposal.

Manpower budget This must take an overall view of the organization's needs for manpower for all areas of activity – sales, manufacturing, administrative, executive, and so on – for a period of years. It leads to two further budgets:

1 Personnel budget: catering for recruitment costs, canteen facilities, first aid, house journals, etc.
2 Training budget: covering all aspects of personnel development from apprentices on the shopfloor to management development programmes.

Purchasing budget Raw materials, consumable items, office supplies and equipment, and the whole range of an organization's requirements, must be considered, along with the questions when, where, at what price, and how often to buy.

Company secretarial budget This will include registration expenses, legal fees, pension fund, insurances, reception facilities, etc.

Services budget Various oddments must not be overlooked, including boiler-house, gatekeeping, night watchmen, security, gardening, and similar activities.

Administration budget Apart from the administrative items included in the secretary's budget, others must be covered as well. EDP, executive salaries, typing pool, and any other expenses should be dealt with in this budget.

Financial budget As we have already seen, this is made up of five individual budgets:

1 Cash budget: concerned with liquidity, must reflect changes between opening and closing debtor balances, and between opening and closing creditor balances, as well as focusing attention on other inflows and outflows of cash (such as those stemming from share issues, or the retirement of debt, or the payment of dividends to shareholders).
2 Budgeted profit and loss account: concerned with profitability. This merely reflects the matching of revenues received during a period with costs incurred during that same period. Nevertheless, it is largely on the basis of this budget that a company forecasts its dividend policy, and determines its ability to obtain debt funding.

3 Budgeted balance sheet: concerned with the structure of assets and the pattern of liabilities.
4 Budgeted funds statement: concerned with the sources of funds and their application in the organization's objective-striving endeavours.
5 Capital budget: concerned with questions of capacity and strategic direction. This must deal with the evaluation of alternate dispositions of capital funds as well as with the choice of the best capital structure.

Taken as a whole, these various different budgets make up the master budget. Clearly there are very many interrelationships and interdependencies. At the end of the budgeting process, however, every item of cost and revenue (along with the activities that result in these costs and revenues, since the financial dimension is simply a method of expressing underlying transactions of one kind or another in a way that permits addition and mathematical manipulation, evaluation, etc.) should have been planned by whoever is responsible for its incurrence/creation. This should include such items as the sale of scrap, which is easy to overlook, and canteen takings which are so often set off against canteen costs and hence hidden.

Agreement should be reached between each successive superior and subordinate as the budgets are consolidated and summarized as they are communicated upwards in the company's hierarchy. Any fundamental error (such as expected sales demand exceeding productive capacity) will be highlighted as the individual budgets are discussed, analysed, and integrated.

It is helpful if a procedure can be established for carrying out the budgeting exercise whenever this is necessary. For example, the time period taken as the basis for budgeting may be the financial year of the company, and it may be decided to review the budget every three months. This will require a procedure for compiling each annual budget from scratch, and also a quarterly review procedure. In a similar manner, the budget period for a company may be of five years' duration, with the first year being planned in great detail and years 2-5 being planned in an increasingly broad way as one gets further and further away from the comparative certainty of the present. As each year passes, a detailed plan can be compiled for the new 'year 1' and another 'year 5' can be added on in outline detail only at the other extreme.

This latter procedure is termed *rolling budgeting* in contrast to the *periodic budgeting* exemplified by the annual profit plan approach so widely adopted. Rolling budgeting can be employed to advantage with an annual planning horizon by encouraging (as well as requiring) every manager to think about the forthcoming period of 12 months. An appropriate procedure could be established whereby every month the budget is revised so that a new month is always being added on 12 months hence as each old month passes. In the case of the capital budget, of course, a much longer time span should be introduced. (Typical projects that might be included in a company's capital budget are the development and launch of a new product, the acquisition of another business, the development of a new factory, etc. Such projects determine to a very significant extent the level of a company's costs – especially its fixed costs – and a careful distinction should be made between the capital budget and operating budgets that exist within the framework and constraints of the capital budget.)

To ensure that the budgeting process, culminating in the creation of a master budget, is accorded its due priority within an organization it should have full support from top management. This can be made effective by appointing a *budget officer* at a senior level. (Very often this is the company's financial controller or chief accountant simultaneously wearing another hat.) Instructions, programmes of action, timetables, etc., can flow through this individual who can also answer queries from those who must compile their own particular budget, and give explanations of what is required, and how, when, where, and to whom it should be given. Such an officer can work through a *budget committee*, which may be composed of senior executives (from both line and staff functions) drawn from all of the company's functional areas. The purpose of a budget committee is to check that the budgets can be integrated in a satisfactory manner; to ensure that all activities are planned in a coordinated way and that none are overlooked; to review levels of anticipated performance; and to evaluate patterns of resource allocation. Any incongruency should be referred back to its source for justification or amendment.

The existence of an effective budget committee should result in a master budget being submitted to the board that is acceptable at that level – assuming that this is in line with specified corporate objectives and bearing in mind that this requires not only arithmetical, but also technical and economic consistency.

Through the budgeting process a business organization can attempt to reach some preferred position in the future, and the budget itself represents an explicit commitment to this end. Even though the future is clouded with uncertainty, it is merely the application of commercial commonsense to realize that *some* thought should be given to the way in which the company's future existence should develop. C. F. Kettering summed it all up magnificently in his statement (cited earlier on p.52):

> I am interested in the future because that is where I intend to live.

If positive steps are taken to map out the type of future that is sought, and the required actions (insofar as they can be identified in advance) are taken to bring this about, then clearly there will be a much greater chance of attaining this preferred future state than if the company ignores the need to plan ahead and simply accepts whatever future may come about.

FIXED BUDGETS

Cost control requires, as a preliminary step, that the *actual* level of costs incurred during a period be compared with a *desired* level of costs for the same period. But this desired level can be looked at from two points of view.

In the first place, the desired level may be related to a specified level of capacity utilization – thus indirect material costs, at 85 per cent of capacity, may be budgeted at £15 000 for a period of 12 months, and this amounts to an average usage of £1 250 per month at that level of capacity for that period of time. If it is expected that 30 000 units of output will be produced evenly during the year in question, then the indirect material charge per unit produced will be £0.50. However, the actual costs may vary from this 'standard' because prices may rise during the year – hence a figure of £17 500 may be incurred, giving a cost variance of £2 500 in total for the given level of activity, or a unit cost of £0.583 for that same level of activity.

The second way of looking at desired cost levels is to consider variations in the level of activity, giving rise to fluctuations in the utilization of available capacity and/or fluctuations in the rate of activity. To continue the above example of indirect material costs, it may have happened that effective demand only led to a level of capacity utilization of 80 per cent over 9 months of the year and then to 95 per cent over the remaining 3 months. It would clearly be inappropriate to compare, on a monthly basis, a 'normalized' cost of £1 250 per month with the costs resulting from the actual pattern of output since this differs most significantly in the rate of activity. But this is exactly what very many organizations do in their use of ***fixed budgets***.

A fixed budget is one that is compiled for a given set of assumed operating conditions and for a clearly specified but estimated level of activity, and which management proposes to leave unchanged during the period to which it relates – regardless of changes in the actual level of activity experienced or in the conditions facing the company during that period.

Figure 8.5 illustrates a fixed budget relating to factory overheads. This has been compiled on the basis of last year's *actual* figures plus, in some instances, an adjustment in accordance with known changes that will affect the forthcoming period (e.g. rates have increased from £1 200 to £1 300).

The right-hand column of this budget statement shows that the annual estimates have been divided up to fit in with a system that works on a four-week cycle. (This has some advantages over monthly reporting systems because the different months vary a good deal in the length of their working portions, but annual and statutory holidays also have a distorting effect on regularized four-week systems.) It is most improbable that conditions will not vary from one four-week period to the next, so the fixed budget divided up into equal periods does not necessarily provide a reasonable estimate of the factory overhead that is

BUDGET—FACTORY OVERHEADS—12 MONTHS TO 31.12.1981

Charge for previous year	*Expense*	*Adjustments*	*Estimate for year*	*4 weeks estimate (1/13)*
£			£	£
1 200	Rent and rates	Increase in rates	1 300	100
260	Lighting	—	260	20
300	Heating	Increase in cost of fuel	325	25
3 000	Indirect wages	Reorganization	2 756	212
600	Depreciation	As plant register	715	55
1 160	Repairs and maintenance	Increase in costs	1 495	115
1 170	Power	25 per cent increase in output	560	120
49	Oil, waste, etc.	25 per cent increase in output	65	5
170	Insurance	Allow for additional plant	195	15
110	Canteen	Allow for additional men	130	10
550	Cranes and hoists	Allow for increase in output	650	50
1 150	National insurance	Allow for additional men	1 300	100
3 200	Works manager's salary	Increase in salary	3 900	300
2 600	Technical costs	—	2 600	200
190	Sundries	Increase in production	325	25
15 709			17 576	1 352

Figure 8.5: Fixed budget

likely to be met in any single period. To be of value, therefore, a fixed budget should be regularly revised, but this is costly and time consuming.

It is important also to realize that budget levels should be set on the basis of what is likely to happen in the future rather than on the evidence of what has happened in the past. There can be no doubt that experience from the past is extremely useful in forward planning, but past mistakes cannot be rectified, and making estimates of the future on the basis of a rule of thumb such as 'last year's figures plus 10 per cent' is not to be recommended. The preferred approach is to consider what needs to be done and then to decide how it is to be done. A cost estimate may then be derived for the specific tasks that have been identified.

If the actual level of activity and operating conditions experienced during a given period do not vary greatly from the pattern assumed in preparing a fixed budget for that period, the fixed budget can be useful in a control sense. But the idea that control over costs can be achieved by comparing performance at one level of activity with a plan that was developed for some other level of predicted activity is both ridiculous and naive. This problem can be overcome however, and flexible budgets have been developed to meet this requirement.

FLEXIBLE BUDGETS

In essence, a *flexible budget* is a set of alternative budget plans appertaining to different expected levels of activity. By comparing the actual results achieved during a period for a *realized* level of activity with the budgeted performance for *that same level of activity* it is possible to evalute performance efficiency in a meaningful way. (It should always be remembered, however, that achieving high efficiency at, say, 80 per cent of capacity utilization is not very good if one wished to operate at 90 per cent of capacity during that period. This highlights the distinction between *effectiveness* – achieving that which is desired – and *efficiency* – doing whatever is done well.)

The flexible budget is based on the fundamental difference in behaviour of fixed costs, variable costs, and mixed costs (i.e. semi-fixed and semi-variable costs) that was discussed in Chapter 1. Since fixed costs do not vary with short-run fluctuations in activity it can be seen that the flexible budget will really consist of two parts: the first is a fixed budget being made up of fixed costs, such as rates and salaries, and the fixed component of mixed costs – such as the rental portion of telephone charges, with the portion relating to calls being a variable cost. The second part is a truly flexible budget that consists solely of variable costs.

Some illustrations should prove useful at this juncture. Three examples are given below.

Example 1

In a medium-sized company the expected level of activity for the forthcoming planning period may be 70 per cent of capacity, and on this basis the various departmental heads may make estimates of overhead costs for the period as shown in Figure 8.6.

The works manager's budget may include a department for which the plan illustrated in Figure 8.7 has been drawn up on the understanding that, whilst 70 per cent may be the most likely level of capacity utilization, other levels may also be achieved. For this reason the range from 50 per cent to 100 per cent has

	Budgeted overheads (£) for year at 70 per cent of capacity
General manager	8 000
Sales manager	20 000
Accountant	12 000
Works manager	408 000
Personnel manager	8 000
	456 000

Figure 8.6: Budgeted overheads

Item	Budget for four weeks					
	Level of activity (per cent)					
	50	60	70	80	90	100
	£	£	£	£	£	£
Chargehands	520	680	680	700	840	880
Setters	144	144	144	160	180	240
Labourers	432	532	632	752	892	992
Loose tools	424	508	592	676	760	844
Plant repairs	180	200	220	240	260	280
Scrapped work	28	32	40	48	52	56
Consumable stores	80	92	92	92	100	100
TOTAL	1 808	2 188	2 400	2 668	3 084	3 392

Figure 8.7: Flexible budget – 1

been considered, and within these figures it should be noted that some items vary directly with the level of activity: for example, loose tools, scrapped work, and plant repairs vary in this way. However, certain other costs remain static when activity is low but increase with overtime working until a sharp rise takes place (e.g. a new setter must be taken on) at 100 per cent of capacity. And still other costs remain relatively unchanged irrespective of the level of activity – consumable stores being a good example.

A control report developed from Figure 8.7 is shown in Figure 8.8. This type of control statement can be compiled for each responsibility centre and it enables a comparison to be made between actual expenditure and the target expenditure for the actual level of activity achieved, along with cumulative figures for the year to date. The extent to which costs are broken down and itemized plays an important part in cost control. In Figure 8.8, for example, if chargehands and setters had not been shown separately, the works manager would not know that the extra cost (£32 for the period, £48 cumulatively) is entirely due to setting. In addition, the extra cost of labourers is seen to be excessive for the activity of the factory, as is the cost of loose tools.

Results for 4 weeks to 29.1.1982						
	Activity this period: 72 per cent			*Activity for year to date: 75 per cent*		
	Budget	*Actual*	*Variance*	*Budget*	*Actual*	*Variance*
	£	£	£	£	£	£
Chargehands	680	680	—	2 040	2 040	—
Setters	144	176	(32)	432	480	(48)
Labourers	632	720	(88)	1 896	2 040	(144)
Loose tools	592	780	(188)	1 776	1 972	(196)
Plant repairs	220	320	(100)	660	840	(180)
Scrapped work	40	160	(120)	120	500	(380)
Consumable stores	92	192	(100)	276	564	(288)
TOTAL	2 400	3 028	(628)	7 200	8 436	(1 236)

Figure 8.8: Flexible budget control report

Example 2

If a company has the information available shown in Figure 8.9, then it is possible to construct a flexible budget (as shown in Figure 8.10) on the basis of it.

	Level of activity per period		
	Up to 140 000 units	*140 000 to 160 000 units*	*160 000 to 200 000 units*
	£	£	£
Sales price per unit	1.00	1.00	0.95
Variable unit costs:			
Materials	0.40	0.39	0.37
Labour	0.20	0.20	0.19
Overheads	0.10	0.10	0.10
Fixed costs	30 000	30 000	35 000

Figure 8.9: Budgeting information

	Level of activity		
	140 000 units	160 000 units	200 000 units
	£	£	£
Selling price per unit	1.00	1.00	0.95
Expected sales revenue	140 000	160 000	190 000
Variable costs:			
Material	56 000	62 400	74 000
Labour	28 000	32 000	38 000
Overhead	14 000	16 000	20 000
	98 000	110 400	132 000
Fixed costs	30 000	30 000	35 000
Total costs	128 000	140 400	167 000
Profit	12 000	19 600	23 000
	140 000	160 000	190 000

Figure 8.10: Flexible budget – 2

The type of budget shown in Figure 8.10 simply illustrates the profit/cost picture that is expected to arise from different levels of activity, but in order to control costs the appropriate level of budgeted costs should be compared with the actual level of activity. If the number of units produced and sold during the period was 180 000, the flexible budget can be interpolated (on the assumption of linearity in cost behaviour within the relevant range) as follows:

			£
Sales revenue	180 000 × £0.95		171 000
Variable costs:			
Material	180 000 × £0.37	66 600	
Labour	180 000 × £0.19	34 200	
Overhead	180 000 × £0.10	18 000	
Fixed costs		35 000	153 800
Profit			17 200

The actual costs and revenue can now be compared with this flexible budget. (Although a real-life example would be much more detailed, this simplified illustration suggests the general approach to adopt.)

Example 3

Flexible budgets can be compiled for areas of activity other than manufacturing despite the fact that they were initially developed for application in controlling factory costs. A flexible budget for a company's sales overheads is shown in Figure 8.11.

	Level of activity		
	£	£	£
Estimated sales	140 000	160 000	180 000
Fixed overheads:			
Sales office salaries	8 000	8 000	8 000
Fixed sales office expenses	6 000	6 000	6 000
Advertising	8 000	8 000	8 000
Salesmen's salaries	16 000	16 000	16 000
Car expenses	8 000	8 000	8 000
Total	46 000	46 000	46 000
Variable overheads:			
Salesmen's commission	5 000	5 700	6 500
Carriage	28 000	32 000	36 000
Agent's commission	4 500	5 144	5 784
Total	37 500	42 844	48 284
Total overheads	83 500	88 844	94 284
Profit contribution	56 500	71 156	85 716

Figure 8.11: Flexible budget – 3

At the end of a period it may be ascertained that the level of sales actually achieved was £100 000, with the result that a flexible budget for this level of activity must be interpolated from the information in Figure 8.11. This is shown in Figure 8.12.

	£	£
Level of sales		100 000
Fixed overheads	46,000	
Variable overheads:		
Salesmen's commission $\frac{100}{140} \times 5000$	3 572	
Carriage 20 per cent of £100 000	20 000	
Agent's commission $\frac{100}{140} \times 4500$	3 216	
Total overheads		72 788
Profit contribution		27 212

Figure 8.12: Interpolated flexible budget

Apart from comparing actual results (in detail) with the budgeted results, management should carefully consider the causes of sales being at such a low level in this example.

Procedure for preparing flexible budget

The procedure for preparing a flexible budget is spelt out below, but actually performing the task is difficult because it must be built on a detailed analysis and understanding of cost behaviour patterns throughout the organization. In addition, there is a major educational obstacle to be overcome when it is first proposed to introduce flexible budgeting into an organization: all those who will be involved in the operation must be trained to appreciate the purpose of flexible budgeting and to perform the necessary steps in the associated planning and control exercise.

Despite these major difficulties, the procedure to follow is given by these five steps:

1 Specify the time period that is to be used. This may be, for example, daily, weekly, monthly, or four weekly, depending on the variability of the activities in question: the more variable they are, the shorter the time period should be.

2 Classify all costs into fixed, variable, and mixed categories.

3 Determine the types of standards that are to be used. Whilst Chapter 10 will develop this topic in some detail, at this point it is necessary to consider whether direct material and direct labour costs will be built up from cost standards, or linked in a broader manner (e.g. as a ratio) to expected activity levels; how tight or loose budget standards should be; and what allowances should be made for changing conditions.

4 Analyse cost behaviour patterns in response to past levels of activity. From this should come an agreed means by which a total cost figure for a given item can be accumulated at any specified level of business activity. Formulae are commonly used for this purpose: thus freight charges may be expressed as being equivalent to £500 per period plus £1.15 per unit. In this instance the fixed costs of the operation are £500 and the variable costs are £1.15 per unit, so for a sales level of 1 000 during a given period the total freight cost will be:

$$£500 + £1\,150 = £1\,650$$

5 Build up the appropriate flexible budget for specified levels of activity (either actual or anticipated)

DANGERS IN BUDGETING

Budgets drawn up along conventional (i.e. static) lines have certain fundamenta drawbacks, such as:

1 They are based on assumed conditions (e.g. rates of interest) and rela

tionships (e.g. product mix held constant) that are not varied to reflect the actual circumstances that came about.

2 They make allowance for tasks to be performed only in relation to volume rather than time.

3 They compare current costs with estimates based only on historical analyses.

4 Their short-term time horizon limits the perspective, so short-term results may be sought at the expense of longer term stability or success.

5 They have a built-in bias that tends to perpetuate inefficiencies. (For example, next year's budget is determined by increasing last year's by 15 per cent, irrespective of the efficiency factor in last year's.)

6 As with all types of budgets the game of 'beating the system' may take more energy than is being devoted to running the business.

7 The fragile internal logic of static budgets will be destroyed if top management reacts to draft budgets by requiring changes to be made to particular items which are then not reflected through the whole budget.

These typical defects are especially apparent in connection with overhead costs, and they point strongly to the need for skill and intelligence to be exercised in tailoring a budgeting system to the particular characteristics, circumstances, and requirements of each individual company.

The business environment is a dynamic one, and a company must not be hindered by its budget from endeavouring to adapt to constantly changing conditions. An unduly rigid framework set up by the budgeting process can interfere with the company's well-being by preventing managers from grasping opportunities that were not predicted when the budget plan was compiled.

Conversely, of course, a budget that fails to give direction (i.e. one that is too loose rather than too rigid) cannot adequately help in coordinating corporate activities in a goal-attaining manner. Under-budgeting, which is the failure to plan ahead in a comprehensive yet flexible way, is as dangerous as over-budgeting, which is exemplified by the rigid situation suggested above in which an excessive degree of inflexibility causes the budget to become meaningless and unduly expensive.

It should be borne in mind that a budget plan represents a means to an end: it is not an end in itself. The desired end is the attainment of specified objectives. It is dangerous, therefore, to allow the budgeted targets to supersede organizational objectives. This danger can be highlighted by considering a situation in which a budget target is maintained as a major goal, irrespective of changing conditions, instead of being varied (along with other dimensions of the budget plan) in accordance with varying circumstances (subject to whatever constraints have been established) in order that the more important company objective might be achieved.

The practice whereby historical levels of expenditure are continued into succeeding periods without proper evaluation can hide – and perpetuate – inefficiencies. Past results do not necessarily reflect a desirable level of performance, so future estimates should not be based on them without a reconsideration of standards and other bases of planning by which policies are translated into numerical terms.

Finally, if budgets are used as pressure devices, the result will be resentment and thus a failure in achieving their intended purpose. One highly desirable way of overcoming suspicion and misunderstanding in budgeting is to involve all those who are concerned actively in ensuring that the company reaches its objectives – the principle of accountability planning as embodied in responsibility accounting.

OTHER APPROACHES TO BUDGETING: ZBB AND PPBS

In order to accommodate the particular needs of non-profit organizations (such as government agencies) as well as providing a focus for more rigorous thinking in relation to *programmed* or *discretionary costs* (i.e. those which are determined purely by managerial discretion – such as R & D, training, and similar outlays), a number of recent developments in budgeting techniques are worthy of mention. In particular, zero-base budgeting (ZBB) and output budgeting (which is also known as a planning-programming-budgeting system, hence the acronym PPBS) have generated considerable interest, so we will take note of them at this point.

Zero-base budgeting

Amongst other failings it is generally agreed that traditional budgeting (or *incremental budgeting* as it is often known due to the tendency to add on a bit more – an increment – to last year's budget level in order to arrive at a figure for next year) is number-oriented, fails to identify priorities, and starts with the existing level of activity or expenditure as an established base, whereas it might be more useful to managers to have a technique that was decision-oriented, helped in determining priorities, and sought to re-assess the current level of expenditures.

It will be appreciated from this last point that in taking as given the current level of expenditure, and the activities that this represents, the traditional approach to budgeting, by looking only at desired increases or, occasionally, decreases, is ignoring the majority of the organization's expenditure. This is rather myopic.

The zero-base budgeting alternative is to evaluate *simultaneously* existing and new ways of achieving specified ends in order to establish priorities amongst them which could mean that there are trade-offs between existing and new activities. For example, a new project A that is considered to be more desirable than an existing project B may be resourced by terminating project B. In essence the approach is carried out in two stages:

1 Decision packages are identified within each decision unit. These decision units are essentially discrete activities that can be described in a way that separates them from other activities of the organization. The decision packages cover both existing and projected incremental activities, and the organizational units responsible for carrying them out are much akin to the responsibility centres that were discussed in Chapter 6. The object is to define for each decision unit the basic requirements that are needed if it is to perform the function for which it was established. Any costs in excess of this basic level are deemed incremental. (It will be seen, therefore, that the title 'zero-base' is something of a misnomer since the base is certainly greater than zero!) In considering what is needed in order to fulfil a particular purpose, over and above the base level, it is probable that alternative ways of achieving the same end will be identified, and these should be described and evaluated as they arise: these are the decision packages.

2 Once the manager of a decision unit has submitted his statement of evaluated decision packages to his superior it is the latter's job to assign priorities to the various submissions from all his subordinates, and to select the highest-ranking decision packages that come within his available budget limit. There are a number of ways in which priorities can be determined, all of which presuppose some explicit criterion of effectiveness in order that competing packages may be ranked.

This approach is logical and has much to commend it in relation to discretionary outlays.

Output budgeting

In the traditional approach to budgeting there tends to be an overall emphasis on the functional areas of an organization. Thus one has the budget for the marketing function, and that for the data processing department. However, no organization was ever established in order that it might have these functions as a definition of what it exists to achieve, so it is helpful to look at the situation from another angle.

In a typical business organization there will be functions such as those shown in Figure 8.13, but the organization really exists in order to achieve various purposes which have been simplified in the 'missions' of Figure 8.14. In developing a business plan the major concern is with the 'missions', subject to the

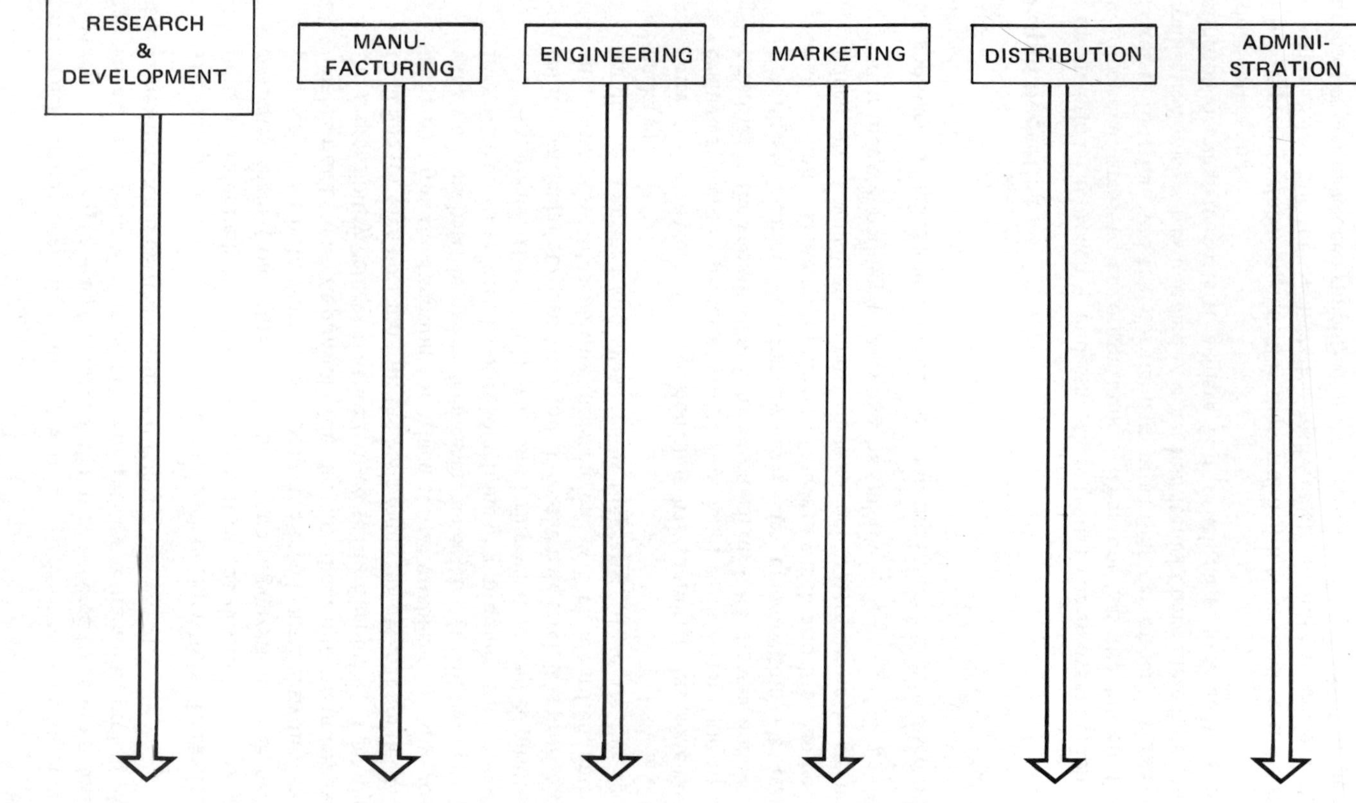

Figure 8.13: Functional activities

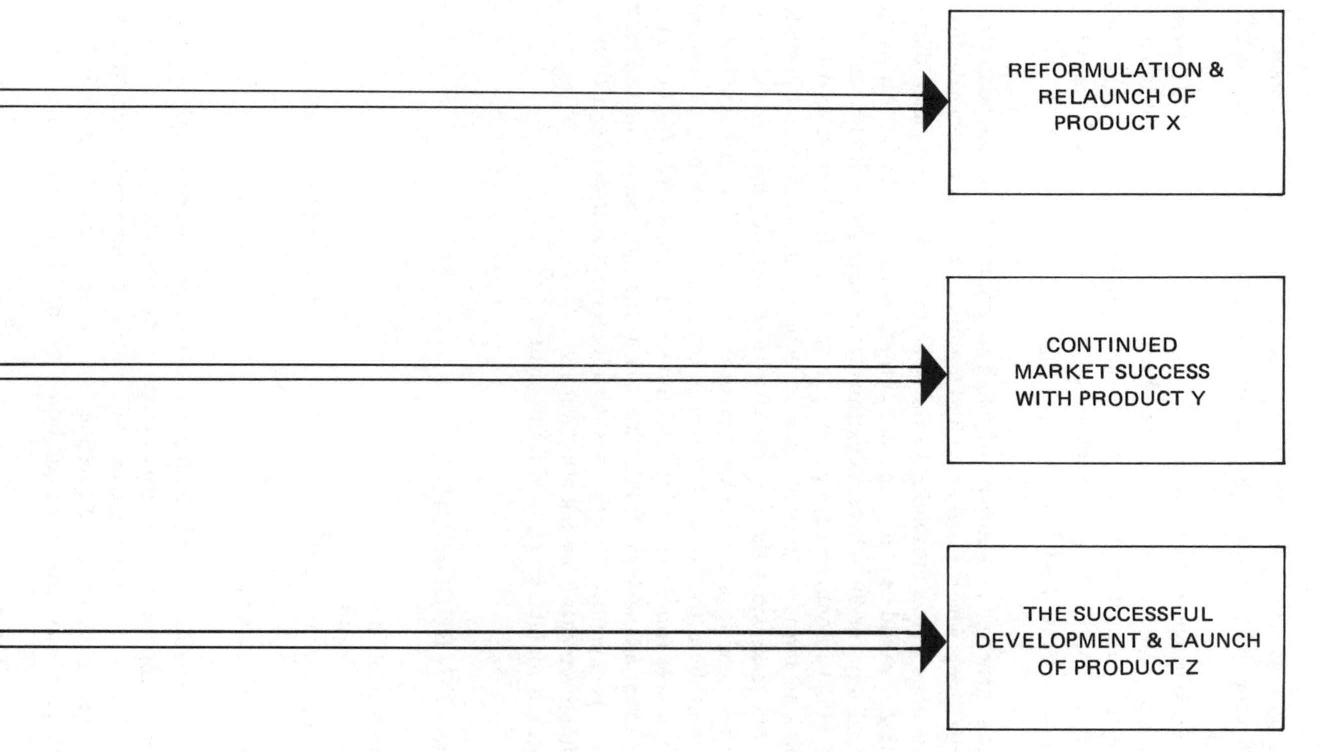

Figure 8.14: Missions

resource limitations within the functions, etc., whereas the development of controls will usually be via the responsibility centres that are contained within the functions.

If we now superimpose the (horizontal) missions over the (vertical) functions we have the crux of the output budgeting approach. What this does is to focus attention on the purposes to be served by the organization, as shown by the missions, and the contribution that each function must make to each mission if the missions are to be successful. Figure 8.15 suggests this in the most simplified manner.

The greatest benefits from output budgeting are probably to be found in non-profit organizations where traditional thinking did not always recognize that different functions were contributing to the same ends. For example, within a local authority it would be part of the conventional wisdom to budget each year in a functional way for the schools department, the recreation department, the police force, etc., without identifying their interactions. However, as soon as one starts to think in terms of missions, such as reducing the incidence of juvenile crime, one will realise that the educational role of schools, the availability of adequate recreational facilities and the presence, and attitudes, of the police all potentially contribute to this end. It makes great sense, therefore, to develop budgets that enable top management to determine the most cost-effective ways of achieving specified missions. If this leads to one function being trimmed back whilst another is expanded then this has the advantage that it can be justified in relation to improvements in overall effectiveness.

This approach contains much food for thought.

CHECKLIST ON BUDGETING

1 Are plans explicit?
2 Are plans understood?
3 Are plans (and the planning function) accepted within the organization?
4 Are plans capable of being adapted to meet change?
5 Are plans (and objectives) compatible with internal and external constraints?
6 Are plans capable of being monitored (i.e. in quantified format)?
7 Is the company's level of activity expanding or contracting?
8 What effect is the answer to question 7 having on manpower requirements?
9 What effect is the answer to question 7 having on financial requirements?
10 What effect is the answer to question 7 having on administrative requirements?
11 Are 'tomorrow's breadwinners' (i.e. new products) being developed? If so, have consumer requirements been carefully evaluated?

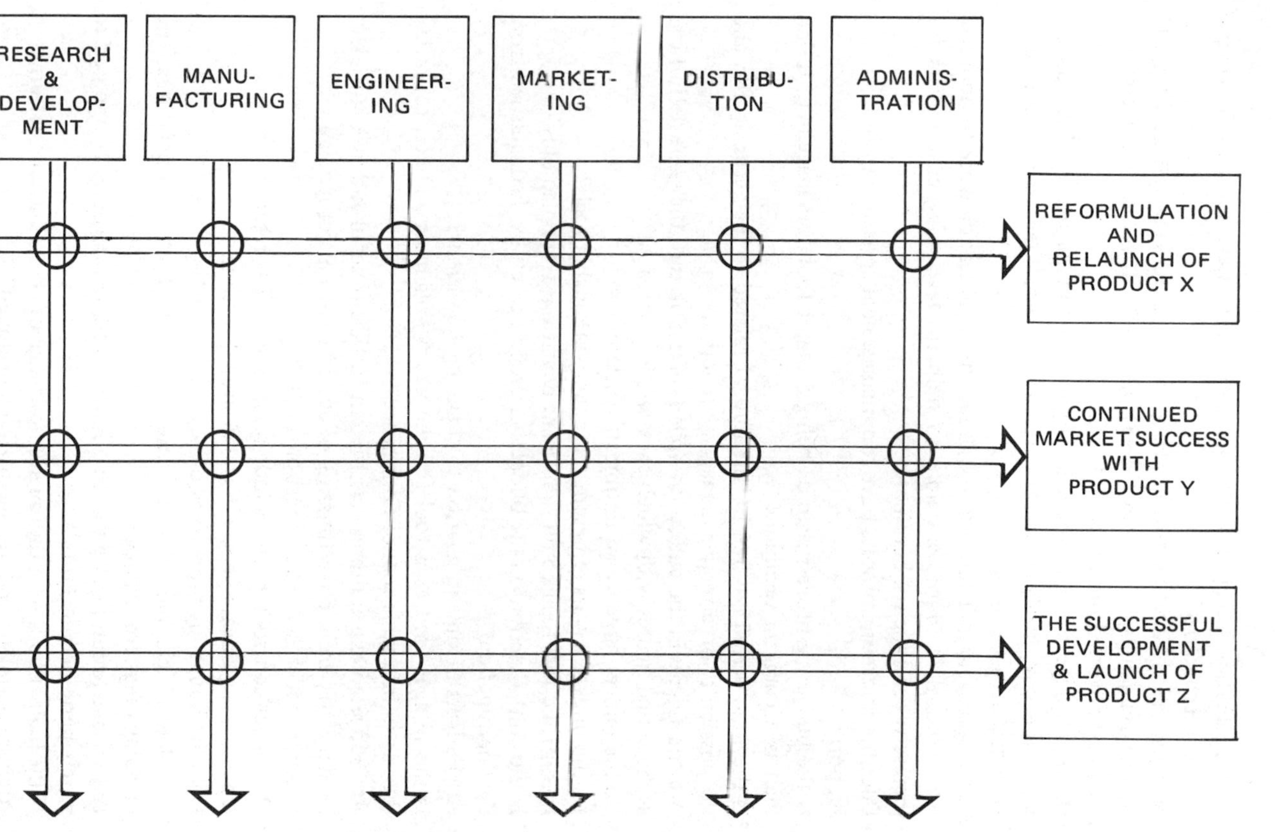

Figure 8.15: A simplified output budgeting format

12 Is consideration being given to the use of new materials, new processes, and new technology?
13 Who will be affected by future plans? How will these people be affected?
14 Is management by objectives (MBO) practised? If so, do managers meet their objectives? If not, why not?
15 Do all employees – and especially supervisors and managers – fully understand the cost implications of their work? Are they able to plan cost expectations accordingly?
16 Can responsible individuals throughout the organization work to budgets?
17 Are responsible individuals able to help in developing cost targets for themselves and their subordinates?
18 Does the budgeting process have top management sponsorship and support?
19 Is the budgeting process seen as being a major tool of management rather than an accounting technique?
20 Is the time period covered by the budget related to the necessity for, and the possibility of, effective management action?
21 Are the figures in the budget compiled on the basis of the same definitions as the actual figures with which they will be compared?
22 Do the budget targets lead to objective attainment?
23 Do the budget targets represent reasonably attainable goals?
24 Is control effort focused on significant deviations from plan only?
25 Is the staff function on the budgeting process carefully distinguished from the line function?
26 Are budgets flexible in relation to changing conditions?
27 Is the budget used as a tool for cooperative planning and control rather than as an inflexible tool of dominance?
28 Are budgeted expenditures classified in sufficient detail and over sufficient headings to permit the estimating of costs by each major item and function under each area of responsibility?
29 Do budget control reports include reasons as well as results?
30 Do budgets motivate people in the desired direction?
31 Does the budgeting process encourage delegation?
32 Is balance achieved between budgeting for short-run operations and planning long-term strategy?
33 Has consideration been given to adopting rolling budgeting as opposed to purely periodic budgeting?
34 Is the budget built on a thorough knowledge of cost behaviour patterns?
35 Are forecasting procedures adequately developed?
36 Is a budget officer employed? If not, why not? If so, are his terms of reference widely known?
37 Does the company have a budget committee?

38 Are the dangers of budgeting understood? Avoided?

39 Is the whole planning/budgeting endeavour based on a careful and continuing evaluation of all major factors (both external and internal) that will affect the future?

40 Is imagination used in identifying alternative courses of action prior to their evaluation in relation to corporate objectives?

SUMMARY

Budgeting is a management tool that is invaluable for short-term planning and control. It aims to anticipate change and enable the company to meet change in an advantageous way. Forecasting is an important dimension of budgeting.

The perspective for budgeting is given by corporate objectives as embodied in the company's long-term strategic plan. These objectives are the end to which the budget provides the means, and each must be clearly specified and quantified if an adequate guide for action is to be given.

Broad approaches to setting budget levels, such as those given by the case-rate principle, ratio analysis, or cost per order aggregates, are grossly inferior to building up the master budget in a grass-roots manner. But whatever approach is selected, it is clear that each element of the budget has major interdependencies with every other element. It is also clear that the future cannot be predicted with certainty, and a sensible precaution is to plan for each likely future outcome instead of placing all one's hopes on just one uncertain outcome. (Programming methods and risk analysis should be used wherever possible).

From a control point of view it is a fruitless exercise to compare a plan for one level of activity (i.e. a fixed budget) with actual results relating to a different level of activity. Control is facilitated by flexible budgeting that enables actual results to be compared with budgeted results for the achieved level of activity. (Programming models, via sensitivity analysis, allow different outcomes to be assessed in advance).

In addition to the budgeting approach that occupies most of this chapter there are other approaches that have applicability in particular situations. Zero-base budgeting is a logical approach to determining the basic requirements of each decision unit within an organization in order that it may carry out its intended function, and proposals beyond this base level are evaluated and then compete for whatever resources are available. As a variation on this theme, output budgeting emphasizes the missions of an organization, and the contribution that each function must make to them if the missions are to be achieved in the most cost-effective manner.

Finally, Figure 8.16 gives an outline job specification for a 'budget director', as propagated by the (US) Budget Executives Institute.

A The function of the budget director is to facilitate the direction and control of the enterprise by:

1 Insuring the generation and dissemination of information needed for decision making and planning to each person in the organization having such responsibilities. The information may include, but is not limited to, forecasts of economic and social conditions, government influences, organization goals and standards for decision making, economic and financial guidelines, performance data, performance standards, and the prerequisite plans of others in the enterprise.

2 Establishing and maintaining a planning system which:

(*a*) channels information (1 above) to each person responsible for planning;

(*b*) schedules the formulation of plans;

(*c*) structures the plans of subsections of the enterprise into composites at which points tests are made for significant deviations from economic and financial guidelines and from goal achievement, and repeats the process for larger segments to and including the enterprise as a whole; and

(*d*) disseminates advice of approval, disapproval, or revision of plans to affected individuals in accordance with established lines of authority and organizational responsibilities.

3 Constructing and using models of the enterprise, both in total and by subsections, to test the effect of internal and external variables upon the achievement of organizational goals.

4 Insuring that performance data be accumulated, related to responsibility centres within the organization, measured against the plans, whether period or project, for each centre, transmitted to each centre, and the analysis of deviations of actual from planned performance.

B The budget director may utilize the services of others in the organization (including but not limited to accountants, data processors, economists, market analysts, financial analysts, and engineers) and/or may perform them himself, but he has the overriding responsibility for insuring that the functions described above are integrated into a consistent and comprehensive system which facilitates the planning and control of the enterprise by those members of the organization bearing such responsibilities.

Figure 8.16: Statement of duties and responsibilities of the budget director*

*Statement prepared by committee consisting of D.R. Borst, Joseph T.Ryerson and Son; W.R. Bunge, Jos. Schlitz Brewing Co.; R. Guthrie, I-T-E Circuit Breaker Co.; H. Mason, S.C. Johnson and Son; A. Moor, United Airlines; and W.E.Thomas, University of Illinois, Chairman. Approved by the National Board as a statement of the Budget Executives Institute, September 1966.

SOME EXAMPLES

ABC Ltd – budgeting

ABC Ltd makes two types of polish, one for floors and one for cars. It sells both types to industrial users only, in one-litre containers.

The specifications for the two products, per batch of 100 litres, are:

Materials	*Floor polish*	*Car polish*
Delta	120 litres	100 litres
Gamma	20 kg	10 kg
Containers—cost per 100	£5	£5
Direct labour:		
Manufacturing	12 man-hours	16 man-hours
Packing	5 man-hours	5 man-hours

During the six months to 30 September, the company expects to sell 15 000 litres of floor polish at 45p a litre, and 25 000 litres of car polish at 35p a litre.

Materials are expected to cost 5p a litre for Delta and 40p a kilogramme for Gamma.

Manufacturing wages in the industry look like being stable at 30p an hour, and packing wages at 20p an hour, throughout the period.

Flexible overhead expense budgets are operated for the manufacturing and packing departments, based on the number of man-hours worked. These budgets for the six months to 30 September are:

Manufacturing department		*Packing department*	
	£		£
5 000 man-hours	2 000	1 700 man-hours	1 300
6 000 man-hours	2 500	1 900 man-hours	1 400
7 000 man-hours	3 000	2 100 man-hours	1 500
8 000 man-hours	4 000	2 300 man-hours	1 600

General administrative overheads are budgeted at £1 850. At the beginning of the period, 1 April, packed stocks will be:

Floor polish: 2 000 litres
Car polish: 3 000 litres

By the end of the period, 30 September, it is desired to increase the packed stocks of the two products to 3 000 litres and 4 000 litres, respectively.

The following are required:

1 A statement of the standard *prime* cost per 100 litres of each product.
2 A sales and production budget (in quantities) for the six months to 30 September.
3 A profit forecast for the period. Show separate gross profits for the two products but do not attempt to allocate overheads between them. No overheads are included in stock valuations.

ABC LTD

1 PRIME COST PER 100 LITRES

	Floor polish	*Car polish*
Materials:		
Delta	120 × 5p = £6.00	100 × 5p = £5.00
Gamma	20 × 40p = £8.00	10 × 40p = £4.00
Labour:		
Manufacturing	12 × 30p = £3.60	16 × 30p = £4.80
Packing	5 × 20p = £1.00	5 × 20p = £1.00
Containers	£5.00	£5.00
	£23.60	£19.80

Note. Assuming 'packing labour' means the process of putting the materials into the containers and not merely parcelling up for delivery.

2 SALES AND PRODUCTION BUDGET (in units)

Sales	15 000	25 000
Closing stocks	3 000	4 000
	18 000	29 000
Less: opening stocks	2 000	3 000
Production requirement	16 000	26 000

3 PROFIT FORECAST

Sales	15 000 × 45p =	£6 750	25 000 × 35p =	£8 750
Less: prime cost	150 × £23.60 =	£3 540	250 × £19.80 =	£4 950
Gross Profit		£3 210	+	£3 800
			£7 010	
		£		
Less: common costs: manufacturing (1)		2 540		
packing (2)		1 500		
			−£4 040	
			£2 970	
Less: general and administrative overhead			−£1 850	
Net Profit			£1 120	

Notes. 1 Calculation of manufacturing hours + overhead
(16 000 × 12/100) + (26 000 × 16/100) = 1 920 + 4 160 = 6 080
Therefore overhead = 2 500 + [(80/1 000) × 500] = £2 540

2 Calculation of packing hours + overhead
(16 000× 5/100) + (26 000 × 5/100) = 800 + 1 300 = 2 100
Therefore overhead = £1 500

BCD Ltd – budgeting

BCD Ltd makes two products, A and B, and the following are the budget forecasts for 1975. Sales of A: 9 000 units at £6 per unit or alternatively 12 000 units at £5.50 per unit. Sales of B: 5 000 units at £9 per unit or alternatively 7 000 units at £8.50 per unit. Other budgeting information is as follows:

1 Direct material and labour at standard (based on expected actual) prices and quantities per unit of output are:

	Standard cost	*Product A*	*Product B*
Materials:			
X	30p per kg	2kg	3kg
Y	10p per m	5 m	6 m
Labour:			
Department 1	40p per hour	6 hours	—
Department 2	25p per hour	—	10 hours

2 Required materials stocks

	Material X	*Material Y*
1 January 1975	3 000 kg	4 080 m
31 December 1975	3 600 kg	5 400 m

3 Required finished stocks

	Product A	*Product B*
1 January 1975	1 000 units	350 units
31 December 1975	1 250 units	500 units

4 Flexible budget for department overheads in 1975

	Department 1 £	*Department 2* £
40 000 direct man-hours	6 500	3 000
45 000 direct man-hours	8 000	5 500
50 000 direct man-hours	10 000	8 000
55 000 direct man-hours	12 000	10 000
60 000 direct man-hours	14 500	11 500
65 000 direct man-hours	17 500	12 500
70 000 direct man-hours	21 000	13 000
75 000 direct man-hours	25 000	13 500

5 Selling and general administration overhead. Fixed cost £12 000 plus variable cost of £1 per 5 units of sales of A or B.

6 Other cost data

(*a*) Assume that work-in-progress is nil at the beginning and end of 1975.

(*b*) It is planned that there should be an even flow of production through 1975.

(*c*) Finished stock is valued at direct standard cost.

(*d*) A man employed works a 45-hour week for 50 weeks of the year, with two weeks' paid holiday.

7 Financial data

BALANCE SHEET OF BCD LTD AS AT 31 DECEMBER 1974

		£				£
Capital			*Fixed assets*			
Issued		50 000	At cost		£120 000	
Profits retained		18 108	Less:			
		68 108	Depreciation		37 000	
						83 000
Loan (repayable in equal instalments over next five years)		20 000	*Current assets*			
			Materials, at standard cost			
			X	£900		
			Y	408		
Current liabilities:					1 308	
For materials	£8 200		Finished stocks, at direct standard cost			
For overheads	7 400	15 600	A	£3 500		
			B	1 400		
					4 900	
			Sales debtors		9 400	
			Cash		5 100	
						20 708
		£103 708				£103 708

a It is expected that at 31 December 1975 debtors will be one-sixth of sales and liabilities for raw materials one-sixth of purchases for 1975.

b Other current liabilities at 31 December 1975 in respect of overheads are estimated at £4 200.

c During 1975 it is expected that further fixed assets will be purchased for £8 000.

d Budgeted overheads for 1975 include depreciation provisions on fixed assets of £12 500.

c Net dividend is to be paid if possible for 1975 of 15 per cent on issued capital.

The following are required:

1 Prepare in physical and monetary terms the following budgets for 1975 on alternative bases so as to take into account the different sales forecasts:

(*a*) Sales
(*b*) Direct cost of sales
(*c*) Income (or profit and loss) account

showing clearly the separate contributions to profits of each product under each of the alternative sales budgets.

2 Select from the alternative budgeted income accounts the one to be preferred and prepare in physical and monetary terms the following further subsidiary budgets in respect of the selected budget:

(*a*) Raw material purchases
(*b*) Direct labour
(*c*) Production

3 Prepare a cash budget for 1975 and the budgeted balance sheet as at 31 December 1975.

Note. All calculations to the nearest £. Ignore taxation.

BCD LTD

Standard direct cost statement (per unit of product)	PRODUCT A Quantity number of units	PRODUCT A Price £ p	PRODUCT A Amount £ p	PRODUCT B Quantity number of units	PRODUCT B Price £ p	PRODUCT B Amount £ p
Materials:						
X	2 kg	0.30	0.60	3 kg	0.30	0.90
Y	5 m	0.10	0.50	6 m	0.10	0.60
Labour:						
Department 1	6 hrs	0.40	2.40			
Department 2				10 hrs	0.25	2.50
Total direct cost per unit			3.50			4.00

7 *Raw material purchases budget*

	Total Amount £	Material X: kg per unit × Number of units =	Quantity in kg	Price £ p	Amount £	Material Y: m per unit × Number of units =	Quantity in m	Price £ p	Amount £
For production of product A	10 175	(2 × 9 250) =	18 500	0.30	5 550	(5 × 9 250) =	46 250	0.10	4 625
For production of product B	10 725	(3 × 7 150) =	21 450	0.30	6 435	(6 × 7 150) =	42 900	0.10	4 290
For increase in stock of raw materials	312		600	0.30	180		1 320	0.10	132
Total raw material purchases	21 212		40 550	0.30	12 165		90 470	0.10	9 047

8 *Direct labour budget*

	Total Amount £	Department 1: Hours per unit × Number of units =	Total number of hours	Rate £ p	Amount £	Department 2: Hours per unit × Number of units =	Total number of hours	Rate £ p	Amount £
For production of product A	22 200	(6 × 9 250) =	55 500	0.40	22 200				
For production of product B	17 875					(10 × 7 150) =	71 500	0.25	17 875
	40 075		55 000	0.40	22 200		71 500	0.25	17 875

Note: Each man works for 45 hours during 50 weeks per year = 2 250 hours per year. Therefore, number of men required in each department is 55 500 divided by 2 250 = 25 in department 1 and 71 500 divided by 2 250 = 32 in department 2.

BCD LTD	*Total at preferred volume*	*PRODUCT A*						*PRODUCT B*					
		Low volume			*High volume*			*Low volume*			*High volume*		
	Amount £	Quantity number of units	Price £ p	Amount £	Quantity number of units	Price £ p	Amount £	Quantity number of units	Price £ p	Amount £	Quantity number of units	Price £ p	Amount £
1 *Sales budget*	113 500	9 000	6.00	54 000	12 000	5.50	66 000	5 000	9.00	45 000	7 000	8.50	59 500
2 *Production budget*			see			see			see			see	
(Units = Production)			over			over			over			over	
For sales (direct cost of sales)	59 500	9 000	3.50	31 500	12 000	3.50	42 000	5 000	4.00	20 000	7 000	4.00	28 000
For stock (direct cost of stock increase)	1 475	250	3.50	875	250	3.50	875	150	4.00	600	150	4.00	600
Total (direct cost of production)	60 975	9 250	3.50	32 375	12 250	3.50	42 875	5 150	4.00	20 600	7 150	4.00	28 600
3 *Departmental overhead budget*													
(Units = Direct man-hours)													
Total units of production		9 250			12 250			5 150			7 150		
Direct man-hours per unit		6			6			10			10		
Total direct man-hours	25 400	55 500		12 250	73 500		23 800	51 500		8 600	71 500		13 150
4 *Variable selling and administration overhead budget* (Units = Sales)	3 200	9 000	0.20	1 800	12 000	0.20	2 400	5 000	0.20	1 000	7 000	0.20	1 400
5 *Fixed selling and administration overhead budget*	12 000												
6 *Budgeted income statement*													
Revenue (per 1)	113 500			54 000			66 000			45 000			59 500
Direct cost of sales (per 2)	59 500			31 500			42 000			20 000			28 000
Gross margin	54 000			22 500			24 000			25 000			31 500
Departmental overheads (per 3)	25 400			12 250			23 800			8 600			13 150
Selling and administration overhead—variable (per 4)	3 200			1 800			2 400			1 000			1 400
Contribution	25 400			8 450			(−2 200)			15 400			16 950
Selling and administration overhead—fixed (per 5)	12 000												
Net profit	£13 400												

Note: The preferred volume is determined by comparison of the above contributions (subject to any consideration not incorporated in the budgets). In this case, low volume is preferred for A and high volume for B. On this basis extensions can be made into the total column.

BCD LTD

BUDGETED CASH ACCOUNT

9(*a*)		£	£	£
	Opening balance of cash			5 100
Inflow	Received from customers: sales (per 1)		113 500	
	Less: Increase in debtors:			
	Closing balance	18 917		
	Opening balance	9 400		
			9 517	
				103 983
	Closing balance—overdraft			7 669
				116 752
Outflow	Paid to suppliers on raw material purchases (per 7)		21 212	
	Add: Decrease in creditors:			
	Closing balance	3 535		
	Opening balance	8 200		
			4 665	
				25 877
	Paid to direct labour (per 8)			40 075
	Paid for overheads:			
	Departmental overhead (per 3)		25 400	
	Variable selling and administration overhead (per 4)		3 200	
	Fixed selling and administration overhead (per 5)		12 000	
			40 600	
	Less: Depreciation		12 500	
			28 100	
	Add: Liabilities in closing balance	4 200		
	Liabilities in opening balance	7 400		
			3 200	
				31 300
	Paid for fixed assets			8 000
	Payment of dividends			7 500
	Repayment of loan			4 000
				116 752

BCD LTD

BUDGETED CASH FLOW STATEMENT

9*(b)*	£	£
Sources		
Trading operations:		
Net profit (per 6)	13 400	
Depreciation	12 500	
		25 900
Applications		
Increase in debtors:		
Closing balance	18 917	
Opening balance	9 400	
		9 517
Decrease in creditors:		
Closing balance	3 535	
Opening balance	8 200	
		4 665
Decrease in liabilities:		
Closing balance	4 200	
Opening balance	7 400	
		3 200
Increase in stocks:		
Raw materials (per 7)	312	
Finished goods (per 2)	1 475	
		1 787
Purchase of fixed assets		8 000
Payment of dividends		7 500
Repayment of loan		4 000
		38 669
CASH OUTFLOW { Closing balance − £7 669 Opening balance + £5 100		−12 769

BCD LTD

BUDGETED BALANCE SHEET

	31 December 1974	Change	31 December 1975
Fixed assets			
Fixed assets			
Cost	120 000	+ 8 000	128 000
Less: depreciation	37 000	+ 12 500	49 500
	83 000	− 4 500	78 500
Current assets			
Raw materials	1 308(7)	+ 312	1 620
Finished goods	4 900(2)	+ 1 475	6 375
Debtors	9 400	+ 9 517	18 917
Cash	5 100	− 5 100	—
	20 708	+ 6 204	26 912
	£103 708	+ £1 704	£105 412
Equities			
Capital and reserves:			
Issued share capital	50 000	—	50 000
Retained earnings	18 108	+ 5 900*	24 008
	68 108	+ 5 900	74 008
Loan (repayable in equal instalments until 1979)	20 000	− 4 000	16 000
Current liabilities:			
Creditors for materials	8 200	− 4 665	3 535
Liabilities for overheads	7 400	− 3 200	4 200
Bank overdraft	—	+ 7 669	7 669
	15 600	− 196	15 404
	£103 708	+ £1 704	£105 412

* (13 400–7 500)

Overall Cost Control

Amongst the items listed on pp.381–3 for further reading, the following are especially recommended:

Hofstede;
Livingstone;
Phyrr;
Thomas;
Welsch.

9

Cost Accounting

THE NATURE OF COST ACCOUNTING

Cost accounting has been conventionally associated with product costing. This is concerned with the determination of the amount of cost to be assigned to each unit of output as a basis for valuing stocks of goods (as shown in a balance sheet) and as a basis for computing the cost of goods sold (which is deducted from sales revenue to show profit). Apart from aiding in these ways in inventory valuation and income determination, product costing is employed in the cost-plus approach to product pricing (e.g. in the contracting and printing industries).

The approach to product costing is generally to assign to each unit of output a 'fair share' of the total cost of operations. This is quite straightforward in a single product (or single service) company, but complexity tends to increase in proportion to the number of product lines manufactured and/or marketed. In a single product company all costs can be seen to be incurred to support that product (e.g. an output of 1 000 000 units at a cost of £5 000 000 gives a unit cost of £5.00). If there are two product lines – or 2 000 product lines – the problem is much more difficult and the cost of any one item from a multi-product line is impossible to measure accurately.

In addition to product costing, cost accounting is also concerned with deriving costs for other units of activity. The products produced by a company are not the only cost units; one can be interested in the cost of operating particular departments; in the cost of operating in certain sales territories; in the cost of serving various industries and customer groups; in the cost of using different channels of distribution; in the cost of servicing orders below a given value; in the cost of hiring a new salesman; and so forth. Many of these topics will be dealt with in Chapters 17 and 18 in the context of distribution cost accounting, but it is important to consider their relevance before embarking further in the context of production cost accounting.

The analysis of segments is usually concerned with measuring the profit from each defined segment of a business firm's market. This usually involves a prior consideration of product-market segmentation: the customers that a company is serving can be classified into various categories ('market segments') according to such criteria as age, occupation, number of children, and income in the case of individual consumers, or size, location, and SIC code in the case of organizational consumers. In order to ascertain the profit consequences of supplying specified products to identifiable market segments it is necessary to match the revenues from the sales made to each segment with the costs of supplying these segments. The revenue aspect is not too difficult, but the cost determination aspect is fraught with problems. For example, to attempt to allocate a proportion of total marketing and distribution costs to each segment in accordance with the percentage of the total revenue attributable to each segment is too simplistic, whilst to attempt to fully apportion each elemental category of cost is likely to be potentially misleading. (This is so because fixed costs are a function of time and variable costs are a function of activity, so to apportion these different categories of costs to segments could be misleading if the object of the exercise was to make decisions relating to which segments to continue to serve. For example, if, on the basis of a 'full cost' calculation, it was decided to withdraw from segment X, it would not follow that the fixed cost element of servicing segment X would be avoided even though the variable costs are likely to be.) It is important, therefore, to consider the purpose for which costs are being computed and the implications of employing different concepts of cost and alternative techniques of analysis.

In addition to segmental analysis, which typically considers the costs associated with parts of an organization's overall operations during comparatively short periods of time (usually one year), it is relevant to introduce at this point the idea of life-cycle costing. This is a technique designed to:

(*a*) provide increased visibility of the total costs of doing business; and
(*b*) highlight areas where resource applications can be improved.

A product's life-cycle begins with the identification of a new consumer need, and this is followed by the various phases identified in Figure 9.1, which represents a logical evolutionary flow. It is quite common for organizations to identify the acquisition costs of a new product idea (e.g. R & D costs, pro-

THE SYSTEM/PRODUCT/PROJECT LIFE CYCLE			
	CONSUMER	IDENTIFICATION OF NEED	'Wants or desires' for products (because of obvious deficiencies/problems, or made evident through basic research results).
	PRODUCER	SYSTEM PLANNING FUNCTION	Marketing analysis; feasibility study; advanced product planning (product selection, specifications and plans, acquisition plan – research/design/production, evaluation plan, product use and logistics support plan); planning review; proposal.
		SYSTEM RESEARCH FUNCTION	Basic research; applied research ('need' oriented); research methods; results of research; evolution from basic research to product design and development.
		SYSTEM DESIGN FUNCTION	Design requirements; conceptual design, preliminary system design; detailed design; design support; engineering model/prototype development; transition from design to production.
		SYSTEM EVALUATION FUNCTION	Evaluation requirements; categories of test and evaluation; test preparation phase (planning, resource requirements etc.); formal test and evaluation; data collection, analysis, reporting, and corrective action; retesting.
		PRODUCTION AND/OR CONSTRUCTION FUNCTION	Production and/or construction requirements; industrial engineering and operations analysis (plant engineering, manufacturing engineering, methods engineering, production control); sustaining production or process operations; plant maintenance; industrial logistics; quality control.
	CONSUMER	SYSTEM USE AND LOGISTICS SUPPORT FUNCTION	Product distribution and operational use; elements of logistics and life-cycle maintenance support; product evaluation; modifications; product phase-out; material disposal; reclamation, and/or recycling.

Figure 9.1: The system/product/project life-cycle activities

duction costs etc.), but these only constitute the tip of the total life-cycle iceberg, as suggested by Figure 9.2. The major benefit of adopting life-cycle costing is that it provides an overall framework for considering total incremental costs over the entire life-span of a product, project, or system, which in turn facilitates the analysis of parts of the whole where cost effectiveness might be improved.

In comparison with the attention that has been given over the years to the costing of physical products there has been relatively little given to the costing of services (such as those supplied to the final marketplace by accounting firms, advertising agencies, management consultants, architects, engineering consultants, or solicitors). In part this is due to the difficulty of being able to define and measure that which is to be costed. For example, is it the audit certificate in the case of an accounting firm, or the television commercial in the case of the advertising agency? By far the largest category of expenditure in service firms is on payroll items, but individuals have different rates of pay, work varying numbers of hours, are capable of different qualities of output, etc., so to cost a service on the basis of, say, staff input hours, is not a very appropriate approach. The increasing size of the service sector of the British economy, in both its commercial and non-profit sectors, makes this a problem area of increasing significance, and we should bear it in mind throughout the following discussion. (There is, of course, a number of internal departments within manufacturing and service organizations that provide services as inputs to the final market offer, and the costing of some of these is considered below.)

Whatever cost unit (i.e. product, department, etc.) is selected as the focus of attention, some costs will be direct (e.g. direct labour and direct materials for a unit of manufactured output, a salesman's salary and expenses for a sales territory) whilst other costs will be indirect (i.e. overheads). Much of this chapter will be concerned with the treatment accorded by cost analysts to overheads.

By definition, overhead costs cannot be traced directly to cost units, so any procedure whereby overheads are assigned to cost units means that the resulting *absorbed cost* is inaccurate to an unknown degree. The assigning of a fair share of cost (made up of direct costs plus a portion of overhead costs the magnitude of which depends upon the costing techniques used) to cost units is at the heart of product costing, but cost accounting exists for other reasons. In particular these are:

1 Control purposes, the aim of which is to assign controllable costs to responsibility centres (as discussed in Chapter 6);
2 Planning purposes, the aim being to collect cost information that can help to indicate the cost implications of alternative courses of action. These decision-making purposes require cost information to answer such questions as:

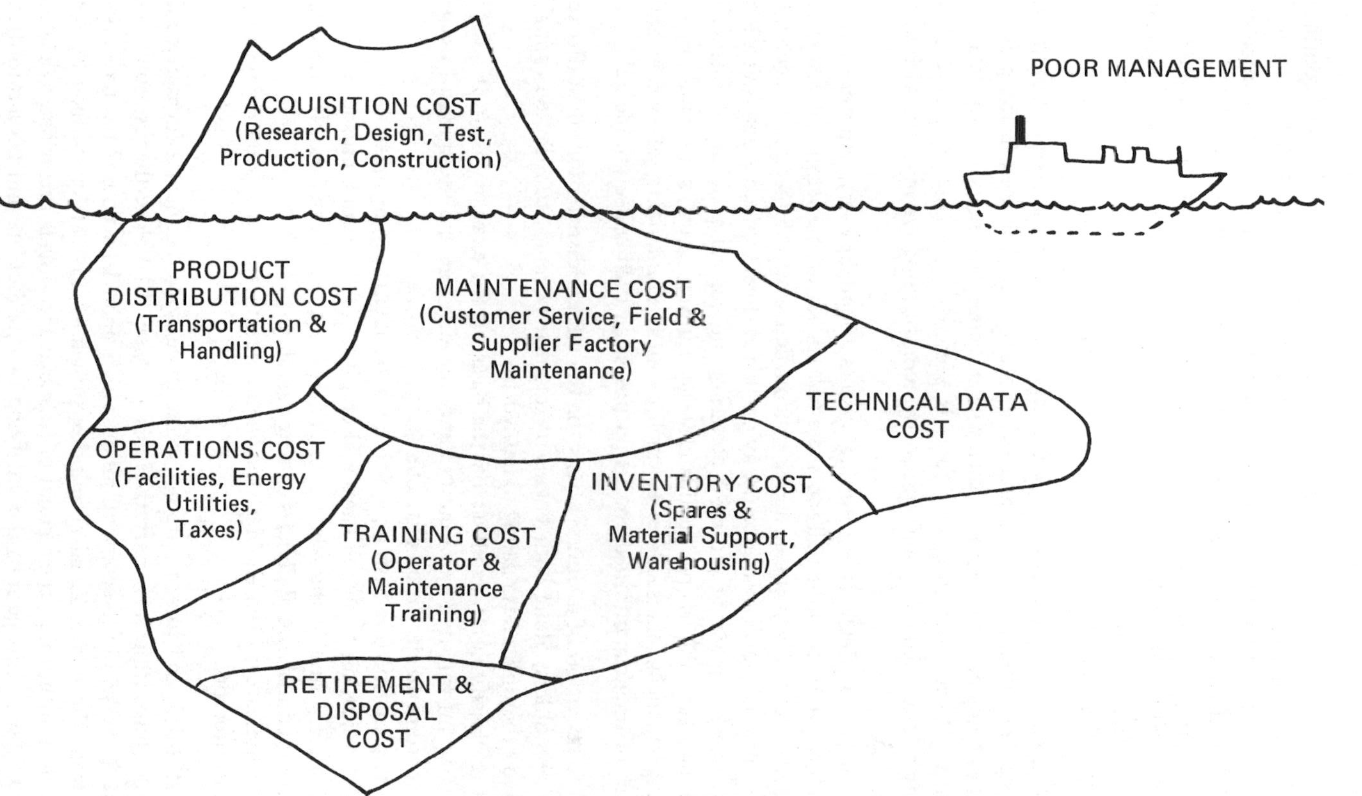
POOR MANAGEMENT
ACQUISITION COST (Research, Design, Test, Production, Construction)
PRODUCT DISTRIBUTION COST (Transportation & Handling)
MAINTENANCE COST (Customer Service, Field & Supplier Factory Maintenance)
TECHNICAL DATA COST
OPERATIONS COST (Facilities, Energy Utilities, Taxes)
TRAINING COST (Operator & Maintenance Training)
INVENTORY COST (Spares & Material Support, Warehousing)
RETIREMENT & DISPOSAL COST

Figure 9.2: Total life-cycle cost

(*a*) What would be the effect on the company's net profit of discontinuing product A and re-allocating the resources to product B?
(*b*) If an order/contract is accepted at a given price, will that price be sufficient to enable the company to earn a profit on the job?
(*c*) Why was last year's profit low despite a major increase in output?
(*d*) What will be the effect of a given wage increase on product costs and hence on profits?
(*e*) What effect will replacing specified equipment have on costs?

In some discussions cost accounting is defined to include management accounting, budgeting, investment appraisal, and other areas, but it is seen in the present context as being narrower in scope than this and complementary to, for instance, budgeting. Cost accounting therefore, is seen to be an essential part of a company's total accounting and control system, but not synonymous with that system.

The orthodox financial accounting system found in every company has a major objective of recording all income and expenditure to permit a measure of profit to be derived which can then be reconciled with the increase or decrease in net worth as shown in the company's balance sheet. Income determination (i.e. the measurement of profit) is certainly the central problem of financial accounting, but the scope of financial accounting extends beyond purely recording financial transactions to include the summarizing, analysing, and reporting of financial information. Its purposes can then be seen to include:

1 The provision of a working basis for the annual distribution of profits to shareholders, along with details of retained earnings, contributed capital, and other measures relating to net worth.
2 The classifying of liabilities on the basis of, for example, maturity, with other information on security, and the division and grouping of assets according to significant characteristics.
3 The provision of a basis on which tax assessments can be made.
4 An indication to shareholders and creditors of the future prospects of the company, and of the relative success of the directors and the effectiveness of broad managerial policies and stewardship.
5 To indicate to shareholders the remuneration that has been enjoyed by the directors.

The first, third, and fourth purposes relate directly to the income measurement problem, illustrating how pervasive this problem is. Nevertheless, solutions must be found within the conventions on which financial accounts are drawn up. Apart from the conventional accounting principles that are prescribed by the professional authorities, the content of financial accounts is prescribed to a large extent by law. This permits the satisfying of shareholders and tax authorities, and good practice in this sphere is largely a matter of learning and applying the relevant law. An outcome of this restriction, from a management control viewpoint, is that financial accounting deals with financial flows classified by *natural* expense headings, whereas other types of accounting consider *functional* flows (see Chapter 2). This accords with the financial accounting imperative to record and interpret financial facts in as objective a manner as possible, but it does not aid in controlling costs or the activities that give rise to costs. Accounting is an expensive activity that in itself has no value: its value is derived from the importance of its objectives and its success in attaining these objectives. Insofar as financial accounting has managerial objectives, these can be thought of as the provision of data to enable management to plan and control operations, but it has been shown that financial accounting is not successful in this endeavour.

The effectiveness of traditional financial accounting lies in its authoritative character rather than in the nature of the information that it produces. The existence of internal controls relating to the financial accounting system acts in a disciplining way on employees and enables the company's financial structure to be depicted in a simple and crude, but overall model that constitutes a huge barrier to chaos. But it can go further.

The intelligent presentation and classification of financial accounts; the provision of comparative figures, percentages and notes; the accompanying of the accounts with tables, graphs, diagrams, and other interpretative devices; and the supplying of supplementary information, such as funds statements and trend tables, enable the financial accountant to make his statements more informative to those who must study and use them. In this way it is possible for financial accounts to be of some limited value in cost control by giving a wide view of events in the recent past, but their value in controlling day-to-day operations is even less, and their relevance to the future is almost nil. Generally, financial accounts are too incomplete, too infrequently-compiled, and too late to be of prime value in cost control.

In contrast to the reliance of financial accounting on standard accounting conventions and legal requirements, cost accounting is governed by the particular characteristics (in the form of products, structure, personalities, processes, policies, etc) of the organization within which it operates. Furthermore, cost accounting is concerned with internal matters whereas financial accounting is largely concerned with dealings between the company and third parties (such as creditors, shareholders, inland revenue, customers, etc.).

Needless to say, the distinguishing feature between cost accounting and financial accounting is not just that the former deals with costs. Cost accounting is concerned with the composition and control of costs, whereas financial accounting deals mainly with income determination. Once financial accountants have (in what purports to be an objective manner) ascertained income, cost accountants (in what they admit to being a subjective approach) proceed to analyse it. The analysis performed by cost accountants enables them to show not only whether a profit has been made on the working of the business as a whole, but whether a profit has been made for each process, job, product, or whatever. Such an analysis aids management in determining the output level and products that should lead to the most desirable level of operations.

The cost accounting function is therefore concerned with:

1 Cost findings (from measurement and estimation).
2 Cost analysis (covering relationships and behaviour).
3 Cost recording (including classification).
4 Reporting.

In overall terms cost accounting's objective is related to the company's profit goals, but accounting (as a service function) is a charge against profits. In relation to its contribution to managerial cost control, therefore, the cost of financial accounting should be minimized and the overhead constituted by cost accounting should be rendered as efficient as possible.

Although the cost accountant must be familiar with managerial problems if he is to perform his duties adequately, he must always be aware of the fact that the actual controlling of costs is a management function rather than an accounting one (i.e. line rather than staff). Control requires both data and action, with the accountant endeavouring to supply the former and with management providing the latter if the control process is to be effective.

COLLECTION OF COST DATA

The type of data that are to be gathered for costing purposes will depend on the type of costing system in force and this will tend to depend on the nature of the type of production being undertaken by the company.

Essentially there are three types of production. These are:

1 **Job production** This involves the manufacturing of a single complete unit. The building of bridges and ships are good examples of the one-off nature of job production. 'Jobbing' is a term used to describe work carried out against a customer's order rather than for stock.

2 **Batch production** This is employed when the number of units to be manufactured of a given product increases. It involves the work being divided into operations, and each operation will be carried out on the whole batch before the next operation is undertaken. Batch production permits the specialization of labour, although the organization and planning required to ensure freedom from idle time are considerable.

In principle, there is little difference between job and batch production.

3 **Flow production** Since the various operations in batch production will inevitably take up different amounts of time, programming the work flow to avoid wasted time is almost impossible. As the scale of operations increases it often becomes possible to establish continuous flow production where there is no wasted time between operations. Such an arrangement requires balancing the times of every operation (including inspection) so that bottlenecks or surplus capacity do not render the line inefficient. Clearly a fault at any stage will have effects on all other stages of the production line.

Prerequisites for satisfactory flow production are:

(*a*) Continuity of demand for the output of the process.
(*b*) Product standardization.
(*c*) Reliable quality of materials and delivery schedules.
(*d*) Balance of activities.
(*e*) All work must conform to quality standards.
(*f*) The maintenance of plant and equipment must be by anticipation and not default.
(*g*) Inspection must be in line with the production.

In parallel with these types of production organization there are different types of costing system:

1 Job/batch costing: this is adopted when each 'job' is to be regarded as a separate cost unit. The job may be one large order (e.g. a bridge) or a batch of like items. All costs relating to the job or batch will be charged to a separate account for that job/batch.
2 Process costing: when units of product are manufactured in large quantities (i.e. flow production) and pass through distinct stages, it is customary to ascertain the cost of each stage.

As will be discussed later, either of these costing systems may be standardized and either may be performed along absorption lines (by which fixed overheads are apportioned) or direct lines. However, attention must be paid to the sources of costing data: labour, materials, and overheads.

Labour – as a source of cost data

The initial point to observe in relation to payroll data is that the cost of employing a man is not just his gross wage or salary. In addition to gross earnings the company must pay its contribution for national insurance, superannuation, and so on.

In a manufacturing or distribution environment time sheets (see Figures 9.3 and 9.4) can be used to record, in summary form, the time that each operative spends on different jobs. Figure 9.3 illustrates a time sheet for an

TIME SHEET							
Name ______ Number ______							
Department ______ Week ending ______							
Date	AM		PM		O/T		Total hours
	In	Out	In	Out	In	Out	
Normal hours ______ @ ______ ______							
Overtime hours ______ @ ______ ______							
Gross earnings ______							

Figure 9.3: Weekly time sheet – 1

operative spending all his time on one job or in one processing department. In contrast, Figure 9.4 is suitable for an operative who spends time on a variety of jobs/batches. A clear indication should be given of overtime (OT) as opposed to normal time (N), and time sheets can usually be designed to facilitate the calculation of gross earnings (e.g. at the foot of Figure 9.3) and the computation of labour cost per job worked on during the week (e.g. on the reverse of Figure 9.4).

Whilst the time sheet refers to the allocation of an individual operative's total time over one or more jobs during the week, the job card (Figure 9.5) refers to the total time spent on a particular job. An operative will be issued with a work ticket (Figure 9.6) by his supervisor (who will receive such tickets from the production control department). Figure 9.6 is designed for small jobs that can be completed at one attempt, but Figure 9.5 is designed for jobs that may involve an operative spending one hour on Monday, three hours on Tuesday, and so on, in accordance with the various demands of the job in question for different operatives' attention, and also in accordance with the demands of other jobs for a particular operative's time.

The onus will often be on an operative to record the time he spends on each job that he works on during a week. This highlights a major danger: unless there is some incentive towards the accurate booking of time, the validity of labour costings will be highly suspect. An operative may attach little importance to tediously recording the time he spends on different tasks if he fails to understand the importance of this function. Further, he may be reluctant to record times accurately because lost time, idle time, and waiting time can reflect partly on himself, partly on his supervisor, and partly on his colleagues.

Name __________ Number __________

Department __________ Week ending __________

Job Number	Mon		Tues		Wed		Thurs		Fri		Sat		Totals
	N	O/T	N	O/T	N	O/T	N	O/T	N	O/T	N	O/T	
Totals													

Figure 9.4: Weekly time sheet – 2

<table>
<tr><td colspan="2">Description of job
....
....
....</td><td colspan="2">Job Number

Name

Time</td></tr>
<tr><td>ON</td><td>OFF</td><td>N</td><td>O/T</td></tr>
<tr><td></td><td></td><td></td><td></td></tr>
<tr><td></td><td>Total time</td><td></td><td></td></tr>
</table>

Figure 9.5: Job card

WORK TICKET

Employee Number ________ Date ________ Job Number ________

Operation ________ Account ________ Department ________

Stop ________ Rate ________ Pieces Worked ________

Rejected ________

Start ________ Amount ________ Completed ________

Figure 9.6: Work ticket

It may be required that the supervisor (i.e. foreman or chargehand) countersigns time sheets, thereby certifying their validity, but this puts a strain on the supervisor and does not necessarily lead to greatly improved accuracy. Activity sampling is another means of validating the data supplied on time sheets. An incentive bonus scheme should lead to more realistic time recording, and this may be one of the most substantial advantages of such a scheme.

So far the discussion has concentrated on the recording of *direct* labour time, but of significant importance is the *indirect* labour time. An analysis of indirect labour hours – especially where reasons can be clearly given – is of great value in pinpointing areas of weakness. Account codes can be drawn up to facilitate the analysis, and each source of indirect labour expense can be recorded against its particular code as it is incurred. For idle time, for example, we may have the following codes:

X123 waiting for orders
X124 waiting for stock
X125 waiting for materials from previous operation
X126 waiting for fitter
X127 waiting for power
X128 waiting for supervisor
X129 waiting for drawings
X130 waiting for maintenance
X131 waiting for jigs
X132 waiting for instructions

If idle time booked to X126 (waiting for a fitter) amounted to, say, £2 500 during the course of a year, a good argument could be put forward for hiring another fitter. A weekly report (Figure 9.7) can be compiled to show how lost time is made up and the proportion it bears to direct labour time.

Materials – as a source of cost data

All issues of materials should be authorized by a requisition (Figure 9.8), but note should be taken that the requisitioned quantity may not always be available, so either a lesser amount will be withdrawn from stores (in which event the requisition must be amended) or the full amount will be issued when available. A material requisition should bear the cost allocation/job number in every instance.

Movements of stocks can be recorded on store cards of the type illustrated in Figure 9.9. In the frequently-met situation in which stock is earmarked in advance, a special stock record (Figure 9.10) can be used to indicate the free stock. (Note that Figure 9.10 is purely in physical terms rather than physical and financial as Figure 9.9.)

A difficulty that arises over material issues is the cost to associate with each

WEEKLY LABOUR REPORT

Date________ Department________

Clock number	Name	Idle time										Total	Direct hours	Per cent
		X123	X124	X125	X126	X127	X128	X129	X130	X131	X132			

Figure 9.7: Weekly labour report

issue. It might appear simple to charge against production *actual* material cost (i.e. the price paid). However, a problem usually arises because the same type of material has been purchased at a variety of prices. 'Actual cost' then has several different meanings and some systematic method of pricing material issues must be selected. It is usual to use the same method for the valuation of material stocks – perhaps adjusted according to the 'lower of cost or market value' convention.

Suppose the following information is available for Material A (given in chronological order):

(a)	Opening stock	100 units	Cost £1.00 per unit =	£100.00
(1)	Issue	75 units		
(b)	Purchase	400 units	Cost £1.10 per unit =	£440.00
(2)	Issue	100 units		
(3)	Issue	50 units		
(c)	Purchase	80 units	Cost £1.20 per unit =	£96.00
(4)	Issue	150 units		
(5)	Closing stock	205 units	(i.e. assuming no wastage)	£636.00

A price per unit is required for issues (1)–(4) and a valuation for closing stock (5).

REQUISITION

Job number__________ Serial number__________

Department__________ Date__________

Authorized__________

Code	Description	Quantity	Rate	Amount

Figure 9.8: Material requisition

STORES CARD

Unit ____________________

Description ____________________ Reorder level ____________________

Code ____________________ Reorder quantity ____________________

Date	Reference	Received			Issued			Balance		
		Quantity	Unit cost	Total cost	Quantity	Unit cost	Total cost	Quantity	Unit cost	Total cost

Figure 9.9: Stores card – 1

STORES CARD

Unit ____________

Description ____________ Reorder level ____________

Code ____________ Reorder quantity ____________

Date	Received		Issued			Balance		
	Ref	Quantity	Ref	Earmarked	Free	Ref	Earmarked	Free

Figure 9.10: Stores card – 2

First in, first out (FIFO) method Assumes that the various units of material are used in the order in which they are received. Closing stock will consist of the last items purchased. Whenever stores are issued the issue price will be calculated by working forwards from the oldest batch in stock.

	Stock (a)	*Purchase (b)*	*Purchase (c)*	
Issue (1)	75 × £1.00			= £75.00
Issue (2)	25 × £1.00 +	75 × £1.10		= £107.50
Issue (3)		50 × £1.10		= £55.00
Issue (4)		150 × £1.10		= £165.00
Stock (5)		125 × £1.10 +	80 × £1.20	= £233.50
	100 units	400 units	80 units	£636.00

This method is easy to operate unless many small purchases at different prices occur. Stock balances represent nearly current costs, and costs are recognized in a manner which should correspond to the physical use of the stock. However, the system is inequitable if a sudden change in price results in similar jobs being charged with different material costs, and where stock turnover is slow and there are substantial price changes, current material costs will not be apparent in the account.

Weighted-average cost method Assumes that all material of a given kind is so intermingled that an issue cannot be made from a particular lot and the cost should therefore represent an average of the entire supply. A new issue price is calculated every time a purchase is made by dividing: (the cost of material received plus the cost of material on hand) by (number of units received plus the number of units on hand).

Issue (1)	75 × £1.000 = £75	
Issue (2)	100 × £1.094 = £109	$\dfrac{(25 \times £1) + (400 \times £1.10)}{25 + 400} = 1.094$
Issue (3)	50 × £1.094 = £55	
Issue (4)	150 × £1.118 = £168	$\dfrac{(275 \times £1.094) + (80 \times £1.20)}{275 + 80} = 1.118$
Stock (5)	205 × £1.118 = £229	
	£636	

Note the calculation may be done on a periodic basis instead of on the occasion of every purchase. Issue and stock pricing would then be recalculated as follows and no entries would be made until the end of the period:

$$\frac{£100 + £440 + £96}{100 + 400 + 80} = £1.093 \text{ per unit}$$

This method is easy to operate, smooths out the sudden jumps likely to occur in pricing under other methods, and gives stock balances that represent relatively current costs. However, the influence of a large purchase on favourable terms may influence stock pricing for many periods if usage is slow.

Last in first out (LIFO) method Assumes artifically that the last items purchased are the first used. Closing stock will be valued at the price of the first goods purchased. Whenever stores are issued the issue price will be calculated by working back from the most recent batch received.

	Stock (a)	*Purchase (b)*	*Purchase (c)*	
Issue (1)	75 × £1.00			= £75.00
Issue (2)		100 × £1.10		= £110.00
Issue (3)		50 × £1.10		= £55.00
Issue (4)		70 × £1.10 +	80 × £1.20	= £173.00
Stock (5)	25 × £1.00 +	180 × £1.10		= £223.00
	100 units	400 units	80 units	£636.00

The only advantage of this method is that it matches recent material cost with current revenue – hence cost of goods manufactured will fluctuate with the market price of material used (unless stock levels are sharply reduced). However, stocks are valued at prices paid for the earliest purchases (including previous periods) which may deviate considerably from current market values.

Conclusion If prices are reasonably stable it matters little which of the above methods is employed. Average cost would probably be best but any of the three applied consistently should be satisfactory.

If prices are not stable the fact that all the above methods (and others) are 'generally acceptable' and therefore are used not only by management internally but for reporting externally is alarming.

Some means of isolating the effect of price changes is essential both from a control point of view and an income reporting point of view. One suggestion is

PURCHASE REQUISITION					
Date ______			Serial Number ______		
Department ______					
Authorized ______					
Quantity	Description	Code	Price	Total	Order Number

Figure 9.11: Purchase requisition

to use LIFO for pricing issues and FIFO for pricing stocks and transfer the ensuing 'difference' to a 'price gains' or 'price losses' account. A far better solution is to employ standard costing whereby all material pricing is based on attainable standards as calculated at the beginning of the period. The effect of unforeseen price changes is then automatically segregated and can be both examined for control purposes and reported separately in income statements.

As well as requisitioning materials from stores (Figure 9.8), requisitions can also be placed on the purchasing department for materials that must be bought out. Figure 9.11 illustrates a simple purchase requisition showing again the need to indicate quite clearly the cost allocation – this is best done at source (i.e. by the individual who raises the requisition).

All invoiced items and petty cash purchases should be coded to ensure they are charged to the correct cost centre. Because of the time lag invariably involved in processing invoices for payment it will be found that some invoices approved towards the end of a month will not be included in the accounts relating to that month. A clear ruling should be made to eliminate any confusion, such as having a well-understood arrangement whereby all invoices approved by a departmental head (or other responsible individual) and passed to the accounting department by, say, the 22nd of the month will be included on that month's cost statement, but that invoices passed on or after the 22nd will be included in the following month's statement.

It is important at this point to grasp fully the significance of approving an invoice for payment. In doing this, the manager is indicating – whether he realizes it or not – that:

1 He accepts the charge and will be responsible for it.
2 The charge itself is correct and is to be paid.
3 He has authority – and sufficient budget – to incur the expense. (If a manager only has authority to spend a maximum of £1 000 on a single item, he cannot authorize expenditure of £1 750 on a single item, and if he only has a budget balance of £800 he is not in a position to spend even £1 000.)

Furthermore, the approval of an invoice for payment affects the remaining budget immediately, the cumulative expense level when recorded, and the cash flow when paid. An apparently simple act is thus full of significance from various viewpoints.

Once purchased, some materials are difficult to control as a result of their physical nature. For example, temperature changes may affect the apparent volume of an issue of a liquid chemical; wastage may arise due to inevitable evaporation or because issues do not correspond with purchases (e.g. galvanized wire may be purchased by the ton but be issued in coils or lengths). These are all examples of *unavoidable* causes and allowances can (and should) be made for such losses and gains. If experience shows that only 19 issues of 10 lbs can be made from a purchase of 200 lbs of material X at a cost of £20, it will be necessary to use the following formula to compute the cost per *usable* pound of material X: $\frac{20}{190}$ (i.e. £0.105 per lb as opposed to $\frac{20}{200}$ or £0.100 per lb).

Avoidable losses are, however, quite a different matter. Further consideration will be given to these in Chapter 16, but suffice it to say at this stage that such losses may result from such causes as:

1 Pilferage.
2 Careless handling.
3 Careless measurement of issues.
4 Incorrect allowances for variations due to evaporation, absorption of moisture, changes in temperature, etc.
5 Unsuitable storage.

Care should be taken in deciding which issues to value on an individual basis and which to value on a collective basis. Items of small value (e.g. nails, nuts, etc.) are of the latter type, and although they are strictly in the nature of direct materials (i.e. their cost can be specifically identified with particular products), it will usually be unnecessarily expensive in terms of clerical labour to do this. The usual procedure, therefore, is to issue such items in bulk and classify them in the overheads as consumable stores rather than issue them at a specially computed price to specific jobs.

Overheads – as a source of cost data

The way in which predetermined (or retrospective) overhead rates can be established will be explained later in this chapter. Indirect (or overhead) labour costs will be obtained from work sheets and labour summaries, and indirect material costs (such as the nails referred to above) will be obtained from requisitions. Further overheads including electricity and other services, supervisory and executive salaries, insurance premiums, depreciation, etc., will be obtained from expense summaries compiled on the basis of either invoices or internal work sheets.

Putting the pieces together

Having discussed labour costs, material costs, and overhead costs, it now remains to consider how these items can be brought together to show the cost of a job/batch/process/department.

Figure 9.12 shows a job cost sheet for a job passing through two departments. Direct material costs are obtained from coded requisitions, the direct labour costs from labour analyses, and the overheads on the basis of whichever costing method is employed (see next section).

In the job costing example shown in Figure 9.12 no attempt is made to compute the cost of running a department, but process costing is based on knowing the cost of operating each processing department. Figure 9.13 gives an example of a cost sheet for a process costing exercise in a company having two processes – X and Y. The cost per unit (ton) can be built up as production progresses from raw materials to the finished product through, initially, process X and then through process Y.

Process costing, as we have seen, is associated with flow production in industries such as chemicals, oil, textiles, plastics, paints, glass, and so on. All costs of each process (i.e. direct material costs, direct labour costs, any direct expenses and overheads) are accumulated and related to the units produced. During any period for which costs are accumulated, it is probable that there will be some incomplete units of product on hand at the beginning of the period, and similarly some partly-processed units will be present at the close of the period. In order to work out a unit cost for the process it is necessary to convert all partly-processed units into the equivalent of fully-processed units. Thus 100 units that were complete in terms of material inputs but only half finished in terms of the labour and overhead input would be converted into *equivalent units* in the following way:

JOB COST SHEET							
Product __________			Date started __________			Order number ________	
Stock __________			Date completed ______			Quantity __________	
Customer ________							
DEPARTMENT A							
Direct material			Direct labour			Overhead	
Date	Code	Cost	Date	Code	Cost	Date	Cost
DEPARTMENT B							
Direct material			Direct labour			Overhead	
Date	Code	Cost	Date	Code	Cost	Date	Cost
SUMMARY							
Selling price							
			Dept A	Dept B	TOTAL		
Costs: Direct material							
Direct labour							
Overhead							
Gross profit							

Figure 9.12: Job cost sheet

PROCESS COST SHEET									Month ________
Details	This month actual		This month budget		Year to date		Budget to date		Remarks
	£	per ton	£	per ton	£	per ton	£	per ton	
Process X Materials Wages Expenses (detail) Overhead allocation Process Y Materials Wages Expenses (detail) Overhead allocation									
Office and establishment overheads Selling overheads									
Cost of sales (A)									
Sales Deduct: outward freight containers									
Net sales (B)									
Profit (B-A)									
Quantity of sales		Tons		Tons		Tons		Tons	

Figure 9.13: Process cost sheet

	£
Material input (total)	600
Labour input (50 per cent)	200
Overhead allocation (50 per cent)	100
	900

The completed units would cost:

	£
Material input	600
Labour input	400
Overhead allocation	200
	1 200

Equivalent units are thus $\frac{900}{1200} \times 100 = 75$ units.

The equivalent output of a process for a particular period will be made up of:

> Units started and completed during this period + Closing equivalent units (i.e. those started but not completed during this period) + Completion of opening equivalent units (i.e. those started in previous periods and completed during this period).

The distinction between process costing and job/batch costing is that the former deals with broad averages and large numbers of like units whilst the latter attempts to apply costs to specific jobs.

Attention can now be turned to considering the costing treatment of overheads.

ABSORPTION COSTING

Both process costing and job costing can be carried out in accordance with overhead absorption principles. The aim of overhead absorption is to ultimately spread the total cost of the company's operations over the jobs, batches, contracts, units, etc., that pass through the company's manufacturing facilities. Dangers abound in attempting to do this: overhead is applied as an average to products that are not average, and this is only partly resolved by subdividing the factory into cost centres.

The basic procedure for applying overhead to manufactured throughput involves developing overhead rates along the following lines:

1 Analyze and classify all costs into their direct and indirect categories. (This can be done as a retrospective exercise using actual costs, or as a predictive exercise using estimated costs.)

2 Relate direct costs to the particular jobs, processes, etc., for which they were/are to be specifically incurred.

3 Of the indirect costs, some will relate to particular production departments through which products pass in the course of the manufacturing cycle, and others will relate (on a responsibility basis) to service or ancillary departments (i.e. non-production departments such as maintenance, production control, stores, costing, etc.). The cost of these service departments is then apportioned to the production departments on some 'fair' basis relating to the benefits enjoyed by different production departments.

The whole question of apportioning service department costs to production departments is complicated by the fact that some service departments render services in a reciprocal manner to each other – the boiler house supplies heating to the stores which in turn supply stores to the boiler house, and the canteen supplies meals for personnel department employees who in turn help in administering the canteen. This problem can be dealt with in various ways:

(*a*) It may be thought best to disregard the cost of any service rendered by one service department to another, and to apportion the total expenses of each service department directly to the manufacturing departments.

(*b*) It may be felt to be most appropriate to first apportion the expenses of that service department that renders services to the greatest number of other service departments but which receives in return the least service from these other departments. The expenses of the next most important provider of services can then be apportioned over the remaining service departments, and so on until all the expenses have been distributed to manufacturing departments.

(*c*) Perhaps the most accurate – and also the most complex – method is to proceed as in item (*b*) above, but with the difference that when the expenses of the second service department are apportioned, some of these expenses may be carried back to the first department, provided that it has benefited from the services rendered by the second department. The whole cycle of apportioning service department expenses in this way will have to be repeated on account of the re-apportionments until the remaining balances are so small that they can be charged directly to manufacturing.

4 An overhead rate can be established for each production department or cost centre, determined by the formula

$$\frac{\text{departmental overheads} + \text{apportioned service overheads}}{\text{level of activity}}$$

and applied to each job, process, or whatever. This is termed the *recovery of overheads*. (A simpler alternative of obvious applicability in a single product company, but also applicable in other circumstances, is to have a single, company-wide overhead rate. However, even in the single product company it will often be desirable to know the cost of each operation through which the work passes, and also to know the cumulative cost of the product as it passes through the various stages of manufacture.)

Overhead rates in practice are generally determined once a year – and preferably in advance rather than retrospectively, but in changing circumstances it will be advisable to revise them as necessary. The level of activity at which a department is expected to operate during a given period is of crucial importance (see Chapter 3), and whenever overhead rates are determined in advance very careful attention must be paid to estimating this dimension.

Items 3 and 4 will now be considered in a little more detail.

APPORTIONMENT OF OVERHEADS

Initially, management must specify the cost centres that are to be used – the company itself as one all-embracing cost centre; major service and production departments; subdepartments; responsibility centres; or some variation of these.

Overhead costs that are directly attributable to the selected centres should be allocated to them. Once this has been done, the objective is to apportion service centre costs to production cost centres on a 'reasonable' basis, which means some basis that seems to reflect the benefits received by each production centre (and service centre if the approach suggested in item 3(*c*) above is adopted), or which is seen to represent a 'fair share' of service centre costs.

It will be seen, of course, that this procedure contradicts the criterion of responsibility discussed in Chapter 6 (that is, a responsible individual – such as a departmental manager – cannot control apportioned costs, and there is a strong argument against apportionments of overhead costs for this reason. However, a certain amount of influence may be brought to bear on such apportioned costs as heating, cleaning, and so forth). It follows, therefore, that the methods generally employed for apportioning and re-apportioning overhead costs among departments for product costing purposes do not give rise to meaningful data for cost control purposes: an individual cannot be made accountable for cost apportionments from a cost centre over which he has no control. A clear distinction must always be made between cost control (by responsibility accounting for instance) and product costing (by overhead apportionment and absorption).

Possible bases for apportioning service department costs are generally related to physical identification (e.g. items 9, 10 and 11 below), facilities provided (e.g. in items 4, 5 and 6 below), or the ease of apportionment itself (e.g. in item 3 below). Before apportioning costs it will usually be necessary to make a survey of the factory to ascertain the floor space per department, the number of employees and their distribution throughout the organization, the investment in plant and equipment per department, the horsepower hours worked by each department, and similar matters. Suggested bases of apportionment for service department costs are:

1 Direct wages paid to production employees.
2 Direct material costs incurred by production departments.
3 Number of employees per department. (This is especially useful for personnel, canteen, welfare, supervision, and costing overheads. But its efficacy is affected by differences in the skilled/unskilled ratio, the rate of labour turnover, the variations in attention given by different services to different production departments irrespective of the number of employees – as when the people using a subsidized factory canteen do not represent a proportional cross section of employees.)
4 Floor area occupied (in square feet). (This is frequently used for apportioning rent, rates, building costs, insurances, and depreciation. However, it presupposes that each square foot of space is of equal value to the organization, and it is complicated by having to find ways of dealing with corridors, stairways, washrooms, etc.)
5 Cubic space occupied. (This modification of 4 can be used for the same purposes, but is more useful for heating overheads.)
6 Capital employed. (Maintenance, depreciation, rates, and insurance costs can all be apportioned on this basis. Care must be taken in deciding on the values to be put on capital assets: replacement value may be more appropriate than written down book value.)
7 Direct labour hours worked. (As a measure of productive activity this can be useful for apportioning personnel, medical, and production planning/control overheads.)
8 Machine hours worked. (As with 7, this can be a good basis for production planning and similar costs, and it is particularly suitable for dealing with maintenance overheads.)
9 Actual measurement/technical estimates. (Electricity, gas, water, oil, compressed air, and steam can either be metered so that the actual consumption per department will be given, or technical estimates can be made with reasonable accuracy.)
10 Units of output. (Materials, handling, production control, stores, maintenance, depreciation, etc., can be spread on the basis of physical output.)
11 Number of requisitions received. (Purchasing, stores, tool-room activity revolves around the processing of requisitions which make the number of requisitions processed a sensible basis for making apportionments. However, it must be borne in mind that differing degrees of attention must be

paid to different requisitions – some materials are easy to obtain whilst suppliers must be sought for others, some items can be issued simply from stores whilst others must be cut before being issued.)

The most important criterion in selecting a base is to relate the overhead cost to its most causal factor: machines require maintenance, space involves paying rates, outputs require inputs. Nevertheless, the whole methodology of apportioning service department costs is plagued by the necessity of having to rely on some arbitrary rules (i.e. relating to 'benefit' or 'fair share') that have been developed in order that service department costs might be rationally spread over production departments. Such apportionments are carried out solely for product costing purposes: the control of individual overhead costs will not be achieved by cost apportionments, and nor will the method of cost apportionment influence cost control.

ABSORPTION OF OVERHEADS

The absorption or recovery of overheads entails computing and applying overhead rates for each production department to products passing through those departments. The absorbed cost of each job or process can be derived by adding the overhead element (calculated on the basis of one of the methods shown below) to the prime cost of the job/process. A more accurate absorbed cost will tend to result from overhead rates developed for each cost centre through which a product passes as opposed to the absorbed cost that results from one company-wide overhead rate. The essential rationale is to consider why one unit of product or a particular job should bear more overhead cost than another, and then to select a suitable basis from the seven given below to reflect the answer. The bases on which production overheads (including apportioned service department costs) may be absorbed are:

1 As a percentage of prime cost. This is given by:

$$\frac{\text{Expected overhead}}{\text{Estimated prime cost}} \times 100$$

Its major failing is in not considering the time factor since overheads tend to be incurred over time. Unless a standard product is being manufactured that requires constant material and labour inputs per unit the absorbed cost computed on this basis will be inaccurate (see items 2 and 3 below).

2 As a percentage of direct labour cost, given by the formula:

$$\frac{\text{Expected overhead}}{\text{Estimated direct labour cost}} \times 100$$

This basis gives some consideration to the factor of time since, for a given grade of labour, the higher the cost the greater the time spent. It has the advantage of simplicity and is economical in that it can be developed directly from payroll data, but it fails to allow for different mixes of labour or for overtime or for payment by results.

3 As a percentage of direct material cost, given by:

$$\frac{\text{Expected overhead}}{\text{Estimated direct material cost}} \times 100$$

Only when output is uniform (i.e. when only one kind of product is manufactured, involving a constant material input for each unit of output) is this method fair. Fluctuations in material prices render it unstable, and because an expensive material may be used on one product in a multi-product company, this does not mean that that product should be expected to recover a proportionately higher amount of overhead.

Items 1–3 will only be acceptable if overheads vary in proportion to the cost base selected – prime cost, direct labour cost, or direct material cost. Any variations in wage rates or material prices will require a change in the overhead rate.

4 As a rate per unit of productive output. This method is appropriate for flow production (i.e. process costing) and separate rates can be developed for each process. The rate is derived by applying the formula:

$$\frac{\text{Expected overheads}}{\text{Estimated output (in units)}}$$

and is only suitable when the units being produced are homogeneous and receive identical (or nearly identical) attention.

5 As a rate per direct labour hour, computed as:

$$\frac{\text{Expected overheads}}{\text{Estimated direct labour hours}}$$

This base depends for its accuracy on proper records being kept of the direct labour time being spent on each activity. It is best suited to labour-intensive operations and may not give very satisfactory results when one group of operatives use machines and another group do not.

6 As a rate per machine hour, given by:

$$\frac{\text{Expected overheads}}{\text{Estimated machine hours}}$$

This complements 5 above in being suitable for capital intensive situations.

7 As a rate per production hour for situations which are neither suitable

for method 5 nor for method 6. The formula is:

$$\frac{\text{Expected overheads}}{\text{Estimated production hours}}$$

Since fixed overhead costs are related to time it is often suggested that time (i.e. methods 5, 6 and 7) is the most important dimension for overhead absorption. There seems to be a very general acceptance that rates based on time or output (i.e. methods 4–7 above) are to be preferred to those based on value (i.e. methods 1–3 above). But whether they are developed in relation to time or output, overhead absorption rates should be based on a consideration of such factors as:

(*a*) The nature of the manufacturing processes – manual versus mechanical.
(*b*) The nature of the materials used.
(*c*) The constancy (or otherwise) of material prices and quality.
(*d*) The differentials in pay rates.
(*e*) The seasonality (if any) of production.
(*f*) The extent to which available capacity is utilized.

There should be some cause and effect link between an overhead cost and the basis of absorption (e.g. if supervisory labour is apportioned to productive cost centres on the basis of direct labour cost, then it should be absorbed into product costs in accordance with direct labour costs).

It is not always necessary to distribute each overhead cost separately: some fixed costs – such as depreciation, rates, insurance premiums, and rent – can be spread collectively on the basis of, say, machine hours (since this factor represents the time during which a product 'rents' the machinery and premises).

Other costs – such as maintenance, certain utilities, operating supplies, and so forth, may be distributed on the basis of units of output. However, those costs that are proportional to direct labour (such as indirect labour, supervision, holiday accruals, overtime premiums, welfare services, personnel department, etc.) can be distributed on the basis of labour cost, manhours, or the number of people employed – whichever seems most appropriate.

Diagrammatically, Figure 9.14 summarizes the apportionment/absorption routine. The first step is to separate service centre costs from production department overheads. The service department overheads are then apportioned over the production departments. Finally, the resulting departmentalized overheads are absorbed into units of production.

It should again be emphasized that when a company produces a heterogeneous range of jobs/products, with each receiving an unequal amount of attention as it moves from one cost centre to another, it is essential to develop and apply departmental overhead rates (rather than one total company-wide overhead rate) to each job if the resulting product cost is to bear any relation to the true (but unknown) full product cost.

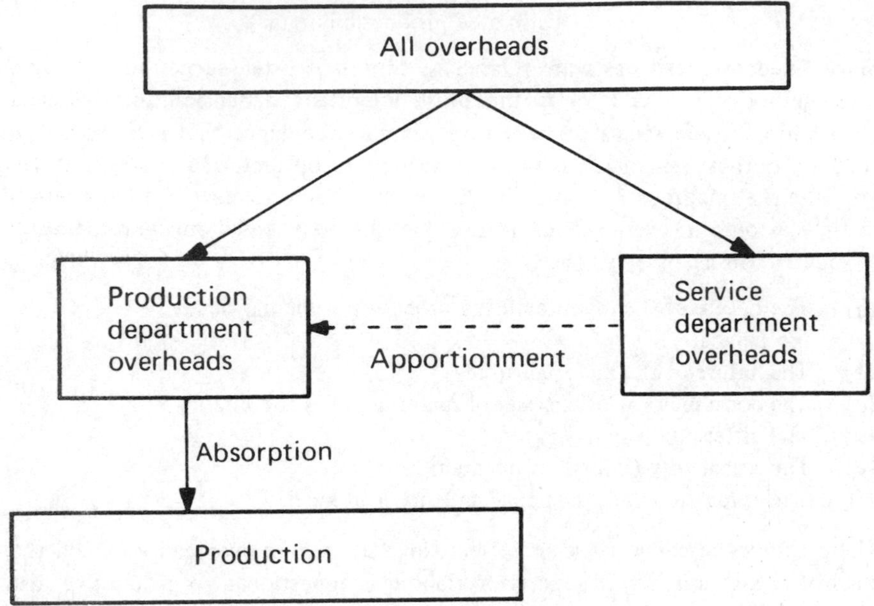

Figure 9.14: Overhead apportionment and absorption

SOME EXAMPLES

The principles given up to this point are (at least to some extent) considered in the following worked examples. The reader is recommended to spend some time following them through.

CDE Ltd – problem

The works overhead cost distribution statement of CDE Ltd, a manufacturing company, for a certain cost period is as follows:

	Total overhead costs	*Production departments X*	*Y*	*Power house*	*Personnel department*	*Plant maintenance*
	£	£	£	£	£	£
Indirect materials	3 602	2 000	1 002	—	100	500
Fuel and power	600	—	—	600	—	—
Foremen	3 550	800	900	550	700	600
Depreciation	1 400	600	450	250	—	100
Rent and rates	1 050	400	350	150	50	100
	10 202	3 800	2 702	1 550	850	1 300
Additional information available:						
Number of persons employed	255	125	100	15	5	10
Power consumed (in kilowatts)	1 500	1 000	500			
Proportion of plant maintenance costs attributable	—	40%	40%	20%		
Machine-hours	—	19 890	8 468			

Job orders worked on by the production department are to be charged with departmental overheads on a machine-hour basis.
The following are required:

1 A calculation of the machine-hour rates to be charged to the products of departments X and Y.

2 A calculation showing what the machine-hour rates would have been if the total power consumption had been 1 750 kilowatts (Department X 1 000; Department Y 500; Plant maintenance 250).

3 A note of any alternative basis of calculation which might have been used in (2) above, having particular regard to their value to management.

CDE Ltd – solution

1	*Total*	*X*	*Y*	*PH*	*PM*	*PD*
	£	£	£	£	£	£
Costs as given	10 202	3 800	2 702	1 550	1 300	850
(a) Allocation of personnel department costs (on the basis of number of employees, ignoring those in the PD)	—	425	340	51	34	(850)
(b) Allocation of plant maintenance costs (on the basis of the proportions given)	—	534	533	267	(1 334)	
(c) Allocation of power house costs (on the basis of the power consumed)	—	1 245	623	(1 868)		
	10 202	6 004	4 198			
Machine-hour rate =		$\frac{6\,004}{19\,890}$	$\frac{4\,198}{8\,468}$			
=		£0.319	£0.496	approximately		

2 The amended pattern of power consumption gives rise to the following two equations, due to the interdependence of power and maintenance:

$$PH = 1\,601 + (1/5)\,PM$$
$$PM = 1\,334 + (1/7)\,PH$$

By substitution

$$PH = 1\,601 + (1/5)\,\{1\,334 + (1/7)\,PH\}$$
$$PH = 1\,601 + 267 + (1/35)\,PH$$

Therefore

$$\tfrac{34}{35}\,PH = 1\,868, \quad PH = 1\,923 \text{ i.e. } (\tfrac{35}{34} \times 1\,868)$$

Similarly by substitution

$$PM = 1\,334 + (1/7)\,\{1\,601 + (1/5)\,PM\}$$
$$\tfrac{34}{35}\,PM = 1\,334 + 229$$

Therefore

$$PM = 1\,609 \text{ i.e. } (\tfrac{35}{34} \times 1\,563)$$

The following is the amended allocation:

	Total	*X*	*Y*	*PH*	*PM*
	£	£	£	£	£
	10 202	4 225	3 042	1 601	1 334
Allocation of PM	—	643	644	322	(1 609)
Allocation of PH	—	1 099	549	(1 923)	275
	10 202	5 967	4 235	—	—

Machine-hour rate = $\frac{£5\ 967}{19\ 890}$ $\frac{£4\ 235}{8\ 468}$

= £0.3 £0.5 approximately

3 Apart from the use of the attrition (or exhaustion) method, which gives the same answer as in (2) above, alternative methods of allocation for part 2 are, for example:

(*a*) to ignore the interdependence of these two service departments
(*b*) to close off first, say, the service department with the smaller amount of costs.

This necessarily means more approximate costing but where the size of the costs involved is relatively small these methods may be sufficient. With method (*a*) the calculations would then be as follows:

	Total	*X*	*Y*	*PH*	*PM*
	£	£	£	£	£
Allocation as in (1) above after allocating personnel department costs	10 202	4 225	3 042	1 601	1 334
Allocation of PM		667	667		(1 334)
Allocation of PH		1 067	534	(1 601)	
	10 202	5 959	4 243	—	—

With method (*b*) the calculation would be as follows:

	10 202	4 225	3 042	1 601	1 334
Allocation of PM		534	533	267	(1 334)
Allocation of PH		1 245	623	(1 868)	
	10 202	6 004	4 198	—	—

Of these two methods (*a*) would seem to give the less exact results but apart from the slightly more involved calculations there seems to be no good reason why the interdependence should not be recognized and use made of simultaneous equations.

DEF Ltd – the treatment of overheads

The following information relating to the month of June is extracted from the cost records of DEF Ltd, which makes mechanical toys, the parts of which are made in Department A and assembled in Department B.

	Total	*Department A*	*Department B*
Direct materials consumed (£)	6 500	5 000	1 500
Direct labour (£)	9 000	4 000	5 000
Direct-labour hours worked	80 000	30 000	50 000
Machine-hours worked	30 000	25 000	5 000
Factory rent, heat, light (£)	1 500		
Supervision wages (£)	600	250	350
Depreciation of machinery (£)	500		
Power (£)	400		
Repairs to machinery (£)	200	160	40
Indirect labour (£)	400	200	200
Machine horsepower (hp)	400	300	100
Book value of plant (£)	5 000	4 000	1 000
Floor space (ft^2)	20 000	10 000	10 000
Number of machines (ratio between departments)		2	1
The costs of batch X252 have been booked as follows:			
Materials (£)	320	270	50
Labour (£)	750	300	450

Direct-labour hours worked on batch X252 were 2 500 in Department A, and 5 000 in Department B. Machine-hours worked on this batch were 1 250 in Department A and 600 in Department B.

You are asked:

1 To advise how overhead expenses might be allocated to batch X252.
2 To consider objections which might be raised against the bases and methods of allocation used.
3 To calculate the cost of each unit in batch X252, assuming there are 1 000 units in the batch.

DEF Ltd

1 The most likely procedure would be to allocate overhead expenses first to departments on 'appropriate' bases, and separating machine costs from others, thus:

DEPARTMENTAL ALLOCATION

Expense	*Basis*	*Total* £	*Dept. A* £	*Dept. B* £
Depreciation	Plant values	500	400	100
Power	Horsepower hours	400	353	47
Repairs to machinery	Actual	200	160	40
Machine costs		1 100	913	187
Rent, etc.	Floor space	1 500	750	750
Supervision	Actual	600	250	350
Indirect labour	Actual	400	200	200
Non-machine costs		2 500	1 200	1 300

In each department, machine costs might now be allocated on the basis of a machine-hour rate, and other costs on the basis of a direct-labour rate.

These rates would be:

	Department A	*Department B*
Machine-hour rate	$\frac{£913}{25\ 000} = 3.65p$	$\frac{£187}{5\ 000} = 3.74p$
Labour-hour rate	$\frac{£1\ 200}{30\ 000} = 4.0p$	$\frac{£1\ 300}{50\ 000} = 2.6p$

This would give an oncost allocation to batch X252 as follows:

Department A:			
Machine costs	1 250 hours @ 3.65p	46	
Other costs	2 500 hours @ 4.0p	100	146
Department B:			
Machine costs	600 hours @ 3.74p	22	
Other costs	5 000 hours @ 2.6p	130	152
Total oncost allocation			£298

2 The allocation of overheads which has been made above on the basis of the information given is open to considerable objection on the grounds of the inappropriateness of the bases in detail and of the whole procedure in general.

As regards thc bases of allocation adopted:

(*a*) A floor-space basis for rent, etc., assumes that every square foot of space gives service of the same value as every other.
(*b*) Spreading supervision evenly over labour-hours assumes that all labour needs the same amount of supervision. This is not often true.
(*c*) The allocation of depreciation on the basis of plant values disregards differences in the extent to which different pieces of plant are subjected to wear and tear.
(*d*) A flat machine-hour rate for power costs within each department assumes that all machines in the department consume equal quantities of power per hour.
(*e*) Similarly, all machines do not need equal amounts of maintenance per hour run.

Some of these objections could be met by breaking the departments down into cost centres, with a separate machine rate for each centre. All machine-hours would then not be treated as being equally costly.

Objections on other grounds are that:

(*a*) No distinction is made between fixed and variable expenses. Avoidable costs will therefore be obscured by the type of calculation shown.
(*b*) A fall in production would result in a rise in the overhead rate. This, if passed on to customers, might cause the fall in business to become cumulative.

3	*Department A*		*Department B*			
	Total	*Unit*	*Total*	*Unit*	*Total*	*Unit*
	£	£	£	£	£	£
Materials	270	0.270	50	0.050	320	0.320
Labour	300	0.300	450	0.450	750	0.750
Overhead	146	0.146	152	0.152	298	0.298
Cost per component	716	0.716	652	0.652	1 368	1.368

EFG Ltd – the allocation of works overheads between jobs on an absorption basis

1 *Non-departmental rates*

The estimated total figures of a factory for a year are budgeted as follows:

	Income account £
Materials	40 000
Labour	60 000
Prime cost	100 000
Overheads	80 000
Total cost	180 000
Profit (10 per cent total cost)	18 000
Sales	£198 000

The total overhead costs are £80 000, the total hours of direct labour are 400 000, and the total number of machine-hours is 320 000, so average overheads per man-hour are £0.20 and per machine-hour are £0.25. Similarly, the total overhead cost is twice the material cost giving an overhead oncost of twice the job's material cost (800/400), and on a labour basis the relationship becomes 133 per cent of the labour cost (with labour being £60 000 and the overheads £80 000).

The 'cost' of a given contract, needing £800 of materials and £200 of labour (requiring 1 100 man-hours and 1 000 machine-hours), may be estimated by one of the following methods. (See table on p.266).

EFG LTD.

NON-DEPARTMENTAL RATES

	(1) *Material* £	(2) *Direct labour* £	(3) *Prime cost* £	(4) *Man-hour* £	(5) *Machine-hour* £
Material	800	800	800	800	800
Labour	200	200	200	200	200
Prime cost	1 000	1 000	1 000	1 000	1 000
Overheads	(2 × £800) = 1 600	($1\frac{1}{3}$ × £200) = 267	($\frac{4}{5}$ × £1 000) = 800	(1100 × £0.2) = 220	(1 000 × £0.25) = 250
Total cost	2 600	1 267	1 800	1 220	1 250
Profit	260	127	180	122	125
Sales	2 860	1 394	1 980	1 342	1 375

2 *Departmental rates*
EFG Ltd might have been organized in two departments, with departmental budgets as follows:

	INCOME ACCOUNTS			
		Department A		*Department B*
		£		£
Materials		30 000		10 000
Labour		40 000		20 000
Prime cost		70 000		30 000
Overheads		60 000		20 000
Total cost		130 000		50 000
Profit		13 000		5 000
Sales		143 000		55 000
Man-hours		200 000		200 000
Man-hour rate	(60 000 ÷ 200 000) =	£0.3	(20 000 ÷ 200 000) =	£0.1
Machine-hours		200 000		120 000
Machine-hour rate	(60 000 ÷ 200 000) =	£0.3	(20 000 ÷ 120 000) =	£0.16

Then the cost of the contract, requiring 750 man-hours and 750 machine-hours in Department A, and 350 man-hours and 250 machine-hours in Department B, would, under methods (4) and (5), be as follows: (See table on p.268).

[*Note.* It should be appreciated that the purpose of this illustration is to show the attempts commonly made in practice to allocate overheads. For the following reasons these attempts, on the bases used, may not be useful:

1 There is an assumption that the particular method of allocation is relevant to all management purposes.
2 Hence it may ignore the characteristics of the particular purpose in mind.
3 Allocations are usually made on an absorption basis rather than an incremental basis, and therefore ignore the problems relating to fixed costs, common costs, etc.
4 It proceeds by way of 'equitable' or 'reasonable' apportionments rather than those based upon economic realities.]

	MAN-HOUR METHOD				*MACHINE-HOUR METHOD*			
		Department A		*Department B*		*Department A*		*Department B*
		£		£		£		£
Materials		600		200		600		200
Labour		120		80		120		80
Prime cost		720		280		720		280
Overhead	(750×£0.3)=	225	(350×£0.1)=	35	(750×£0.3)=	225	(250×£0.16)=	40
Total cost		945		315		945		320
Profit		95		31		95		32
Sales		1 040		346		1 040		352

OVER AND UNDER RECOVERY

The actual overhead costs of a particular period will only be equal to the applied overheads of that period (i.e. predetermined overhead rate × number of units produced) by chance (unless, of course, the period's costs and activities were all rigidly determined in advance, or the forecaster was in the improbable position of having a perfect view of the future).

If more overheads are applied to units of output than are actually incurred, then overheads are said to be over-absorbed (or over-applied or over-recovered). Conversely, if too little overhead is applied to units of output, then overheads are said to be under-absorbed (under-applied, under-recovered). The degree to which overhead costs are over- or under-absorbed is a useful piece of management information. A record should be kept of the extent to which the overheads of each cost centre are over- or under-absorbed, and this can be a guide that indicates when overhead recovery rates require adjustment. (Because over- and under-absorbed overhead costs are charged directly to the profit-and-loss account, they are not reflected at all in any product cost. Clearly this is unsatisfactory in an absorption costing system that exists purely for product costing reasons.)

An over- or under-absorption of overheads may arise because the actual level of overhead costs has varied from the amount anticipated, or because the level of activity actually experienced during a period has differed from the level predicted. Either of these causes – or the two of them acting together – can render the predetermined overhead recovery rate inappropriate. (It is also possible for these two causes to act together in such a way that the overhead rate remains appropriate: thus an expected level of activity of 10 000 direct labour hours in conjunction with a predicted level of overhead costs of £20 000 gives an overhead rate per direct labour hour of £2.00. If costs actually amount to £25 000 and the level of activity was 12 500 direct labour hours, the effective overhead recovery rate remains £2.00 per direct labour hour.)

The explanations behind the major causes of over- and under-recovery are price rises, an expanding level of general economic activity, poor marketing, and so on. If plant capacity along with materials are available but sales volume is so low as to create an under-recovery of overheads, then this may be considered to be a marketing responsibility. However, if there is a backlog of orders and under-absorbed overhead costs results from the ineffective use of manufacturing facilities, then it becomes a manufacturing responsibility.

As suggested in Chapter 3, normalized overhead rates save having to make minor changes every month in attempting to recover precisely 100 per cent of overhead costs during a year. For example, if overheads are expected to be £60 000 for a forthcoming year in which a company is expected to produce 120 000 units of output at an uneven rate, then a monthly over-or under-recovery is bound to occur if a normalized rate of $\frac{£60\,000}{120\,000}$ = £0.50 per unit is chosen. However, over the full year it should even out.

Figure 9.15 illustrates this more fully, with cumulative figures for over- and under-recovered overheads balancing out over the whole period of 12 months. The effect of different monthly production levels of a more extreme nature is shown in Figure 9.16. If a normalized rate (of £3.715) is not used, the overhead per unit of product will vary from £51.00 at one extreme to £2.00 at the other, depending on the month in which the product was made (August or April). These extremes are unacceptable because they are not representative of the typical, or normalized, production circumstances which have a horizon beyond the end of the current month.

Apart from highlighting the need to use normalized overhead recovery rates for seasonal products, these examples further illustrate the point that the product costing imperative to absorb all overheads is of no value in controlling costs since cost control cannot operate under a regime that is confined to apportionments and absorption.

FIXED AND VARIABLE OVERHEAD RATES

So far the discussion has focused exclusively on deriving overhead rates that do not distinguish fixed from variable costs, but an important refinement of absorption costing is to derive different rates for both variable overheads and for fixed overheads.

Consider, for instance, a labour-intensive cost centre having estimated fixed overheads of £40 000 for a period, and estimated variable overheads of £30 000 for the same period, with an expectation of working 20 000 direct labour hours. A fixed overhead recovery rate of $\frac{£40\,000}{20\,000}$ = £2.00 per direct labour hour, and a variable overhead recovery rate of $\frac{£30\,000}{20\,000}$ = £1.50 per direct labour hour can be readily derived. If the actual figures for the period in question are:

Fixed overheads	£41 500
Variable overheads	£31 500
Direct labour hours	19 500

then the fixed overhead will be under-applied by £1 000 [i.e. £40 000 – (19 500 × £2.00)] whilst fixed overhead prices have risen by £2 500 [i.e. £41 500 –(19 500 × £2.00)]. Variable overheads to the extent of £29 250 (i.e. 19 500 × £1.50) will have been absorbed, but the actual variable overheads incurred (£31 500) are made up of price changes and inefficiencies of £2 250 (i.e. £31 500 – £29 250). (Chapter 11 will deal at greater length with this topic.)

To take a slightly more involved example, Figure 9.17 shows a flexible

Month	*Production units*	*Annual overhead rate (£)*	*Monthly applied overhead (£)*	*Monthly actual overhead (£)*	*Over-applied overhead (£)*	*Under-applied overhead (£)*	*Cumulative balance over (under) (£)*
January	6 000	0.5	3 000	4 200	—	1 200	(1 200)
February	5 500	0.5	2 750	4 100	—	1 350	(2 550)
March	8 000	0.5	4 000	4 600	—	600	(3 150)
April	11 000	0.5	5 500	5 200	300	—	(2 850)
May	16 000	0.5	8 000	6 200	1 800	—	(1 050)
June	19 000	0.5	9 500	6 800	2 700	—	1 650
July	11 000	0.5	5 500	5 200	300	—	1 950
August	8 000	0.5	4 000	4 600	—	600	1 350
September	10 500	0.5	5 250	5 100	150	—	1 500
October	13 000	0.5	6 500	5 600	900	—	2 400
November	7 000	0.5	3 500	4 400	—	900	1 500
December	5 000	0.5	2 500	4 000	—	1 500	—
Total	120 000	0.5	60 000	60 000	6 150	6 150	0

Figure 9.15: Over- and under-recovered overheads

Month	*Total budgeted overhead (£)*	*Units to be produced*	*Monthly rate per unit (£)*	*Annual rate per unit (£)*
January	70 000	20 000	3.50	3.715
February	80 000	30 000	2.67	3.715
March	90 000	40 000	2.25	3.715
April	100 000	50 000	2.00	3.715
May	65 000	15 000	4.33	3.715
June	60 000	10 000	6.00	3.715
July	55 000	5 000	11.00	3.715
August	51 000	1 000	51.00	3.715
September	55 000	5 000	11.00	3.715
October	60 000	10 000	6.00	3.715
November	65 000	15 000	4.33	3.715
December	70 000	20 000	3.50	3.715
	821 000	221 000	—	3.715

Figure 9.16: Monthly and annual overhead rates

budget for a machining department of a company for anticipated monthly levels of activity. This budget gives a variable overhead rate of £1.70 per direct labour hour. If variable overhead costs have been properly analysed and classified, and if the estimates forming the basis of the flexible budget are accurate, then this rate should be valid over the relevant range.

Standard direct labour hours	8 000	9 000	10 000	11 000
Variable factory overhead:				
Material handling	£8 000	£9 000	£10 000	£11 000
Idle time	800	900	1 000	1 100
Rework	800	900	1 000	1 100
Overtime premium	400	450	500	550
Supplies	3 600	4 050	4 500	4 950
Total	£13 600	£15 300	£17 000	£18 700
Variable overhead rate = £1.70 per direct labour hour				

Figure 9.17: Flexible overhead budget

Fixed overheads cannot be absorbed on the basis of this type of flexible budget, but must be absorbed on the basis of some predetermined estimate of capacity utilization – such as normal capacity (as discussed in Chapter 3). Let us suppose that normal capacity is 10 000 direct labour hours, and that the combined flexible budget is shown in Figure 9.18.

At normal capacity of 10 000 direct labour hours, the fixed overhead recovery rate is given by $\frac{£10\,000}{10\,000}$ = £1.00 per direct labour hour.

The combined overhead rate (at a normal level of output of 10 000 direct labour hours) is thus a variable rate of £1.70 per direct labour hour and a fixed rate of £1.00 per direct labour hour, amounting to £2.70 per direct labour hour.

WHY ABSORB OVERHEADS?

The simple answer to this question is 'product costing'. Overheads are applied to products because management needs to have some idea of the fully absorbed cost of each product as a guide, perhaps, for pricing decisions, as a basis for inventory valuation, and hence as a prerequisite to income measurement (i.e. the determination of profit). *But* flexible budgets require the predetermining of overhead rates also, and the purpose of flexible budgets is to control costs.

			Normal capacity	
Standard direct labour hours	8 000	9 000	10 000	11 000
Variable factory overhead:				
Material handling	£8 000	£9 000	£10 000	£11 000
Idle time	800	900	1 000	1 100
Rework	800	900	1 000	1 100
Overtime premium	400	450	500	550
Supplies	3 600	4 050	4 500	4 950
Total	£13 600	£15 300	£17 000	£18 700
Variable overhead rate = £1.70 per direct labour hour				
Fixed factory overhead:				
Supervision	1 700	1 700	1 700	1 700
Depreciation—plant	2 000	2 000	2 000	2 000
Depreciation—equipment	5 000	5 000	5 000	5 000
Rates	1 000	1 000	1 000	1 000
Insurance	300	300	300	300
Total	£10 000	£10 000	£10 000	£10 000
Fixed overhead rate for normal capacity = £1.00 per direct labour hour				

Figure 9.18: Combined flexible overhead budget

If a company has estimated the level of sales for the next operating period, and if the planned overhead costs have been spread over the planned output along with the expected prime costs, then management may tend to feel that as long as the company sells the budgeted level of output of each product at a price that is at least equivalent to the sum of prime cost plus overhead element plus required profit margin, the company will achieve at least its planned level of profit. This way of thinking focuses attention on 'full' cost, but since different expenses are aggregated in overhead recovery rates, it is difficult to see what is implied in a unit overhead cost figure, and hence in a unit 'full' cost figure. The very fact that any one of several bases may be used for both apportioning and absorbing overhead costs, with the resulting full cost differing under each method, demonstrates the lack of accuracy and meaning that may be exhibited. However, when a company must base its prices on cost plus a desired profit margin (as in contracting), then overheads must be allocated to jobs. Yet pricing on the basis of full costs in other circumstances can be distinctly damaging. For instance, the higher the level of activity, the lower will be the unit full cost. (That is, direct material cost per unit, direct labour cost per unit, and variable overhead cost per unit are all assumed to be constant within the limits of the relevant range, but fixed overhead costs are lower per unit the more units over which they are spread.) This means that a company using full cost as its basis for pricing will tend to have lower prices the higher the level of activity and higher prices the lower the level of activity. Let us assume that a company bases its prices on full cost plus 25 per cent, that fixed overhead costs are £10 000 per period, and that the level of sales may vary from 100 000 units (giving a unit fixed overhead element of £0.10) to 50 000 units (giving a unit fixed overhead element of £0.20).

Assume that direct material cost is £0.25 per unit, direct labour cost is £0.30 per unit and variable overhead cost is £0.15 per unit. Then the price per unit can be calculated as in Figure 9.19.

	High sales 100 000 units	*Low sales 50 000 units*
Direct material cost	0.25	0.25
Direct labour cost	0.30	0.30
Variable overhead cost	0.15	0.15
Fixed overhead cost	0.10	0.20
Full cost	0.80	0.90
Profit @ 25 per cent	0.20	0.225
Selling price per unit	£1.00	£1.125

Figure 9.19: Cost-plus pricing

The outcome of cost-plus pricing may be to depress sales when it is desired to encourage sales because prices rise as demand falls. Cost-plus pricing is unable to respond to market conditions, and for this reason – along with a general dissatisfaction with overhead allocations – marginal costing has been more and more widely adopted in recent years. Whilst absorption costing aims to ascertain the 'full' cost of jobs and processes, marginal costing aims to deal with the effects of changes in either the volume or type of output.

MARGINAL COSTING

Marginal – or direct – costing is concerned with differences in aggregate cost (i.e. direct labour + direct material + direct expense + variable overhead) caused by producing one unit more or one unit less (where a 'unit' will usually – but not always – refer to a unit of manufactured output).

Marginal costing is essentially short run in nature and is concerned with variable costs. In contrast, differential costing (also known as incremental costing or relevant costing – see next section in this chapter) is concerned with longer-run questions (e.g. adding or dropping a product line, make-or-buy decisions, lease-versus-own decisions, etc.), and since these questions involve a consideration of the costs of following one course of action rather than another, fixed costs are important.

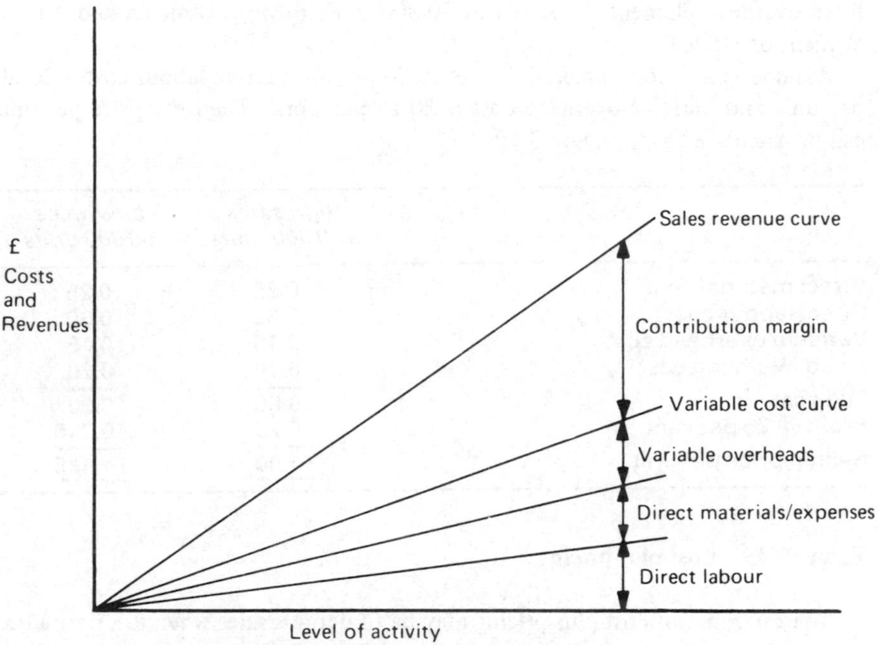

Figure 9.20: Contribution margin

In direct costing systems, fixed overheads are viewed as being *period costs* and are charged directly to the profit-and-loss account as costs of a period of time instead of being spread over processes and units of output as product costs. Fixed costs are thus treated as costs of being in business rather than as operating costs related to manufacturing given product lines. This approach facilitates the analysis of the effects of changes in the volume and type of output by means of the cost-volume-profit (or break-even) technique. The fundamental distinction between variable costs and fixed costs is here seen to be of great significance yet again in controlling costs – for flexible budgets, in cost-volume-profit analysis, and in marginal costing.

The highlight of marginal costing is the contribution margin (i.e. the excess of sales revenue over variable cost). This margin represents the contribution that the item in question makes to fixed costs and profit. In Figure 9.20 it is the distance between the variable cost curve and the revenue curve.

In simple equation form:

Contribution = sales revenue − variable costs
Since: sales revenue = fixed costs + variable costs + profit
By substitution: contribution = fixed costs + profit

A contribution margin per unit can be easily worked out. If the selling price of a product is £1.00 and its variable cost amounts to £0.60 then the contribution margin will be £0.40. The immediate implication of this is that for every increase in sales, 40 per cent of that increase for this product is the contribution towards fixed costs and profit. If the level of fixed costs is £100 000 and it is sought to make a profit of £50 000, how many units should be sold? The answer can be readily determined by substituting known variables into the basic equation:

Sales revenue = fixed costs + variable costs + profit
Let R = desired sales revenue, and it is already known that FC = £100 000.
P = £50 000, and VC = 0.60R.
Then: $R = 100\,000 + 0.60R + 50\,000$
Therefore $0.40R = 150\,000$
Therefore $R = 375\,000$ @ £1.00 = £375 000

Or more simply: $$\frac{\text{Fixed costs + profit}}{\text{Contribution margin}} = \frac{150\,000}{0.40} = 375\,000$$

Two detailed examples will help to illustrate the role of cost-volume-profit analysis.

FGH Ltd – cost-volume-profit analysis

The operating results of FGH Ltd for the past two years have been as follows:

	1973	1974
	£	£
Sales	300 000	360 000
Operating expenses	290 000	326 000
Net income	10 000	34 000

The company sells only one product at a price of £0.75 per unit. As the result of a study of operations, the company concludes that all variable costs are a linear function of output. At normal capacity the plant is capable of turning out 600 000 units a year.

The following are required:

1 At what volume of sales (in £) does the company break even?
2 What is the average total unit cost at 75 per cent of capacity?
3 At what volume would a profit of £50 000 be made?
4 At what volume would a profit of £40 000 be secured after income taxes at a 30 per cent rate are paid?
5 Due to generally improved economic prospects for 1975 the company anticipates that its profit showing for 1975 will be improved. However, it is attempting to choose from among the following alternative policies. For each case determine what profits would be. (In all cases changes are changes from 1974 figures.)

   (*a*) With no change in price or product, unit sales will increase by 5 per cent.
   (*b*) If unit price is increased by 10 per cent, unit sales will decline by 5 per cent.
   (*c*) If unit price is cut by 5 per cent, unit sales will increase by 15 per cent. cent.
   (*d*) If improved materials are used and sales price is unchanged, unit sales will increase by 20 per cent. The improved materials will increase variable costs by 5 per cent.
   (*e*) If advertising expenditures are increased by £25 000 and unit price is advanced by 10 per cent, unit sales will be unchanged.

Variable costs = 36 000/60 000 = 60 per cent, so p/v = 40 per cent (i.e. sales have increased by £60 000 and costs – all of which are variable – by £36 000 so p/v = 40 per cent). Since $R = VC + FC + P$, using the 1973 data we have: £300 000 = 0.6(300 000) + FC + £10 000.
Therefore fixed costs = £110 000.

Therefore 1 $0 = 0.4R - 110\,000$

$R = 275\,000$

2 T (total unit cost) $= 0.6(0.75) + \frac{110\,000}{450\,000}$

$= 0.45 + 0.24 = 0.69$

3 $50\,000 = 0.4R - 110\,000$

$400\,000 = R$

4 $P = \frac{p}{v}R - FC - \left(\frac{r}{1-r}\right)P$ where r is rate of income tax

$40\,000 = 0.4R - 110\,000 - \frac{0.3}{0.7}40\,000$

$417\,857 = R$

5 $P = \frac{p}{v}R - FC$

(*a*) $P = [0.4(1.05)\,360\,000] - 110\,000$

(*b*) $P = [\frac{0.4 + 0.1}{1.0 + 0.1}\,360\,000(1.10)(0.95)] - 110\,000$

(*c*) $P = [\frac{0.4 - 0.05}{1 - 0.05}\,360\,000(0.95)(1.15)] - 110\,000$

(*d*) $P = [\frac{(1 - (0.60 + 0.03))}{1.00}\,360\,000(1.2)] - 110\,000$

(*e*) $P = [\frac{0.4 + 1}{1 + 0.1}\,360\,000(1.1)] - (110\,000 + 25\,000)$

GHI Ltd – cost-volume-profit analysis

Assume the following:

Present sales: £400 000
Variable cost: £0.75 per £ of sales
Fixed cost: £80 000

1 Find the effect on profit of:

(*a*) A decrease of 20 per cent in sales.
(*b*) An increase of 20 per cent in sales.

2 Same as (1) above except that the variable costs equal £0.60 per £ of sales.

3 Assuming the same data as in (1), what is the effect on profit at present unit volume of:

(*a*) An increase in sales price of 10 per cent, other factors remaining the same?
(*b*) A decrease in sales price of 10 per cent, other factors remaining the same?

4 Assuming the same data as in (1), what is the effect on profit at present unit volume of:

(*a*) An increase of 6 per cent in the variable cost?
(*b*) A decrease of 6 per cent in the variable cost?

5 Assuming the same data as in (1), what is the effect on profit at present unit volume of:

(*a*) An increase of 10 per cent in the fixed cost?
(*b*) A decrease of 10 per cent in the fixed cost?

Revenue = variable cost + fixed cost + profit

$$R = VC + FC + P$$

1 (a) $400\,000(0.8) = 0.75(400\,000)(0.8) + 80\,000 + P$
therefore $P = 0$

(b) $400\,000(1.2) = 0.75(400\,000)(1.2) + 80\,000 + P$
therefore $P =$ £40 000 (profits doubled)

2 (a) $P =$ £48 000

(b) $P =$ £112 000

3 (a) $400\,000(1.1) = \frac{0.75}{1.10}(400\,000)(1.1) + 80\,000 + P$
therefore $P =$ £60 000 (profits tripled)

(b) $400\,000(0.9) = \frac{0.75}{0.90}(400\,000)0.9 + 80\,000 + P$
therefore $P = -$ £20 000

4 *(a)* $400\,000 = 0.795(400\,000) + 80\,000 + P$
therefore $P = £2\,000$
(b) $400\,000 = 0.705(400\,000) + 80\,000 + P$
therefore $P = £38\,000$
5 *(a)* $400\,000 = 0.75(400\,000) + 1.1(80\,000) + P$
therefore $P = £12\,000$ (profits reduced by 40 per cent)
(b) $400\,000 = 0.75(400\,000) + 0.9(80\,000) + P$
therefore $P = £28\,000$ (profits increased by 40 per cent)

Alternative calculations for solving problems 5(*a*) and 5(*b*) may be based on the equation:

$$\text{Profit} = \tfrac{P}{V}R - FC$$

thus:

(*a*) $P = 0.25(400\,000) - 1.1(80\,000)$, and
(*b*) $P = 0.25(400\,000) - 0.9(80\,000)$.

Determining total contribution

It is important to determine how much contribution exists for a given product line, and whether the total contribution from all product lines is sufficient to cover fixed costs and leave a satisfactory profit. Let us take the example of a company producing three products – A, B and C – with aggregate cost, profit, and sales figures as shown in Figure 9.21.

	Product A	*Product B*	*Product C*	*Total*
	£	£	£	£
Direct materials	20 400	35 600	16 000	72 000
Direct labour	6 000	12 200	1 800	20 000
Overheads	6 600	13 500	1 900	22 000
Total cost	33 000	61 300	19 700	114 000
Profit	2 000	3 700	300	6 000
Sales revenue	35 000	65 000	20 000	120 000

Figure 9.21: Cost, profit and sales revenue summary

It would seem from Figure 9.21 that product A is making a profit of £2 000, and if product A is deleted from the range it may be thought that total profit would fall to £4 000 from its current level of £6 000. But the allocation of overheads (of £6 600) to product A includes various fixed overhead costs amounting to, say, £5 500 that would still need to be paid even though product A was no longer in the range. Let us suppose that £5 275 of this amount is transferred (i.e. re-allocated) to product B and the balance of £225 is re-allocated to product C. The outcome of deleting product A and transferring the fixed charges is given in Figure 9.22.

	Product B £	*Product C* £	*Total* £
Direct material	35 600	16 000	51 600
Direct labour	12 200	1 800	14 000
Overheads	18 775	2 125	20 900
Total cost	66 575	19 925	86 500
Profit or (loss)	(1 575)	75	(1 500)
Sales revenue	65 000	20 000	85 000

Figure 9.22: Revised cost, profit and sales summary – 1

Figure 9.22 shows that the deletion of product A causes a reduction in profit of £7 500 (i.e. from a profit of £6 000 to a loss of £1 500). To think that the fall in profit would only be £2 000 is clearly erroneous because it ignores the fixed costs that must be re-allocated once A is deleted. Mistaken assumptions can be avoided if fixed overheads are separated from variable overheads (in accordance with Figure 9.23) in such a way that the contribution that each product makes to common fixed overheads and profit is evident. The contribution approach is highlighted in Figure 9.24.

	Product A £	*Product B* £	*Product C* £	*Total* £
Direct materials	20 400	35 600	16 000	72 000
Direct labour	6 000	12 200	1 800	20 000
Variable overheads	1 100	6 600	1 625	9 325
Marginal cost	27 500	54 400	19 425	101 325
Fixed overheads	5 500	6 900	275	12 675
Total cost	33 000	61 300	19 700	114 000

Figure 9.23: Revised cost, profit and sales summary – 2

If a product is not covering its marginal cost (i.e. it is making a negative contribution), it would be essential to ensure that its selling price is not too low (given its quality in relation to competitive products) and that the production methods and materials are appropriate. In cases where a product's sales revenue is below its marginal cost but prices cannot be increased and production methods cannot be improved, careful consideration should be given before it is

	Product A £	*Product B* £	*Product C* £	*Total* £
Sales	35 000	65 000	20 000	120 000
Marginal cost	27 500	54 400	19 425	101 325
Contribution	7 500	10 600	575	18 675
Total fixed costs				12 675
Profit				6 000

Figure 9.24: Contribution margin statement

deleted lest the picture of Figure 9.21 is found.

An illustration of marginal costing and pricing is given below.

HIJ Ltd – marginal costing

HIJ Ltd manufactures a product which costs:

Fixed (per month)	£1 000
Variable (per unit)	£0.10

Sales are currently 10 000 units per month at £0.30 per unit. The company's sales manager proposes that the company should sell in a foreign market where demand for an additional 5 000 units per month is expected. However, in order to do this it will be necessary to absorb additional shipping costs and duties amounting to £0.12 per unit.

1. Will the foreign business be profitable?
2. A domestic chain store has offered to take 5 000 units per month at £0.18 per unit. Should this order be accepted in place of the foreign order?
3. The sales department proposes that the selling price of the company's product be reduced to increase sales. It submits the following estimates of sales volume anticipated at various prices:

£0.30 per unit (present price)	10 000 per month
£0.25 per unit	14 000 per month
£0.20 per unit	19 000 per month

   (*a*) Assuming the above estimates are correct, should the price be reduced?

   (*b*) What effect will price reduction have on the rate of profit on sales?

1

		£
Marginal revenue per unit		0.30
Marginal cost per unit:		
Variable cost	0.10	
Additional shipping costs and duties	0.12	0.22
Net Revenue for each additional unit sold		£0.08

The foreign business would therefore be profitable on the basis of the information given. If expectations are realized then profit will increase (or losses diminish) by 5 000 × 12 × £0.08 = £4 800 per annum.

2

	£
Marginal revenue per unit	0.18
Variable cost per unit	0.10
Additional net revenue per unit	£0.08

On the basis of the information given, and assuming that it could not accept both, the company would be indifferent to whether it accepted home or foreign business. A decision on which alternative to take should be made in the light of the company's further knowledge of the different markets. In principle, the company would be concerned about whichever of the two markets is likely to be the more profitable to exploit in the long run. In this connection the company would be concerned with such matters as:

(*a*) Which of the two markets offered the best growth prospects economically.
(*b*) Which of the two markets (home or foreign) was more subject to economic fluctuations from the points of view of the economy in general and the specific industry in particular.
(*c*) The likelihood of exchange rate fluctuations.
(*d*) Foreign trade is more subject to the influence of international political considerations.
(*e*) The possibility of tariffs and duties on exports from the home country and imports into the foreign market.
(*f*) An increase in the supply of the product on the home market may be more likely to have price repercussions for the company if the company has a much bigger share of the home market than of the foreign market.
(*g*) The firm's name may be better known at home.
(*h*) If the foreign market is to be. further expanded, greater additional sales effort per added sale may be required, etc.

3(*a*)

	Estimate 1 (£0.3)		Estimate 2 (£0.25)		Estimate 3 (£0.2)	
Revenue per month		£3 000		£3 500		£3 800
Costs per month:						
Fixed	1 000		1 000		1 000	
Variable	1 000		1 400		1 900	
		2 000		2 400		2 900
Net revenue		£1 000		£1 100		£900

Net revenue is greatest at a price of 25p per unit and, accordingly, the price should be reduced to that amount.

3(*b*)

	Estimate 1	*Estimate 2*	*Estimate 3*
Percentage profit to sales (approximately)	33.33	31.43	23.68

It should be noted that the point at which net profit percentage to sales is greatest is not necessarily the point at which total net profit is greatest in absolute terms.

Margin of safety

Within the context of marginal costing and cost-volume-profit analysis, a useful concept is that of the *margin of safety*. This refers to the amount by which sales revenue can fall before a loss is incurred. For instance, if a company can break even at 50 per cent of expected sales, then it has a margin of safety of 50 per cent. The expected sales level may be 1 000 units, and the break-even volume may be sales of 500 units, so sales can fall by 500 units or 50 per cent before a loss will be made and the margin of safety is given by the formula:

$$\frac{\text{Actual sales} - \text{break-even sales}}{\text{Actual sales}}$$

$$\text{Margin of safety} = \frac{1\,000 - 500}{1\,000} = 0.5 = 50 \text{ per cent}$$

Summary of the value of marginal costing

The following points summarize the value of the contribution approach of cost-volume-profit analysis and marginal costing to management planning and control:

1. A change in either the selling price of a product or its variable cost rate will alter the break-even point and the contribution margin ratio (i.e. the proportion of sales revenue that is left when variable cost is deducted).
2. When sales are above the break-even point, a high contribution margin ratio will result in greater profits than will a small contribution margin ratio.
3. A low contribution margin ratio will require a large increase in sales volume to create a significant increase in profit.
4. If other factors stay constant, a change in total fixed costs will alter the break-even point by the same percentage and the net profit will vary by the same amount as the change in total fixed costs.
5. A large margin of safety will mean that a major fall in sales can occur before losses are incurred.

ABSORPTION COSTING VERSUS DIRECT COSTING

There are various advantages of using marginal costing, amongst the most important of which are the following:

1. Marginal costing systems are simpler to operate than are absorption costing systems because they do not involve the problems of overhead apportionments and recovery. This makes costs easier to identify and accumulate, and it does not confuse product costing with cost control.
2. Marginal costing avoids the difficulties of having to explain the purpose and basis of overhead absorption to management that accompany absorption costing. Fluctuations in profit are easier to explain because they result from cost-volume interactions and not from changes in inventory. (In absorption costing systems a varying element of fixed overhead will be contained in the cost of inventories, and fluctuations in inventory levels can affect profit due to the fixed cost element. However, marginal costing introduces a direct relationship between sales volume and marginal income (i.e. the contribution).)
3. It is easier to make decisions on the basis of marginal cost presentations. For example, marginal costing shows which products are making a contribution and which are failing to cover their avoidable (i.e. variable) costs. Under absorption costing the relevant information is difficult to gather, and there is the added danger that management may be misled by reliance on unit costs that contain an element of irrelevant fixed costs.

However, on the other side of the coin are various disadvantages of using marginal costing. For example:

1 Economic selling prices over the long run cannot be set without some attention being paid to fixed costs. Each product line/job must not just cover its marginal costs, but collectively the contributions of all jobs must cover at least all costs if a profit is to be made.
2 The importance of time tends to be overlooked in marginal costing: two jobs may have the same marginal cost, but one may take twice as long to complete as the other and hence its 'true' cost will be more. This aspect of capacity-utilization is not brought out in marginal costing (but see the example – LMN Ltd – later in this chapter).
3 The difficulties and dangers of spreading fixed overhead costs do not mean that they should be ignored: they are just as vital as are direct wage costs, etc. In fact, as production becomes more automated and greater in volume, more costs will tend to be fixed, and hence they should not be overlooked.

The choice between using absorption costing and marginal costing will be determined by such factors as:

1 The system of financial control in use (e.g. responsibility accounting is inconsistent with absorption costing).
2 The production methods in use (e.g. marginal costing is favoured in simple processing situations in which all products receive similar attention; but when different products receive widely differing amounts of attention, then absorption costing may be more realistic).
3 The significance of the prevailing level of fixed overhead costs.

How a cost system is to be used is more important than its form, since a technique *per se* does not achieve anything. From the point of view of cost control, a costing system should be able to promptly show costs that are running out of control, guide corrective action, indicate the effects of alternative decisions, and focus on helping to secure control rather than being the perfect systems design.

The two examples that follow should reinforce many of the points made in this section.

IJK Ltd – direct costing

The following data refer to certain operations of IJK Ltd for the year 1974:

	1st quarter	*2nd quarter*	*3rd quarter*
Sales	800 000 units	800 000 units	800 000 units
Production	800 000 units	1 000 000 units	600 000 units

Selling price per unit is £2.50. Labour, material, and variable overhead cost per unit is £1.20. Fixed manufacturing overhead cost per quarter is £800 000. Fixed overhead is charged to jobs at a rate based on capacity of 1 000 000 units. Under-absorbed overhead is treated as an addition to cost of goods sold.

The following are required:

1 Prepare gross profit tabulations for each quarter under (*a*) absorption costing methods and (*b*) direct costing methods.
2 Prepare reconciliations of the gross profit figures for each quarter.

1 (*a*) *Absorption costing*

	1st quarter £	*2nd quarter* £	*3rd quarter* £
Sales	2 000 000	2 000 000	2 000 000
Cost of goods sold:			
Opening inventory	0	0	400 000
Production costs	1 600 000	2 000 000	1 200 000
	1 600 000	2 000 000	1 600 000
Ending inventory	0	400 000	0
Cost of goods sold	1 600 000	1 600 000	1 600 000
Under-absorbed overhead	160 000	0	320 000
Total cost of goods sold	1 760 000	1 600 000	1 920 000
Gross profit (absorption basis)	£240 000	£400 000	£80 000

The cost per unit on an absorption basis is:

Labour, materials, and variable overheads	1.20
Fixed overheads $\frac{800\,000}{1\,000\,000} = 0.8$ per unit	0.80
Production cost	£2.00

Since only 800 000 units are produced instead of the capacity volume of 1 000 000 units there is an under-absorption in the first quarter of 0.8(1 000 000 – 800 000) = £160 000. In the second quarter the total fixed overhead of £800 000 is absorbed by the capacity production, while there is a further under-absorption of 0.8(1 000 000 – 600 000) = £320 000 in the third quarter. Because there is a closing inventory at the end of the second quarter of 200 000 units, it will be evident that these units contain 200 000 × £0.8 = £160 000 of fixed overheads that are carried forward to the third quarter. In direct costing, fixed overheads are written off during the period in which they were incurred, and not carried forward.

1(*b*) *Direct costing*

	1st quarter £	*2nd quarter* £	*3rd quarter* £
Sales	2 000 000	2 000 000	2 000 000
Direct cost of goods sold:			
Opening inventory	0	0	240 000
Direct production costs	960 000	1 200 000	720 000
	960 000	1 200 000	960 000
Ending inventory	0	240 000	0
Direct cost of goods sold	960 000	960 000	960 000
Marginal income	1 040 000	1 040 000	1 040 000
Fixed costs	800 000	800 000	800 000
Gross profit (direct basis)	£240 000	£240 000	£240 000

2 *Profit reconciliation*

	£	£	£
Gross profit on direct costing basis	240 000	240 000	240 000
Change in fixed costs in inventory	0	+160 000	−160 000
Gross profit on absorption costing basis	£240 000	£400 000	£80 000

JKL Ltd – absorption and direct costing

JKL Ltd absorbs manufacturing overheads by means of departmental overhead rates. Stocks of materials and parts are valued at average full cost, including absorbed overhead. The overhead rates in the company's three factory departments are:

Machining: £1.00 per £1.00 of direct labour.
Wiring: £1.50 per £1.00 of direct labour.
Assembly: £2.00 per £1.00 of direct labour.

The company now has an opportunity to submit a bid covering the requirements of a local authority for 1 000 units of a custom product. This product is an assembly of four parts, two of which are now carried in stock. The analysis of the most recent job cost sheets for these two parts was as follows:

Cost per unit	*Base number 101* £	*Subassembly number 463* £
Materials	0.30	1.80
Labour		
Machining	0.12	0.50
Wiring	—	2.50
Assembly	0.04	0.50
Overhead allocation	0.20	5.25
Total	£0.66	£10.55

The remaining two parts, a gauge and a cover, can be purchased from an outside supplier at a unit price of £2.50 and £1.80 respectively.

To manufacture this custom product, JKL Ltd will have to attach the gauge to the subassembly in the wiring department and assemble this with the base in the assembly department. The estimated labour costs of these operations are £0.10 and £0.30 respectively.

The following are required:

1 Prepare a cost estimate for this custom product, following the absorption costing principle.

2 Assuming that variable overheads per direct labour £ in the three departments are £0.50, £0.70, and £1.00 respectively,

(*a*) Compute the stock value of the two manufactured parts if JKL Ltd followed the direct costing principle.

(*b*) Prepare a cost estimate for the custom product based on the direct costing principle.

3 Assuming that from inside information it is known that the lowest rival bid of equal quality is £15 per unit, how should JKL Ltd react? (Make any assumption you consider necessary.)

1 *Cost estimate – absorption costing*

	£	
Base (as given)	0.66	
Subassembly (as given)	10.55	
Gauge (at cost)	2.50	
Cover (at cost)	1.80	
Attaching conversion cost		
(0.1 × 1.5) + 0.1	0.25	
Assembly conversion cost		
(0.3 × 2.0) + 0.3	0.90	
Unit cost	£16.66	× 1 000 = £16 660

2(*a*) *Cost estimate (parts) – direct costing*

	Base £		*Subassembly* £	
Materials (at cost)	0.30		1.80	
Labour	0.16		3.50	
Variable overhead				
Machining	0.06	(0.5 × 0.12)	0.25	(0.5 × 0.5)
Wiring	—		1.75	(0.7 × 2.5)
Assembly	0.04	(1.0 × 0.04)	0.50	(1.0 × 0.5)
	£0.56		£7.80	

2 (*b*) *Cost estimate (whole product) – direct costing*

	£	
Base (as in 2(*a*) above)	0.56	
Subassembly (as in 2(*a*) above)	7.80	
Gauge (at cost)	2.50	
Cover (at cost)	1.80	
Attaching conversion cost		
(0.1 × 0.7) + 0.1	0.17	
Assembly conversion cost		
(0.3 × 1.0) + 0.3	0.60	
Unit cost	£13.43	× 1 000 = £13 430

3 *Reaction*

Assuming that capacity is available, any quotation accepted above £13 430 will make some contribution to fixed costs and thus add to profit. To quote £15 000 or higher would be pointless assuming the information concerning competition is reliable. JKL Ltd may also with to anticipate future cost increases in formulating its bid. The decision depends mainly on other opportunities of using available capacity (perhaps contributing more to profit). There may be a step to further more lucrative business with the local authority. Absorption cost in any case is irrelevant.

RELEVANT COSTING

The question of whether absorption or marginal costing is 'best' emphasizes the relevance of *purpose* in cost accounting. Different costs are required for different purposes: for cost control purposes, absorption costing has little relevance, whilst marginal and differential costing have great relevance. In fact, a ***relevant costing*** approach is the most desirable from a cost control viewpoint.

For rational decision-making and effective control, management must have reports showing the interrelationships of costs, volume, and profit. This involves distinguishing fixed from variable costs, controllable from uncontrollable costs, and joint from separable costs. Given these distinctions, the relevant costing approach shows differences between alternatives as a basis for choice. Absorption costing is inadequate when considering, for example, a change in the level of sales and the impact of this on profit, because overheads will have been spread on the basis of a normalized level of activity which is inappropriate as a basis for making decisions relating to alternative levels of activity.

The relevant costing approach is shown in the examples that follow.

KLM Ltd – cost analysis

KLM Ltd consists of three departments, grinding, turning, and milling, all of which have the same productive capacity. The overheads budget for the next cost period of 1 000 machine-hours' capacity for each department is as follows:

	Fixed costs	*Directly variable costs (per machine-hour)*
	£	£
Grinding	2 000	0.25
Turning	1 000	0.20
Milling	750	0.375

A tender by the company is invited in respect of each of three contracts, X, Y, and Z, and it appears to the management that no other work is likely to become available during the cost period in question.

The works manager has studied the specifications relating to these three contracts and makes the following calculations with regard to costs and production times:

	Contract X	*Contract Y*	*Contract Z*
	£	£	£
Direct materials costs	1 800	1 610	1 240
Direct labour costs (rate per hour) which differ due to the varying skills involved:			
Grinding	0.30	0.25	0.45
Turning	0.20	0.25	0.40
Milling	0.15	0.20	0.225
Use of capacity (in machine-hours):			
Grinding	660	400	400
Turning	760	500	420
Milling	864	400	320

It will be necessary to employ three men in each department for the number of hours during which machine facilities are used on the work in respect of each of the three contracts.

The following are required:

1. A comparative statement showing the minimum amount at which the firm could afford to accept each of these contracts.
2. Would it make any difference to your calculations if you were informed that it was necessary to employ at least one man (included under direct labour) in each department regardless of the level of activity? If so, indicate the necessary amendments to your computations under (1) above.
3. Assuming that each of the three tenders would be accepted by the customer concerned if the manufacturer quoted the following prices: contract X £4 100, Y £3 200, Z £2 650, advise the manufacturer what he should do concerning contracts to be accepted, if any, if the circumstances are (a) as in (1) above, and (b) as in (2) above.

1 *Avoidable costs of the jobs*

		Contract X £		*Contract Y* £		*Contract Z* £
Materials		1 800		1 610		1 240
Labour:						
Grinding	198		100		180	
Turning	152		125		168	
Milling	130		80		72	
	480×3=1 440		305×3=915		420×3=1 260	
Directly variable costs:						
Grinding	165		100		100	
Turning	152		100		84	
Milling	324		150		120	
		641		350		304
Minimum amount on unavoidable cost basis		£3 881		£2 875		£2 804
2 The wages for one worker would now be a fixed cost and should therefore be deducted from the avoidable costs		3 881 480		2 875 305		2 804 420
Revised avoidable cost		3 401		2 570		2 384
3(*a*) Contract prices		4 100		3 200		2 650
Avoidable costs as in (1) above		3 881		2 875		2 804
Net revenue (or loss)		219		325		(154)

Capacity is sufficient to undertake each of the three contracts separately or contracts Y and Z combined. It will pay the manufacturer to accept contract Y only on the basis of the above calculations.

3(*b*)				
	Contract prices	4 100	3 200	2 650
	Avoidable costs as in (2) above	3 401	2 570	2 384
	Net revenues	699	630	266
			Combined profit 896	

In these circumstances it would be preferable to accept contracts Y and Z combined, since capacity is sufficient and the total net revenue exceeds that from contract X.

LMN Ltd – profit maximization

LMN Ltd is considering adding to its product line and concludes that products X, Y and Z are the most desirable additions on the grounds of the firm's present technical abilities, its knowledge of markets, and also on the grounds of productive flexibility. (These three products can all be made on the same kind of plant as that already in use and, therefore, as regards production, all products can be readily substituted.) It is, however, considered necessary to build further plant to cater for this added production.

The following estimates concerning costs, revenues, and production are made in respect of the new products:

	Product X £	*Product Y* £	*Product Z* £
1 Average variable cost per unit (materials, labour, and variable overhead)	20	32	28
2 Selling price per unit	35	42	37
3 Demand in units per cost period (on the basis of the above selling prices)	200	125	750
4 Machine-hours required per unit of production	15	5	3

The manufacturer considers that initially he can build extra plant facilities to operate at the following five different levels of activity, namely 1 800, 2 300, 2 800, 3 300 and 3 800 machine-hours per cost period. The fixed overhead costs for a cost period relevant to these five different plant sizes are estimated at £1 500, £2 000, £2 600, £3 300, and £3 900 respectively.

The following are required:

Computations to show which product or products should be made and in what quantities at each of the five contemplated levels of activity in order to maximize profits at each level and also to show the size of plant that seems most desirable.

The manufacturer should concentrate on the products giving the biggest contribution towards fixed costs *per machine-hour*.

Contributions in £s per machine-hour:

$$X = \frac{35 - 20}{15} = 1 \qquad Y = \frac{42 - 32}{5} = 2 \qquad Z = \frac{37 - 28}{3} = 3$$

The table on p.296 shows the feasible alternatives available to LMN Ltd.

It would therefore appear that additional capacity of 2 800 hours would maximize profits according to the information given. Other matters would, however, have to be taken into consideration in a capital budgeting decision of this nature, for example:

1 Possibilities of raising prices when demand is apparently unsatisfied.
2 The return on the capital to be invested as compared with the cost of such capital.
3 Possible long-run changes in conditions.

STANDARD COSTING

A logical step onwards from either absorption costing or marginal costing, especially in view of the fact that both approaches already involve a considerable amount of prediction of future cost levels, is to institute a system of standard costs. This topic will be developed in the next chapter, but the principle is to develop a complete specification of all expenditure levels from which standards are derived. (Chapter 10 deals with the determination of standards, and Chapter 11 deals with the variances that arise when standard costs and actual costs differ.)

A predetermined standard can be established for each element of cost at each stage of production. For direct materials, the standard cost would indicate the estimated amount of each kind of material and the cost per kilo (or other unit). For labour, the standard would show the number of hours in each department or cost centre; the hourly rate, and the total cost in each department.

The standard cost for overheads in each department would indicate the number of hours of machine time, direct labour hours, or whatever; the standard overhead recovery rate; and the total expense (i.e. hours × rate). When all the cost elements (direct materials, direct labour, direct expenses, fixed and variable overheads) have been accumulated, the standard should indicate the desired cost

Additional capacity (machine-hours)	*Contribution of products towards fixed costs*			*Total contri-butions*	*Fixed costs*	*Profit*
	X *(maximum 200 units = 3 000 hours)*	Y *(maximum 125 units = 625 hours)*	Z *(maximum 750 units = 2 250 hours)*			
1 800	—	—	3 × 1 800 = 5 400	5 400	1 500	3 900
2 300	—	2 × 50 = 100	3 × 2 250 = 6 750	6 850	2 000	4 850
2 800	—	2 × 550 = 1 100	3 × 2 250 = 6 750	7 850	2 600	5 250
3 300	*425 × 1 = 425	2 × 625 = 1 250	3 × 2 250 = 6 750	8 425	3 300	5 125
3 800	*925 × 1 = 925	2 × 625 = 1 250	3 × 2 250 = 6 750	8 925	3 900	5 025

* Includes incomplete units of X on the assumption that they can be completed in the following period.

of all elements of a unit of productive output.

The standard cost of materials shows what the cost *should* be if the correct types of material are used in the right quantities with the minimum of waste. Similarly, the standard labour cost shows what labour *should* cost if the job is performed at a specified level of efficiency by properly trained operatives of the appropriate grade working for agreed rates of pay. The standard overhead cost for a unit of output will be based upon standard fixed overhead rates and standard variable overhead rates developed in relation to particular assumed circumstances.

Standard costing differs from conventional absorption costing because the latter aims to charge units of output with a 'fair' share of the *actual* costs (either predictively or retrospectively) of making the product. In contrast, standard costing is based (either wholly or in part) on the principle that the costs to be charged to units of output are the costs that *should* have been incurred.

Direct or marginal costing systems can be developed along standard costing lines, in which event fixed overhead costs are not standardized but all direct costs, along with variable overheads, are standardized.

When a standard costing system is in operation, it can be operated in an integrated manner with the budgeting system, since both are concerned with what costs ought to be, what they actually are, and the reasons for the differences that arise. In other words, both standard costing and budgeting are concerned with cost control.

CHECKLIST ON COST ACCOUNTING

1 Is the company's costing system tailored to the company's needs?
2 Have cost centres been clearly defined?
3 Are the benefits of the system commensurate with its costs?
4 Are all costs classified into their direct and indirect, fixed and variable, controllable and uncontrollable, and separable and joint categories?
5 Is the behaviour of different costs understood in relation to changes in the level of activity?
6 Are cost reports made available promptly? How often? How quickly?
7 Could statements be presented earlier if more estimates were used? (Are estimating procedures reliable?)
8 Are figures rounded so that the results are more easily understood?
9 Can any figures of small value (as shown on the chart of accounts) be grouped?
10 Are the descriptions of reported items clear?
11 Are unusual items adequately explained?
12 Will further (or less) mechanization affect the overhead of cost accounting?

13 Can the effectiveness of cost accounting procedures be improved?
14 Has sufficient thought been given to the type of costing system to use? (That is, standard costing, absorption costing, or marginal costing.)
15 Has the purpose for which costing is being performed been fully considered? (For example, pricing, product costing, cost control.)
16 Is the costing system adequate in determining the relative efficiencies and profitability of divisions, processes, product lines, jobs, etc?
17 Is the costing system adequate for the needs of EDP and operations research analysts?
18 Are ratios, graphs, etc., used to supplement the figures produced by the costing system?
19 Is a satisfactory procedure being operated to price material issues from stores?
20 Are all withdrawals of stock and ordering of goods from outside suppliers duly authorized by requisitions?
21 Are job allocation numbers recorded against labour time, material usage, etc., in all cases?
22 Do employees understand the importance of recording the allocation of time to jobs? How are they encouraged to do this accurately?
23 What is the basis for the apportionment of each service department's costs? Is the most suitable basis selected in every case?
24 How are overheads absorbed into productive output? Is the most suitable basis used?
25 What action is taken on the basis of over- or under-recovery of overheads?
26 Are normalized overhead recovery rates used? If not, why not? For example, is the level of activity stable from month to month?
27 Have separate overhead rates been developed for fixed overhead costs and variable overhead costs?
28 Why are overheads absorbed (if they are absorbed)?
29 Is the contribution margin concept understood within the company?
30 Is cost-volume-profit analysis undertaken?
31 Is marginal costing undertaken?
32 Has the company's margin of safety ever been worked out?
33 Are the comparative advantages and disadvantages of marginal costing versus absorption costing fully appreciated?
34 Is the costing system closely geared to the type of production processes operated?
35 What role does cost accounting play in relation to special decision-making?

SUMMARY

Cost accounting is principally concerned with product costing (for pricing, inventory valuation, and income determination purposes), and only concerned in a secondary manner with cost control.

Data for product costing (and cost control) is derived from many sources, such as labour summaries, weekly time sheets, job cards, material requisitions, stock cards, and expense summaries. The pricing of material issues from stores is a particularly difficult topic in times of rising prices.

The type of costing system – and hence the nature and source of much costing data – will be determined by the structure of the organization and its methods of production. Job costing and process costing have been developed to deal with job/batch production and flow production respectively.

Conventional absorption cost accounting requires that all overheads be spread in some way over the productive output of the company. This is achieved by apportioning service department overheads to production departments, and then absorbing these accumulated production + service overheads over units of output. Many different bases exist for both apportioning and absorbing overheads, and the most suitable will be that which characterizes a cause-and-effect relationship between the activities and the outputs.

Overhead rates can be developed for fixed and variable overheads, but when the actual level of activity differs from the estimated level, there will be an over- or under-recovery of overheads. This may signal the need to revise overhead recovery rates.

For various reasons the apportioning/absorbing of overheads is dangerous (or at least gives misleading results) and marginal costing has developed to overcome these problems. Attention centres around the contribution margin, and the interrelationships of cost-volume-profit are a focal point for decision-making. Whilst marginal costing is a short-run function, relevant (or differential) costing is more suited to longer-run decisions in which fixed costs may vary in addition to changes in variable costs.

Standard costing is a normative refinement of either absorption or marginal costing that can be usefully integrated with budgeting in attempting to control costs.

Amongst the items listed on pp.381–3 for further reading, the following are especially recommended:

Anton, et al.;
Dearden;
Solomons;
Tucker.

10

Standards

THE NEED FOR STANDARDS

The purposes for which cost standards can be used are to identify areas of inefficiency, to measure these inefficiencies, and to bring the inefficiencies to the attention of those who have authority to take corrective action. In addition, from an accounting viewpoint, standard costing makes for great economy in book-keeping.

Standard costs are costs that should be obtained under efficient operations. They are predetermined costs and represent targets that are an essential feature of cost control. An important measure of performance is derived from a comparison of actual performance and standard performance. For example, if the standard material input for a unit of production is 50p and the actual cost is 48p, then the variance of −2p is the appropriate measure of performance, and – assuming a satisfactory quality level – the actual performance is an improvement on the standard. It is better to compare actual costs with a cost standard than with, say, comparative figures from the company's previous financial results. The main reason for this is that a comparison between current results and previous results presupposes that the previous results were at a level of efficiency that was sufficiently suitable to be emulated: this will rarely be the case. The future is a much better perspective, and future circumstances will almost certainly differ from past circumstances. If this year's profit is £3m and last year's profit was £2m, this may be seen as a remarkable improvement and a highly desirable state of affairs ... but maybe this year's profit should have been £5m.

The establishing of standards as a basis for setting standard costs is an important part of the work of the industrial engineer. Without standards, a company's management has no way of knowing if the company's overall performance, or the performance of one of its divisions, etc., was average, below average, exceptional or whatever.

Whilst standards are closely related to budgets, the two are not identical. A budget is a prediction of probable future results that has been formalized into a plan (see Chapter 8) whereas a standard is a cost level that should be achieved by efficient working under prevailing conditions. (Budgets are also authorities to spend, or to limit spending, and are prepared for all departments and operations of a company, but standards are simply benchmarks that tend to be used mainly for manufacturing activities.)

BASES FOR SETTING STANDARDS

Technical and engineering considerations underlie many standards, subject to these standards being agreed by those whose performance is to be judged. A major issue in standard costing is in determining the tightness of standards which may range from a desire for engineering perfection to very slack practices. Possible bases are:

1 Ideal standards that represent a maximum level of efficiency, hence a perfect level of operating performance. Such standards will represent the minimum costs that are possible given the company's product specifications, its productive facilities, operating conditions, and so forth. Since it is essential in control terms for standards to motivate individuals towards their attainment (and therefore to secure control over operations and operating costs), ideal standards can be seen to be of dubious value due to the rare likelihood of their ever being reached. Where they are found, ideal standards are more likely to be set for direct material costs and usage rather than for direct labour or overhead costs.
2 Basic standards are those that are set and maintained at their initial level, thereby providing a constant benchmark (albeit of questionable utility) through succeeding periods. This facilitates the identification of trends through an analysis of the variances (i.e. standard costing analysis of variance as opposed to statistical analysis of variance) over time, but changes in production methods, new products, variations in price, etc., will all render this approach generally unacceptable. Basic standards point the wrong way in emphasizing the past instead of adopting a future

orientation: they tend accordingly to take no account of the improvements in operations and conditions that can be achieved or expected.

3 Currently attainable standard costs are those costs that should be incurred under efficient forthcoming operating conditions. Allowances must be made in compiling currently attainable standards for normal spoilage, unavoidable idle time, unavoidable machine breakdown, set-up time, etc., so to this extent (at least) ideal standards will differ from currently attainable standards. But currently attainable standards must be set at a level that reflects operators' aspirations: they should be sufficiently tight to enable a sense of achievement to be experienced when they are met. Standards compiled on this basis are essential for labour, and are also most effective for materials, although it may be thought best to have an ideal standard for material quantities and a currently attainable standard for material prices.

Since cost control is achieved through maintaining the actual level of performance at (or near to) a standard level of performance, if the standards are tighter than the level of performance that is currently attainable (given a desired level of efficiency) this may prove to be discouraging (i.e. it will fail to motivate individuals to reach standard levels of performance because they are beyond those individuals' aspiration levels). Conversely, a standard that can be met by poor performance has the effect of hiding inefficiency, which contradicts the standard costing objective of encouraging efficiency.

Other bases on which standards may be set, in addition to ideal standards, basic standards, and currently attainable standards, include:

1 An average of historical cost levels.
2 The lowest historical cost.
3 Estimated cost at normal activity level.
4 Estimated cost at expected activity level.
5 Cost at average good performance.

When standards are of a current nature, they will become inaccurate due to improved production facilities, etc., and the need therefore exists for standards to be revised from time to time. The dangers and disadvantages of out-of-date standards are great enough to warrant at least an annual review of standards, but the frequency with which revisions are made will depend on the circumstances of each organization. A total revision of standards involves a considerable amount of work and thus should not be undertaken unless it is necessary, but the amount of work involved should not be allowed to act as a deterrent if the existing standards are sufficiently out-of-date to be no longer useful as a basis for cost control. Once it is decided to revise standards, this exercise should be completed before the commencement of the period during which the new standards are to be operational.

A revision of standards will have an immediate effect on the value of stocks since they will be valued at one standard at one point in time and at another standard thereafter. The difference that arises due to this revaluation can be charged against profit in either the period relating to the old standards or the period relating to the new ones.

A clear need for the revision of standards is seen in price increases and the inability of operatives to meet standards. This latter cause may be due to delays in receiving materials, lack of suitable training, excess set-up time, and so forth. On the other hand, of course, standards may be too slack, and this can cause problems when attempts are made to tighten them with a consequent effect on the level of earnings an operative may achieve.

SETTING STANDARDS

Within the production sphere standards can be set for the following:

1 Physical output (e.g. units per hour).
2 Direct materials:
 (*a*) Usage per unit of physical output
 (*b*) Price per unit of input
 (*c*) Yield from mixing raw materials
 (*d*) Mix of materials
 (*e*) Value of scrap
 (*f*) Quantity of scrap/wastage.
3 Direct labour:
 (*a*) Labour rates of pay
 (*b*) Labour input per unit of output
 (*c*) Grades of labour
 (*d*) Rates of production per hour.
4 Variable overheads:
 (*a*) Cost per unit of output
 (*b*) Cost/consumption for a given level of output.
5 Fixed overheads:
 (*a*) The total cost
 (*b*) The cost per unit at normal activity (or whatever base may be used).

The use of standards has certain measurement advantages. For instance, if a standard hourly wage rate is 50p, it is known that £5.00 represents 10 standard hours and also that 20 standard hours are equivalent to a standard labour cost of £10.00. In the same way, finished stock can be expressed in terms of the quantity or value of raw materials necessary to make it, and vice versa, as well as the hours/cost of labour involved in its manufacture, and vice versa.

Let us consider a product that is composed of 3 kilos of raw material and 5 hours of direct labour, with material costing £1.00 per kilo and labour costing £0.50 per hour. The standard direct cost of this product is therefore:

3 kilos material	@ £1.50	£3.00
5 hours labour	@ £0.50	£2.50
Standard direct unit cost		£5.50

Since the labour element is 5/11 of the total, it is possible to compute the labour component of the standard direct cost of, say, 100 units:

100 units	@ £5.50	=	£550.00
Labour element	= 5/11 × £5.50	=	£250.00

This is made up of (100 × 5) = 500 standard hours of labour (which is also equivalent to $\frac{250}{0.50}$).

Similarly, direct material cost will be 6/11 of the total cost: 6/11 × £550 = £300.00. This consists of 100 × 3 = 300 kilos (alternatively given by $\frac{300}{1.00}$).

However, great care must be taken in developing standard rates/costs for labour, materials, and overhead costs, such as those shown in the standard cost sheet of Figure 10.1.

Overhead standards can be developed along the lines suggested in section headed 'Fixed and Variable Overhead Rates' in Chapter 9. Ideally, separate rates should be developed for variable overhead costs and fixed overhead costs. It will usually be found to be more difficult to set standards for overhead items than for direct items. Typical problem areas are:

1 The responsibility for controlling overhead items is spread over a greater area of the organization than is the case with direct items. Thus a production manager cannot control many of the overhead items that are charged to his department.

2 Manufacturing overheads consist of items having a wide variety of characteristics, and each must be analysed to determine its behaviour as a prelude to establishing overhead standards (i.e. fixed, variable, and mixed cost behaviour patterns must be identified).

3 The accuracy of overhead standards varies over a wide range depending upon the number of variables involved and the availability of data. Payroll items are easily made into standards, whereas service charges, repair costs, etc., are more variable and consequently more complex.

In setting overhead standards, a balance must be achieved between accuracy and the costs (of analysis, etc.) involved in setting standards. When standards

Product			Unit price	Per ten
Material:				£
100 kilos alloy to BSS			25p per kilo	25.00
Packing material: 10 cartons			10p each	1.00
Labour:				
Shop number 1 :	lathe A	50 hrs	60p per hour	30.00
	lathe B	10 hrs	55p per hour	5.50
Shop number 2 :	miller F	20 hrs	70p per hour	14.00
	grinder	8 hrs	45p per hour	3.60
Inspection		0.5 hrs	50p per hour	0.25
				79.35
Less: standard scrap recovery: 10 kilos @ 5p				0.50
Direct standard cost for 10 units				78.85
Overheads:				
Standard Allowances				
Fixed: 75 hours @ £1.50				112.50
Variable: 75 hours @ £1.00				75.00
Standard cost for 10 units				266.35

Figure 10.1: Standard cost sheet

of this type are first introduced into a company it may be necessary to sacrifice accuracy in order to obtain full coverage of all elements of cost. However, when this is the case it must be recognized that standards and controls must be improved at the first opportunity.

The following guidelines are useful in controlling overhead costs in this context:

1 Overhead cost standards should be set for both operating and non-operating departments.
2 The responsibility for all items should be assigned at the level of most effective control.
3 Overhead standards should represent the best currently attainable performance level that can be secured with existing facilities under standard conditions.
4 The determinant of each overhead item should provide the most accurate measure of that item that is consistent with accuracy/cost criteria.
5 The accuracy of overhead standards should be improved as rapidly as is realistic.

Turning to consider direct cost standards, it will be appreciated that *physical standards* are the foundation of a standard costing system. Physical standards are constructed from systematic observation, measurement, and controlled experimentation, or alternatively result from careful planning. Cost standards are developed by multiplying physical standards by cost factors (e.g. cost per kilo, litre, metre, etc., for materials, or rate per hour/piece for labour). Money is the only common denominator for standards, and the use of a monetary measure in addition to a physical measure draws attention to expensive items, since these need more managerial attention than do less expensive ones.

Material costs are affected by two major factors – cost and usage. The company cannot control (in most situations) the price of bought-in materials and components in the same way that it can control their usage. But this does not mean that price standards should not be set – indeed, if standards are not set so that price variations can be isolated, it will be impossible to identify usage variations.

A material price standard will tend to be set on the basis of anticipated prices (for the period during which the standard is to be applied) or, possibly, current prices (i.e. at the time when the standard is set). The company's purchasing department is responsible for most material prices (for a given quality and quantity of a specified material), and should be actively involved in setting standards (which essentially involves predicting future price levels for the materials in question, although prices can be negotiated in advance so that prices are certain).

Amongst the advantages of standard costing in connection with purchasing is that purchasing executives, in setting and agreeing material price standards, have to stop the malpractice of using favouritism/social *bonhomie* in selecting suppliers and turn to efficiency as a central criterion. However, a failure to meet price standards may be due to an urgent requisition being placed on the purchasing department, or unexpected increases in the volume of productive activity, and in these instances the purchasing officer cannot be held responsible for failing to meet established standards. But when material price variances *are* due to purchasing department errors, it may point to a change of supplier or a consideration of alternative materials.

Material quality and quantity standards can be more closely controlled by the company. Engineering and technical specifications are the basis for determining quality standards, and quantity standards are based on product specifications, production methods, normal spoilage (in storage), normal (i.e. unavoidable) waste (in manufacture). The nature of materials in use will determine the precise nature of the standards to be used: for a bought-out component, for example, the ideal standard is equal to the currently attainable standard and is given by the market price of the component; but for bulk materials, or materials that need machining or processing in some other way, the currently attainable standard is *not* equal to the ideal standard and an allowance must be made for spoilage, waste, etc.

As with direct material standards, there are price and quantity aspects of direct labour standards. The control of direct labour rates (i.e. the price factor) is partly in the hands of the works committee since negotiation with trades unions is necessary. But immediate control will rarely be possible because negotiations will be ultimately finalized at national level in many cases, or local demand and supply conditions may mean that the 'invisible hand' controlling market forces has control over labour rates.

Labour rates become cost standards once they have been applied to physical labour standards, and standards must be amended whenever rates change. To allow for different rates being paid to different grades of labour, standard costs may be based either on an average rate or on the understanding that particular tasks will be performed by particular grades of labour (see Figure 10.1) in which case specific rates for particular tasks can be used. (The treatment of overtime and incentive bonus payments deserves special attention.)

The most difficult standard to set relates to direct labour time, and work study techniques (time and motion study especially) are frequently applied in setting standards. Consideration must be taken of equipment, production methods, material flow, material handling, support services (e.g. machine setting, quality control, etc.), degree of training of operatives, and other conditions in setting direct labour time standards. Furthermore, allowances must be made for idle time due to fatigue, personal needs, machine breakdowns, delays caused by waiting for materials, etc. Whenever any change occurs in underlying conditions, direct labour standards should be revised.

The steps involved in setting a labour time standard are, in outline:

1 Study the motions being made by the operative.
2 Improve the motions and determine the best method by improving the layout of the factory, eliminating the delays that exist, determining the best sequence of motions for the right and left hands, and instructing the worker in the improved methods.
3 Observe and record the time required to perform each element of the task in question.
4 Establish the time standard by averaging the element times, rating the worker who has been observed for skill and effort, and computing allowances for delays. All exceptional times noted in step 3 should be discarded as being too long or too short, and the pace at which an average operative can work should be carefully evaluated.

Once set, labour standards (for both set up and operations) can be incorporated into routing sheets and work tickets so that supervisors and operatives are fully aware of what is expected. Figure 10.2 illustrates a typical routing sheet that gives standard times for all operations and set ups.

ROUTING SHEET				
Part: Fuel pump body with bushings *Stock specifications:* Grey iron casting				*Part number:* B-489 *Standard quantity:* 200
Operation number	*Department number*	*Standard time allowed (in minutes)*		*Description of operation*
		Set up	*Operation (per unit)*	
20	27	90	10.2	Drill, bore, face, chamfer and ream
25	29	18	0.7	Face and chamfer hub
30	29	12	1.5	Mill eng. fit pad
35	31	18	8.0	Drill and tap complete
40	29	12	1.5	Mill clearance
45	29	—	1.8	Clean and grind hose connection
50	29	12	2.3	Press in 2 bushings G-98 and face flange on mandrel
	13			Inspect
	21			To stockroom

Figure 10.2: Operations routing sheet

NON-PRODUCTION STANDARDS

The emphasis in the discussion so far has been on setting production standards, but it is important to realize that standards can be established in other areas of business activity. In Chapter 14 cost and time standards in the context of administration and office management will be discussed. At this point it can be observed that standards for, say, marketing activities, can be set for the same reasons as production standards are set.

Such standards can be derived to cover such items as:

1 Cost to create £1.00 of sales
2 Cost per customer serviced
3 Cost per sales transaction
4 Cost to create £1.00 of gross contribution
5 Average selling cost of each unit sold
6 Selling prices
7 Discount structures
8 Sales mix
9 Gross sales per salesman

10 Selling expenses per salesman
11 Contribution per salesman
12 Contribution per sales region
13 Contribution per channel of distribution
14 Contribution per order
15 Sales administration costs.

Performance in relation to sales cost standards can reveal that too much sales effort is devoted to small-account customers, and so on. Studies can be made of sales territories and their potential in order to set standards in the form of sales quotas, time per call, and call frequency. Control of the sales force through standards should provide means of determining and influencing performance to ensure that the target profit contribution is attained.

Let us consider a simple example of standards for sales force control. The essential control data for monitoring sales force profitability for Abacus Associates is:

(*a*)	Average total cost of each salesman	£15 000 p.a.
(*b*)	Average number of calls	1 000 p.a.
(*c*)	Average cost per call ((*a*) ÷ (*b*))	£15
(*d*)	Order: call ratio	1:10
(*e*)	Average cost per order ((*c*) × (*d*))	£150
(*f*)	Average order size (total sales/orders)	£5 000
(*g*)	Product mix percentage gross contribution	25%
(*h*)	Average profit contribution per order ((*f*) × (*g*))	£1 250
(*i*)	Average number of orders ((*b*) ÷ (*d*))	100
(*j*)	Average profit contribution per salesman ((*h*) × (*i*))	£125 000

If the average contribution per salesman (see (*j*) above) is unsatisfactory, attention can be directed towards the constituent elements (such as order: call ratio, and average order size) to see if these can be improved.

The figure given in (*a*) above for the average total cost of a salesman can be readily broken down into its fixed and variable components. For example, typical fixed costs are:

(*a*) salaries;
(*b*) depreciation on cars;
(*c*) fixed car expenses (road tax, insurance); and
(*d*) superannuation and other payroll expenses.

On the other hand, variable sales force costs include:

(*a*) commissions;
(*b*) travelling expenses (including car running costs); and
(*c*) entertaining.

Sales quotas can be classified into two categories: those that reflect a desired level of performance which may not be achieved, although it acts as a strong motivator; and those that are geared to actual expectations. Management must be quite clear which philosophy it wishes to adopt before standards/sales quotas are drawn up.

In general, in order to establish any cost standard, one needs to identify the activity for which a standard is sought and then to measure the inputs to that activity at some acceptable efficiency level. Figures 10.3 – 10.8 illustrate the range of functions (or activities) within the marketing/distribution domain for which standards might be developed, along with the work units (or inputs) that can be used for developing these standards.

TOLERANCE LIMITS

Before turning (in Chapter 11) to consider causes of variations from standard, let us look again at the question of tolerance limits. (The reader is recommended to re-read the section headed 'Statistical Quality Control' in Chapter 5 in which this topic was first introduced.)

Management by exception is an approach that is recommended throughout this book, and this hinges upon the identification and analysis of significant variances. But what is a 'significant' variance?

Answering this question requires a consideration of random deviations or variances (i.e. those that arise purely due to chance) on the one hand, and statistically significant deviations (i.e. those that are unlikely to have arisen due to chance) on the other. Random deviations are uncontrollable, whereas statistically significant deviations have assignable causes, and once these causes have been discovered it is possible to eliminate them and thereby bring operations back into control.

Given that the magnitude of a deviation is important in determining whether it is worthy of investigation, how can 'small' be distinguished from 'large'? To some extent this will depend on the amount from which a given deviation deviates, thus a deviation of £10 000 from a standard of £1 000 000 is not as large (in percentage terms) as is a deviation of £10 000 from a standard of £20 000. Conventional accounting procedures are only able to produce (i.e. measure) deviations, but cost control must be based on some measure of the importance of these deviations. Statistical method provides means by which a range for a particular cost item can be established in such a way that deviations falling within this range are considered to be acceptable whereas deviations beyond the range (i.e. outside the tolerance limits) are deemed worthy of investigation. The basis of one of the most widely-used statistical techniques

FUNCTION	WORK UNITS
Salesmen's salaries	Sales call Salesmen's hour
Commissions and bonuses	Net sales £ Product units sold Sales call Sales order Sales transaction
Subsistence	Days subsisted
Entertainment	Customer
General sales office expense and supervision salaries	Salesmen Sales transaction Sales order Salesmen's hour Customer account
Salesmen's travelling expense	Miles travelled Days travelled Call Customer Sales order
Salesmen's equipment	Sales call
Telephone solicitation	Telephone call Order received
Salesmen's training and education	Number of salesmen Number of salesmen's calls
Routing and scheduling of salesmen	Number of salesmen Number of salesmen's calls
Making quotations	Quotations made
Payroll insurance and taxes and supplemental labour costs	Payroll £
Handling sales adjustments and returns	Adjustments and returns handled
Total direct selling	Cost per unit of product sold Cost per sales transaction Cost per sales order Cost per customer served

Figure 10.3: Bases for direct selling standards

FUNCTION	*WORK UNITS*
Direct media costs newspapers	Sales transaction Newspaper inches Gross or net sales (where this is chief medium used)
Outdoor billboards and signs	Billboard and other outdoor sign units
Radio and television	Minute of radio or television time Number of set owners
Letters, circulars, calendars and other direct mail	Gross or net direct mail sales Item mailed or distributed Inquiry received
Demonstrations	Demonstration
Technical and professional publications	Inquiry received Unit of space
Samples distribution	Samples distributed
Directories, house organs and theatre programmes	Unit of space Inquiry received
Catalogues	Page or standard space unit Gross or net catalogue sales when identifiable
Store and window displays	Day or window trimming and display
Advertising allowances to dealers	Unit of product cost Net sales
Dealers' help	Pieces or units Customers
Entertainment of visitors at plants	Visitors
Advertising administration (salaries, supplies, rent, miscellaneous administrative expenses)	Cost per £ of net sales Cost per £ of all direct advertising and sales promotional costs
Total advertising and sales promotion	Sales transaction Prospect obtained Net sales Product unit sold

Figure 10.4: Bases for advertising and sales promotion standards

FUNCTION	*WORK UNITS*
Receiving	Purchase invoice line Weight or number of shipping units Shipment £ of merchandise purchased
Pricing, tagging and marking	Warehouse unit handled Invoice line
Sorting	Physical unit stored £ of average inventory Order
Assembling stock for shipment	Order Order line Item Shipment Sales transaction
Handling returns	Return
Packing and wrapping	Order Order line Physical unit shipped Shipment
Taking physical inventory	Warehouse unit £ of average inventory
Clerical handling of shipping orders	Order Item Shipment Sales transaction Order line
Total warehousing and handling	Shipment Order line Item handled Physical unit of goods handled (product, weight or weighted factor)

Figure 10.5: Bases for warehousing and handling standards

FUNCTION	*WORK UNITS*
Planning and supervision	Sales £ Route Customer served Ton-mile Unit shipped
Transportation clerical work entries in shipping records	Shipment Delivery
Preparing shipping documents and recording shipment	Shipment Unit of product shipped Weighted unit of product shipped
Transportation bills	Unit audited Shipment
Handling claims	Claim handled Shipment Entry
Loading and unloading	Pounds loaded
Drivers' and helpers' wages	Truck hours of operation Truck miles Cubic foot space
Gasoline, oil, repair and maintenance	Mile Truck miles
Total transportation	£ of shipments as delivered Unit of product shipped as delivered Weighted unit of product Unit of classes of product

Figure 10.6: Bases for transportation standards

FUNCTION	*WORK UNITS*
Credit investigation and approval	Sales order Account sold Credit sales transaction
Credit correspondence, records and files	Letter Account sold Sales order Item
Preparing invoices – handling	Invoice
Preparing invoices – line item	Order line Invoice line
Posting charges to accounts receivable	Number of postings per hour Invoice Shipment
Posting credits to accounts receivable	Number of postings per hour Remittances Account sold
Preparing customers' statements	Statement Account sold
Making street collections	£ collected Customer
Handling window collections	Collection
Total credit and collection	Sales order Credit sales transaction Account sold

Figure 10.7: Bases for credit and collections standards

FUNCTION	*WORK UNITS*
General accounting including auditing fees, salaries of general bookkeepers and accounting supplies	General ledger posting Customers' orders Invoice lines
Sales analyses and statistics	Order Invoice line
Financial expense	Ratio of total distribution cost to sales Ratio of average distribution investment to sales Ratio of inventory turnover
Personnel expense	Number of employees Number of persons employed, discharged and reclassified
Filing and maintaining order and letter files	Order Letter Units filed
Mail handling	Number of pieces in and out
Vouchering	Number of vouchers
Sales auditing	Number of sales slips
Punching cards	Number of cards
Tabulating	Number of cards run
Cashiering	Number of transactions
Fixed administration and market research	Time spent

Figure 10.8: Bases for general distribution standards

for cost control is to determine the probability distribution for each cost item at different levels of activity, and to establish tolerance limits from this.

This methodology is beyond the scope of this volume, but any manager requiring advice in this area should seek it from a statistician/operations researcher rather than from, say, a company accountant whose quantitative skills are of the traditional variety.

SUMMARY

Standards are developed as a benchmark for measuring performance, and represent the level of performance that should be achieved at a given level of efficiency under expected conditions. (Other bases – such as ideal standards – are rather unrealistic for general use, although they are of value in particular circumstances.)

It is usually in the production sphere that standards are set, covering the price/rate and quantity/usage/efficiency aspects of direct labour, direct materials, and overhead items. Standard direct labour times present perhaps the greatest difficulties because such standards often determine a man's earning capacity, with the result that union agreement may be a vital ingredient.

Non-production areas – such as marketing and distribution activities, research and development work, and administration – can all benefit from having standards developed.

Management by exception focuses the attention of responsible individuals on significant deviations from standard, and 'significance' in this context is a statistical concept rather than an accounting one.

Amongst the items listed on pp.381–3 for further reading, the following are especially recommended:

Horngren;
Rayburn;
Shillinglaw.

11

Variance Analysis

PURPOSE OF VARIANCE ANALYSIS

The computation and classification of variances (as a starting point for analysis and corrective follow-up) is a vital feature of standard costing and cost control. What causes variances? There are many causes, some of which are indicated below:

1. Labour rates/salary levels may change due to union negotiations, policy decisions, merit increases, progression along a scale, or changing composition of the workforce with regard to length of service.
2. Selling prices may change.
3. In a multi-product company, the product sales mix may vary, and if (as is likely) different product lines have different margins, the overall profit contribution will vary.
4. The improving of systems can bring about reductions in costs.
5. Changes in productivity (i.e. the level of effort) on the part of operatives, supervisors, management, and clerical staff can help or hinder cost levels.
6. Investment in new capital equipment, and scrapping of old equipment/processes/methods can have immediate effects on direct operating cost levels (direct labour and direct material inputs) as well as on overhead items (such as depreciation charges and insurance premiums).

7 Bought-out materials and components can vary in price.
8 Changes in product design will alter the cost inputs.
9 Policy decisions of various kinds relating to, for example, organization structure, may affect cost levels.
10 The value of money is constantly changing.
11 Longer or shorter hours may be worked.
12 The amount of (e.g.) idle time may vary due to production hold ups strikes, power failures, etc.

If a variance is significant (see section headed 'Statistical Quality Control' in Chapter 5 and section headed 'Tolerance Limits' in Chapter 10) it signals the need for managerial investigation: it is essential to fully appreciate that the identification of a variance is of no value in itself – the value lies in ascertaining the cause of the variance and acting to correct it. The cause of variances can be personalized, so variance analysis operates in accordance with the principles of responsibility accounting: production foremen will be responsible for direct labour time variances, marketing management for sales price and sales mix variances; the purchasing department for material price variances, and so on.

Even though specific variances may be seen to be the responsibility of specific individuals, the existence of any variance is only a prima facie indication of good or poor performance. The truth of the situation may be a standard that was set at the wrong level in the first place.

DIRECT MATERIAL VARIANCES

Four direct material variances will be considered: price variance, usage variance, mix variance, and yield variance.

The first of these, the ***direct material price variance***, can be illustrated by means of a material X that has a standard cost of 50p per kilo, and 100 kilos are bought for £53.00. This gives a material price variance of £3.00 in total or £0.03 per kilo, and it is a straightforward matter to isolate this total variance immediately the material is invoiced, with the result that material X is booked into stock at its standard cost per kilo of 50p, and so the company's stock records can be kept in either monetary units or kilos in the knowledge that they are interchangeable.

In formula terms, material price variance (*MPV*) is given by:

$$MPV = (AP - SP) \times AQ$$

where SP = standard price per unit
AP = actual price per unit
AQ = actual quantity bought

therefore $MPV = £(0.53 - 0.50) \times 100 = +£3.00$

Let us now suppose that the standard direct material input of material X into product A is 4 kilos per unit, so that the standard direct material cost per unit is:

$$4 \times £0.50 = £2.00$$

If the purchase of 100 kilos of material X is fully used up in producing 24 units of product A, then a *direct material usage* (*or quantity*) *variance (MUV)* can be calculated by applying the formula:

$$MUV = (AQ - SQ) \times SP$$

where SQ = standard quantity
AQ = actual quantity used
SP = standard price per unit

therefore $MUV = (100 - 96) \times £0.50 = +£2.00$

This adverse variance has arisen because 4 kilos too much have been used, but usage variances may arise due to other causes such as:

1 Materials may deteriorate in poor storage conditions.
2 Purchases may be of a substandard quality.
3 The wrong materials may be issued.
4 Machinery may not be properly set or poorly maintained.
5 Tools/jigs may be faulty.
6 An inadequately trained operative may cause a high rate of scrap to result from poor work, etc.

Both the direct material price variance and the direct material usage variance can be derived from Figure 11.1.

Alternatively, the picture can be seen in Figure 11.2, which analyses the total variance in a graphical manner.

Management can analyse the direct material price and usage variances and then investigate them by asking:

1 Why has excess material been used? ($MUV = +£2.00$).
2 What is the difference between actual and standard costs for the material? ($MPV = -£3.00$).

In certain processing industries where raw materials are mixed together in standard proportions, it is sometimes found that there is a temporary shortage of one type of material and so a substitute must be used. This involves varying the standard mix of materials which also happens if the standard materials are blended in non-standard proportions. Since different materials have different costs, the cost of an actual (i.e. non-standard) mix will vary from the standard cost of the standard mix and thus give rise to a *direct materials mix variance*.

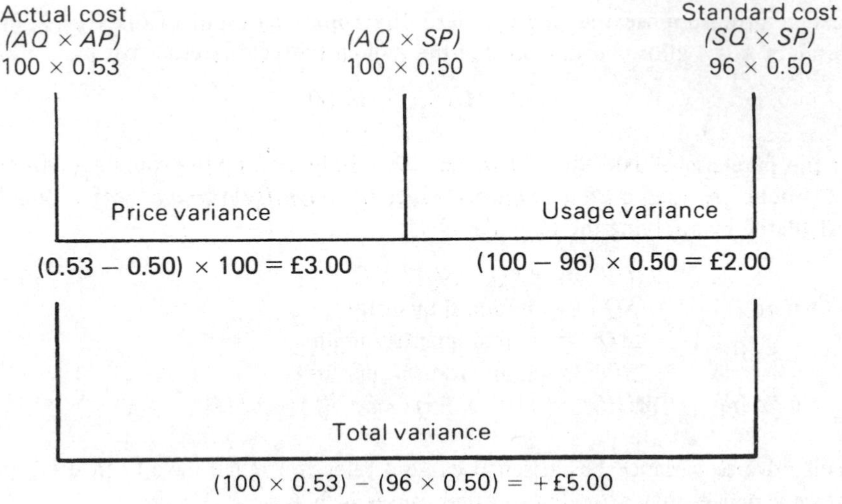

Figure 11.1: Direct material variances – 1

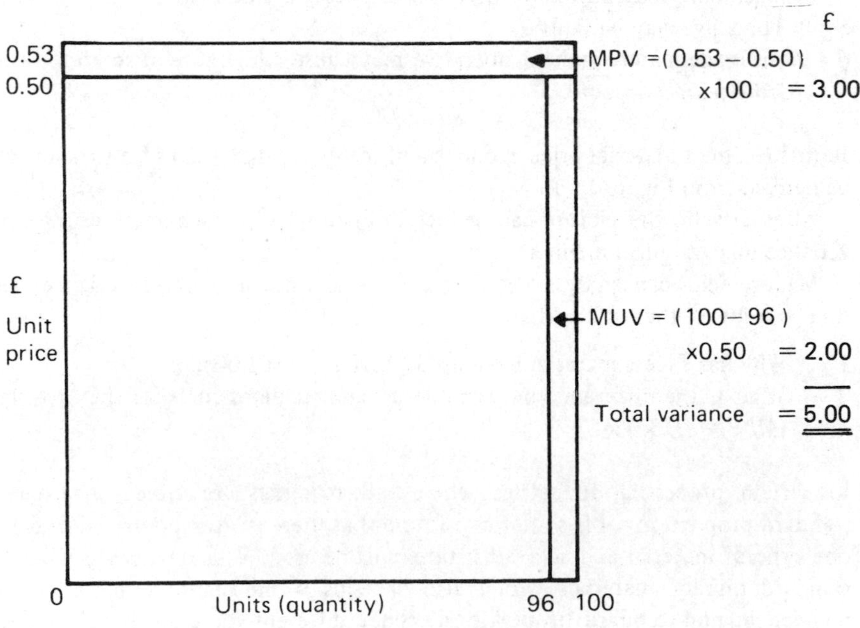

Figure 11.2: Direct material variances – 2

To take an example, if the production of 100 litres of product Z requires a standard mix of:

Material A	30	litres @ standard cost £0.50	=	£15.00
Material B	50	litres @ standard cost £1.00	=	£50.00
Material C	20	litres @ standard cost £0.25	=	£5.00
	100			£70.00

the standard cost of this materials mix is therefore £70.00. However, material C may be in short supply, so the mix may be varied to the following:

Material A	40	litres @ £0.50	=	£20.00
Material B	50	litres @ £1.00	=	£50.00
Material C	10	litres @ £0.25	=	£2.50
	100			£72.50

Varying the mix in this way gives rise to a direct materials mix variance of £(72.50 – 70.00) = +£2.50.

It could have happend that, as a result of some chemical reaction, the non-standard materials mix shown above may only have produced 95 litres of product Z. Such an outcome -- the output is less than the input – is common in chemical processing and, insofar as it is 'normal', can be allowed for in a control system. But unexpected outcomes produce ***direct material yield variances.***

Continuing with the above example, in which it is assumed that the non-standard mix of materials A, B, and C produced 95 litres of product Z, the yield variance (YV) is given by:

$$YV = (AY - SY) \times SC$$

where
SY = standard yield
AY = actual yield
SC = standard cost of standard mix per unit of output

therefore $YV = (95 - 100) \times £0.70 = +£3.50$

The actual cost per litre under these circumstances is $£(\frac{72.5}{95}) = £0.76$ as opposed to a standard cost per litre of $£(\frac{70.00}{100}) = £0.70$. The total variance of (76 – 70)p = 6p per litre is made up of:

Material mix variance per litre	2.5p
Material yield variance per litre	3.5p
Total variance per litre	6.00p

Mix and yield variances should not be confused with material usage variances because their causes are quite different: a materials mix variance may be due to a lack of availability of the correct materials; a materials yield variance may be due to the processing of a standard mix of standard materials at the wrong temperature; and a material usage variance may be due to an excessive number of rejected units of output.

DIRECT LABOUR VARIANCES

The variances stemming from differences between actual labour costs and standard that will be discussed are direct labour rate variance, efficiency variance, mix variance, idle time variance, and calendar variance.

The direct labour rate variance is equivalent to the direct material price variance (in the same way that the direct labour efficiency variance is analogous to the direct material usage variance).

Whilst the factor of time does not generally affect any direct material variances, it can have an impact on direct labour variances. As a result of payments to labour being related to the length of time spent on various processes, etc., any variations in amounts paid can be seen to be related to the degree of efficiency exhibited as well as to the rates of pay in force.

When devising a standard labour time for a job, if a worker of a higher grade than was initially intended is used for the job, then a ***direct labour rate variance*** will arise. For example, a job may have a standard time of 10 hours and may be intended to be performed by a particular grade of operative at a standard hourly direct labour rate of £0.65, giving a standard direct labour cost for the job of £6.50. However, an operative from a more highly skilled grade earning £0.75 per hour may actually do the work, with a resultant cost (assuming he took 10 hours) of £7.50 and an unfavourable direct labour rate variance (*LRV*) of £1.00. The formula for computing this variance is:

$$LRV = (AR - SR) \times AH$$

where SR = standard direct labour rate per hour
AR = actual direct labour rate per hour
AH = actual direct labour hours

therefore $LRV = £(0.75 - 0.65) \times 8 = +£0.80$

Taking this example further, if the skilled operative had done the job in 8 hours rather than 10, a *direct labour efficiency variance (LEV)* would have arisen, as shown by applying the formula:

$$LEV = (AH - SH) \times SR$$

where SH = standard hours allowed
AH = actual hours taken
SR = standard direct labour rate per hour

therefore $LEV = (8 - 10) \times £0.65 = -£1.30$

This is a favourable variance, and the combined effect of a job for which SR = £0.65 and SH = 10 being done with AR = £0.75 and AH = 8 is shown in Figure 11.3.

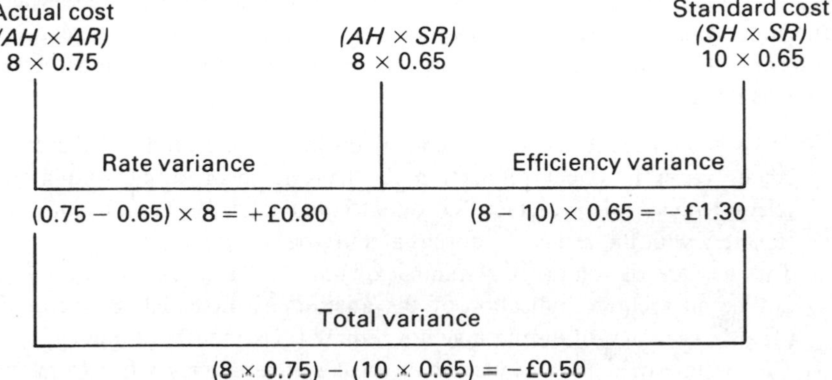

Figure 11.3: Direct labour variances – 1

As with direct material price and usage variances, a graphical analysis of direct labour rate and efficiency variances can be made (see Figure 11.4). The net outcome of the favourable LEV and the unfavourable LRV is a favourable total direct labour variance of £0.50.

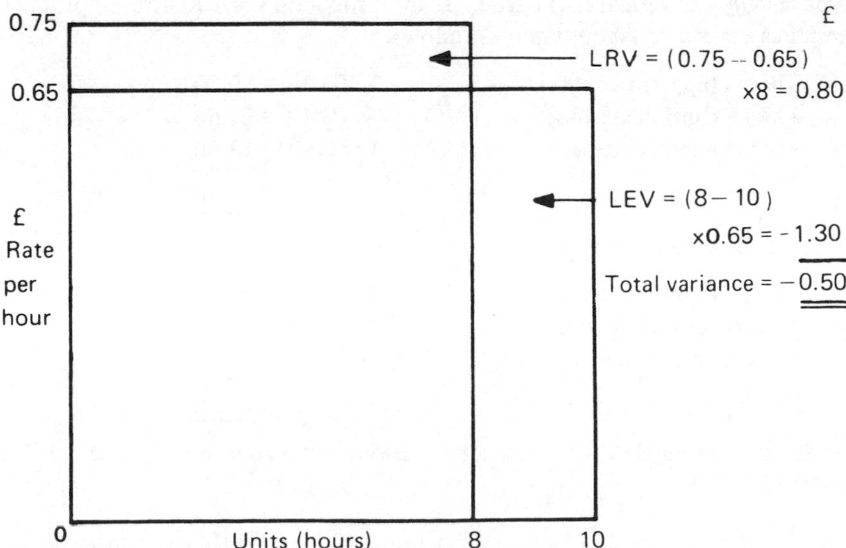

Figure 11.4: Direct labour variances – 2

Labour efficiency variances are not simply due to the amount of effort that a worker puts into his job, but can be caused by many other factors amongst which are the organization of the flow of work; the adequacy of materials, jigs, etc.; the efficiency of support services (e.g. set-up time taken may be excessive, maintenance may be needed, training/inspection/instruction may be needed); and so on. The following points should also be noted (although the list is far from exhaustive):

1. The standard labour cost for a unit of output is only valid if the cost of labour varies in direct proportion to the volume of output within the relevant range. (It is certain that direct labour costs do not vary proportionately with the volume of output at all levels of production.)
2. The measure of volume (e.g. number of units, kilos of output, etc.) may not be an accurate indication of the amount of direct labour required. (That is, each unit of output may not require the same labour input.)
3. The volume used to generate labour cost standards may differ from the volume that was experienced and which gave rise to the actual direct labour cost of a period.
4. The items included in standard direct labour costs (e.g. holiday accruals, overtime premiums, etc.), may not be included in actual costs.

As with the example given in the previous section for materials mix, so the standard mix of different grades of direct labour may not be achieved and so a *direct labour mix variance* will arise. If the production of 100 litres of product Z requires a standard labour input as follows:

2 hours (apprentice rate)	@ £0.25	= £0.50
4 hours (unskilled rates)	@ £0.40	= £1.60
6 hours (skilled rates)	@ £0.60	= £3.60
		£5.70

and if the actual labour input is:

4 hours (apprentice rate)	@ £0.25	= £1.00
2 hours (unskilled rates)	@ £0.40	= £0.80
6 hours (skilled rates)	@ £0.60	= £3.60
		£5.40

then it can be seen that there is a direct labour mix variance of £(5.40 – 5.70) = –£0.30.

A mix variance is due to a lack of availability at a particular point in time of a particular type of labour, but *idle time variances* are due to a lack of work. When direct production workers are prevented from being productive for known reasons, these reasons should be noted, the cost of the enforced idleness they cause recorded, and remedial action taken. There is a close relationship between idle time and labour efficiency since the causes of idle time lead to inefficiency but idle time should be isolated and treated as an overhead cost whereas direct labour efficiency variances are not overheads. If the lack of availability of raw materials causes the loss of 200 direct labour hours at a standard rate of £0.65, this gives an adverse idle time variance of £130.00.

When a budget is compiled on the basis of an assumed number of working days – hence hours – per month, the occurrence of a public holiday will alter the calculations, and this can lead to a *calendar variance*. The formula for working this out is simply the total number of hours lost due to the holiday multiplied by the standard hourly rate.

Direct cost variances – labour and materials – are summarized in Figure 11.5.

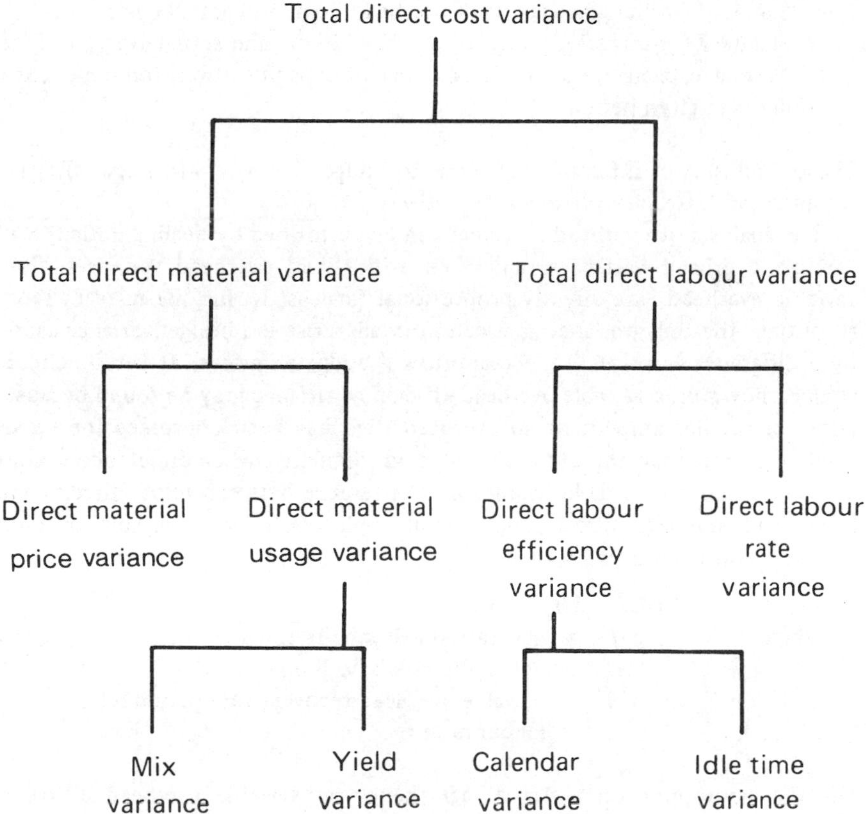

Figure 11.5: Direct cost variances

The use of standard costing variance analysis (and variance analysis related to budgeted versus actual costs) should enable the accountant to report the following matters to management in connection with direct material costs and direct labour costs:

1 Which variances have arisen?
2 Who is responsible?
3 Why have the variances arisen?

OVERHEAD VARIANCES

Overhead cost variances arise in any company employing an absorption costing system when there is a difference between:

1 Standard (or budgeted) costs of overhead items and actual costs.
2 Standard (or budgeted) usage of overhead items and actual usage.
3 Normal capacity and the actual level of capacity utilization experienced during a given period.

These three sets of differences give rise to budget (or cost) variances, efficiency variances, and capacity variances respectively.

The analysis of overhead variances can be performed by dealing initially with variable overhead variances, and then with fixed overhead variances. Since variable overheads are directly proportional (at least within the relevant range) to output, the only variance that can normally arise is a budget variance caused by a difference in prices (i.e. actual prices $\neq$ budgeted prices). In certain circumstances, however, a variable overhead efficiency variance may be found because a larger or smaller amount of an overhead item has been consumed for a given level of output than the quantity budgeted. Similarly, when direct labour hours are used to absorb variable overheads, a difference between actual direct labour hours and standard direct labour hours will result in a variable overhead efficiency variance given by the formula:

$$(AH - SH) \times VR$$

where
SH = standard direct labour hours
AH = actual direct labour hours
VR = variable overhead recovery rate per direct labour hour

On the assumption that $AH = SH$ (hence no variable overhead efficiency variance), Figure 11.6 shows a simplified analysis of variable overhead variances.

A great improvement would be to indicate on this report the probability of the variances shown actually occurring, thereby incorporating statistical analysis (see section headed 'Tolerance Limits' in Chapter 10) into cost control.

Department: ____________ *Month ending:* ____________

Variable overhead items	Actual	Budget for 800 standard hours	Variance	Explanation
	£	£	£	
Materials handling	8 325	8 000	325 U	Wrong grade of worker
Idle time	850	800	50 U	Machine breakdown
Rework	825	800	25 U	Apprentice used
Overtime premium	250	400	150 F	Closed two Saturdays
Supplies	4 000	3 600	400 U	Substitute cutting materials
	14 250	13 600	950 U	

Budgeted rate: £1.70 per standard hour
Standard hours allowed: 8 000

U = Unfavourable
F = Favourable

Figure 11.6: **Variable overhead variance report**

In connection with fixed overheads, the variances that can be identified are the budget variance (where the actual expenditure on fixed overhead items differs from the standard or budgeted expenditure) and the capacity variance. This latter variance is only associated with fixed overheads and it occurs when the level of activity used to spread fixed overhead costs over production (i.e. normal capacity or whatever other method may be chosen) differs from the level actually experienced. The fixed overhead capacity variance is a measure of the benefit of working above, or the cost of working below, normal capacity, and it is given by:

$$(\text{normal activity (in hours)} - AH) \times \text{fixed overhead rate.}$$

It is inevitable, given the nature of fixed cost behaviour and the problem of absorbing fixed costs over production, that capacity variances will frequently occur because it is unlikely that management will be able to operate continually at normal capacity which is the only way to avoid capacity variances (other than revising the fixed overhead recovery rate so that fixed costs are fully absorbed by the level of output achieved). The causes of a fixed overhead capacity variance (i.e. the reasons why actual activity is not equal to normal activity) may be poor production scheduling that leads to bottlenecks and low output; unexpected machine breakdowns; strikes; a shortage of skilled operatives or materials; acts of God (such as floods); and so forth. Figure 11.7 summarizes a fixed overhead variance report.

Department: ______________ *Month ending:* ______________

Fixed overhead items

	Actual	*Budget*	*Variance*		Explanation
	£	£	£		
Supervision	1 700	1 700	—		
Depreciation—plant	2 000	2 000	—		
Depreciation—equipment	5 000	5 000	—		
Rates	1 150	1 000	150	U	Increased assessment
Insurance	350	300	50	U	Increased cover
	10 200	10 000	200	U	

Normal capacity: 10 000 standard hours. Budgeted rate: £1.00 per SH
Actual level: 8 000 standard hours U = Unfavourable

Figure 11.7: Fixed overhead variance report

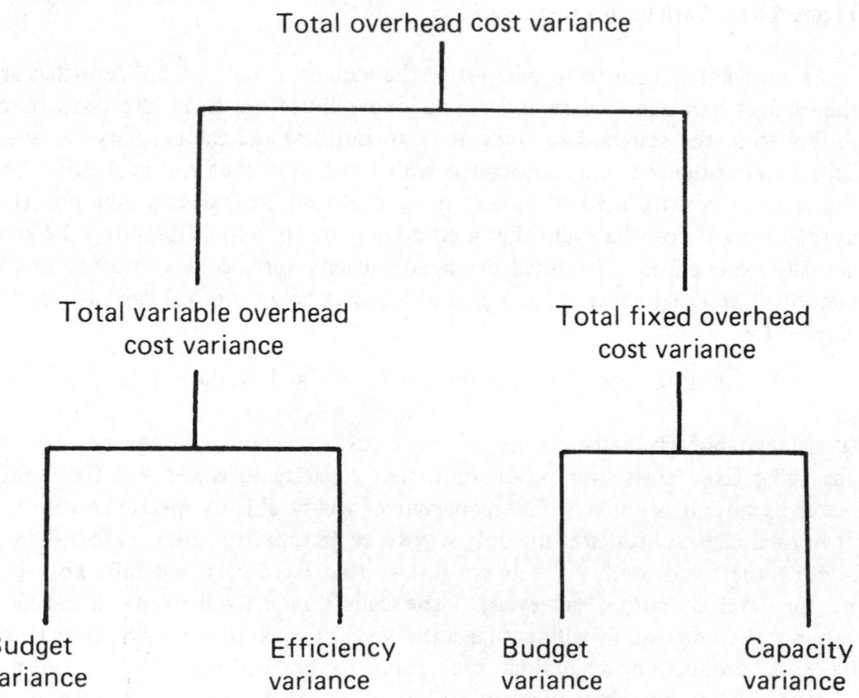

Figure 11.8: Overhead cost variances

From Figure 11.7 it can be calculated that the total fixed overhead variance is £2 200 made up as follows:

Actual fixed overheads incurred	£10 200
Overheads applied ($AH \times SR = 8\,000 \times £1.00$)	£8 000
Total variance (adverse)	£2 200

Of this total, the budget variance is £10 200 – £10 000 = +£200, and the capacity variance is (10 000 – 8 000) × £1.00 = +£2 000, both of which are adverse variances and which together account for the total fixed overhead variance of £2 200 (adverse).

Overhead variances – both fixed and variable – are summarized in Figure 11.8. (Together with Figure 11.5, Figure 11.8 summarizes the major direct and overhead cost variances.)

The analysis contained in Figures 11.6 and 11.7 can be combined as shown in Figure 11.9 in a most valuable manner for appreciating the overall situation with regard to overhead costs. Figure 11.9 shows exactly where overhead variances arose and the explanations for fixed and variable variances are shown in Figures 11.6 and 11.7.

An overall summary of direct and overhead cost variances is shown in Figure 11.10. Included in this summary are three further variances relating to fixed overheads (efficiency, idle time, and calendar variances) that are analogous to their direct labour equivalents. Also an additional direct material variance for scrap is shown, but it is straightforward.

SALES VARIANCES

In the same way that standards can be set for non-production items (see section headed 'Non-Production Standards' in Chapter 10) so variance analysis can be carried out for non-production items.

When actual selling prices differ from standard selling prices, a *sales price variance* can be computed. Standard selling prices will be used in compiling budgets, but it may be necessary to adapt to changing market conditions by raising or lowering prices, so it becomes desirable to segregate variances due to price changes from variances due to quantity and product mix.

Quantity and mix are the two components of *sales volume variances*, and variations in profit can be explained to some extent by analysing sales quantity and sales mix.

The formulae for computing sales variances are:

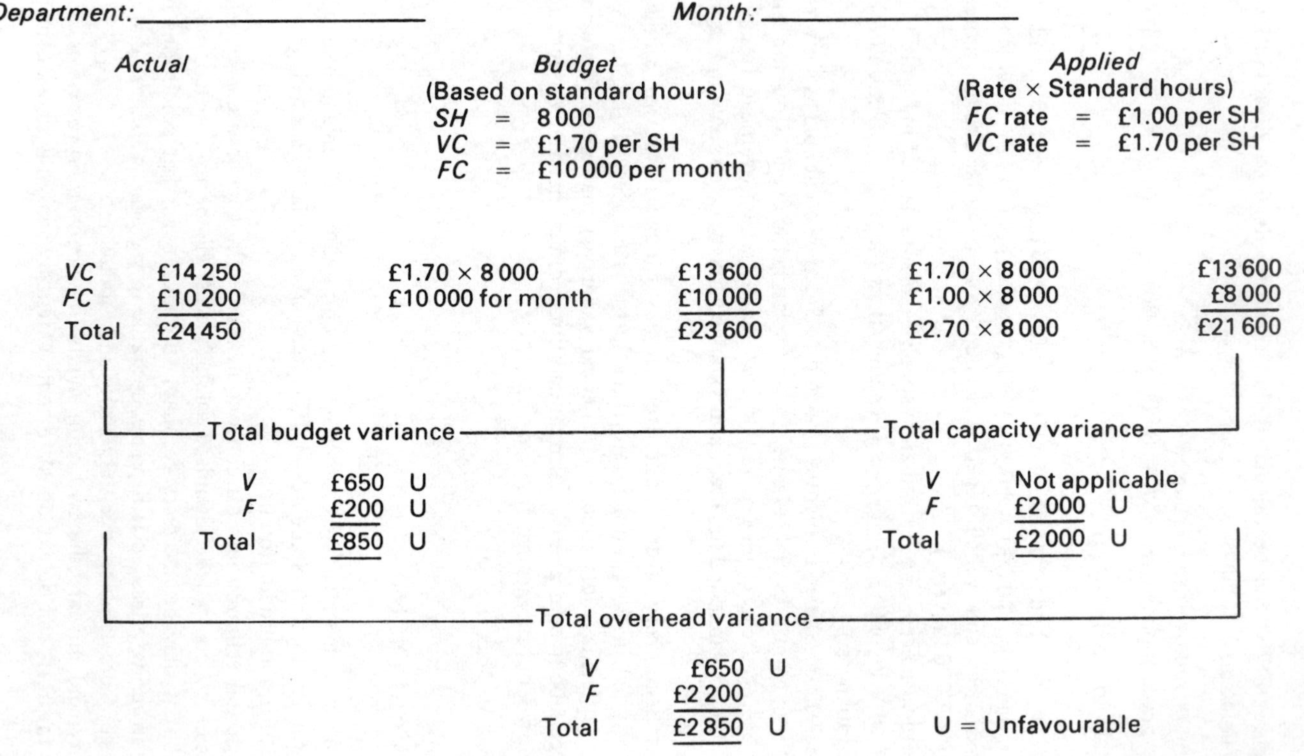

Figure 11.9: Fixed–Variable overhead analysis

Type of variance	*Cause of cost variation*	*Primary responsible individual*
1 *Direct material*		
(a) Price variance	Increase/decrease in actual cost	Chief buyer
(b) Usage variance	Increase/decrease in actual usage	Production manager
(c) Yield variance	Increase/decrease in actual output	Production manager
(d) Mix variance	Increase/decrease due to material mix differing from standard mix	Production manager or chief chemist
(e) Scrap variance	Increase/decrease in actual scrap	Production manager
2 *Direct labour*		
(a) Rate variance	Increase/decrease in actual rates	Production manager
(b) Efficiency variance	Increase/decrease in rate of output	Production manager
(c) Mix variance	Increase/decrease due to labour mix differing from standard mix	Production manager
(d) Idle time variance	Standard labour cost of abnormal idle time	Production manager
(e) Calendar variance	Standard labour cost of lost time due to paid holidays	Uncontrollable
3 *Variable overheads*		
(a) Budget variance	Increase/decrease due to price changes	Chief buyer
(b) Efficiency variance	Change in consumption per unit of output	Production manager
4 *Fixed overheads*		
(a) Budget variance	Increase/decrease in actual costs	
(b) Capacity variance	Increase/decrease in budgeted output	Analysis of specific causes needed to determine responsibility
(c) Efficiency variance	Increase/decrease in budgeted rate of output for hours worked	
(d) Idle time variance	Standard fixed overhead cost lost due to abnormal idle time	
(e) Calendar variance	Standard fixed overhead cost lost due to paid holidays	

Figure 11.10: Direct and indirect overhead cost summary

Sales price variance = actual units sold × (actual price − standard price)

Sales volume variance = sales quantity variance + sales mix variance

Sales quantity variance = budgeted profit on budgeted sales − expected profit on actual sales

Sales mix variance = expected profit on actual sales − standard profit on actual sales

'Expected profit on actual sales' is calculated as though profit increases or decreases proportionately with changes in the level of sales. 'Standard profit on actual sales' is the sum of the standard profit per unit for all units sold. (For a single product firm, or in one where the profit per unit of sales is constant over the product range, the standard profit on actual sales is equal to the expected profit on actual sales, and the sales mix variance will necessarily be nil.)

The following example should make the methodology clear. Budgeted sales of a company's two products for a forthcoming period were as follows:

Product A 500 units @ £2.00 per unit
Product B 700 units @ £1.50 per unit

and their costs were:

Product A £1.75 per unit
Product B £1.30 per unit

Actual sales for the period were.

Product A 560 units @ £1.95 per unit
Product B 710 units @ £1.40 per unit

Budgeted sales revenue	= £[(500 × 2.00) + (700 × 1.50)] =	£2 050	
Actual sales revenue	= £[(560 × 1.95) + (710 × 1.40)] =	£2 086	
Budgeted profit	= £[(500 × 0.25) + (700 × 0.20)] =	£265	
Actual profit	= £[(560 × 0.20) + (710 × 0.10)] =	£183	
Total sales variance			−£82
Sales price variance	= £[560 × (1.95 − 2.00)] + [710 × (1.40 − 1.50)] =		−£99
Sales volume variance:			
Quantity variance	= £265 − [$\frac{2086}{2050}$ × 265] =		+£4
Mix variance	= £269 − [(560 × 0.25) + (710 × 0.20)] =		+£13
Sales volume variance			+£17
Total sales variance			−£82

VARIANCE ANALYSIS FOR DISTRIBUTION COST CONTROL

As with production costing, the analysis of cost variances in distribution costing is the first step toward the goal of identifying the factors that caused the difference between the standard and actual costs so that any inefficiencies can be eliminated. To do this, each enterprise will have to decide what specific variance analyses it may want to use. Often companies only compute a net variance for their distribution costs and do not attempt to break the variance down into causal factors. This practice is not to be encouraged, however, since it tends to hide inefficiencies. If the analysis is to be meaningful the variance must be further explained in terms of price and efficiency components. Such price and quantity or efficiency variances can be computed for distribution activities. The price variance is given by:

$$(\text{Standard price} - \text{Actual price}) \times \text{Actual work units}$$

and the quantity (or efficiency) variance is given by:

$$(\text{Budgeted work units} - \text{Actual work units}) \times \text{Standard price}$$

A variance reporting example

The distribution costs of the Hill Company are analyzed by territories: data for the southern territory is shown in Figure 11.11. The warehousing and handling function's standards are:

	Total standard for direct and indirect costs (£)
Variable costs:	
Receiving	21 per shipment
Pricing, tagging and marking	6 per unit handled
Sorting	5 per order
Handling returns	10 per return
Taking physical inventory	0.50 per unit warehouse unit
Clerical handling of shipping orders	2 per item
Fixed costs:	
Rent	600 per month per territory
Depreciation	450 per month per territory

The following units of variability were budgeted and recorded for the month of January 1982:

HILL COMPANY –

Expense variance report –
January

	Units of variability	(1) Actual cost (actual @ actual price)
Detailed function:	Shipment	
Receiving:		
direct costs		£ 6,400
indirect costs	(420/(500 × £2,500	2,100
Total		£ 8,500
Pricing, tagging and marking:	Unit handled	
direct costs		1,115
Sorting: direct costs	Order	565
Handling returns:		
direct costs	Return	680
Taking physical inventory	Warehouse unit	880
Clerical handling of shipping orders:		
direct costs	Item	£ 500
indirect costs	(780/(900 × £1,223)	1,060
Total		£ 1,560
Total variable expense		£13,300
Fixed expense:		
rent		650
depreciation		445
Total warehousing and handling		£14,395

F = favourable; U = unfavourable

Figure 11.11: Distribution cost variances

SOUTHERN TERRITORY

warehousing and handling
1982

(2)	*(3)*	*(2 – 1)*	*(3 – 2)*	*(3 – 1)*
Actual units @ standard price	*Budgeted costs (budgeted units @ standard price)*	*Price variance*	*Efficiency variance*	*Net variance*
£8,820 (420 × £21)	£ 8,400 (400 × £21)	£320 F	£420 U	£100 U
1,338 (223 × £6)	1,200 (200 × £6)	223 F	138 U	85 F
540 (108 × £5)	500 (110 × £5)	25 U	10 F	15 U
710 (71 × £10)	700 (70 × £10)	30 F	10 U	20 F
815 (1,630 × £0.50)	800 (1,600 × £0.50)	65 U	15 U	80 U
1,560 (780 × £2)	1,500 (750 × £2)	0	60 U	60 U
	£13,150	£483 F	£633 U	£150 U
	600			50 U
	450			5 F
	£14,200			£195 U

	Budgeted	Actual
Shipments	400	420
Units handled	200	223
Orders	110	108
Returns	70	71
Warehouse unit	1 600	1 630
Item	750	780

Southern territory's actual direct costs for the month of January 1982 were as follows:

Receiving	£6 400
Pricing, tagging and marking	1 115
Sorting	565
Handling returns	680
Taking physical inventory	880
Clerical handling of shipping orders	500
Rent	650
Depreciation	445

The company allocates the following actual indirect costs to its southern and northern territories:

Receiving (allocated on actual shipments: southern 420, northern 80)	£2 500
Clerical handling of shipping orders (allocated on actual items: southern 780, northern 120)	1 223

Efficiency variance

Shipments received is the unit of variability chosen for the receiving function. There were a total of 420 shipments made, while only 400 shipments were budgeted. This results in an unfavourable efficiency variance because actual shipments exceeded those budgeted. (It should be noted here that care must be used in analyzing distribution cost variances because it is easy to misinterpret the results associated with such costs. Each cost variance is considered favourable or unfavourable as far as that individual detailed function is concerned, not for its effect on the overall company.) The efficiency variance in this case is unfavourable because 20 more shipments were made than planned. Hence, orders of larger quantities should be encouraged to save costs in receiving.

Price variance

The actual cost of £20.238 (i.e. £8 500 total actual cost of receiving as shown in Figure 11.11 ÷ 420 actual units) for each shipment received is less than the standard price of £21.00, which results in a favourable price variance. This difference in price is multiplied by the actual shipments to give a total favourable price variance of £320. It is not necessary to compute the actual cost per unit using the format illustrated in Figure 11.11, since the price variance can be determined by comparing total actual cost to the actual units at standard price shown in Column 2.

Efficiency and price variances are computed for variable costs only. Only a net variance is computed for the two fixed expenses shown in Figure 11.11. This measures the difference between budgeted costs (budgeted units at standard price) and actual costs (actual units at actual price).

A STANDARD COSTING EXAMPLE

MNO Ltd – Standard Costing

MNO Ltd operates a system of standard costs. For a given four-week period, budgeted for sales of 10 000 units at £5 per unit, actual sales were 9 000 units at £5.125 per unit. Costs relating to that period were as follows:

	Standard £	*Actual* £
Materials	25 000	25 740
Wages	7 500	7 087
Fixed overhead	2 000	1 881
Variable overhead	1 000	925
Semivariable overhead	270	243
Standard hours	50 000	–
Actual hours	–	40 500

Notes.

1 The standard material content of each unit is estimated at 25 kg at 10p per kg; actual figures were 26 kg at 11p per kg.

2 The standard wages per unit are 5 hours at 15p per unit; actual wages were 4.5 hours at 17.5p.

3 Semivariable overhead consists of five-ninths fixed expense and four-ninths variable.

4 There were no opening stocks and the whole production for the period was sold.

5 The four-week period was a normal period.

You are required to draft a statement reconciling the standard net profit for the period with the net profit actually realized.

MNO Ltd – statement reconciling 'standard net profit' with 'realized net profit'

	Unfavourable	Favourable	
			£
Budgeted sales			
(10 000 units at £5 per unit)			50 000
Standard cost of sales			
(25 000 + 7 500 + 2 000 + 1 000 + 270)			35 770
Standard net profit (1.4230 per unit)			14 230
Variances:	Unfavour-able	Favour-able	
	£	£	
1 Sales volume:			
(10 000 – 9 000) × 1.4230	1 423		
Sales price:			
9 000 × £0.125		1 125	
2 Material price:			
26 × 9 000 × 1p	2 340		
Material usage (or efficiency):			
1 × 9 000 ×10p	900		
3 Labour rate (or price):			
4.5 × 9 000 × 0.025	1 012		
Labour efficiency:			
(45 000 – 40 500) × 15p		675	
4 Variable overhead expenditure (or budget):			
£1 033 – 9 000 × £0.112			
or £1 033 – 45 000 × £0.0225	25		
5 Fixed overhead budget (or expenditure):			
£2 016 – £2 150		134	
Fixed overhead efficiency:			
£0.043 (40 500 – 45 000)		193	
Fixed overhead volume:			
0.043 (50 000 – 40 500)	408		
	6 108	2 127	£ 3 981 unfavourable
Realized net profit			
(9 000 × £5.125) – £35 876 = £10 249			£10 249

Notes

1 Budgeted hours 10 000 units × 5 hours = 50 000 standard hours
Actual hours 9 000 units × 4.5 hours = 40 500 hours
Actual output 9 000 units × 5 hours = 45 000 standard hours

2 Variable overhead rate:

$$= \frac{\text{Budgeted variable overhead}}{\text{Budgeted hours}} = \frac{1\,000 + (4/9 \times 270)}{50\,000} = 0.0225$$

3 Fixed overhead rate:

$$= \frac{\text{Budgeted fixed overhead}}{\text{Budgeted hours}} = \frac{2\,000 + (5/9 \times 270)}{50\,000} = 0.043$$

Some of the main causes of overhead variances are:

1 Volume variances:
(*a*) Decreases in consumer demand
(*b*) Excess plant capacity
(*c*) Plant stoppages due to poor scheduling or input bottlenecks
(*d*) Calendar fluctuations that have not been allowed for.

2 Efficiency variances:
(*a*) Waste of materials
(*b*) Poor labour performance
(*c*) Employees not being properly fed with work
(*d*) Machine breakdowns
(*e*) Lack of inputs (e.g. operatives, tools, materials, instructions)
(*f*) Use of wrong grades of material and labour.

3 Budget variances:
(*a*) Unforeseen market price changes
(b) An inability to obtain the most favourable prices.

It is evident, therefore, that standard costing variance analysis provides a basis from which to investigate changes in costs but is not sufficiently subtle to analyse variances by detailed causes.

SUMMARY

The measurement of variances is a mechanical task that has no importance in itself. The value of variances comes from an analysis of significant variances, the identification of their causes, and the correction of these causes.

A large number of reasons are at play in causing variances – indeed, any agent of change is a potential source of a variation between an actual outcome and a desired (standard or budgeted) outcome. By classifying variances as direct material, direct labour, or overhead variances, attention is focused on possible causes of deviations.

Variances can be readily computed by means of simple formulae or by simple graphical analysis. Their significance is a statistical question that is not necessarily directly related to their magnitude.

In addition to standard costing variances, it is also possible to analyse variances in other areas of business activity. A variance is merely a difference between two observations, so variance analysis can be performed whenever an actual result can be compared with a planned result and it is sought to explain their difference. An obvious extension of the analysis of production variances is the analysis of sales variances, and variance analysis is an essential feature of budgetary control which stretches to every part of a company's operations.

Amongst the items listed on pp.381–3 for further reading, the following are especially recommended:

Anthony and Dearden,
Bierman and Dyckman;
De Coster and Schafer.

12

Ratio Analysis

THE ROLE OF RATIO ANALYSIS

Cost control endeavours can be aided considerably by using ratio analysis techniques. In principle, ratio analysis is a variation on the theme of budgeting and standard costing, although it tends to be concerned with broader issues than those that are the subject of, say, direct labour cost standards.

The rationale behind ratio analysis is that management must take a greater interest in *relative* as opposed to *absolute* figures in order to control costs. In other words, knowing how much has been spent is, in itself, not very informative; but knowing both how much *should* have been spent and the difference between this and how much *was* spent is informative and can help in securing control over costs.

It is possible to compute a great many ratios pertaining to liquidity, profitability, capital structure, stock market tests, etc., but this book is primarily concerned with operating cost ratios. A general factor applies, however, no matter what type of ratio is being computed: only significant factors (in a control sense) should be measured because the behaviour of insignificant factors will respond to the control of more significant ones. Since ratios can be worked out for the relationship between any two items, discretion should be carefully applied in identifying the items that are important in terms of control. Thus the ratio of:

$$\frac{\text{Motor insurance costs}}{\text{Direct labour hours worked}}$$

is unlikely to be of significant managerial value whereas:

$$\frac{\text{Indirect labour cost}}{\text{Output}} \times 100$$

is a helpful indicator of an important factor input.

In using ratio analysis it is imperative that when a ratio's actual value differs significantly from its expected value a cause is sought. The extent to which a variance (i.e. the difference between an actual ratio value and a desired ratio value) causes investigation will be determined – as with other variances – by the item in question, the tolerance limits, the size of the variance, and its statistical significance. Management by exception principles should be applied (as in Chapters 10 and 11) by which minor variances are ignored and only major variances are analysed in order to find and eliminate their cause.

Perhaps the biggest danger in using ratio analysis, assuming that the right ratios are being computed, is that stemming from the use of averages. The value of a ratio of indirect labour cost to output, measured monthly, may be acceptable (i.e. the variance may be minor and statistically insignificant) but it may conceal high and low values that arose in particular weeks that warrant remedial attention. For instance, a standard ratio for indirect labour cost to output may be £0.05 per unit of output. In a given month consisting of four weeks the ratio may be:

$$\frac{£500}{10\,000} = £0.05$$

This suggests that all is well, but if the ratios for the individual weeks are as shown in Figure 12.1 it is very evident that all is not well.

Week	*Indirect labour cost* £	*Output (units)*	*Ratio*
1	100	2 000	£0.05
2	150	5 000	£0.03
3	50	1 000	£0.05
4	200	2 000	£0.10
Total	500	10 000	£0.05

Figure 12.1: Ratio averages

All averaging suffers from the problem of compensating deviations. Very high performance (week 2) and very low performance (week 4) are, for very different reasons, both unsatisfactory, yet the monthly averaging process conceals their existence, and weekly averages conceal daily variations, and daily ones conceal hourly ones, and so on. The straightforward solution is to establish tolerance limits and time spans that fit each situation, and then to measure the ratio at the predetermined frequency so that the ratio is representative of the activity in question.

One major advantage of ratios is that they can facilitate the comparison of results on a common basis over time. Index numbers (of consumer prices, etc.) are a good example since they measure each year's prices in relation to a base of 1963 = 100. Because the base is constant, it is possible to see the relative increases/decreases from period to period.

The example that follows (NOP Ltd) shows a simple case of financial analysis in which all items in the company's balance sheet and profit and loss account for three years are expressed in terms of their absolute and relative values.

NOP Ltd—Financial analysis

		Balance sheet Year 1	Per cent	Balance sheet Year 2	Per cent	Balance sheet Year 3	Per cent
1	*Basic information*						
	Short-term financial assets	2 000	20	2 000	16	3 000	20.0
	Stocks	2 000	20	3 000	24	4 000	26.7
	Current assets	4 000	40	5 000	40	7 000	46.7
	Fixed assets	6 000	60	7 500	60	8 000	53.3
	Total assets	£10 000	100	£12 500	100	£15 000	100
	Current liabilities	2 000	20	4 000	32	5 000	33.3
	Capital	8 000	80	8 500	68	10 000	66.7
		£10 000	100	£12 500	100	£15 000	100
(a)	*Balance sheet trends* (Year 1 = 100)						
	Stocks	2 000	100	3 000	150	4 000	200
	Current assets	4 000	100	5 000	125	7 000	175
	Current liabilities	2 000	100	4 000	200	5 000	250

(b)	*Liquidity ratios*			
	Short-term assets	2 000	2 000	3 000
	Short-term financial liabilities	1 000	2 000	2 500
	Liquidity ratios	200%	200%	120%
(c)	*Working capital ratios*			
	Current assets	4 000	5 000	7 000
	Current liabilities	2 000	4 000	5 000
	Working capital ratios	200%	125%	140%
(d)	*Stock position*—Stocks as proportion of current assets	50%	60%	57.1%
(e)	*Long-term financial stability*			
	Capital	8 000	8 500	10 000
	Current liabilities	2 000	4 000	5 000
	Proprietary ratios	400%	212.5%	200%

NOP Ltd—Financial analysis—*continued*

	Profit and loss account		*Profit and loss account*		*Profit and loss account*	
	Year 1	*Per cent*	*Year 2*	*Per cent*	*Year 3*	*Per cent*
2 *Basic information*						
Gross sales·	10400		11160		12000	
Less: Sales returns and other deductions	400		1160		1000	
Net sales	10000	100.0	10000	100.0	11000	100.0
Less: Cost of sales	6500	65.0	6400	64.0	6600	60.0
Gross profit	£3500	35.0	£3600	36.0	4400	40.0
Less:						
Selling costs	1500	15.0	1650	16.5	1650	15.0
Administrative costs	600	6.0	600	6.0	605	5.5
Finance costs	50	0.5	50	0.5	55	0.5
Operating profit	1350	13.5	1300	13.0	2090	19.0
Add: Non-operating revenue	200		250		220	
Net profit (before tax)	1550	15.5	1550	15.5	2310	21.0
Less: Taxation	450		420		770	
Net profit (after tax)	£1100	11.0	£1130	11.3	£1540	14.0

(a) *Analysis of profitability* (as in trading account)						
Sales revenue	10 000	100	10 000	100	11 000	100
Cost of sales	6 500	65	6 400	64	6 600	60
Gross profit	£3 500	35	£3 600	36	£4 400	40
(b) *Profit and loss account trends* (Year 1 = 100)						
Net sales	10 000	100	10 000	100	11 000	110
Cost of sales	6 500	100	6400	98.5	6 600	101.5
(c) *Return on total funds employed*						
Profit (before tax and interest)	1 350		1 300		2 090	
Average funds employed	10 000		11 250		13 750	
Return	13.5%		11.5%		15.2%	
(d) *Return on proprietorship capital*						
Net profit (before tax)	1 550		1 550		2 310	
Average proprietorship capital	8 000		8 250		9 250	
Return	19.4%		18.8%		25%	

THE RATIO PYRAMID

A hierarchy of ratios can be seen to exist starting with the final measure of financial performance – the rate of return on capital invested (ROI) which is also known as the rate of return on capital employed (ROCE). This is the *primary ratio* and forms the apex of the ratio pyramid (or hierarchy), and consequently it is a highly aggregated measure. ROI is given by the formula:

$$\frac{\text{Net profit}}{\text{Capital invested}} \times 100 = \text{ROI}$$

The primary ratio is made up of two *secondary ratios*, each of which is also highly aggregated and broad:

$$\text{Profit ratio} = \frac{\text{Net profit}}{\text{Sales}}$$

$$\text{Capital turnover ratio} = \frac{\text{Sales}}{\text{Capital invested}}$$

These two secondary ratios are related in a very simple way to produce the primary ratio:

$$\frac{\text{Net profit}}{\text{Sales}} \times \frac{\text{Sales}}{\text{Capital invested}} = \frac{\text{Net profit}}{\text{Capital invested}}$$

which gives:

$$\text{Profit rate} \times \text{Capital turnover} = \text{Return on investment}$$

(This approach was introduced in Chapter 6, pp.127–30).

The general cause of any deviation in ROI from standard may be found by computing the profit ratio and the capital turnover ratio, but this is only a starting point. Before corrective action can be taken, a study of specific causes must be made, and hence *tertiary ratios* need to be worked out.

Tertiary ratios are those that constitute the secondary ratios. The profit ratio reflects the relationship between the gross profit rate, the level of sales, and overhead costs (i.e. net profit + overheads = gross profit) whilst the rate of capital turnover is affected by the level of sales and the capital structure mix (of fixed and working capital, etc). From these details it is a simple step to compute four tertiary ratios as follows:

1 $\frac{\text{Gross profit}}{\text{Sales}}$

2 $\dfrac{\text{Sales}}{\text{Overheads}}$

3 $\dfrac{\text{Sales}}{\text{Fixed assets}}$

4 $\dfrac{\text{Sales}}{\text{Working capital}}$

Many other levels of the ratio pyramid can be identified, and the process of decomposing broad ratios into their component parts can be continued further and further until the reasons for variances are known. If, for example, the tertiary ratio of sales to working capital (4 above) was broken down further, it will be seen to be made up of two ratios, which themselves are made up of many more subordinate ratios. Thus:

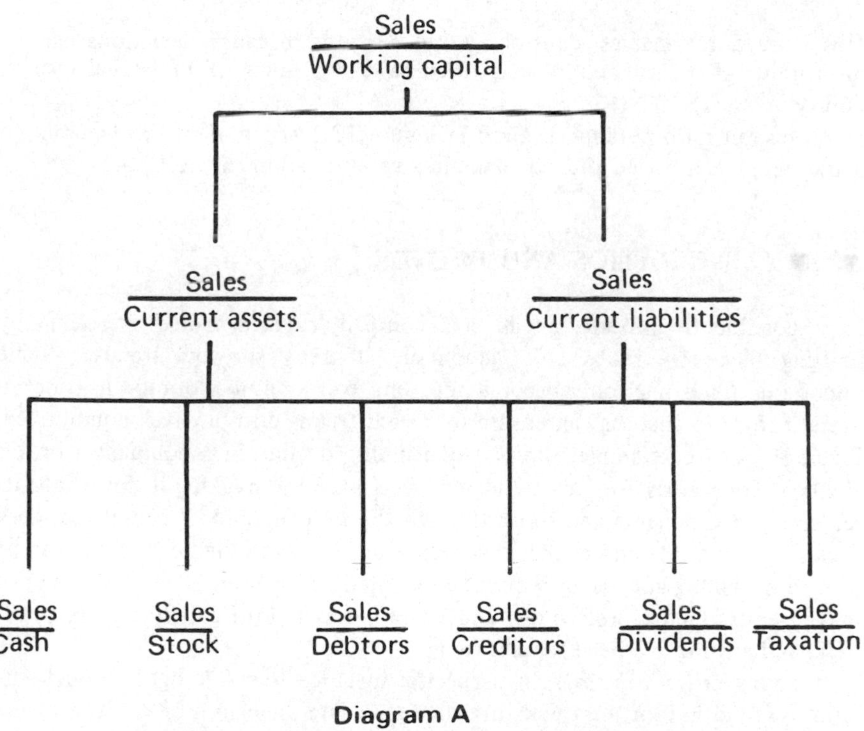

Diagram A

The decomposition can still go on because, for instance, the ratio of sales to stock is made up as follows:

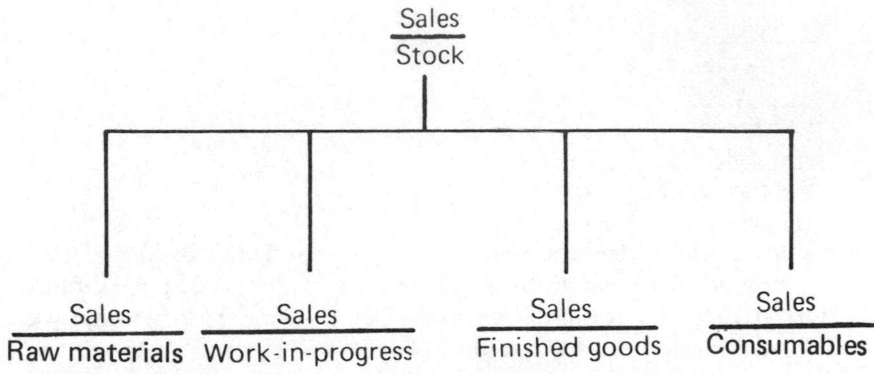

Diagram B

This procedure enables control to be exercised because deviations can be specifically identified and related (eventually) to areas of individual responsibility.

An overall ratio pyramid is given in Figure 12.1 and part of this (relating to marketing) is developed and examined in greater detail in Figure 12.3.

ANALYZING RATIOS AND TRENDS

It is possible to indicate trends in a company's performance over time by plotting successive ratios on a graph and thereby showing trends. Some important trends may only become apparent over a number of months (or even years) and ratio analysis can ensure that such trends do not develop unnoticed. Figure 12.4, for example, shows a continuing decline in a company's profitability. The causes for this trend may be found by breaking it down into its secondary components and so on through the ratio pyramid. These secondary trends – profit rate and capital turnover – are shown in Figure 12.5 and can be seen to be falling and rising respectively. Figure 12.6 then takes the former of these trends (falling profit rate) and decomposes it into a falling gross profit trend and a rising overhead to sales trend.

It could prove necessary in a specific instance to work right through the ratio pyramid in plotting trends in order to isolate the causes of variations from the desired trend line in high levels of the ratio hierarchy, and it may also be necessary to apply some imagination and common sense. This last mentioned requirement can be illustrated in two ways. First, the declining ROI noted in Figure 12.4 may be thought, prima facie, to be due to the falling net profit to

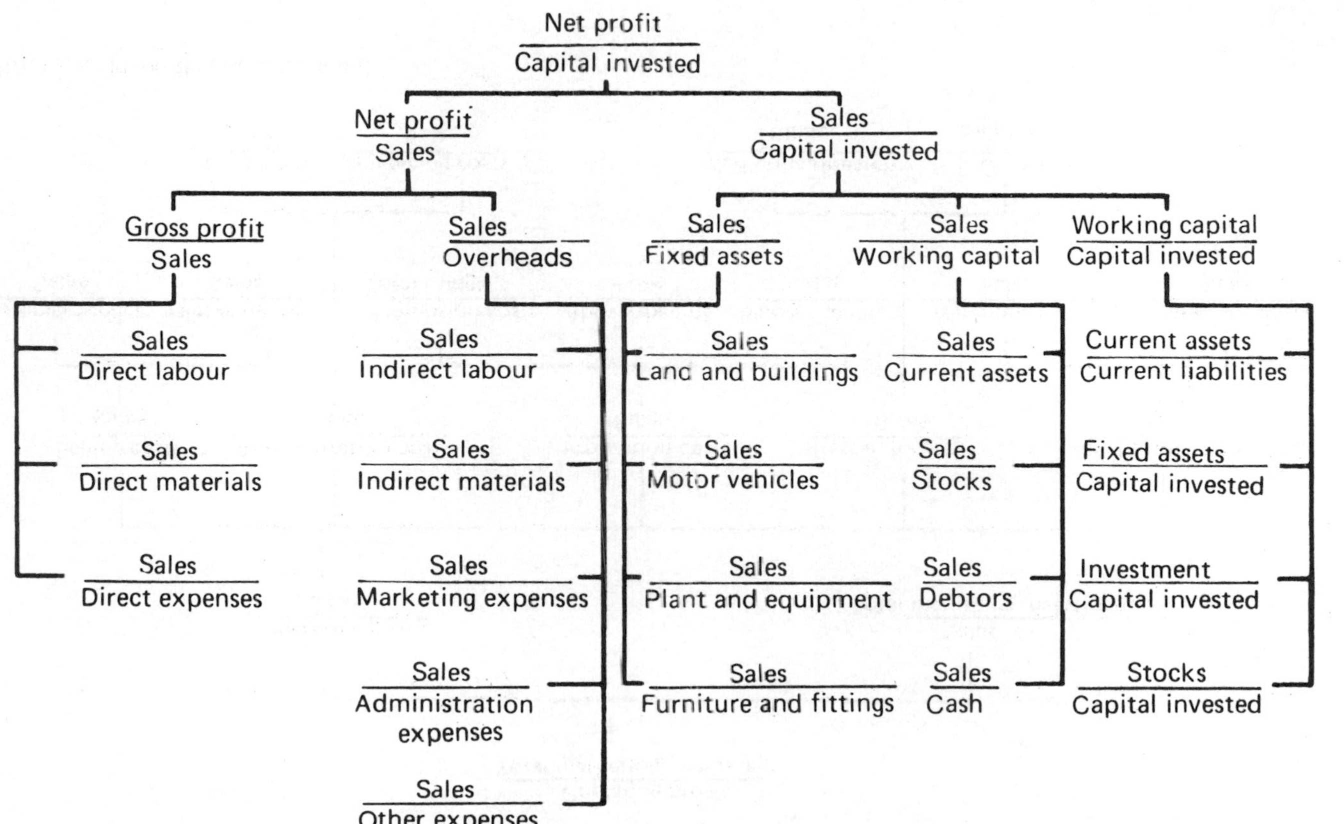

Figure 12.2: Ratio pyramid

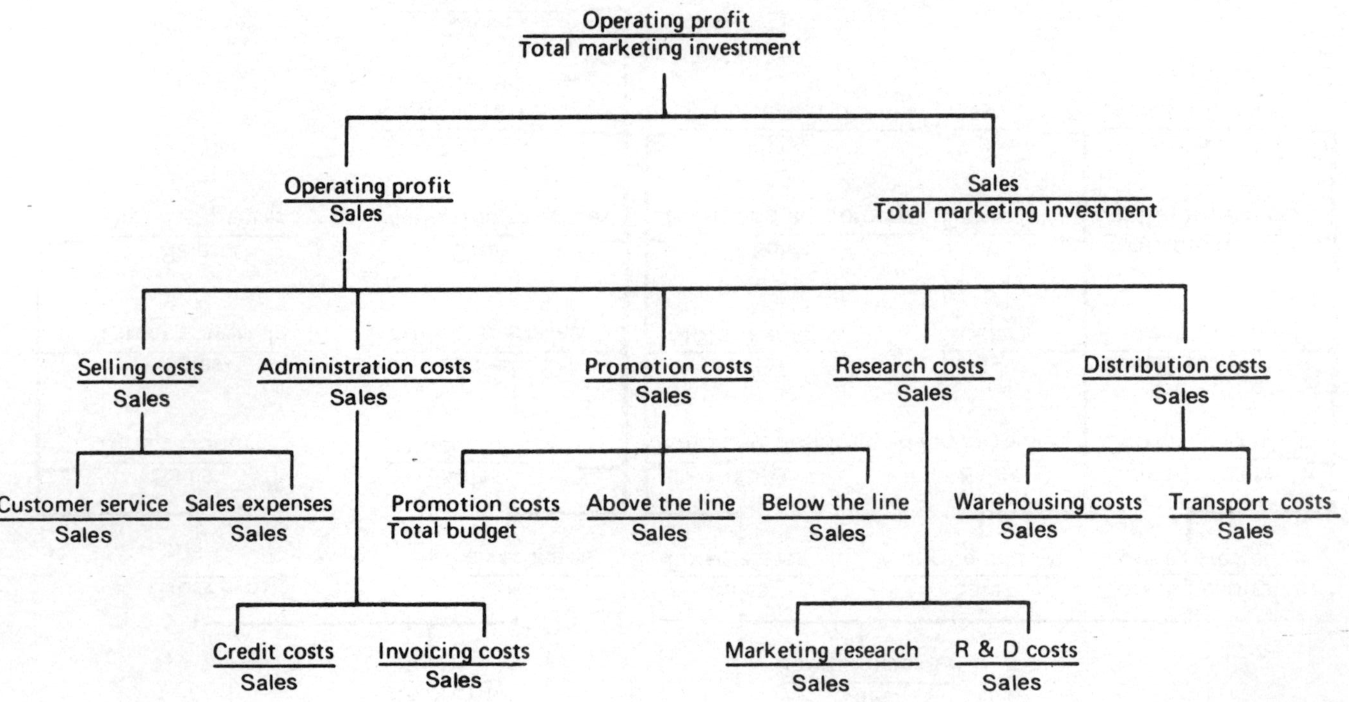

Figure 12.3: Marketing ratio pyramid

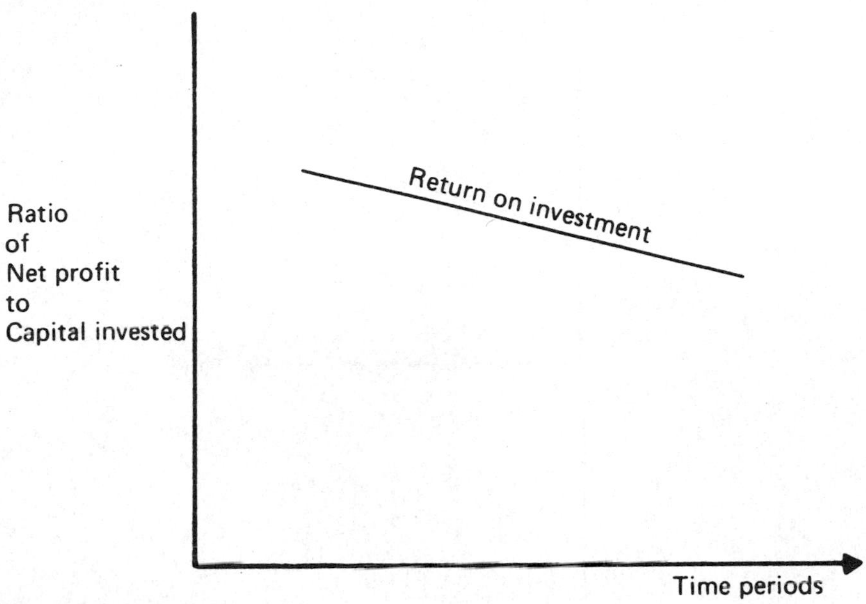

Figure 12.4: Primary trend

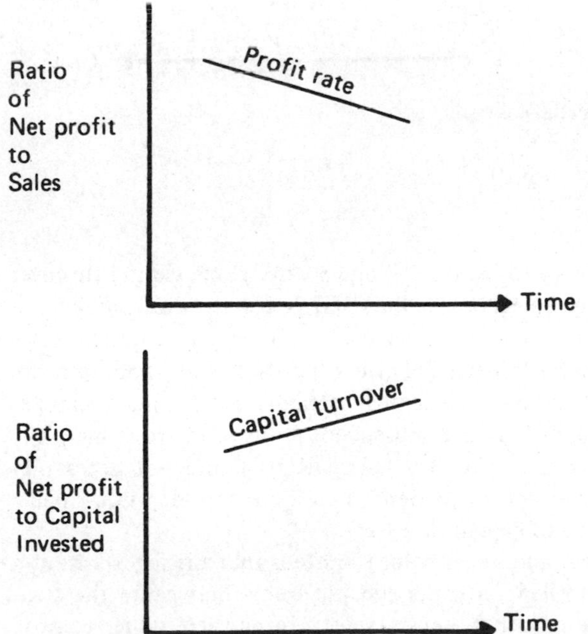

Figure 12.5: Secondary trends

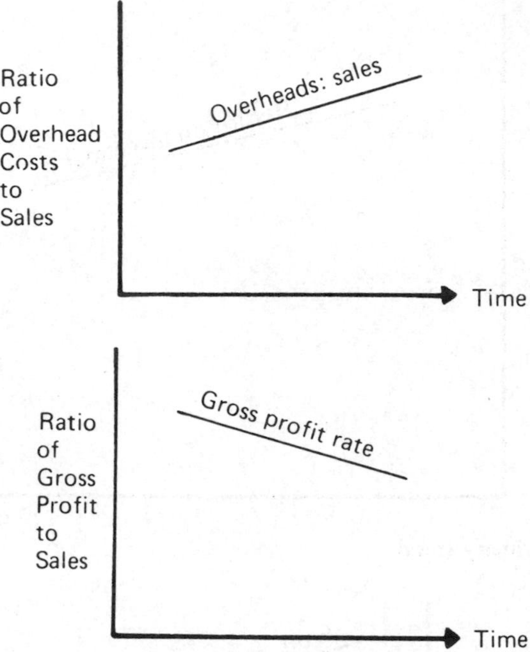

Figure 12.6: Tertiary trends

sales trend shown in Figure 12.5, and so the rising capital turnover trend as in Figure 12.5 may be ignored. But ROI is clearly the combined outcome of a particular level of profit and a particular quantity of capital investment, so any variation in either will inevitably affect the ROI. Furthermore, a rising aggregate trend of capital turnover will almost certainly conceal many more compensating highs and lows in tertiary and subsequent levels of the ratio hierarchy. It follows that attention in the light of a falling ROI should not necessarily be focused exclusively on the net profit trend, but some consideration should be given to the rate and trend of capital turnover.

The second commonsense point to note is that a rising overhead to sales trend cannot be controlled until the specific items that cause the trend have been identified and appropriate steps taken to bring them under control. Of course, the extent to which the decline of the profit rate (a secondary trend) is caused by either of its constituent tertiary trends should be carefully established.

RATIOS AND INTERFIRM COMPARISON

In many industries – and especially in those in which production methods, technology, product characteristics, and general operating conditions are very similar – it is helpful to have comparative figures for one's own company and for other companies within the industry. From published accounts it is possible to see the primary, secondary, and tertiary ratios (hence trends) of competing companies, but no reasons for divergences between one's own company's results and other companies' results can be discerned from such accounts due to a lack of detail relating to the lower part of the ratio pyramid (i.e. below the tertiary level), and therefore there is no guidance for future actions.

One major cause of divergence between the results of any two companies can be found in their use of differing accounting techniques and definitions. This will be seen, for example, if two companies purchase a similar asset each at the same point in time and one company chooses to depreciate the asset over four years whilst the other company chooses to take a 100 per cent depreciation allowance in the first year. It follows, therefore, that a meaningful comparison must be based on common definitions and usage, and this can best be achieved (for comparative purposes) by a central organization and for this reason the Centre for Interfirm Comparison was set up.

The British Institute of Management has published a *Management Information Sheet* (number 3 in a series) on the topic of interfirm comparisons, and the content of this is reproduced (with permission) below.

1 Objectives – management's need for comparative data It is now generally accepted that a firm can, by comparing certain of its accounting, costing and other performance data with those of other firms in its industry, discover otherwise unnoticed weaknesses in its policy and operations. This implies that a firm can use figures of other firms as an instrument of self-diagnosis, as a means of evaluating its own profitability and productivity, and as a basis for setting targets of performance.

Comparative yardsticks of performance of this kind become available through interfirm comparisons (IFC) of management ratios. The term 'IFC' refers to an organized pooling amongst firms of an industry of certain business figures on an anonymous, voluntary, confidential and agreed uniform basis.

2 The Centre for Interfirm Comparison Ltd The Centre for Interfirm Comparison was set up in 1959 as an independent, autonomous and non-profit-making organization by the BIM in association with the British Productivity Council in order to meet the demand of industry and trade for an expert body to conduct interfirm comparisons of management ratios (see section 3) on a confidential basis as a service to management. This service is available (for an agreed fee) both to members and non-members of the sponsoring organizations. Each company taking part receives a confidential report showing how its overall success compares with that of others in the same industry, and *why* it differs from theirs. The tables which form part of these reports do not only show averages, but present, anonymously, the actual ratios of each participating firm. In conducting these IFCs every care is taken to ensure that participants cannot be identified and that the figures contributed by them are strictly comparable.

The Centre's reports are prepared with the needs of the managing director in mind: they alert him to those major aspects of policy and performance which require his special attention, and indicate the direction in which improvements should be made. In other words, the Centre's IFCs are not statistical surveys but provide each of the firms taking part with a valuable aid to self-diagnosis. So far, the Centre has prepared or conducted interfirm comparisons in some 60 industries and trades. Most of them were carried out in cooperation with the trade association concerned. A list of these industries is available on request from the Centre for Interfirm Comparison. Facilities for setting up new comparison groups are offered by the Centre to companies who do not operate in industries covered by IFC.

3 Management ratios Interfirm comparison is concerned with the individual firm, its success, and the part played by general management in making it successful. It is the Centre's policy to ensure that the content of its interfirm comparisons appeals to those at general management level in participating firms because:

(*a*) The results of an IFC provide a stimulus to self-criticism: if self-criticism starts at the top, it will have the strongest impact on the development of the firm concerned.

(*b*) General management is in the best position to decide on remedial action, and to see to its implementation.

This means that an IFC will have the greatest impact if it deals with matters of concern to the men who are not primarily concerned with any one major function or department of the business, but who are responsible for ensuring that through proper coordination of the manufacturing, marketing, financial and other major operations of the business, a satisfactory profit is earned on the capital it employs.

This concern determines the choice of the principal data (management ratios) used by the Centre in its interfirm comparisons; i.e. these comparisons often take as a starting point the ratio of operating profit/operating assets which reflects the earning power of the operations of a business, and shows whether profitable use has been made of its assets. This is the 'primary ratio' used by the Centre in an IFC for general management.

The other ratios of a properly constructed set of management ratios are selected to show in successive stages and in a systematic logical manner why the above mentioned primary ratio differs from those of other firms. These 'explanatory' ratios will cover all major cost/sales and sales/asset relationships which determine the primary ratio and which, therefore, have to be taken into account by management in the control and planning of the business as a whole. Such a set of management ratios was devised by the Centre some years ago specially for general management use, and because it can be presented diagrammatically in the form of a pyramid it is now commonly called a 'pyramid of ratios'. Examples of pyramids can be obtained from the Centre for Inter-firm Comparison Ltd.

4 Interpretation of management ratios It is not the object of an IFC to compare 'firms' as such, but to reveal what effect certain differences in their features and practices have on their performance. In fact, if there were no differences between the firms taking part they could learn nothing from the comparison. Therefore, the Centre takes special care to *explain* to participating firms why their pyramid ratios differ from those of others in their industry. Such explanations are, for instance, given by providing subsidiary data which are selected because they will reflect the impact of such factors as size; labour productivity; degree of mechanisation; plant capacity utilization; type of market supplied; distribution methods; stock policy.

5 Conclusion As the foregoing shows:

(*a*) An IFC for management must be based on a comprehensive set of management ratios so as to enable participants to see:

  (*i*) how their success and performance compare with those of other firms,
  and
  (*ii*) why they differ.

(*b*) The accounting data of the firms covered must be comparable. This means that figures taken from published accounts are not suitable for IFC.

(*c*) The IFC report must provide background data which a firm taking part needs in order to understand the reasons for differences between its pyramid ratios and those of other participants.

A brochure is available from the Centre which gives further information under such headings as 'What does the Centre do?'; 'Confidentiality'; 'Comparability';

'What participation involves for a firm'. The brochure gives a figure example illustrating how a particular company can benefit from participation in an IFC and also refers to the seminars which the Centre conducts both in London and other major cities. The brochure, and other papers on various aspects of IFC are available free of charge from the Centre for Interfirm Comparison Ltd, 25, Bloomsbury Square, London WC1A 2PJ.

Example of the use of interfirm comparison

Whilst interfirm comparison figures are expressed in relation to quartiles and the median, (i.e. if all results are ranked in descending order of size, the first quartile is represented by the figure that comes one quarter of the way down, the median is the figure that comes half way down, and the third quartile is three quarters of the way down) and the following example (OPQ Ltd) simplifies this by just giving the general approach to interfirm comparisons. The necessary steps in such an exercise are:

1 Ensure that the reports, etc., that are to be compared incorporate figures that have been prepared on a comparable basis.
2 Compute the required ratios, percentages, and key totals from submitted reports.
3 Compare the results of each company with the aggregate results.
4 Introduce intangible or qualitative factors that may aid in interpreting the results of each individual company in the light of the whole picture.
5 Examine the numerator, denominator, and lower ratios in instances where a ratio differs significantly from the external standard (or average, median, or whatever).
6 Determine the adjustment (if any) that is required to bring a given company's divergent ratio into line with the aggregate norm.

OPQ Ltd – ratio analysis

The following is a simple example of interfirm comparison. Here are the ratios of OPQ Ltd, a firm in a light engineering industry, for the two years 1980 and 1981:

Table 1 OPQ's own figures:

	Ratio	Unit	1980	1981
1	Operating profit / Assets employed	%	8.25	10.0
2	Operating profit / Sales	%	5.5	6.1
3	Sales / Assets employed	times	1.5	1.65
3(a)	Assets employed / Average daily sales	days*	249	222
4	Production cost of sales / Sales	%	71.0	70.4
5	Distribution and marketing expenses / Sales	%	17.7	17.7
6	General and administrative expenses / Sales	%	5.8	5.8
7	Current assets / Average daily sales	days*	215	188
8	Fixed assets / Average daily sales	days*	34	34
9	Material stocks / Average daily sales	days*	49	45
10	Work-in-progress / Average daily sales	days*	53	46
11	Finished stocks / Average daily sales	days*	52	39
12	Debtors / Average daily sales	days*	61	54

*Days required to turn the asset item over once.

This looks like a success story. Profit on assets employed has gone up from 8.25 per cent to 10 per cent due to an increase in the firm's profit on sales (ratio 2) and the better use it seems to have made of its assets (ratios 3 and 3a). The higher profit on sales seems to have been achieved through operational improvements which resulted in a lower ratio of cost of production (ratio 4). The firm's faster turnover of assets (ratio 3) is due mainly to a faster turnover of current assets (ratio 7) and this in turn is due to accelerated turnovers of material stocks (ratio 9), work-in-progress (ratio 10), finished stock (ratio 11), and debtors (ratio 12).

The firm's illusion of success was shattered when it compared its ratios with those of other light engineering firms of its type. The following table is an extract from the results – it gives the figures of only 5 of the 22 participating firms. OPQ Ltd's figures are shown under letter C.

Table 2 The interfirm comparison

	Ratio		*Firm*				
			A	*B*	*C*	*D*	*E*
1	Operating profit / Assets employed	(%)	18.0	14.3	10.0	7.9	4.0
2	Operating profit / Sales	(%)	15.0	13.1	6.1	8.1	2.0
3	Sales / Assets employed		1.20	1.09	1.65	0.98	2.0
3(a)	Assets employed / Average daily sales	*	304	335	222	372	182
4	Production cost of sales / Sales	(%)	73.0	69.4	70.4	72.5	79.0
5	Distribution and marketing expenses / Sales	(%)	8.0	13.1	17.7	13.7	15.0
6	General and administrative expenses / Sales	(%)	4.0	4.4	5.8	5.7	4.0
7	Current assets / Average daily sales	*	213	219	188	288	129
8	Fixed assets / Average daily sales	*	91	116	34	84	53

9	Material stocks / Average daily sales	*	45	43	45	47	29
10	Work-in-progress / Average daily sales	*	51	47	46	60	52
11	Finished stocks / Average daily sales	*	71	63	39	94	22
12	Debtors / Average daily sales	*	36	84	54	18	26

* Days required to turn the asset item over once

In this year the firm's operating profit on assets employed is well below that of two other firms, and this appears to be due to its profit on sales (ratio 2) being relatively low. This in turn is mainly due to the firm's high distribution and marketing expenses (ratio 5). In the actual comparison further ratios were given helping firm C to establish to what extent its higher ratio 5 was due to higher costs of distribution and warehousing; higher costs of advertising and sales promotion; or higher costs of other selling activities (e.g. cost of sales personnel).

SUMMARY

Ratio analysis is an extension of other methods of cost control by which a desirable ratio is predetermined and actual performance is compared with the standard and corrective action taken if the deviation is statistically significant.

Whilst relative figures are more valuable than many absolute figures, dangers exist in covering operations with a blanket of averages: ratios should be measured for important variables only and at frequent intervals to avoid the possibility of compensating variances.

A ratio pyramid, with ROI at the apex, can be compiled for any company, with similar ratio hierarchies being applicable in different functional areas. The identification of a ratio variation can initiate an investigation throughout the pyramid until the specific causes for variation are known and corrected.

Ratios permit comparisons over consecutive periods of time and hence the monitoring of trends. The reasons for trends can be found by tracing them through lower and lower levels of the ratio hierarchy. It is possible – and necessary for effective cost control – to trace variances to responsible individuals.

Comparative figures for a company and its (anonymous) competitors can be obtained in over 60 industries through participation in interfirm comparison programmes based on uniform accounting techniques and definitions.

Overall Cost Control

Amongst the items listed on pp.381–3 for further reading, the following are especially recommended:

Boyce and Christie;
Ingham and Harrison;
Tucker;
Westwick.

13

Management Audit

INTRODUCTION

As business becomes more and more complex, the manager becomes increasingly dependent on the established systems of recording, processing and reporting information for planning and control purposes. But the existence of a good set of control and information systems, even with good supervision, does not necessarily mean that no other management tools are required.

If all supervisors (departmental managers, for example) were highly trained and competent, if all employees were always careful and diligent, if plans and policies worked as originally envisaged and were always fully understood, and if the systems themselves were well designed, then it could be that no other management tools would be necessary. Unfortunately, this situation is idealistic, and is not to be found in practice.

The need arises, therefore, for some means of ensuring that the established systems, plans, etc., are appropriate and that they are being adhered to. This, in a nutshell, is the nature and task of internal auditing.

INTERNAL AUDITING

An increasingly useful service to management is being provided by the internal audit function. This activity is not closely related to the external audit (i.e. the annual financial audit) in principle, but in many organizations it tends to live under the shadow of that activity.

The US-based Institute of Internal Auditors (which is active in this country, as evidenced by the existence of a UK chapter) publishes various guide-lines for members, and the current Statement of Responsibilities is shown in Figure 13.1.

NATURE

Internal auditing is an independent appraisal activity within an organization for the review of operations as a service to management. It is a managerial control which functions by measuring and evaluating the effectiveness of other controls.

OBJECTIVE AND SCOPE

The objective of internal auditing is to assist all members of management in the effective discharge of their responsibilities, by furnishing them with analyses, appraisals, recommendations and pertinent comments concerning the activities reviewed. The internal auditor is concerned with any phase of business activity where he can be of service to management. This involves going beyond the accounting and financial records to obtain a full understanding of the operations under review. The attainment of this overall objective involves such activities as:

- reviewing and appraising the soundness, adequacy and application of accounting, financial and other operating controls, and promoting effective control at reasonable cost;
- ascertaining the extent of compliance with established policies, plans and procedures;
- ascertaining the extent to which company assets are accounted for and safeguarded from losses of all kinds;
- ascertaining the reliability of management data developed within the organization;
- appraising the quality of performance in carrying out assigned responsibilities; and
- recommending operating improvements.

RESPONSIBILITY AND AUTHORITY

The responsibilities of internal auditing in the organization should be clearly established by management policy. The related authority should provide the internal auditor full access to all the organization's records, properties and personnel relevant to the subject under review. The internal auditor should be free to review and appraise policies, plans, procedures and records

The internal auditor's responsibilities should be:

- to inform and advise management, and to discharge this responsibility in a manner that is consistent with the Code of Ethics of The Institute of Internal Auditors; and

— to co-ordinate his activities with others so as to best achieve his audit objectives and the objectives of the organization.

In performing his functions, an internal auditor has no direct responsibility for, nor authority over, any of the activities which he reviews. Therefore, the internal audit review and appraisal does not in any way relieve other persons in the organization of the responsibilities assigned to them.

INDEPENDENCE

Independence is essential to the effectiveness of internal auditing. This independence is obtained primarily through organizational status and objectivity.

— The organizational status of the internal auditing function and the support accorded to it by management are major determinants of its range and value. The head of the internal auditing function, therefore, should be responsible to an officer whose authority is sufficient to assure both a broad range of audit coverage and the adequate consideration of and effective action on the audit findings and recommendations.
— Objectivity is essential to the audit function. Therefore, an internal auditor should not develop and install procedures, prepare records, or engage in any other activity which he would normally review and appraise and which could reasonably be construed to compromise his independence. His objectivity need not be adversely affected, however, by his determination and recommendation of the standards of control to be applied in the development of systems and procedures under his review.

Figure 13.1: Responsibilities of the internal auditor

However, the concept of 'internal control' is more appropriate in this context as it has wider coverage in that its scope embraces not only internal audit and internal check, but also encompasses the whole system of controls, financial and otherwise, established by management to facilitate orderly operations, protection of assets, and accuracy and reliability of records. In fact, internal control comprises the plan of organization, and all of the co-ordinating methods and measures adopted within the business to promote operational efficiency and encourage adherence to prescibed managerial policies.

Some of the more obvious points that internal control procedures should be designed to prevent and cover will usually include:

(*a*) the combination of duties that could enable one person to conceal irregularities;
(*b*) the possibilities of collusion, especially between related persons, among employees;
(*c*) the possible conflict of interests that may arise in the case of a responsible employee having other business interests;

(*d*) the extent to which those in positions of trust, especially where cash is concerned, fail to take regular holidays; and

(*e*) the operation of systems during times of absence (due to holidays, sickness and lunch breaks).

To cope successfully with these matters, the following principles of internal control have been developed:

1 Personnel should be reliable, and given duties commensurate with their abilities. Using low calibre staff for responsible tasks is grossly inefficient in either control or productivity terms.

2 The record-keeping function should be separated from the physical handling of assets. Thus the cashier should not maintain the cash book, those who handle incoming deliveries of goods should not keep the records of such deliveries, and those handling other assets should not have access to the relevant records.

3 The organizational structure should be appropriate and known by all. In this way, every employee will have and know he has a supervisor who will oversee his work and appraise his performance.

4 Responsibility should be delegated to individuals as far down the line as possible. The psychological impact of fixing responsibility in this way is to promote care and efficiency.

5 The establishing of routine procedures permits the division of duties and facilitates specialization, which results in automatic checks as each person involved validates the work done in earlier stages of the routine. Thus the authorization to pay a supplier for goods will require independent confirmation from several sources that the goods were ordered, delivered in the correct quantity, were of the right quality, and were invoiced at the specified price.

6 All documents must be controlled in such a way that information is recorded immediately, completely, and cannot be subsequently removed or altered without authorization. Cash tills, receipts and serially numbered documents all help in this control effort.

7 All employees should take their holiday entitlement, giving others the opportunity to ensure that everything is in order. In addition, job rotation is advisable for certain clerical jobs, especially those relating to debtors' and creditors' records and payments.

8 All phases of activity should be subjected to periodic review by 'outsiders'. For instance, bank reconciliations should not be performed by the cashier, and physical stocks should be counted periodically and compared with the records by non-stores personnel.

9 Physical safeguards should be available and used. Safes, security officers, restricted access and similar precautions can pay dividends.

10 The cost of internal control should not outweigh the benefits. The aims of accuracy and reliability in the records, and the safeguarding of the firm's assets and efficiency, cannot be achieved completely without conflicting with the criteria of speed and economy. The practical compromise is to make it as difficult as is practical, rather than impossible, for employees to be either dishonest or careless.

The internal audit staff who have to develop the internal control procedures, must be not only *au fait* with the firm's organizational structure, systems and managerial plans and policies at one time: they must also be kept informed of every change. This will cover, for instance, changes in the allocation of staff duties including promotions, dismissals, resignations and new appointments. Beyond this, however, the internal audit staff should be familiar with the firm's background, its competitors, production methods, products, marketing methods, principal customers, channels of distribution, principal suppliers and the industry itself.

From this background, the internal auditor's investigation will often follow the conventional professional auditor's general procedure. This is composed of three phases:

(*a*) ascertainment of the systems and procedures actually in use, which may differ significantly from those prescribed by management;
(*b*) testing the workings of selected parts of the systems in depth, to ensure that transactions are properly authorized and fully recorded; and
(*c*) assessing the effectiveness of the systems, their adequacy, and the extent to which employees adhere to them.

The work of the internal auditor will inevitably overlap with the work of the external auditor, since they are both concerned with such matters as the accuracy of financial records, the adequacy of accounting systems and the effectiveness of internal checks.

However, the internal auditor is primarily concerned with activities that are determined by top management, because these activities provide a valuable service to management. In contrast, the external auditor's tasks are prescribed by statute, and his first obligation is to the shareholders. As a result, the external auditor is more independent; but the internal auditor can be made independent of most managerial and other influences if he reports directly to, say, the managing director.

Irrespective of these differences, the means of performing their duties are similar, and they can help each other considerably. It is, in fact, desirable that they co-operate to prevent unnecessarily duplicated effort.

Apart from investigating and reporting on conformance to departmental and corporate policies and procedures in this way, the internal auditor can also examine such matters as adherence to schedules, quality control standards and budget allowances. In addition, reports and records can be reviewed to ensure that they are timely, accurate and complete. However, in the case of a function such as manufacturing, departments such as production planning, stock control, progressing and inspection exist to maintain checks on the physical activities involved. These departments perform duties that are beyond the scope of internal audit, but their records are within the scope of the internal audit department's authority, and hence are subject to investigation and appraisal.

A valuable practical aid in internal control is the internal control questionnaire. This specifies a list of points to be investigated for a particular area of operations, in order that the effectiveness of internal checks can be determined. Questionnaires should be drawn up for the following basic areas:

(*a*) general financial arrangements;
(*b*) payables;
(*c*) receivables;
(*d*) cash transactions;
(*e*) computer systems;
(*f*) fixed assets;
(*g*) investments;
(*h*) stocks (including work-in-progress); and
(*i*) wages and salaries.

However, techniques such as flow charts and questionnaires are only as useful as the thought and effort put into them enables them to be. The design of a suitable internal control questionnaire is a skilled task if it is to indicate weaknesses in the system of internal check and permit amendments to be made.

The precise system and techniques of internal control adopted by a firm will vary in accordance with its particular circumstances. There is no absolute standard of internal control, and any system for securing internal control must be balanced with the risks it is designed to check. Thus the checking of additions and extensions on suppliers' invoices for sums below a specified amount may not be tenable on a cost/benefit basis.

MANAGEMENT AUDITS

Internal control is concerned with the efficiency of systems, and not with the efficiency of performance or with effectiveness. The emergence of management auditing in recent years has complemented traditional internal control by focusing attention on the efficiency of performance.

Management auditing exists to appraise and review critically the firm's management process, covering the extent and effectivness of the system of delegation, channels of communication, harmony of co-ordination, the adequacy of the methods of planning and control, the skill in supplying management information as a guide to action and, in general, the competence of supervisory and specialist teams.

This is a wide range of matters to review and appraise, but at all times the auditor must bear in mind that he is not the manager: his function is to supply a service to management, and he can only adequately discharge this service by remaining independent and free of executive responsibility. Nevertheless, it is vital that the management auditor has a management perspective, lest he becomes obsessed with the accuracy of figures rather than with the managerial implications of inefficient practices.

A particularly significant development within the field of management auditing is the operational audit. This is totally removed from any financial audit concept, since the procedure is to select an activity for study, review and appraisal. The following are three examples: the marketing audit, the distribution audit and the retail audit.

The marketing audit

The marketing audit exists to help correct difficulties and to improve conditions that may already be good. While these aims may be achieved by a piece-meal examination of individual activities, it is better achieved by a total programme of evaluation studies. The former approach is termed a 'vertical audit' as it is only concerned with one element of the marketing mix at any one time. In contrast, the latter approach, the 'horizontal audit', is concerned with optimizing the use of resources, thereby maximizing the total effectiveness of marketing efforts and outlays. As such, it is by far the more difficult of the two, and hence rarely attempted.

No matter which form of marketing audit is selected, top management (via its audit staff) should ensure that no area of marketing activity goes unevaluated, and that every aspect is evaluated in accordance with standards that are compatible with the total success of the marketing organization, and of the firm as a whole. This, of course, requires that all activities be related to the established hierarchy of objectives.

The distribution audit

In the planning and control of costs and effectiveness in distribution activities the management audit can be of considerable value. Not surprisingly, however, it entails a complex set of procedures right across the function if it is to be carried out thoroughly. The major components are the channel audit, the PDM audit, the competitive audit, and the customer service audit. Each of these will be considered briefly in turn.

(*a*) *The channel audit*
Channels are made up of the intermediaries (such as wholesalers, factors, retailers) through which goods pass on their route from manufacture to consumption. The key channel decisions include:
- choosing intermediaries;
- determining the implications (from a PD point of view) of alternative channel structures; and
- assessing the available margins.

It follows from the nature of these decisions that the main focus of a channel audit will be on structural factors on the one hand and on cost/margin factors on the other.

(*b*) *The PDM audit*
There are three primary elements within this audit: that of company profile (which includes the handling cost characteristics of the product range and the service level that is needed in the light of market conditions); PDM developments (both of a technological and contextual nature); and that of the current system's capability.

Cost aspects exist in each of these elements, but operating costs loom largest in the last since it is predominantly concerned with costs and capacity. For example some of the items that will be subjected to audit will include those shown in Figure 13.2.

Capacity utilization	– Warehouse – Transportation – Flexibility and expansion scope
Warehouse facilities	– Total costs – Age and maintenance costs – Flexibility throughput/period – Total throughput/period – Returns handled – number – recovery time – Picking accuracy – Service levels/back orders – Cube utilization – Cost of cube bought out

Inventory	– Total inventory holding costs
	– Product group costs
	– Service levels – total
	        – plant
	        – field

	– Field inventory holding costs – Transfers – number – volume – Stock out effects – loss of business – rectification costs
Transportation	– Total costs – Production to field units – Field units to customers – Vehicle utilisation – Vehicle cube utilisation – Total volumes shipped – Cost per mile – volumes shipped – cases/pallets shipped – Costs of service bought out – Costs by mode/comparisons
Communications	– Total costs – Order communication times – method – cost – Time and costs per line item per order method for: – order processing and registration – credit investigation – invoice and delivery note preparation – statement preparation – Number and cost of customer queries – Salesmen's – calls/day – calls/territory/day – calls/product group/day – calls/customer group/day – Salesmen's use of time – selling – inventory checking – merchandising - order progressing
Unitization	– Total costs – Volumes shipped – Unitization method/proportions of: – pallets – roll pallets – containers – Costs of assembly and handling by load type
Service achieved	– Total costs
(By market segment)	– Service levels operated/costs – Delivery times – Delivery reliability – Order processing and progressing – Order picking efficiency – Claims procedure/time/cost

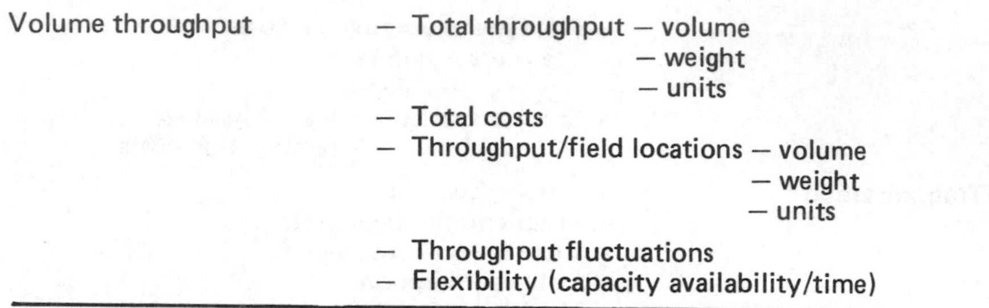

Volume throughput
– Total throughput – volume
– weight
– units
– Total costs
– Throughput/field locations – volume
– weight
– units
– Throughput fluctuations
– Flexibility (capacity availability/time)

Figure 13.2: System capability factors

(*c*) *The competitive audit*
Through this phase it should be possible to ascertain the quality of competitors' distribution policies, etc., and especially the level of service that competitors are able to offer (and maintain). Within the competitive audit regard should also be had to channel structures, pricing and discount policies and market shares.

(*d*) *The customer service audit*
Given that the level of service is at the centre of physical distribution management it is essential to monitor regularly its cost and quality characteristics.

A very thorough approach to the distribution audit is that developed at the Cranfield School of Management by Martin Christopher and his colleagues which is cited at the end of this chapter (see p.380).

The retail audit

As in marketing and distribution, the management audit can be developed to evaluate retail activities. The main steps of a retail audit are shown in Figure 13.3. These consist of the following:

1 Determining who is to do the audit. There are basically three alternatives:
 (*a*) company specialists (i.e. internal auditors with particular expertise in retail and in the organization in question;
 (*b*) departmental managers on a do-it-yourself basis; and
 (*c*) outside specialists on a consulting basis.
 The relative costs, degree of objectivity and expertise, plus the scope for combining 'vertical' audits into a 'horizontal' one will influence the choice.

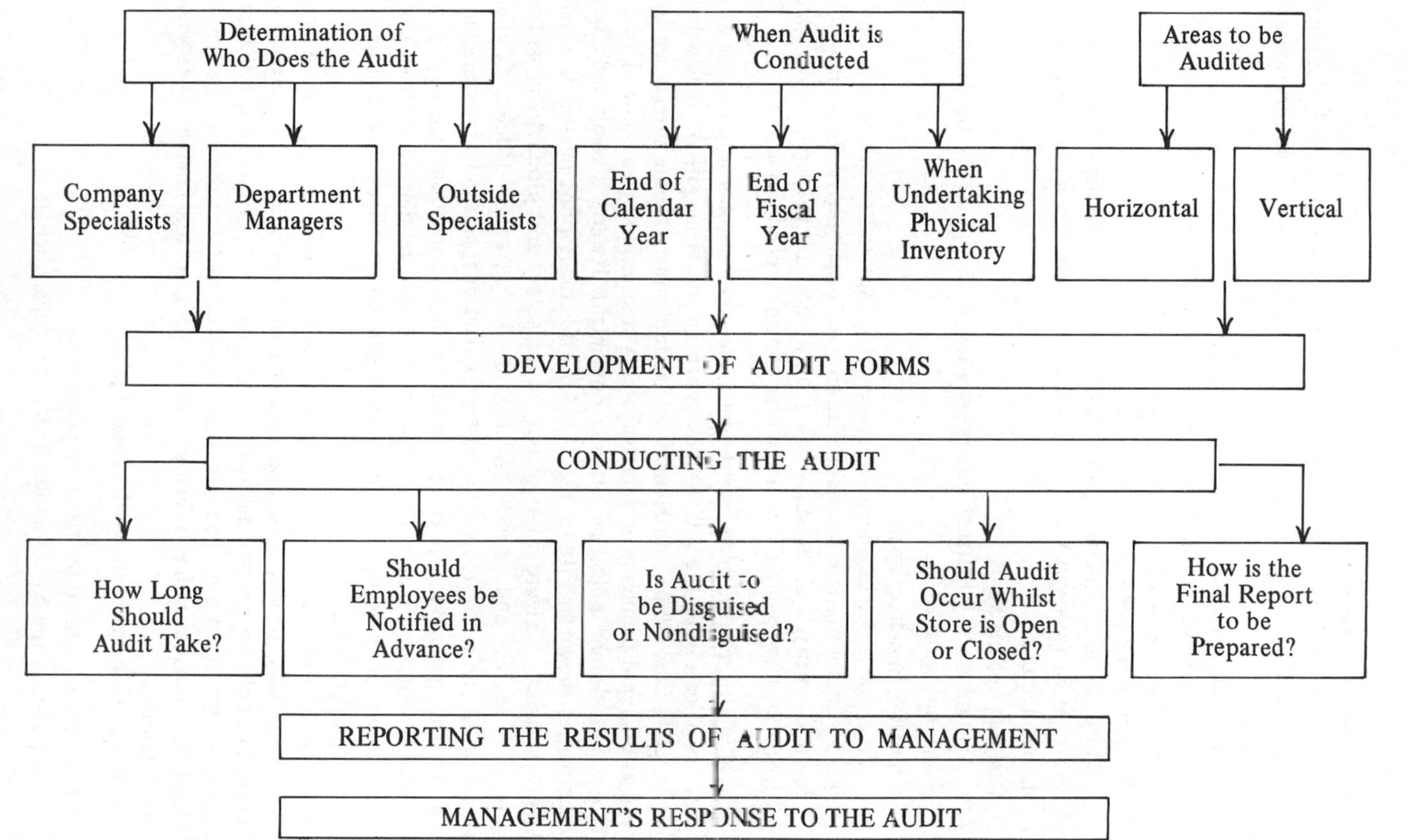

Figure 13.3: The retail audit process

2 Determining when and how often the audit is to be conducted.
Various 'obvious' times suggest themselves (see Figure 13.3). Annual audits are, however, rather too infrequent to be of significant operational benefit.

3 Determining which areas are to be audited.
In other words, should the audit be specific to one factor ('vertical'), or an across-the-board assessment ('horizontal')?

4 Developing the audit forms.
These detailed questionnaires should cover all the aspects worthy of investigation (given the aims of the audit). Examples will be given later in this chapter.

5 Carrying out the audit.
A number of important questions arise in this phase of the audit (as shown in Figure 13.3).

6 Reporting to management.
Once the audit has been completed it is essential to present the findings (with appropriate recommendations) to management. It is only as a result of managerial decisions based on a carefully prepared report that action leading to improvements in cost control procedures is likely.

In proceeding through these stages it is inevitable that a number of problems will be met. Not least of all the audit will be expensive, in terms both of money and time, but there are human problems (such as individuals feeling threatened by investigations) and problems of data availability and accuracy to contend with.

To give a clearer indication of how one might develop a retail audit the questionnaires shown in Figures 13.4 – 13.6 offer suggestions relating to small retailers' activities. Figure 13.4 focuses on budgetary and productivity issues; Figure 13.5 on cash and finance, and Figure 13.6 on credit policies. Similar questionnaires can be developed for customer relations, personnel management, stock control, purchasing, pricing, advertising and promotion, display equipment and layout, and many other aspects of a small retailer's activities. Collectively a set of questionnaires developed along these lines will facilitate a systematic, horizontal audit.

The specific needs of large retailers will need to be met by questionnaires designed especially to suit their organizational and operational characteristics.

Other examples of operational audits would include the purchasing function, covering the full spectrum of activities and procedures from the time an item is required and ordered until it is finally received, paid for, and charged to expense in the accounts.

The integral aspects of the study would include:

(*a*) the factors required for effective purchasing;
(*b*) co-operation and co-ordination with other departments;

1 Do you express your plans in terms of a budget, covering sales, stocks, mark-ups and expenses?
2 Do you set up your budget for relatively short periods?
3 Do you make an organized effort to determine the potential sales of your merchandise lines in your community and to calculate your market share?
4 In controlling your operations, do you frequently compare actual results with the budget projections you have made; and do you then adjust your merchandising, promotion and expense plans as indicated by deviation from these projections?
5 Do your key employees have a voice in formulating budget plans concerning them?
6 Do you study industry data and compare the results of your operation with them?
7 Do you think in terms of ratios and per cents, rather than exclusively in pounds and pence?
8 Do you use a variety of measures of productivity, such as:
   (*a*) net profit as a per cent of your net worth;
   (*b*) stockturn (ratio of your sales to the value of your average inventory);
   (*c*) gross profit margin per pound of cost investment in merchandise (pounds of gross margin divided by your average inventory at cost);
   (*d*) sales per square foot of space (net sales divided by total number of square feet of space); and
   (*e*) selling cost per cent for each salesperson (remunerations of the salesperson divided by that person's sales)?

Figure 13.4: Management audit for small retailers: budgetary control and productivity

1 Does someone other than the cashier or bookkeeper open all mail and prepare a record of receipts that will be checked against deposits?
2 Do you deposit all of each day's cash receipts in the bank without delay?
3 Do you restrict the use of your petty cash funds to payment of small expenditures (not exceeding a stated amount) and limit them to the amount needed for a short period of time – a week or two?
4 Do you require adequate identification of 'cash-take' customers who want to pay by cheque and those who ask you to cash cheques?
5 Have you taken adequate steps to protect your cash from robbery?
6 Is your postage metered?
7 Are your cheques prenumbered?
8 Are you careful to lay aside cash for all amounts withheld from employees wages for taxes, national insurance etc. and for all VAT collected and to remit these sums as required to the appropriate authorities?
9 Do you calculate your cash flow regularly (monthly, for example) and take steps to provide enough cash for each period's needs?

10 Have you established, in advance, a line of credit at your bank, not only to meet seasonal requirements but also to permit borrowing at any time for emergency needs?
11 Do you consistently avoid drawing cheques to 'cash' and signing blank cheques?
12 Have you taken out indemnity insurance on your cashier and other employees who handle cash and securities?
13 Do you keep company securities under lock and key, preferably in a safe deposit vault?
14 Do you control your liabilities with the same degree of care you devote to your assets?
15 To permit modernization and expansion of your premises (if you rent them), have you seriously considered your landlord as a source for the additional capital you will need?
16 Do you maintain a close personal relationship with your local bank?

Figure 13.5: Management audit for small retailers: cash and finance

1 Do you have a credit policy?
2 Do you set definite credit limits and explain your rules carefully to all credit applicants?
3 When customers do not make payments as agreed, do you follow up promptly?
4 If you have your own credit plan, do you have a simple method of identifying credit customers and authorizing their purchases?
5 Have you introduced a revolving credit plan whereby customers can complete payment for merchandise by means of a number of monthly, or weekly, payments and are privileged to buy more at any time within a set limit?
6 Are your bad-debt losses comparable with those of other similar stores?
7 Periodically, do you review your accounts to determine their status?
8 Are you a member of a retail credit bureau, and do you actively use the information it provides?

Figure 13.6: Management audit for small retailers: credit

(*c*) controls;
(*d*) purchase authorization;
(*e*) selection of suppliers;
(*f*) negotiation of terms;
(*g*) issue of official purchase orders;
(*h*) follow-up of order;
(*i*) receipt and inspection of delivered goods; and
(*j*) stores procedures.

Similarly, studies can be done on the efficiency and weaknesses of every function in the company, and should lead to cost savings and profit improvement in all cases.

Although similar to O & M studies in some respects, operational audits are concerned with improvements in managerial processes rather than purely paper flows. They are more comprehensive than other forms of control, but nevertheless are best used as supplementary control devices, and not as primary ones.

As with marketing research and operations research studies, the initial outcome of the management audit is a report. If this is poorly written, or fails to include all pertinent details, it may cause damaging decisions to be made. The need for skill and patience in drawing up reports can hardly be exaggerated, as the overall effectiveness of any study depends mainly upon the report, the distribution it receives, and the effectiveness of the follow-up action.

SUMMARY

Internal audit exists to ensure that established procedures and policies are being adhered to, and that other forms of control are being effective. It is helpful to consider internal auditing in the broader context of internal control (which comprises the plan of organization and all the co-ordinating methods adopted within the business). A set of principles of internal control can be put forward.

Whilst the internal and external audits have much in common, one development from the former that focuses on effectivness, rather than on minimum compliance with legal requirements etc., is the management, or operational, audit. Appropriate approaches can be developed for any functional activity, such as marketing, distribution, or purchasing. Flow-charting and internal control questionnaires, which are basic tools in internal auditing, can also be applied in the carrying out of operational audits.

FURTHER READING

American Management Association, *Analyzing and Improving Marketing Performance*, New York: A.M.A., 1959.
(Despite its age this is the standard work on marketing audits.)

Christopher, M.G., Walters, D.W. and Gattorna, J.L., *Distribution Planning and Control*, Aldershot: Gower, 1977. (This readable book contains a detailed, operational guide to carrying out a distribution audit.)

Schofield, A. and Husband, T., *The Wage and Salary Audit*, Aldershot: Gower, 1977.
(This practical guide aims to help managers apply a number of simple techniques to the analysis of their organization's wage and salary structures.)

Smith, A.C., Russell, A.G. and de Paula, F.C., *Internal Control and Audit*, London: Pitman, 2nd ed. 1968.
(A standard work on the subject, which inevitably adopts an accounting orientation.)

FURTHER READING FOR PART TWO

Anderson, D.R., Schmidt, L.A. and McCosh, A., *Practical Controllership*, Homewood, Illinois: Irwin, 3rd ed., 1973.
(A readable and practical book.)

Anthony, R.N. and Dearden, J., *Management Control Systems*, Homewood, Illinois: Irwin, 4th ed., 1980.
(A valuable text that brings together many control techniques in the context of a realistic organizational setting.)

Anton, H.R., Firmin, P.A. and Grove, H.D. (eds), *Contemporary Issues in Cost & Managerial Accounting*, Boston: Houghton Mifflin, 3rd ed., 1978.
(A comprehensive selection of articles on aspects of cost and management accounting, with suggestions as to further reading on specialist topics.)

Bentley, T.J., *Report Writing in Business*, London: ICMA, 1977.
(A practical, how-to-do-it guide.)

Bierman, H. and Dyckman, T.R., *Managerial Cost Accounting*, New York: Macmillan, 2nd ed., 1976.
(A comprehensive and rigorous treatment that emphasizes analytical techniques.)

Boyce, R.O. and Christie, N.D., *Integrated Managerial Controls*, London: Longmans, 2nd ed., 1975.
(A well-written and practical approach to the subject.)

Boyce, R.O. and Eisen, H., *Management Diagnosis: A Practical Guide*, London: Longmans, 1972.
(A similar book to Boyce and Christie – clear and helpful.)

Dearden, J., *Cost Accounting and Financial Control Systems*, Reading, Mass.: Addison-Wesley, 1973.
(An excellent text by an excellent author.)

DeCoster, D.T. and Schafer, E.L., *Management Accounting – A Decision Emphasis*, New York: Wiley, 1976.
(A splendid text that relates accounting to managing.)

Emery, J.C., *Management Planning & Control Systems*, New York: Macmillan, 1969.
(A technical, computer-oriented treatment of the subject, but containing many good ideas for the more general reader.)

Goodman, P.S., *New Perspectives in Organizational Effectiveness*, San Francisco:

Jossey-Bass.
(This throws a broader slant on to the question of effectiveness than one usually gets.)

Goodman, S.R. and Reece, J.S. (eds), *Controller's Handbook*, Homewood, Illinois: Irwin, 1978.
(A compilatioń that is full of helpful checklists and techniques, although the depth of coverage varies from author to author.)

Hofstede, G., *The Game of Budget Control*, London: Tavistock, 1968.
(A classic study of the behavioural aspects of budgetary control. To be recommended.)

Horngren, C.T., *Cost Accounting*, Englewood Cliffs, N.J.: Prentice-Hall, 4th ed., 1977.
(The standard international text.)

Ingham, H. and Harrington, L.T., *Interfirm Comparison*, London: Heinemann, 1980.
(A very useful guide by two long-standing experts from CIFC. However, less comprehensive than Westwick – see below.)

Livingstone, J.L. (ed.), *Management Planning and Control Models*, New York: McGraw-Hill, 1970.
(A rigorous set of evaluations of a batch of quantitative articles. Excellent for those of quantitative inclination.)

Pfeffer, J. and Salancik, G.R., *The External Control of Organizations*, New York: Harper & Row, 1978.
(An excellent; highly relevant book – although unusual in some respects. Recommended.)

Phyrr, P.A., *Zero-Base Budgeting*, New York: Wiley, 1975.
(The book by the man who has made his name from this technique.)

Rayburn, G.L., *Principles of Cost Accounting with Managerial Applications*, Homewood, Illinois: Irwin, 1979.
(A reasonable introductory text: see especially Chapter 13, pp.437–474.)

Shillinglaw, G., *Managerial Cost Accounting*, Homewood, Illinois: Irwin, 5th ed., 1982.
(Another standard text book that is even more comprenehsive than Horngren.)

Solomons, D. (ed.), *Studies in Cost Analysis*, London: Associated Business

Publishers, 2nd ed., 1968.
(An advanced collection of key articles on aspects of cost analysis.)

Thomas, W.E. (ed.), *Readings in Cost Accounting, Budgeting & Control*, Cincinnati, Ohio: South-Western, 5th ed., 1978.
(The longest-established compilation of articles in the field – but regularly revised – and one which probably has greatest appeal to the non-specialist.)

Tucker, S.A., *Profit Planning through the Break-even System*, Aldershot: Gower, 1980.
(Still valuable after more than 20 years.)

Tucker, S.A., *Profit Planning through the Break-even System*, Aldershot: Gower, 1980.
(This shows how to apply break-even analysis to a wide range of business situations.)

Welsch, G.A., *Budgeting*, Englewood Cliffs, N.J.: Prentice-Hall, rev. ed., 1976.
(The standard work on the subject: a detailed and comprehensive treatise.)

Westwick, C.A., *How to Use Management Ratios*, Aldershot: Gower, 1973.
(An excellent guide to the subject, based on the author's eight years at CIFC.)

Part Three

DEPARTMENTAL COST CONTROL

INTRODUCTION

Any attempt to try and deal with all the specific situations in which cost control procedures need to be applied would be doomed to failure. Each company has different needs, and its individual circumstances and operating environment cannot be reflected in a handbook of this type. Nevertheless, on the basis of the discussion of costs in Part One and cost control techniques in Part Two, an attempt is made in Part Three to cover generally applicable situations. The particular requirements of a particular company can be met by relating the general methodology to the requirements of the specific problem.

With this constraint in mind, following the Preamble, the first area to be examined will be that of administration.

Preamble to Part Three

Implementation Impacts

It is a generally valid element of experience that suggests that our ability to carry out a particular task will be better at the second attempt than it was at the first, and better again, up to a certain optimum point, on each successive attempt. (This gives rise to the adage: 'practice makes perfect'.) This phenomenon applies to groups working together on a common task in the same way that it applies to individuals.

The explanation behind this phenomenon is given in the *learning curve theory*. This was initially developed in the US aircraft industry when it was observed that the man-hours spent in building planes declined at a regular rate over a wide range of production, which contradicts the widespread tendency to compile budgets and standards on the assumptions of level performance and constant costs.

Human beings have the capacity to learn, and this enables them to avoid earlier errors in subsequent attempts at a task and, as a result, to become more efficient in the execution of their jobs. In general, the greater the frequency of repetition of tasks the greater will be the efficiency of performance. In diagrammatic terms this is shown in Figure V: the more units produced, the lower is the man-hours input per unit.

Evidence suggests that a predictable decrease in man-hours will be found. For example, within the aircraft industry the pattern that has been observed is that each subsequent production run only required 80 per cent of the previous run, on a recurring basis. It also seems to be the case that in connexion with

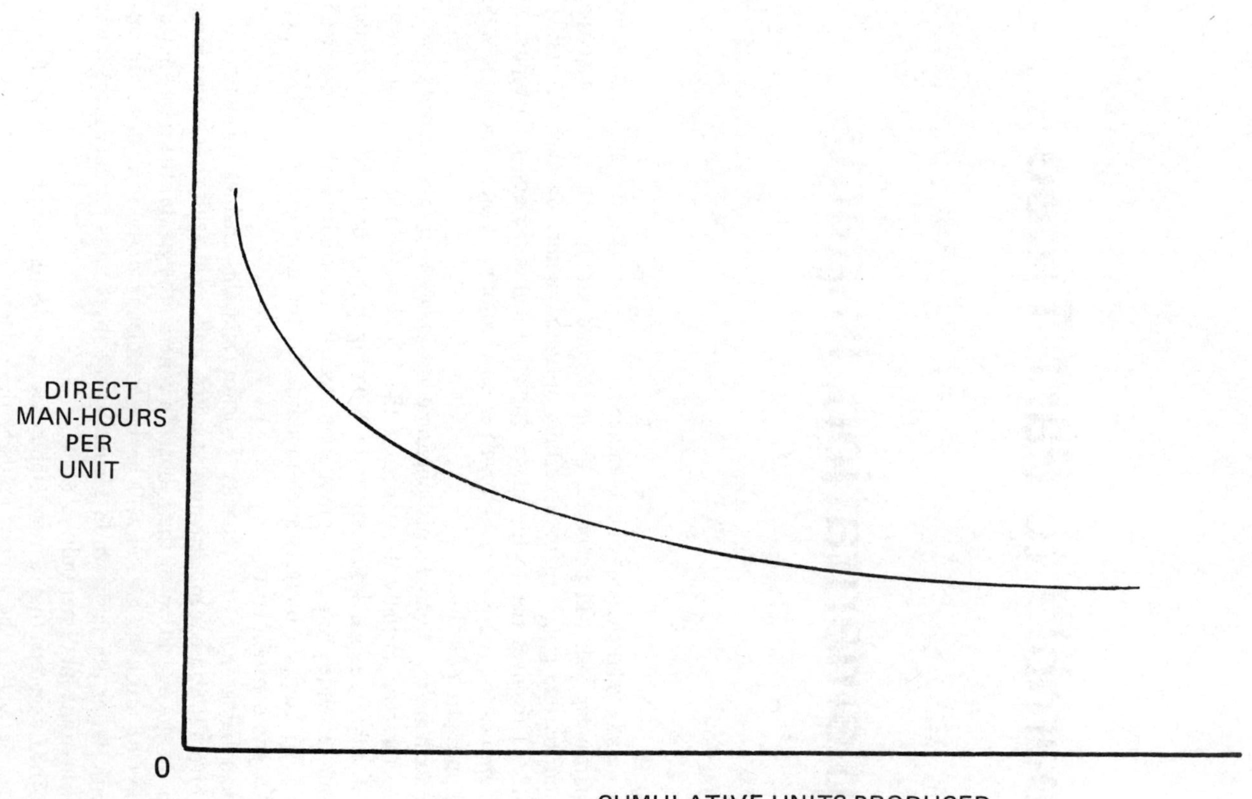

Figure V: The learning curve

more complex tasks there is greater scope for learning and that a larger reduction in inputs in successive attempts at a given task will be found than is the case with simpler tasks.

It will be apparent that proper training will enable an individual to increase his skill in a task more rapidly than if he is left on his own to struggle with it.

If we take this line of argument out of its production-oriented setting and consider the ways in which individuals can be rendered more effective in controlling costs it will be appreciated that familiarity and practice in preparing budgets, repeated analyses of performance reports, plus a well-designed training programme are amongst the factors that are likely to lead to successful cost control.

Training should not be restricted to operating personnel: it is essential that top managers, as well as managers in other ranks, have a clear understanding of the techniques of cost control that are in use if these techniques are to be successfully implemented. There is a collective learning experience to be undertaken each time a new technique is to be employed.

One of the most challenging problems confronting top management in any organization is that of motivating their staff towards the efficient accomplishment of goals. Thus to find that budgets are either viewed or operated as pressure devices by a bureaucratic management is not likely to be a happy discovery. Budgets should be developed to help managers reach a preferred future position (e.g. reflecting higher profits, a larger market share, etc.). If they are not viewed, and used, in this way they are likely to inhibit motivation, and this highlights the need for some remedial training effort. (This same argument applies, of course, to cost control techniques other than budgeting.)

Individuals will be motivated to achieve a particular outcome if there is some identifiable reward associated with working towards that end. For chief executives and other top managers there may be share options, and for managerial personnel generally there may be profit-sharing bonuses, which are variations on the shorter-horizon commissions payable to salesmen and piece-rate bonuses payable to production operatives. But these conspicuous financial rewards are only the tip of the iceberg of rewards, and punishments, that exist in most organizations to help in motivating employees. Extrinsic rewards are those that are paid for performance and visible achievement. They include wages and salaries, bonuses, merit increases, promotion, increased job security, and various other forms of corporate recognition. On the other hand we can also identify intrinsic rewards which cover the internally-generated rewards for successful task-attainment. (These cover pleasure, feelings of self-worth and personal attainment.)

If any system of cost control is to be effective in aiding motivation it must be seen to help in linking the effort that individuals exert in task accomplishment to the system of rewards – both extrinsic and intrinsic – that each individual perceives. This is no mean task! Such fairness requires, amongst other things, that those whose performance is to be assessed should be involved in determining appropriate standards of performance. In other words, the principles of accountability planning and responsibility accounting that were discussed in Chapter 6 need to be adopted.

Apart from the key issue of motivation there are many other important behavioural matters that should be taken into account in devising, implementing and using techniques of cost control. (Guidance can be found in the further reading items listed at the end of this Preamble.) One of these matters is the concept of the *level of aspiration*. This refers to the tendency for us to strive to achieve success in a task when that task is perceived as being within our capability. If we achieve it we will probably aspire to a higher level next time, and if we do not quite achieve it we may still consider it a worthwhile and achievable aim and try again. On the other hand, if a task is seen as being too easy we will not be motivated to repeat it.

It is necessary also to consider failure: if a task is well beyond our capability we may revise our aspirations downwards, or possibly give up altogether, depending upon such factors as our progress in the performance of the task in question.

The aspiration level is identifiable in a cost control context as the standard or budget that managers are expected to achieve. If it is set at the wrong level it will not encourage managers to strive to attain it, and their resultant behaviour may be any of a number of different patterns. This becomes particularly significant when profits are being squeezed and there is a pressing need to improve profit performance.

Figure VI shows a situation in which the prevailing scope for profit (i.e. the distance between the total revenue curve R_1 and the total cost curve C_1) is limited, but it can be improved by marketing actions (to shift R_1 to R_2) and by cost reduction actions (to shift C_1 to C_2). Cost control methods can then be applied, as outlined in earlier chapters, to ensure that cost levels are kept within desired limits.

We will not pursue marketing tactics at this point, but it is relevant to say a few words about cost reduction. Contrary to a commonly-held view, cost reduction studies are not limited to short-run crisis situations. It is highly desirable for a cost reduction philosophy to be built into planning and control routines on a continuing basis. This should result in a systematic attempt to eliminate all forms of waste without damaging the organization's ability to generate revenue.

Within the office environment the array of techniques covered by O & M can be applied to reducing costs, and in the production domain it is possible to increase cost effectiveness by means of value analysis, work simplification, improved layouts, standardization, replacement of old plant, incentive

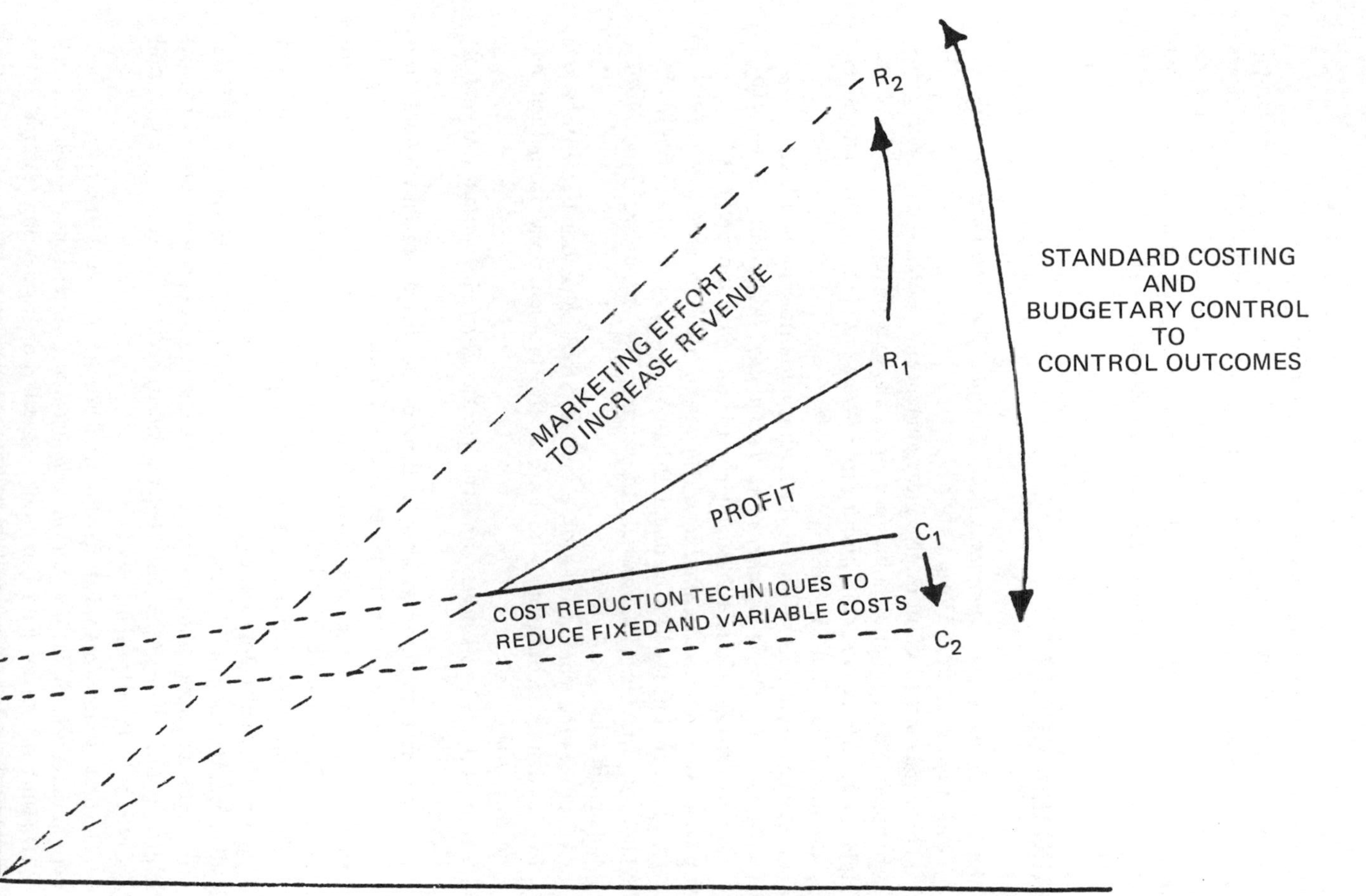

Figure VI: Profit improvement chart

schemes, etc. Some valuable references are cited below.

These issues that have been briefly touched upon – training and the learning curve, behavioural matters (especially motivation), and establishing cost levels that exclude avoidable waste – are worthy of consideration through the remainder of Part 3. They are aspects of implementing cost control systems that have a profound effect on their likelihood of success.

FURTHER READING

Adair, J., *Training for Communication, Training for Decisions, Training for Leadership*, Aldershot: Gower, 1978.
(These re-launched editions give clear guidance for establishing training programmes in a way that combines principles and experience.)

Caplan, E.H., *Management Accounting and Behavioral Analysis*, Reading, Mass.: Addison-Wesley, 2nd ed., 1981.
(A scholarly synthesis by one of the leading authorities in the USA.)

Dick-Larkam, R., *Profit Improvement Techniques*, Aldershot: Gower, 1973.
(This workbook offers a thorough guide to cost reduction methods.)

Hopwood, A.G;. *Accounting and Human Behaviour*, London: Haymarket, 1974.
(An excellent introduction by one of Britain's leading authorities in this field.)

Livingstone, J.L. (ed.), *Managerial Accounting: The Behavioral Foundations*, Columbus, Ohio: Grid, 1975.
(An interesting compilation of essays by five behavioural scientists and five academic accountants who look at five problem areas from their respective corners.)

McKenna, E.F., *The Management Style of the Chief Accountant*, Aldershot: Gower, 1978.
(An empirical study, undertaken in Britain, that helps explain why organizations get the type of accounting service they do.)

National Industrial Conference Board, *Administration of Cost Reduction Programs*, (Studies in Business Policy, no. 117), New York: NICB, 1965.
(This report gives a broad picture of US practice, including the pros and cons of alternative approaches.)

Radke, M., *Manual of Cost Reduction Techniques*, London: McGraw-Hill, 1972.
(A systematic programme of immediate and effective cost reduction methods.)

Schiff, M. and Lewin, A.Y. (eds), *Behavioral Aspects of Accounting*, Englewood Cliffs, N.J.: Prentice-Hall, 1974.
(The best available compilation of journal articles on this theme.)

Vernon-Harcourt, A.W., *Rewarding Management*, Aldershot: Gower, annual.
(Drawing on survey data this book suggests how to develop rewards in the light of the current legal position and employment situation.)

14

Administration

INTRODUCTION

In this chapter some specific aspects of the administrative function (office work, forms control, personnel management, and training) will be discussed.

Administrative costs are, in the main, incurred for the benefit of the organization as a whole, but under the responsibility criterion these costs are within the control (to a greater or lesser extent) of specific individuals within the organization. (Unless one is looking at the organization itself as being one large cost unit, administration costs can be seen to be of an overhead or indirect nature.) Since administration costs are incurred for the communal good, the question inevitably arises as to whether or not they should be apportioned – as with other service department costs – to departments that benefit from them. Three bases of apportionment exist:

1 If administrative costs are small in relation to manufacturing overheads, they may be apportioned over the various departments within the factory and thereby included within factory overhead rates.
2 It may be considered appropriate to apportion administrative costs between the manufacturing function on the one hand and the sales and distribution function on the other, in which event only part of the administration overheads will end up within the factory overheads.
3 Finally, it may be desired to make a separate charge for administration

on each job passing through the factory, and this can be achieved by adding an agreed percentage (oncost) to the works cost (i.e. direct labour + direct material + direct expense + apportioned factory overhead) of each job.

However, from the point of view of actually controlling administrative overheads, apportioning them over production is irrelevant: managers cannot be held responsible for apportioned costs. Value may be derived from indicating to each manager the approximate administration burden that is incurred in support of his department. In this way all managers will realize the scale of costs that exists and hence appreciate the implications of their own activities on other managers' budgets (and vice versa).

OFFICE WORK

The functions of the office are essentially:

1 Receiving information, which involves sorting, distributing, filing, recording, etc.
2 Processing information, involving analysis, indexing, etc.
3 Communicating information, by means of typing, duplicating, mailing, telephoning, etc.
4 Control and protection of the company through such activities as inspection, internal auditing, etc.

In a typical factory situation there exists a production control department that has the tasks of establishing production plans, drawing up schedules (or production programmes) and coordinating the various activities that are involved in producing finished goods. This approach has rarely been applied in the same way to office work, yet there are close parallels between the throughput of a factory and the throughput of an office. The basic requirements for cost control in either instance are:

1 A target level of performance.
2 A measure of actual inputs (costs) in terms of hours spent by different individuals and machines on particular jobs, material usage, etc.
3 A measure of output in terms of goods produced, reports prepared, invoices typed, etc.

Reasons why more rigorous controls have not been applied to office work include the general absence of standard times for clerical operations; the huge variety of tasks performed by the average office; the usual presence of established procedures that tend to suggest that detailed controls are unnecessary;

clerical tasks are non-repetitive or irregular; work units are often not defined; and there is no tradition of control. But for maximum efficiency – and the control of costs – office work should be coordinated, scheduled with regard to both time and the order of performance, and controlled.

Control can be exercised over quality of work, quantity of work, and the time taken. Accuracy and effectiveness are the primary criteria of quality, and quality standards must be established and made known to those who are to be bound by them. Poor quality – a badly-typed letter, a mistake in an invoice, a misplaced file – leads to waste and hence higher costs than should be necessary.

Many errors are unavoidable and arise due to external causes, but blame should never be assigned without ensuring that the correct cause is known. Bad organization, poor management, and inadequate systems may be more at blame than the ignorance of clerical staff. The level of accuracy obtained will depend to a large extent upon the skill and training of the clerical staff as well as that of management. More particularly, causes of errors may arise from:

1 Clerical causes:
   (*a*) Too much haste
   (*b*) Lack of method
   (*c*) Lack of knowledge
   (*d*) Inexperience
   (*e*) Poor writing
   (*f*) Lack of supervision
   (*g*) Illness/tiredness.

2 Managerial causes:
   (*a*) Poor training
   (*b*) Bad selection of staff
   (*c*) Vague instructions
   (*d*) Lack of control
   (*e*) Poor organization
   (*f*) Low morale
   (*g*) Complexity of tasks
   (*h*) Poorly-designed forms
   (*i*) Poor working conditions (lighting, heating, noise, ventilation, etc).

Since these factors cannot all be taken into consideration in setting standards for clerical work, one solution is to observe what happens and to measure quality levels, and then take steps to improve these levels. By proceeding in this way it should be possible to determine the level at which quality in a given task begins to level off, and this could be deemed an attainable current standard. (For example, correctly filing 99 out of every 100 index cards may be the highest currently attainable standard of accuracy.) It is advisable to express quality levels in percentage terms to facilitate comparisons amongst individuals and time periods as well as between actual and standard.

Checking the accuracy of work done is an expensive exercise, so care must be taken in choosing the means of checking. There are three methods:

1. A total 100 per cent check, which amounts to doing everything twice.
2. Statistical quality control as discussed in Chapter 5.
3. Sampling. One method of sampling involves checking a specified sample of work done (say 10 per cent) and accepting the entire batch if the quality of the sample is acceptable. If the quality of the sample is below standard, however, a larger sample will then be taken, and so on until all the batch has been checked. (A particular clerk's work may demand that larger samples be taken if quality is known to be frequently below standard.)

Once discovered, errors should be brought to the attention of those responsible. Control charts (such as that in Figure 14.1 for correspondence errors) can be used to motivate staff to keep error rates down, and can be compiled for individuals as well as for whole departments.

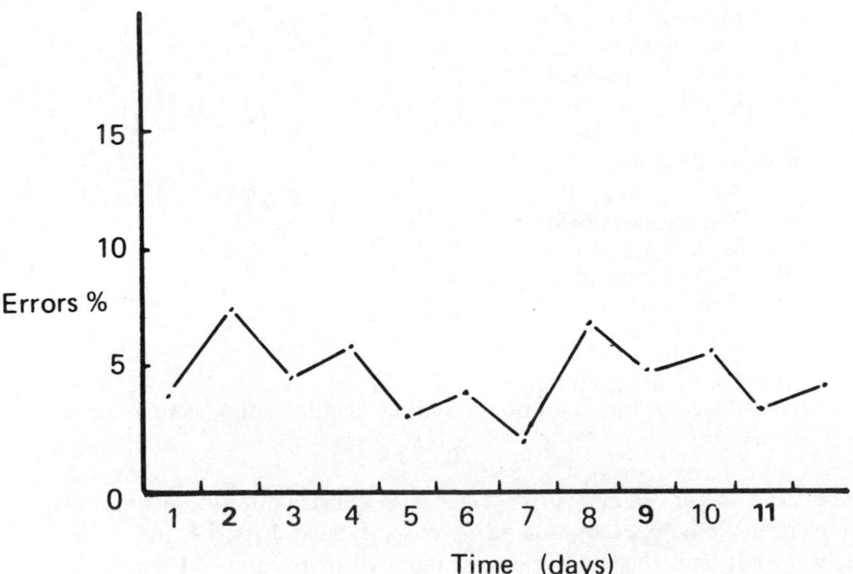

Figure 14.1: Control chart for correspondence errors

To control the quantity of work done, it is necessary to be able to measure the amount of work performed. This control must be exercised to ensure that the proper service is being given, and requires that fairly detailed work plans have been compiled in conjunction with schedules of the available man-hours of each grade of clerical employee. From this base it becomes relatively simple to transfer staff as necessary from one section to another, or to arrange for either temporary staff or overtime. Office work can usually be scheduled with a high degree of success once measurements have been taken of how long particular jobs should take, or how many clerks will be required to do a given task within a specified time limit. It is quite surprising how much office work can really be measured: one estimate puts the amount as high as two-thirds.

For each major activity a work schedule can be drawn up on the basis of:

1. The normal volume of work in terms of the number of units per day (where the unit may be a ledger posting, an invoice, a batch of 100 purchase orders, etc.).
2. The standard time per unit.
3. The total standard time per day – (1) × (2).
4. The required time of completion of the work.
5. The time when the work can be started.
6. The number of clerks who will be needed to complete the work within the available time.

The plan that stems from the scheduling of office work should allow for the completion of the budgeted amount of work to a timetable that also allows for contingencies (as well as making every effort to reduce the effects of peaks and troughs in the flow of work through the office). Within this plan lies the required level of performance. Comparing actual performance with target performance is easy in the case of activities such as payroll or sending out monthly statements, but it is not so easy in the case of continuing activities – such as passing purchase invoices for payment. However, it should not prove too difficult (on the basis of past experience and outstanding orders) to forecast with tolerable accuracy the number of purchase invoices that will be received during a particular month, although it is impossible to predict either the number or the complexity of those arriving on a specific day and hence the daily work load in processing them. Nevertheless, the monthly work load (in terms of required man-hours) can be planned and the processing of purchase invoices thus spread over the month in accordance with urgency and the demands of other tasks.

The objective of work scheduling is to ensure that work is performed strictly in accordance with the timing on the schedule itself (see Chapter 15). Thus it should be possible to control a job so that it is commenced at a predetermined time and is completed at a predetermined time, and so fits in with the demands of related tasks.

The next consideration is the budgeting process with reference to office work. Clerical costs, along with other office expenses, should be budgeted in some detail. The size of the office staff will depend on the anticipated work load, and it should be specified in terms of so many staff of each grade (i.e. A, B, C, D, E and F – see Chapter 6). It is then fairly simple to apply rates of pay to the staff establishment to build up a clerical payroll budget. An allowance for overtime costs and the costs of temporary staff can be included in accordance with anticipated fluctuations in the volume of work to be done: this will ensure that budget variations are associated directly with particular tasks – such as the preparation of annual accounts, or a quarterly revision of cost standards.

In addition to budgeting gross rates of pay, it is essential that other payroll costs be allowed for. The employer's national insurance contribution and payments into a pension or superannuation fund must be included in the final budgeted figure. (It is essential, of course, in any budgeting activity to have supporting schedules for the budget figures that explain how these figures were arrived at. For example, a salary estimate should be supported by a list of personnel showing job title, salary, and any changes that are envisaged during the budget period.)

Whilst administration costs do not vary greatly with changes in the level of sales or productive activity during a period (at least, not within the relevant range) they cannot be considered to be fixed. Accordingly, since the level of activity that is expected will determine the level of many administrative costs, it is essential that some reference be made to this level in terms relevant to office procedures. These may be expressed in such ways as the following:

> Payroll section: budget based on 1 000 weekly paid and 500 monthly paid employees.
> Sales invoicing: budget based on 250 invoices per week and 500 statements per month.
> Accounts office: budget based on 150 active accounts in the bought ledger and 750 active accounts in the sales ledger.
> Cashier's office: budget based on 500 cash book entries per week with a weekly reconciliation.

As we have already seen, the control of office costs is generally less rigorous than is the control of other types of cost – even though office costs may be high. Often it may be found that the office manager is unable to justify his costs in detail and *operation costing* has been developed to resolve this problem.

It is important that office costs (as an input) are not simply measured as a realized amount because to be of real value in a control context requires that this amount be related to some level of output – such as the service given, or the performance of the business. There should be an awareness of whether or not a given amount of office expense is reasonable, or whether it is capable of being reduced.

In building up overall budgets it is very helpful if all clerical activities have been studied and costed. Timing such activities in order to either set standards or measure performance against a standard must be carried out in accordance with the vagaries of clerical work, and in the case of setting standards this will involve the averaging of several observations. It may be found, for instance, that the operations involved in preparing sales invoices are those shown in Figure 14.2.

Operation	*Standard time per 100 (mins)*	*Job grade*	*Standard rate per hour*	*Standard cost per 100*
1 Receive, control and sort copy despatch notes	60	A	30p	0.30
2 Price	120	C	50p	1.00
3 Check prices	90	D	60p	0.90
4 Extend and calculate discount	240	B	40p	1.60
5 Check extension	180	C	50p	1.50
6 Type invoice	600	C	50p	5.00
7 Check invoice	300	D	60p	3.00
8 Prepare for post	100	A	30p	0.42
Total labour				13.72
Stationery				
100 invoice sets @ 2p	£2.00			
100 envelopes	£0.25			
100 postage stamps @ 3½p	£3.50			
Total materials				£5.75
Supervision allowance (10 per cent of labour)				£1.37
Total cost per 100 sales invoices				£20.84

Figure 14.2: Operation costing of sales invoicing

By incorporating into this operation costing exercise the clerical gradings and rates of pay it is a simple matter to compute a standard cost for preparing sales invoices (£20.84 for 100, £0.21 for one). This approach is better than the alternative whereby one divides the total sales invoicing section's costs by the number of invoices produced during a period. This is because the latter approach fails to show the elemental steps involved. It is possible, with the help of detailed costings, to charge other departments with work done on their behalf: thus the sales department could be charged £0.21 per invoice, and any variance would show up in the invoicing department's costs.

All office costs, however, cannot be treated in this way, and any activity that is non-routine or non-repetitive raises immediate difficulties. The preparation of, say, final accounts, cannot be treated for cost control purposes in the same way as producing an invoice. (It should be possible, nevertheless, for the financial controller to estimate an overall figure for the activities concerned and then to attempt to work within that figure. This would entail the keeping of work diaries on the part of non-clerical staff.)

The detailed costing of operations enables the office manager to check that he has based his plans on known facts and provided a basis for comparison. The maintaining of detailed records relating to actual performance for purposes of comparison can be expensive in all but the larger offices, so operation costing may be best employed in helping to set budget levels that lead to broader controls (e.g. clerical costs must not exceed 10 per cent of turnover) as opposed to helping control each clerical activity.

Whilst similar problems exist in relation to clerical work in the factory as in clerical work in the office, and similar techniques can be applied to their control, the general level of efficiency of clerical staff in the factory environment is much lower than their counterparts in the office block.

The reasons for this lower degree of efficiency are:

1 The small size of many factory offices means that clerical staff within them are often under-employed.
2 Physical conditions are often poor in the factory (e.g. fumes, noise, etc.) and this discourages efficiency, and the lack of size of many factory offices noted above causes their frequent inability to justify labour-saving office equipment.
3 Because of the nature of factory life and the scattered location of factory offices, supervision will often be poor and supervisors who are factory-oriented may not appreciate how to run an office effectively: in addition, many of the staff in factory offices will have moved there from the shop floor without the benefit of proper training.

By centralizing factory office work it should be possible to apply cost control techniques fully and to increase efficiency. Centralization permits better staff supervision and higher productivity; it eliminates under-employed staff and encourages job rotation and training; and it tends to result in the provision of better facilities in the office itself.

FORMS CONTROL

The purposes of forms are:

1 To make clear what information should be gathered and communicated.
2 To provide a specific location for each item of information needed.
3 To eliminate the need for recopying standard information.
4 To facilitate the use of multiple copies.
5 To identify records and facilitate filing and future reference.

It has been estimated that the cost of processing forms may average 17 times the cost of producing and filing them. It follows, therefore, that forms control is an important adjunct to cost control in making sure that forms are efficient and economical in design as well as in use. More particularly, forms control aims to:

1 Ensure forms are designed to lead to maximum clerical efficiency.
2 Eliminate obsolete forms.
3 Consolidate forms to minimize the duplication of effort.
4 Minimize printing costs, and produce forms by the most appropriate and economical method.
5 Distribute copies of forms only to those who have a justifiable reason for having them.
6 Study all proposed new forms or revised old forms for essentiality.
7 Evaluate forms design primarily on the amount of time required to use the forms.
8 Review periodically all forms in use to keep them in line with the current system requirements of the office.

The *existence* of particular forms will follow from the existence of particular systems (rather than the other way around), but the *design* of forms must be considered in conjunction with office procedures.

The design of forms should be evaluated primarily on the amount of time required to use the forms. Forms are important in being the carriers of information, and if their design is poor they will impede the vital function of communication. Furthermore, poorly designed forms are difficult to complete, lead to clerical errors, produce incorrect decisions, and thereby result in inefficiency and increased costs.

Closely related to forms design and control is the control of office stationery. Especially following the worldwide shortage of paper that began in late 1973, tighter control should be exercised over the range of stationery items held, the level of stationery stocks, etc. Guidelines for the management of stationery include:

1. Efficient purchasing – the right items of the right quality in the right quantities at the right price at the required time.
2. The carrying of the minimum stock consistent with usage and economical purchasing.
3. Storing facilities that prevent deterioration, make effective use of available space, etc.
4. Issuing arrangements that prevent pilfering and wasteful consumption.
5. General arrangements to cover the proper control of the use of office stationery.

Figure 14.3 illustrates a requisition that is suitable for reordering, revising an order, or initiating an order for stationery. In a company of any appreciable size, an efficient system of requisitioning is necessary to ensure that only authorized stationery items are ordered, and also that all withdrawals from stock are authorized. Consumption of stationery should be kept to a minimum, and the responsibility for stationery consumption must be placed on those who sign requisitions.

Standardization of stationery can lead to greater efficiency. It is sensible practice to aim for:

1. Standard paper sizes
2. Standard carbon paper
3. Standard equipment (for duplicating, etc.)
4. Standard stock levels, reorder quantities, etc.
5. Standard style and design (logos, etc.)
6. Standard procedures for issuing/ordering stationery.

Every form should be raised/created/ordered for a clearly-defined purpose in such a way that it meets the requirements of both user and printer. Moreover, standards can also be set for the retention of records in both active and inactive files, for microfilming when appropriate, for classifying if necessary, and for eventual destruction.

CHECKLIST ON FORMS CONTROL

1. Ensure that the form will suit the purpose for which it is required.
2. Ensure that the cost of using the form is as low as possible for a given purpose.
3. Reduce the number of different types of form in current use in order to attain a simple system of recording information.
4. Reduce the number of forms in use and the number of copies made of each by designing each form to serve more than one purpose.

Requisition for ordering forms

To: Print department manager *Date:*________________

( ) 1 REPRINT attached form on same type of paper.

(a) Quantity to be printed ________________

(b) Quantity used monthly ________________

(c) Quantity on hand ________________

( ) PRINT ( ) MIMEO ( ) OFF-SET

( ) 2 REPRINT attached form with revisions.

(a) Quantity to be printed ________________

(b) Quantity used monthly ________________

(c) Quantity on hand ________________

(d) Purpose of revision ________________

____

(e) Paper colour ________________

(f) Paper weight ________________

(g) Ink colour ________________

( ) PRINT ( ) MIMEO ( ) OFF-SET

( ) 3 PRINT new form as attached sample.

(a) Quantity to be printed ________________

(b) Quantity to be used monthly________________

(c) Purpose of form ________________

____

(d) Paper colour ________________

(e) Paper weight ________________

(f) Ink colour ________________

( ) PRINT ( ) MIMEO ( ) OFF-SET

Authorized by:____________________ Allocation code: __________________

Figure 14.3: Stationery requisition

5 Reduce the number of operations necessary in the use of the form.
6 Make the form easy to use and read.
7 Where a form is to be used with other documents, relate the form to those documents by designing the layout in a similar way.
8 Restrict the information on a form to that for which there is a definite, continuing requirement.
9 Where information has to be transcribed from one form to another, ensure that the order and arrangement of entry spaces on each form is identical.
10 Establish economic order quantities, and reorder levels for stationery stock items.
11 Determine the appropriate quality of paper in relation to the purpose of the form.
12 Agree sizes of forms to obtain best purchasing terms (e.g. standardize on A4, etc.) but ensure that the chosen sizes fit office machines in use.
13 Are all forms in use necessary?
14 Do forms improve or facilitate operations?
15 Do forms reduce clerical effort?
16 Are all copies of each form essential?
17 Can similar forms be combined?
18 Have all those who will use the form been consulted over its content, design, routing, etc?
19 Is there justification for using paper of a colour other than white, or ink other than black?
20 Are vital records stored in fireproof cabinets?
21 What are the company's filing costs?
22 Do different forms have clearly specified retention periods?
23 Are there any controls over filing several copies of the same item in different locations?
24 What controls exist over the distribution of written communications?
25 Is there an adequate procedure for coding or classifying forms/reports/incoming correspondence, etc?
26 Should microfilming be employed?
27 Could a centralized filing system save costs?
28 Does the company have a forms control programme?
29 Are forms printed internally when it may be more economical to buy them out?
30 Does information from forms flow easily into reports?
31 Are forms designed in accordance with equipment requirements?
32 Is stationery ordered centrally in bulk?
33 Can print quantities be economically justified?
34 What procedures exist for authorizing the creation of new forms?

35 Is the circulation list for each form/report reviewed regularly to determine each recipient's needs?

PERSONNEL COSTS

The routine costs of running the personnel department will be susceptible to the control procedures already outlined. In this section let us concentrate on one particular aspect of personnel concern – the problem of labour turnover (LTO).

If it is to survive, a company must be capable of recruiting and retaining employees of the necessary type and calibre for efficient operations. (Moreover, it must attend to employees' training needs, and this is dealt with later in this chapter.) If a company proves unable to retain employees – especially those in key positions – it runs a grave risk of failure, so LTO is a most serious topic to consider, as well as being a most expensive element of payroll-related costs.

A trend towards increasing rates of LTO is encouraged by full employment and the patterns of social and manpower mobility of recent years. Some of the reasons for LTO are listed below, some of which are controllable and some of which are not, but more than one is likely to operate in any given case:

1 Personal betterment
2 Dissatisfaction with job
3 Dissatisfaction with supervisor
4 Dissatisfaction with immediate colleagues
5 Dissatisfaction with remuneration
6 Dissatisfaction with working conditions
7 Accidents
8 Transport problems
9 Housing difficulties
10 Retirement
11 Death
12 Leaving the area
13 Illness
14 Marriage
15 Pregnancy
16 Redundancy
17 Insufficient to do in present job
18 Insufficient discipline
19 Poor scheduling of work flow
20 Poor equipment

21 Uncertainty as to future prospects in present company
22 Poor staff facilities and fringe benefits
23 Oversold when interviewed and appointed
24 Better rewards, conditions, hours, etc., elsewhere
25 Fired.

It can reveal significant causes if those who are about to leave are interviewed before their final departure in order to identify their reasons. The true reasons are usually hard to isolate, but the attempt may be rewarding. Helpful pointers are given by analysing reasons (as given above) as well as:

1 Leavers analysed by department
2 Leavers analysed by age
3 Leavers analysed by sex
4 Leavers analysed by length of service
5 Leavers analysed by travelling time
6 Leavers analysed by level of earnings.

The costs that stem from LTO are formidable. Included within the long list are to be found such cost items as:

1 Recruiting replacements: agency fees
2 Advertising
3 Screening
4 Interviewing
5 Testing
6 Induction
7 Training – employee's and trainer's time and costs
8 Travelling and subsistence allowances
9 Temporary staff whilst vacancies exist
10 Overtime premiums whilst vacancies exist
11 Reduced output initially of new recruits
12 Medical examinations
13 Costs of termination of previous incumbent
14 Cost of lost output whilst vacancies exist
15 Increased wastage and spoilage by new recruits
16 Reduced morale caused by new recruits' inability to immediately acquire, accept, and reflect the company's traditions.

Even at shopfloor level, it will be readily appreciated that to recruit one employee may cost £250 when there is a good market for shopfloor workers. When there is a poor market (i.e. excess demand) as at present exists for secretarial staff in central London, then the cost of LTO of the scarce grade of employee can be astronomical. Any effective reduction in the rate of LTO can be the source of huge cost savings.

To compute a company's (or department's) LTO, the following formula can be applied:

$$\text{LTO} = \frac{\text{Number of employees leaving during a period}}{\text{Average number employed during that period}} \times 100$$

The personnel covered by this index should consist of terminations and additions to or from the total strength, and not transfers of staff from one department to another. Temporary employees should be excluded, but seasonal workers should be included.

An annual LTO rate is more often found than is a monthly rate because the former smooths away the latter's fluctuations. But wide divergences from month to month may have more than seasonal significance and should not be dismissed without thought.

Various arguments against the crude, net LTO rate formula given above have been put forward. For example, some terminations are inevitable (retirement) or otherwise uncontrollable by the company (death), so the rate should be determined by a modified formula:

$$\text{LTO} = \frac{\text{Avoidable terminations}}{\text{Average number employed}} \times 100$$

Alternatively, since the first formula given above provides no information about the length of service of those leaving, it is biased in that every company suffers from a fringe of short-term employees who only stay for a matter of days or weeks with the company and hence inflate the LTO rate in what may be an essentially stable organization. This stability can be reflected by using another LTO formula:

$$\text{LTO} = \frac{\text{Number of employees with over 12 months' service}}{\text{Number of employees at beginning of the year}} \times 100$$

The converse rate (i.e. those who leave within the 12 months) can be easily computed, and further analyses can reveal how many employees have been with the company for 2 years, for 3 years, for 4 years, and so on. A departmental analysis along these lines will clearly reveal those departments in which employees seem unable or unwilling to settle.

A high rate of LTO may be due to a basic instability of the labour force, although this is most unlikely. It is more probably due to poor recruitment, or bad management, or to full employment with excess demand for staff. Since high LTO causes high expenditure of time and money in filling vacancies, causes should be identified and remedial steps taken.

A study carried out in 1968 in the food industry showed that, if it costs 20 per cent of annual salary to replace a member of staff, the total costs for different rates of labour turnover are as shown in Figure 14.4.

Forms suitable for analysing labour turnover are given in Figures 14.5(a), 14.5(b) and 14.6. It will be seen that these are very straightforward, and that Figure 14.6 is simply a variation on the theme of Figure 14.5(a) showing an alternative way of presenting the same information by varying the design of the form.

Annual labour turnover rate						
Annual payroll cost	5%	10%	15%	20%	25%	30%
£	£	£	£	£	£	£
50 000	500	1 000	1 500	2 000	2 500	3 000
100 000	1 000	2 000	3 000	4 000	5 000	6 000
200 000	2 000	4 000	6 000	8 000	10 000	12 000
300 000	3 000	6 000	9 000	12 000	15 000	18 000
500 000	5 000	10 000	15 000	20 000	25 000	30 000
1 000 000	10 000	20 000	30 000	40 000	50 000	60 000
2 000 000	20 000	40 000	60 000	80 000	100 000	120 000

Figure 14.4: Cost of labour turnover

In preparing a budget for personnel costs, the question of how much to allow for almost every personnel activity is an imponderable. There is no established means by which the personnel manager can decide how much to spend. A specified amount per employee may be budgeted, but this does not get around the basic question of determining *how much* per employee to set aside.

Predicting recruitment costs, LTO rates, redundancy and other termination payments, and welfare expenses (if these are within the scope of the personnel manager's activities) is a most difficult task, but it is the sort of problem faced in such areas as advertising, marketing research, and R & D. Past experience is bound to be relied on heavily, although full cognizance must be taken of anticipated and known future situations (e.g. factory closures, establishing a new corporate planning department, etc.).

Some activities/facilities will be comparatively easy to budget for, including canteen facilities, sports/social club, medical facilities, holiday (payroll) costs, concessions for housing, transport, suggestion scheme and long-service awards, and so on, not forgetting the direct costs of personnel department employees.

Only by drawing up a personnel department budget is a benchmark provided for cost control purposes. However, top management should be aware of the difficulty of deriving meaningful estimates of some items, so some large variances will be expected (but this most certainly does not render the budgeting endeavour a waste of effort).

MONTH:									*ANALYSIS OF LEAVERS*														*COMPANY:* *DEPARTMENT:*		
Cumulative length of service	SEX	*Reasons for leaving*																							TOTAL
		A—Discharges					*B—RESIGNATIONS*																		
		1	2	3a	3b	3c	4	5	6	7	8a	8b	9	10	11	12	13	14	15	16	17	18	19	20	
Less than 1 month	M F																								
1-3 months	M F																								
4-12 months	M F																								
1-5 years	M F																								
Over 5 years	M F																								
TOTAL	M F																								

Monthly LTO =

$$\frac{\text{Number of leavers during month}}{\text{Average number employed during month}} \times 100$$

Total number of leavers in month	M	
	F	
Total new starters in month	M	
	F	
Total employees at beginning of month	M	
	F	
Total employees at end of month	M	
	F	
Average employees during month	M	
	F	

Figure 14.5(a): Monthly analysis of labour turnover—1
(see Figure 14.5(b) for key to reasons for leaving)

REASONS FOR LEAVING

A DISCHARGE

1 Unsuitable
2 Disciplinary reasons
3 Redundancy:
   (a) Shortage of materials
   (b) Seasonal fluctuation
   (c) Other

B RESIGNATION

4 Remuneration
5 Hours of work
6 Physical working conditions
7 Dissatisfaction with job
8 Relationship with:
   (a) Fellow workers
   (b) Supervisors
9 Personal betterment
10 National service
11 Transport difficulties
12 Housing difficulties
13 Domestic responsibilities
14 Illness or accident
15 Marriage
16 Pregnancy
17 Move from district
18 Retirement
19 Death
20 Cause unknown

(Record major reason when there is more than one reason given)

Figure 14.5(b): Reasons for leaving

CHECKLIST ON PERSONNEL CONTROL

1 Does each employee have a job description?
2 Do all employees understand their roles and know how their performance will be measured?
3 Does a well-defined salary structure exist? If so, is it fair in relation to responsibility differentials, other companies' rates of pay, etc.?
4 Are regular performance and salary reviews carried out?
5 Are rates of pay sufficient to retain skilled personnel?
6 Do all employees have a good understanding of the company's activities, structure, policies, and products?
7 Is there a full induction programme for all new employees?

CUMULATIVE LENGTH OF SERVICE														
M=Male F=Female	Less than 1 month		1–3 months		4–12 months		1–2 years		2–5 years		Over 5 years		Total	
	M	F	M	F	M	F	M	F	M	F	M	F	M	F
Discharged employees 1 Unsuitable 2 Disciplinary reasons 3 Redundant														
Resignation (uncontrollable) 4 Changes in personal circumstances Domestic (eg, pregnant) Illness/accident Death/retirement Relocation Housing problems Travelling														
Resignation (controllable) 5 Dissatisfaction with job Remuneration Nature of work Prospects Hours Conditions Human relations														
Totals														

FORMULAE:

Monthly LTO=

$$\frac{\text{Number of leavers in month}}{\text{Average number employed}} \times 100$$

Annual equivalent=Monthly LTO×12

LABOUR TURNOVER CALCULATIONS:

Monthly LTO: Male %. Female % Annual LTO : Male %. Female %		
Total leavers	=	Male Female
New engagements	=	Male Female
Total employed at begining of month	=	Male Female
Total employed at end of month	=	Male Female
Average number employed during month	=	Male Female

Figure 14.6: Monthly analysis of labour turnover – 2

8 What methods are used for attracting recruits and selecting new employees? Are they satisfactory?
9 Are the fringe benefits that the company offers in line with current practice?
10 Do working conditions within the company compare favourably with those offered by other organizations both locally and elsewhere within the same industry?
11 What is the level of labour turnover within the company? Has this been analysed amongst departments, etc? Are there any differences?
12 Are the reasons for labour turnover known?
13 Are the costs of labour turnover known?
14 What steps are being taken to reduce the rate of labour turnover?
15 Is the company clear about the type of individual it is seeking when it advertises a vacancy?
16 Are the company's personnel policies regularly reviewed?
17 Are such techniques as job evaluation and merit rating in use? If not, why not?
18 What incentive schemes are in operation? What is their effectiveness?
19 Is there a definite programme for management development and promotion?
20 Are man-power requirements forecast and plans compiled?
21 Are office rules, etc., enforced? What disciplinary action can be taken?
22 Is morale high or low? Why?
23 How successful are the company's welfare facilities?
24 Is the canteen subsidized? Sports club? Social club? With what result?
25 Is a complete personnel budget prepared?

TRAINING COSTS

Whilst training activities can be very expensive, off-setting grants will often be claimable from the relevant Industrial Training Board (ITB). This factor should be allowed for in budgeting training costs, but it should not be overlooked that there will be a significant time lag between cost incurrence and obtaining an ITB rebate.

In order to obtain the maximum ITB grant it is imperative that all training costs be recorded in relation to their purpose (i.e. nature of course, dates, employees attending, etc.) distinguishing between specific costs such as course fees, and delegates' subsistence and travelling expenses.

The management (including cost control) of a training programme is a joint responsibility of the training (or personnel) department and the user departments. However, this is not an argument for apportionment, although many costs can be directly allocated to a particular department (for example, if Mr Green of purchasing goes on a one week course on value engineering that costs £450 in fees and £200 in travelling and subsistence costs, there is no ambiguity whatsoever about the reason for the expenditure or the amount, and so the whole £650 can be directly charged to the training section of the purchasing department's budget. Alternatively, the training department's budget may be compiled to cater for all charges such as these. The point to note is that charging out a portion of the training manager's salary, etc., is of no value in a strict control sense.)

Apart from budgets providing a means of controlling training costs, due regard should be paid to the *purpose* of training. In the case of factory operatives, for instance, the effectiveness of training may be determined by measuring such factors as:

1 Increases in the rate of output following training.
2 Reductions in the time required to complete a task.
3 Increases in the number of operatives who meet the standards of production.
4 Decreases in the time required for new employees to reach the expected standard.
5 Reductions in the number of accidents.
6 Reductions in the level of absenteeism.
7 Reductions in the rate of labour turnover.
8 Decreases in the breakage of machine tools.
9 Decreases in the amount of scrap/wastage.
10 Increases in the level of morale.

The emergence of these benefits may not warrant an incentive scheme for participating employees, but incentives for those who successfully complete training courses can be highly motivating.

From a cost control point of view, training is an investment that must be justified. The preparation of a training budget enables top management to compare the expected cost of training with its perceived benefits in the light of particular needs. Questions to be asked will relate to how economical the chosen training methods are, how much *should* be spent on training, how training cost trends are developing, how future results might benefit from current investment in training, and so on.

The costs of training are essentially the following:

1 Trainees' wages and salaries during formal training.
2 Trainees' travelling and subsistence expenses for the duration of the training (if paid).
3 Cost of fees, books, equipment, etc., to be supplied by the company to the trainee.

4 Trainers' wages and salaries.
5 Loss of output due to the performance of those under training being less than that of experienced workers.
6 Wastage, spoilage, or provision of special materials.
7 Special training facilities, accommodation, equipment, record-keeping, etc.
8 Training department overheads.
9 Consultants' fees.
10 Outside speakers' charges, fees, hire of films, etc.
11 Awards to trainees, examination fees, incentive bonuses.
12 Training board levy.

When the overall cost level has been computed it should be compared with the expected benefits to see if the suggested programme makes economic sense. Even an effective training programme could possibly produce a result that could be achieved by a less expensive means.

If a company thinks that by failing to carry out any training it is saving the costs of training, then the management of such a company should reflect on the thought that the costs of *not* carrying out training in a systematic manner can exceed the costs of a full training programme. Whenever a new employee is taken on there will be learning needs, and if the new employee's needs are not met in a planned way, it will be apparent that they will of necessity be met in a haphazard, unplanned way. This latter approach involves the incurrence of costs of the following types:

1 Low production whilst the new employee is operating at an inefficient level (and the learning curve in an unplanned learning situation will have a lower slope than in a planned learning programme).
2 Increased wastage due to untrained employees.
3 Under-used plant because the company will be operating below optimum capacity.
4 Lost time of established employees due to constant interruption from the queries of untrained newcomers.
5 Low morale leading to higher rates of labour turnover (with consequent higher costs of recruitment, etc.) and a detrimental effect on the company's image in the labour market.

The higher the level one considers, the greater will be the costs of not offering training facilities to staff. Untrained managers are likely to make poor decisions.

If training is carried out in a systematic manner, the costs relating to each individual's training programme can be compiled on a form of the type shown in Figure 14.7. (This form is merely an indication of some of the information to be collected: further analyses of costs are desirable.)

NAME:			DATE OF BIRTH			
DEPARTMENT:			DATE OF JOINING COMPANY:			
Dates		Nature of course (Purpose, method, etc.)	Location	Cost	Result	
From	To					

Figure 14.7: Individual training record

CHECKLIST ON TRAINING CONTROL

1 What are the areas of the company's activities that are covered by the training programme?
2 How deeply involved are managers/supervisors in defining training needs and drawing up the training programme?
3 How is success determined following participation in training courses?
4 To what extent is top management committed to systematic training?

5 At what level in the organization is the training programme determined?
6 Do training plans have a degree of built-in-flexibility?
7 How up-to-date is the company's knowledge of training methods?
8 Are training methods related to individual needs?
9 What are the objectives of the training activities?
10 What resources are available for training?
11 What barriers are there to achieving desired training objectives?
12 Where should training resources be allocated to achieve the desired results?
13 Are investment appraisal (cost/benefit) techniques applied to training expenditures?
14 What are the benefits of investment in training?
15 How can benefits be measured?
16 What is the cost effectiveness of the training strategies pursued?
17 What are the actual costs of training?
18 What are the costs and consequences of *not* training?
19 How are variances between intended training outcomes and actual outcomes dealt with?
20 Is it known what effect training has on company performance?
21 Are the scheduled future staff requirements (hence training needs) of each department known for 1 year ahead? Five years ahead?
22 Is training directly related to the knowledge, skills, and attitudes needed for specific jobs?
23 What proportion of leavers depart before, during, or shortly after induction training?
24 Do changes in personnel policies (e.g. in connection with selection procedures) indicate a need for different training?
25 When changes are planned (e.g. relating to products, processes, procedures, policies, etc.) is a programme drawn up to explain these to all personnel?
26 Is industrial relations training provided for all managers, supervisors, shop stewards, etc?
27 How urgent is the need for training?
28 How many people are to be trained? In what? What training organization is needed to deal with this function?
29 Should training be in-company, on or off the job, or external? Why?
30 Is training to be an on-going activity for all employees, or will it be restricted to induction training?
31 Is it known which training methods are most effective in given situations?
32 Are adequate records maintained for the evaluation of training, and decision-making with regard to future training?

SUMMARY

This chapter has looked at some aspects of administration: office work, forms control, personnel management, and training. Cost control principles, as discussed in preceding chapters, are applicable in all these areas, but their application must take into account the particular needs of individual departments within unique organizations. (An important part of any company's training endeavours should relate to training all managerial and supervisory staff in the requirements and methods of cost control.)

Whilst administrative costs are incurred for the benefit of the entire organization, it is not in the general interests of cost control to apportion these costs over other departments and productive output.

Office costs should be controlled with regard to time and quality as well as to cost. Budgeting and operation costing are applicable, and it is essential in any control effort to establish some standard of comparison.

The importance of forms – and hence the need for their control – is great. Not only do forms cost money to design, print, and store, but, of greater significance, they are the focus for recording and processing information, and this information on forms is the basis of managerial decisions. It follows that the control of forms should be taken seriously.

Within the context of personnel management, attention was directed to the rate of labour turnover since this is the determinant of the level of many personnel costs – including recruitment, selection, and training costs. To survive, a company must be able to adapt, and it should therefore predict its manpower requirements for some years ahead and ensure that the labour turnover rate does not outpace particular manpower needs.

As is the case with personnel costs (apart from the routine administrative items) many aspects of budgeting training costs are open to question because the bases for making some of the estimates are weak, but this is not to suggest that an attempt should not be made.

Specific objectives for training activities should be established, and performance evaluated in relation to these objectives.

FURTHER READING

Albert, K.J. (ed.), *A Handbook of Business Problem Solving*, New York; McGraw-Hill, 1978.

(A useful compendium of guidelines for an array of relevant issues.)

Denyer, J.C., *Office Administration*, London: Macdonald & Evans, 5th ed., 1980.

(A basic text on the subject.)

Administration

Company Administration Handbook, Aldershot: Gower, 5th ed., 1982.
(Each of the 34 chapters has been contributed by a specialist on his subject, and basic principles as well as practical systems are covered.)

Mills, G. and Standingford, O., *Office Administration*, London: Pitman, 3rd ed., 1977.
(Another basic text on the subject.)

15

Research and Development

INTRODUCTION

By examining the research and development (R & D) function it is possible to see how current outlays can affect – in profound ways – future benefits. For example, within the long term, expenditure on fundamental research can change the entire nature of an organization's activities. Since an organization's products will tend to determine its customers, and hence the markets in which it operates, its competitors, its suppliers, its channels of distribution, and so forth, it will be apparent that a change in the range or type of product offered (which will be determined, at least in part, by research expenditure somewhere along the line) will affect the organization's role. Furthermore, the technological parameter of a company's activities is the cornerstone of all other parameters in the long term: technology determines materials that will be available, processes that can be used, techniques that can be employed, consumer needs that must be satisfied, and products that can be profitably manufactured. By deriving an appropriate R & D strategy, therefore, a company is simply applying commonsense to its future survival.

In order for benefits to accrue it is not always necessary to consider the long term alone: modifications to existing processes, the substitution of one material for another, and the up-dating in minor ways of existing products can all give a pay-off. Therefore, whether it is the long or the short term, or research or development that is being considered, the problem is essentially an investment decision whereby resources are allocated to R & D at this point in time in anticipation of rewards (in the form of major technological breakthroughs, increased productivity through streamlining the technology of production processes, or whatever) at future points in time.

R & D is a fairly essential area of corporate activity but it is difficult to specify how much should be spent on R & D and how the results should be evaluated. (In this respect one can draw obvious parallels between the control of R & D and the control of, say, advertising or public relations.) Two obvious ways to approach these problems are in terms of clearly specified projects on the one hand, and clearly specified responsibilities on the other.

PROJECT CONTROL

In the last 15 years or so project management has emerged to play an important role in technical operations, and a major tool of the project manager is network analysis.

A project manager will generally have full responsibility – managerially, financially, and technically – for directing a particular project. The mix of his project team will depend on the specific characteristics of the job in hand. When the project is complete, the team members – who are only 'lent' to the project – will return to their functional bases, or move on to another project with another mix of specialists. Thus each project team is separately constituted and hence the organization can exhibit a much greater degree of flexibility than is typically found.

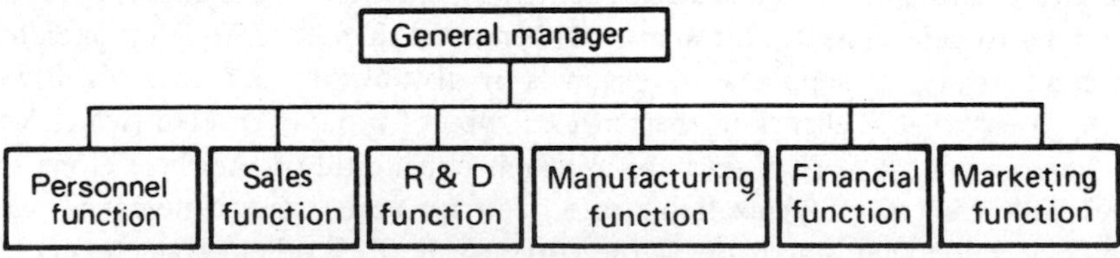

Figure 15.1: A simple functional organization

Figure 15.1 shows a basic, conventional, functional organization design, but the project (or matrix or systems) design of Figure 15.2 is much more in line with adjusting work groups to the particular manpower requirements of a given task. (The product management function, developed from the marketing concept, is a good example of project management in which the role of the project head is to coordinate all activities that are relevant to achieving the project's objectives.) Line responsibility of each sales representative, project engineer,

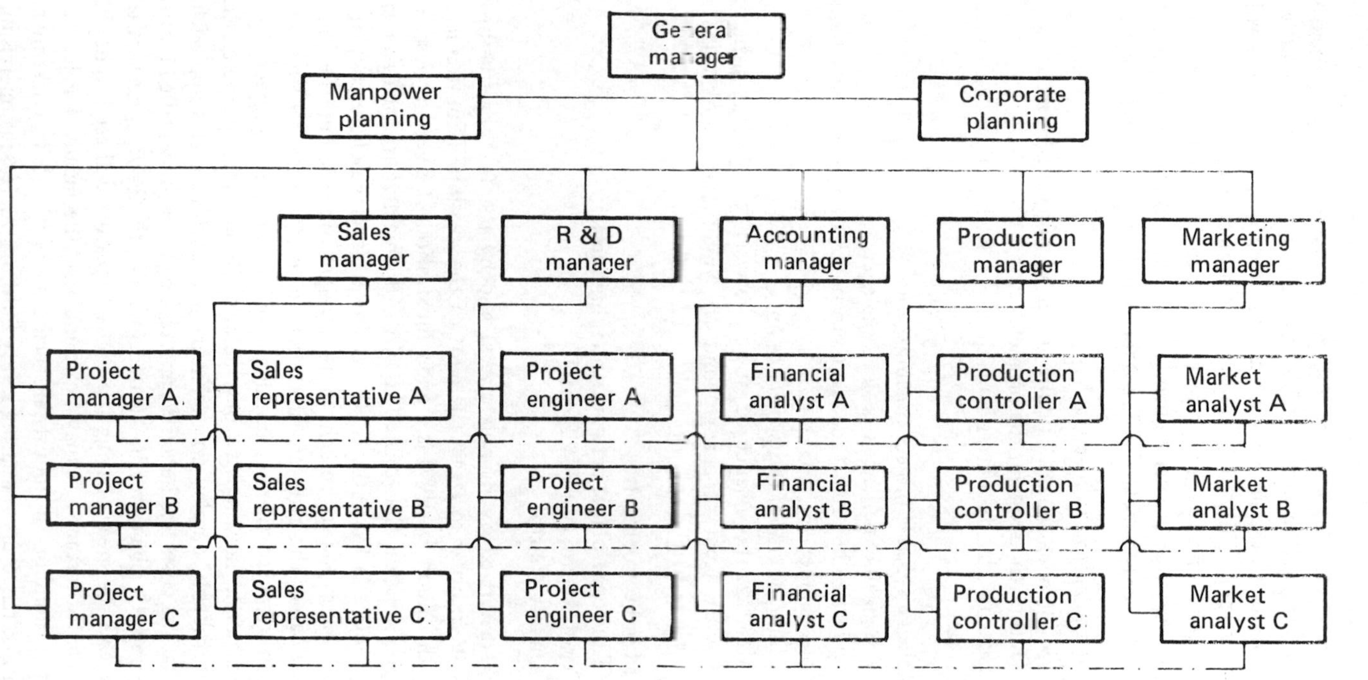

Figure 15.2: Project management structure

financial analyst, production controller, and market analyst, is permanently to the respective functional heads (i.e. sales manager for sales representative, etc.) but for the duration of the project each analyst, engineer, and so forth, will have temporary line responsibility to the appropriate project manager.

Because of the great diversity of projects that exist it is difficult to prescribe general rules for project management. However, the following points have emerged from the experience of the aerospace and construction industries:

Guideline 1 Define the project's objectives:
- (*a*) Define management's intentions in pursuing the project.
- (*b*) Outline the scope of the project.
- (*c*) Specify the desired end result along with performance measures.

Guideline 2 Establish a suitable project organization:
- (*a*) Assign an experienced project manager.
- (*b*) Organize the project manager's responsibilities in an unambiguous manner.
- (*c*) Limit the size of the project team.
- (*d*) Maintain the balance of power between the project manager (as an agent of change) and the functional manager (as a seeker of stability).

Guideline 3 Install project controls:
- (*a*) Time control (via networking techniques).
- (*b*) Cost control (via PERT/cost).
- (*c*) Quality control.

A project is characterized by its objective(s) and by the fact that the project team only exists in order to attain the aims of the mission. (For example, putting a man on the Moon by 1970 is a good illustration of a very large-scale, exceedingly complex mission that related to NASA's objective following President Kennedy's directive in the early 1960s. Other projects may have comparatively insignificant aims and be much more straightforward, but the basic principle is still the same: the project team is set up to attain the mission, and once this has been achieved there is nothing more to hold the project team together.) In considering how it is to best achieve its intended purpose, the project team will probably employ *cost-effectiveness analysis*. This approach, briefly, requires that the costs and benefits appertaining to each identified means of attaining the project's objectives be related in order to derive a measure of cost effectiveness, and the means having the highest measure will tend to be the one selected. Thus, for instance, it may be found that the means that lead to a reduction in the number of industrial accidents (with their consequent losses) include an insistence upon wearing safety clothing, increased supervision, and training of all operatives in safety procedures. To achieve a given result (e.g. a reduction of 25 per cent in 6 months of the number of accidents) it may be estimated that the provision (at the company's expense) of safety clothing will cost an extra £5 000 during the period; the increased supervision may cost an extra £3 500; and the training may cost £7 000. *On the single criterion of cost effectiveness in achieving a given result*, increased supervision can be seen to be the best means *of those taken into consideration*. (This rather simplistic example ignores the other dimensions of the problem of course, such as how desirable it is to increase safety supervision without improving operatives' awareness of occupational risks via training.)

This missions approach requires that the whole spectrum of R & D activities be related to other corporate activities since they do not exist in a vacuum. The other approach to controlling R & D expenditure – via responsibility accounting – requires a breakdown of R & D activities in functional terms. Reference to Figure 15.2 will show that the *horizontal activities* accord with the missions approach whilst the *vertical activities* accord with the conventional functional approach, thus illustrating clearly the two ways of approaching this problem. From either point of view, however, it is important to be aware of the nature of the tasks encompassed by the expression R & D. There are four major task groups (see Figure 15.3) – basic research, applied research, development, and technical support. Planning and controlling the first of these is especially difficult because of the large element of creativity involved: research scientists cannot realistically be expected to create in accordance with a timetable. For a variety of reasons basic research may be viewed as being speculative in nature, and since it will invariably be a long-term activity it will be akin to other long-term investment outlays. (This contrasts it with short-term charges against profit.) Whether top management decides to allocate funds to basic research or not will inevitably be dependent upon the availability of, and alternative uses for, investment funds. Long-term corporate objectives (which act as a frame of reference for mission aims) will have a very strong influence on the allocation of funds, but even with well-formulated objectives there will be no definitive way of determining a basic research budget.

Applied research is more amenable to programming (i.e. it is generally possible to plan the activities and outcomes of a period's applied research endeavours – provided there is a clear distinction between basic research and applied research). Controlling development tasks is usually even more straightforward than is the control of applied research: target requirements can be specified and detailed statements of timing, costs, and expected benefits can usually be compiled. (This leads to a problematical situation in that those activities that have the greatest significance in terms of an organization's strategic future – namely pure, fundamental, and exploratory research, along with some applied research – lead to the greater problems of decision-making

TYPE OF ACTIVITY	*DISTINGUISHING CRITERIA*				
	People	*Place*	*Purpose*	*Process*	*Proceeds*
Basic research Fundamental research Pure research Exploratory research	Creative, curious, unrestrained individuals motivated by scientific tradition	University or non-profit foundation, government laboratories and a few industrial laboratories	To understand the unknown and to contribute to new knowledge	Investigating new scientific phenomena, discovering secrets of nature, and verifying theories of the physical world	New knowledge to be presented or distributed to, and evaluated by, a group of scientific peers
Applied research Invention Technological research	Creative, curious individuals of varied backgrounds externally directed by market needs	Industrial, university, government, and commercial research laboratories	To explore practical possibilities of creating new products and processes. To satisfy previously unsatisfied wants	Creating, inventing or discovering new components, devices, compounds or processes or modifying and combining existing materials, devices, compounds or processes to produce a new application	Theories or knowledge about natural or industrial materials processes and potential products, tests of all areas of uncertainty, and proof of technical feasibility

Development New product development New process development Major improvements or new uses Evolutionary inventions Testing Evaluation	Individual effort often reinforced by teams of scientists and engineers, with planning and organizing skills, who work well together	Industrial laboratories and pilot plants	To creat reliable and satisfactory new or greatly improved products or processes	Using professional teams with varied skills and greater resources to resolve major technological aspects of new or greatly improved products or processes	Technical specifications and production requirements for greatly improved products or processes
Technical support Application engineering Cost reduction Product maintenance Product engineering Foreign intelligence Technical information Quality control	Scientists, engineers, and technicians	Industrial laboratories and production facilities or in the field	To aid in maximizing the return on current products or product lines	Using highly trained people and substantial resources to meet varying requirements of the marketing and producing departments	Technical services or reports as appropriate

Figure 15.3: Types of R & D and distinguishing criteria

and resource allocation, whilst less significant activities can be planned and controlled with relatively fewer and smaller difficulties.)

Technical support is an aspect of the R & D function that links short-term and long-term horizons in the sense that it is an on-going activity for which there is a continuing demand from many segments of the organization. Its nature renders it more controllable than the other categories of R & D.

Throughout this discussion it should be borne in mind that R & D costs are *discretionary costs*, or *managed costs*, that the organization voluntarily incurs in order to preserve its competitive technological (hence competitive, and, in turn, its financial) viability on a continuing basis. R & D costs are incurred to protect future profitability and survival objectives, and it is against these longer-term aims that the control effort should be exercised.

OVERALL COST CONTROL

Reference has already been made to the two major ways by which R & D activities may be controlled – by project and by responsibility. The latter tends to be rather aggregated and fails to focus on the purpose of the activities in question: without relating in some way to purpose the control exercise cannot be fully effective. (That is it is more meaningful to state that a particular outcome should be achieved subject to a limit of expenditure of, say, £5 000 than it is to focus exclusively on the comparison of actual versus standard costs and omit the object of the expenditure. Cost is simply an input that respresents a *means* to a desired end rather than being that end, so a preoccupation with cost rather than control – which relates to objective attainment – is clearly the wrong perspective to adopt.)

Responsibility accounting in the R & D area is in line with the principles that have already been discussed (see Chapter 6 especially). This will involve the planning, accumulating, and controlling of costs by individual responsibility and the nature of the expenditure: occasionally this criterion of responsibility will coincide with the project basis when the responsibility centre and the project group are the same.

Flexibility is an essential ingredient in the context of R & D, and it will reveal itself when an excessively rigid responsibility budget causes ineffective research work. The degree of uncertainty that prevails within the research environment demands that a certain degree of freedom exists to enable resources to be re-allocated between different uses (albeit subject to an overall limit). If this flexibility is not allowed for it is possible that wastage of effort (and resources) will be high. Discretion must thus be accorded to the project manager, etc., to do that which is necessary without over spending in aggregate terms. (It is to be hoped that this discretionary licence will ensure effective results are produced, but as will be seen later in this chapter, measuring the efficiency of R & D activities is far from simple.)

Regardless of whether the detailed control of costs (i.e. at the operational or project level) is attempted via responsibility accounting or project control techniques there is a need to consider at some early stage the *scale* of the R & D programme. This involves determining the total amount of money (and resources that this represents) which must be devoted for a given time span to R & D as a whole, and the way that this total should be broken out amongst competing claims (i.e. fundamental research, technological research, evolutionary inventions, etc.).

The general emphasis on (or away from) research will stem from corporate policies as laid down by top management. This emphasizes again the importance of objective-orientation: as with so many other activities, R & D can only be sensibly evaluated (in terms of either needs before the event, or accomplishment afterwards) in relation to organizational objectives.

As a prelude to determining the overall R & D appropriation it is helpful to view the constituent elements of the overall R & D programme. These are likely to consist of:

1 A continuing research programme that is concerned with research in the area of non-current methods, materials, and products. This programme will provide ideas that will be expected to increase the organization's future profitability and thereby ensure its long-term survival.
2 A programme of substantial development projects that will often take the form of new product ideas that require substantial funding to take them from the laboratory stage to full commercialization. (This theme will be discussed in some detail later in this chapter.)

Basic and applied research effort, development effort, and technical support are all potentially necessary for both these categories, and one of the values of distinguishing them is to assist in establishing priorities in planning the appropriation for R & D. An approach to setting the overall appropriation involves the following steps:

1 Having distinguished continuing research from development categories (i.e. the two points above) a list of suggested projects should be drawn up. This list will consist of projects-in-progress and new suggestions.
2 As many of these projects as are amenable to financial analysis should be evaluated. The essential information required for each project will include:
   (*a*) An initial feasibility study
   (*b*) Title of project
   (*c*) Statement of the project's objectives

(*d*) A listing of criteria for success (including required completion date)
(*e*) Anticipated cost (of a non-capital nature)
(*f*) Anticipated capital outlays
(*g*) Review dates (financial and technical)
(*h*) Priority rating
(*i*) Expected benefits (e.g. through cost reduction, profitable new products, etc.).

3 An overall limit for the programme budget should be derived. At its maximum this will be sufficient to undertake all the suggested and on-going projects listed. Some notice may be taken of competitive rates of R & D expenditure, the percentage of sales revenue that has been spent on R & D in the past, the ROI from R & D outlays, and the amount that the company feels it can afford to spend on R & D. However, these latter rule of thumb guides have major weaknesses: the nature of continuing research requires a long-term commitment rather than a wildly fluctuating series of short-term appropriations; R & D tends to create rather than result from sales levels, so to base the R & D budget on sales is inappropriate; different companies operate in different circumstances so competitive parity is meaningless; and 'affordability' is far too imprecise.

4 A priority listing of available projects from step 3 should then be drawn up to allocate the total budget.

5 Detailed project budget summaries can then be compiled for cost control purposes. Items within a project budget will be:
(*a*) Manpower requirements
(*b*) Direct expenditure on materials/equipment
(*c*) Overhead expenditure that can only be apportioned to individual projects
(*d*) Capital outlays
(*e*) Subcontracted work and charges for using outside facilities.

By drawing up a list of suggested projects, evaluating them, and assigning priorities to those that are acceptable, it is possible to come up with a total budget requirement. This is likely to be much higher than the current level of spending, so some projects will usually have to be cut or postponed in order to bring the budget total into line with the amount that the company is willing to commit to R & D for the period under consideration. (Some balance must obviously be struck between the existing R & D organization and corporate R & D requirements over, say, the next 5 or more years.)

In finalizing the selection of projects that are to be included within the R & D programme attention should be paid not only to the priority rating of individual projects (and hence to their compatibility with corporate aims) but also to their riskiness (i.e. to the likelihood of some acceptable pay-off) and to possible interactions between projects. An ever-present danger of treating the evaluation of projects in isolation is that both beneficial and damaging (i.e. wasteful) interactions or overlapping may be overlooked.

In the final analysis, the main factor in selecting projects to fit into the R & D programme may not be a financial one: it may turn out to be the result of a compromise between the stated needs of the company and the desire by the R & D department to maintain a balanced level of scientific development for the future. To recap, the reasons for this may include one or more of the following:

1 A lack of financial data of sufficient accuracy to gain the confidence of management as a basis for project selection.
2 The inertia that tends to be found in R & D departments that militates against making dramatic changes in research programmes in the short term.
3 The need for the R & D staff to look at likely developments in scientific knowledge beyond the range of short-term corporate activities.
4 The existence of a status quo in R & D that predetermines in many cases the approach made to problems.

PROJECT COST CONTROL

The accounting aspects of R & D projects do not differ in any significant way from accounting in other areas. In principle the accumulation of the costs of a project is a simple application of job costing (as discussed in Chapter 9), but in practice difficulties do arise due to the nature of R & D activities. Working habits will be flexible within R & D, with the result that records of material usage, labour times, etc., may be incomplete. Rigid recording systems should not be allowed to inhibit creative research effort and this strongly suggests that accounting control should emphasize the authorizing of expenditure *before* resources are obtained rather than requiring detailed record keeping that will – in this context – lead to wasted effort in attempting to analyse variances. Supplies are usually relatively minor and could be made available on a self-service basis.

The major R & D costs relate to salaries/wages and facilities, and the control effort should be directed towards the effective utilization of both time and facilities. *Time* is the basic commodity of R & D, and staff should be encouraged to keep time sheets of the effort that is devoted to each project. Only if this is done can results be evaluated with any degree of accuracy. Hourly rates can be derived for each category of research worker to include an allowance for usage of consumable materials if this is thought to be satisfactory in compiling cost reports.

Project budgets facilitate control insofar as they supplement the project leaders' awareness of project objectives and planning schedules. Such budgets should specify (in addition to the normal ingredients of a budget) the critical points in terms of time, money, and resources beyond which the project should not proceed unless there is a satisfactory outcome from previous stages. A risk will always exist that a project may be abandoned after any review and in the light of this factor those who are involved should understand fully the distinction between the expenditure on different projects during a given year and the possible final cost of each project over a number of years. Any revision in project budgets/time schedules may lead to a revised priority rating and/or cancellation.

Two specific approaches to project control will now be discussed: the first will focus on authorization/cost accumulation, whilst the second will emphasize the scheduling aspects.

From the viewpoint of project authorization and cost accumulation it is necessary to develop a system that has the following features:

1 A procedure for numbering projects
2 A project application form
3 A project authorization form
4 A procedure for accumulating costs by project
5 A regular reporting cycle.

PROJECT APPLICATION		
DEPARTMENT:	LOCATION:	NUMBER:
DATE:	☐ SPECIAL ☐ NORMAL	PRIORITY:
Objective and description of project: Estimated resource requirements: Estimated costs: Estimated benefits:		
Submitted by: Authorized by:		

Figure 15.4: Project application form

The first of these features is necessary for identifying each project, whilst the second requires a statement of the objectives of the project, a description of the project, resource requirements (e.g. man-days, etc.) estimated costs, and estimated benefits. Figure 15.4 illustrates a project application form.

Where appropriate (i.e. when the project application has been approved) this should be followed up by a project authorization as shown in Figure 15.5.

PROJECT AUTHORIZATION		
DEPARTMENT:	LOCATION:	NUMBER:
TITLE OF PROJECT:		
Justification of amount required: Original date started: Cost to date:		 Amount requested:
Submitted by: Approved by: Authorized by:		Date: Date: Date:

Figure 15.5: Project authorization form

For each authorized project a cost record must be maintained to ensure that the amount spent at any time is within the authorized total. Typical items that should be recorded are:

1 Hours worked (by project) for technical and non-technical staff
2 Materials/supplies used
3 Purchases of special equipment, etc.
4 Commitments
5 Overhead allocation (e.g. rate × hours).

Costs can be accumulated via cost summaries and thence to project cost cards. An example of the latter is given in Figure 15.6.

PROJECT COST CARD

PROJECT TITLE: PROJECT NUMBER:

LEADER: TOTAL AUTHORIZED: £
SPENT TO DATE: £
BALANCE AVAILABLE: £

Date	Labour charges		Special purchases	Material issues	Over-head	Total	Out-standing commit-ment
	Technical	Non-technical					

Figure 15.6: Project cost card

A monthly report can readily be compiled by analyzing or abstracting information from the cost card.

This covers the outline of a system of project authorization and cost accumulation, but it will be noticed that this system does not cater for scheduling considerations. This can be done by means of network analysis.

NETWORK ANALYSIS

For any task or project, no matter how complex, provided it has an identifiable start and finish (related to the attainment of some known objective) it is possible to make use of one of the various techniques of network analysis.

Network analysis, in brief, is a method of problem solving that is based on systematically and logically analysing the relationships and time factors involved in carrying out a particular project. An appropriate project is any activity that can be considered to have a definable beginning and end, and this includes:

1 Building a new factory.
2 The maintenance programme for a factory.
3 Developing and launching a new product.
4 Product modification projects.
5 Large-scale promotional campaigns.
6 Installing new processes or plant.
7 Laying out workshops.
8 Designing and making production aids.
9 Testing equipment.
10 Very small activities that would benefit from a more rigorous approach.

At present, network techniques are used most frequently on construction projects, major maintenance projects, and research projects (e.g. developing a Polaris submarine).

Two techniques that were developed during the late 1950s made the application of network analysis possible. These techniques are critical path analysis (CPA) and programme evaluation and review technique (PERT). Networks developed by the application of these techniques show the relationships amongst all the activities that must be performed in terms of time in completing the project in question. A very simple illustration of this is the toasting of three pieces of bread in a toaster that can take two pieces of bread at a time and only toast one side of each at one time. One schedule for this task may be:

	Seconds
Toast one side of pieces A and B	30
Toast other side of pieces A and B	30
Toast one side of piece C	30
Toast other side of piece C	30
Total time	120

However, it is easy to see that this can be improved:

	Seconds
Toast one side of pieces A and B	30
Toast one side of C and other side of A	30
Toast other side of B and C	30
Total time	90

This saving of 30 seconds results from employing the optimum sequence of events, and network analysis aims to produce similar savings by using a rigorous and logical discipline. Almost any task can be speeded up, of course, if more people are employed, but this costs money and when a project is composed of a series of connected tasks it is necessary for the total time for the entire project to be shortened if additional expenditure is to be justified.

The network analyst wishing to apply CPA must study each task within the project in order to ascertain the sequence in which tasks must be performed (since some tasks will need to be completed before others are commenced) and to establish which tasks can proceed in parallel. The time each task will take must be estimated, and this is usually done by making three estimates:

1 The optimistic time (i.e. the shortest possible time in which the activity can be accomplished if nothing goes wrong).
2 The pessimistic time (i.e. the longest length of time the task may take if all goes wrong).
3 The most likely time (i.e. the weighted average time).

By manipulating the possible times for each task, and by considering the logical sequence of activities, the whole project can be laid out along a diagrammatic timescale. Figure 15.7 illustrates such a sequence (with the timescale omitted for the sake of simplicity).

The network shown in Figure 15.7 is drawn by using three basic symbols:

1 A solid line represents an *activity*.
2 A circle represents an *event* or intersection between activities.
3 A dotted line represents a *dummy* activity that exists as a means of showing logical relationships that are not physical activities (such as transfers of information between events).

When a network is first drawn it is usual to omit duration times for reasons of simplicity in identifying the correct sequence of events and their interdependencies. Once times have been incorporated it becomes possible to find the overall project time which is determined by the activities that are in sequence – the critical path. This critical path is the longest path (in terms of time) through the network, and it indicates a series of tasks that must be performed in sequence and which will take longer than the other sequences of tasks that can be proceeding at the same time. (A certain amount of time – or 'float' – will usually be available on those activities that are not on the critical path to permit flexibility in executing the project.) The reason why the critical path is so called lies in the fact that the time spent on the tasks that lie along this path must be reduced if the total time spent on the whole project is to be reduced.

One criticism that has been made of CPA is that the emphasis on the critical path activities obscures the fact that some activities on a second path may be very close to being critical and would become so with slight changes in time estimates. Such a possibility can always be alleviated by specifying the first most critical path, the second most critical path, etc., and then determining the critical activities within this broader context.

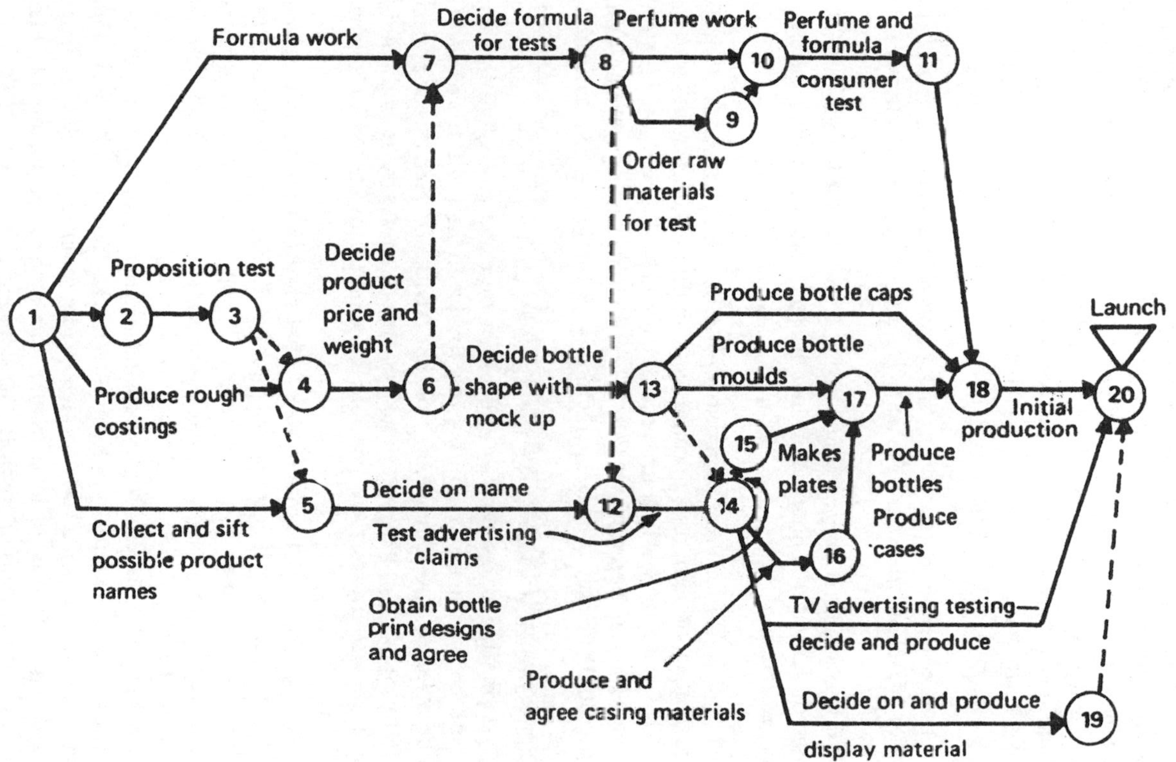

Figure 15.7: Network for launching a new product

Basic CPA and PERT networks only cater for the time dimension, so further analysis requires the introduction of a cost dimension. This is the role of the PERT/Cost technique, which has the aim of determining the optimum combination of manpower and costs to meet a directed project completion date. As an integrated management system, PERT/Cost is made up of a basic procedure for planning and controlling schedules of activities and cost levels, evaluating cost and activity performance, and predicting cost and time overruns. In addition, there are two supplementary procedures:

1 The time-cost option procedure that displays alternative time-cost-risk courses of action which are available for achieving the objectives of the project.
2 The resource allocation procedure that determines the lowest cost allocation of resources among individual project tasks to meet a specified project duration.

Both PERT and PERT/Cost are designed for use in single, large-scale projects, but the technique of resource allocation and multi-project scheduling (conveniently abbreviated to RAMPS) has been developed to deal with the problems of allocating resources to several projects when a number of projects are being undertaken simultaneously and when there is a restriction on the availability of resources.

In building a detailed network the first stage should be to draw up a list of activities, personnel, and resources in order that time and cost allocations can be made without any ambiguity during the course of the project, and also to enable those involved to readily identify all the activities covered by the project.

In its early stages the network should be drawn to clarify responsibilities and to establish cost centres. A framework showing the overall stages is shown in Figure 15.8.

In controlling a project it is preferable to use an *activity-based cost system* rather than the traditional budgetary control method. The steps in this activity-based system, which is based on coordination amongst accounting, administrative, and project management personnel as well as on a time-based network, are shown in Figure 15.9.

When all steps in this control system have been completed the project manager will be able to control both time and cost factors, and it is possible by this approach to keep total costs within a predetermined sum. Furthermore, this approach enables costs to be attributed directly to measurable activities which gives a sensitive means of control. The steps are:

1 Allocate resources to activities by carefully listing all resources required for each activity prior to costing. For example:

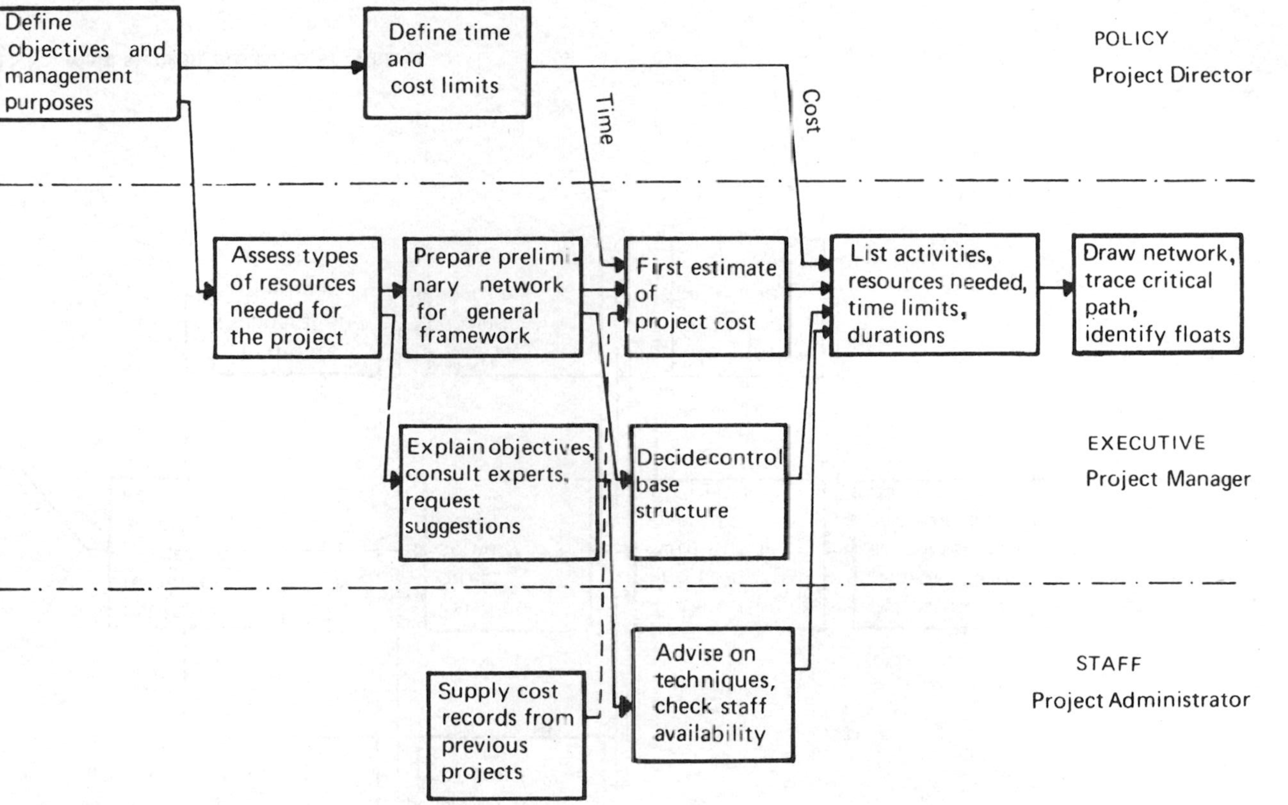
Define objectives and management purposes
Define time and cost limits
Time
Cost
POLICY
Project Director
Assess types of resources needed for the project
Prepare preliminary network for general framework
First estimate of project cost
List activities, resources needed, time limits, durations
Draw network, trace critical path, identify floats
Explain objectives, consult experts, request suggestions
Decide control base structure
EXECUTIVE
Project Manager
Supply cost records from previous projects
Advise on techniques, check staff availability
STAFF
Project Administrator

Figure 15.8: Project planning framework

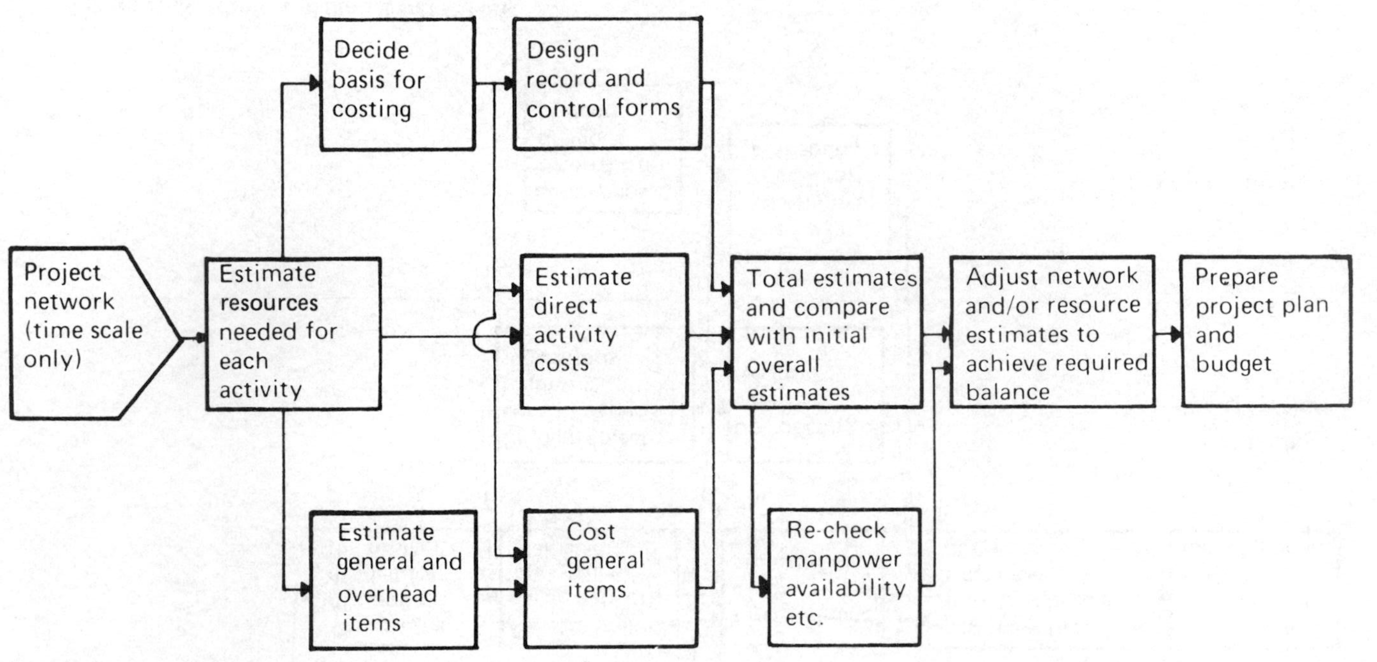

Figure 15.9: Main steps in project cost control

Activity: Design internal transport system.
Planned duration: 15 working days

Resources required:		
	Project manager	1 day
	Data analyst	15 days
	Statistician	3 days
	Clerk	15 days
	Technical assistant	7½ days
	Draughtsman	5 days
	Computer data preparation	12 hours
	Computer time	3 hours

2 List all resources and costs not related to specific activities. These are the general items such as rent, administrative costs, head office charges, etc., and must be allowed for in drawing up the total project budget.

3 Attach costs to all activities – including general items. This can be done on the basis of daily rates for each grade of personnel by activity, and on agreed bases for general items – possibly as an overhead rate to be applied to the payroll costs.

4 Summate the activity cost estimates – see form illustrated in Figure 15.10.

5 Compare estimated costs (step 4) with agreed overall cost made when total budget was divided amongst individual projects. If the estimate exceeds the budgeted figure, it becomes necessary to appraise the activities involved in the project, and make appropriate adjustments.

6 Make a forecast of manpower loadings and total requirements, trimming cost forecasts if required. This step should ensure that there are no overlapping demands for the same resource.

7 Adjust network for revised resource allocations to achieve the required balance.

8 Calculate activity costs by unit of time – Figure 15.11 below, and aggregate into monthly totals to control the completion of the project within specified limits. A project cost profile (Figure 15.12) can be constructed to aid further in the control effort.

The reports that are produced by either of these two approaches to project control can be a starting point for the review of a project. A technical report should supplement cost reports whenever a project has exceeded its time/cost authorization in order that the project may immediately be reviewed as a basis for authorizing additional work or rescheduling priorities. Furthermore, a regular review should be made of *all* projects to ensure that their objectives still have the significance originally ascribed, or that their probability of success has not changed. In the event that a basic parameter has changed it will be necessary to amend the priority rating of the project.

COST ESTIMATING SUMMARY SHEET				
PROJECT:		NUMBER:		
Allocation number	Description	First estimate	Second estimate	Final estimate
	Direct activity costs General costs			
	Total			

General costs as percentage of total:	
First estimate	
Second estimate	
Final estimate	

Budget figure £ ________	Prepared by:	
Contingency included in budget £ ________	Checked by:	
	Date:	

Figure 15.10: Cost estimating summary sheet

ACTIVITY		PROJECT NO:												POSITION AT END:					Remarks
Allocation	Description	Total to end May	Jun	Jul	Aug	Sept	Oct	Nov	Dec	Jan	Feb	Mar	Apr	May	Total budget	Amount spent	Percentage spent	Percentage complete	Value of work done

Figure 15.11: Monthly summary report

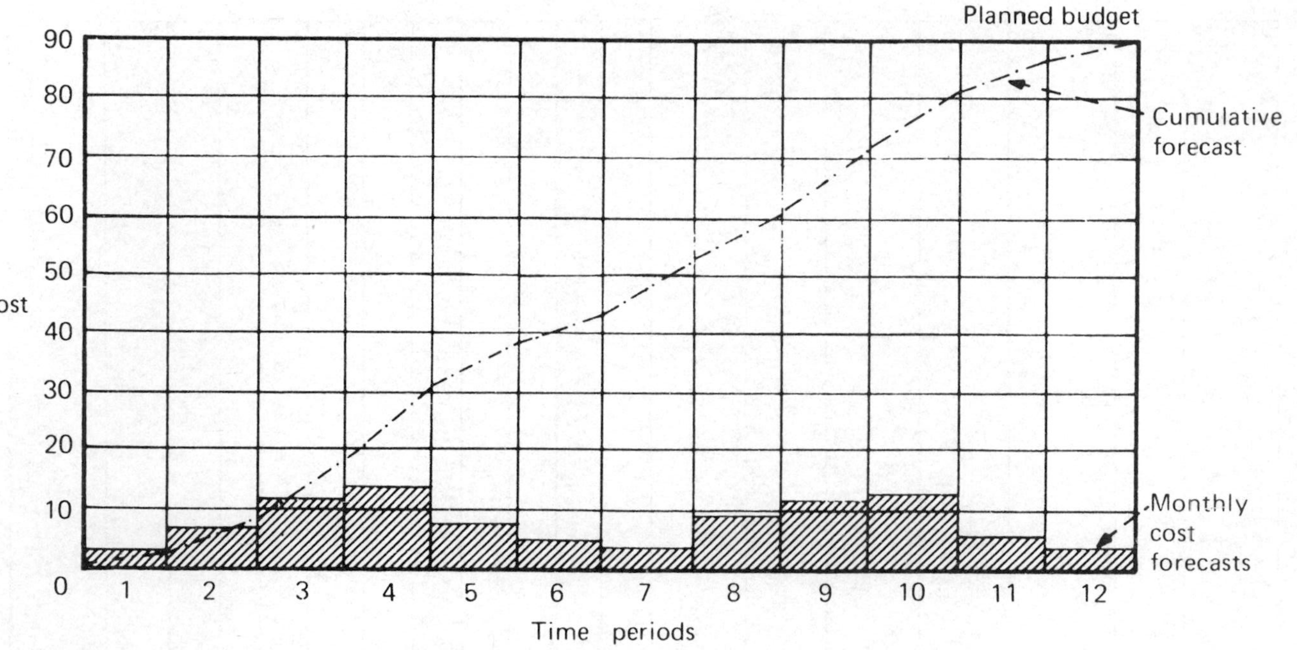

Figure 15.12: Project cost profile

BAR CHARTS

Early in the twentieth century, a charting system was developed by Gantt to show the relationship between time and the functions within a production programme. The principle behind the Gantt chart is that a programme should be seen as a series of interrelated events. This was, in fact, the first formal scheduling system to be used by management, and in addition to showing planned performance, a Gantt chart can also show actual performance and hence variances (in the form of over-production and under-production).

Whilst CPA and PERT techniques are applicable to one-off projects, the Gantt chart was designed for, and is most successfully applied to, highly repetitive production operations. But there is no reason why a Gantt chart should not be used in connection with one-off projects. The advantage of repetitive work is that time standards can be derived and used with confidence, but the absence of a high degree of confidence in particular estimates (as in one-off projects) does not make techniques such as the Gantt chart irrelevant. Two examples will show one approach to scheduling by Gantt charts.

Let us suppose that plans for a house have been drawn up and approved by the appropriate planning authority, and the objective is to execute the construction of the house in the minimum time. Figure 15.13 shows the minimum information that is necessary for compiling a Gantt chart. By skilfully

Activity		*Time required (days)*	*Notes*	*Subcontractor selected*
1	Survey the site	1		
2	Excavate	3	Can start immediately after activity 1	21
3	Masonry	10	Immediately after 2	48
4	Carpentry	34	Start 6 days after start of 3	113
5	Plumbing: piping	9	8 days after 4 starts	88
6	Plumbing: set fixtures	5	7 days after 11 ends	88
7	Heating: piping	9	Start with 5	34
8	Heating: set radiators	2	Finish with 5	34
9	Electric wiring	7	2 days after 7 starts	236
10	Electric fixtures	2	1 day after 12 ends	236
11	Plastering	7	2 days after 9 starts	3
12	Painting	11	1 day after 11 ends	27
13	Paper hanging	5	7 days after 11 ends	7
14	Clean up	3	1 day after 13 ends	—
	Total time	108	working days	

Figure 15.13: Scheduling information

manipulating the starting times of the 14 activities of Figure 15.13 so as to avoid conflicts and interruptions, the total of 108 working days is compressed into a period of 45 days in Figure 15.14. A conveyance completion can be offered on that date that is 45 + contingency days hence – subject to materials, labour, etc., being available. If each subcontractor knows of the schedule (Figure 15.14) there may be more likelihood of achieving the objectives because each will see how his own role is important to the roles of others.

For the second illustration of bar charts, let us consider the problem of moving one piece of plant (X) to a new site and installing in its place another piece of plant (A). The objective is to have X and A in their new locations, tested, and ready to run, in the minimum time.

The major activities connected with X are:

1 Clear site for X
2 Remove X from old location
3 Install X in new location
4 Text X in new location.

The similar activities for A are:

1 Prepare site for A
2 Clear rubbish
3 Remove A from old location
4 Install A in new location
5 Obtain tools for A
6 Test A
7 Obtain material handling equipment.

These various activities are shown in a network in Figure 15.15 with optimistic (E) and pessimistic (L) times being given for each event and the duration of activities being given also.

This network can be translated into the bar chart of Figure 15.16 which bears a very close resemblance to it.

It may appear that the interrelationships within any project are sufficiently apparent through using a Gantt chart that nothing can be gained by CPA or PERT networks, and this may be true in the case of simple, small-scale projects. But when many people are involved, and when projects are large, complex, or expensive, networks become essential if control is to be successfully achieved. It is only through networks that interdependencies become clearly apparent, and in other than very simple cases, Gantt charts are inadequate in showing interdependencies and fail altogether in showing the critical path. Since the critical path is at the heart of CPA and PERT, thereby enabling these techniques to focus on the time span that must be reduced if the project duration is to be shortened, they have a distinct advantage over bar charts.

Building: House
Site: 35 Park Lane

Architect: A. B. Partners
Owner: Abacus Associates

Contract number: 1234
Completion date: 8.3.1982

Activity	S.C. No.	W/E 4/1	W/E 11/1	W/E 18/1	W/E 25/1	W/E 1/2	W/E 8/2	W/E 15/2	W/E 22/2	W/E 1/3	W/E 8/3	W/E 15/3
		MTWTF	MTWTF	MTWTF	MTWTF	MTWTF	MTWTF	MTWTF	MTWTF	MTWTF	MTWTF	MTWTF
1 Survey												
2 Excavate	21											
3 Masonry	48											
4 Carpentry	113											
5 Plumbing	88											
6 Plumbing	88											
7 Heating	34											
8 Heating	34											
9 Electric	236											
10 Electric	236											
11 Plastering	3											
12 Painting	27											
13 Paper hanging	7											
14 Cleaning	—											
Total 45 days												

Figure 15.14: Schedule

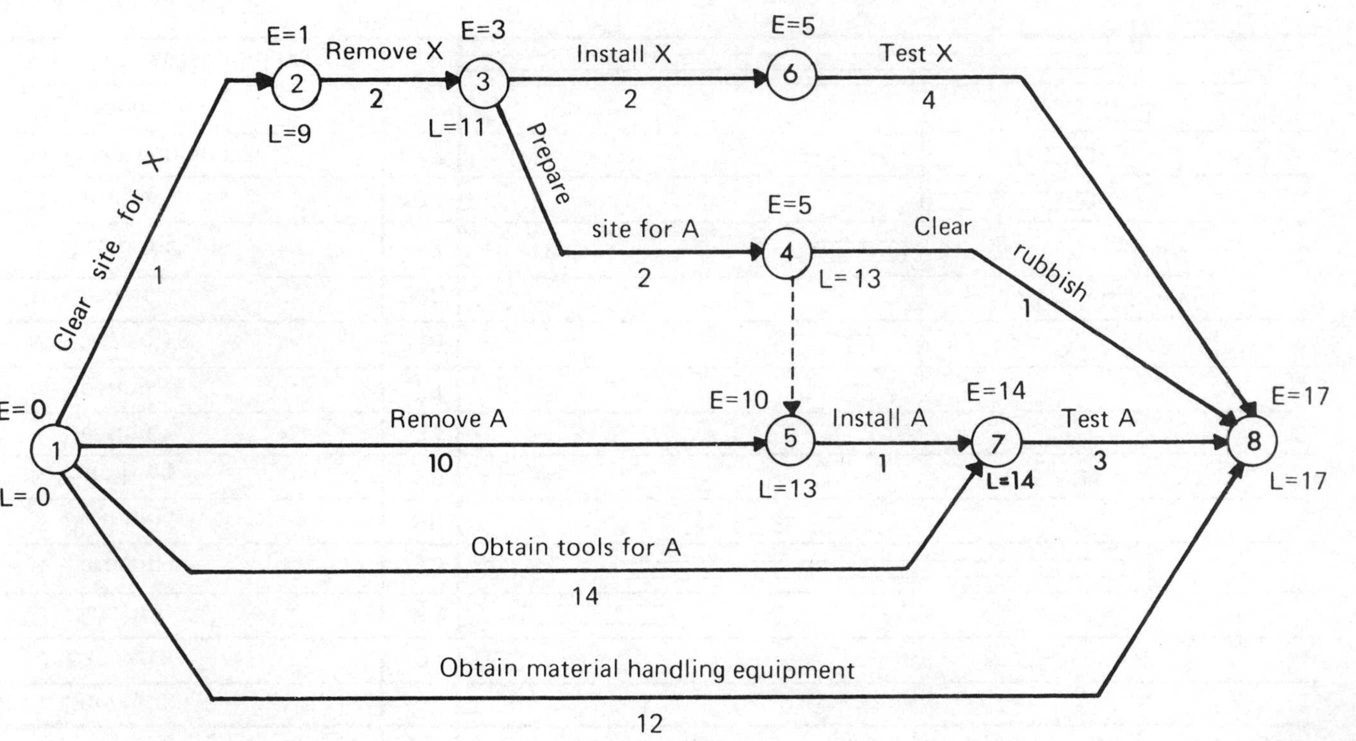

Figure 15.15: Network

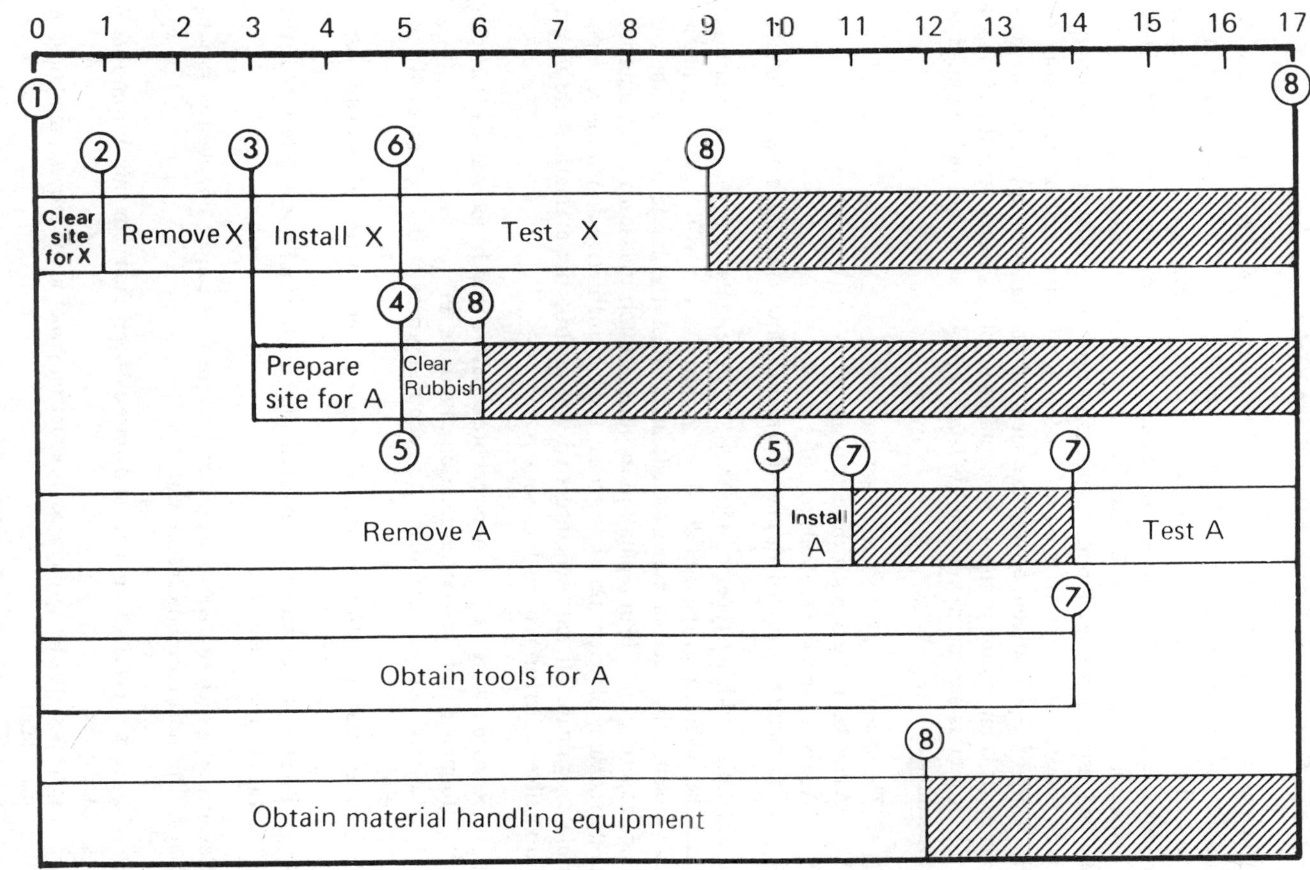

Figure 15.16: Bar chart

EVALUATION OF R & D EXPENDITURE

The commercial justification for spending money on R & D activities is the anticipated improvement in future profitability, and it is against this benchmark that one would expect R & D outlays to be evaluated. However, basic research can rarely be justified on economic grounds: since it is not related to specific products it must be justified on the basis of judgement. In contrast, applied research and development work can usually be evaluated on an economic basis (subject to the provisos on p.427–9). A formal evaluation made prior to the start of a project can, as we have seen, be the basis for appraising the outcome. (It is important in this to make all assumptions underlying the appraisal of a project as explicit as possible.) Whether a project should be discontinued or not will be affected by:

1 The issue of a patent to a competitor.
2 A change in the competitive situation.
3 A need to re-allocate funds to other areas.
4 The success achieved during the period since the project's last review.

A difficulty with all types of research and development is that of measuring (and then evaluating) the usefulness (or success) of the work. Both qualitative and quantitative factors are involved, and whilst the image of the company may benefit from a high reputation in pure research that leads to an improved understanding of scientific phenomena, such a qualitative dimension is impossible to evaluate. It has been suggested that quantitative evaluations are almost impossible to perform for such reasons as:

1 Research work is of a non-repetitive nature and hence standards of performance that facilitate evaluation cannot be set.
2 Research workers are unable to adequately predict the outcomes of their efforts.
3 The creative nature of research work prevents accurate estimates being made of time schedules.
4 There is an uncertain commercial value of original research results at the time of their discovery.

Nevertheless, quantitative measures of performance can be obtained in various ways. The most useful means are via:

1 Increased profits from new and improved products stemming from R & D activities.
2 Increased profits through cost reduction (whether of process, methods, or materials).
3 Savings on royalty payments.

R & D EVALUATION							
Product	Code	Average for last 5 years			Budget for next year		
		Net sales	Net profit	R & D expense	Net sales	Net profit	R & D expense

Figure 15.17: R & D evaluation

4 Royalties received from others.
5 Increases in the goodwill value of the organization.

Figure 15.17 illustrates a form that can be used to show product-related R & D effort and results (in terms of sales and profits) over the last 5 years along with a forecast of the expected relationships over the next year.

When a project is completed it is possible to evaluate it in technical terms as well as in financial terms. An attempt might be made, for instance, to list the outcomes of the project in terms of:

1 Patents licensed.
2 Products, materials, or processes already exploited (or being exploited).
3 New fundamental research areas of potential value brought to light as a result of the work.
4 Subsequent applied research and development projects initiated to extend the knowledge acquired.

Such a listing will help in arriving at an overall rating for the project that blends quantitative with qualitative dimensions.

NEW PRODUCT DEVELOPMENT

In a rather simplified way one can view the principal factors contributing to profit in the following way:

A		B		C		
A good product	×	Efficient manufacturing	×	Effective marketing	=	Profit

The three factors A, B and C are all essential for profit, and the importance of A over B and C can be demonstrated in a number of ways, for instance:

1 There can be no manufacturing or marketing without a product, so the product must come first.
2 The magnitude of the manufacturing and marketing effort is determined by the market potential of the product.
3 The nature of the manufacturing and marketing effort must be adjusted to the requirements of the product.
4 The ceiling on profit potential is set by consumer acceptance of the product.

As manufacturing and marketing methods are made increasingly efficient, profit will approach its maximum for the product. Further increases in profit can only result from changes in the product, the introduction of further products, or the substitution of a new product. This indicates most clearly the importance of products and the need to relate R & D effort to the constant improving of the product line.

A new product is one that opens up an entirely new market, replaces an existing product, or significantly broadens the market for an existing product. However, it is not always necessary to create entirely new products in order to rejuvenate the product line and improve profits – existing products may be modified and thereby have the desired effect.

Modifying a product will involve a change in some characteristic of the product or of its pack. Such changes may be in quality, style, or features, but do not extend to changes merely in the marketing programme. Product modifications stem from technological improvements (e.g. materials, processes) and competitive response, and are in the province of applied research and development. New products, in contrast, will stem from basic and applied research.

The management of new product development is best done, perhaps, by means of the missions approach (i.e. venture management or project management) whereby a clear objective (or mission) is specified and the whole process from conception of new product ideas through to commercialization is seen as one project and handled by a small team that has responsibility for the full process. This approach aims to make innovation more predictable and less random than it might otherwise be by managing new product development as a continuing commitment (made up of a series of on-going projects) rather than as a sporadic or periodic crash programme.

To be most effective, the missions approach requires that each project be subjected to a rigorous multi-stage evaluation procedure. At each stage in this procedure the project must be subjected to a go/no go decision to determine its eligibility to proceed to the next stage. The stages of the process are:

1 Idea generation: is the concept acceptable?
2 Screening: is the concept compatible with objectives?
3 Business analysis: is the product likely to be profitable?
4 Product development: is the product technically sound?
5 Market testing: is the product acceptable to consumers?
6 Commercialization: is the product successful?

Figure 15.18 shows how these stages relate to one another. Somewhere between the first and the final stages of this process it is probable that those ideas that are incompatible with either corporate objectives or resources will be identified and eliminated. Special attention should be paid to the company's:

1 Technological ability to develop a particular idea into a working product.
2 Financial ability to fund the project from inception to full commercialization.

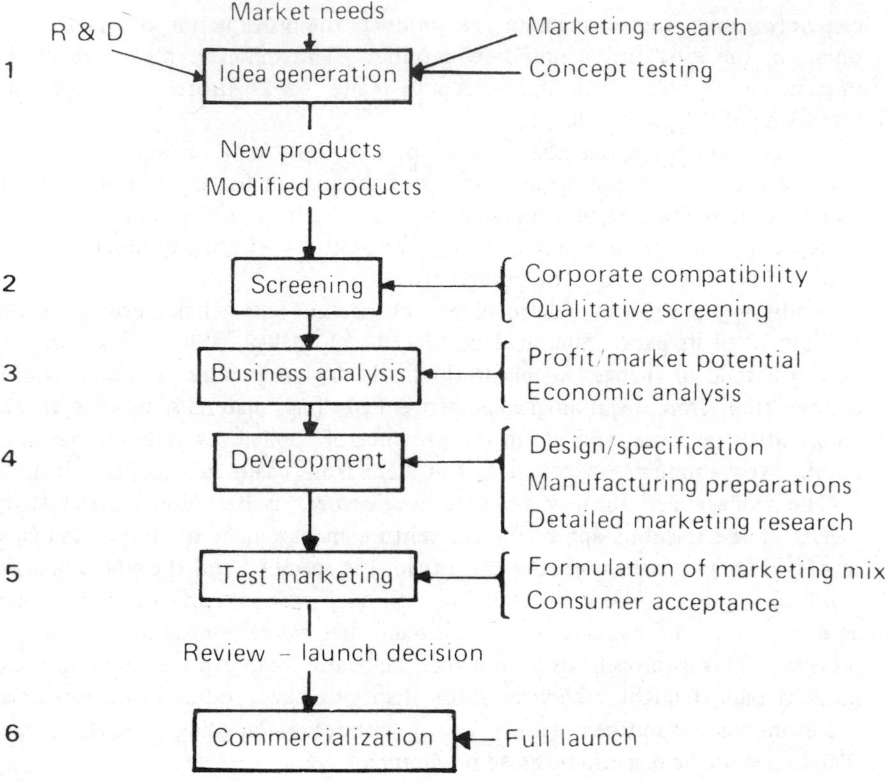

Figure 15.18: New product development cycle

3 Manufacturing ability to physically produce the goods in an efficient manner.

4 Marketing and distributive ability to successfully promote and sell the product at a satisfactory return, after allowing for competitive activity.

Since each stage of the evaluation process is more refined than the previous one, these ideas that are eventually marketed should have a high probability of success. A new idea may be subjected to a corporate compatibility screening (i.e. stage 2) as shown in Figure 15.19.

Each dimension in Figure 15.19 that is important in terms of determining product fit is listed in the left-hand column and given a weight (A) to show its relative importance (i.e. R & D compatibility with a weight of 0.20 is considered to be twice as important as financial compatibility with a weight of 0.10). The product idea is then evaluated against each dimension and is found

Sphere of performance	(A) Relative weight	(B) Product compatibility value											Rating (A x B)
		0.0	0.1	0.2	0.3	0.4	0.5	0.6	0.7	0.8	0.9	1.0	
Company personality & goodwill	0.20							✓					0.120
Marketing	0.20										✓		0.180
R & D	0.20								✓				0.140
Personnel	0.15							✓					0.090
Finance	0.10										✓		0.090
Production	0.05									✓			0.040
Location & facilities	0.05				✓								0.015
Purchasing & supplies	0.05										✓		0.045
Total	1.00												0.720

Figure 15.19: Evaluation matrix

to be a good fit in relation to marketing, for example, but a poor fit in relation to location, with scores of 0.90 and 0.30 respectively. By multiplying the weights (A) by the compatibility scores (B) an overall rating of 0.720 is arrived at. This can be interpreted against a generalized scale:

Score	*Rating*
0.00	Totally incompatible
0.01–0.40	Poor
0.41–0.70	Fair
0.71–0.99	Good
1.00	Perfect compatibility

A minimum acceptance score of 0.71 may be required before an idea is taken further.

Let us accept that an idea is to be evaluated up to commercialization. But what is to happen after that? It is relatively easy for management to recognize the profit implications of design changes, product obsolescence, price variations, and so on in isolation for a particular product, yet insufficient acceptance of the concept of the *product life cycle* as a basis for planning the overall strategy for a product seems to exist.

A product life cycle is a way of portraying (either before or after the event) the cash flow/profitability/sales level of a product. In Figure 15:20 a product's life cycle is represented in terms of funds flows: prior to its launch all funds flows are negative due to R & D and related activities. Even after the launch it takes some time for positive funds flows to counteract the heavy initial promotional and other launch outlays. When the product is deleted, funds cease flowing altogether.

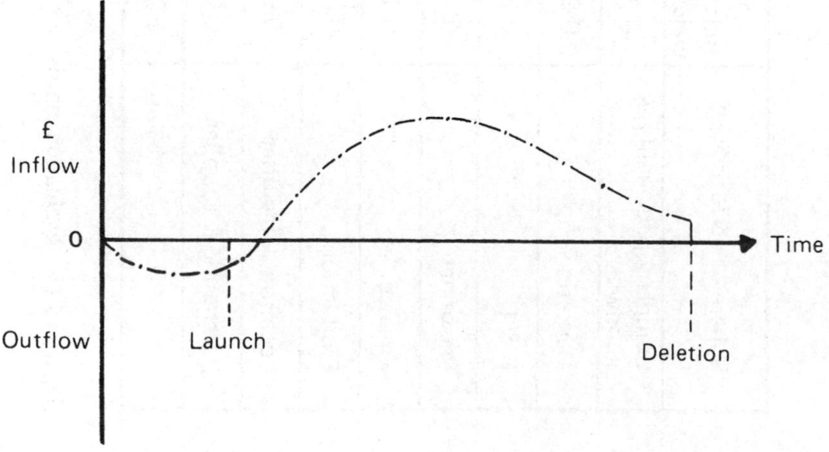

Figure 15.20: Product life cycle – 1

Figure 15.21 looks at the product life cycle in a slightly different way: it not only separates revenue and profit, but it also identifies different phases of the life cycle. The development phase may last about 6 years on average, and the post-launch period will last for a similar length of time. Within the development phase, of course, are the various screening stages from concept testing to test marketing, and these exist in parallel with laboratory work, pilot plant activity, and main-line production planning (including methods and materials).

In the introduction phase costs will be high, sales revenue low, and profits probably negative. The skill that is exhibited in testing and launching the product will rank high in this phase as a critical factor in securing success and initial market acceptance.

Following a successful launch is the growth phase during which the product's market penetration – hence sales – will increase. Since costs will be lower than in the earlier phases the product will start to make a profit contribution. Following the consumer acceptance in the launch phase it now becomes vital to secure wholesaler/retailer support.

As growth levels out we reach the phase of maturity. This is characterized by stable prices and profits and the emergence of competitors. However, as the market becomes saturated pressure is exerted for a new product and sales (along with profit) begin to fall. Intensified marketing effort may prolong the period of maturity – but only by increasing costs disproportionately. (Saturation and decline stem from a range of very similar competitive offerings that do not offer the consumer a differentiated choice in terms of value or technological superiority.)

Growing price competition as sales decline will reduce profitability until it reaches zero, at which point the product's life is commercially complete. Cost control is especially important in the period of decline in order that the product may be deleted before it begins to incur losses.

An appreciation of the concept of the product life cycle is useful in any cost control exercise relating to R & D, marketing, manufacturing, distribution, or finance in that it brings out some general guidelines. These are:

1 That products have finite lives and pass through the cycle of development, introduction, growth, maturity, decline, and deletion at varying speeds.
2 Product cost, revenue, and profit patterns tend to follow predictable courses through the life cycle: profits first appear during the growth phase and, after stabilizing during the maturity phase, decline thereafter to the point of deletion.
3 Products require different functional emphases in each phase – such as an R & D emphasis in the development phase and a cost control emphasis in the decline phase.

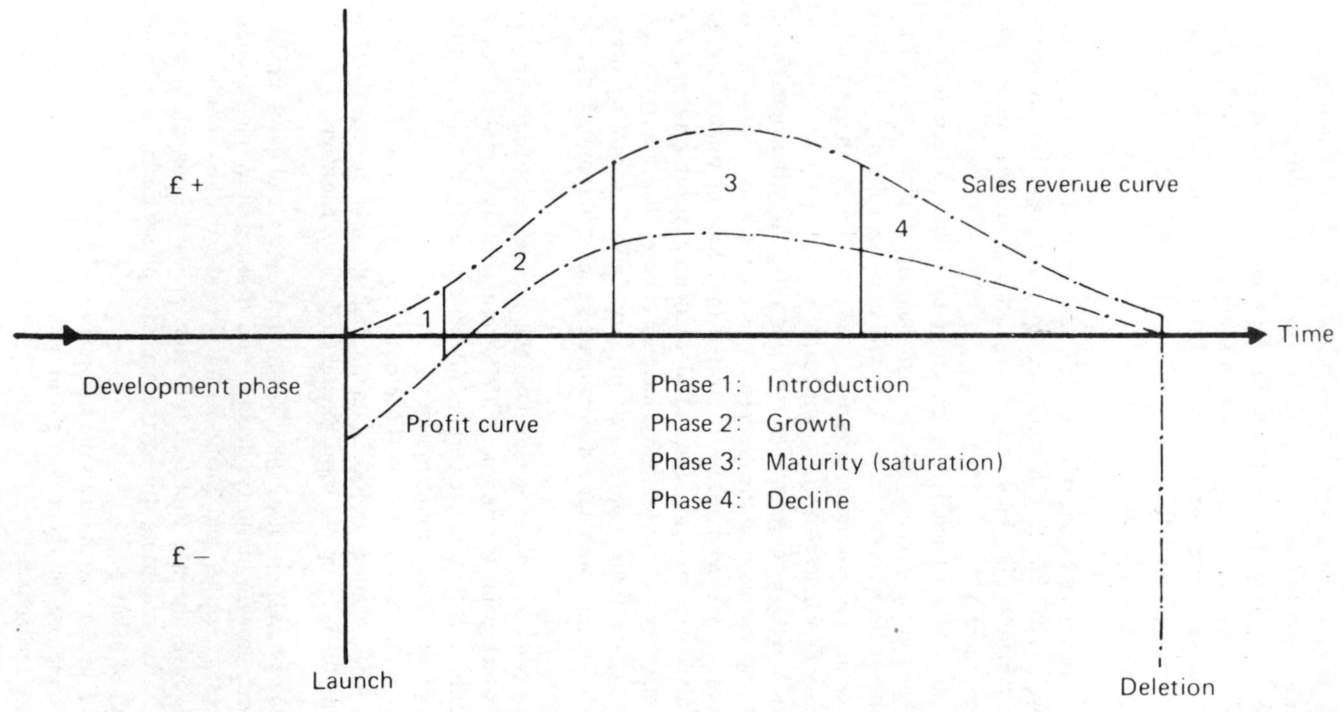

Figure 15.21: Product life cycle – 2

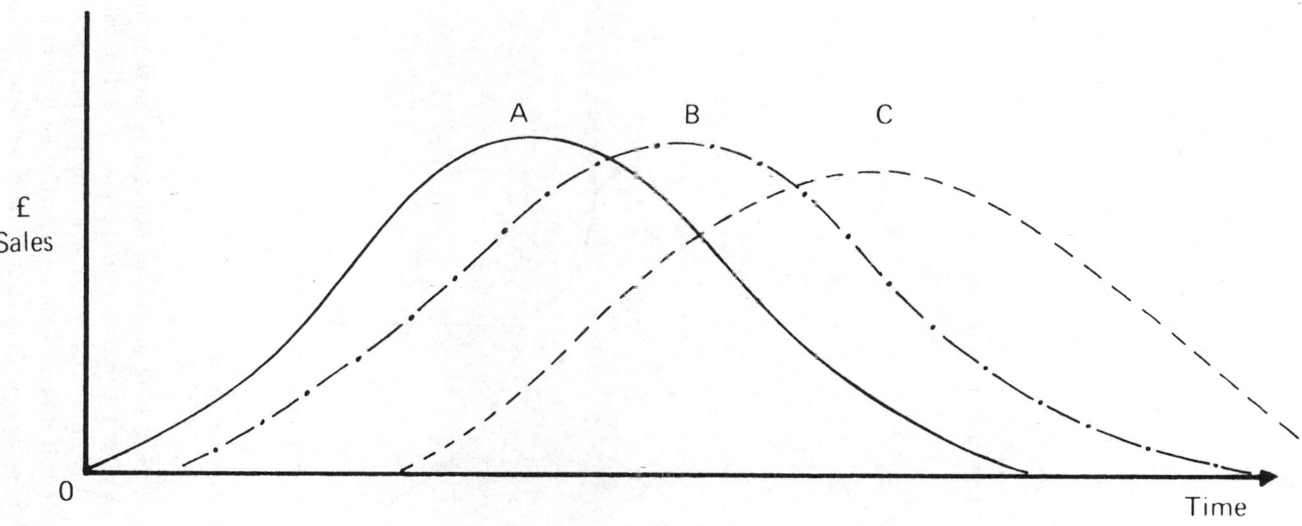

Figure 15.22: Life cycle phasing

These general guidelines can be used to help in controlling the development of both new and existing products. They indicate that introducing a new product so that it reaches its earnings peak as other products decline is helpful in maintaining at least a constant level of profits. Alternatively, as a product reaches its peak, a major modification may help to prolong this phase; or it may be promoted to new markets, or for new uses, or for more frequent use. Figure 15.22 shows the way in which product B can be introduced to take over from the declining product A, and so on. The other case is shown in Figure 15.23 in which a single product has its life prolonged – and performance improved – by being promoted to new market segments.

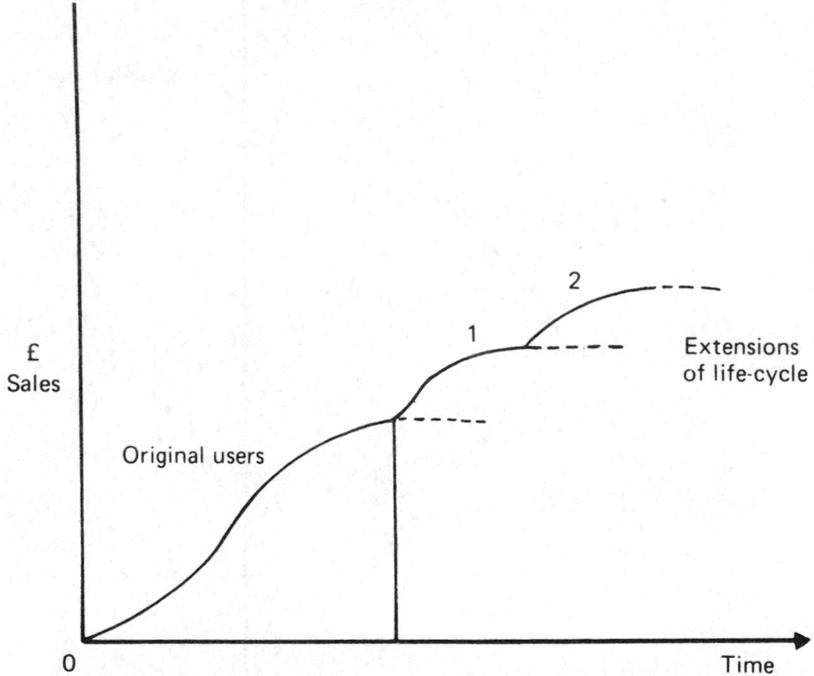

Figure 15.23: Life cycle extensions

The final topic that we will look at in this context of new product development is complementary to the product life cycle: it is the pattern of new product acceptance. Any innovation, such as a new product, will take time to gain wide acceptance but if it is possible to identify the type of individual who is adventurous in adopting new products it may be possible to plan one's marketing programme (and thus have a basis for planning cost/revenue patterns) in relation to adoption rates.

Studies have shown that individual consumers differ in their willingness to try new products and also in the extent to which others view them as 'opinion leaders' (i.e. those from whom information is sought, or whose behaviour tends to be imitated). Consumers have accordingly been categorized into five groups (see also Figure 15.24):

1 Innovators represent, perhaps, 2½ per cent of the population and due to their venturesomeness are first to try new products.
2 Early adopters represent 13½ per cent or so of the population, and adopt new products fairly rapidly but with more discretion than is exhibited by the innovators.
3 Early majority, making up 34 per cent of the total, and characterized by deliberate behaviour, follow the opinion leaders (i.e. (1) and (2)).
4 The late majority display scepticism, and make up a further 34 per cent of all consumers.
5 Finally, the laggards have a dominant value of tradition and constitute the remaining 16 per cent of the total number of adopters.

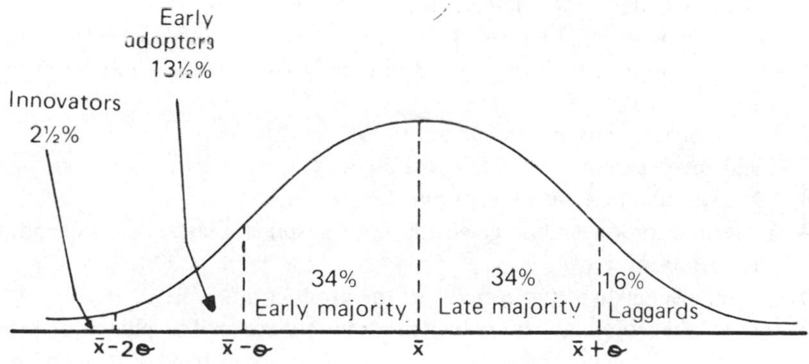

Figure 15.24: The adoption process

The adoption process can reasonably be represented by a normal distribution (thus Figure 15.24 follows the statistical principles outlined in Chapter 5), when plotted over time. From the outset the rate of adoption is slow – innovators – but then it picks up as the early adopters begin to purchase the innovative product. A peak is reached with the early majority and then, with fewer people left to use the product for a first time, the rate of adoption declines. This parallels the general shape of the product life cycle.

CHECKLIST ON R & D

1. Are R & D objectives clearly defined? (Are they restricted to particular products?)
2. Is there an effective product diversification programme? (What economic criteria are used in devising this programme?)
3. Is there a balanced R & D programme made up of both long-term and short-term projects?
4. Is there clear policy on when projects should be terminated?
5. Is the R & D programme diversified amongst projects concerning products, processes, and materials?
6. Is a time span established for the recovery of development costs from profits resulting from R & D efforts? (What criteria are employed? How does R & D ROI compare with ROI from other areas of activity?)
7. Are specific budgets compiled and authorized for each project?
8. How are projects determined and approved? What criteria are used for determining priorities?
9. Are costs allocated to specific projects? If so, how?
10. Are reports prepared regularly and appropriate control effort taken?
11. Are development efforts related to redesigning existing products/processes for lower costs?
12. Do managers appreciate the nature of the different categories of research and development?
13. Is a stimulating research environment provided?
14. Are new product ideas given the same systematic attention as candidates for deletion?
15. Is full use made of the concept of the product life cycle?
16. Does the company know which products are in the phases of growth, maturity, decline? Are appropriate strategies in hand for extending life cycles?
17. Is high investment in technology needed to enter the company's business? How easy is it for new competitors to enter?
18. Is the life cycle of the industry known?
19. What licensing agreements are in force? What are their costs?
20. How much is paid in the form of royalties? How much is received in the form of royalties?
21. Do the answers to Question 19 and Question 20 indicate that the company should (or should not) spend more (or less) on R & D?
22. What benefits can (does) the company receive from licensing agreements?
23. What patents does the company have? (When do they expire? What will happen then?)

24 How far ahead of (behind) competitors is the company's technological capability?
25 Is this technological capability used to its full advantage? (Is it necessary?)
26 Is obsolescence built into the company's products?
27 Are modifications planned for style/quality/features in a structured way? (Are modifications given appropriate consideration *vis-à-vis* new products?)
28 Have safety features been considered in product/process design?
29 Have installation problems been dealt with?
30 Are standard parts used wherever possible? (Does this facilitate repair/replacement?)
31 Has the need for maintenance been minimized?
32 Are the best materials (with regard to functional efficiency, texture, finish, colour, etc.) used?
33 Does the product need instruction sheets, etc? If so, who is to prepare them? Are they adequate?
34 How is R & D linked to quality control?
35 Is an effective screening process for new products in existence?
36 Is a project management approach employed?

SUMMARY

The long-term survival of a company will tend to be closely related to its commitment to a continuing R & D programme. Technology is the most fundamental characteristic of any organization: it determines products, and products determine processes and materials; and it determines uses which in turn determine markets.

Various categories of R & D can be identified – basic and applied research and development, plus technical support. Different criteria will determine the role of each in any given situation. R & D projects are best controlled as missions, each mission having a clearly-defined objective. (Whilst these missions are wholly discretionary they have the utmost strategic significance.) Time is the basic commodity (insofar as this represents the application of expertise to problems) and its utilization should be the focus of control efforts at the project level. In consequence, networking techniques are more relevant than are control methods lacking a strict time dimension.

Although drawing up a valid network for a project is difficult, the procedure demands thorough and systematic analysis, and the discipline that this requires means that relationships which might otherwise have been overlooked are included. Furthermore, it specifies the sequence of decisions that must be made, and this provides a framework for control as well as permitting planning and scheduling.

Network analysis is of great value in ensuring that resources are not wasted, and the efficiency that is thereby encouraged is a vital complement to other cost control procedures. Network analysis can fail in practice for such reasons as a lack of top management support, the use of excessive detail, bad charting, a failure to update charts/networks/schedules, and an absence of feedback information.

The range of projects to which network analysis can be successfully applied is limitless, and wide use has been made of the techniques of, for example, PERT and CPA in the construction industry and in industries pursuing advanced technological research and product development.

Early networks consisted of bar charts (or Gantt charts named after Henry Gantt who first used such devices), but more complex projects, involving more interrelationships, required the emergence of PERT and CPA. These newer techniques only portrayed interrelationships over time, and so PERT/Cost was developed to introduce the financial dimension.

Project management and networking are closely related aspects of modern administration. New patterns for organizational design have appeared to cater for rapidly-changing environments that are typical of the project management situation. Flexibility is very necessary in order that organizations may adapt promptly to change, and also initiate change via project management itself.

Beyond the level of the individual project is the R & D programme. The overall budget cannot be definitively specified so one must attempt to relate priorities to corporate objectives. R & D effectiveness can only be determined in relation to objectives, but this is extremely difficult.

New product development is helped by adopting a missions approach, and is helped by an awareness of the concept of the product life cycle and the adoption process.

FURTHER READING

Kharbanda, O.P., Stallworthy, E.A. and Williams, L F. *Project Cost Control in Action*, Aldershot: Gower, 1980.
(A splendid book in terms of its practical, commonsense coverage of the subject matter. Very helpful.)

Staffurth, C. (ed.), *Project Cost Control Using Networks*, London: Heinemann (for ICMA). 2nd ed. 1980.
(A valuable, albeit brief, book that constitutes a handy checklist.)

Urban, G.L. and Hauser, J.R., *Design & Marketing of New Products*, Englewood Cliffs, N.J.: Prentice-Hall, 1980.
(This is a thorough book that covers all aspects of new product development from a number of analytical viewpoints. Very high quality content.)

Villers, R., *Research and Development: Planning and Control*, New York: Financial Executives Research Foundation, 1964.
(This is rather old now, but it covers the practices of leading US companies and offers a lot of good advice that is still highly relevant.)

16

Manufacturing

INTRODUCTION

Efficiency within the province of manufacturing will tend to depend on the adequacy of impersonal factors such as:

1 The nature of the manufacturing process
2 The purchasing process
3 Inventory management
4 Routing and scheduling procedures
5 Progressing and expediting
6 Working conditions

It will also depend upon the adequacy of such personal factors as:

1 Training
2 Supervision
3 Morale
4 Motivation
5 Labour relations (i.e. management-trade union relations).

Insofar as cost control principles can be applied, these have largely been covered in earlier chapters. Budgeting, for example, was discussed in Chapter 8, and it was assumed that the major aim of the production function is to provide finished goods of a specified quality to meet the demands of the marketing function. The distribution budget will specify the stock levels for finished goods inventory, and these can be related to the sales budget to give detailed production requirements.

Following from this it is necessary to consider a series of subsidiary budgets relating to raw materials, bought-out components, work-in-progress, direct labour, manufacturing capacity, and manufacturing overheads. Beyond these budgets it is necessary to consider: the aggregation of the direct labour and indirect manufacturing labour budgets with the other constituent elements of the manpower budget (including the training budget); the aggregation of the direct materials and consumable materials budgets with the purchases budget; the maintenance budget; and the impact of the total manufacturing budget on the organization's financial position (covering cash flow, funds flow, capital commitments, profitability, etc.).

A prerequisite to the effective control of manufacturing costs is a knowledge of cost behaviour patterns. Within the context of budgeting, for example, it is impossible to compile a meaningful flexible budget without previously having analysed costs into fixed, variable, and mixed categories. (It was emphasised in Chaper 8 that fixed budgets leave a great deal to be desired and that flexible budgets should be employed wherever possible.)

In order that cost control may be precise it is helpful to plan and report costs in some detail rather than as aggregated measures. In this respect cost standards can be most useful, and the installation of a standard costing system should make the compilation of budget data more straightforward. Apart from helping to secure book-keeping economy, the purposes for which cost standards can be used (as mentioned in Chapter 10) are to identify areas of inefficiency, to measure these inefficiencies, and to bring the inefficiencies to the attention of those who are in a position to take corrective action.

Standard costs are those that should be obtained under efficient operations: they are predetermined and represent targets that are an essential feature of cost control. A cost standard can be established for each element of cost at each stage in the manufacturing process, and this can also be adjusted to reflect different possible levels/rates of activity. The range of possible standards that can be set within the production sphere was discussed in the section headed 'Setting Standards' in Chapter 10. Cost and usage (which are equivalent to price and quantity) are the principal physical characteristics affecting standards, and they apply whether one is dealing with labour, material, or overhead factors of production.

Whilst standards are closely related to budgets, it must be pointed out that the two are not the same. A budget is a prediction of probable future results that has been formalized into a plan, whereas a standard is a level of cost that should be achieved under efficient working in prevailing conditions. (Budgets are also authorities to spend, or to limit spending, and are prepared for all departments of an organization, but standards are simply benchmarks that tend to be restricted in their application to manufacturing activities.)

When standards are being established due attention must be paid to their degree of attainability in the same way that a measure of capacity must be carefully selected if it is to be a suitable basis for comparative purposes. In conjunction with establishing standards, it is necessary to determine tolerance limits: without tolerance limits it is not possible to practise *management by exception* since *every* variation would be treated as exceptional rather than using tolerances to specify those that are *significant*.

The computation and classification of variations from either budget or standard is a vital feature of manufacturing cost control. Once a variance has been noticed and is seen to be significant it signals the need for managerial investigation. (The actual measurement of variances is a rather mechanical exercise that is of no value in itself: the value of variance measures comes from the identification of causes and the correction of these causes.) A large number of reasons can account for variances and careful analysis is required to pinpoint particular causes for particular variances. (Chapter 11 deals with variance analysis.)

Cost accounting – the subject dealt with in Chapter 9 – is very much concerned with product costing which has rather different needs to those of cost control, so care must be taken in seeking the *purpose* for which a cost figure has been compiled before using it in an inappropriate way. Cost control, for instance, is not facilitated by apportioning overhead costs or joint costs over processes or units of manufactured output, whereas many methods of product cost determination rely on cost apportionments. However, a company's costing system will be able to provide a large quantity of information that is of immense value in planning and controlling costs. (The type of information that is provided will, of course, depend on the type of costing system in force, and this in turn will tend to depend upon the nature of the production process – job production, batch production, or process – or flow – production.)

The recording of labour data was covered in Chapter 9, but it can be observed at this point that a fundamental distinction between labour and materials is that labour cannot be stored, and since labour costs accumulate over time it becomes imperative to control the allocation and effective utilization of time.

Material costs and usage were also discussed in Chapter 9 (and in Chapter 18 in the context of inventory control). A vital aspect that should not be overlooked is that the cost of materials is not limited to the amounts shown on suppliers' invoices: it is made up of invoiced amounts plus such items as the following:

		Per cent
1	Losses due to pilfering, evaporation, and other wastage	5
2	Storekeeping costs	3
3	Stock recording	2
4	Rent of storage facilities	1
5	Insurance	1
6	Interest on borrowed funds	15
7	Foregone return on funds invested	18
	Annual material cost addition	45

These hypothetical figures show that material costs should be viewed in a wide setting and controls applied to the broader picture.

Issues should not be made from stores without an authorized requisition and all materials should be *specified* (i.e. each stocked item should be accurately and unambiguously described and numbered). In setting standards for materials it will often be necessary to allow for spoilage, scrap, and waste, with rectification being treated as an overhead item. The key to controlling these items is first to distinguish normal from abnormal spoilage, scrap, or waste (where 'normal' refers to the unavoidable loss that is to be expected under efficient operations for a given process in specified conditions and 'abnormal' is anything above or below 'normal') and second to distinguish the categories themselves. This can be done in the following way

1. Spoilage relates to production units that are unsatisfactory (for reasons of dimension, etc.) for normal use and for rectification. It will generally be found that, say, for every 100 satisfactory units of output it is necessary to manufacture 105 units of which 5 will represent normal spoilage. The standard cost of 100 good units will thus be based on manufacturing 105 units (i.e. the normal spoilage cost will be built in to the standard).
2. Rectification (or rework) is carried out on unsatisfactory units of output that are capable of being rectified. Such units will go into the 100 good units mentioned in (1) above, but the additional costs incurred in rectification work will be treated as a direct cost of the batch of 100 units rather than as an overhead charge.
3. Scrap refers to residual material that has either a resale value or a re-use value. Certain shavings can be sold as scrap, whilst some residual material in chemical processing can be put to use in another process or batch. An allowance for scrap can be made in setting a standard material cost figure with the residual value being set-off against the gross material cost.
4. Waste is residual material that has no resale or re-use value (and may have disposal costs – such as is the case with radioactive waste). Allowances can be made in setting standards for a 'normal' amount of waste.

The treatment of overheads has been discussed at length in earlier chapters, and it should be clear to the reader that such costs can only be controlled if they are classified by field of responsibility: absorption costing is not a basis for effective cost control.

Ratios can be employed as a means of securing control. A ratio can be a standard for comparison and can be made up of items extracted from the budget, or standard cost and output figures. Chapter 12 suggested that ratio analysis is an extension of these other types of cost control, and a pyramid of ratios of particular interest to manufacturing management can be compiled in the same manner that Figure 12.3 was compiled for marketing management.

Network analysis (Chapter 15) deals with ways in which costs can be controlled in a project setting over time, and this has obvious applicability in a large variety of one-off manufacturing situations.

This brief summary of some earlier sections of the book that have immediate relevance to manufacturing cost control serves to avoid a high degree of repetition. One area that has not been touched on in any detail, however, and which warrants close attention, is that of the purchasing function and supplier evaluation; this will now be discussed and then attention will be turned to maintenance activities, productivity issues, and the control of energy costs.

PURCHASING

The overall aim of the purchasing function will be to obtain the right goods at the right place in the right quantities at the right price and at the right time. This presupposes to a large extent that the purchasing department is able to obtain information on new products, processes, materials, and services; that it is able to locate suppliers and select the best (in relation to some definition of, say, reliability); that it is in a position to advise on probable prices, delivery dates, and performance of items under consideration by the design, R & D, and estimating departments; and that it is competent in negotiating with suppliers.

The work of purchasing is affected by the way in which the timing of the purchase order and the schedule for deliveries into stock are determined. Reorder levels can initiate the placing of orders, in which event the accuracy of the lead-time figure and the adequacy of the buffer stock will dictate the degree of disruption that could arise if delivery dates are not met. Purchasing exists as a service to other departments of the organization and the planned levels of cost incurrence of these departments can be disrupted by a failing in the purchasing process. For example, a failure in relation to delivery dates may cause idle time to be incurred, or a rush order – at high cost – may have to be placed with one supplier because another supplier has not delivered in time.

In selecting a supplier the purchasing department must look at more than the price dimension. It was emphasized in Chapter 5 that cost (= price) must be related to a level of quality, and then there are the other aspects of reliability (such as ability to meet delivery schedules, after-sales service, and so forth) that must be taken into account. A potential supplier's labour relations record will increasingly be a major determinant of selection, as will that source's financial stability if it is being evaluated with a view to a long-term agreement.

Characteristic	*Weight*	0.1	0.2	0.3	0.4	0.5	0.6	0.7	0.8	0.9	1.0	Total
Price	0.25											
Quality	0.20											
Delivery	0.15											
After-sales	0.05											
Labour relations	0.10											
Financial stability	0.05											
Credit terms	0.10											
Flexibility	0.05											
Technical support	0.05											
Total	1.00											

Figure 16.1: Evaluation matrix

For existing suppliers it is possible to evalute their performance and to this end a variety of schemes have been developed. A simple one is linked to an evaluation matrix (Figure 16.1). In this matrix are listed the most important characteristics of a supplier (left-hand column) and each of these is given a weight to show its relative importance. In turn each characteristic for a given supplier will be evaluated on a scale of 0.00 to 1.00 (useless to perfect) and the weighted score shown in the right-hand column. The sum of the scores gives an overall evaluation for the supplier, and if this exercise is repeated for other suppliers it is possible to see their relative performance. (In using this type of measure it will be meaningless to compare directly the performance of, say, a supplier of standard stocked items with the performance of a commodity broker, but comparing the relative performance of two suppliers of castings will generally be quite acceptable.) This approach is similar to the approach suggested in Chapter 15 for evaluating new product ideas – see Figure 15.19.

A rather more elaborate scheme for evaluating suppliers involves computing an overall supplier performance rating from individual measures for each supplier's performance over time on each selected dimension. Let us take price, quality, and delivery as being the relevant dimensions of performance with weights given as follows:

Dimension	*Weight*
	Per cent
Price	20.0
Quality	50.0
Delivery	30.0
	100.0

Now let us attempt to compare the performance of two suppliers (ABC Ltd and XYZ Ltd) who each supply two components (α and β) and the comparison will be made over a two-year period (1982 and 1983).

Supplier	*Year*	*Item*	*Quantity*	*Average unit price*	*Supplier*	*Year*	*Item*	*Quantity*	*Average unit price*
ABC	1982	α	2 000	£1.00	ABC	1982	β	1 000	£0.50
XYZ	1982	α	9 000	£0.95	XYZ	1982	β	6 000	£0.45
ABC	1983	α	1 250	£1.25	ABC	1983	β	1 250	£0.60
XYZ	1983	α	7 000	£1.00	XYZ	1983	β	10 000	£0.55

Figure 16.2: Supplier price evaluation

The data to enable us to assess performance of the price dimension are given in Figure 16.2. From this figure it can be seen that the value of orders in 1983 from ABC Ltd amounted to:

Item α	1 250 @ £1.25	=	£1 563
Item β	1 250 @ £0.60	=	£750
	Total	=	£2 313

Weights can be simply derived in the form of percentages showing the relative amount spent on each item. Thus:

Item α	$\frac{1\,563}{2\,313} \times 100$	=	68
Item β	$\frac{750}{2\,313} \times 100$	=	32
	Total	=	100%

Similarly for supplier XYZ Ltd the value of orders in 1983 is as follows:

Item α	7 000 @ £1.00	=	£7 000
Item β	10 000 @ £0.55	=	£5 500
	Total	=	£12 500

and the weights as:

Item α	$\frac{7\,000}{12\,500} \times 100$	=	56
Item β	$\frac{5\,500}{12\,500} \times 100$	=	44
	Total	=	100%

The relative performance of ABC Ltd and XYZ Ltd on the price dimension can be given by indices computed from this data.

For ABC Ltd:

$$\left(\frac{1.25}{1.00} \times 68\right) + \left(\frac{0.60}{0.50} \times 32\right) = 123.4$$

and for XYZ Ltd:

$$\left(\frac{1.00}{0.95} \times 56\right) + \left(\frac{0.55}{0.50} \times 44\right) = 117.2$$

This comparison shows that the performance of ABC Ltd has fallen (i.e. prices have risen) by 23.4 per cent between 1982 and 1983 whilst in the case of XYZ Ltd they have risen by the smaller figure of 17.2 per cent. (1982 = 100). The general formula is the sum of the weighted indices

$$\left(\text{i.e. } \sum\left[\frac{\text{Latest price}}{\text{Previous price}} \times \text{Weight}\right]\right)$$

for each item being supplied.

Turning to the quality dimension the data in Figure 16.3 are given as a starting point. From the data in Figure 16.3 it is a very straightforward task to work out the indices of performance from the general formula:

$$\frac{\text{1983 performance}}{\text{1982 performance}} \times 100 = \text{Index}$$

(1) Year	(2) Supplier	(3) Items delivered (units)	(4) Rejects	(5) Rejects as percentage of deliveries (4) ÷ (3) × 100
1982	ABC	3 000	75	2.5
1982	XYZ	15 000	300	2.0
1983	ABC	2 500	125	5.0
1983	XYZ	17 000	425	2.5

Figure 16.3: Supplier quality evaluation

This gives, for ABC Ltd (with 1982 = 100):

$$\left(\frac{5}{2.5} \times 100\right) = 200$$

showing that quality has fallen by as much again as in 1982, and for XYZ Ltd:

$$\left(\frac{2.5}{2} \times 100\right) = 125$$

showing that quality in 1983 is 25 per cent down on the 1982 figure.

SUPPLIER ABC				SUPPLIER XYZ			
Year	Number of deliveries	Total days late	Average days late	Year	Number of deliveries	Total days late	Average days late
1982	8	28	3.5	1982	10	45	4.5
1983	7	35	5.0	1983	12	36	3.0

Figure 16.4: Supplier delivery evaluation

Our final dimension is delivery. Figure 16.4 shows the respective delivery patterns for both companies in the two years under review. As with the quality index, a delivery index for each supplier (with 1982 = 100) can be derived from the formula:

$$\frac{\text{1983 performance}}{\text{1982 performance}} \times 100 = \text{Index}$$

Thus for ABC Ltd the index is:

$$\left(\frac{5.0}{3.5} \times 100\right) = 143$$

and for XYZ Ltd the index is:

$$\left(\frac{3.0}{4.5} \times 100\right) = 67$$

It follows, therefore, that ABC's performance has fallen by 43 per cent whilst XYZ's has improved by 33 per cent.

Now it only remains to combine these three different performance dimensions into one overall comparative index. We have already specified weights for price, quality and delivery, and the formula to apply is:

$$\begin{array}{ll} & (\text{price index} \quad \times \quad \text{price weight}) \\ + & (\text{quality index} \quad \times \quad \text{quality weight}) \\ + & (\text{delivery index} \quad \times \quad \text{delivery weight}) \\ \hline = & \text{overall performance index} \end{array}$$

The two indices are:

ABC Ltd $(123.4 \times 0.2) + (200 \times 0.5) + (143 \times 0.3) = 167.58$
XYZ Ltd $(117.2 \times 0.2) + (125 \times 0.5) + (67 \times 0.3) = 106.94$

Since 1982 the overall performance of ABC Ltd has declined by 67.58 per cent but the performance of XYZ Ltd has only fallen by 6.94 per cent. This shows a strong argument in favour of supplier XYZ Ltd.

This method of supplier evaluation thus gives us a useful means of comparing a single supplier over time and two or more suppliers over time. Subjective judgement is involved in determining the weights that are to be assigned to each dimension, but other than this the index is objectively determined.

CHECKLIST ON PURCHASING

1 Are quotations obtained from a sufficient number of sources?
2 What alternative materials have been considered?
3 Are suppliers' financial position and credit standing vetted?
4 Are suppliers heavily committed to other (especially competing) buyers?
5 What credit terms are offered? (How do these compare with other suppliers' credit terms? How do they compare with the supplier's cash flow needs?)
6 Does the supplier have the resources (capacity, distribution system, etc.) to meet delivery dates?
7 What are the cost implications of overdue deliveries?

8 Can the supplier meet quality standards?
9 Are the items being supplied patented? If not, can they be reproduced more cheaply by another source of supply?
10 Are spares involved? If so, are they allowed for in plans and schedules?
11 Is there sufficient information on cost elements to know the reasonableness of prices charged?
12 Are make-or-buy studies undertaken?
13 Are prices competitive (given quality levels)?
14 What controls do suppliers have over their activities? (For example, is standard costing employed? What are the quality control arrangements)?
15 Are all purchase requisitions/purchase orders properly authorized?
16 Does a policy exist for inviting bids (or estimates or tenders)?
17 Are safeguards in existence to prevent the purchasing of excessive quantities?
18 Is the purchasing department given a sound forecast of materials and other requirements in good time to enable them to be bought on favourable terms?
19 Are some components currently being made-in that could be bought-out at less cost?
20 Is due consideration given to balancing ordering costs against stock-holding costs?
21 Do buyers have the authority to speculate in commodity markets?
22 Are economic factors other than price considered in selecting suppliers?
23 Are materials ordered in amounts and sizes that permit their utilization with minimum wastage?
24 What effect does storage have on materials? (Could the supplier hold stocks on behalf of the buying company?)
25 Is the supplier carrying out unnecessary operations on the components he is supplying? (Are there operations that he could perform more economically than the buyer?)

MAINTENANCE

The maintenance department has the task of keeping all physical property in as good condition as can reasonably be expected at all times. This involves the protection and care of manufacturing machinery and equipment, service equipment, factory buildings, yards, and all other facilities that form part of the physical property of the organization. (The maintenance function obviously extends beyond the manufacturing sphere to include repairs, maintenance, and 'house-keeping' in all parts of the organization, but it is convenient to deal with it in the context of manufacturing for reasons that I hope are self-evident.)

In a manufacturing setting consideration should be given to preventing the occurrence of breakdowns that will interfere with production schedules as well as to handling emergency repairs that might arise. The importance of a first-rate maintenance facility increases with the amount of fixed investment in plant and machinery: unless this equipment is kept in proper working order the investment is wasted. Only with a well-organized approach to maintenance is it possible to obtain maximum efficiency in manufacturing.

Maintenance costs are easy to cut without creating immediate problems. For instance, preventative inspection/maintenance may be curtailed and reliance placed upon prompt repair when a machine actually breaks down.

In many cases it may well be cheaper to allow this to happen *in the short term* but due regard should be had to the consequences. A breakdown at an inopportune time might lead to serious production delays and heavy financial losses. To avoid this risk it may prove necessary (in the absence of a programme of planned maintenance) to do one of the following:

1 Hold large inventories of finished goods to allow demand to be satisfied whilst repairs are being carried out.
2 Own duplicate (or adaptable) equipment that can be substituted for the broken down machine.
3 Have skilled labour and replacement parts on continuous standby duty in anticipation of breakdowns.

These alternatives are all expensive and all indicate that profits will be affected sooner or later if planned maintenance is ignored.

The behaviour pattern of maintenance costs will vary in accordance with the approach adopted – either crisis repairs or planned prevention. A break-even chart could be compiled to show which approach is cheaper for a particular set of circumstances, but it should be borne in mind that maintenance costs will not be strictly proportional to levels of production. Reasons for this include:

1 New machines require relatively little attention whereas old machines require a good deal.
2 Unused machinery should be maintained in operating conditions so that it can be used when needed.
3 Maintenance work is often done when a department is not in operation to avoid disrupting production.

If a programme of maintenance work is planned and agreed for a period, it should be treated as a fixed cost of that period.

Maintenance work is a service to manufacturing. Just sufficient maintenance should be carried out to provide the required level of service. At the extreme this level of service may specify a total freedom from breakdowns, but generally

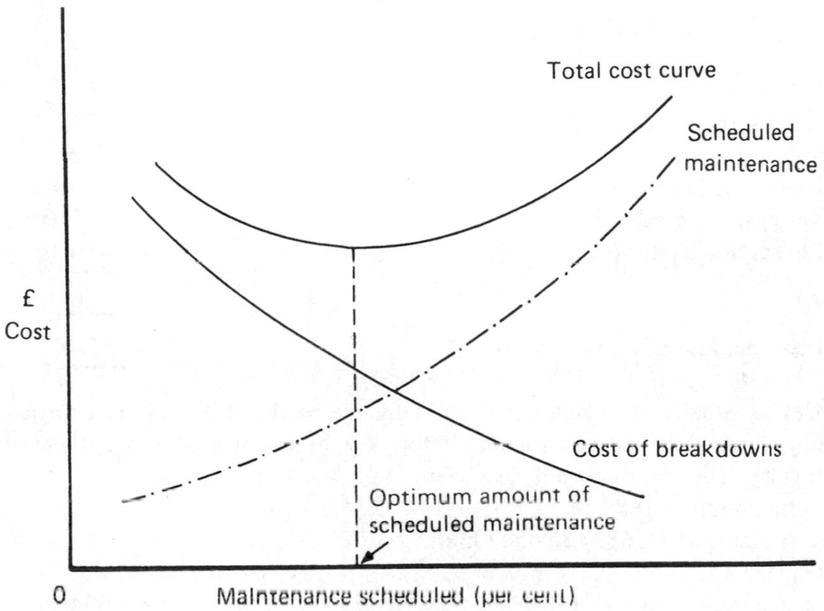

Figure 16.5: Optimum maintenance chart

one would aim to find some optimal balance between.

1 Preventative, planned maintenance (e.g. over a weekend, or between batches, thereby involving no loss of production).
2 Breakdowns (inevitably leading to a loss in productive output).

Figure 16.5 illustrates the optimal situation.

The point of optimum scheduled maintenance is the point of lowest total cost and it is from this point that the maintenance programme should be developed.

A view should also be taken of the impact of maintenance cost levels on production costs. It is possible, for instance, for product costs to be reduced by increasing the volume (hence the cost) of maintenance. An example should make this clear.

Example

A plant produces continuously at maximum capacity of 3 kilos per hour. Raw material costs £1.00 per kilo of output and direct labour costs are £4.00 per hour. A mechanical defect causes the loss of 10 productive hours.

Production for week = (168 – 10) = 158 hours.
Output = 158 × 3 = 474 kilos.

		£
Cost of material = 474 × £1.00	=	474
Cost of direct labour = 168 × £4.00	=	672
Normal cost of maintenance	=	20 (say)
Cost of repairing breakdown	=	154 (say)
Total losses due to stoppage	=	450 (say)
TOTAL		1 770
Total cost per kilo of output = $\frac{£1\,770}{474}$	=	£3.74

Now let us suppose that additional maintenance costing £20 had been carried out (e.g. inspection and adjustment) before the breakdown occurred (thereby avoiding it). The picture would have been:
Production hours = 168
Productive output = 168 × 3 = 504 kilos.

		£
Cost of material = 504 × £1.00	=	504
Cost of direct labour = 168 × £4.00	=	672
Normal maintenance cost	=	20
Additional maintenance cost	=	20
TOTAL		1 216
Total cost per kilo of output = $\frac{£1\,216}{504}$	=	£2.41

This shows a reduction of £1.33 per kilo of output for a slight increase in maintenance. (Refined operations research techniques exist to determine optimum allocations for maintenance, such as the number of engineers or fitters that should be on hand at any time to deal with breakdowns in such a way that costs are minimized for a given level of service.)

Maintenance costs often give rise to problems in assigning responsibility: if such costs are considered to be wholly the responsibility of the maintenance department then it is possible that supervisors/managers in other areas may make excessive demands for maintenance services. On the other hand, if maintenance costs are charged out to those requesting maintenance facilities, the tendency to request less may arise *against* the interests of sound plant maintenance. The departmental foreman can influence the amount of required maintenance work by the amount of maintenance he requests on a regular basis (i.e. by the care he takes of his equipment). Some aspects of maintenance, of course, such as repainting, cleaning up, etc., are required to be carried out on a regular basis irrespective of foremen's actions.

Possible approaches to charging out maintenance work are:

1 To apportion maintenance costs to operating departments on the basis of the number of maintenance labour hours devoted to each.
2 To charge operating departments a prescribed amount for each type of job carried out.
3 To charge each department on the basis of the number of machine hours it operates (as a percentage of total productive machine hours).

Whichever procedure is adopted must be related to the requirements of a particular company's circumstances. The total budget should be planned in advance and a programme drawn up. (Network analysis is very useful for planning maintenance activities in a programme format.) Clearly it will be inappropriate to allocate all maintenance facilities to planned maintenance since then there would be no spare capacity with which to tackle emergencies. Bearing this in mind, an annual plan could be drawn up to utilize, say, 75 per cent of maintenance resources. Such a plan could be expressed in the form of major projects which might include:

1 Statutory requirements, which cover the washing and painting of walls, ceilings, and staircases, the inspection and maintenance of lifts and hoists, steam boilers, travelling cranes, fire equipment, weighing machines, etc.
2 Maintenance of company vehicles.
3 Maintenance of office equipment.
4 Plant and equipment in operating department A.
5 Plant and equipment in operating department Z.
6 External paintwork, gardens, etc.

The projects can be individually worked up in CPA format, and collectively they could be shown (as in Figure 16.6) on a Gantt chart.

From a cost control viewpoint there are many other points that should also be considered appertaining to maintenance. A stores facility, for instance (and procedures) must be established and controlled within the overall maintenance budget. Also the maintenance aspect of plant selection should not be overlooked. (For example, this will entail examining proposed purchases of plant to assess the accessibility of parts for adjustment and repairs, the availability of replacement parts, the likelihood of particular faults arising, and so forth.)

CHECKLIST ON MAINTENANCE

1 Does the company have a programme of preventative maintenance?

Project	Jan	Feb	Mar	Apr	May	Jun	Jul	Aug	Sep	Oct	Nov	Dec
1												
2												
3												
4												
5												
6												
7												

Figure 16.6: Maintenance schedule

2 Are maintenance records/reports used in equipment replacement decisions?
3 Is there a procedure for charging out maintenance costs to user departments?
4 Are all buildings, items of equipment, etc., regularly inspected from the point of view of maintenance, safety, fire protection, and theft?
5 Is there an effective control against excessive maintenance? (If this is not contained in the budget, why is it not?)
6 Are depreciation charges adequate in writing off the value of equipment over its useful life? (Should cost price or replacement price be used as the basis for depreciation?)
7 Are too many external maintenance services being bought?
8 Are company vehicles operated in accordance with a preventative maintenance schedule?
9 Is full advantage taken of suppliers' service and warranty agreements rather than carrying out all repairs at the company's expense?
10 Can local suppliers be relied upon for spares/consumable items rather than holding a separate maintenance stock?
11 Are there established standards for maintenance tasks?
12 Are the costs of maintenance known in detail and by cause? (What are their behaviour patterns over time and over different levels of output?)
13 Are the costs of a *lack* of maintenance known? (e.g. idle time due to machine breakdown).
14 Is management satisfied with maintenance and housekeeping performance?
15 Are maintenance objectives specified?
16 Are all regulations and statutes adhered to?
17 Could maintenance costs be reduced by tackling with the company's staff those tasks that are contracted out?
18 Could certain tasks (e.g. window cleaning) be contracted out more economically than being performed internally?
19 Are the man-hours invested in maintenance consistent with the actual man-hour requirements for the job to be performed?
20 Are maintenance activities scheduled via networks?

PRODUCTIVITY SCHEMES

Productivity improvements are vital to improvements in living standards as well as to reductions in cost levels. The link is, of course, through profits: lower costs mean higher profits, and higher profits mean greater economic well-being. It is possible to take actions that lead to improvements in productivity without any attempt being made to measure the change. However, it is not possible to control that which one cannot monitor, so some form of measurement is highly desirable. This should not suggest that measuring productivity changes is an easy matter: on the contrary there are innumerable complexities of definition and measurement to be resolved before one can devise adequate productivity improvement schemes.

In the simplest of terms productivity measures seek to divide outputs from a system by the inputs to that system in order to derive an index. This index then provides a comparative measure for relating actual to desired productivity for a period, or for relating last period's productivity to that of this period, etc. If a particular system had only one input factor and one output there would be little problem in measuring productivity, but systems typically have multiple inputs and outputs which must be reduced to a common base if they are to be related to one another.

The idea of an index that relates physical output to an input of direct labour hours is one that is frequently met, not least of all on an economy-wide basis. It might be argued that man-hours is the basic resource, but it is by no means the only input to productive processes. Capital, management, materials, equipment etc., all contribute to the attainment of outputs in addition to direct labour inputs. Furthermore, any attempt to reduce a group of inputs to the lowest common denominator, which is invariably a monetary one, presupposes that a real measure can be found (i.e. one that overcomes the problems of inflation).

Different types of organizations operating in different types of industry will almost certainly need to determine appropriate definitions and measures of productivity that suit their own circumstances. However, certain general questions can be posed as a means of guiding managers towards some answer:

1 How complex a measure should be developed? (For what purpose is it desired?)
2 How can the impacts (on outputs as well as other inputs) of major input factors be identified?
3 How will productivity measures for the functional components of the organization be tied to productivity measures for the organization as a whole?
4 How can productivity measures be linked to measures of profitability?
5 How will measures reflect changes in capacity utilization?
6 How, if at all, are changes in the qualitative characteristics of the system's outputs to be shown?

When developing productivity measures it makes greatest sense to do this in a way that starts with a framework within which one can analyse the various inputs and outputs in order to identify how each contributes to the overall system's output. (This is analogous to the approach contained within the ratio pyramids of Chapter 12.) A number of dangers must be avoided in developing an analytical framework, such as confusing the role of qualitative and quantitative factors, or quantifying peripheral as opposed to central factors. It is also necessary to ensure that the selected numerator and denominator relate to the same sectors of activity and to properly linked time periods; and that the inputs actually contribute to the outputs in a causal manner.

One approach to meeting these requirements is given in Figure 16.7 which identifies six components of a *network of productivity relationships*. Three of the components are input requirements per unit of output for labour, materials, and capital investment respectively. (Capital invested is then compared with productive capacity – which reflects the potential of that capital – rather than with output since this facilitates a subsequent comparison between that potential and the extent to which it is being utilized under prevailing market conditions.)

The remaining three components cover the extent to which the first three are combined, including the extent to which one input factor may be substituted for another. An important consequence of this approach is to be found in the way it highlights the fact that a change in, say, output per man-hour may arise due to changes initiated elsewhere within the network (i.e. in a passive way) rather than through consciously-planned changes to output or man-hours. Thus the substitution of more machines for man hours would cause a reduction in man hours and, for an assumed constant rate of output, an increase in the output per man-hour ratio.

The physical characteristics of productivity measures must be integrated with financial measures if control and decision making are to be improved. This can be helped by superimposing the structure of costs onto the network of productivity relationships shown in Figure 16.7. This is done in Figure 16.8.

Within this expanded framework the importance of going beyond the assumption that input prices are constant is highlighted, so attention is now focused on the impact of changes in input requirements (and their associated costs) on changes in outputs. This is not only done for individual inputs, of course; it is done for the whole mix of inputs, since a change in the price of one input factor is likely to lead to a change in the quantity consumed of another, with a possible change in the price of the latter, and so on. The central measure given in Figure 16.8 is the ratio of profit to total investment (i.e. ROI) which is seen to depend on interactions amongst five factors:

(*a*) average revenue per unit of output;
(*b*) total cost per unit of output;
(*c*) the rate of capacity utilization;
(*d*) the capacity available relative to fixed investment; and
(*e*) the proportion of fixed investment to total investment.

These interactions are reflected in Figure 16.9 and show that any attempt, say, to increase profitability does not depend solely on any one interaction.

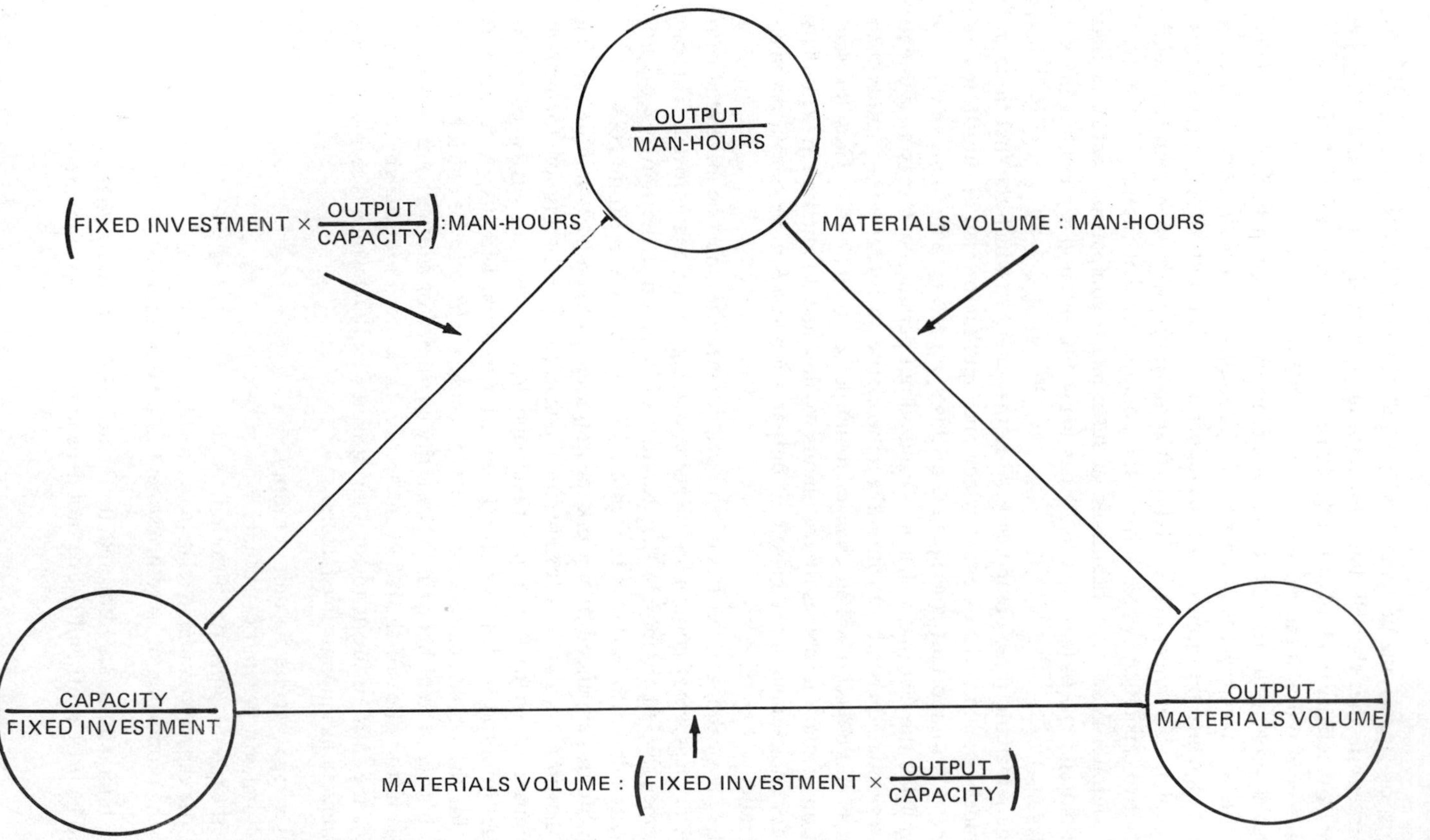

Figure 16.7: The network of productivity relationships among direct input factors

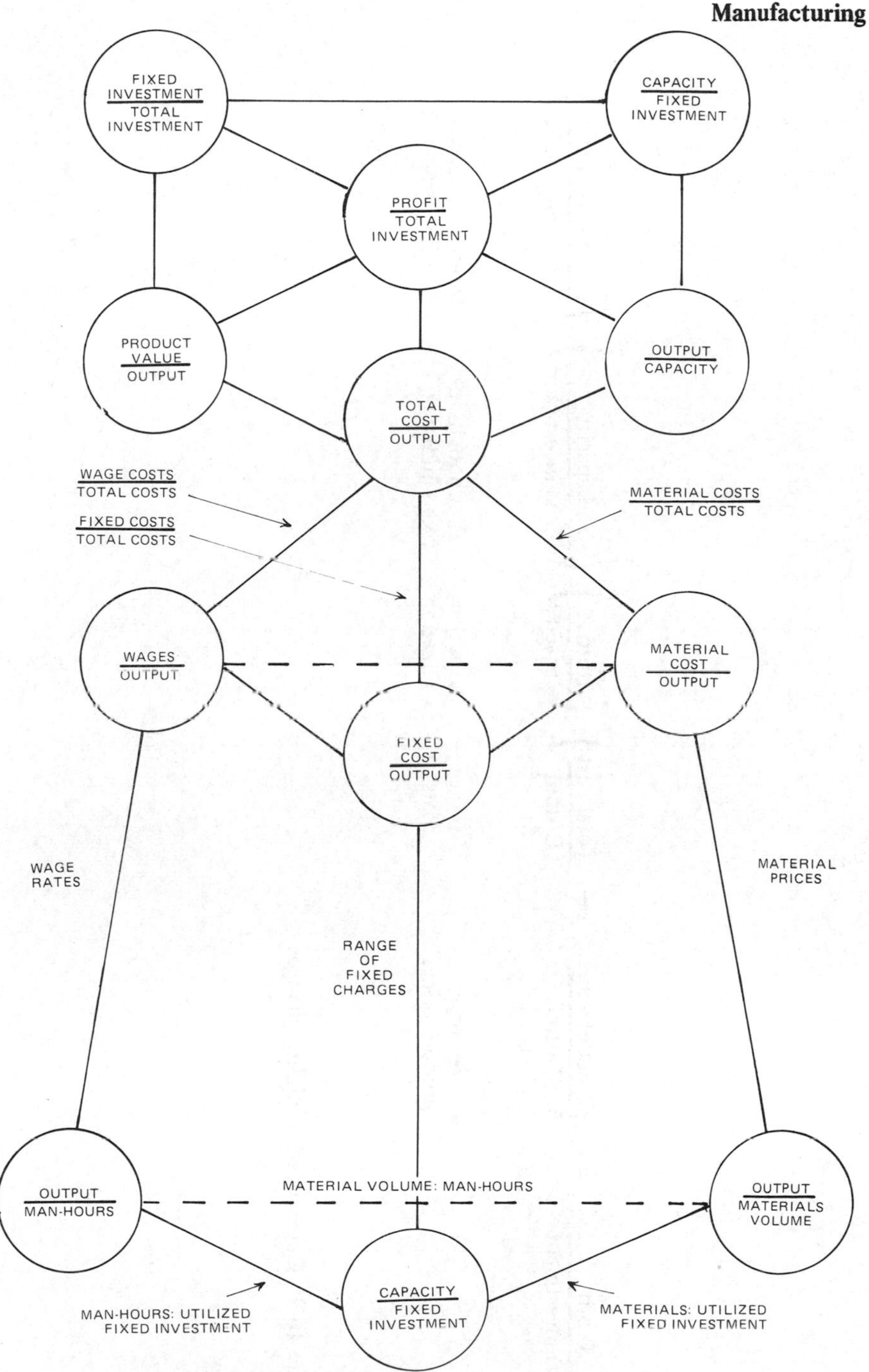

Figure 16.8: Productivity network, cost structure and managerial control ratios

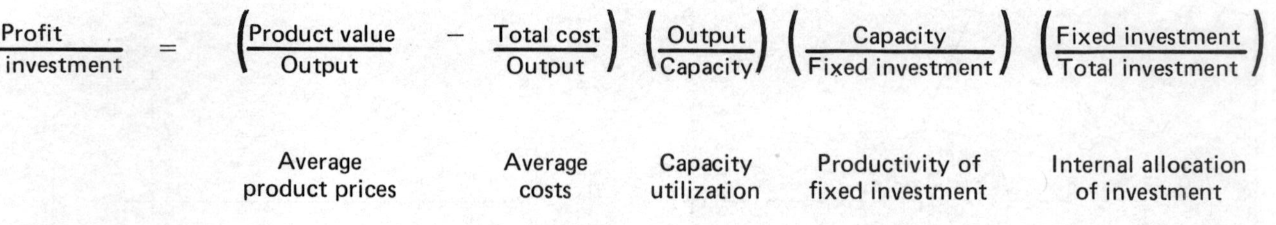

$$\frac{\text{Profit}}{\text{Total investment}} = \left(\frac{\text{Product value}}{\text{Output}} - \frac{\text{Total cost}}{\text{Output}}\right)\left(\frac{\text{Output}}{\text{Capacity}}\right)\left(\frac{\text{Capacity}}{\text{Fixed investment}}\right)\left(\frac{\text{Fixed investment}}{\text{Total investment}}\right)$$

Average product prices	Average costs	Capacity utilization	Productivity of fixed investment	Internal allocation of investment

Figure 16.9: Causes of profitability changes

It may be the case, for example, when viewed from the level of the organization as a whole, that it is better to try to improve profitability by increasing revenue relative to costs (rather than seeking to reduce costs relative to physical output). Indeed, as one takes an increasingly broader view across an organization it will invariably be the case that a productivity measure based on *financial* inputs and *financial* outputs becomes most useful, whereas measures relating *physical* inputs to *physical* outputs are likely to be more meaningful at lower levels. Within a framework such as that presented here it is possible to see the relevance of physical *and* financial aspects of productivity, and this should help in achieving integrated control of performance.

ENERGY COST CONTROL

The impact of energy costs is all-pervasive, and it influences the design, functioning and manufacture of products, as well as the design and location of manufacturing and distribution facilities, plus a good deal more. One increasingly hears the advice being given that organizations should set up high-powered *energy committees* to oversee their *energy programmes*, covering the planning and control of all aspects of energy needs. In handling information on energy matters it becomes necessary to think in terms of energy measures rather than purely financial ones. Thus the British thermal unit (BTU) becomes the key unit of measure for planning and control purposes, at least in the first instance.

The BTU is defined as the amount of energy needed to raise one pound of water through one degree Fahrenheit, and an equivalence can readily be established between BTUs and units of energy sources. This is illustrated in Figure 16.10.

Source	*Unit*	*BTUs per unit*
Electricity	Kwh	3 413
Natural gas	Mcf	1 000 000
Fuel oil	Gal.	140 000
Gasoline	Gal.	130 000
Propane	Gal.	91 000
Coal	Ton	24 000 000
Steam	100lb	100 000

Figure 16.10: Energy conversion factors

Budgets can be compiled for each location to show the overall energy needs at different levels of activity, and also at different times of year. It will hardly have escaped anyone's attention that energy needs arise for heating/air conditioning reasons, depending on the weather, as well as for productive processes and service activities, as shown in Figure 16.11:

Manufacturing
- Process heat
- Machinery motive power

Ancillary
- Background heating and lighting
- Materials handling equipment motive power
- Cleaning and maintenance facilities
- Safety and standby operations
- Control equipment power
- Office needs

Transport
- Motive power for goods movement by road, rail, water, and air

Figure 16.11: Major energy uses

In compiling energy budgets initially it is helpful in developing a view of the usage pattern to analyse consumption in recent periods, although one should do this in a critically curious way rather than merely accepting the historical usage pattern as being 'reasonable'. From this base an energy plan can be devised, taking into account whatever is known about the availability of alternative energy sources, their likely costs, anticipated governmental regulations etc. This should cover additional capital equipment needs, engineering skills that will be required, and projections of energy consumption by source, location etc.

Two approaches that have been discussed in earlier chapters have an important role to play in preparing the energy budget and plan. The first is to carry out an *energy audit* (a variation on the management audit of Chapter 13), and the second is to see energy requirements in the context of *life-cycle costing* (introduced in Chapter 9).

If one breaks energy usage into the groupings suggested by Figure 16.11 this will give a more manageable basis for attempting to control energy costs. However, it may well be the case that total energy costs for a particular site are known, but that the usage by various cost centres is not. Until it is known how much energy is being consumed by different users it is not really possible to motivate users to consume less. It becomes desirable, therefore, to instal measuring devices rather than to use one of the cruder apportionment exercises (such as spreading heating costs according to the cubic space occupied by each cost centre).

GENERAL CHECKLIST

1 Do adequate standards exist?
2 Are performance records adequate?
3 Are variances promptly reported and fully investigated?

4 If some employees perform both direct and indirect activities, is the system for distinguishing the time spent on each adequate?
5 Are all processing operations necessary?
6 Could alternative processes be used to advantage?
7 Could existing processes be simplified?
8 Is the sequence of operations the best possible?
9 Is idle time between operations at a minimum?
10 Can operations be performed in different departments to avoid handling delays?
11 Do any operations result in excessive rejects?
12 Are supply costs of consumable production materials properly isolated from general maintenance costs?
13 Are supplies purchased in economic quantities?
14 Are there safeguards against overstocking?
15 Do excessive material shortages arise?
16 Are obsolete supplies disposed of?
17 Is there adequate protection against pilferage, wastage, etc?
18 Are containers compatible with storage, materials handling, etc?
19 Is the most suitable materials handling equipment used?
20 Can materials be moved best by gravity or on rollers? Is a conveyor justified?
21 Are fork-lift trucks and pallets used to advantage?
22 Are the materials handling and manufacturing functions effectively co-ordinated?
23 Where should in-coming and out-going materials be located with respect to work stations? (Can operations be combined at one work station to reduce materials handling?)
24 Are containers uniform to permit stacking?
25 Could lighter or lower cost packaging be used?
26 Is packaging design coordinated with materials handling?
27 Do all items really need packages?
28 Are scrap and waste materials dealt with effectively?
29 Are containers marked/coloured for easier segregation/identification?
30 Could materials be purchased in sizes or quantities that would make for easier materials handling?
31 How much capital is tied up in obsolete materials/components?
32 Could excess stocks be sold in bulk with special discounts, or is it cheaper to allow high stocks to run down through normal usage?
33 Is the inventory of maintenance spares adequate?
34 Are shortages excessive in the light of the total investment?
35 How much of inventory investment is in work-in-progress?
36 What are the costs of carrying each type of inventory?

37 What are the costs of reordering items for inventory?
38 Are order points developed for each item on the basis of lead times, rates of usage, and safety stocks?
39 Has an analysis been carried out to verify lead times used in reordering?
40 Where sales are seasonal is it more advisable to produce in accordance with demand, or to produce at an even rate and use stocks as a buffer?
41 What costs are associated with the alternatives in 40 above?
42 Are required completion dates shown on production orders?
43 In scheduling production is sufficient lead time allowed to enable:

  (*a*) The accumulating of small orders for special processing?
  (*b*) The minimizing of set-up costs?
  (*c*) The scheduling of labour more efficiently?

44 Are alternative processing methods developed and used for scheduling standard operations in bottleneck areas?
45 Are cost differences between alternate processing methods known?
46 Are machine loadings used for production scheduling?
47 Are workloads planned sufficiently far in advance to permit workforce and machines to be balanced?
48 How much idle time and overtime occurred last year? (How much was anticipated?)
49 How much subcontracting was done last year? (Why was this required?)
50 Is scrap/spoilage a significant element of production cost?
51 Is there a sound procedure for disposing of scrap? (Is scrap sold on the basis of bids?)
52 Are records of spoilage maintained for control purposes?
53 If of value, are returnable containers properly accounted for and controlled?
54 Are incoming goods examined for quantity, quality and conformance to order?
55 Are all categories of cost in the manufacturing sphere planned in advance? (Are they all the specified responsibility of named individuals?)
56 Does the company employ a flexible budgeting procedure?

SUMMARY

The principles of cost control that can be applied in the manufacturing sphere have been dealt with at length in earlier chapters of the book: cost accounting (Chapter 9), budgeting (Chapter 8), standard costing (Chapter 10), variance analysis (Chapter 11), ratio analysis (Chapter 12), and network analysis (Chapter 15). A good deal of available literature on cost control and cost accounting focuses very heavily on the manufacturing area and it is important to distinguish between product costing on the one hand and cost control on the other.

Purchasing is concerned with providing the right goods in the right quantities, of the right quality, at the right price, in the right place at the right time. Suppliers must be evaluated in order to select the best, and two approaches have been dealt with (both of which take into account weighted evaluations of each major performance dimension).

Maintenance must find a balanced route between planned maintenance that saves repairs but interferes with production and emergency repairs that also disrupt production. It may be helpful to have a procedure for charging out maintenance costs so supervisors are aware of the cost but the danger exists that this may discourage them from requesting maintenance. Network techniques are useful in controlling major maintenance projects.

The definition and measurement of productivity is a major problem area, but it is vital to recognize that output per man-hour is a very poor base on which to build compensation schemes for workers since output depends upon much more than a single input factor. A suitable framework within which one might analyse productivity includes physical and financial elements, and it resembles a ratio pyramid through which one seeks to identify causal relationships.

An increasingly significant manufacturing cost is that relating to energy. This can be planned and controlled as any other resource provided it is done by suitably qualified individuals on the basis of adequate information. Responsibility accounting and budgeting methods are equally applicable to energy.

FURTHER READING

Bailey, D., and Hubert, T. (eds), *Productivity Measurement*, Aldershot: Gower, 1980.
(A collection of conference papers that review the whole field.)

Dick-Larkham, R., *Cutting Energy Costs*, Aldershot: Gower, 1978.
(This looks at each major source of fuel and usage, and suggests simple ways to improve efficiency.)

Eilon, S., Gold, B., and Saesan, J., *Applied Productivity Analysis for Industry*, Oxford: Pergamon, 1976.
(A concise and rigorous treatment of the subject. Recommended to those who wish to take the matter seriously.)

Lockyer, K.G., *Factory and Production Management*, London: Pitman, 1974.
(An excellent introductory text, written in a lucid way.)

17

Marketing—Order-Getting

INTRODUCTION

There are two sides to the control of marketing costs. The first of these is concerned with the costs of obtaining orders through such activities as selling, advertising and sales promotion. These costs tend to vary with changes in the level of sales, but sales volume will be the dependent variable and order-getting costs will be the independent variable. In other words, sales volume will respond to the level of order-getting costs, and variations in the level of order-getting costs will be made in anticipation of sales being at a predicted level. In this sense, positive management action is needed to permit order-getting costs to increase with increases in sales volume, and in contrast to manufacturing circumstances, a policy of cost minimization in marketing is unlikely to be desired because of the causal relationship between marketing outlays and sales levels. But the relationship between order-getting costs and sales volume may not be directly linear. For example, a company may increase the amount it is to spend on advertising when sales fall on the basis of the wholly reasonable argument that declining sales require counteractive promotional support to reverse an adverse trend. On the other hand, some companies may maintain the amount to be spent on advertising at some predetermined level (giving it the characteristics of a committed rather than a managed or programmed cost), whilst still others may unwisely raise advertising expenditure as the level of sales rises and decrease advertising expenditure as sales decline.

The other side of marketing expenditure relates to order-filling activities – warehousing, transport, shipping, invoicing, credit control, etc. These are dealt with in the context of physical distribution management in Chapter 18.

Furthermore, the vital, and central, function of new product development, was dealt with in the context of research and development activities in Chapter 15. In this present chapter it is proposed to look at some general aspects of cost control in marketing, including distribution cost accounting and an introduction to marketing programming, and then to look more particularly at sales activities and advertising, and at some cost aspects of pricing.

It was emphasized throughout Chapter 9 that the control unit from the point of view of factory cost accounting is occasionally the department or the process, but more usually the job, batch, or product. In contrast, the control unit in marketing may be the product, the product line, the salesman, the sales territory, the order, the order size, the customer, the customer (or industry) group, or the channel of distribution. Given the control unit for a particular purpose, however, individual categories of marketing expenditure can be divided into fixed and variable types, their behaviour patterns can be established, and standards can be set via budgets or standard costs. It is therefore possible for comparisons to be made between actual outlays and desired (or standard) outlays as in any other area of cost control. A general understanding of cost behaviour, cost-volume-profit relationships, and relevant costing is a fundamental prerequisite to the control of any category of cost. Within the marketing sphere, however, the influence of external factors is more strongly felt and this raises measurement problems relating both to the prediction of outcomes in the face of very many internal-external interactions, and to the identifying of causal relationships when attempting to evaluate, for instance, the effectiveness of advertising outlays. The key to controlling marketing activities lies in the very careful planning of marketing activities, provided that plans are flexible and drawn up in accordance with the principles of contingency planning (for example, if it is expected that product X will secure a 10 per cent share of its market segment which, in total, is expected to amount to sales of 100 000 units during the next period, a detailed plan should be compiled that not only gives consideration to this size and share but which also considers 'what if . . .?' questions. What if the market demand is 75 000 units, or 125 000 units? What if our share with product X is 12 per cent or 8 per cent?).

The example just given highlights the importance of sales forecasting in the planning of order-getting cost levels. Order-getting budgets are also affected by:

1 Specific marketing objectives that must be achieved.
2 Anticipated competitive behaviour.
3 Other anticipated environmental factors.

4 Past experience.
5 Funds available.

This final point – the money available with which to carry out a plan – is widely used as a basis for budgeting advertising and promotional outlays. It can be derived as follows:

Expected sales revenue		£250 000
Works cost	100 000	
Administration and other overheads	75 000	
Required profit	50 000	
		225 000
Money available for promotions		£25 000

Behind this simplistic approach is a belief that advertising is more important in achieving success than is manufacturing, but it is an unsatisfactory approach for reasons other than this. It places too much emphasis on the *residual* amount (i.e. the funds remaining after all other costs have been covered) rather than on the amount that is required to achieve a specified result, and it fails to consider adequately the *effectiveness* of the expending of this amount. Cost control must look at both the actual and the desired patterns of expenditure *and* the effectiveness (which is equivalent to quality) of the expenditure, and this is far from being an easy task. To what extent, for example, is a given level of sales due to the ability/personality of the salesman, the characteristics of the customer, features of the product itself, competitive offerings, general business conditions, or the effect of advertisements and other promotional activity?

MARKETING EXPERIMENTATION

One way of overcoming the difficulties referred to above is to plan and control the conditions under which information is collected instead of trying to overcome the limitations of historical information. This can be achieved through marketing experimentation.

In a marketing experiment attempts are made to identify all the controllable factors that affect a particular dependent variable, and these factors are then manipulated systematically in order to isolate and measure their effects on the performance of the dependent variable.

It is not possible, of course, to plan or control all the conditions in which an experiment is conducted: for example, the timing, location, and duration of an experiment can be predetermined, but it is necessary to measure such uncontrollable conditions as those caused by the weather and eliminate their effects from the results. Irrespective of these uncontrollable influences, the fact that experiments are concerned with the deliberate manipulation of controllable variables (i.e. such variables as price and advertising effort) means that a good deal more confidence can be placed in conclusions about the effects of such manipulation than if the effects of these changes had been based purely on historical associations.

Studies of marketing costs can provide the ideas for experiments. Questions such as the following are fairly representative of the type that can be answered as a result of marketing experimentation:

1 By how much (if any) would the net profit contribution of the most profitable products be increased if there were an increase in specific marketing outlays, and how would such a change affect the strategy of competitors in terms of the stability of, say, market shares?
2 By how much (if any) would the net losses of unprofitable products be reduced if there were some decrease in specific marketing outlays?
3 By how much (if any) would the profit contribution of profitable products be affected by a change in the marketing effort applied to the unprofitable products, and vice-versa, and what would be the effect on the total marketing system?
4 By how much (if any) would the total profit contribution be improved if some marketing effort were diverted to profitable territories or customer groups from unprofitable territorial and customer segments?
5 By how much (if any) would the net profit contribution be increased if there were a change in the method of distribution to small unprofitable accounts, or if these accounts were eliminated?

Only by actually carrying out properly-designed marketing experiments can management realistically predict with an acceptable degree of certainty the effects of changes in marketing expenditure on the level of sales and profit of each differentiated product, territory, or customer segment in the multi-product company.

Experiments must be conducted under conditions that resemble the real-life conditions of the market place (insofar as this is possible). It is pointless, for example, carrying out an experiment to prove that the sale of £1's worth of product X in Southampton through medium-sized retailers adds more to profit than does the sale of £1's worth of product Y through small retailers in Newcastle if the market for product X is saturated and no re-allocation of marketing resources can change the situation. This points to the danger of confusing what is happening now with what might happen in the future: ascertaining that product X is more profitable than product Y may be the right answer to the wrong question.

The correct style of question should be: 'what will happen to the dependent variable in the future if the independent variables are manipulated now in the following way?'. If the concern is with the allocation of sales effort, the aim of an experiment may be to show how changes in the total costs of each sales team can be related to changes in the level of sales. In such a simple case in which only one type of marketing effort is being considered, this effort should be re-allocated to those sales segments where an additional unit of effort will yield the highest contribution to net profits and overheads.

The experiment can be designed to show which sales segment produces the highest value when the following equation is applied to each in turn:

$$\frac{\text{Additional sales} - \text{additional variable costs}}{\text{Additional expenditure}}$$

If an additional budget allocation of £1 000 to the London sales force results in extra sales of £5 000 with additional variable costs amounting to £2 000, then the index of performance is

$$\frac{5\,000 - 2\,000}{1\,000} = 3$$

It may happen that the same index computed for the Midlands sales force of the same company has a value of 4, in which case selling effort should be re-allocated to the Midlands *provided* due consideration has been given to the expected level of future demand.

As a result of the high costs involved, experiments must usually be conducted with small samples of the relevant elements. This is generally valid so long as the samples are properly determined and representative. However, it is believed by some that marketing experimentation is not a feasible means by which information can be obtained as a basis for making important decisions.

There are certainly a lot of difficulties to be overcome in planning and executing experiments, and the need to keep special records and make repeated measurements is both expensive and time consuming. The risk is always present that the results of an experiment will not be of any value because they may not be statistically significant. A further risk is that even temporary and limited experimental variations in the marketing mix may damage sales and customer relationships both during and after the experiment.

COST ANALYSIS

Control in marketing must be concerned with the allocation of total marketing effort to products, customer groups, and sales territories, along with the profitability of these allocations. It is generally found, however, that companies do not know the profitability of regions, product groups, etc., in marketing terms. Useful computations of marketing costs and profit contributions in the multi-product company require the adoption of analytical techniques that are not difficult in principle but which are not widely adopted on account of, *inter alia*, the preoccupation with factory cost accounting that exists.

It is clearly essential for management to know the cost implications of different courses of action if the best is to be selected. In the pricing decision, for example, products may be priced in such a way as to give a specified rate of return. However, if costs are inappropriately allocated to products, then some products will be overpriced and some underpriced. (This is not intended to be an argument in favour of cost-plus pricing.)

The fact that most companies do not know what proportion of their total marketing outlay is spent on each product, area, or customer group may be due to the absence of a sufficiently refined system of cost analysis, or it may be due to vagueness over the nature of certain costs. For instance, is the cost of packaging a promotional, a production, or a distribution expense? Some important marketing costs are hidden in manufacturing costs or in general and administrative costs, including finished goods inventory costs in the former and order-processing costs in the latter.

Since few companies are aware of costs and profits by product (or other segment) in relation to sales levels, and since even fewer are able to predict changes in sales volume and profit contribution as a result of changes in marketing effort, the following errors arise:

1 Marketing budgets for individual products are too large, with the result that diminishing returns become evident and benefits would accrue from a reduction in expenditure.
2 Marketing budgets for individual products are too small and increasing returns would result from an increase in expenditure.
3 The marketing mix is inefficient, with an incorrect balance and incorrect amounts being spent on the constituent elements – such as too much on advertising and insufficient on direct selling activities.
4 Marketing efforts are misallocated amongst products and changes in these cost allocations (even with a constant level of overall expenditure) could bring improvements.

Similar arguments apply in relation to sales territories or customer groups as well as to products. The need exists, therefore, for control techniques to indicate the level of performance required and achieved as well as the outcome of shifting marketing efforts from one segment to another. As is to be expected, there exists great diversity in the methods by which manufacturers attempt to obtain costs (and profits) for segments of their business, but much of the cost data is inaccurate for such reasons as:

1 Marketing costs may be allocated to individual products, sales areas,

customer groups, etc., on the basis of sales value or sales volume, but this involves circular reasoning. Costs should be allocated in relation to causal factors, and *it is marketing expenditures that cause sales to be made* rather than the other way round: managerial decision determines marketing costs. Furthermore, despite the fact that success is so often measured in terms of sales value achievements by product line, this basis fails to evaluate the efficiency of the effort needed to produce the realized sales value (or turnover). Even a seemingly high level of turnover for a specific product may really be a case of misallocated sales effort. (An example should make this clear: if a salesman concentrates on selling product A which contributes £5 per hour of effort instead of selling product B which would contribute £12 per hour of effort, then it 'costs' the company £7 per hour he spends on selling product A. This is the *opportunity cost* of doing one thing rather than another and is a measure of the sacrifice involved in selecting only one of several alternative courses of action.)

2 General overheads and administrative costs are arbitrarily (and erroneously) allocated to segments on the basis of sales volume.

3 Many marketing costs are not allocated at all as marketing costs as they are not identified as such but are classified as manufacturing, general, or administrative costs instead.

Distribution cost accounting (or analysis) has been developed to help overcome these problems and aims to:

1 Analyse the costs incurred in distributing and promoting products so that when they are combined with production cost data overall profitability can be determined.

2 Analyse the costs of marketing individual products to determine their profitability.

3 Analyse the costs involved in serving different classes of customers and different areas to determine their profitability.

4 Compute such figures as cost per sales call, cost per order, cost to put a new customer on the books, cost to hold £1's worth of inventory for a year, etc.

5 Evaluate managers according to their actual controllable cost responsibilities.

6 Evaluate alternative strategies or plans with full costs.

These analyses and evaluations provide senior management with the necessary information to enable them to decide which classes of customer to cultivate, which products to delete, which products to encourage, and so forth. Such analyses also provide a basis from which estimates can be made of the likely increases in product profitability that a specified increase in marketing effort should create. In the normal course of events it is far more difficult to predict the outcome of decisions that involve changes in marketing outlays in comparison with changes in production expenditure. It is easier, for instance, to estimate the effect of a new machine in the factory than it is to predict the impact of higher advertising outlays. Similarly, the effect on productive output of dropping a production worker is easier to estimate than is the effect on the level of sales caused by a reduction in the sales force.

The methodology of distribution cost analysis is similar to the methodology of product costing. Two stages are involved:

1. Marketing costs are initially reclassified from their natural expense headings into functional cost groups in such a way that each cost group brings together all the costs associated with each element of the marketing mix.
2. These functional cost groups are then apportioned to control units (i.e. products, customer groups, channels of distribution, etc.) on the basis of measurable criteria that bear a causative relationship to the total amounts of the functional cost groups.

Whilst costs can be broken down in a microscopic manner, there are dangers and limitations which should not be overlooked since they can hinder the control of marketing costs. If the outcome of functionalizing all marketing costs is to compute a unit cost on every activity, then this can be misleading. At the least a distinction should be made between fixed and variable costs, and the focus should be on the *purpose* for which a particular cost is to be derived and not simply on the *means* by which a figure is computed. Thus costs and units can be looked at separately, thereby avoiding myopic confusion.

An important distinction to make in distribution costs analysis – beyond the basic fixed-variable split – is that between separable fixed costs and non-separable fixed costs. A sales manager's salary is a fixed cost in conventional accounting, but insofar as his time can be linked to different products, sales territories, customers, etc., his salary (or at least portions of his salary) can be treated as being separable fixed costs attributable to the segments in question in accordance with time devoted to each. In contrast, corporate advertising expenditure that is concerned with the company's image is not specific to any segment, hence it is non-separable and should not be allocated. Any non-specific, non-separable cost allocations would inevitably be very arbitrary, and such costs should therefore be excluded from all detailed cost and profit computations.

If one is concerned purely with measuring profit by segment, then even separable fixed costs should be omitted from the calculations since they are not direct deductions from the sales revenue of specific segments. However, distribution cost analysis is concerned also with the most effective use of marketing effort, and this form of analysis requires the inclusion of separable fixed costs. (This highlights the important difference between product costing and distribution cost analysis: the former is very much concerned with the compiling of product costs whereas the latter is concerned with the cost and revenue implications of different marketing actions and activities.)

There are many different bases for analysing and apportioning marketing costs to control units, but it is important to observe that some costs vary with the characteristics of one type of control segment only. Thus inventory costs depend on the characteristics of the products rather than on those of the customers, whereas the cost of credit depends on the financial integrity and number of customers rather than on sales territory factors. Accordingly, all functional costs should not be apportioned indiscriminately to products, customers, territories, etc., but only to whichever segments exhibit a cause-and-effect relationship with the cost factor in question.

The cost control of marketing activities can now be seen to depend on the generation and analysis of information to realistically attach costs to the activities to which they relate, and this in turn constitutes the basis on which the margin of contribution may be calculated – the size of which will tend to determine whether or not the activity under consideration is deemed satisfactory.

Introducing distribution cost analysis to an organization

It must be remembered when using distribution cost analysis that any cost allocation involves a certain degree of arbitrariness, and this means that an element of error is contained within each apportionment. Furthermore, it remains necessary to supplement the analysis of distribution costs with other relevant information and with managerial judgement. Distribution cost analysis is the joint responsibility of the financial controller and the marketing manager, with the former supplying most of the information and the latter supplying most of the judgement. Nevertheless, the marketing manager must be fully aware of the methodology and limitations of distribution cost analysis in the same way that production managers should understand product costing.

The high costs involved in establishing and maintaining a distribution costing system are justified by the benefits derived from increasing the efficiency of marketing effort. The risks involved in adopting a full system of distribution cost analysis before the benefits have been demonstrated can be reduced by initially confining the analysis to a sample of products, customers, or territories, and by making periodic rather than continuous analyses. An illustration is given below of the way in which a particular product line can be analysed in order to test the applicability of detailed cost analysis.

Let us consider a company that has a product line made up of nails, screws, nuts and bolts. Figure 17.1 shows an analysis of overheads (both production, administrative and marketing) and direct costs in relation to product types. This analysis differs from most statements of this nature in three ways:

1 It shows marketing expenses as *costs* rather than as deductions from gross profit.

2 It analyses the cost/profit profile of the four product types (and note that all four show a profit).
3 It shows costs in some detail rather than as aggregates.

(£'000s)	*Total*	*Nails*	*Screws*	*Bolts*	*Nuts*
Sales revenue	3 500	1 400	825	560	715
Direct material	1 000	600	100	120	180
Direct labour	625	149	230	86	160
Set-up costs	60	12	30	12	6
Supervision-factory	30	7	11	4	8
Tool maintenance	30	9	6	4	11
Tooling costs	40	16	12	6	6
Power	65	19	15	11	20
Maintenance	35	12	6	4	13
Payroll preparation	30	7	11	4	8
Production control	25	5	8	7	5
Time study	20	4	7	6	3
Purchasing	40	12	18	6	4
Cost accounting	30	10	12	5	3
Depreciation	215	65	60	49	41
Freight	225	103	30	27	65
Warehousing	85	17	33	25	10
Sales management	20	5	7	3	5
Field sales costs	380	190	50	50	90
Sales invoicing	20	4	10	3	3
Promotions	55	11	28	10	6
Administration	110	43	26	18	23
Total conversion cost	2 140	700	610	340	490
Total cost	3 140	1 300	710	460	670
Profit (loss)	360	100	115	100	45
Profit (loss) (per cent)	10.3	7.2	14.0	17.9	6.3
Minutes of standard time	17 850	4 400	6 500	2 300	4 650

Figure 17.1: Distribution plus product costs

A more detailed analysis is given in Figure 17.2 which shows the breakdown of the figures relating to bolts in accordance with the source of the orders received: regular orders from customers, special orders from customers, orders for spare parts, and internal orders for stock. By analysing product and distribution costs in accordance with order types it can be seen that losses are made on special orders and orders for spares. (These losses are £29 000 and £38 000 respectively.)

If this analysis is taken a stage further and the cost per 1 000 standard minutes for each expense head by product line is shown the results shown in Figure 17.3 are obtained.

(£'000s)	*Bolts*	*Regular*	*Special*	*Spares*	*Stock*
Sales revenue	560	390	84	30	56
Direct material	120	84	18	12	6
Direct labour	86	60	12	9	5
Set-up costs	12	4	4	2	2
Supervision-factory	4	2	1	1	—
Tool maintenance	4	2	1	1	—
Tooling costs	6	2	2	2	—
Power	11	7	2	1	1
Maintenance	4	2	1	—	1
Payroll preparation	4	1	1	—	1
Production control	7	2	2	3	1
Time study	6	1	2	2	1
Purchasing	6	1	2	2	1
Cost accounting	5	1	2	1	1
Depreciation	49	34	7	3	5
Freight	27	13	8	3	3
Warehousing	25	5	10	6	4
Sales management	3	1	1	1	—
Field sales costs	50	13	25	12	—
Sales invoicing	3	1	1	1	—
Promotions	10	4	4	2	—
Administration	18	4	7	4	3
Total conversion cost	340	160	95	56	29
Total cost	460	244	113	68	35
Profit (loss)	100	146	(29)	(38)	21
Profit (loss) (per cent)	17.9	35	(3.7)	(12.7)	3.7
Minutes of standard time	2 300	1 600	350	230	120

Figure 17.2: Order analysis

This information can now be used as a starting point for cost reduction as well as a tool for cost control. For example, Figure 17.2 showed the losses on special orders and spares orders amounted to £67 000, but this could be due to several factors – such as high costs or low prices. Figure 17.3 gives assistance in connection with the cost aspects of the situation by showing that, for example, in the case of bolts the following items are above the norm:

Item	*Total*	*Bolts*	*Percentage above norm*
Set-up costs	3.36	5.22	55
Production control	1.40	3.04	117
Time study	1.12	2.61	132
Warehousing	4.76	10.87	128
Depreciation	12.04	21.32	77

It may well be that these differences are entirely justifiable, but it is important to be aware of their nature and magnitude with a view to improvements.

As a concluding comment on distribution cost analysis, since a fundamental objective of this technique is to increase the productivity of marketing outlays (and not necessarily to reduce them) the manager who wishes to introduce distribution cost analysis must emphasize the desire to make better use of existing funds rather than to reduce the magnitude of future budgets. The integration of distribution costing with marketing research can assist in this matter. Confining any costing system to data provided from accounting records forces that system to be historical, but marketing research can provide estimates of future sales resulting from variations in marketing effort (with or without experimentation and the building of complex models) that enable the efficiency of alternative expenditure patterns to be predetermined and evaluated in accordance with corporate aims.

Any cost analyses must be presented in some form of report, and the whole reporting structure can be strengthened by the presence of cost analysts within the marketing department who would be responsible for extending and summarizing analyses for marketing management in accordance with their needs.

(£'000s)	*Total*	*Nails*	*Screws*	*Bolts*	*Nuts*
Minutes	17 850	4 400	6 500	2 300	4 650
Direct labour	35.05	33.86	35.38	37.39	34.41
Set-up costs	3.36	2.73	4.62	5.22	1.29
Supervision-factory	1.68	1.59	1.69	1.74	1.72
Tool maintenance	1.68	2.05	0.92	1.74	2.36
Tooling costs	2.24	3.63	1.85	2.61	1.29
Power	3.64	4.32	2.31	4.78	4.30
Maintenance	1.96	2.72	0.92	1.74	2.80
Payroll preparation	1.68	1.59	1.69	1.74	1.72
Production control	1.40	1.14	1.23	3.04	1.07
Time study	1.12	0.91	1.08	2.61	0.65
Purchasing	2.24	2.73	2.77	2.61	0.88
Cost accounting	1.68	2.27	1.85	2.17	0.65
Depreciation	12.04	14.78	9.23	21.32	8.82
Freight	12.60	23.40	4.61	11.74	13.96
Warehousing	4.76	3.87	5.08	10.87	2.15
Sales management	1.12	1.14	1.08	1.30	1.07
Field sales costs	21.28	43.18	7.69	21.74	19.35
Sales invoicing	1.12	0.91	1.54	1.30	0.65
Promotions	3.08	2.50	4.31	4.35	1.29
Administration	6.16	9.77	4.00	7.82	4.95
Total conversion costs	119.89	159.09	93.85	147.83	105.38

Figure 17.3: Conversion costs per 1 000 minutes

Such analysts can help greatly in presenting relevant information for marketing decision-making. (For example, by associating costs with physical units rather than with the value of sales, any distortions arising from price variations can be automatically eliminated.) In addition, the existence of marketing cost analysts could help in securing uniformity in the measures used by both marketing management and the financial controller's department – especially in relation to salesmen's activities. These measures might include standards for cost per call, cost per new customer, cost per order serviced, break-even order size, sales per call, etc., and such standards could shed light on profitability, work load assignments, sales quotas, and compensation problems.

A variety of cost and profit reports can stem from accounting-marketing collaboration. A few examples can be given.

The most common control report relates to product profitability and may cover any period from a day to a year. However, the suitability of such reports for decision-making is not increased by unnecessary and arbitrary cost allocations.

Figure 17.4 illustrates a simple, aggregated cost/profit statement for a product line.

Products ______ *Period* ______	*Actual*	*Budget*	*Variance*
Net sales			
LESS:			
1 Cost of goods sold:			
(a) Cost of sales			
(b) Distribution expenses			
TOTAL			
2 Research and development costs			
3 Marketing costs:			
(a) Administrative			
(b) Selling			
(c) Advertising and promotion			
TOTAL			
4 General and administrative expenses			
TOTAL OPERATING EXPENSES			
OPERATING PROFIT			

Figure 17.4: Product profit statement – 1

This type of report can be produced for each sales territory, region, or the whole country, and further columns can be added to accommodate budget revisions, or further categories of cost can be specified to permit detailed cost control. A more detailed statement is illustrated in Figure 17.5, and a further variation which provides for the separation of direct and allocated (or separable and non-separable) costs is shown in Figure 17.6.

A few words of warning should perhaps be given in connection with using cost reports for decision-making. Any decision that requires a knowledge of cost-volume-profit behaviour must be based on an analysis of manufacturing and marketing costs into their fixed and variable components. Moreover, if the performance of marketing executives (such as product managers) is based on net profit reports of the types illustrated in Figures 17.4, 17.5, and 17.6, it must be recognized that any given marketing executive will not be able to control all the functions since many of the costs will be allocated. Full-cost reports (of the type shown) necessitate the allocation of *all* costs which can easily lead to the incorrect use of sales value for allocating certain administrative costs. Because this allocation procedure tends to obscure the meaning and thereby reduce the reliability of the reported net profit figure, it may be a more desirable proposition to use contribution margin statements instead.

MARKETING PROGRAMMING

Programming is a form of analytical modelling that is useful when it is desired to allocate funds (or other resources) in the best way. The most widely used technique is that of linear programming which aims to determine the optimum allocation of effort in a situation involving many interacting variables: in other words, it produces the solution which maximizes or minimizes a particular outcome in accordance with given constraints. (For example, how should sales effort be allocated amongst regions to maximize the level of sales subject to a maximum availability of 10 000 units of product per period? Or which product mix should be sold – subject to demand – in order to achieve the maximum level of profit?)

In carrying out his duties the marketing manager will be interested in making the best use of his limited resources, and the constraints that exist will set the upper limit to the level of performance that is possible. For example, the company cannot spend more on advertising than the amount which it has in its advertising appropriation, thus:

PRODUCT PROFIT REPORT						
PRODUCT ________			PERIOD ________			
Description	*Actual amount*	*Percentage of net sales*	*Budget amount*	*Percentage of net sales*	*Variance amount*	*Percentage of net sales*
Gross sales						
Less: deductions						
Net sales		100		100		100
Cost of sales						
Gross profit						
Less: Marketing costs						
Advertising						
Consumer promotions						
Trade deals						
Field sales						
Product research						
Marketing management						
Product management						
Marketing research						
Sales accounting						
Administration						
Warehousing						
Traffic management						
Stock control						
Freight						
Total marketing costs						
Profit						

Figure 17.5: Product profit statement – 2

QUARTERLY PRODUCT PROFIT REPORT				
PRODUCT ____________	PERIOD ____________			
Item	*Direct*	*Allocated*	*Total*	*Per cent*
Gross sales				
Less: Cash discounts				
Net sales				
Cost of goods sold				
Standard cost				
Special direct charges				
Engineering				
Other costs				
Total				
Actual gross profit				
Other operating expenses				
Sales promotion				
Product management				
Advertising				
Trade deals				
Market research/testing				
Merchandising management				
Inventory/warehousing				
Freight				
Administration				
Corporate R & D				
After-sales service				
Field sales activity				
Total				
Profit				

Figure 17.6: Product profit statement – 3

$$a_1\,(W) + a_2(X) + a_3(Y) + a_4(Z) \leqslant A$$

where:

$\leqslant$ means 'equal to or less than'
A is the total advertising appropriation
a_1 (W) is the amount spent on advertising product W
a_2 (X) is the amount spent on advertising product X
a_3 (Y) is the amount spent on advertising product Y
a_4 (Z) is the amount spent on advertising product Z

Similarly, a constraint exists in relation to every fixed budget or limited resource such as sales force time or warehouse space:

$$b_1(W) + b_2(X) + b_3(Y) + b_4(Z) \leqslant B$$

where:

B is the total available sales force time
$b_1(W)$ is the time devoted to selling product W, etc.

and:

$$c_1(W) + c_2(X) + c_3(Y) + c_4(Z) \leqslant C$$

where:

C equals the available warehouse space
$c_1(W)$ is the space occupied by the inventory of W, etc.

The basis on which resources should be allocated is the *marginal response.* If the expenditure on advertising of, say, £100 000 results in sales amounting to £500 000, then the *average response* is 5/1, and if an increase in advertising expenditure of £1 000 produces additional sales totalling £10 000, this gives the measure of marginal response which is equal to 10/1. Marginal response can thus be seen to be a measure of the value of available opportunities..

If a company's advertising budget is set at £100 000 for a period, the optimal allocation to each of the company's three products (A, B and C) is given by equating the marginal responses because this gives the situation where it will not be beneficial to re-allocate funds from one product to another. The requirement, therefore, is to find the best solution to the equation:

$$a_1(A) + a_2(B) + a_3(C) = £100\ 000$$

where:

$a_1(A)$ is the advertising budget for product A
$a_2(B)$ is the advertising budget for product B
$a_3(C)$ is the advertising budget for product C

The solution is given when: $\dfrac{\Delta s_1}{\Delta a_1} = \dfrac{\Delta s_2}{\Delta a_2} = \dfrac{\Delta s_3}{\Delta a_3}$

where s_1, s_2, s_3 are the sales of products A, B and C; and

$\dfrac{\Delta s_1}{\Delta a_1}$ is the marginal response for product A

measured as: $\dfrac{\text{change in sales}}{\text{change in advertising outlay}}$

and so on for products B and C.

Linear programming must be applied in the absence of uncertainty, which means that uncertainty must be evaluated and eliminated before variables are quantified and put into a linear programming format. Moreover, all the relationships within problems that are to be solved by means of linear programming are assumed to be linear, and this may not apply under all conditions. For example, costs rarely rise in direct proportion to increases in sales. But even with this disadvantage, linear programming is still able to indicate the best direction for allocating resources to segments.

SALES OPERATIONS

A major aid in controlling selling costs is to personalize them: if a salesman knows that all the costs he incurs will be recorded against his budget, he will tend to be more cost conscious. Control is not facilitated by the averaging of such costs (e.g. entertaining, samples, travelling, telephone, stationery, etc.) over products sold.

Attention should not be drawn narrowly towards cost minimization but the aim should be to get the maximum returns from the available resources. Salesmen should be directed towards increasing their sales activity per hour and to pushing the most profitable lines. Profit contribution will be the ultimate measure of sales success rather than cost minimization, and this means that salesmen should avoid spending large amounts on entertaining and travel for small orders, quoting unrealistic prices, promising impossible delivery dates, creating confusion that leads to administrative difficulties, or maximizing sales volume (as so often happens) regardless of profit contribution. A high level of sales volume does not necessarily carry with it an increasing rate of profitability. It follows, therefore, that sales effort should be directed towards those customers having greatest profit potential. If sales managers focus their attention exclusively on expense reports, the result may well be that a high level of efficiency is achieved, but if no attention is paid to the allocation of effort it may prove to be the case that the level of effectiveness is low (e.g. through servicing a large number of small accounts).

The preoccupation with sales volume that is found amongst sales personnel causes an order for £10 000 to be viewed as being better than an order for £5 000 despite the fact that the former may be only half as profitable as the latter (or which may have taken five times as long to secure). Similarly, a preoccupation with gross margins may cause 150 orders of £100 each with a 25 per cent margin to be viewed more favourably than an order of £1 000 000 with a 1 per cent margin. The cost of processing an order for £1 is unlikely to differ from the cost of processing an order for £1 000 000 but apart from not knowing the cost of processing orders, relatively few companies know the profitability of different orders, or of different accounts. It has been suggested that 50–75 per cent of customers in most instances contribute to losses rather than to profits., so each account should be analysed to see if it makes a positive contribution. An easy way to do this is shown in Figure 17.7.

Annual salary per salesman	£7 000	
Average expenses (including car)	£6 200	
Total cost	£13 200	
Number of days spent selling	220	
Cost per day	£60	
Average calls per day	5	
Average cost per call	£12	
	Sales account A	*Sales account B*
Annual sales volume	£1 600	£4 800
Sales calls per year	6	8
Cost per call	£12	£12
Total call cost	£72	£96
Commission rate	5%	5%
Commission paid	£80	£240
Account profit (loss)	£(28)	£96

Figure 17.7: Account contributions

This simple method of computing the contribution made by different accounts is easy to apply and can readily show those that are incurring higher costs than the revenue they produce. A fuller analysis can be carried out within the framework of Figure 17.8. Customer analysis of this type enables relative profit contributions and the distribution of marketing effort to be attached to order size groups. The outcome is a most straightforward schedule of profitable versus unprofitable order-size groups, and these can be investigated further to see if any particular order-size group contains a preponderance of specific customer types. If so, the management must decide if it can make these groups more profitable, if it should stop selling to them, or what other course of action may be appropriate.

From top management's point of view, the information that is required on the financial dimensions of sales operations consists of:

1. The contribution from sales and its comparison with the requirements of the budget.
2. The extent to which variances have arisen from changes in the volume of sales, the varying of sales margins, or the mix of products sold.
3. The extent of cost variances.
4. The volume of orders placed for future delivery in relation to available productive capacity.

Customer volume group: amount of annual purchases (£)	*Number of accounts percentage of total*	*Number of calls percentage of total*	*Sales percentage of total*	*Gross profit percentage of total*	*Selling expenses percentage of sales*	*Operating profit percentage of sales*
0– 5						
6– 10						
11– 25						
26– 50						
51– 100						
101– 150						
151– 200						
201– 250						
251– 300						
301– 400						
401– 500						
501– 750						
751–1 000						
Over 1 000						
No sales			—	—	—	—
Total of averages	100.00	100.00	100.00			

Figure 17.8: Customer analysis

This information is essential (and in itself sufficient) to indicate whether the company is keeping in line with the budgeted objectives. It also shows the factors causing deviations from plan insofar as the sales function is concerned.

From this it is possible for further studies to be carried out at lower managerial levels to pinpoint and remedy basic causes.

The cost of credit

Allowance in planning and controlling cost levels should always be made for the costs of providing credit, the costs of giving cash or trade discounts and the losses due to debts turning out to be bad. The estimating of the amounts to allow for these items will tend to be influenced by past experience, current practice and future expectations. Compare, for instance, the sale to a normal customer amounting to £1 500 in value with a sale to an occasional trade customer who expects a trade discount of 33⅓ per cent, giving a value for the same order of only £1 000. Also consider the sale of goods to the value of £1 000 on 90 days credit terms with an average bad debt rate of 2 per cent:

Value of sale		£1 000
Interest cost: 90 days @ 16 per cent pa	£40.00	
Bad debt risk: 0.02 × £1 000	£20.00	
Related costs		£60.00

In contrast, let us assume that a cash discount of 5 per cent is allowed for settlement within 14 days:

Value of sale	£1 000
Cash discount @ 5 per cent	£ 50
Net sum due	£ 950

It can be seen that the cost of granting credit (ignoring the additional book-keeping and administration costs that this causes) exceeds the cost of a generous cash discount, and there is no risk of debts turning out to be bad or cost of extending credit when all sales are on a cash basis.

The cost of a salesman

Turning to the costs of the salesman himself, these can easily be classified into fixed and variable categories in preparing budgets, standards, etc. The fixed cost items will typically include:

1 Salary
2 Depreciation of motor car
3 Fixed car expenses (e.g. insurance, road fund)
4 Superannuation.

Variable costs will cover:

1 Commissions (which is best related to profit contribution – or net sales – rather than to gross sales volume)
2 Travelling expenses
3 Entertaining costs; etc.

A *vehicle record* is a useful report. It can be submitted weekly or monthly by each salesman and show his daily mileage, split between business and private mileage, petrol consumption, servicing costs, new tyre requirements, etc. This type of report is a helpful supplement to the weekly *expense claim form*, an example of which is shown in Figure 17.9.

The expense claim form gives details of all business expenses incurred in the course of the salesman's work (and can be used by other personnel also). Whenever expense claim systems are in operation, those who are affected by them should be left in no doubt as to what is and what is not valid business expense. To this end a set of notes for guidance should be compiled and circulated to all concerned. A specimen set is shown below.

Expenses – notes for guidance

1 **General** The general aims in relation to expenses incurred on company business are:

1 From the company's point of view, to exercise economy in respect of the nature and level of expenses.
2 From the individual's point of view, to minimize the inconvenience of being out of pocket.

Within this framework there is a good deal of scope for personal discretion, but it is expected that commonsense will be applied at all times.

Expenses should be approved by your immediate superior: this is a prerequisite for reimbursement.

Sales representatives should submit expense claims weekly with their call reports to the sales manager, and will be reimbursed every fortnight by credit transfer into their bank accounts.

Other staff should claim reimbursements on a monthly basis and payment will be made as promptly as possible after the submission of a claim. The exception to this is in the case of senior executives where special arrangements have

EXPENSES CLAIM FOR MONTH ENDING: ______________			
NAME: ______________	BUSINESS MILEAGE		
DEPARTMENT: ______________	PRIVATE MILEAGE		
	TOTAL MILEAGE		

CODE		£	£
	Entertaining—Details to be specified		
	Travelling expenses Fares Hotels Meals		
	Motor expenses Petrol & oil Repairs Servicing		
	Less private motoring charge @ 10p per mile		
	Other expenses—Details to be specified		

ALL VOUCHERS ARE TO BE ATTACHED		*TOTAL* £	
JOURNEYS ARE TO BE DETAILED ON REVERSE		*ACCOUNTS OFFICE*	
SIGNATURE:	DATE:		
AUTHORIZED:	DATE:		

Figure 17.9: Expense claim form

been made for deferred reimbursement.

In exceptional circumstances, with the consent of the individual's superior, it will be possible to arrange either advances or immediate repayments.

When submitting expense claims, all relevant sections of the standard expense form should be completed and vouchers (i.e. receipts) attached. In the absence of vouchers, full details should be given of the nature of, and reason for, the expenditure.

2 Hotels and meals Unless arrangements have been made with the accounting department for the forwarding of hotel bills, these should be paid on departure by the individual and included (net of any items of personal expenditure) on the next expense claim.

Receipts should be obtained for all meals as well as for payments to hotels. Preference should generally be given to table d'hôte rather than à la carte menus (where the choice exists) and a responsible attitude should be adopted in relation to the level of expense being incurred.

When employees are engaged on company business away from home and do not expect to arrive home before 9.00 pm, it is in order for them to charge the cost of an evening meal either en route or where they have been working.

Reasonable gratuities are allowable in the absence of specified service charges.

3 Travel

(a) Public transport. All air travel undertaken on company business should be by tourist class.

Rail travel should be covered by warrants obtainable from the personnel department. In accordance with the general principle of sensible economy, warrants are issued for second-class travel to all company employees whatever their seniority. If the circumstances of the journey (e.g. crowding in second-class compartments, or being accompanied by customers) suggest it, employees are at liberty to travel first class, paying the supplement and reclaiming it from the company.

In London, it is clearly preferable in financial terms (and usually also in terms of time) to use the underground, but wherever taxis are used details should be given if the daily cost exceeds £5.

(b) Travel by car. (See also 'Regulations for Users of Company Vehicles'). All charged motor expenses must be covered by receipts. In the case of company-owned vehicles, it is requested that receipts be obtained for all petrol purchased and that both the mileage covered during the month on business and pleasure be noted. A payment of 10p per private mile will then be deducted from the expense claim as a contribution towards the cost of private motoring.

In the case of privately-owned vehicles, allowances will be paid on the following scale for authorized use on company business:

Up to	1200 cc	20p per mile
	1200 to 1500 cc	25p per mile
Over	1500 cc	30p per mile

Each employee using a company-owned car is responsible for the car being serviced in accordance with the manufacturer's recommendations, cleaned regularly, and maintained in sound mechanical order. Faults should be rectified when they occur, with approval being obtained from the field sales manager in the case of the sales force, and from the individual's immediate superior in the case of other users of company vehicles, for expenditure in excess of £50 and for the purchase of new tyres.

Car hire without prior approval from an employee's superior should only be undertaken in a real emergency and authority obtained as soon after the event as is practicable.

4 Telephones In the case of employees who must use their private telephone for company calls, they should pay their accounts in full and submit the receipted account with their next expense claim. The company will pay for the installation of telephones in approved cases, quarterly rentals in approved cases, and for business calls only. It will be necessary, therefore, for the claim for reimbursement to be made not of private calls.

5 Entertaining Since the expense for entertaining persons other than overseas customers is disallowed for taxation purposes, special care should be taken in relation to expenditure under this heading. Receipts (where applicable) should be obtained and a record submitted with each expense claim stating who was entertained. Reasonable expenditure on drinks at the bar will be accepted in relation to entertaining. It should not necessarily be required of us to entertain all visitors since there is always room for reciprocity.

When executives travel or eat out with other members of the company, the senior person will normally pay and note for whom he has paid on his expense claim. Under normal circumstances it should not be expected that claims will be made for the entertaining of colleagues.

It should always be possible to relate expenses under the heading of entertainment to specific individuals.

If a particular company prefers to give fixed expense allowances to salesmen, instead of operating the expense reimbursement system, then it is prudent to require an account from each recipient of how his allowance has been used. Complications can arise over the tax aspects of expense payments if procedures are not established and carefully followed. The obvious inland revenue problem arises in the form of Form P11D which must be completed by employers for each of their employees who received (in the form of remuneration – salary, commission, etc – and expenses) the sum of £8 500 or more during the last tax year. In detail, the figures that have to be declared in this respect are:

Expenses payments made and benefits, etc., provided by employer

£

1 **Entertainment** Enter all payments made exclusively in respect of entertaining, including:

(a) Amount of any round sum allowance

(b) Specific allowances for entertaining

(c) Sums reimbursed

(d) Sums paid to third persons

(Show all sums paid under the headings notwithstanding that they will fall to be disallowed in computing the employer's tax liability where they do not relate to the entertainment of 'overseas customers'.)

2 **General expenses allowances** (Enter the amount of any round sum allowance not exclusively for entertaining.)

3 **Travelling and subsistence**

(a) Fares, hotels, meals, etc. (excluding payments for travel between home and normal place of employment).

(*b*) Payments for travel between home and the normal place of employment.

4 **Cars**

(a) Car owned or hired by employer and provided for or used by director or employee:

(i) Annual value of the use of the car (if owned, 12½ per cent of the cost of the car when new; if hired, the amount of the hire charges).

(ii) Running and overhead expenses borne by the employer, e.g. chauffeur's wages, licence, insurance, petrol, oil and repairs (including cost of work done or petrol, etc., supplied by the employer).

(b) Car owned or hired by director or employee:

(i) Allowances to the director or employee in respect of the use of the car and running and overhead expenses borne by the employer, e.g. chauffeur's wages, licence, insurance, petrol, oil and repairs (including the cost of work done or petrol etc. supplied by the employer).

Total carried forward

Total brought forward £

(ii) Sum contributed towards the purchase price, depreciation, or hire.

5 **House, flat or other accommodation provided for director or employee:**

(a) Address and nature of accommodation . . . .
. . . .
. . . .

(b) Gross value for rating of the property.

(c) If rented by the employer, rent, repairs and insurance borne by him.

(d) Expenses borne by the employer which are the liability of the director or employee, e.g. rates, heating, lighting, upkeep of gardens, wages, keep and accommodation of domestic or other staff, hire of furniture.

(e) Annual value of the use of furniture and fittings owned by the employer.

6 **Subscriptions**

7 **Private medical, dental, etc., attention and treatment**

8 **Goods and services supplied free or below market value** Enter the market value or the cost to the employer, whichever is the higher, less the sum, if any, paid by the director or employee. (If goods are supplied under discount facilities available to employees generally the price payable may be taken as market value.)

9 **Work carried out at the director's or employee's own home or on his property or assets** (Enter cost to the employer, including wages of his own workmen and contractors.)

10 **Wages and insurance, keep, etc., of personal or domestic staff** (if not included above).

11 **Cars, property, furniture, etc., and other assets given or transferred to the director or employee:**

(a) If the asset has belonged to the employer and during his ownership it was used or had depreciated, enter the market value at the date of transfer, less the sum, if any, paid by the director or employee.

Total carried forward

Total brought forward £

(b) In all other cases, enter the market value at the date of transfer or the cost to the employer, whichever is higher, less the sum, if any, paid by the director or employee.

12 **Other expenses and benefits, etc.,** if not included above, e.g. national insurance contributions, holidays, home telephone, education of family, etc., private legal, accountancy, secretarial, etc. expenses, sporting facilities (shooting, fishing, horseracing), contributions towards house purchase, rates and other household and gardening expenses. Descriptive particulars and amounts of any–

(a) Expenses payments (including payments to the director or employee, payments made on his behalf and not repaid, and sums put at his disposal)

. . . .

. . . .

. . . .

. . . .

(b) Benefits (including benefits provided for the director's or employee's family, etc.)

(i) Emoluments given to the director or employee otherwise than in money (enter the market value or the cost to the employer whichever is the higher).

(ii) Annual value of the use of any asset belonging to the employer.

(iii) Expenses incurred in or in connection with the provision for the director or employee of benefits or facilities of whatsoever nature:

. . . .

. . . .

. . . .

Total (items 1 to 12)

Less *(a)* So much of the expenses and benefits entered above as have been made good by the director or employee (if not already deducted in arriving at the amounts stated at 8 and 11 above)

. . . .

(b) Amounts included above from which tax has been deducted under Pay As You Earn

. . . .

Net Total

Figure 17.10: Form P11D

It makes good sense to design the expense claim form along the lines of Form P11D, since this will enable time to be saved and will also help in avoiding confusion.

By combining fixed and variable costs for a salesman, along with the percentage contribution rate for the budgeted product mix, it is possible (Figure 17.11) to construct a break-even chart for controlling sales operations.

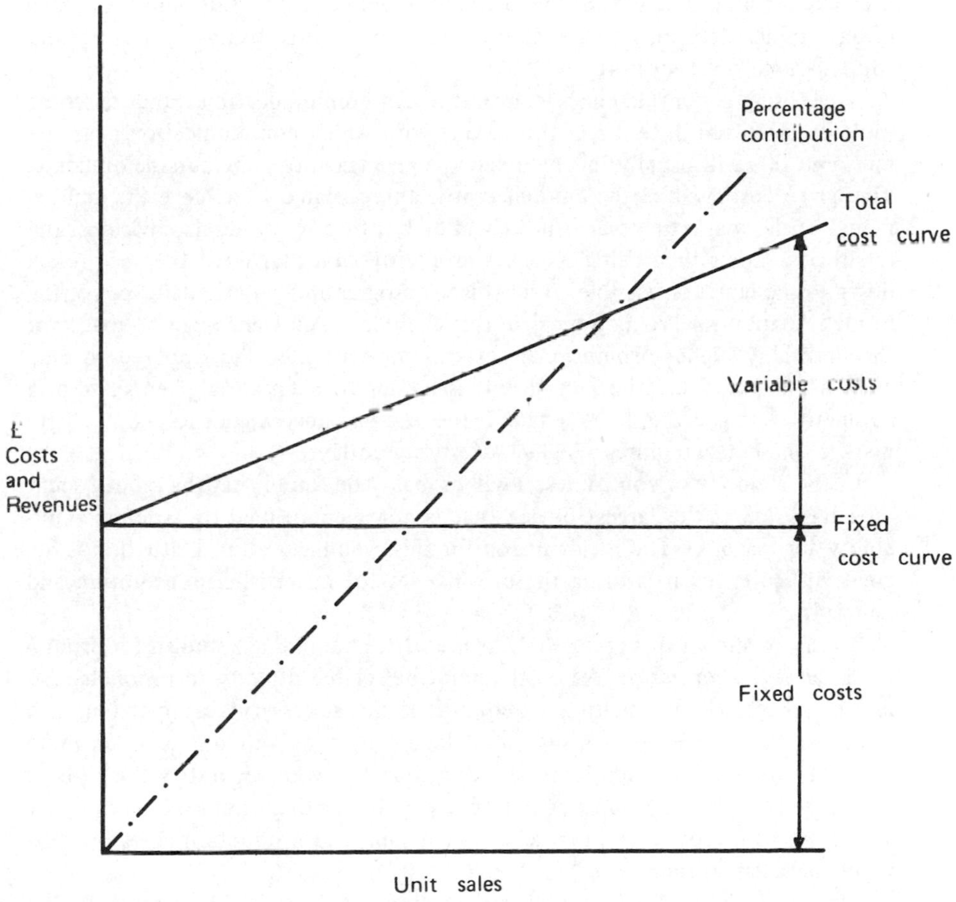

Figure 17.11: Sales force control chart

An extension of this form of analysis can show how many salesmen are necessary for a given level of sales activity. The break-even point can be used as the starting point for paying commission (although complications arise when different rates of commission are payable on different product lines).

ADVERTISING

Advertising can be viewed as an addition or as an alternative to other forms of order-getting activity – notably direct selling and sales promotion. The cost clearly exists, therefore, of not being able to do something else with the money that is being spent on advertising. It follows, as ever, that the investment of funds in advertising must be made in anticipation of some beneficial pay-off. This pay-off should be seen in the relationship between total sales and advertising outlays rather than in, say, the relationship between advertising expenditure and total marketing expenditure.

Advertising is conspicuously concerned with communications, and its results must be measured in terms of the success with which communication goals are met, and this will usually involve relating a given cost to a measurable outcome. The 'given cost' will be the amount that is appropriated to achieve the requirements of the marketing plan, and it will be built up by products, divisions, and territories, rather than being specified as a lump sum that must then be broken down (although it is possible to do this via programming methods – see section headed 'Marketing Programming' in this chapter). Allowance can be made for the inevitably higher promotional costs of new products (as opposed to established ones) and for the fact that it is harder to maintain a given share of a competitive or growing market than is the case in a declining or less competitive market, and hence requires a higher advertising outlay.

In the majority of companies, it will probably be found that the money spent on advertising is the largest outlay that is not accompanied by strict accountability for reasons. The major reason for this seemingly absurd situation is the great difficulty of measuring the effectiveness of advertising expenditure and its results.

The form shown in Figure 17.12 is useful for compiling a budget for promotional activities *ab initio*. All costs cannot be related directly to products, and in the process of formulating a budget it is not necessary to apportion such costs, so Figure 17.12 is a summary document that will be based on more detailed schedules for such items as exhibitions (showing separately the costs of space, design, fittings, transport, staff, etc.) and distinguishing between space and production costs for press advertising, time and production costs for television advertising, and so on.

Figure 17.13 is of a rather different nature. It is built up on the fact that flexibility is a key ingredient in promotional planning, and it is thus vital to know what proportion of the available funds are uncommitted, committed but cancellable, spent (i.e., invoiced or committed and uncancellable) and so forth, in order that available funds may be switched from one proposed use to another. If it is desired to exceed the budget level, the foot of the form enables authorized overspends to be distinguished from unauthorized overspends.

	Unallocated	*Product A*	*Product B*	*Product C*	*Total*
Advertising agency fees					
PR agency fees					
Press advertising					
Television advertising					
Radio advertising					
Poster advertising					
Direct mail advertising					
Departmental expenses					
Exhibitions					
Literature					
Photography					
Films					
Research					
Editorial publicity					
Packaging design					
Sales aids					
Manuals					
Point of sale					
Trade deals					
Consumer promotions					
Gifts					
Christmas cards					
Miscellaneous					
Contingency					
TOTAL					

Figure 17.12: Promotion budget form

Period ________ *Division/product* ________	*Budget*	*Revised budget*	*Invoiced*	*Committed*		*Uncommitted*	*Total*
				Cancellable	*Uncancellable*		
Above-the-line							
TV time							
TV production costs							
Trade press space							
Trade press production costs							
Consumer press space							
Consumer press production costs							
Poster sites							
Poster production costs							
Below-the-line							
Exhibitions							
Point of sale							
Premium offers							
Gifts							
Sales literature							
Total							
Authorized over-budget							
Unauthorized over-budget							

Figure 17.13: Promotion control report

THE ROLE OF COSTS IN PRICING: THE CASE OF BIDDING

Within this section it is not proposed to elaborate on the dangers of basing the price of standard lines too closely on costs. (The circular reasoning implicit in this is well known: if costs are used as the basis of pricing the resulting price will have some impact on demand which, in turn, will influence the extent to which capacity is utilized, and this will be reflected in the level of costs . . . and so on. The key variables here – cost, price, and demand – have an interdependence, but this approach pays insufficient attention to competitive activities, and this includes the ways in which the company in question can seek to influence demand other than by means of price.) Instead, the main concern will be with the role of costs in arriving at competitive bid prices.

Three basic approaches to price-setting in practice are readily identifiable:

1 Cost-oriented pricing:
   (*a*) mark-up pricing;
   (*b*) target pricing.
2 Demand-oriented pricing.
3 Competitive-oriented pricing:
   (*a*) going-rate pricing;
   (*b*) sealed-bid pricing.

It will be evident that bidding for a contract is but one means by which a price may be set. The usual pricing problems are met in determining the value of a bid, but some problems peculiar to bid pricing are also met – those relating specifically to having to price in advance, with no opportunity to revise this price, and those relating also to uncertainty and the great significance of competition.

Bid pricing embodies the characteristics of competitive pricing in that the approach does not seek to maintain a rigid relationship between price and costs or demand. Costs or demand may change – but the firm must maintain its price because competitors maintain their prices. Conversely, the firm will change its price in response to competitors, regardless of cost or demand.

Two kinds of competitive bidding can be envisaged:

1 Closed bidding, where two or more bidders submit independent bids for a contract.
2 Auction, or open bidding, in which two or more bidders continue to bid openly on an item until nobody is willing to increase the bid.

In the former case, of course, the lowest bid will probably be the winner, whereas in the latter case, the highest bid will probably be the winner. In this section, however, our interest is in the closed bidding situation.

Bidding, as a pricing mechanism, is necessary because all firms do not face mass markets. In those sectors having only a small number of prospective customers there will be a limited number of selling opportunities, and success will tend to be strongly dependent upon bidding strategy. Any firm engaged in marketing industrial goods, for example, must take note of the opportunities presented by nationalized industries, and local or central government. To obtain a share of this large and growing market the firm must master the art of bidding or tendering.

Since bidding strategy is based on expectations of how one's competitors will bid (rather than on costs or demand) the open bid situation can be a trap to snare the responsible firm into unprofitable contracts and tempt the small, inexperienced firm into bankruptcy. Consequently, bidding objectives must be agreed upon within the firm, and explicitly stated.

Bidding objectives

The major tactical objective in bidding is to obtain the contract. But this may only be achieved if a low bid is submitted. Consequently, we must look at wider objectives.

The most likely aim would seem to be the maximizing of total expected profits on both the contract in question and on other available contracts during the period with which we are concerned. Alternatively, the aim may be to minimize expected losses, or to minimize the profits of competitors, or even to keep production lines working although this may result in a loss.

We will assume that the maximizing of total expected profits is our objective, as this is commonly met in practice, and is relatively simple to handle for purposes of exposition.

The relevance of probability theory to competitive bidding should be obvious: the higher the bid, the lower the probability of obtaining the contract. But we can accommodate this factor by the use of our concept of expected profit. This concept will be examined in a later section, but suffice it to say at this stage that the expected profit is the product of the profit that could be made on a particular contract and the probability of being awarded that contract.

Following from the specification of bidding objectives is the 'bidding problem', or the determination of the actual bid price. We will consider the analytical methods that help us to find the right balance between payoff and risk, but the bidding problem is especially complex because:

(*a*) information needs vary from facts to intangibles to unknowns, e.g. from costs to attitudes to specific competitive bids; and
(*b*) the manipulating and interpreting of this data must be performed by one person, involving the collection of information, the considering of interactions, and the determining of a bid price.

Operations research approaches

The manipulation of the relevant data is more easily performed if it can be quantified in a model that describes the relationships pertinent to the problem.

This will relieve the manager of the task of computation, and permit him to concentrate on the application of judgement. Additionally, a formal quantitative approach helps by ensuring:

(*a*) a systematic gathering of data;
(*b*) a consideration of all factors thought to be relevant;
(*c*) minimization of emotional irrationality;
(*d*) a systematic evaluation of interactions;
(*e*) an analysis geared to management's objectives; and
(*f*) an equitable division of burden between the manager and the model.

Operations research developments in the field of pricing involve no new economic concepts, but apply the accepted concepts in a usable framework. The management scientist attempts particularly to formulate pricing problems in a way that is amenable to mathematical treatment. But even when one cannot solve mathematically the models formulated by OR specialists, such models frequently illuminate the problem, thereby enabling one to deal more effectively with practical situations.

A competitive bidding model is helpful in understanding many other pricing situations, as bidding situations make the proper role of cost considerations unusually clear, and help to sharpen the concept of demand. In this sense, competitive bidding can be thought of as being scientific because the bid price, when determined, results from rigorous, formal analysis.

On the other hand, OR cannot remove the need for judgement on the part of marketing management. To the extent that the manager must evaluate customers, competitors, and risks in deriving his bid price, competitive bidding is also an art.

In attempting to construct an appropriate bidding model, the management scientist must be *au fait* with the bidding objective and strategy. This strategy will be dependent upon the firm's current economic position, including such matters as, for example, the order-book situation. Once this information is known, decisions about what price to bid for a contract include the following:

1 How much would it cost to fulfil the terms of the contract?
2 Who else will bid for the contract?
3 How much will they bid?
4 How much should we bid?

Expected profit

As we have seen, the lower the bid price, the greater the probability of success in winning the contract, but also the lower the probability of this being profitable. These two opposite pulls are best described by the expected profit of a particular bid. This is illustrated in Table 17.1:

Firm's bid	*Firm's profit*	*Assumed probability of getting contract with this bid*	*Expected profit*
£ 9 500	£ 100	0.81	£ 81
10 000	600	0.36	216
10 500	1 100	0.09	99
11 000	1 600	0.01	16

Table 17.1

As the bid price increases, the expected profit decreases, and the best bid in this example would be £10 000, giving an expected profit of £216. However, there may be times when a firm will accept a low expected profit to increase the likelihood that it will get *some* profit. To illustrate this point, it will be appreciated that a small profit multiplied by a high probability can give the same expected profit as a high profit multiplied by a low probability. The option chosen will inevitably depend upon the need of the firm for income, and upon the attitude of management towards risk-taking.

So far the possibility of failure has not been considered. The following example makes this explicit.

For a contract, the estimated cost c is £20 000, and the bid price x has a success probability of 0.3 at £40 000, and 0.7 at £30 000.

If the contract is obtained, the profit is either:

(*a*) £40 000 – £20 000 = £20 000, or
(*b*) £30 000 – £20 000 = £10 000

In case (*a*), the probability of a profit of £20 000 is 0.3, and the probability of zero profit is 0.7, i.e. 1 – 0.3. It follows that the expected profit on a bid of £40 000 is:

$$0.3\,(20\,000 + 0.7\,(0)\,) = \text{£}6\,000$$

If the bid price is £30 000, the expected profit is:

$$0.7\,(10\,000 + 0.3\,(0)\,) = \text{£}7\,000$$

Under these circumstances the bid of £30 000 is the one that should be submitted.

The relevant formulae, therefore, are:

1 If contract awarded, profit $= x - c$
2 If contract not awarded, profit = 0
3 If probability of obtaining the contract is p, then the probability of not obtaining the contract is $1 - p$.
4 Expected profit $= p(x - c) + (1 - p)\,(0) = p(x - c)$, since $(1 - p)\,(0) = 0$.

The recognition of a relationship between the probability of award and the size of bid can be expressed as a probability distribution function. If it is assumed that the firm is to bid on a contract that will cost an estimated £8 000 to fulfill, the relationship between the size of the bids and the probabilities of success at each bid price may be as shown in Table 17.2.

Bid x	*Probability of success p*
£ 7 000	1.00
8 000	0.95
9 000	0.85
10 000	0.60
11 000	0.30
12 000	0.10
13 000	0.00

Table 17.2

This is such a probability distribution function, showing that as the bid gets larger the probability of success decreases. It indicates that a bid of £7 000 would be certain to secure the contract, but that a bid of £8 000 would only be successful 95 times out of 100 in the same circumstances. This is explained by the fact that there is a $1.00 - 0.95 = 0.05$ probability that a competitor would bid below £8 000. (In this example, with large steps of £1 000, such a bid would be £7 000, but in practical bidding situations it could be at any level below £8 000.)

By repeating this reasoning, we can convert the probability distribution function into a probability density function, as in Table 17.3.

Bid x	*Probability of bid*
£ 7 000	0.05
8 000	0.10
9 000	0.25
10 000	0.30
11 000	0.20
12 000	0.10
13 000	0.00

Table 17.3

The probabilities total 1 due to the fact that one must occur, and no other is possible. This is merely a different way of looking at the data in Table 17.2.

We must, however, be able to calculate the expected profit. If the firm bids £9 000 with estimated costs of £8 000, and obtains the contract, its profits will be:

$$x - c = £1\,000.$$

But the probability (from Table 17.2) of obtaining the contract with such a bid is 0.85. The expected profit, therefore, is:

$$p(x - c) = 0.85\,(9\,000 - 8\,000) = £850.$$

By applying the formula for expected profit to the other bid levels, we obtain the figures in Table 17.4 which is an expanded illustration of the principle portrayed in Table 17.1.

Bid x	*Expected profit*
£ 7 000	1.00 (7 000 – 8 000) = – £1 000
8 000	.95 (8 000 – 8 000) = £ 0
9 000	.85 (9 000 – 8 000) = £ 850
10 000	.60 (10 000 – 8 000) = £1 200
11 000	.30 (11 000 – 8 000) = £ 900
12 000	.10 (12 000 – 8 000) = £ 400
13 000	.00 (13 000 – 8 000) = £ 0

Table 17.4

From a bid of £10,000, the maximum expected profit is £1 200, and this is the bid that should be submitted.

Expected profits can also be plotted graphically, and would be of the form shown in Figure 17.14.

From this curve, it is a simple matter to identify that bid price that maximizes expected profit. However, the difficulty lies in determining the curve itself, which in turn depends on the probability of winning as a function of the bid price.

A word of warning is called for at this point. In a strict statistical sense the expected profit represents the average return per bid under the following conditions:

(*a*) the firm repeats the same bid on a large number of contracts with precisely the same costs; and

(*b*) the probability of its being awarded the contract remains at p for each bid x.

If these conditions are not approximately met, the concept of expected profits and the methodology pursued in the remainder of this discussion are not valid. Consequently, this approach is only of major use in large firms which bid frequently, and which are not particularly concerned about any specific contract. If a firm bids rarely, or has a special interest in a particular contract, then the expected profit criterion is probably not very useful. For example, it does not distinguish adequately between a £1 000 profit with a success probability of 0.1 and a £125 profit with a success probability of 0.8. Although they both give the

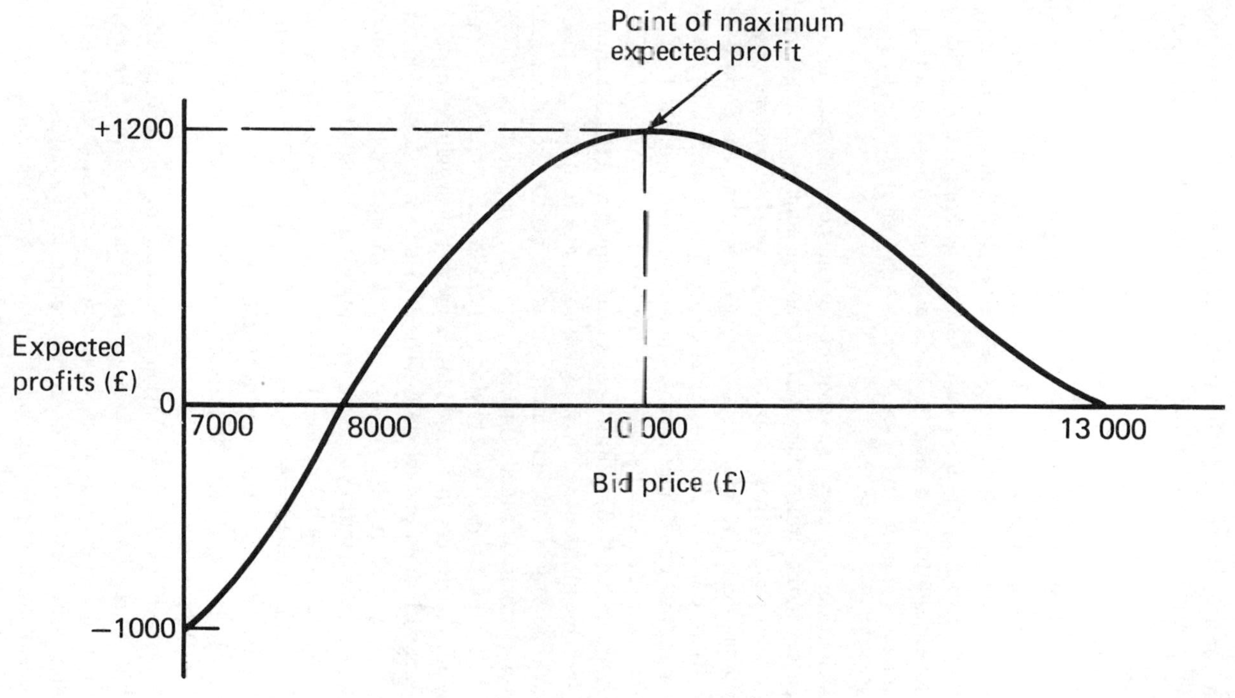

Figure 17.14: Expected profits

same result in terms of expected profit, the latter is preferable, but the money value of expected profit, as already observed, may not reflect its utility value.

The role of costs

There can be no doubt that the firm should have some idea of its costs for performing a particular contract. Guidance can be given by collected data indicating the relationship between the actual costs incurred on contracts awarded, and the estimates of those costs used in determining the bid price. This can be done easily by recording the ratio of estimated costs to actual costs for each completed contract. As a result, a distribution of these ratios can be made, as shown in Figure 17.15.

Such a distribution indicates the reliability of our cost estimates as a guide to greater accuracy in the future. However, it must be emphasized that marginal costs, as opposed to any other measure of costs, such as average costs, are relevant to bidding decisions. But it is not suggested that one should necessarily set one's bid at the level of marginal costs. These costs clearly indicate the very minimum that one should accept. Indeed, the future of the firm would be brief if all bids were made at the marginal cost level!

Some recognition of the opportunity costs of bidding on a contract should be incorporated into the bid floor set by marginal costs, and then the firm must ask itself how much more than that amount it is likely to get for the job. To aim to bid below competitors, provided this is above marginal cost, is the wrong approach, as it confuses *probabilities* with *certainties*. In addition, it fails to take into account differences in the amount of profit that would be made if one won the contract with other possible bids. The choice becomes one of balancing the pay-off (or expected profit) against the risk (or probability of success), which requires that consideration be given to competitors' possible bids.

Before considering competition, the 'problem of bidding' must be discussed. Whereas the 'bidding problem' refers to the level of bid price to submit, the 'problem of bidding' relates to the decision whether or not to bid on a particular contract. The solution would appear to rest within the alternatives of placing a bid, or refraining from bidding.

This problem is worthy of consideration on account of the costs involved in preparing a bid. Especially in the case of non-standard items, the cost of preparing the data on which the bid is based can be substantial, and it is rarely possible to follow a strategy of bidding on every contract that arises.

This problem of bidding is intrinsically related to the bidding problem, since the decision whether or not to place a bid will depend to a large extent on the value of the bid.

The combined problem can be approached by adjusting the cost estimates for the contract by the cost of bidding. (This, of course, would only be applic-

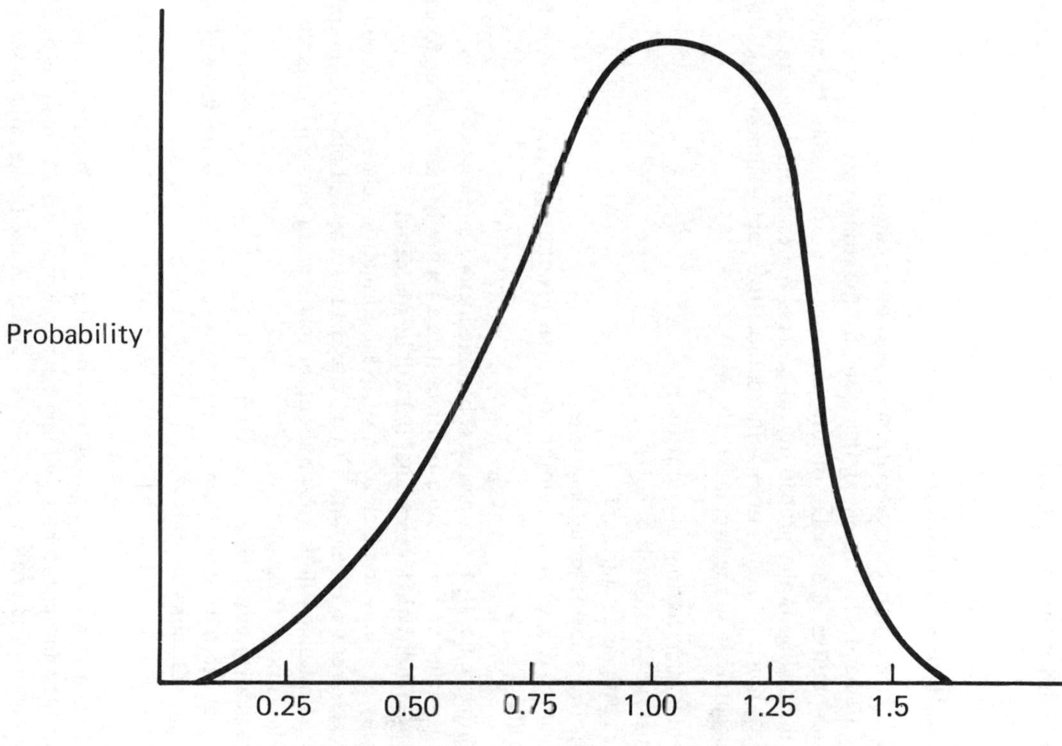

Figure 17.15: Distribution of cost ratios

able in cases where a bid is to be placed, and irrelevant when no bid is to be made.) In such a case, the profit if the contract is lost is negative, not zero, which would affect the calculation of expected profit that was used in an earlier example.

Consideration of competition

Bid pricing is based more on expectations of how one's competitors will bid than on costs or demand. It is essential, therefore, for the firm to estimate the likelihood of competitors' bids being of any particular size. Certainly the biggest unknown in bidding is the probability of success for each bid level, and this depends very much on competition. But competitive data is almost impossible to obtain accurately, so the firm must rely on:

(*a*) past bidding behaviour of competitors;
(*b*) estimates of their levels of costs;
(*c*) trade gossip and conjecture;
(*d*) competitors' needs for business; and
(*e*) the nature of current and future commitments of competitors' productive capacity.

If the firm has details of competitors' bidding history and knows which competitors it is facing on a particular contract it is a relatively easy matter to calculate the probability that a particular bid will be successful.

Frequently the only available competitive information relates to announcements of those contracts for which they have made successful bids. In normal circumstances nothing will be known about the relationship between competitors' costs and the value of these bids.

The prospective buyer may state which firms have been invited to bid for a contract, what are the value of bids so far received, and what is the value of the accepted bid. If none of this data is made available, the bidding problem becomes very much more difficult, and the process must necessarily be less scientific.

As a competitive weapon, flexibility in bidding certainly has its merits. A rigid consistency in approaching bidding situations will make it relatively easy for competitors to forecast one's own firm's actions in the future, and care must be taken with this in mind.

Now we must formulate bidding strategies for various competitive possibilities. We have seen how to determine the most profitable bid, in terms of expected profit, given the distribution of probabilities of success as a function of the bid price. However, initially this distribution must be determined. The following cases will be considered:

(*a*) one known competitor;
(*b*) several known competitors; and
(*c*) unknown competitors.

One competitor

The type of data which would be useful in the case of one known competitor might be as in Table 17.5:

Potential competitive bid			*Likelihood*
Less than		£9 500	0.1
9 500	–	9 999	0.3
10 000	–	10 499	0.3
10 500	–	10 999	0.2
11 000 and over			0.1
			1.0

Table 17.5

This informs us that the firm in question, competitor A, is unlikely (0.1) to bid less than £9 500, so if we bid £9 499 we have a probability of success of 0.9. On the other hand, we are almost certain to lose if we bid over £11 000, as a probability of 0.9 exists that competitor A will bid below this level. Similarly, if we bid £10 000, we have 6 chances in 10 of obtaining the contract.

However, before such a table can be compiled we must collect data relating to every successful bid that competitor A has made, and for which we possess cost estimates, i.e. estimates of our own costs, prepared as a basis for bidding. From this data, the ratio of A's bid price to our cost estimates for each common contract can be calculated. (Our cost data has the advantage of providing a constant basis for comparison.) The resulting figures may be as shown in Table 17.6.

Contract	*Estimated cost*	*A's bid*	*Ratio*
1	£ 8 500	£10 200	1.2
2	22 000	33 000	1.5
3	11 000	15 400	1.4
4	35 000	38 500	1.1
5	9 000	9 000	1.0

Table 17.6

All the information on A's bid can then be summarized as in Table 17.7, which indicates the frequency with which each ratio has arisen.

Ratio of A's bid to our cost estimates	*Frequency*
0.9	1
1.0	3
1.1	5
1.2	11
1.3	15
1.4	8
1.5	4
1.6	3
	50

Table 17.7

Thus out of 50 bids, made by both A and our firm, the former has bid successfully at 90 per cent of our cost estimate on one occasion, etc. This gives a relative frequency of 1/50, or 0.02. The plotted relative frequencies are shown in Table 17.8.

Ratio of A's bid to our cost estimates	*Probability of ratio*
0.9	0.02
1.0	0.06
1.1	0.10
1.2	0.22
1.3	0.30
1.4	0.16
1.5	0.08
1.6	0.06

Table 17.8

The relative frequencies give us a probability density function, comparable with Table 3. From it we can define the probability distribution function of A, showing the likelihood that a particular bid, expressed as a multiple of our cost estimate, will be lower than A's bid. For instance, there is a probability of $1.00 - 0.02 = 0.98$ that a bid of 0.9 times our cost estimate will be lower than A's bid. To eliminate the possibility of equal bids, our firm's bid could be lowered a little. Consequently, a bid of 0.89 times our cost estimate has a probability of 1.00 of being lower than A's bid. Similarly, a bid of 0.99 times our cost estimate will have a probability of $1.00 - 0.02 = 0.98$ of being lower than A's bid. This situation is represented in Table 17.9.

Bid, as multiple of our cost estimates	*Probability that bid is lower than bid of A*
0.89	1.00
0.99	0.98
1.09	0.92
1.19	0.82
1.29	0.60
1.39	0.30
1.49	0.14
1.59	0.06
1.69	0.00

Table 17.9

This gives the necessary probability distribution function. Its use can be demonstrated as follows:

Let bid x be 1.09 × cost estimate $= 1.09c$
Probability $= 0.92$ that contract will be won.
Profit from contract $= 1.09c - c = 0.09c$.
Expected profit $= p(x - c)$
But $x = 1.09\,c$
Then expected profit $= 0.92\,(0.09c) = 0.0828c$

In the same way, the following can be calculated:

Bid, as multiple of our cost estimates	*Expected profit where A is the only competitor*
0.89	$1.00\,(0.89c - c) = -0.11c$
0.99	$0.98\,(0.99c - c) = -0.0098c$
1.09	$0.92\,(1.09c - c) = 0.0828c$
1.19	$0.82\,(1.19c - c) = 0.1558c$
1.29	$0.60\,(1.29c - c) = 0.1740c$
1.39	$0.30\,(1.39c - c) = 0.1170c$
1.49	$0.14\,(1.49c - c) = 0.0786c$
1.59	$0.06\,(1.59c - c) = 0.0354c$

Table 17.10

A bid of $1.29c$ will give us the greatest expected profit of $0.174c$.

Several known competitors

If there are several known competitors, the same analysis as above can be extended. However, the probability of winning the contract is smaller, even if the data for each competitor are identical.

The ratios of competitors' previous successful bids to our cost estimates can be plotted as illustrated by Figure 17.16.

Probability distribution functions can be described, as in the case of the single known competitor, and the result may be as shown in Table 17.11.

Bid, as multiple of our cost estimates	*Probability that bid is lower than bid of*	
	A	*B*
0.89	1.00	1.00
0.99	0.98	0.94
1.09	0.92	0.83
1.19	0.82	0.68
1.29	0.60	0.37
1.39	0.30	0.20
1.49	0.14	0.10
1.59	0.06	0.03
1.69	0.00	0.00

Table 17.11

It can be seen from this table that a bid of 1.09 times cost estimate will be lower than A's bid with a probability of 0.92, and lower than B's bid with a probability of 0.83. But this considers the bids of A and B separately. The probability will be 0.76 (i.e. 0.92 × 0.83) that a bid of 1.09 times the cost estimate will be simultaneously lower than both the bids of A and B. The probability for other bids is shown in Table 17.12.

Bid, as multiple of our cost estimates	*Probability that bid is simultaneously lower than bids of A and B*
0.89	1.00 × 1.00 = 1.00
0.99	0.98 × 0.94 = 0.92
1.09	0.92 × 0.83 = 0.76
1.19	0.82 × 0.68 = 0.56
1.29	0.60 × 0.37 = 0.22
1.39	0.30 × 0.20 = 0.06
1.49	0.14 × 0.10 = 0.01

Table 17.12

As stated, the probability of our bid of $1.09c$ being simultaneously lower than the bids of A and B is 0.76, thereby giving an expected profit of $0.76\ (1.09c - c) = 0.0684c$. Such a procedure can be adopted for any number of known competitors.

A variation on this procedure is feasible, indicating also the probability that we will win the contract with a bid of any given size. Table 17.13 illustrates the point:

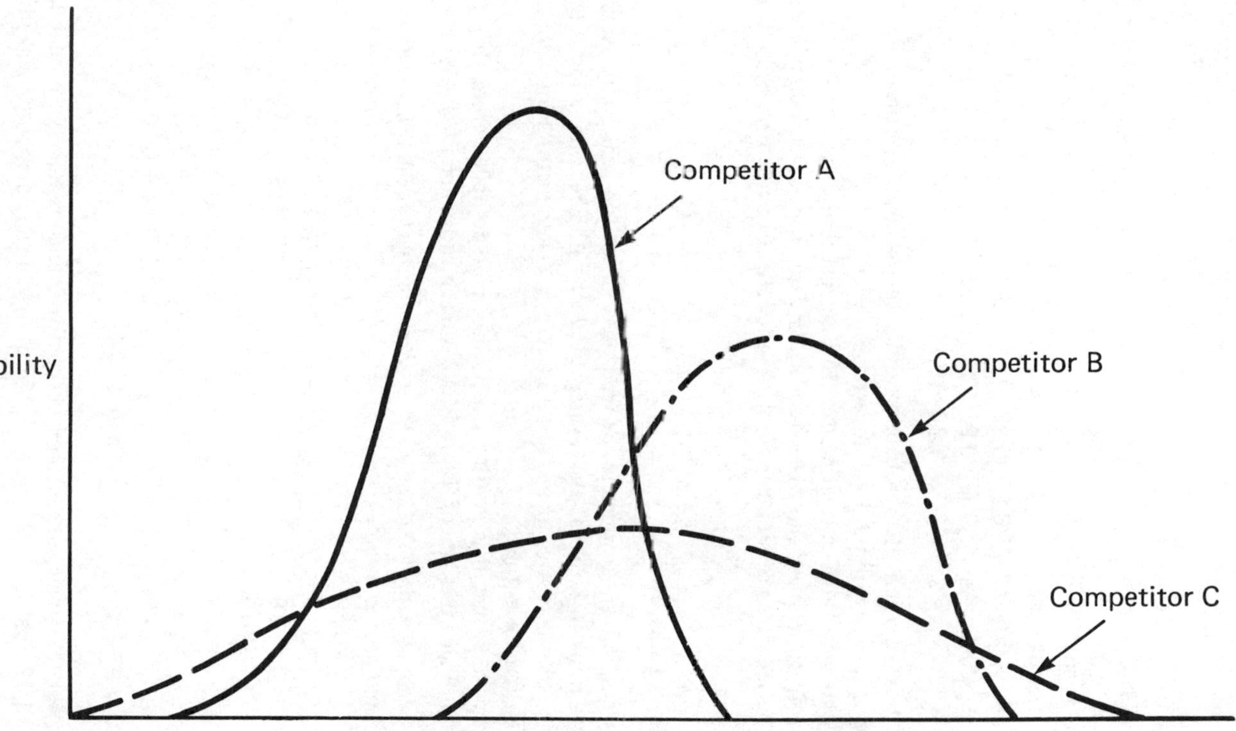

Figure 17.16: Distribution of competitors' bid to cost ratios

Potential bid	Competitor X	Y	Either X or Y	Cumulative probability of a bid by Either X or Y	Probability of getting the award with comparable bid
Under £9 500	0.1	0.1	0.19	0.19	0.81
9 500 – 9 999	0.3	0.3	0.45	0.64	0.36
10 000 – 10 499	0.3	0.3	0.27	0.91	0.09
10 500 – 10 999	0.2	0.2	0.08	0.99	0.01
Over £11 000	0.1	0.1	0.01	1.00	–

Table 17.13

By use of this variation, the probability of success is given by considering the cumulative probability of bids by competitors at each level.

The key to success lies in treating the resulting distribution as if it was that of a single competitor, even though it represents data from several competitors. This is so because we are interested only in the lowest competitive bid on each contract.

Competitors unknown

When it is not known how many, or who the competitors will be, it becomes necessary to think in terms of the 'average' bidder. All previous ratios of competitive bids to our cost estimates are plotted as a single distribution function. Figure 17.17 illustrates this.

An averaged probability density function can be compiled from this non-specific data. Using the data of Table 17.12, we can construct Table 17.14.

Bid, as multiple of our cost estimates	*Probability that bid is lower than bid of 'average' competitor*
0.89	1.00 (1.00 + 1.00 ÷ 2)
0.99	0.96 (0.98 + 0.94 ÷ 2)
1.09	0.88 (0.92 + 0.83 ÷ 2)
1.19	0.75 (0.82 + 0.68 ÷ 2)
1.29	0.48 (0.60 + 0.37 ÷ 2)
1.39	0.25 (0.30 + 0.20 ÷ 2)
1.49	0.12 (0.14 + 0.10 ÷ 2)

Table 17.14

This table, for the single, unspecified competitor, tells us that the probability of a bid of 1.19*c* being lower than the bid of any single competitor picked at random is 0.75.

In that case where the identity of competitors is not known, but their number is, the data of Table 14 can be used to determine the probability of success for each bid by proceeding as in the case of known competitors. A bid

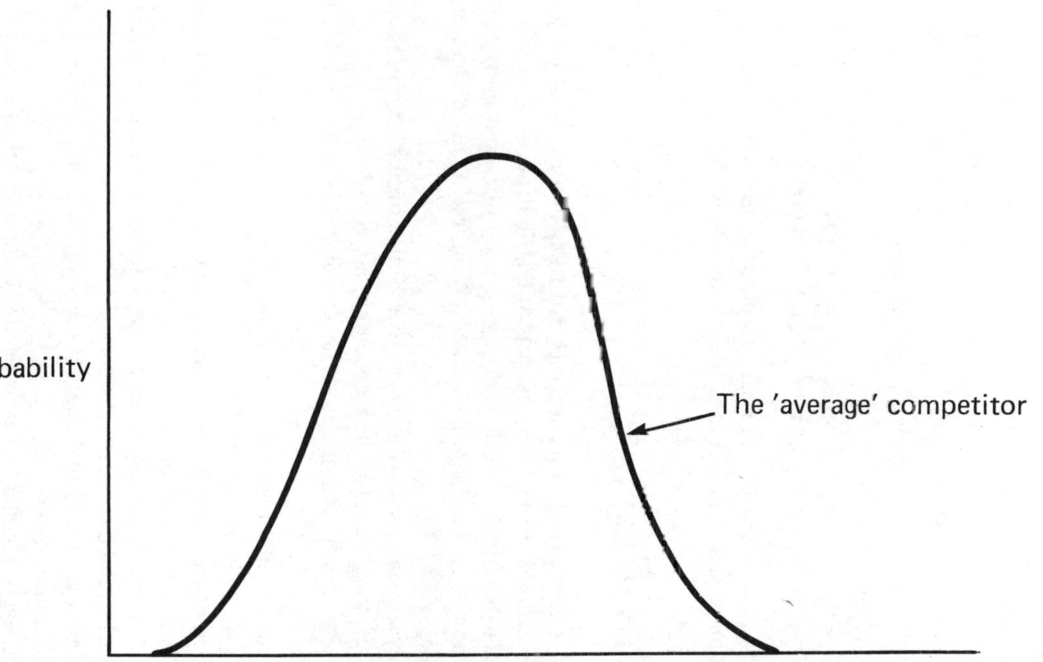

Figure 17.17: Distribution of averaged bid to cost ratios

of $1.19c$, as shown, has a probability of 0.75 of being lower than the bid of a single random competitor. If there are two such competitors, the probability of such a bid being simultaneously lower than bids of both competitors is $0.75 \times 0.75 = 0.563$. In the case of three competitors, the probability is $0.75 \times 0.75 \times 0.75 = 0.422$, and so on.

It will be evident that such probabilities are the same as the probability of winning the contract in the face of one, two or more competitors. From them, the expected profit for each bid can be computed as demonstrated, assuming three competitors:

Bid $x = 1.19c$
Expected profit $= 0.422\,(1.19c - c) = 0.0802c$
If $c =$ £8 000, expected profit $= 0.0802 \times 8\,000 =$ £641.6

To use this technique when the number of competitors is unknown, however, requires that some means of estimating their number be found.

CHECKLIST ON MARKETING

1 Are costs, expenses and revenues analysed to show profitability by areas, products, customer groups and channels of distribution?
2 Are regular reports produced showing sales, profits and costs for each product, area, customer group, channel? Are these related to budgets and market share data?
3 Have analyses been made to see how many small orders are processed that fail to cover costs? Do discounts encourage larger orders?
4 Are salesmen concentrating on those customers who are known to be profitable?
5 Are salesmen's movements known, planned and controlled? Are sales areas appropriately determined?
6 Do compensation schemes for salesmen result in profitable new business rather than extra volume alone?
7 Are cash discounts resulting in more rapid debt collection, or should they be increased or discontinued?
8 Are records kept of broken delivery promises with a view to their improvement? Are causes known?
9 Are stock levels adequate to provide the planned level of service? How often do shortages arise?
10 What pricing policies exist? Are these in line with market conditions?
11 Is an attempt made to obtain a profit as a percentage of sales, or as a rate of return on investment based on anticipated volume levels?
12 How do price changes compare with cost changes? Are the likely effects of price increases on forecasted volume and profits taken into consideration?

13 Do some products incur unusually large selling and servicing costs that are not taken into account in product pricing?
14 Are market shares known? What are the trends?
15 How do competitive prices compare?
16 Are price differentials based on quality differentials?
17 How do competitors compare in such areas as product quality, customer service, etc?
18 Could higher quality, better service – and the related higher costs – lead to higher profits?
19 In which marketing areas is the company strongest? Can other areas benefit by following their example?
20 Are sales forecasts developed by product lines, regions and customer groups? Do sales plans take due account of productive capacity and stock levels?
21 Since they represent a vital volume parameter, are sales forecasts regularly reviewed, updated and compared with actual results?
22 Is market research data used (via distribution cost analysis) to show product, area, and customer group performance?
23 Are distribution costs related to production costs to give a full cost picture?
24 Are the functions of advertising and promotion departments clearly defined?
25 Is the promotions department adequately staffed to perform its functions effectively?
26 Do catalogues portray the quality of the company's products as well as the desired image?
27 Is the promotional budget based on present sales levels or on projected sales levels?
28 Has a thorough analysis been made of all media and are budgets built up in relation to the importance of different media in selling more products?
29 Is the promotional programme disrupted without fully considering the consequences?
30 Does the company have sound economic reasons for participating in trade fairs?
31 Are budget and actual figures compared on a regular basis? Are variances investigated?
32 Is printed matter bought in the most economic manner? Could the company save money by establishing its own print department?
33 Does the company have specific goals for advertising and sales promotion within its marketing strategy? Are these quantified and are results capable of being measured?
34 On what basis did the company select its advertising agency?
35 Does the promotion budget include a sum for measuring the effect of promotions?

SUMMARY

This chapter has dealt with some topics in the sphere of order-getting costs. Other aspects of cost control relating to marketing activities are dealt with in Chapter 15 and Chapter 18.

Order-getting costs determine in large part the scale of the company's activities because they influence the level of sales. Whilst most costs follow from a given level of demand, order-getting costs help to create that level of demand.

The control of marketing costs is made possible through careful planning and this involves analysing costs into their fixed and variable categories as a starting point. In studying the behaviour of marketing costs, marketing experimentation and distribution cost analysis are valuable techniques.

Experiments are expensive to carry out, but they can help to allocate marketing effort in the most effective manner to product lines, customer groups, channels of distribution, sales territories, and so on. (This highlights a problem of marketing control: the existence of so many possible control units.) Most companies do not know the profitability or cost levels of their market segments (i.e. regions and customer groups, as well as order size, product lines, etc.).

Cost analysis in marketing can indicate the cost implications of different courses of action, and help to avoid the misallocation of effort (i.e. resources). But the danger of over-allocating costs must be avoided in distribution costing, or the outcome will be so arbitrary as to be valueless. The objective of distribution cost analysis is to increase the productivity of marketing outlays and this cannot be achieved by over-allocations.

Programming techniques can be put to good use in allocating marketing resources, but a framework of cost control is still necessary. Budgeting, ratio analysis, standard costing, variance analysis, network analysis, cost-volume-profit analysis, etc., all contribute to controlling marketing costs. Effectiveness is more important than cost minimization, but this is unlikely to come from the frequently-encountered obsession with sales volume maximization, so sales operations should be re-oriented to take profitability into consideration.

In relation to pricing decisions the role of costs is by no means insignificant. Variable cost represents the lower limit at which a (short-run) price should be set, and competitors' prices represent the higher limit. A good deal of help is available from the operations research domain for building competitive bidding models based on the analysis of costs.

FURTHER READING

Montgomery, D.B., and Urban, G.L., *Management Science in Marketing,* Englewood Cliffs, N.J.: Prentice-Hall, 1969.
(A thorough coverage of the interface of management science technology and marketing problems.)

Sevin, C.H., *Marketing Productivity Analysis*, New York: McGraw Hill, 1965.
(A masterly synopsis of techniques for reducing marketing costs by this late pioneer of the subject.)

Wilson, R.M.S., *Management Controls and Marketing Planning*, London: Heinemann (for the Institute of Marketing and the CAM Foundation), 2nd ed., 1979.
(A modelling approach is adopted in explaining, with lots of examples, how to control marketing activities.)

Wilson, R.M.S. (ed.), *Financial Dimensions of Marketing: A Source Book*, (2 vols), London: Macmillan (for ICMA), 1981.
(This is the definitive compilation on the subject.)

18

Distribution—Order-Filling

INTRODUCTION

Physical distribution management (PDM) is composed of a number of activities that are essential in linking marketing, manufacturing, and administration, but which had received little co-ordinated study until recent years. A major reason for this is that attention has been directed from time to time to elemental parts of the distribution process (such as, say, inventory control) without viewing the parts in the context of the whole process. (In a similar way, it is an over-simplification to extract, say, advertising from its order-getting setting of marketing, and so on in other areas.)

The activities encompassed by the order-filling PDM function include:

(i) order processing,
(ii) inventory management,
(iii) warehousing,
(iv) materials handling,
(v) traffic management,
(vi) transport facilities,
(vii) packaging,
(viii) customer services (e.g. credit control),

(ix) depot/warehouse location,
(x) selecting channels of distribution.

The costs of these activities constitute a major part of total marketing costs. Estimates suggest that the non-manufacturing portion of the prices consumers pay for their purchases amounts to 60 per cent, and of this a large element relates to distribution costs. It follows that an examination of physical distribution activities – and their costs – is likely to be a worthwhile exercise if efficiency is to be improved and/or costs reduced.

A close parallel may be drawn between the control of many order-filling costs and the control of production costs. Flexible budgets (based on the separating of fixed and variable costs) can be compiled for order-filling costs with any one of various activity measures as their base – units of product, tons, cases, sales value, etc. – depending on the purpose of the analysis. The best base in a given situation is that which represents a causal relationship with cost levels. For example, the following activities may be related to cost levels through the units of measurement shown alongside them:

Activity	*Unit of measurement*
Warehouse labour	Kilos handled per day
Packaging labour	Units packed per hour
Despatch/picking labour	Items loaded/picked per hour
Invoicing	Lines typed per hour
Posting sales debtors	Postings per hour

As with many other standards (both in the factory and in the office) many order-filling cost standards will be developed under average conditions and variances will thus arise whenever conditions depart from the average. Variances must obviously be interpreted in this light, and the costs of developing more accurate standards should be related to the expected benefits in the control endeavour.

Cost behaviour patterns must be analysed and understood as a starting point both for control and prediction. Whilst many distribution expenses (including packaging, freight charges and insurance) will tend to vary with the level of sales, other costs will tend to have more complex behaviour patterns. There is unlikely to be a close degree of correspondence between the level of manufacturing expenses and the level of distribution expenses, although a graph of their respective and combined behaviour patterns can indicate the optimal level of output – as in Figure 18.1.

Distribution costs will tend to rise *per unit of output* as the company has to service consumers living further and further away from its factories and warehouses. This explains the increasing slope of the distribution cost curve in

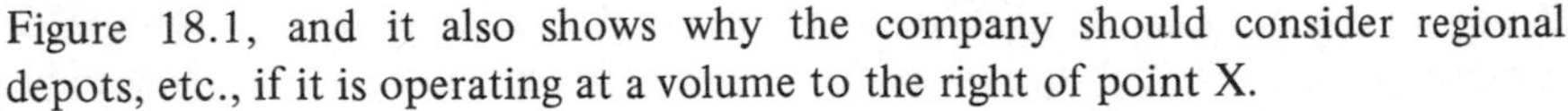

Figure 18.1, and it also shows why the company should consider regional depots, etc., if it is operating at a volume to the right of point X.

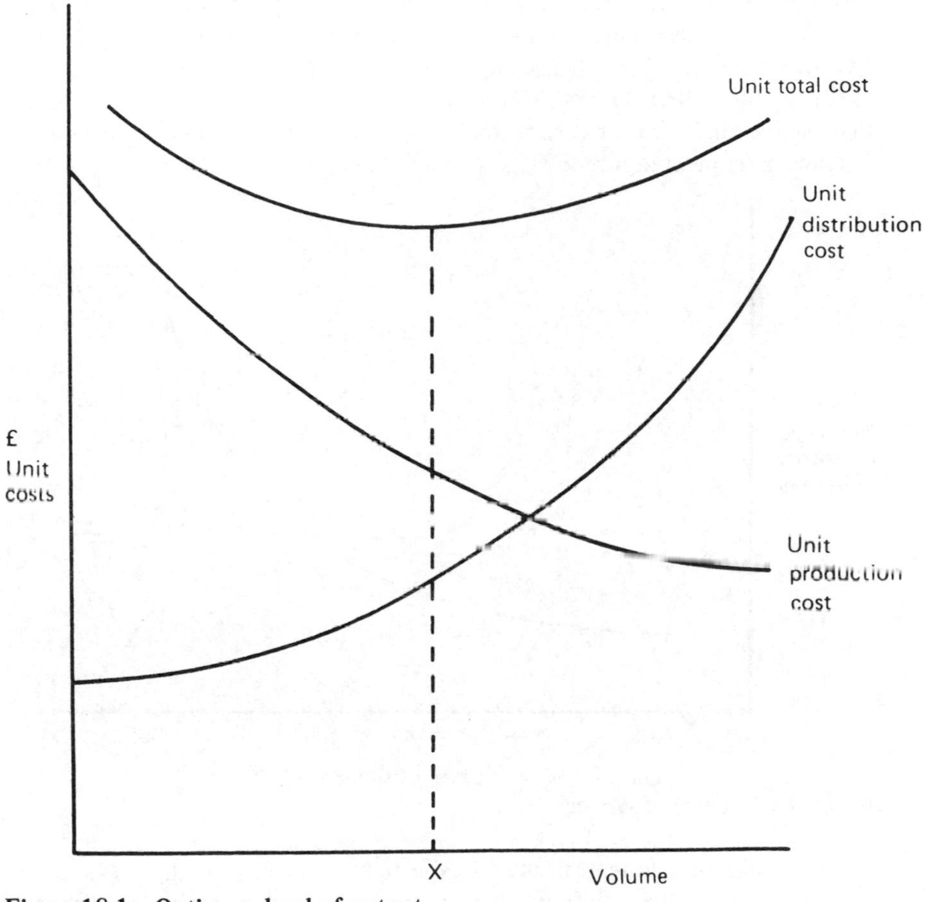

Figure 18.1: Optimum level of output

In general the level of a company's distribution costs will be affected by:

1 The bulk, weight and quantity of goods sold.
2 The nature of these goods and hence their packaging requirements.
3 The location of customers (and hence the destination of the goods).
4 The means of transport employed.
5 The degree of service expected by customers.

The *level of service* is an important determinant of distribution policy and may be defined in terms of either the number of days that it takes the company to deliver an order, or as the proportion of orders that can be filled from stock at any point in time. In order to maximize the level of service offered, a company must have high inventory levels, a large number of warehouses, and a very fast transport facility. This clearly involves a huge commitment of funds, so many companies more economically attempt to comply with the prevailing level of service offered by their competitors.

Taking the definition of the level of service as being the percentage of orders that can be filled from existing stocks, the relationship between this and the required investment in inventory is shown in Figure 18.2.

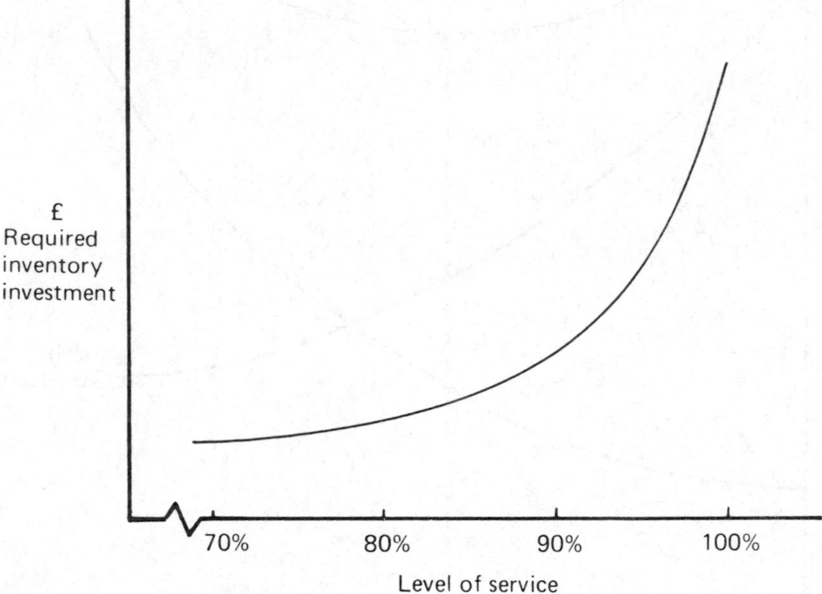

Figure 18.2: Level of service

No company could realistically be expected to provide – at all times – a 100 per cent level of service, but an *efficient* level of service could be established at a more modest point. Efficiency is a more appropriate reference point in this context than are maximum and minimum concepts. To be efficient in PDM requires that costs be looked at as a whole since a reduction of costs in one area may require in compensation a proportional increase in costs in another area. It may, for example, prove to be much less costly, in *total* terms, and more efficient, in terms of achieving a specified level of service (days required to deliver), to use an expensive form of transport (e.g. air freight) than to maintain a number of local warehouses with related inventory costs and administrative expenses.

It is often found that orders are delivered after the promised date, and since this may involve penalties as well as a loss of consumer goodwill, it is easy and helpful to analyze delivery delays as shown in Figure 18.3. Such an analysis serves as a measure of performance and also indicates the size of the control problem – especially if it is related to lost orders and penalties arising from delays.

Delivery pattern	*Number of orders*	*Percentage of total*
As promised	186	37.2
Late: 1 day	71	14.2
2 days	49	9.8
3 days	35	7.0
4 days	38	7.6
5 days	28	5.6
6 days	14	2.8
7 days	13	2.6
8 days	10	2.0
9 days	8	1.6
10 days–2 weeks	17	3.4
2 weeks–3 weeks	15	3.0
3 weeks–4 weeks	10	2.0
4 weeks–5 weeks	6	1.2
TOTAL	500	100.0

Figure 18.3: Delivery control statistics

Apart from the delivery and availability aspects of service, there are several other dimensions which need considering within the combined order-getting and order-filling function. Technical service is an obvious example, as is the arranging of finance for consumers and also the provision of credit. The granting of credit – and the subsequent debt collection process – involves a good deal of screening of acceptable credit risks, late payers/bad debts and so on. (If a company operates on a net profit margin of 5 per cent of sales, a bad debt of £100 due to carelessly extending credit is equivalent to the net profit on sales of £2 000.)

When credit is offered, related costs are the discounts that are offered to encourage prompt payment and the finance charges (i.e. average amount outstanding × interest rate) on the funds outstanding. (See page 513).

Costs of order-filling constitute part of the difference between gross profit and net profit and are not integral product costs. (The tendency is for many order-filling costs to vary with the level of sales activity rather than the level of productive output.) When it comes to budgeting in the area of PDM, the basic data requirements will depend on the distribution methods in use and also on the characteristics of the products being distributed. Typically, however, the following data will be required.

1 Volume of anticipated sales by product line
2 Staffing requirements and rates of pay
3 Distribution methods
4 Distribution expenses, by type of expense
5 Packaging methods and materials.

Standard costs can be developed to cover various categories of labour (being based on standards for each cost centre through which items – or their documentation – pass, or alternatively on an overall distribution labour cost centre); packaging and shipping materials (taking care to distinguish between products that must be dealt with in the normal way and those that must be dealt with specially in accordance with either customers' instructions or, say, export requirements); transport and freight costs that can be directly related to throughput; and distribution overheads, such as rent, rates, insurance, etc.

In this chapter we will look at transport costs and at warehousing costs and consider how they might be controlled. Finally, a brief glance will be given to packaging and evaluating channels of distribution.

TRANSPORT COST CONTROL

Transport activities make up an important segment of the total distribution function, the costs of which (especially since the 1974 oil crisis) have been rising at a faster rate than have other costs. In many companies, transport costs are hidden within general overheads, or expressed as a percentage of production costs. Alternatively, too much attention may be paid to *total* transport costs and too little to unit costs (such as cost per ton, per litre, per ton-mile, ratio of transport cost to turnover and so on). Some companies may seek to provide a high level of service and in so doing overlook the optimum utilization of time and vehicle capacity: this can lead to increases in delivery costs, a reduction in the profit rate and hence a reduction in the level of service.

The imperative urge to control transport costs and operating efficiency in order to remain profitable has caused management in many companies to begin looking more closely at their transport procedures. As with other activities, relevant and regular control information is needed, along with standards of performance as a basis for comparison. This could take the form of cost statements (of the type shown in Figure 18.4) for each vehicle (or group of like vehicles), for workshop activities, and for other overheads. (The content of Figure 18.4 could, of course, relate to costs in total, or to unit costs – i.e. per mile, per ton, etc., – for the period.)

VEHICLE COST STATEMENT						
VEHICLE NUMBER____ TYPE____ PERIOD____						
DEPOT____ PAYLOAD____						
Cost category	*This period*			*Year to date*		
	Actual	*Budget*	*Variance*	*Actual*	*Budget*	*Variance*
1 *Fixed costs* Licences Insurance Depreciation Garaging 2 *Variable costs* Fuel Oil Tyres Maintenance Repairs Other 3 Wages 4 Overheads TOTAL						
TONS CARRIED						
MILES RUN						

Figure 18.4: Vehicle control report

In this discussion it is assumed that the company operates its own distribution service, so no consideration will be given to the policy questions of whether to have one's own fleet or to use outside contractors, although full attention must be paid to the comparative costs of the alternatives. However, whether 'owning' is taken to mean using vehicles under contract hire, leasing them, or owning them outright is immaterial. It will be appreciated that operating a fleet of vehicles involves dealing with a relatively inflexible cost structure regardless of whether one has to contend with monthly lease payments on the one hand, or monthly depreciation charges on the other. Once the decision to operate a vehicle has been made, the costs of licensing, taxing and insuring the vehicle, as well as depreciation (or lease payments) must be met irrespective of the work done. Furthermore, a driver must be employed, and a substantial part of his wages (plus employer's national insurance contribution, etc.) must be paid no matter how much – or how little – work is done. Maintenance is a semi-variable cost depending on both time and mileage, and repairs are difficult to classify. This only leaves fuel, oil, and tyres that are truly variable, so once a decision is made to put a vehicle on the road management automatically limits to a large degree its ability to vary the level of costs that will be incurred due to the existence of the vehicle.

This fact brings us back to the realization that management's contribution to the cost effectiveness of transport activities must be related to maximizing utilization rather than minimizing (or attempting to reduce) costs.

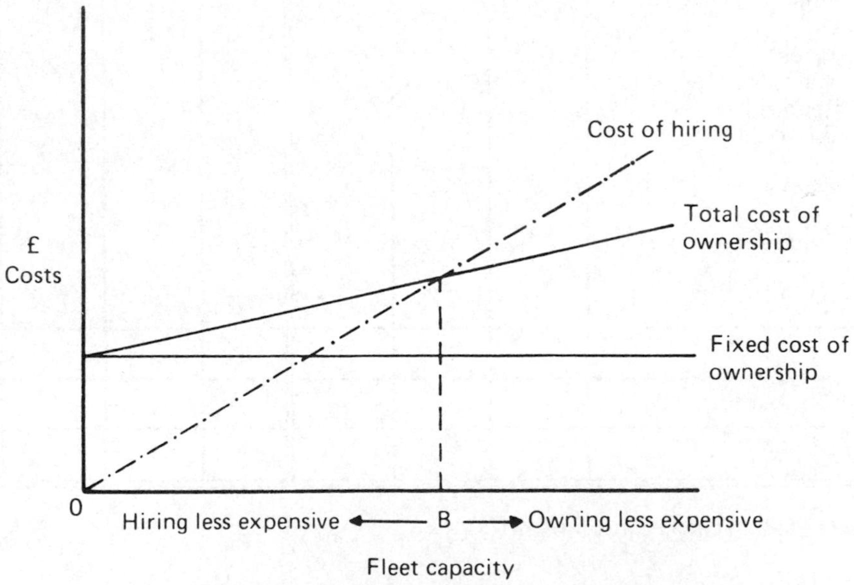

Figure 18.5: Break-even chart for transport

In the usual situation, the transport department within a company will not be in control of the quantity of work that is to be carried out, so the need may arise from time to time for additional transport facilities. This need for extra capacity can be met through the hiring of outside contractors to supplement the company's own fleet, and improving the utilization of company vehicles can help to keep down the cost of outside hire.

Figure 18.5 illustrates the way in which a break-even chart can be used to show the extent to which hiring a vehicle is more favourable (or less favourable) than owning a vehicle. A time dimension must be added for a full analysis to show, for instance, that the capacity owned is fixed at any given point in time: but in principle, as demonstrated via point B in Figure 18.5, there is a range within which it is cheaper to hire required capacity (i.e. the range OB), and beyond which it becomes cheaper to own (i.e. to the right of point B).

Transport operating costs can be classified under the following main headings:

1 Vehicle costs: these can, as we have seen, be split into fixed, mixed and variable costs.
2 Driver costs: apart from payroll-related items, this category will include living-out expenses. Difficulties in recruiting drivers, plus the legal 10 hour limit per day, have caused wages to become much more fixed than used to be the case.
3 Workshop costs: rent, rates, power, fitters' wages and so forth can be built up into a maintenance cost rate and applied to all maintenance and repair jobs. Time is the key factor, so overheads should be related to labour hours, and direct material costs (i.e. spares) added to this. From time to time it is useful to compare one's own workshop rates with outside rates to ensure that benefits are outweighing outside charges in running an in-company vehicle maintenance department.
4 Overhead costs: a fleet of any size will have spare trailers, lorries (i.e. tractors), administration expenses, tarpaulins, ropes, sheets, etc., that are not associated with particular vehicles (hence they are indirect). Such costs can be spread over the fleet on a simple *pro rata* basis. For example, if a company has 5 spare tractors that are additional to its fleet (consisting of 40 tractors) and which cost £3 000 annually to own and maintain, then the cost to apportion to each tractor served would be £3 000 ÷ 40 = £75. Similarly, if there were 20 spare trailers (annual cost £2 400) serving 40 tractors, the apportioned cost per trailer would be £2 400 ÷ 40 = £60. Furthermore, 5 standby drivers costing £6 000 per year and serving 40 tractors would give a cost apportionment of £6 000 ÷ 40 = £150 per unit.

The overhead costs that have just been discussed (i.e. spare trailers, etc.) are quite specific to the transport function, but it is sometimes advocated that other, more general corporate overheads can be apportioned if an attempt is being made to show the profitability of a haulage company's activities for instance. One way in which general overheads can be apportioned is on the basis of payload (i.e. on the basis of relative carrying – hence earning – capacity). If a company has 6 lorries with the following payloads:

2 vehicles @ 20 tons each	=	40 tons
2 vehicles @ 15 tons each	=	30 tons
1 vehicle @ 10 tons	=	10 tons
1 vehicle @ 7 tons	=	7 tons
Total		87 tons

and general overheads amounting to £8 700, then the apportionment per vehicle is:

20-ton vehicle: £ $\frac{8\,700}{87} \times 20 \times 2 =$ £4 000
15-ton vehicle: £ $\frac{8\,700}{87} \times 15 \times 2 =$ £3 000
10-ton vehicle: £ $\frac{8\,700}{87} \times 10 \times 1 =$ £1 000
7-ton vehicle: £ $\frac{8\,700}{87} \times 7 \times 1 =$ £700
Total £8 700

A simpler method, of course, is to spread these general overheads on the basis of the number of vehicles: thus

$$\text{apportionment} = \frac{\text{general overheads}}{\text{number of vehicles}} = \frac{8\,700}{6} = £1\,450$$

However, this is extremely unrealistic since it burdens a 7-ton lorry with the same amount of general overhead cost as a 20-ton lorry.

The above argument has assumed implicitly that the fleet capacity is fully utilized, but this may not be the case. If 100 per cent of capacity is not to be used, some allowance must be made for this. Figure 18.6 shows how this might be done.

Vehicle	*Capacity*	*Budgeted capacity utilization*	*Budgeted payload*	*Overhead apportionment*
	tons	per cent	tons	
1	20	85	17	17/75 × £8 700 = £1 972
2	20	85	17	17/75 × £8 700 = £1 972
3	15	86	13	13/75 × £8 700 = £1 508
4	15	86	13	13/75 × £8 700 = £1 508
5	10	90	9	9/75 × £8 700 = £1 044
6	7	86	6	6/76 × £8 700 = £696
Totals	87		75	£8 700

Figure 18.6: Fleet capacity utilization and apportionment

The budgeted degree of capacity utilization can be determined from the projected vehicle activity based on orders (or historical data). Return journeys are a frequent source of lost capacity.

Again the discussion has highlighted the importance of output (i.e. activity) over cost in securing efficient operations. Physical loads rather simplify the picture because they suggest that the end result of the transport activity is the same as the end result of the production process, but this is not so. Essentially, what the transport function does is to change the location of goods and thereby create a particular level of utility as opposed to creating the goods themselves.

The measurement of the 'output' of the transport activity requires the combining of the distance over which the goods are transported and the quantity and nature of the goods moved to each delivery point. It will be appreciated, however, that the relationship between these factors and the level of operating costs is complex. For example, the greater the distance over which goods are moved, the greater the cost is likely to be; but the cost of running a vehicle is affected by both distance *and* time, thus it may cost the same to run a lorry 200 miles in 4 hours on a motorway as it does to run the same lorry 150 miles in 5 hours on ordinary roads. (The availability of the vehicle and the driver are not considered to be variable in this context. From this it will often follow that a journey taking, say, 90 per cent of a driver's legal working day limit will mean that no further work can be done that day, and a journey that just extends into a second working day will cause a disproportionate increase in cost due to paying for a driver's lodging and also the disruption of the second day's work.)

Mileage charges can readily be computed for each type of vehicle in use in the following way:

Fuel: cost per gallon ÷ miles per gallon
Oil: cost per pint ÷ miles per pint
Tyres: cost ÷ average mileage
Maintenance: budgeted cost ÷ average annual mileage

These costs are the ones that have some variability with mileage, but the costs that vary with time can be related to time (on a cost per day or cost per hour basis):

Road licences: annual cost ÷ operating days/hours
Insurance: annual cost ÷ operating days/hours
Depreciation: annual cost ÷ operating days/hours
Garaging: annual cost ÷ operating days/hours
HP interest: annual cost ÷ operating days/hours
Fleet overheads: annual cost ÷ operating days/hours
General overheads: annual cost ÷ operating days/hours

Whenever cost estimates are being prepared, due allowance should be given to inflationary and other expected cost increases. In this respect, for example, depreciation rates should be based on replacement values rather than on book or original cost figures.

Apart from cost per mile and cost per day figures, the quantity of goods moved also has an effect on costs (although this may be complex). The size of each delivery is one aspect of this situation: it obviously costs more to deliver 100 tons of products to 20 customers than to a single customer. Similarly, the nature of the product has a bearing on its transportation costs: bulky products tend to be comparatively expensive to transport since they prevent effective utilization of space and may require extensive packaging.

Care must be taken in attempting to establish any rate. An obvious example is that of a rate per mile, which is given by dividing expected costs by expected mileage (as with fuel, oil, etc., shown above). But the higher the mileage run the lower is the cost per mile. If a vehicle travels 40 000 miles during one year, the number of operating days is 242, and the total vehicle cost is £4 840, then the average daily mileage will be 40 000 ÷ 242 ≑ 165 miles. The rate per mile is £4 840 ÷ 40 000 = 12.1p, giving a daily cost rate of £19.96 for 165 miles. However, if the annual mileage differs, the daily budget will vary, and clearly the cost per mile will vary. Examples are (for a year of 242 working days):

Annual mileage	*Daily mileage*	*Annual cost*	*Cost per mile*
40 000	165	£4 840	12.1p
24 200	100	£4 840	20.0p
20 086	83	£4 840	24.2p
12 100	50	£4 840	40.0p

(It is assumed that all costs are fixed, which over-simplifies, but the general point is clearly made.)

To be effective as a measure of efficiency, a unit of measure (of performance) that takes account of at least the most significant of the variable factors should be used. The classic ton-mile is one such unit that seeks to give effect to the variations in both weight and distance: its use can be valuable when dealing with the movement of goods, in full vehicle loads, between a limited number of points.

Figure 18.7 shows an example of a ton-mile calculation, and it is evident that the more drops on a delivery run, the more difficult is the computation.

Destination	*Miles*	*Tons moved*		*Ton miles*	
		Period 1	*Period 2*	*Period 1*	*Period 2*
Birmingham	110	500	700	55 000	77 000
Leeds	190	800	800	152 000	152 000
Manchester	184	700	550	128 800	101 200
Newcastle	273	600	550	163 800	150 150
		2 600	2 600	499 600	480 350

Figure 18.7: Ton-mile computation – 1

The detail that is necessary in computing every delivery in a multi-drop route is highlighted in Figure 18.8.

Destination (1)	*Miles* (2)	*Tons delivered* (3)	*Load (tons)* (4)	*Ton miles* (2) × (4)
A	10	2	17	170
B	15	5	15	225
C	25	1	10	250
D	5	7	9	45
E	10	2	2	20
Base	15	0	0	0
		17		710

Figure 18.8: Ton-mile computation – 2

One way of simplifying the analysis is to record deliveries by ***area*** rather than by specific destination. This can be transformed into a ton-mile approximation if the quantity for the area is multiplied by the distance from the central point (or major city) in the previous area to the corresponding point in the current area. This is illustrated in Figure 18.9.

Area	*Tons delivered*		*Miles*	*Product (ton miles)*	
	Period 1	*Period 2*		*Period 1*	*Period 2*
A	50	70	20	1 000	1400
B	70	70	50	3 500	3 500
C	50	40	70	3 500	2 800
D	80	100	90	7 200	9 000
E	150	120	100	15 000	12 000
	400	400		30 200	28 700

Figure 18.9: Ton-mile computation – 3

In addition to cost and quantity measures of the types discussed above, work-study techniques can be applied to derive standard times for each of the main factors that make up a vehicle's working day. Representative examples are:

1 Running times (minutes per mile either as an average, or specific standards for different areas/types of road).

2 Delivery times (perhaps expressed as a time per delivery plus an allowance per ton or per pack delivered).

3 Loading times. (Apart from timing considerations of the work-study variety, loading should not be done during delivery hours – it is cheaper to do it early in the morning, or during the evening or night; and labourers rather than drivers should carry out the loading).

A further measure is to derive a 'cost per standard hour', and a whole range of ratios of one kind and another can be produced.

Having appreciated the need for setting desired levels of performance, and having established appropriate standards, it remains to design a reporting system that will permit cost control and facilitate future planning. Such a system will probably include reports of the following nature:

1 Daily log sheet, showing details of times, destinations, tons carried, miles run, drops made, fuel/oil used, etc.
2 Fuel and oil report, showing quantities, price, etc., for each vehicle and the relationship with mileage.
3 Repairs and maintenance report, showing the nature of faults, regularity of servicing, labour and parts charges, etc.
4 Vehicle record sheet, summarizing 1–3 above, and also including driver's wages and expenses, and any other data thought relevant.
5 Vehicle cost sheet, being a cost summary of 4.
6 Fleet cost sheet, being the summation of vehicle cost sheets for the whole fleet analysed to show fixed and variable costs separately.
7 Workshop operating statement, giving details of maintenance time, costs, etc.
8 Expense statement, which is a combined overall summary setting out direct and indirect fleet costs along with any general overhead apportionment. As with other reports, budget comparisons should be shown.

Ratio analysis, which was discussed at length in Chapter 12, can be applied to the control of transport costs. As an example we can consider the scheme operated by the Centre for Interfirm Comparison for members of the Road Haulage Association, which fits the current context of transport cost control. Figure 18.10 outlines the ratios that influence a road haulier's major costs. By working logically through the constituents of this pyramid, and by associating it with the broader range of comparative ratios within the CIFC/RHA scheme, it should be possible to gain a better understanding of how high one's haulage costs are and why they are at this level. From that point it is possible to consider how the situation can be improved.

CHECKLIST ON TRANSPORT

1 Have the costs of having a company-owned transport function been compared with the costs of using outside contractors?
2 Are the best means of transport (from both cost and service viewpoints) used for different products?
3 Are increases in transport costs considered to be unavoidable and thus

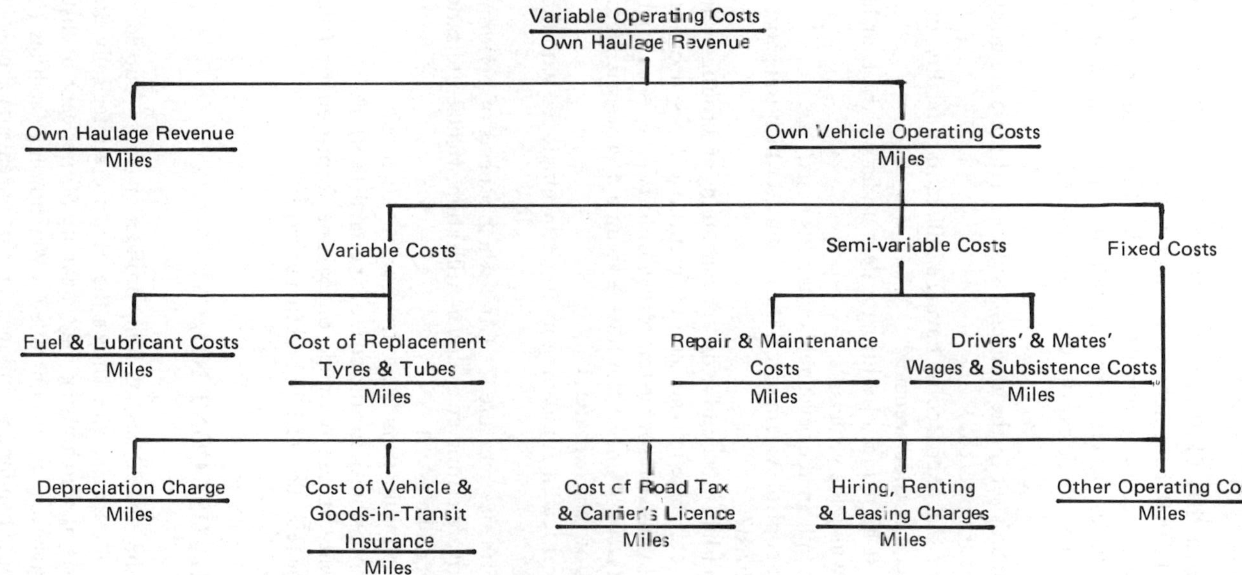

Figure 18.10: Road haulage ratios

passed on to customers without studying the efficiency of transport activities?

4 Is it appreciated that £100 saved in transport costs will be equivalent to extra sales of £1 000 if the net profit margin is 10 per cent?

5 Are *all* transport costs accounted for under the heading of transport?

6 Can those vehicles having disproportionately high operating costs (in relation to other vehicles of the same make, age, and capacity) be identified?

7 How are standards set in the transport sphere? (If there are no standards, should they be introduced?)

8 Is control over fuel exercised by having a bulk storage facility, or does the company rely on outside agencies?

9 Could any cost be reduced by hiring a fleet under contract, or leasing it, rather than owning the vehicles?

10 Is maintenance planned or available on a crisis basis?

11 Does the cost control system reveal the extent to which transport facilities are under-utilized?

12 Does an established procedure exist for scheduling and routing vehicles?

13 Does routing, etc., take into account different road types, urban areas, etc?

14 Is the most expensive resource (e.g. driver or lorry) the focus of attention?

15 Is the capacity constraint of the fleet a volume or a weight factor? (Are the right sizes of vehicle in use?)

16 Can mechanical loading/unloading methods be employed with the type of vehicles in use?

17 How is performance measured? (And which aspects of performance are measured? Driver performance, driver utilization, vehicle utilization, delay time, etc., can all be used.)

18 What follow-up results from the extraction of variances?

19 Who takes responsibility for the cost of special deliveries?

20 To what extent can use be made of existing forms/reports (such as log sheets, mileage records, etc.), in building up costs?

WAREHOUSING COST CONTROL

An emphasis on the economics of long production runs coupled with the demand for a high level of service shows the need for strategically-sited warehouses, and the costs of warehousing may make up 50 per cent of distribution costs, so they must be carefully controlled. Warehousing facilities (including their location, layout, handling techniques, and management) should be suited to the particular requirements of the company and its products. Budgets can be prepared along the lines suggested in, for example, Chapter 8, and standard costs can be used – especially in high-volume situations. Let us take an example of the use of standard costing for warehouse labour. If a standard rate of 5p per 100 kilos handled exists (being based on fixed costs of £1 800 per month plus variable costs of 2p per 100 kilos) and if 7 000 000 kilos were handled in the warehouse during a given month at a total cost of £3 400, the analysis is as follows

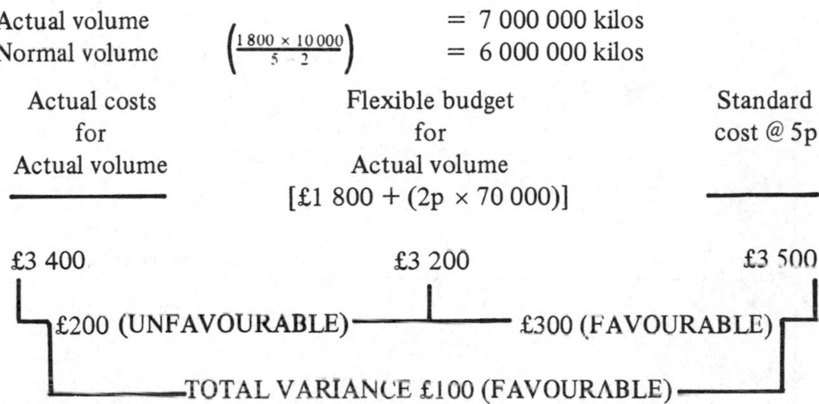

This analysis employs the flexible budget method, and the total variance of £100 (favourable) is seen to be made up of an unfavourable budget variance of £200 and a favourable capacity variance of £300 (due to operating at a higher level than 'normal' capacity).

Cost-volume-profit analysis can be employed in connection with warehousing activities. For example, when deciding whether to own or lease warehouse space it is obvious that variable space requirements favour leasing (whereby only sufficient for a given period is leased) whilst stable demand tends to favour ownership. Figure 18.11 illustrates a simple analysis of the cost patterns involved. Ownership costs are partly fixed and partly variable, and leasing costs are wholly variable: the outcome is that if the inventory level (as shown in Figure 18.11) is required (or expected) to be less than OB it is cheaper to lease warehousing space, but if the inventory level is likely to exceed OB, then it is cheaper to own the facilities. (Obviously there are further considerations other than purely the one of cost.)

A link exists between transport and warehousing in that regional warehouses should be established if savings in direct delivery costs from a central warehouse to customers, plus an increase in patronage from faster local delivery, exceed the incremental costs of operating the warehouse.

Within the warehouse, materials handling has absorbed a good deal of time and money in recent years (and in some cases its comparative importance has gradually come to equal that of the production process, although the fully auto-

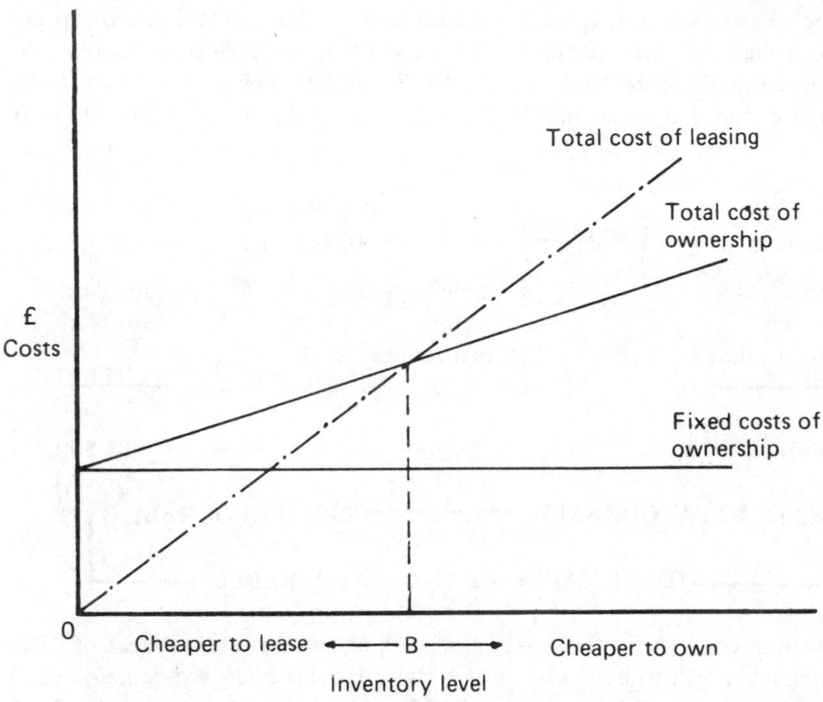

Figure 18.11: Break-even chart for warehousing

mated warehouse remains something of a rarity).

Strictly, materials handling is one branch of work study and many of its problems can be resolved by applying work study techniques. The importance of cost control in the materials handling function becomes apparent when one realizes that handling materials increases their costs without adding to the value of the materials handled. It follows that the cheapest way to handle materials is not to handle them – or at least not to handle them unnecessarily. Materials handling, dealing as it does with moving raw materials and despatches to customers, plus all stages in between, is the backbone of the manufacturing-distribution cycle. At least 25 per cent of the finished cost of a product will normally be attributable to material handling activities. (In fact, the quickest and cheapest way to improving productivity may well be found in improving materials handling methods.) If the need for handling materials can be controlled and reduced, then the costs of this function can also be controlled and reduced. This can be achieved if all unnecessary and indirect movements are eliminated and if the most effective handling methods are used for the inevitable movements.

Expensive labour (e.g. drivers) should not be used to load lorries: labourers should be used. Single items should be moved in batches rather than individually. (The grouping together of a quantity of items to form a single unit – ideally of the same dimensions and other physical characteristics as will optimize the cost of handling and transport throughout the distribution chain – constitutes a *unit load*. This concept really starts at the product design stage and ends at the point of delivery to the consumer. The range of methods of unitization is large – containers at one extreme, through pallets to cartons and shrink-wrapped groupings at the other extreme. Whichever means is best in a given situation will depend on the circumstances of that situation.)

Poor material handling practices cause congestion in the warehouse, which leads to wasted time and all of this adds to cost. Suitable equipment, in the form of fork-lift trucks, gravity conveyors, power conveyors, lifts, hoists, cranes, monorails, etc., can be used to cost-saving advantage. Considerations involved in selecting materials handling equipment include, of course, its cost, but also the characteristics of the goods to be moved, the speed of the equipment, the quantity of goods to be moved, the storage procedures currently in use, the reliability/capacity of the equipment and its compatibility with existing equipment/facilities.

Inventories and their control

For any asset (cash, inventories, machines) there is an optimum level of investment below which opportunities are lost through having too little of the asset, and above which more opportunities are lost through idleness of excess assets or an inability (due to inflexibility) to transfer one type of asset into another use (e.g. excess inventories would have to be sold, and the resulting funds applied to buying new plant if this was seen as being a more favourable allocation of resources, but this takes time). Idle assets or non-existent assets (as exemplified by inventories that are too high or too low) cannot earn a return, which involves the cost of lost opportunities. Inventory management should aim to facilitate the manufacturing-distribution-marketing cycle at minimum cost for a given level of service.

The costs that can be associated with inventories that are too large are:

1 Loss of a return on the capital tied up in excess stocks
2 Risks from obsolescence
3 Storage costs
4 Handling costs
5 Clerical costs
6 Insurance premiums.

On the other hand, if inventories are too low, production may be disrupted by short runs for urgently required items, and sales may be lost due to the lack of availability of goods when they are required. The costs that stem from low inventories include:

1 The profit element in foregone sales
2 Foregone purchase discounts
3 Loss of customer goodwill
4 Increased unit costs of purchasing and transportation
5 Extra costs of uneconomic production runs.

In formulating an inventory policy for finished goods, management must take into account at least the following points:

1 The perishability of the goods
2 The demand pattern (i.e. sales requirements)
3 The length of the production/order cycle
4 Storage facilities (including capacity)
5 Carrying costs
6 Capital requirements
7 The risks due to possible shortages/price increases/price reductions/ technological obsolescence/change in tastes/theft.

Following this, two major questions must be answered:

1 How much to order
2 When to order.

The first question will now be discussed. The amount of inventory to be ordered (either as a call on productive output or via a purchase order to an outside supplier) will directly influence the frequency of ordering (i.e. an annual demand of 20 000 units may require one order of 20 000 units for stock, 20 000 orders of one unit, or something in between). Since placing an order involves costs (stamps, order forms, envelopes, machine accounting time, clerical and supervisory time in raising and checking the order, and so on, when an order is to be placed with an outside supplier, and set-up costs for manufacture, order forms, machine accounting time, clerical and supervisory time, etc., when the order is an internal one) and holding inventories also involves costs (the larger the inventory the larger are the costs of storage capacity, capital charges such as interest, rates, insurance, depreciation, etc.), the decision as to how much to order must come from a balancing of two opposing effects.

Figure 18.12 shows the inventory carrying cost curve rising with the amount of inventory (i.e. size of order) and it also shows the cost of ordering falling the larger the order size (i.e. the fewer the number of orders per period).

If the two costs are summated into a total inventory cost curve, the optimum order size is given by this curve's lowest point: the answer to the question how much to order is given by point X (as shown in Figure 18.12).

In addition to this graphical analysis, a simple formula can be employed to compute the economic order quantity (EOQ) given by point X. The formula is:

$$X = \sqrt{\frac{2QP}{S}}$$

where

X = economic order quantity (in units)
Q = annual usage (in units)
P = cost of placing an order
S = annual storage cost per unit

The number of orders required per period is given by $Q \div X$. Clearly, from this equation, X will increase as either Q or P grows larger, or as S decreases, and vice versa. Furthermore, the true reorder quantity (X) is determined by means of this formula regardless of discrete periods of time. This can be illustrated by Figure 18.13 (p. 568) which shows a hypothetical reorder situation.

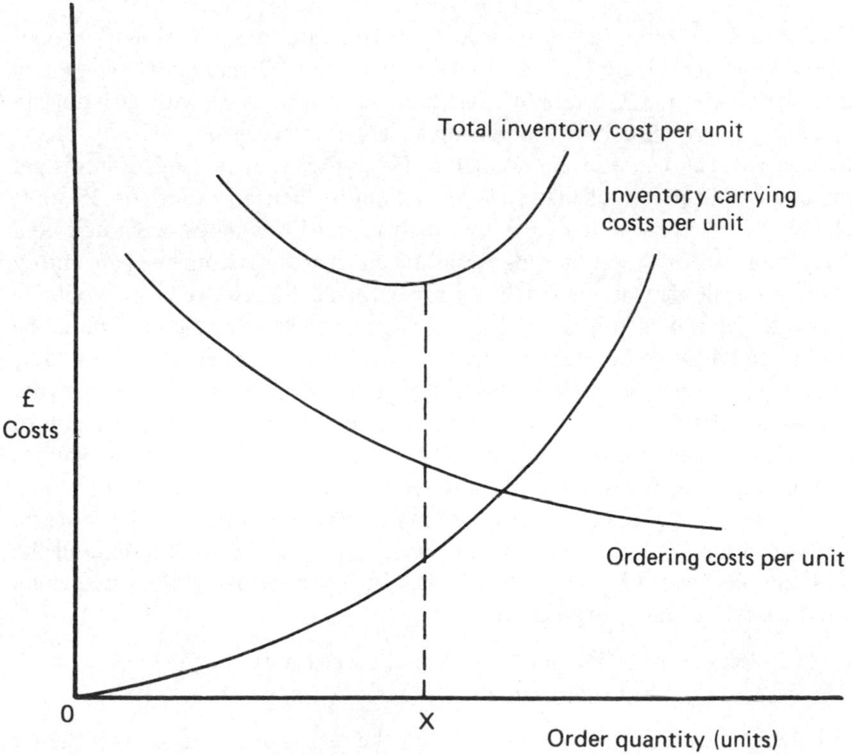

Figure 18.12: Inventory cost curves

The best frequency of ordering appears to be 4 orders per annum giving a total inventory cost of £1 700. However, it may be the case that the optimum situation is not given in Figure 18.13 because it falls outside the specified frequencies or order size (e.g. it may be 3½ months' supply) and the formula method will precisely identify the solution.

Number of months' supply per order	1	2	3	4	6	12
Orders per annum	12	6	4	3	2	1
Average inventory costs	£1 500	£3 000	£4 500	£6 000	£9 000	£12 000
Annual order costs @ £200	£2 400	£1 200	£800	£600	£400	£200
Annual carrying costs @ 20%	£300	£600	£900	£1 200	£1 800	£3 600
Total costs	£2 700	£1 800	£1 700	£1 800	£2 200	£3 800

Figure 18.13: Annual inventory costs

The second question, 'when to order', requires a study of the rate of usage of the item under consideration. In the formula above Q represents the annual usage, but variations in the rate of usage during the year, along with variations in lead time (i.e. the time between placing an order and receiving delivery of the items ordered) can cause severe problems. If usage is steady at, say, 50 units per month, and delivery is reliable at twice a month, then an order for 25 units could be placed every half month in anticipation of the goods being delivered before the inventory ran out: this would mean that the last units of inventory were used on the day the new delivery arrived, and the reorder point would be an inventory level of 25 units (in other words, a new order for 25 units would be placed when the last order was delivered, and the usage between orders would be exactly equal to the quantity of each delivery). This, however, is somewhat unrealistic: variations will be unavoidable in delivery schedules and the rate of usage, with the result that stock-outs will arise from time to time as well as situations involving overstocking. To counter the disruptive danger of stock-outs, it is common practice to have a safety stock. An order will therefore be placed when the level of inventory has fallen to the safety stock level, and the size of the order will be given by the EOQ. The relationship between usage rate and lead time is given by the formula:

Reorder point (in units) = rate of usage (units per day) ×
lead time (days) + safety stock (in units)

Figure 18.14 illustrates the reorder point in the usual conditions of uncertainty in which a safety stock is needed. An order will be placed at point X and

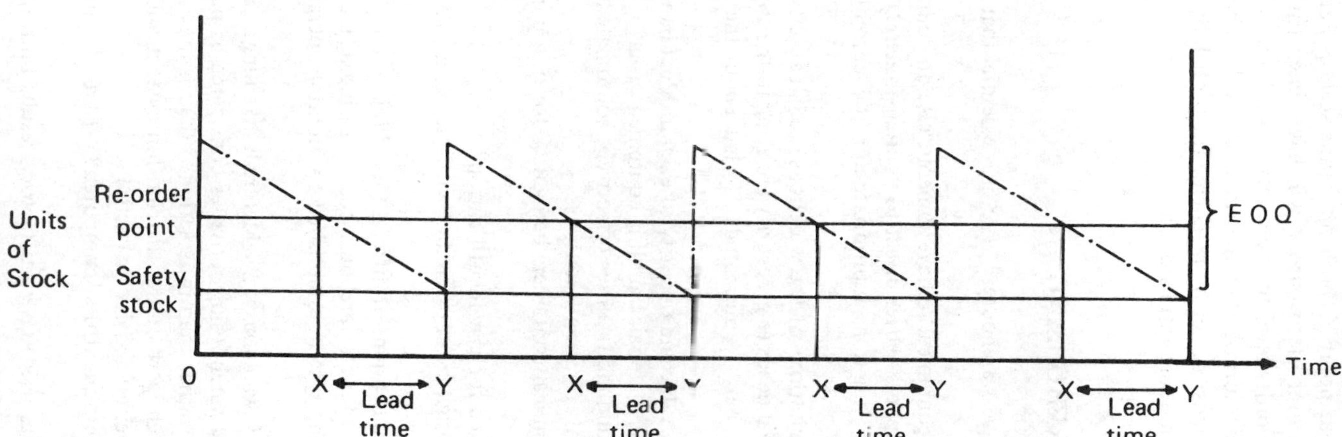

Figure 18.14: Reorder points

delivery will be expected at point Y (both on a time scale). Between ordering and receiving goods the level of inventory will have fallen (in conditions of normal usage) from the reorder level to the safety stock level. If, however, the rate of usage is greater than normal, then the stock level will be below the safety level, so the safety stock must be set by balancing the probability of a high rate of usage with the costs of holding extra stocks.

CHECKLIST ON WAREHOUSING

1 Is it necessary to have warehouses? (i.e. is it essential that finished goods stocks be held?)
2 Would it be more economical to have someone else do your stockholding? (e.g. could your suppliers deliver direct to your customers?)
3 Is the warehousing function appropriate for the current (and future) distribution system?
4 Are the physical limitations of the warehouse (e.g. capacity) appreciated, along with any special needs (e.g. security) relating to the stock?
5 Is order-picking manual or automated? (What about the preparation of picking lists?)
6 Are the size, weight, value and quantity of each product handled known?
7 Is the most economic materials handling equipment used?
8 Are the materials handling facilities effectively coordinated with both the manufacturing and distribution functions?
9 Are the most economical containers being used for transporting each type of product?
10 Are containers marked for easy identification?
11 Could packaging design be coordinated with materials handling? (Do all items need packaging?)
12 What are the cost implications of different handling systems?
13 Are budgets prepared for all warehouse costs – including maintenance, etc?
14 Is a suitable reporting system established to monitor operations and their costs?
15 What is the aim of warehousing? Materials handling? Stock control?
16 Are the costs of all warehousing activities considered as part of the total cost of distribution rather than in isolation? (e.g. is the cost relationship known between each part of the distribution system and the effect of various different levels of activity on each?)
17 Are economic order quantities computed? (Are the underlying data reliable?)
18 Do reorder points (as used) give satisfactory results both in cost terms as well as in the level of service?

19 Is one manager responsible for the whole of the warehousing/stock control system?
20 Have attempts been made to develop standard costs within the warehousing function?

OTHER ASPECTS OF DISTRIBUTION

In this section one or two aspects of packaging and channel evaluation will be covered in brief. The remaining activities within distribution (such as order-processing and administration) can be treated under the suggestions of Chapter 14.

Packaging is an important element in physical distribution management, and decisions connected with designing a new pack (or modifying an old one) should not be taken without considering the impact that this might have on all other parts of the distribution system.

In addition to the obvious marketing requirement that a pack should help promote the product, there are other features of packaging that should be borne in mind. For example, the structure of the package should ensure that the product (or the handler) is protected: water vapour, grease, pilferage, infestation, odour, contamination, light, and so on, must all be taken into account in matching packaging characteristics and strengths with product requirements.

Pack design can secure significant savings in transport and warehousing costs, but this requires that packaging questions be related to the overall requirements of the distribution system. A cheap pack will save on packaging costs but may double some other costs in the system. An adequate pack for its purpose must be provided – irrespective of cost.

There can be a certain amount of ambiguity over the purpose of a pack in some instances: is the pack an integral part of the product, a marketing feature, or a distribution requirement? Obviously the answer will vary depending on the nature of the product. If a product is incomplete without a pack (e.g. a can of peas, a bar of chocolate, or a box of matches) then the pack can be treated as a manufacturing cost and becomes part of the prime cost of production. Special wrappers (e.g. on banded packs) are a marketing expense and packages that are only required for distribution (e.g. cartons for despatching items requested from a mail order house) are clearly a cost of distribution. Standards and budgets can be developed for all packaging materials and the associated labour and related expenses.

Channels of distribution (i.e. the sequence of intermediaries between the manufacturer and the final consumer), once selected and established, involve the company in relatively long-term commitments to other organizations (such as wholesalers and retailers) as well as affecting in a very significant manner every other major marketing decision. It is important, therefore, to ensure that the implications of each alternative channel are carefully evaluated. In particular, this will mean considering:

1 Economic criteria, which are perhaps the most important, and which determine the pattern and levels of costs, sales and profit. As each alternative channel is likely to produce different levels of sales and costs, the best alternative is not that producing the most or the least respectively, but the one that produces the best relationship between the two – profit.
2 Control criteria, which relate to the degree of influence, motivation, and conflict amongst channel participants. An agent who handles many different manufacturers' lines will probably not be seen favourably by manufacturer A because the agent will put his own interests ahead of A's in endeavouring to sell *any* line – not just A's – and this can lead to friction.
3 Adaptive criteria, by which the manufacturer is able to preserve his flexibility in response to changing conditions. Long-term franchise agreements are antithetical to adaptive behaviour within channels of distribution.

Whilst accepting that a variety of criteria are relevant in choosing a channel of distribution, the economic criteria can be evaluated broadly by means of a break-even chart. In Figure 18.15 the choice between using a sales agent and establishing a branch sales office is depicted. The level of fixed costs of the former (in the form of a retainer) will probably be less than the fixed costs of the latter (in the form of rent, salaries, etc.) but the variable cost of the agent (i.e. commission) will be greater per unit sold than will be the case with the

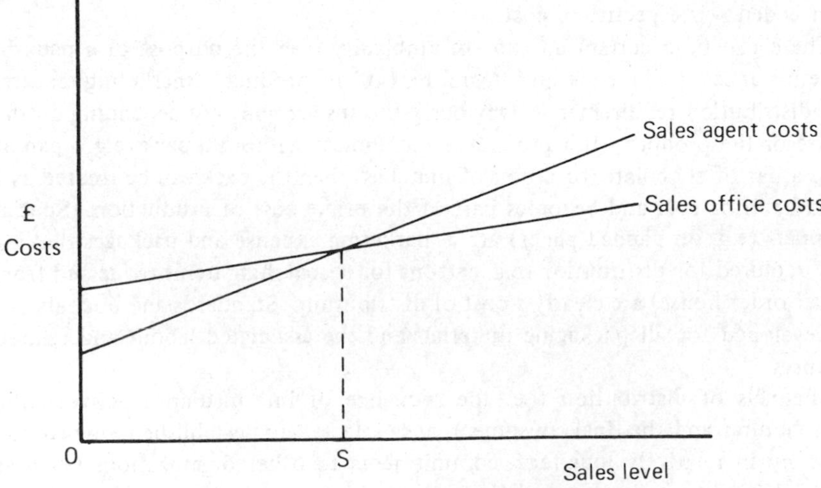

Figure 18.15 : Break-even chart for channel decisions

branch office's variable costs. If the level of sales is expected to be below point S on the horizontal scale, then a sales agency arrangement is preferable financially, but otherwise a branch office is to be preferred.

If a company has, say, four channels of distribution in operation, the cost pattern of each can be identified by means of the relevant costing approach. This requires that the variable and separable fixed costs appertaining to each channel be allocated to them, and the result will be contribution (by channel) to the non-separable fixed costs. A hypothetical set of figures is given in Figure 18.16.

Figure 18.16 demonstrates that channel C is distinctly unprofitable and channel B is neither profitable nor unprofitable (i.e. a break-even situation). By eliminating channel C the variable and separable fixed costs incurred in connection with this channel will be eliminated – as will the sales revenue – and net profit will improve by £1 000 (as shown in Figure 18.17).

Eliminating channel B would bring no benefit, and if some new initiatives can be taken within channel B it may be possible to make it profitable (e.g. by improving efficiency and thereby reducing costs and improving its contribution).

		Channels			
	Total	A	B	C	D
Sales revenue	37 000	6 000	7 000	5 000	19 000
Variable costs	15 000	1 000	3 000	4 000	7 000
Separable fixed costs	14 000	3 000	4 000	2 000	5 000
Contribution	8 000	2 000	0	−1 000	7 000
Non-separable costs	5 000				
Net profit	£3 000				

Figure 18.16: Channel profitability – 1

		Channel		
	Total	A	B	D
Sales revenue	32 000	6 000	7 000	19 000
Variable costs	11 000	1 000	3 000	7 000
Separable fixed costs	12 000	3 000	4 000	5 000
Contribution	9 000	2 000	0	7 000
Non-separable costs	5 000			
Net profit	£4 000			

Figure 18.17: Channel profitability – 2

GENERAL CHECKLIST

1 What information is available on transport costs? (e.g. are figures available for fleet costs, postal charges, rail transport, road transport, sea transport, air freight, forwarding agents' fees, etc?)
2 Are distribution costs broken down into home and export markets?
3 What information is available on warehouse costs? (e.g. can costs be compiled for handling goods received; holding stocks; ordering stock; locating, retrieving and picking; etc?)
4 Are packing and packaging costs known?
5 Are materials handling costs known?
6 Can *all* PDM costs be identified?
7 Is it appreciated that concentrating on the control (or reduction) of costs in one area of distribution without considering all other distribution costs is a mistake?
8 Are standards, budgets, etc., prepared for all distribution costs on the basis of cost behaviour studies?
9 What level of service is to be given? And what cost constraint is to prevail?
10 How do stock levels (hence inventory costs) respond to different levels of service?
11 Are forecasting procedures adequate for efficiently planning distribution activities?
12 Is the existing organization structure capable of ensuring coordinated PDM? And is PDM integrated with manufacturing and marketing?
13 Are packages designed for the characteristics of their contents and the requirements of the distribution process?
14 Do packaging materials give the required protection and are they structurally adequate and readily available?
15 Can packages be formed, filled, and closed with existing equipment? (Would it be better to change package sizes/form rather than buy new equipment?)
16 Is the unit pack suitable for making up into cases? Is the pack convenient for wholesalers, retailers, and consumers?
17 Does the pack have all the required consumer benefits? (i.e. size, disposability, use when empty, storage, visibility of contents, resealing, etc.)
18 Is the package cost in proper proportion with the use to which it is put? (Does this include congruence with the market image of the product showing that the pack has been considered from the point of view of identifying the product, informing potential consumers of the product's attributes and inviting attention?)
19 Is a credit policy properly formulated?
20 How and on what basis are bad debts provided for in budgets? Is this basis valid?

21 How much working capital is to be allowed for credit extension? On what terms?
22 Are all new accounts screened for credit status and existing accounts re-evaluated regularly?
23 Are credit limits established for every account?
24 How many days, on average, are one day's credit sales outstanding?
25 Is there a routine for dealing with creditors who fail to pay, or overreach their credit limit? Does this include using an agency and regular court proceedings?

Finally, regard should be paid to the pyramid method of ratio analysis which can be applied to the distribution function. The Centre for Interfirm Comparison has demonstrated this in the series of Distribution Cost Comparisons which it has been conducting since the early 1970s.

The comparison was initially designed for manufacturers of fast moving consumer non-durables (food, drink, tobacco, pharmaceuticals/toiletries, household goods, etc.), where the requirements of customer service as well as the physical scale and cost of the operation make distribution one of the most important functions in the company, rather than a 'Cinderella' function.

The series of comparisons still continues for manufacturers in the consumer non-durable sector but the Centre has found that the techniques can be applied to other product categories, and also to carriers providing distribution services.

The aims of the comparison are to enable firms to find out how their distribution costs compare with those of other firms; to discover the reasons for differences in performance; to identify areas of weakness; and to encourage firms to take action in the right areas to reduce costs or to increase the effectiveness of the distribution function.

The first stage in this process involves the preparation by the Centre of an extremely detailed report showing each company how its distribution performance compares with that of fifteen to twenty other similar but anonymous companies. This report leads on to plans for remedial action, following discussion of the comparison results with the Centre's staff and probably also after further internal investigations by the company itself.

The initial report showing the results of the comparison is presented in seven tables, with the first three being devoted to a detailed cost analysis. Comparative cost information is provided in the form of an integrated pyramid or ratios. The primary ratio of total distribution costs per unit of throughput is calculated in three ways: in terms of tonnage, the number of cases delivered, and the volume in cubic feet. Differences between each company's primary ratios can be explained with the help of the subsidiary ratios which become progressively more detailed, thus allowing a systematic analysis of performance to be made.

An example of the method of making a progressively more detailed analysis is shown in Figure 18.18. The large pyramid shows the initial breakdown of the principal cost areas. A similar diagram (inset) shows how one of these cost headings – delivery costs – can be further analyzed into a number of explanatory ratios. For example, taking delivery costs per tonne, it can be shown that there is a simple arithmetic relationship between this and two further ratios which measure costs on the one hand and output on the other (i.e. delivery costs per mile and tonnes delivered per mile). The tonnes per mile ratio can be further analyzed into two ratios where there is again a simple arithmetic relationship: the size of the average drop and the distance between drops. These ratios build up into a simple integrated pyramid where the ratios at the higher levels can be explained by the values of the subsidiary ratios.

In industries where distribution is an important part of the marketing effort, its effectiveness cannot be measured purely in terms of cost. It must also be viewed in the context of the service levels provided, the types of outlets used, typical drop sizes, and other factors such as the degree of capital investment with which the distribution function is provided. The Centre's comparisons therefore include information on these and on other relevant items.

It should be noted that the CIFC scheme excludes inventory costs and the costs of 'communications' (such as order-processing, invoicing and credit control), and to this extent it offers only a partial analysis of distribution costs.

SUMMARY

Physical distribution management should be seen as an integrated set of activities which are vital in linking manufacturing and marketing.

Cost control requires budgets and standards for comparison and establishing these is relatively straightforward within the various aspects of PDM.

The level of service sets a basic parameter for distribution activities and the higher the level of service the higher will be the level of costs. It is imperative that *all* costs be taken into account in planning to achieve the target level of service: a change in one cost element in isolation of a consideration of repercussions throughout the system is incorrect and shortsighted.

Transport services have a good deal in common with some features of production, as have warehousing activities. With transport costs the aim should be to maximize utilization rather than to minimize costs. This is made difficult because, in servicing manufacturing and marketing, the distribution manager has no direct control over the level of activity. Control can be exercised by analysing costs into fixed and variable categories and then relating them to the vehicles, the drivers, and the maintenance workshop. Indexes of performance are given by such measures as cost per ton-mile which is a more meaningful measure than is the single dimensional cost per mile.

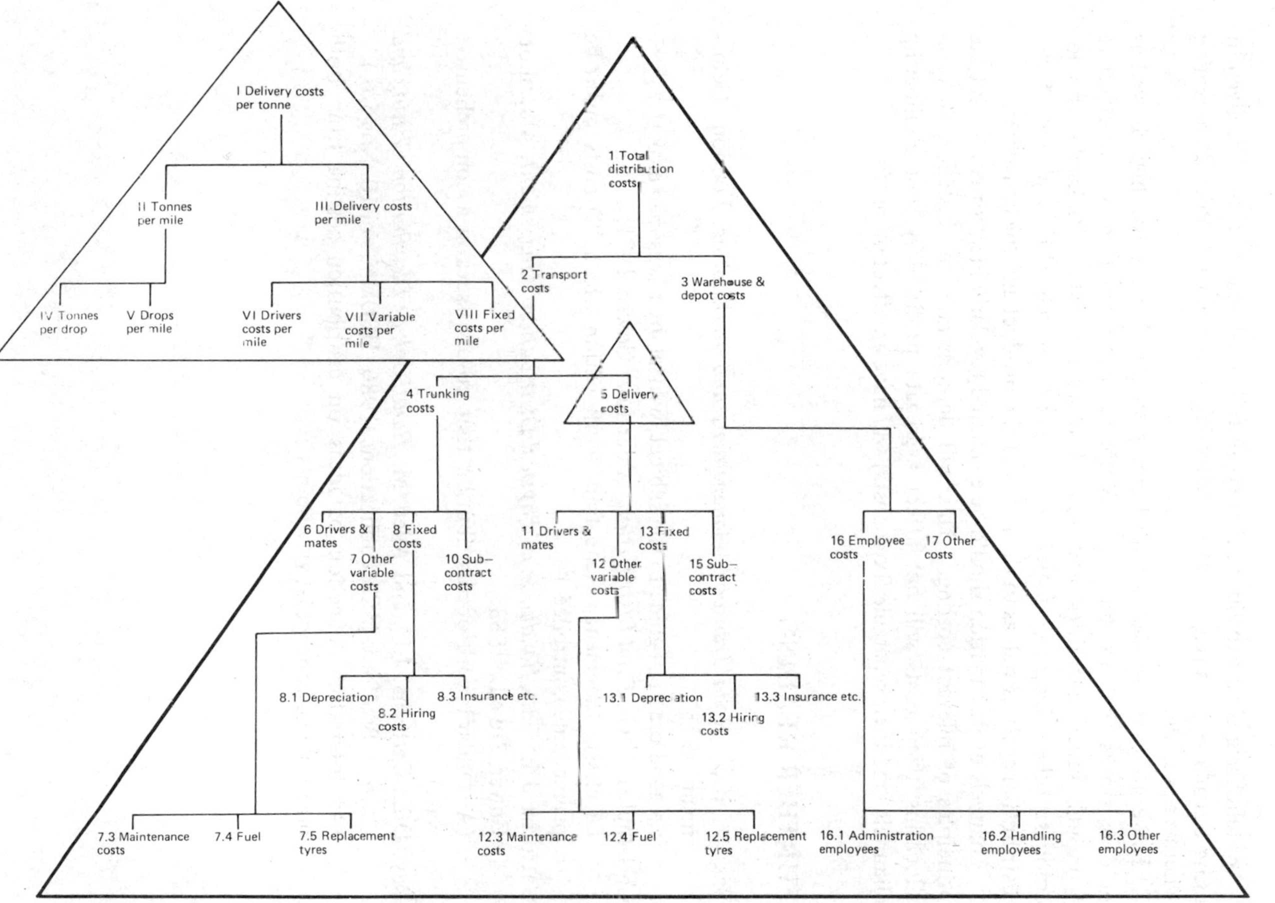

Figure 18.18: CIFC pyramid of distribution cost ratios

Warehousing is an expensive acitivity, so full consideration should be given to using outside services (e.g. suppliers delivering to customers) rather than owning wherever possible.

There are costs associated with holding stocks that are too high as well as holding stocks that are too low. Simple analysis can lead to cost-effective economic order quantities and related reorder points. Packaging should, amongst other things, be suited to the needs of the various phases of the distribution cycle as well as to the needs of the product and the consumer.

Channels of distribution should be evaluated regularly in accordance with the principles of relevant costing. This will demonstrate, for instance, that re-allocating fixed costs will not affect aggregate profitability, but eliminating channels (and their separable fixed costs) will have an effect on profit.

FURTHER READING

Bassett, R.G., *Road Transport Management and Accounting*, London: Heinemann, 1975.
(A good practical guide to the subject, written by a seasoned expert.)

Christopher, M.G., *Total Distribution* Aldershot: Gower, 1971.
(A classic statement of the framework within which PD costs might be planned and controlled.)

Gattorna, J.L. (ed.), *Handbook of Physical Distribution Management*, Aldershot: Gower, 3rd ed., 1983.
(A standard work on distribution that covers issues in a comprehensive way.)

Ray, D.L., Gattorna, J.L., and Allen, M., *Handbook of Distribution Costing and Control*, Bradford: MCB Publications, 1980 (IJPDMM Vol.10. Nos 5/6.)
(An interesting collection of ideas on distribution costing from both practical and conceptual viewpoints.)

Glossary

Abandonment cost The costs incurred in closing down a department or a division, or in withdrawing a product or ceasing to operate in a particular sales territory, etc.

Absenteeism The deliberate withholding of labour on an individual basis that shows the extent to which work is temporarily intolerable (ie, equal to wages foregone). This is not the same as certified sickness.

Absorbed cost That cost that is made up of direct costs plus overhead costs, the latter having been allotted to cost units by means of overhead absorption rates.

Absorption costing The practice of charging all costs – both variable and fixed, and both direct and indirect – to operations, products, or processes.

Accounting period That period of time over which costs and revenues are 'matched' in order to arrive at a profit figure, or the period of time between sets of accounts (eg, 1 year, 1 month, etc.). This will also relate to the future periods for which budgets are compiled.

Accrued charges Charges that are known but not yet due for payment. (Opposite of payment in advance.)

Acid test The ratio of liquid assets (ie, current assets net of stock) to current liabilities that represents an organization's ability to meet its immediate financial commitments.

Activity costing The process of determining costs for activities (or segments) of a business other than manufacturing.

Activity sampling A technique in which a large number of instantaneous observations are made, over a period of time, of a group of machines, processes, or workers.

Actual cost The cost incurred in carrying out an activity, running a process, manufacturing a product, etc, that is compared with a standard cost in order to determine a measure of efficiency.

Algorithm A set of explicit rules (ie, a procedure) for solving a (mathematical) problem.

Allocation The charging of whole items of cost to cost centres or cost units. (This follows the responsibility criterion since allocated costs are direct costs of the cost centre or cost unit.)

Apportionment The charging of proportions of items of cost to cost centres or cost units. (This is not in accordance with the responsibility criterion. Indirect costs need to be apportioned – eg, in absorption costing systems.)

Appropriation The funds allocated to a particular purpose (eg, advertising appropriation, R & D appropriation) for a given period. Such funds represent the total budget for their purpose and are programmed costs.

Assets The resources owned by an organization (both tangible and intangible) that are put to use in achieving organizational objectives.

Audit An inspection of records, assets, activities, and transactions in order to verify and validate their existence and accuracy.

Average cost An aggregate measure given by dividing total cost by the number of units (or other denominator).

Weighted average cost A measure that weights each constituent element of the total in accordance with the proportion which that element bears of the total.

Avoidable cost (escapable cost) A cost that will not be incurred if an activity is not undertaken or discontinued. (Avoidable costs will often correspond with variable costs.)

Balance sheet A classified statement of assets, liabilities, and ownership interest in an organization. This statement characterizes the 'accounting identity': $A = C + E$, where
A = assets
C = claims (or liabilities)
E = equity (or ownership)

Basic standard A standard that is established for use in unaltered form for an indefinite period of time.

Batch costing The technique and process of ascertaining costs for a group of identical items that maintains its identity throughout one or more stages of production.

Bias An influence (or prejudice) that prevents an objective point of view being taken. **Intentional bias** arises when one is conscious of the subjectivity of one's point of view. **Perceptual bias** is beyond our control and beyond our conscious awareness, and arises through our tendency to filter out many signals, etc.

Bidding An approach to determining price in a competitive situation which involves either: (a) open-bidding (ie, auction) in which the highest bid will usually be the successful one; or (b) sealed-bidding in which the lowest bid will usually be the successful one.

Book value *see* Written Down Value

Breakeven analysis *see* Cost-volume-profit analysis.

Break-even point The level of activity (output) at which profit is nil (ie, total revenue is equal to total cost).

Budget A financial and/or quantitative statement, prepared and approved prior to a defined period of time, of the policy to be pursued during that period for the purpose of attaining a given objective.

Budgetary control The process of establishing financial limits to component parts of individual enterprises so that responsibilities are related to the requirements of policy, and the continuous comparison in accounting for outlays, etc., between actual and budgeted results so that remedial action, if necessary, may be taken at an early stage.

Buffer stock A minimum holding of stock as a safety measure against increased usage or delayed deliveries from suppliers.

Burden *see* Overhead rate

By-product By-products are joint products that have minor sales value. They differ from scrap in that they may be subjected to further processing beyond the split-off point.

Capacity The level of output that can be achieved with existing facilities in a given period of time.

Capital employed The sum of share capital, reserves, and loan capital. (This is equivalent to total assets net of current liabilities and is also termed 'net worth'.)

Capital expenditure Outlays on assets that are required and held for the purpose of generating income (eg, plant and machinery, motor vehicles, premises). Contrast with revenue expenditure.

Cash flow In its simplest sense, the change in an enterprise's bank account during a period. More precisely, the cash flow is the after-tax earnings of the enterprise, net of dividends, plus depreciation charges of the period.

Ceteris paribus From the Latin: 'other things being equal'. Thus one examines the impact of changes in variable X on output A, holding variables Y and Z constant in a situation in which $A = f(X,Y,Z)$.

Chart of accounts A classified statement of account headings that represents the framework of the accounting system. Such a chart is the basis for a coding scheme.

Charts Bar charts, component bar charts, frequency polygons, multiple bar charts, ogives, pictograms and pie charts are described in Chapter 7.

Coding A procedure that facilitates the classifying and collecting together of like items by assigning descriptive letters and/or numerals. The structure of the coding system will follow from the chart of accounts.

Committed cost A cost that is primarily associated with maintaining the organization's legal and physical existence (and over which management has little, if any, discretion).

Common cost An indirect cost that is incurred for the general benefit of a number of departments (or for the whole enterprise) and which is necessary for present and future operations.

Constraint Limitation to freedom due to a scarcity of resources. The constraint that provides the greatest restriction is termed 'the limiting factor'.

Contingent liabilities *see under* Liability

Contract costing A variation on Job Costing in which the order is of a long duration and undertaken to a customer's special requirements.

Contribution The difference between sales revenue and the marginal cost of sales (ie, a contribution towards fixed costs and profit).

Contribution margin *see* Contribution

Control A process that entails a set of organized, adaptive actions directed towards achieving a specified goal in the face of constraints.

Controllable cost A cost that can be influenced and regulated during a given time span by the actions of a particular individual within an organization.

Controller An organization's principal accounting officer who has the responsibility for planning and controlling the recording of financial data and the production of financial reports.

Control limits The points beyond which it is unlikely that an observation will fall if a process is under control.

Conversion cost The cost incurred in transforming raw materials into finished goods (or in transforming a material from one state to another).

Cost The amount of sacrifice (or outlay) attributable to a given item, process, etc. This may be actual or notional.

Cost unit An item or quantity of output, a period of time, an area of activity, a process, etc., in relation to which a cost may be ascertained or expressed.

Cost accounting The techniques and processes of ascertaining the amount of expenditure (actual or notional) incurred in, or attributable to, particular products, processes, or services. This involves collecting, classifying, processing and analyzing costing data for either cost control or product costing purposes.

Cost-benefit analysis(CBA) The systematic comparison of the cost of carrying out a service or activity and the value of that service or activity (quantified as far as possible, with all costs and benefits being taken into account).

Cost centre A location, individual, item of equipment, etc, for which costs may be ascertained and used for purposes of cost control or product costing. This is not essentially a personalized concept.

Cost control The regulation by executive action of the costs of operating an undertaking. The control process essentially involves the setting of cost standards and the study of significant deviations from standard.

Cost-effectiveness analysis The procedure whereby alternative courses of action are analyzed to ensure that, in making a particular decision, costs are not incurred unnecessarily and that maximum value (benefit) is obtained from those costs that are incurred.

Cost reduction The process of seeking ways to achieve a given result through improved design, better methods, new layouts, incentive schemes, etc (ie, the establishing of new standards).

Cost-volume-profit analysis (CVP analysis, break-even analysis) The study of the inter-relationships of cost behaviour patterns, levels of activity, and the profit that results from each alternative combination.

Critical path analysis (CPA) *see* Networking techniques

Critical path method (CPM) *see* Networking techniques

Critical success factor (key variable,

key results area) Those factors on which the success of the organization as a whole critically depends. Such factors vary from industry to industry.

Current assets Assets that will turn into cash during the next accounting period (eg, debtors, stocks, etc).

Current liabilities Claims that must be met during the next accounting period (eg, trade creditors, bank overdraft, etc).

Current ratio (working capital ratio) The ratio of current assets to current liabilities. A measure of the short-term ability of an undertaking to meet its obligations, but a measure that has serious weaknesses.

Currently attainable standard A standard that should be capable of being achieved consistently under current operating conditions and in those conditions expected in the near future.

Cybernetics The study of communication and control in animals and machines. (In effect this is the study of self-regulating, complex systems.)

Decision package In zero-base budgeting a definable project, activity, or function for which funding is sought.

Depreciation The diminution in the value of a fixed asset due to use and/or the passage of time.

Differential cost The difference in aggregate outlays between one course of action and another.

Differential costing The process of measuring differential cost.

Direct cost A cost that can be identified specifically and wholly with a particular cost unit.

Direct costing The process of charging all direct costs to products, processes, or services, leaving all indirect costs to be written off against profits in the period in which they arise.

Discounted cash flow (DCF) A technique of investment appraisal in which an appropriate rate of discount is derived to reduce forecasts of incremental costs and revenues over the life of a project to zero in present value terms.

Discretionary cost A programmed cost that is subject both to management discretion (ie, free choice) and management control.

Distribution cost analysis (DCA) (distribution cost accounting) A set of procedures for allocating, apportioning, and controlling the costs of distribution (where 'distribution' refers to the set of activities more commonly termed 'marketing').

Downtime *see* Idle time

Economic order quantity (EOQ) (economic batch size) The optimum size of either a normal outside purchase order or an internal production order that minimizes total annual holding and ordering costs of inventory.

Effectiveness The accomplishment of a desired objective or outcome.

Efficiency This is the ratio of a system's outputs to inputs, and is strictly a limiting example of the idea of productivity in that an efficient system is one in which this ratio is optimal. Two categories of efficiency should be noted:
Economic efficiency, which arises when the cost of inputs is minimized for a given level and mix of outputs; and **Technical efficiency**, which arises when the output is maximized for a given volume and mix of inputs.

Equifinality describes the way in which an open system can follow many different routes to arrive at a given end state.

Equity See also net worth. The claim that the owners of a business have on that business. (This is typically represented by ordinary shares, share premiums, and accumulated reserves.)

Equivalent unit A means of expressing partly processed units of production in terms of completed units. (Thus 100 units that are half-processed will be equivalent to 50 completed units.)

Escapable cost *see* Avoidable cost

Establishment cost see Fixed cost

Expected activity This is a measure of the expected production volume for a forthcoming period, and may be expressed in terms of anticipated units of input or output, or as a percentage utilization of capacity.

Expected value This is simply a weighted arithmetic average.

Feedback The flow of information on the outcome of an event that facilitates comparisons of actual with standard outcomes. **Negative feedback** requires corrective measures to counteract deviating outcomes. **Positive feedback** requires corrective measures to amplify deviating outcomes.

Fiduciary role *see* Stewardship

Financial accounting A process and set of procedures for recording, summarizing, classifying, analyzing, and reporting financial transactions.

Financial leverage *see under* Leverage

First-in-first-out (FIFO) A method of valuing inventories based on the assumption that the earliest purchases are used first and hence the inventory value is made up of the most recent purchases at the most recent prices.

Fixed (tangible) assets The long-term physical assets of a business (such as plant, equipment, motor vehicles) by means of which it generates productive activities.

Fixed budget A budget that is designed to remain unchanged irrespective of the level of activity actually attained.

Flexible budget A budget that recognizes the difference in behaviour pattern of fixed and variable costs, and which is designed to change in relation to the level of activity actually attained.

Fixed cost (period cost) A cost that tends to be unaffected by changes in the level of activity during a given period of time.

Frequency distribution A means of classifying data so that the number of observations of a given value (or within a specified range) is shown for a sequence of values (or ranges).

Full cost *see* Absorbed cost

Functional cost A cost incurred within a particular section (or function) of an organization (eg, marketing or manufacturing). Alternatively, this may be defined as the cost of performing a particular function (eg, typing a letter).

Funds Funds may be defined as cash, or as working capital, or as liquid assets.

Funds flow The movement of funds into, out of, and within the organization.

Funds flow statement A statement showing the movement (ie, sources and dispositions) of funds over a given period of time.

Futures Forward sale or forward purchase (often by speculators), especially in commodity trading, made in an endeavour to avoid increases in costs.

Game theory A method for the study of decision-making in situations of conflict in which none of the 'players' has complete control over the factors influencing the outcomes.

Gantt chart A simple visual tool used in scheduling resources over time. It permits the portraying of several activities at once, and actual performance can be recorded against scheduled performance for control purposes.

Gearing This refers to the extent to which a company employs debt capital: a highly-geared company has a high ratio of debt to total capital, whilst a low-geared company will have most of its capital in the form of shareholders' funds (ie, equity).

Going concern This describes an organization that is assumed to be continuing its operations on an indefinite basis (ie, having an infinite life).

Goodwill The difference between

the value of the going concern and the value of the component parts of the organization. Goodwill is an intangible asset that relates to an enterprise's reputation.

Gross profit The excess of sales revenue in a given period over the cost of goods sold plus the expenses of acquiring those goods (such as carriage.)

Group capacity assessment A work measurement technique employed in clerical/administrative situations to evaluate the input requirement (in terms of staffing) to produce a given output, or to measure the level of efficiency of existing activities.

Heuristic A rule of thumb whereby a problem is solved in a suboptimal way by trial and error.

Histogram A bar chart that represents (in graphical form) a frequency distribution.

Historical cost Actual cost, determined after the event.

Historical costing The process whereby costs are ascertained after they have been incurred.

Homeostasis The state of dynamic equilibrium that is characteristic of viable, adaptive, purpose, living systems.

Ideal capacity The maximum possible capacity that could conceivably be available in a given situation.

Ideal standard The standard that relates to the most favourable conditions conceivable.

Idle time Time for which payment is made to employees because the cause of their idleness is beyond their control (eg, due to non-availability of components, poor scheduling, power cut, etc.).

Income measurement The process whereby net profit is determined for a given period of time.

Incremental cost The extra cost of taking one course of action rather than another (= differential cost).

Incremental costing The process whereby incremental costs are ascertained.

Index number A device for comparing the general level of magnitude of a group of distinct, but related, variables in two or more situations (eg, over time).

Indirect cost A cost that cannot be allocated but which can be apportioned to cost centres or cost units. Overhead costs are indirect costs.

Inflation The phenomenon whereby prices in general rise, with the result that the distinction between, say, *real* increases in costs or profits and *monetary* increases becomes confused, and this is compounded by the fact that all prices do not rise at the same rate.

Intangible assets Assets that do not have a physical presence (such as goodwill and patent rights) but which, nevertheless, facilitate the carrying out of business activities.

Inter-firm comparison The exchange of comparative information among firms with the aim of helping management to improve their individual firms' efficiency.

Internal audit The independent appraisal activity within an organization for reviewing accounting, financial, and other operations as a basis for protective service to management.

Internal control The process of, and procedures for, safeguarding the accuracy and reliability of an organization's accounting data, promoting operational efficiency, and encouraging adherence to prescribed managerial policies.

Internal check The arranging of work tasks in such a way that the work of one individual independently verifies that of another individual.

Internal rate of return (IRR) The rate of discount at which the present value of future income expected from a project equals that of future outlays. (This is the same as DCF.)

Interpolation Where the values of known observations form an incomplete series, it may be necessary to estimate the value of a new observation between two known observations' values. This is the process of interpolation.

Invariable cost *see* Fixed cost

Inventory A schedule of items held at a particular point in time. (This is synonymous with stock.)

Inventory control The management of stocks so that costs are minimized for a given level of service.

Investment appraisal A means of assessing whether expenditure on a capital project would show a satisfactory rate of return (either absolutely or in relation to alternative uses of funds), and of indicating the optimum time to commit expenditure.

Investment centre A personalized location for which a named individual is responsible for both the investment base and the rate of return on this investment base. (Compare cost centre and profit centre.)

Job analysis The collection and analysis of any type of job-related information.

Job cost The cost of a cost unit (= job) consisting of a single order (ie, a single item or a single batch of like items).

Job costing The process whereby a

job cost is ascertained.

Job evaluation A method of determining the relative standing, for pay purposes, of jobs within an organization.

Joint costs The costs of either a single process or a series of processes that simultaneously produce two or more products of significant relative sales value.

Joint products Two or more manufactured items produced by a single process (or sequence of processes) but which are not identifiable as individual products until they reach a split-off point beyond which they require individual treatment.

Last-in-first-out (LIFO) A method of valuing inventories based on the assumption that the most recent purchases are used first and hence the inventory value is made up of the earliest purchases at the earliest prices.

Lead time The period that elapses between placing an order and receiving the ordered goods into stock.

Learning curve A mathematical (graphical) portrayal of the decreasing rate of increase in costs of labour whilst experience is being gained in a new task.

Level of resolution This is concerned with the spatial and temporal 'focus' through which one analyzes systems (and hence problems).

Level of service The percentage of orders that can be filled immediately from stock, or the number of days (on average) that is taken to deliver an order. (This expression is generally related to the distribution function, but can be used in other senses in other settings.)

Leverage *see* Gearing. **Financial leverage** The ratio of total debt to total assets. **Operating leverage** The ratio of fixed costs to total costs.

Liability A claim by an outsider on the assets of the enterprise. **Current liabilities** are those claims that must be met within the next period. **Long-term liabilities** are claims that need not be met until after the next period. **Contingent liabilities** are those that may not fall to be met at all since their existence will be probabilistic.

Life cycle costing (terotechnology) A technique designed to provide increased visibility to the total costs of doing business and to highlight areas where resource applications can be improved.

Limiting factor *see* Constraint

Linear programming (LP) A type of mathematical programming for solving allocation problems so that limited resources are assigned to a number of uses in order to achieve maximum effectiveness.

Line of balance (LOB) *see* Networking techniques

Liquidity This relates to a firm's cash position and its ability to meet obligations at the appropriate time.

Liquidity ratio The ratio of liquid assets to current liabilities.

Liquid assets Cash or near-cash resources (such as debtors, stocks, etc.).

Long-range planning (strategic planning, corporate planning) The process of deciding upon objectives, on the resources to be used to attain these objectives, and on the policies that are to govern the acquisition, use, and disposition of these resources.

Long-term liabilities *see under* Liability

Managed cost A cost that stems from current operations but which must continue to be incurred into the future, at some level determined by management, to ensure the continued existence of the enterprise.

Management accounting The application of accounting knowledge to the purpose of producing and of interpreting accounting and statistical information designed to assist management in its functions of promoting maximum efficiency and in formulating and coordinating future plans and subsequently in measuring their execution.

Management audit The systematic assessment of standards and techniques of management.

Management by exception The process by which only significant variations from plan (ie, standard or budget) are referred to management, other cases being dealt with according to laid down procedures in a routine matter.

Management by objectives A technique whereby targets (or 'objectives') are established for individuals and departments/divisions as a basis for achieving greater effectiveness throughout the whole organization.

Management control The process whereby resources are obtained and used effectively and efficiently in the accomplishment of the organization's objectives.

Management science An approach to management problem-solving based on the scientific method. Essentially management science encompasses operations research and computer applications.

Marginal cost The amount at any given volume of output by which aggregate costs are changed if the volume of output is increased or decreased by one unit.

Marginal costing The process of ascertaining marginal costs and of the effects of changes in volume or type of output on profit by differentiating between fixed and variable costs.

Marginal revenue The amount at any given volume of output by which aggregate revenue is changed if the volume of output is increased or decreased by one unit.

Margin of safety The excess of budgeted (or actual) sales over the break-even sales volume.

Market value The value an asset has if offered for sale on the open market in its present condition, less any costs incurred in disposing of that asset.

Master budget The summary budget that incorporates the key figures and totals of all other budgets.

Mathematical programming A group of mathematical techniques for maximizing the effectiveness (or minimizing the cost) in allocating scarce resources amongst different uses. (One such technique is linear programming.)

Matrix organization An organizational design that focuses attention on projects (or missions) rather than on the traditional functions.

Mean (arithmetic average) The total value of a number of observations divided by that number.

Median The value that exceeds in magnitude half the values in a series of observations and which is exceeded in value by the other half. **Mode** is the value around which most observations in a series are concentrated. **Moving average** is an approach to smoothing observed data by revising average measures as each new observation is available and deleting the oldest observation so that the average does, in fact, move forward each period.

Merit rating The systematic evaluation of personnel by their superiors involving the use of forms and procedures that have been developed for the purpose.

Method study The critical study of existing and proposed ways of doing work as a means of developing and applying easier and more effective methods and reducing costs.

Methods time measurement An approach to predetermining time standards that breaks the elements of each task down and establishes a time for each element and hence a time for the overall task.

Mission A task that is characterized by its end rather than its means, such as 'put a man on the moon by 1970'.

Mixed cost Typified by semi-fixed and semi-variable costs, mixed costs are those whose behaviour patterns are representative of neither fixed costs nor variable costs, but a combination (stepped) of both.

Model A simplified representation

of reality that may be in the form of a mathematical equation, a chart/flow diagram, a 3-D representation, etc., that can help in defining and solving problems.

Mutatis mutandis From the Latin: 'when the appropriate changes have been made'. (Thus one would consider changes in *all* inputs and outputs of a system rather than focusing on only one of each.)

Natural expense An outlay that is classified by its nature (eg, salary, rent, etc.) rather than by its function (such as marketing, etc.).

Negative feedback *see under* Feedback

Net assets see Total assets

Net present value The present value of income arising from a project, less the present value of expenditure on the project, arrived at by discounting at a given rate of interest (usually the cost of capital).

Networking techniques (network analysis) Methods for planning the undertaking of a project in a logical way by analyzing the project into its component parts and representing them on a network that is then used for planning and controlling the inter-related activities over time in carrying the project to completion.

Net worth *see* Capital employed

New product development The process whereby ideas for new products are collected, developed, evaluated, and eventually launched as competitive market offerings.

Normal activity That level of activity (eg, of productive output) that can be expected to be attained over a future period of time covering the business cycle.

Normal distribution This is a statistical distribution that is bell-shaped, symmetrical, and asymptotic in both directions to the x-axis, and depends only on the two parameters $\bar{x}$ and σ.

On-cost *see* Overhead

Operating budget The annual budget that is composed of the programme of activities to be performed during the period, the forecast costs and revenues, and a statement of responsibilities.

Operating cost The non-capital cost of running a particular process, activity, department, or enterprise for a given period of time.

Operating costing The procedures by which costs are ascertained for a process or activity, whether of a manufacturing, administrative, or other functional nature.

Operating leverage *see under* Leverage

Operating statement A summary of

the operating costs (and, where appropriate, of the revenue and profit margins) of the whole or part of the activities of an enterprise for a given period.

Operations research (OR) The application of scientific methods, techniques, and tools to problems involving the operations of a system so as to provide those in control of the system with optimal solutions to the problems.

Opportunity cost The maximum amount that could be obtained at any given point of time if a resource was sold or put to the most valuable alternative use that would be practicable.

Opportunity costing The process whereby opportunity costs are ascertained.

Optimization The process of selecting the 'best' course of action from amongst alternatives. ('Best' only has relevance in the context of some desired end which must be specified.)

Order-filling costs Costs of distribution (being mainly composed of the costs attributable to warehousing, transport, order-processing, and inventory management).

Order-getting costs Costs of marketing (being mainly composed of the costs attributable to advertising, sales promotion, personal selling, and product PR).

Organization chart A pictorial model that represents the formal relationships amongst individuals within an enterprise, the main lines of communication, the division of responsibility, and the delegation of authority.

Organization & methods (O & M) A service giving advice on the structure of an organization, its management and control, and its procedures and methods.

Out-of-pocket cost A cost that will necessitate a corresponding outflow of cash.

Over-absorbed cost (over-recovered overhead) The excess of the amount of overhead absorbed (ie, output × overhead rate) over the amount of overhead cost autually incurred.

Over-capitalized An excess of capital for the scale of operations being undertaken. **Under-capitalized** A deficiency of capital for the scale of operations being undertaken.

Overhead (burden, oncost) The aggregate of indirect material costs, indirect labour cost, and indirect expenses.

Overhead rate The expression of overhead in relation to some specific characteristic of a cost centre as a means of providing a basis for its apportionment or absorption.

Over-trading Carrying on operations with a deficiency of working capital.

Pareto's law (the 80/20 rule) This refers to the frequently-encountered phenomenon in which most (80%) of one variable's behaviour is caused by a small (20%) amount of another factor, (eg, 80% sales revenue arises from 20% products; 20% customers contribute 80% of profit, etc.).

Payback period The length of time it takes an investment to generate sufficient extra net income to repay the additional capital and other outlays involved.

Payment-by-results (PBR) *see* Piece-work

Pay-off The benefit (in whatever form) that accrues through pursuing one chosen course of action in relation to a specified objective. A measure of performance.

Period cost *see* Fixed cost

Periodic budgeting The process whereby budgets are prepared at fixed intervals (usually annually) and allowed to run their course before the next period's budget is devised and instituted.

PERT *see* Networking techniques

PERT/COST *see* Net-working techniques

Physical distribution management (PDM) An integrated and coordinated approach to order-processing, materials handling, warehousing, inventory control, transportation, packaging, depot location, customer service, etc.

Piece-work The arrangement whereby operatives are paid on the basis of the amount of work (ie, number of pieces) they produce.

Piece-rate The amount payable for each piece produced.

Pie chart *see* Charts

Planning, programming, budgeting system (PPBS) (output budgeting) A system for analysing expenditure by reference to particular (output) objectives instead of under (input) headings such as natural and functional cost classifications.

Positive feedback *see under* Feedback.

Practical capacity The maximum volume that can be produced in regularly scheduled hours.

Present value The value today of a future payment, receipt, or stream of payments and/or receipts, discounted at an appropriate discount rate.

Primary ratio This is the apex of the ratio pyramid: the rate of return on investment =

$$\frac{\text{net profit}}{\text{capital invested}}$$

Prime cost The aggregate of direct material cost, direct labour cost, and direct expenses.

Probability The probability of a particular outcome of an event is simply the proportion of times this outcome would occur if the event were repeated a great number of times.

Problem solving The process that starts with the definition of the problem that is to be resolved, and which identifies and evaluates alternative possible solutions. Problems can be classified into three exhaustive groupings: **Problems of analysis** which are essentially problems of *prediction.* (Thus, given a system's structure, how will it behave?) **Problems of synthesis** which are essentially problems of *explanation*. (Thus, given the desired behaviour of a system, how can it be structured to produce that behaviour?) **Black box problems** are those that cannot be classified under either of the previous headings since knowledge about them is very limited.

Process costing The procedures whereby the costs of operating a manufacturing process are ascertained. This involves dealing with broad averages and large numbers of like units.

Product cost The aggregate of costs that are associated with a unit of product. Such costs may or may not include an element of overheads depending upon the type of costing system in force – absorption or direct.

Product costing The process by which product costs are ascertained.

Productivity The rate of output per unit of time.

Product life-cycle The pattern of expenditure, sales levels, revenue, and profit over the period from new idea generation to the deletion of a product from the product range.

Profit centre A form of responsibility centre in which a manager is held responsible for both revenue and costs, and hence for the resultant level of profit.

Profit & loss account (income statement, revenue account) A statement in which revenues for a period are summarized along with the costs incurred in securing those revenues. The difference is a profit (if positive) or a loss (if negative). A formalized operating statement.

Profit plan A fully developed set of budgets that show which activities are to be carried out and how each is to contribute to profit.

Profit-volume ratio The proportion of each additional unit of sales revenue that consists of contribution (to fixed costs and profit).

Profit-volume chart (profitgraph) A diagram showing the expected relationship between cost and revenue at various volumes with profit being the residual. A break-even chart.

Programmed cost A cost that is subject both to management discretion and management control but which has little immediate relevance to current operations although it is generally incurred to ensure long-term survival.

Programming *see* Mathematical programming and linear programming

Project (venture, mission) A set of inter-related activities that have a recognizable beginning and end, and which exists in order to attain a stated objective.

Project management An approach to managing complex ventures in uncertain conditions.

Quality control The systematic examination of errors in order to show what might be done (by such means as improved training) to reduce the incidence of errors and to reveal ways of improving procedures, etc., in order to eliminate the causes of error.

RAMPS *see* Networking techniques

Ratio analysis The examination of significant relationships between reported statistics of cost, revenue, profit, assets, liabilities, and capital structure, with a view to better control.

Ratio pyramid A hierarchy of ratios showing how each ratio is made up and how it relates to other ratios.

Relevant cost An incremental (or differential) cost. (ie, one that is expected to differ among alternative future courses of action).

Relevant range The range of activity within which particular cost behaviour patterns are known (or presumed) to exist (eg, the range within which a fixed cost is actually fixed).

Reorder level That level of stock availability when a new order should be raised. (Reorder level = rate of usage × lead time + buffer stock.)

Reorder point *see* Reorder level

Replacement cost The cost replacing an asset at any given point in time, either now or in the future (excluding any element attributable to improvement).

Residual income The difference between actual net income and a specified target figure, with the target reflecting the cost of capital.

Residual value The value of an asset at the end of its useful (economic or technological or physical) life. This will be equivalent to the proceeds of sale net of any disposal costs.

Responsibility accounting An approach to cost control whereby every item of expenditure is made the responsibility of that individual who can best influence it by his actions.

Responsibility centre A personalized

group of cost centres under the control of a 'responsible' individual.

Retained earnings The accumulated balance of net profit (after tax) that is undistributed (in the form of dividends) and unappropriated to another use.

Return on investment (ROI) (return on capital employed (ROCE)) The primary ratio that relates net profit to the capital invested in the enterprise as a whole, or in divisions of the enterprise.

Revenue account *see* Profit & loss account

Revenue centre A responsibility centre in which a manager is only held responsible for the level of revenue.

Revenue expenditure That which is incurred in the normal course of business, the benefit of which is received during the period in which the expenditure is made (ie, non-capital expense).

Re-work *see under* Scrap

Risk The situation in which a number of outcomes of a decision are possible, but this number can be identified and the probability of each occurring is known.

Rolling budget A budget that always accommodates a specified period. Thus a 12 month rolling budget will be amended every month to delete the month that has just passed and to add on the new month that is 12 months hence.

Sample A number of observations taken from a (larger) population of observations with a view to identifying characteristics of the population by examining characteristics of the sample.

Scattergraph A diagram on which a series of observations is recorded in order to identify significant relationships between the variables represented on the axes.

Scrap Residue material that has a recovery value. **Spoilage** Production that fails to meet quality or dimensional requirements. **Re-work** Spoilt units of output that can be rectified and thus become good units.

Secondary ratios The constituent elements of the primary ratio, namely:

$$\text{Capital turnover} = \frac{\text{Sales}}{\text{Capital invested}}$$

$$\text{Profit margin on sales} = \frac{\text{Net profit}}{\text{Sales}}$$

Segment A responsibility centre (division, department, etc.) of an organization (or, alternatively, a portion of the market for a given product in which all consumers have important characteristics in common).

Semi-variable cost *see* Mixed cost

Semi-fixed cost *see* Stepped cost

Sensitivity analysis A technique that identifies key variables in a system and then assesses the sensitivity of the output of that system to variations in the input variables.

Separable cost *see under* Split-off point

Service costing A variation on process costing in which the focus of interest is the cost of service outputs (rather than the cost of physical outputs).

Service department A department serving the organization as a whole that is not directly productive: examples include boilerhouse, personnel department, maintenance, etc.

Set-up cost The cost incurred in adjusting machinery, etc., before a production task can be undertaken.

Shutdown costs The costs incurred in relation to the temporary closing of a department/division/enterprise. Such costs include those of reopening as well as those of closing.

Simulation The representation of a system by a model which will react to change in a similar way to that which is being simulated. This enables a decision-maker to predict the outcome of a particular decision through testing it via the model.

Split-off point The point beyond which joint products can be processed individually but prior to which they must be treated jointly. **Separable costs** Costs incurred beyond the split-off point (such that they can be identified with specific products).

Spoilage *see under* Scrap

Standard cost A predetermined cost that is calculated on the basis of a desired level of operating efficiency.

Standard costing The process whereby standard costs are developed and used as a comparison for actual costs so that variances can be isolated, investigated if significant, and remedial action taken when deemed necessary.

Standard deviation A measure of dispersion about a central point given by applying the formula:

$$\sigma = \sqrt{\sum \frac{(x - \bar{x})^2}{N - 1}}$$

Start-up costs The costs incurred in commencing a business.

States of nature are the various environmental factors that constitute constraints (or stimuli) to an organization's purposive behaviour.

Statistical control chart A diagrammatic device incorporating control limits and onto which observations are recorded. Any observation falling beyond the statistically determined control limits is subject to investigation.

Statistical quality control (SQC) An

approach to quality control based on the selection and inspection of samples (of a statistically predetermined size), and the analysis of results in accordance with statistical principles.

Stepped (semi-fixed) cost A cost the behaviour pattern of which is characterized by steps (ie, sudden changes) at intervals in accordance with the level of activity, but between these steps the behaviour pattern is typically of a fixed cost nature.

Stewardship That function of accounting that involves the maintaining of records, etc., on behalf of the (absent) shareholders.

Strategy in a management context refers to an available course of action that an organization needs to identify and evaluate with a view to pursuing it.

Structure The set of rules and roles (ie, organizational relationships) that determines patterns of power, resource allocation, and behaviour within organizations.

Sub-optimize To obtain a result from a particular solution which is not the 'best' in relation to a particular problem.

Sunk costs Those costs that have been invested in a project and which will not be recovered if the project is terminated.

System An assemblage of interacting and interdependent elements that functions as a purposive whole. The most important of the various sub-classifications are: **Closed systems** (which are those having no interactive exchanges with their environment), and: **Open Systems** (which are those that survive by means of inter-active exchanges with their environments).

Systems analysis The process of analysing the workings of enterprises (or segments thereof) with a view to ascertaining objectives and prescribing how these might be met.

Technocracy The collective noun for all persons who bring specialized knowledge, talent, or experience to group decision-making within complex organizations.

Tertiary ratios The constituent elements of the secondary ratios:

$$\frac{\text{Gross profit}}{\text{Sales}} \qquad \frac{\text{Sales}}{\text{Overheads}}$$

$$\frac{\text{Sales}}{\text{Working capital}} \qquad \frac{\text{Sales}}{\text{Fixed assets}}$$

Time study (time & motion study) A technique for recording the times and rates of working for the elements of a specified job carried out under specified conditions, and for analysing the data so as to obtain the time necessary for carrying out the job at a defined level of performance.

Tolerance limit *see* Control limit

Total assets The sum of fixed assets and current assets. **Net Assets** *see* Capital employed

Trade-off The sacrifice that is involved in choosing one course (or dimension) of action rather than another (eg, it may be necessary to trade cost for quality).

Trading account The account in which an enterprise's gross profit is shown by matching sales revenue with the cost of those sales.

Transfer price The 'price' at which goods are transferred from one division/department of an enterprise to another division/department of that same enterprise.

Treasurer The company officer who has responsibility for monitoring the inflow and outflow of cash (and who also may have responsibility for insurance matters and investor relations/financial PR).

Trial balance A schedule of balances, both debit and credit, extracted from the accounts contained in an enterprise's ledgers.

Turnover The total value of sales during a period. Alternatively, in relation to stock, it is cost of sales ÷ aveage inventory of finished goods; and in relation to capital it is sales revenue ÷ capital invested in the enterprise.

Uncertainty The situation in which the outcomes of a decision cannot be identified in advance, nor probabilities given to the likelihood of any outcome occurring.

Uncontrollable cost A cost that is beyond the control (ie, is uninfluenced by the actions) of a given individual during a given period of time.

Under-absorbed cost (under-recovered overhead) The deficit in the amount of overhead absorbed (ie, output × overhead rate) compared with the amount of overhead cost actually incurred.

Under-capitalized *see under* Over-capitalized

Uniform costing The use by several undertakings of the same costing principles and/or practices.

Unit cost The total of a specified cost factor divided by a given volume of units to give an average cost. The unit in question may be of output, of time, etc., depending on the reason for the computation.

Utility The power to satisfy human wants.

Value This is a measure of preference (eg, for buying an asset rather than holding cash) which reflects the benefits that one expects to receive from owning the asset.

Value added The difference between the value of an enterprise's outputs and the value of its inputs.

Value analysis The comparison of the cost of an item with the value obtained from it as a basis for determining whether or not the value justifies the outlay. This technique focuses on basic design rather than on, say, manufacturing methods.

Value engineering The application of value analysis techniques at the original decision-making stage (ie, when new expenditure is being planned).

Variable cost A cost that tends to vary in accordance with the level of activity (within the relevant range, and within a given period of time).

Variable costing *see* Direct costing

Variable factor programming A technique for improving the work flow of indirect (eg, administrative) departments and eliminating idle time that proceeds by measuring the time each activity a given worker performs takes, setting targets, and devising 'programmes' without interruptions.

Variance The difference between a planned (ie, budgeted or standard) outcome and the actual outcome of an event.

Variance analysis The investigation and explanation of variances with a view to controlling operations.

Variety is the measure of a system's complexity and is expressed by the number of different states that each variable within the system can exhibit, on an interactive basis.

Variety reduction (variety control) An approach to cost reduction by eliminating those varieties (of components and finished goods) that absorb a disproportionate amount of attention in relation to their profitability.

Venture *see* Project

Venture capital Funds that are invested in (high-risk) projects in expectation of high rewards.

Venture management *see* Project management

Waiting time A type of idle time spent pending the arrival of work (in the form of materials, instructions, etc.).

Waste Material loss during production or storage due to eg, evaporation, chemical reaction, unrecoverable residue, shrinkage, etc.

Wasting asset A fixed asset that is depleted by use (eg, a mine or quarry).

Weighted average *see* Mean

Working capital An enterprise's investment in short-term assets net of short-term liabilities.

Working capital ratio *see* Current ratio

Work-in-progress (work-in-process)

Partly-processed units.

Works cost The sum of direct and indirect manufacturing costs.

Work simplification A technique for analysing operations and procedures with a view to finding easier ways of performing the work involved.

Work study A generic term for those techniques (especially method study and work measurement) that are used in the examination of human work, and which lead systematically to the investigation of all factors affecting the efficiency of the situation being reviewed as a basis for making improvements.

Work measurement The application of techniques designed to establish the time for a qualified, representative worker to carry out a specified job at a defined level of performance.

Work sampling *see* Activity sampling

Written down value (WDV) (book value) The value, net of depreciation, that an asset has as shown in the enterprise's books of account. Only by chance will this accord with the economic or market value of that asset.

Yield The rate of return on an investment.

Zero-base budgeting An approach to budget review and evaluation that requires a manager to justify the resources requested for all activities and projects (including on-going ones) in rank order.

Z-chart A chart showing three sets of statistical data consisting of:

1 The original data line (eg, monthly or weekly observations)
2 A cumulative curve of data from 1
3 A curve showing moving annual totals.

Index

Index